Models
for
Writers

Short Essays for Composition

SEVENTH EDITION

Alfred Rosa
Paul Eschholz

University of Vermont

BEDFORD/ST. MARTIN'S
Boston ◆ *New York*

For Bedford/St. Martin's

Developmental Editor: Leah Edmunds
Senior Production Supervisor: Dennis J. Conroy
Marketing Manager: Brian Wheel
Project Management: Books By Design, Inc.
Text Design: Books By Design, Inc.
Cover Design: Lucy Krikorian
Cover Art: Paul Klee, *Blossoming,* 1934. Oil on canvas, 31⅞ × 31½ in. (81½ × 80 cm). Kunstmuseum Winterthur, Inv. No. 1184. Gift of Clara and Emil Friedrich-Jezler, 1973.
Composition: Pine Tree Composition
Printing and Binding: Haddon Craftsmen, an R. R. Donnelley & Sons Company

President: Charles H. Christensen
Editorial Director: Joan E. Feinberg
Editor in Chief: Nancy Perry
Director of Marketing: Karen R. Melton
Director of Editing, Design, and Production: Marcia Cohen
Manager, Publishing Services: Emily Berleth

Library of Congress Control Number: 00-105364

Manufactured in the United States of America.

6 5 4 3 2 1
f e d c b a

For information, write: Bedford/St. Martin's, 75 Arlington Street, Boston, MA 02116   (617–399–4000)

ISBN: 0–312–25569–1
        0–312–39476–4 (high school edition)

Acknowledgments
Acknowledgments and copyrights are continued at the back of the book on pages 521–25, which constitute an extension of the copyright page.

Diane Ackerman. "Why Leaves Turn Color in the Fall." From *A Natural History of the Senses* by Diane Ackerman. Copyright © 1990 by Diane Ackerman. Reprinted with the permission of Random House, Inc.

Preface

Models for Writers provides students and instructors with high-interest, readable essays that model rhetorical elements, principles, and patterns. But *Models for Writers* is much more than a collection of essays, important as it is for students to read as they are learning to write college-level essays. The questions and activities that accompany each selection focus attention on how the essay is structured and allow students to see how rhetorical strategies and techniques enhance what the author is saying. In addition, writing activities and assignments help students stitch the various rhetorical elements together into coherent, forceful essays of their own. This approach, which over the course of six editions has helped a generation of students to become better writers, remains at the heart of this new edition. *Models for Writers* combines the best collection available of examples for student writers with the most useful and abundant support to help them master the writing skills needed for their college classes.

In this new edition, the classic features of *Models for Writers* that have won praise from teachers and students alike continue to be emphasized.

Favorite Features of *Models for Writers*

• **Lively Examples.** Most of the selections in *Models for Writers* are comparable in length (two to three pages) to the essays students will write themselves, and each clearly illustrates a basic rhetorical element, principle, or pattern. Just as important, the essays deal with subjects that we know from our own teaching experience will spark the interest of most college students. Drawn from a wide range of sources, the essays represent a variety of popular contemporary prose styles.

• **Rhetorical Organization.** Each of the eighteen chapters in *Models for Writers* is devoted to a particular element or pattern important to college writing. Chapters 1 through 7 focus on the concepts of thesis, unity, organization, beginnings and endings, paragraphs, transitions, and effective sentences. Chapter 8 illustrates the importance of controlling diction and tone, and Chapter 9, the uses of figurative language. Chapters 10 through 18 explore the types of writing most often required of college students: illustration, narration, description, process analysis, definition, division and classification, comparison and contrast, cause and effect, and argument.

- **Abundant Study Materials.** To help students link reading to their writing, every essay is accompanied by ample study materials.

For Your Journal activities precede each reading and prompt students to explore their own ideas and experiences regarding the issues presented in the reading.

Questions for Study and Discussion focus on the content, the author's purpose, and the particular strategy used to achieve that purpose, with at least one question in each series focusing on a writing concern other than the one highlighted in the chapter to remind students that good writing is never one-dimensional.

Vocabulary sections identify several words from each reading that students will find worth adding to their vocabularies, with exercises asking students to define each word as it is used in the context of the selection and then to use the word in a new sentence of their own.

Classroom Activities provide brief exercises enabling students to work in the classroom (often in groups) on rhetorical elements, techniques, or patterns. These activities range from developing thesis statements to using strong action verbs and building argumentative evidence. Classroom Activities help students apply concepts modeled in the readings to their own writing.

Suggested Writing Assignments provide two writing assignments for each essay, one encouraging the use of the reading selection as a direct model and the second asking students to respond to the content of the reading.

- **Flexible Arrangement.** Each chapter is self-contained so that instructors can easily follow their own teaching sequences, omitting or emphasizing certain chapters according to the needs of their students. Whatever sequence is followed, thematic connections among the selections can be made by referring to the alternate Thematic Contents at the beginning of the book.

- **Useful Introduction.** The book opens with an introduction that shows students how the text can be used to improve their writing. Included in the introduction are four student essays demonstrating the major types of writing students need to master—a personal narrative, two expository essays, and an argumentative essay.

- **Concise and Helpful Chapter Introductions.** Users have been generous in their praise for the chapter introductions, which explain the various rhetorical elements and patterns. In each one, students will find numerous illuminating examples of the feature or principle being discussed.

- **A Glossary of Useful Terms.** Whenever possible in the questions or writing assignments throughout the book, we refer students to this helpful list, which covers rhetorical and literary terms, and we encourage them to connect the terms with concrete examples.

- **Instructor's Resource Manual.** In the manual that accompanies *Models for Writers,* we offer insights into the rhetorical features of each essay as well as advice on how best to use the materials in class. Suggested answers for study questions, vocabulary, and classroom activities are included.

Highlights of the Seventh Edition of *Models for Writers*

New Readings. The twenty-one new essays in the seventh edition of *Models for Writers* cover topics of current interest such as doublespeak, drunk driving, technology, competitive sports, horror movies, computers and minorities, and the death penalty. We chose these essays with an eye toward critical thinking and writing as well as for their brevity, clarity, and suitability for student writers. Among the new readings included in this edition are essays by popular writers such as N. Scott Momaday, Natalie Goldberg, Diane Ackerman, Ellen Goodman, and Stephen King.

Revised Chapter Introductions, Including Student Examples. The chapter introductions offer clear explanations of the different rhetorical elements, principles, and patterns, and now include student writing as well as professional examples. New writing samples, charts and visual aids, definitions of unfamiliar terms, and cross-references to other chapters help students focus on their writing goals.

A New Appendix on Writing a Research Paper. A brief, helpful appendix, including a sample documented student essay, offers guidance on conducting research using print and online sources; evaluating, quoting, and integrating sources; and using the MLA citation style.

New Student Essays. Four full-length student essays in the Introduction (three of the essays new to this edition) and a full-length documented essay in the Appendix on Writing a Research Paper demonstrate to students how the rhetorical methods they learn are employed by their peers.

A Strengthened Emphasis on Combining Rhetorical Strategies. Throughout the chapter introductions and study materials, students are encouraged to observe how writers have used effective combinations of rhetorical patterns to fulfill their purposes and to use these combinations in their own writing.

New Paired Argument Essays. Opposing viewpoints in the argument chapter promote analytical thinking and help students consider difficult issues, contrast opposing viewpoints, and establish their own stance.

Acknowledgments

In response to the many enthusiastic users of this book, we have kept the solid foundation of previous editions of *Models for Writers* while adding fresh readings and writing topics to stimulate today's student writers.

We are indebted to many people for their criticism and advice as we prepared this seventh edition of *Models for Writers*. We are especially grateful to Laurie Bucholz, Porterville College; Judith L. Burken, Kellogg Community College; Merry Caston, Lane Community College; Robert Corrigan, Baltimore City Community College; Tracy Dougherty, Georgia Military College; Carole Fickert, Holyoke Community College; Moselle Alden Ford, Amarillo College; Sandra Jerinsky, Rockland Community College; Ilka Luyt, Jefferson Community College; Sally Peltier Harvey, Yuba College; Barbara Peterson, Isothermal Community College; Ruth Port, Waubonsee Community College; Gordon Roadcap, American River College; Linda Schmidt, Iowa Western Community College; Rod Siegfried, American River College; Neal Snidow, Butte Community College; Carrie Vogel, Northern New Mexico Community College; Donna Weyrich, Columbus State Community College.

It has been our good fortune to have the editorial guidance of Leah Edmunds, Nancy Perry, and Emily Berleth of Bedford/ St. Martin's as we worked on this new edition.

Thanks to our colleagues Sue Dinitz, Brian Kent, Dick Sweterlitsch, and Alex Vardamis, who have shared with us their experiences using *Models for Writers* in the classroom. Thanks also go to Mark Wanner and Betsy Eschholz for their cheerful and prompt editorial assistance with the text and to Betsy Eschholz for preparing the Instructor's Resource Manual for this new edition. Our greatest debt is, as always, to our writing students, for all they have taught us over the years.

Alfred Rosa
Paul Eschholz

Contents

part one **The Elements of the Essay**

I Thesis   29

2 Unity   47

ix

16 Comparison and Contrast 373

17 Cause and Effect 394

18 Argument 420

Thematic Contents

Men and Women

The Minority Experience

Science and Technology

Health and Medicine

Writers and Writing

Introduction

Models for Writers is designed to help you learn to write by providing you with a collection of model essays, essays that are examples of good writing. We know that one of the best ways to learn to write and to improve our writing is to read. By reading we can begin to see how other writers have communicated their experiences, ideas, thoughts, and feelings. We can study how they have used the various elements of the essay—words, sentences, paragraphs, organizational patterns, transitions, examples, evidence, and so forth—and thus learn how we might effectively do the same. When we see, for example, how a writer like James Lincoln Collier develops an essay from a strong thesis statement, we can better appreciate the importance of having a clear thesis statement in our writing. When we see the way Lisa Brown uses transitions to link key phrases and important ideas so that readers can recognize clearly how the parts of her essay are meant to fit together, we have a better idea of how to achieve such clarity in our own writing.

But we do not learn only by observing, by reading. We also learn by doing, by writing, and in the best of all situations we engage in these two activities in conjunction with one another. *Models for Writers* encourages you, therefore, to write your essays, to practice what you are learning, as you are actually reading and analyzing the model essays in the text.

The kind of composition that you will be asked to write for your college writing instructor is most often referred to as an essay—a relatively short piece of nonfiction in which a writer attempts to develop one or more closely related points or ideas. An effective essay has a clear purpose, often provides useful information, has an effect on the reader's thoughts and feelings, and is usually a pleasure to read.

All well-written essays also share a number of structural and stylistic features that are illustrated by the various essays in *Models for Writers*. One good way to learn what these features are and how you can incorporate them into your own writing is to look at each of them in isolation. For this reason we have divided *Models for Writers* first into three major sections and, within these sections, into eighteen chapters, each with its own particular focus and emphasis.

"The Elements of the Essay," the first section, includes chapters on the following subjects: thesis, unity, organization, beginnings and endings, paragraphs, transitions, and effective sentences. All of these elements are essential to a well-written essay, but the concepts of thesis, unity, and organization underlie all the others and so come first in our sequence.

Briefly, "Thesis" shows how authors put forth or state the main ideas of their essays and how they use such statements to develop and control content. "Unity" shows how authors achieve a sense of wholeness in their essays, and "Organization" illustrates some important patterns that authors use to organize their thinking and writing. "Beginnings and Endings" offers advice and models of ways to begin and conclude essays, while "Paragraphs" concentrates on the importance of well-developed paragraphs and what is necessary to achieve them. "Transitions" concerns the various devices that writers use to move from one idea or section of an essay to the next. Finally, "Effective Sentences" focuses on techniques to make sentences powerful and to create stylistic variety.

"The Language of the Essay," the second major section of the text, includes a chapter on diction and tone and one on figurative language. "Diction and Tone" shows how carefully writers choose words either to convey exact meanings or to be purposefully suggestive. In addition, this chapter shows how the words a writer uses can create a particular tone or relationship between the writer and the reader—one of irony, for example, or humor or great seriousness. "Figurative Language" concentrates on the usefulness of the special devices of language—such as simile, metaphor, and personification—that add richness and depth to writing.

The final section of *Models for Writers*, "Types of Essays," includes chapters on the various types of writing most often required of college writing students: "Illustration" (how to use examples to illustrate a point or idea); "Narration" (how to tell a story or give an account of an event); "Description" (how to present a verbal picture); "Process Analysis" (how to explain how something is done or happens); "Definition" (how to explain what something is); "Division and Classification" (how to divide a subject into its parts and place items into appropriate categories); "Comparison and Contrast" (how to demonstrate likenesses and differences); "Cause and Effect" (how to explain the causes of an event or the effects of an action); and "Argument" (how to use reason and logic to persuade someone to your way of thinking). These types of writing are referred to as *rhetorical patterns.*

Studying the rhetorical patterns and practicing using them are very important in any effort to broaden one's writing skills. In *Models for Writers* we look at each pattern separately; we believe this is the simplest and most effective way to introduce them. However, this does not mean that a well-written essay is necessarily one that chooses a single pattern and sticks to it exclusively and rigidly. Confining oneself to comparison and contrast throughout an entire essay, for instance, might prove impractical and may yield a strained, unnatural piece of writing. In fact, it is often best to use a single pattern to organize your essay and then to use other patterns as your material dictates. When you read the student essays that follow, notice how, for example, Trena Isley's essay is basically a narrative but also includes comparison and contrast. James Duffy's essay is an argumentative one that makes its point with strong illustrations and vivid narrative examples. As you read the model essays in this text, you will find that in the service of the dominant pattern a good many of them utilize a combination of other patterns.

Combining rhetorical patterns is probably not something you want to plan or even think about when you first tackle a writing assignment. Rather, such combinations will develop naturally as you organize, draft, and revise your materials. Such combinations of patterns will also enhance the interest and impact of your writing.

All of the chapters are organized in the same way. Each opens with an explanation of the element or principle under consideration. These introductions are intended to be brief, clear, and practical. Here you will also usually find one or more short examples of the feature or principle being studied. Following the introduction, we present three or four model essays (Chapter 18, with nine essays, is an exception), each with a brief introduction of its own, providing information about the author and directing your attention to the way the essay demonstrates the featured writing technique. Every essay is followed by study materials in four parts: *Questions for Study and Discussion, Vocabulary, Classroom Activity,* and *Suggested Writing Assignments.*

Models for Writers, then, provides information, instruction, and practice in writing essays. By reading carefully and thoughtfully and by applying what you learn, you can gain more control over your own writing. Trena Isley, Zoe Ockenga, Carrie White, and James

Duffy, four of our own writing students at the University of Vermont, found this to be true, and their work is a good example of what can be achieved by studying models.

Four Model Student Essays

After reading several personal narratives — Helen Keller's "The Most Important Day" and Dick Gregory's "Shame" in particular — and discussing in general significant changes in life that are signaled by memorable events, Trena Isley decided to write a narrative of her own. Trena focused on the day that she told her father she no longer wished to participate in sports. Recalling that event led her to reconsider her childhood experiences of running track. Trena welcomed the opportunity to write about this difficult period in her life. As she tried to make her dilemma clear to her classmates, she found that she clarified it for herself. She came to a deeper understanding of her own fears and feelings about striking out on her own and ultimately to a better appreciation of her difficult relationship with her father. What follows is the final draft of Trena's essay.

On the Sidelines

Trena Isley

Point of View: First person

It was a Monday afternoon, and I was finally home from track practice. The coach had just told me that I had a negative attitude and should contemplate why I was on the team. My father greeted me in the living room.

"Hi honey. How was practice?"

"Not good, Dad. Listen, I don't want to do this anymore. I hate the track team."

Opening: critical dialogue between writer and her father highlights conflict

"What do you mean *hate*?"

"This constant pressure is making me crazy."

"How so?"

"It's just not fun anymore."

"Well, I'll have to talk to Coach —"

"No! You're supposed to be my father, not my coach."

"I am your father, but I'm sure . . ."

"Just let me do what I want. You've had your turn!"

He just let out a sigh and left the room. Later he told me that I was wasting my "God-given abilities." The funny part was that none of my father's anger hit me at first. All I knew was that I was free.

My troubles began the summer I was five years old. It was late June, and the sticky weather had already settled over Vermont. My father was yanking my hair into a ponytail in preparation for the first day of the summer track and field season.

Flashback: writer returns to beginning of her story and sets context

As our truck pulled into the upper parking lot I could look down on the scene below. The other kids resembled ants against the massive black track, all of them parading around with no obvious purpose. I stepped out of the truck, never taking my eyes off the colony beneath me, and fell. As I stood there, both knees skinned and bleeding, the last thing I wanted to do was join the other kids. My father quickly hushed my sobs and escorted me down into the throng of children. Around the track we ran, each step stinging my knees as the water in my eyes contin- ued to rise. Through blurred vision I could see my father on the sidelines, holding his stopwatch in one hand and wearing a grin from ear to ear.

Echo of Title

For most of my childhood I was content to let my father make me a track star. As my collec- tion of blue ribbons grew, I was perfect in my father's eyes. By the time I was ten, college

Organiza- tion: chrono- logical sequence of events

coaches were joking with me about scholarships. So I continued to run. It was fun in the beginning, and Dad always had nice things to say about me. I can remember him talking to my grandmother over the holidays: "Trena's got a real shot at winning the 200 meters at the state meet this year, but she's got to train hard."

I began to alter my opinion of competition as I entered my teenage years. At this point I wasn't having fun anymore. My father took me to the gym for "training" sessions four days a week before school. I knew my friends weren't getting up at 5:00 a.m., so I didn't understand why I had to. At thirteen years old all I wanted was to be considered normal. I wanted to fit in with the other kids and do regular teenage stuff.

My father didn't understand my waning interest in track. He still looked forward to my competitions and practice every morning. When my alarm would go off, I would not get out of bed right away, often claiming that I didn't feel well or pretending to oversleep. I began not winning all or even most of my races. My father pushed me to work harder. He would talk incessantly about other competitors and how often they practiced. He never stopped trying to coax me into practicing by buying me breakfast or taking me out to lunch. He tried endlessly, but I just didn't care about track. I resented him more and more with each attempt. I needed to do something that I was truly interested in. And I needed to do it alone.

Dialogue: shows instead of tells

"Hey Dad, what do you think about me trying out for the school play this term? I was told I have a good shot at a part."

"I don't think you'd have time. Track practice is every day isn't it? I've been talking with the coach, and he says the team is looking strong this year. He tells me the state meet should be tough, though. Do you need new spikes?"

"No, Dad. The ones I have are fine, but I just thought . . ."

"Great, 'cause you'll need good spikes when you run on some of those dirt tracks."

So that was that. It got so bad that my father didn't hear me unless "track" was in the sentence. I was starving for my own identity. The mold "Trena the track star" that my father had created for me was crumbling rapidly. Sadly, he wasn't noticing; however, I knew I wanted to quit the track team, but I was afraid that if I gave up sports there would be nothing left for me to be good at. The worst thing someone could be in my family was average.

When I finally did it—told my father the pressure was making me crazy and that I was quitting—I felt three times lighter. I came to find out, though, that this freedom did have its price. I got to sleep late, but Dad didn't ask me how my day was anymore. He didn't ask me much of anything except when I'd be home at night and whom I was going out with. He wasn't my coach anymore—he was my warden. Every night I was grilled for details. He needed to know everyone I was with and what we were doing. When I'd tell him, he never seemed to believe me. My dreams of living on a farm and building my own house were laughed at. In the same conversation my younger sister could tell my parents that she was hoping to work for the United Nations, and she would be

Return to Opening Scene

applauded. The shift had been made. I gained my
personal and creative independence but lost a
parent.

Organiza-
tion: time
reference

It has been five years since I retired from
athletics and slipped out of my father's graces.
Presently my father and I do speak, but it's all
on the surface. I now realize that I didn't need
the extra morning practices to be good at some-

Ending:
reflections
on mean-
ing of rela-
tionship

thing. This transition was normal and healthy. It
happened quickly, so quickly that I left my father holding the remains of our relationship. The
problem was that neither of us bothered to rein-
vent one for our future as adults. It's not hard
for me to understand why we still have a hard
time relating to each other. We really don't know
each other very well.

Eventually we'll be able to talk about my
quitting track as just that, a small incident
that marked the turn of a page in both our lives.
We both have unresolved feelings that are standing in the way of our friendship. I need to stop
blaming him for my blemished self-image, and he
needs to realize that I can succeed without his
coaching. In the end we both have to forgive each
other.

For an assignment following the James Lincoln Collier reading in
the chapter on thesis, Zoe Ockenga tackled the topic of anxiety. In
her first draft, she explored the anxiety she felt the night before her
first speech in a public speaking class and how in confronting that
anxiety she benefited from the course. Zoe read her paper aloud in
class, and other students had an opportunity to ask her questions and
to offer constructive criticism. Several students suggested that she
might want to relate her experiences to those that Collier recounts in
his essay. Another asked if she had other examples that she could include to bolster the point she wanted to make. At this point in the

discussion, Zoe recalled a phone call she had had with her mother regarding her mother's indecision about accepting a new job. The thought of working outside the home for the first time in more than twenty years brought out her mother's worst fears and literally threatened to keep her from accepting the challenge. Armed with these valuable suggestions, Zoe went back to work. In subsequent drafts, Zoe worked on the Collier connection and developed the example of the anxiety surrounding her mother's decision. What follows is the final draft of Zoe's essay, which incorporates the changes she made based on the peer evaluation of her first draft.

The Excuse "Not To"

Zoe Ockenga

Title: indicates main idea of the essay

I cannot imagine anything worse than the nervous, anxious feeling I got the night before my first speech in public speaking class last spring semester. The knots in my stomach were so fierce that I racked my brain for an excuse to give the teacher so that I would not have to go through with the dreaded assignment. Once in bed, I lay awake thinking of all the mistakes that I might make while standing alone in front of my classmates. I spent the rest of the night tossing and turning, frustrated that now, on top of my panic, I would have to give my speech with huge bags under my eyes.

Beginning: captures readers' attention

Anxiety is an intense emotion that can strike at any time or place, before a simple daily activity or a life-changing decision. For some people, anxiety is only a minor interference in the process of achieving a goal. For others, it can be a force that is impossible to overcome. In these instances, anxiety can prevent the accomplishment of lifelong hopes and dreams. Avoiding the causes of stress or fear can make us feel secure and safe. Avoiding anxiety, however,

Thesis — may mean forfeiting a once-in-a-lifetime window of opportunity. Confronting anxiety can make for a richer, more fulfilling existence.

First Example: continues story introduced in opening paragraph to support thesis

    The next day I trudged to class and sat on the edge of my seat until I could not stand the tension any longer. At this point, I forced myself to raise my hand to volunteer simply to end my suffering. As I walked to the front of the room and assumed my position at the podium, the twenty-five faces of the classmates I had been sitting beside a minute ago suddenly seemed like fifty. I probably fumbled over a word or two as I discussed the harmful aspects of animal testing, but my mistakes were not nearly as severe as I had imagined the night before. Less than five minutes later the whole nightmare was over, and it had been much less painful than I had anticipated. As I sat down with a huge sigh of relief to listen to the next victim stumble repeatedly over how to milk dairy cows, I realized that I had not been half bad.

    Although I still dreaded giving the next series of speeches, I eventually became more accustomed to speaking in front of my peers. I would still have to force myself to volunteer, secretly hoping the teacher would forget about me, but the audience that once seemed large and forbidding eventually became smaller and much more human. A speech class is something that I would never have taken if it had not been a requirement, and I can honestly say that I am better off because of it. I was forced to grapple with my anxiety and in the process became a stronger, more self-confident individual. Before this class I had been able to hide out in large lectures, never offering any comment or insights. For the first time at college I was forced to participate, and I realized that I could effectively speak in front of strangers and, more importantly, that I had something to say.

The insomnia-inducing anticipation of giving a speech was a type of anxiety that I had to overcome in order to meet my requirements for graduation. In the short essay "Anxiety: Challenge by Another Name" by James Lincoln Collier, the author tells of his own struggles with anxiety. He tells of one particular event that happened between his sophomore and junior years in college when he was asked to spend a summer in Argentina with a good friend. He writes about how he felt after he made his decision:

> I had turned down something I wanted to do because I was scared, and had ended up feeling depressed. I stayed that way for a long time. And it didn't help when I went back to college in the fall to discover that Ted and his friend had had a terrific time. (27)

The proposition of going to Argentina was an extremely difficult one for Collier as it meant abandoning the comfortable routine of the past and venturing completely out of his element. Although the idea of the trip was exciting, the author could not bring himself to choose the summer in Argentina because of his uncertainties.

The summer abroad that Collier denied himself in his early twenties left him with such a

Second Example: cites essay from Models for Writers *to support thesis*

feeling of regret that he vowed to change his approach on life. From then on, he faced challenges that made him uncomfortable and was able to accomplish feats he would never have dreamed possible: interviewing celebrities, traveling extensively through Europe, parachuting, and even learning to ski at age forty. Collier emphasizes that he was able to make his life fulfilling and exciting by adhering to his belief that anxiety cannot be stifled by avoidance; it can only be stifled by confrontation (28).

Third Example: introduces mother's dilemma

Anxiety prevents many individuals from accepting life's challenges and changes. My own mother is currently struggling with such a dilemma. At age fifty-three, having never had a career outside the home, my mother has been recommended to manage a new art gallery. The River Gallery, as it will be called, will be opening in our town of Ipswich, Massachusetts, this spring. An avid collector and art lover as well as a budding potter, my mother would, I believe, be exceptional at this job.

Anticipating this new opportunity and responsibility has caused my mother great anxiety. Re-entering the workforce after over twenty years is as frightening for my mother as the trip to Argentina was to Collier. When I recently discussed the job prospect with my mother, she was negative and full of doubt. "There is no way I could ever handle such a responsibility," she commented. "I have no business experience; I would look like a fool if I actually tried to pull something like this off. Besides, I'm sure the artists would never take me seriously." Just as my mother focused on all the possible negative aspects of the opportunity in front of her, Collier questioned the value of his opportunity to spend a summer abroad. He describes having second thoughts about just how exciting the trip would be:

> I had never been very far from New England, and I had been homesick my first few weeks at college. What would it be like in a strange country? What about the language? And besides, I had promised to teach my youngest brother to sail that summer. (27)

Quotation: quotes Collier to help explain mother's indecision

Focusing on all the possible problems accompanying a new opportunity can arouse such a sense of fear that it can overpower the ability to take a risk. Both my mother and Collier found out that dwelling on possible negative outcomes allowed them to ignore the benefits of a new experience and thus maintain their safe current situation.

In an article published in *Cosmopolitan* magazine, Lucinda Bassett, author of "From Panic to Power," relates how anxiety prevented her from achieving her potential at one stage in her life.

Quotation: cites outside source to provide insight into anxiety as an excuse

> My anxiety was my excuse "not to." Not to change careers, not to take risks, I used anxiety to justify my unhappiness and my weakness. [. . .] I see now that I was afraid of the shame of failure and also of the responsibility of success. If I maintained my excuses not to try, then I wouldn't have to face either of these painful issues. (4)

Currently my mother is using anxiety as an excuse "not to." To confront her anxiety and take an opportunity in which there is a possibility of failure as well as success is a true risk. Regardless of the outcome, to even contemplate a new challenge has changed her life. The summer forgone

by Collier roused him to never again pass up an exciting opportunity and thus to live his life to the fullest. Just the thought of taking the gallery position has prompted my mother to contemplate taking evening classes so that if she refuses the offer she may be better prepared for a similar challenge in the future. Although her decision is unresolved, her anxiety has made her realize the possibilities that may be opening for her, whether or not she chooses to take them. If in the end her answer is no, I believe that the lingering feeling of "what if" will cause her to re-evaluate her ex-
Conclusion pectations and goals for her future.

Anxiety can create confidence and optimism or depression, low self-esteem, and regret. The outcome of anxiety is entirely dependent on whether the individual runs from it or embraces it. Some forms of anxiety can be conquered merely by repeating the activity that causes them, such as giving speeches in a public speaking class. Anxiety brought on by unique opportunities or life-changing decisions, such as a summer in a foreign country or a new career, must be harnessed. Opportunities forgone due to anxiety and fear could be the chances of a lifetime. Although the unpleasant feelings that may accompany anxiety may make it initially easier to do nothing, the road not taken will never be forgotten. Anxiety is essentially a blessing in disguise. It is a physical and emotional trigger that tells us when and where there is an opportunity for us to grow and become stronger as human beings.

WORKS CITED

Bassett, Lucinda. "From Panic to Power." 1 Jan.
    1996 <http://nrstglp.djnr.com/cgi-bin/
    DJInteractive?cgi=WEB_FLAT_PAGE&page=
    wrapper/index&NRAUTOLOG=012q9ZtDlrsXv75hb1774
    RXZEwuAAA&NRLBRedirect=nrstag2p&entry_
    point=1>.

Collier, James Lincoln. "Anxiety: Challenge by
    Another Name." Models for Writers. Ed. Al-
    fred Rosa and Paul Eschholz. 6th ed. New
    York: St. Martin's, 1998. 26-29.

Family photographs fascinated Carrie White, and she sought in one of her essays to explain why she valued them so much. She started by making a list of information, memories, and specific family pictures she might include in her essay. Soon Carrie discovered that the items on her list clustered into several key groups that helped explain why she treasured family photographs. She was then able to develop the following preliminary thesis: "Photographs have played an extremely important role in my life by allowing me to learn about my past and to stay connected with my family in the present." This thesis, in turn, helped Carrie decide to organize her examples chronologically. What follows is the final draft of Carrie's essay.

Family Portraits

Carrie White

I haven't always liked photographs. I can
still remember squinting into the sun's glare,
annoyed as my Mom straightened my shirt and said,
"Hold still." Photographs have incredible capabilities: to document history, to tell the absolute truth, to capture a moment. But to me they
mean more. By allowing me to learn about my past   *Thesis: an-*
and that of my family before, during, and after I   *nounces*
was born, photographs have played an extremely   *focus of*
important role in my life. Only recently have I   *essay*

appreciated the immeasurable value of photographs.

*Organi-
zation:
presents
first in a
series of
reasons
why pho-
tographs
are im-
portant*
Photographs have let me know my parents before they were married, as the carefree college
students they were, in love and awaiting the rest
of their lives. I have seen the light blue Volkswagen van my dad used to take down the coast of
California when he went surfing, and the silver
dress my mom wore to her senior prom. Through
pictures I am able to witness their wedding,
which has shown me that there is much in their
relationship that goes beyond their children. I
am able to see the look in their eyes as they
hold their first, newborn daughter, as well as my
sister's jealous expression at my birth a few
years later. There is something almost magical
about viewing an image of yourself that you are
too young to remember, such as a second birthday
or a first trip to the beach.

*Organi-
zation:
second
reason*
Photographs can take you to places you've
never been and times before you were born. I can
visit my grandmother's childhood home in Vienna,
Austria, and walk down the high-ceilinged, iron
staircase by looking through the small, white
album my Grandma treasures. I also know of the
tomboy she once was, wearing Lederhosen instead
of the Dirndls worn by her friends. I have seen
the beautiful young woman who traveled with the
Red Cross during the war, uncertain of her future. It is the photograph that rests in a red
leather frame on my Grandma's nightstand that has
allowed me to meet the man she would later marry.
He died before I was born, but I've been told
that I would have loved his calm manner, and I
can see for myself his gentle smile and tranquil
expression.

Photographs are always honest. While they may not always document an image as it is remembered, they usually reflect a scene or situation accurately. School portraits can be a painful reminder of the past, but they undoubtedly document growth and change. I distinctly remember school portrait day each year in elementary school. I can still hear the "One-two, one-two-three . . . smile" of Sterling, the photographer who dutifully came back year after year to take our pictures, always telling each of us how much we'd grown. Each portrait of mine represents a phase in my life, often one that I'd otherwise forget about. Catching a glimpse of the faded green corduroy jumper in my second-grade school picture reminds me of the time I was first allowed to dress myself each day, wearing the same outfit three days a week if I chose to do so. Most of us probably have certain periods in our lives which make us shake our heads when we reflect on them. Whether it is an awkward growth phase or a unique fashion statement, a picture shows you as you were then and reminds you of the progress you've made.

The summer after I was in fifth grade my family went to Greece. My Mom carefully documented the trip and took her camera wherever we went. There is not a single picture in which my older sister, Jamie, is smiling. Instead she displays an unpleasant scowl in each one. I distinctly remember that "non-smiling" stage in her life, when she was a teenager, unsure of the way she felt about anything. While she may not like to remember that particular time, the pictures serve as an honest reminder.

Often, photographs are all that there is to go on. I never realized this until coming to

Organization: third reason

Paragraph Development: examples support topic sentence

Organization: fourth reason

college here in Vermont, over five thousand miles
from home. At first I felt like I was living in
two completely separate worlds. The only bridge I
had to connect the two places was photography. It
was very important to me for the people at college to know my family and friends at home, and
for everyone at home to know my friends here at
school. Documenting the first snowfall of freshman year on film, for which purpose I excitedly
ran outside in my pajamas, allowed my family at
home to feel as if they had experienced it, too.
Similarly, showing my friends at school photographs of my dad's sailboat or the white sand
of Lanikai Beach gives them an idea of what my
home is like. I have done my best to capture both
places through pictures, and by sharing them I
feel as though my worlds have been brought closer
together. When my family came to Vermont for
Christmas this year, my friends told me that my
family was "just as they had imagined from the
pictures."

Examples: support topic sentence of paragraph

Photographs have an incredible capacity to
capture mood. As much as you are expected to
smile when being photographed, if you don't feel
like it or aren't in the mood, it is certain to
be evident when the film is developed. Further,
the overall tone of a gathering of people or a
situation can be shown through a photo. Just as
pictures can show emotions, they can also capture
chaos, tranquility, or bliss. Each year in elementary school my older sister and I would participate in the May Day Pageant. We always had to
wear an outfit that matched that of our classmates, as well as a head lei made out of plumeria
flowers. On such mornings my Mom would always
have Jamie and me stand against a wall in the en-

Organization: fifth reason

tryway of our house, and she would take our picture. For some reason, the chaotic events of such
mornings almost always resulted in at least one
of us being in tears. But my Mom always insisted
on getting our picture anyway. While her coaxing
or my Dad's attempts to make us laugh would usually make both of us attempt a feeble smile, each
of the photos shows at least one red, tear-
streaked face.

Some of my most prized possessions are photo
albums, not because of the material objects they
contain, but because of all they represent. Photographs have documented my life and serve as reminders of so many things I have done, people
I've met, and places I've been. They capture my
birthday party in first grade, my awkward stage
in sixth grade, and my first experience making a
snowball, and they allow me to share these moments with the people in my life—those I grew up
with, as well as those who came later. When I
look at my photo albums, I well up with an overwhelming feeling of both pride in all I have accomplished and sadness that so much of my life
has passed, leaving little behind but the photos.

Conclusion: summa- rizes the reasons for valu- ing pho- tographs, especially the way they cap- ture the past

One of the few truly irreplaceable things in
this world is the past. The more time goes by, the
fainter memories and feelings become. So much can
be learned from our pasts if we will only recollect
them. Old mistakes can be avoided. Experiences and
their lessons can be remembered. By sharing our experiences with others, we can aid in their understanding of us, and shared memories grant us a deep
and unique understanding of those we love.

The past should never be forgotten. Photographs help us remember.

James Duffy's assignment was to write a thesis-driven argument, and, like Trena and Carrie, he was free to choose his own topic. He knew from past experience that to write a good essay he would have to write on a topic he cared about. He also knew that he should allow himself a reasonable amount of time to find the topic and to gather his ideas. A pre-medical student, James found himself reading the essays in *Models for Writers* with a scientific bent. He was particularly struck by Barbara Huttmann's essay, "A Crime of Compassion," because it dealt with the issues of the right to die and treating pain in terminally ill patients, issues that he'd be confronting as a doctor.

James began by brainstorming about his topic. He made lists of all the ideas, facts, issues, arguments, opposing arguments, and refutations that came to mind as a result of his own firsthand experiences with the topic. Once he was confident that he had amassed enough information to begin writing, he made a rough outline of an organizational plan that he believed would work well for him. James then wrote a first draft of his essay. Together with his teacher, he examined this draft carefully, assessing how it could be improved.

James wrote this particular essay in the second half of the semester, after he had read a number of model essays and had learned the importance of such matters as good paragraphing, unity, and transitions in his earlier papers. The final draft of James's essay illustrates that he has learned how the parts of a well-written essay fit together and how to make revisions that emulate some of the qualities in the model essays he has read and studied. The following is the final draft of James's essay.

One Dying Wish

James Duffy

Opening: anecdote focuses attention on the problem

It was an interesting summer. I spent most of my time assisting post-doctoral students doing research in Cincinnati. One day I came across a file I will never forget. Within the thick file was the story of a fifty-something cancer patient. The man's cancer had metastasized and now was spread throughout his entire body. Over a period of two months he went under the knife seven

times to repair and remove parts of his battle-
weary body. He endured immeasurable pain. The
final surgery on record was a spinotomy. In an
effort to stop the pain, the man's spinal cord
was intentionally severed.

Terminally ill patients experience in-
tractable pain, and many lose the ability to live
a life that has any real meaning to them. To
force these people to stay alive when they are in
pain and there is no hope for recovery is wrong.
They should have the choice to let nature take
its course. Forcing people to live in pain when
only machines are keeping them alive is unjust.

Thesis: clear statement of position

The hospital I was working at that summer
had a policy that as long as someone was alive,
they would do anything to keep them living. The
terminal cancer patient whose file I stumbled
across fit into this category. He was on nar-
cotics prescribed to alleviate his pain. The
problem was that the doctors could not prescribe
above a certain dosage, a level far below what
was necessary to manage the patient's pain. In
such a situation, the doctors can't raise a dose
because they risk sedating the patient to the
point of heart failure.

Presentation of Opposing Argument

The hospital I was working at had fallen on
hard times; the last thing they needed was to
lose a large malpractice suit. If a doctor pre-
scribes above the highest recommended dosage, his
or her hospital is at risk if the patient dies.
Keeping patients on life support at low dosages,
however, is cruel. The doctors at many hospitals
have their hands tied. They can't give dosages
high enough to treat the pain without putting the
hospital at risk, and the other option, stopping
life support, is forbidden by many hospitals.

When I was fifteen, my Aunt Eileen, who was thirty-four, was diagnosed with a malignant skin cancer. The disease was caught late, and the cancer had metastasized throughout her body. At the time, Eileen had been married for eight years and had a four-year-old daughter and a six-year-old son. They were and are adorable children. When Eileen learned of the disease she was devastated. She loved her husband and children very much and could not bear the thought of not being with them. Eileen fought the disease fiercely. She tried all the conventional treatments available. Her father and brother were both doctors, so she had access to the best possible care, but the disease did not succumb to the treatment. She tried nonconventional methods, seeking out any possible help, but it was too late. The disease had an unshakable grip on her. She had wasted away to below one hundred pounds; a tumor had grown to the size of a grapefruit on her stomach. It was the end, and everyone knew it. Luckily Eileen was able to get into a hospice center. While she was there she was able to make peace with herself and God and die a calm death without pain.

If Eileen had been forced to keep living, her pain undertreated and her body resuscitated again and again, the damage to her and her family would have been enormous. It would have been almost impossible to make peace with herself and God if she had been in pain so intense she couldn't think. The hospice managed the pain and gave her peace a hospital could not have, and helped her and her family avoid the devastating results of a prolonged and painful death.

In "A Crime of Compassion," Barbara Huttmann, a registered nurse, recounts her hospital's disregard for a patient named Mac. Mac's story is one of a prolonged and painful death, without options. Mac came into the hospital with a persistent cough and walked out with a diagnosis of lung cancer. He battled the disease but lost ground fast. Over the course of six months, Mac lost "his youth ... his hair, his bowel and bladder control, and his ability to do the slightest thing for himself." Mac wasted away to a mere sixty pounds. He was in constant pain, which the hospital was unable to manage. His young wife now looked "haggard and beaten." Mac went into arrest three times some days. Every time his wife broke down into tears. The nurses ordered "code blue" every time it happened, and the hospital staff resuscitated Mac. This situation repeated itself for over a month. During one month, Mac was resuscitated fifty-two times. Mac had long ago realized the battle was over. He pleaded with his doctors and nurses to let him die. The problem was that the hospital did not issue no-code orders. A no-code order meant that if Mac went into arrest again they would let him die. Days passed as Barbara, the nurse, pleaded for a no-code order. Each time he went into arrest his wife, Maura, took another step toward becoming psychologically crippled. As Barbara worked to resuscitate Mac she'd look into his eyes as he pleaded for her to stop. Finally, Barbara decided enough was enough. Mac went into arrest and she did not call the Code Blue until she was certain he could not be resuscitated. For granting Mac his dying wish, Barbara was charged with murder (233-36).

Evidence: example from reading

The situation of Mac illustrates the death
many people are forced to endure. These situations constitute an irony in today's society.
Many complain that executions are inhumane or
cruel and unusual. A principle argument of these
people is that the death is not pain free. People
also think that regardless of the situation a patient should not be allowed to die and should
definitely not be medicated to the point of
death. Mac was forced to live on the brink of
dying for over a month, watching as his wife was
also destroyed by his illness. The treatment Mac
received can only be described as inhumane. To
force a man to live in pain when there is no reasonable hope he will ever get better is truly
cruel and unusual. Had Mac the option of a peaceful and pain-free death it would have saved his
wife and himself the pain of being forced to live
on the edge of death for such an extended period
of time. Maura must have looked into Mac's tor-
tured eyes and wondered why he had no choices
concerning his life or death. Any choice would
have been better.

Conclusion: summarizes argument and cites needed actions

Society needs to re-evaluate the right of
the terminally ill to die. Keeping people in agonizing pain for a long period is wrong. Everyone
would agree with that. Many people do not understand, however, that prolonging the life of a
terminally ill patient with unmanageable pain is
the same thing. Laws need to be passed to protect
doctors who accidentally overmedicate a terminally ill patient in the interest of pain management. Patients also deserve the right to
determine if they want to go off life support, no

matter what hospital they are in. Until people
take action to resolve this issue, the terminally
ill will continue to suffer.

WORKS CITED

Huttmann, Barbara. "A Crime of Compassion." Mod-
    els for Writers. Ed. Alfred Rosa and Paul
    Eschholz. 6th ed. New York: St. Martin's,
    1988, 233-36.

The Elements
of the Essay

Thesis

The *thesis* of an essay is its main idea, the point it is trying to make. The thesis is often expressed in a one- or two-sentence statement, although sometimes it is implied or suggested rather than stated directly. The thesis statement determines the content of the essay: everything that the writer says must be logically related to the thesis statement.

Because everything you say in your composition must be logically related to your thesis statement, the thesis statement controls and directs the choices you make about the content of your essay. This does not mean that your thesis statement is a straitjacket. As your essay develops, you may want to modify your thesis statement. This urge is not only acceptable, it is normal. One way to develop a working thesis is to determine a question that you are trying to answer in your paper. A one- or two-sentence answer to this question often produces a tentative thesis statement. For example, one of our students wanted to answer the following question in her essay:

Do men and women have different conversational speaking styles?

Her preliminary answer to this question was this:

Men and women appear to have different objectives when they converse.

After writing two drafts, she modified her thesis to better fit the examples she had gathered:

Very often, conversations between men and women become situations in which the man gives a mini-lecture and the woman unwittingly turns into a captive audience.

The thesis statement should not be confused with a purpose statement. Whereas a thesis statement makes an assertion about your topic, a purpose statement describes what you are trying to do in the paper. Here is an example of a purpose statement:

> I plan to explain the different objectives men and women have when they converse.

A thesis statement should be (1) more general than the ideas and facts used to support it, (2) appropriately focused for the length of your paper, and (3) the most important point you make about your topic. A thesis statement should not be a question, but an assertion — a claim made about a debatable issue that can be supported with evidence.

Another effective strategy for developing a thesis statement is to begin by writing *What I want to say is that . . .*

> *What I want to say is that* unless the university administration enforces its strong anti-hazing policy, the well-being of many of its student-athletes will be endangered.

Later you can delete the formulaic opening, and you will be left with a thesis statement:

> Unless the university administration enforces its strong anti-hazing policy, the well-being of many of its student-athletes will be endangered.

Usually the thesis is presented early in an essay, sometimes in the first sentence. Here are some thesis statements that begin essays:

> One of the most potent elements in body language is eye behavior.
>
> –Flora Davis

> Americans can be divided into three groups — smokers, nonsmokers, and that expanding pack of us who have quit.
>
> –Franklin E. Zimring

> Over the past ten to fifteen years it has become apparent that eating disorders have reached epidemic proportions among adolescents.
>
> –Helen A. Guthrie

Clutter is the disease of American writing. We are a society strangling in unnecessary words, circular construction, pompous frills,
and meaningless jargon.

–William Zinsser

Each of these sentences does what a good thesis statement should
do: it identifies the topic and makes an assertion about it.

Often writers prepare readers for a thesis statement with one or
several sentences that establish a context. Notice in the following example how the author eases the reader into his thesis about television
instead of presenting it abruptly in the first sentence:

With the advent of television, for the first time in history, all
aspects of animal and human life and death, of societal and individual behavior have been condensed on the average to a 19-inch diag-
onal screen and a 30-minute time slot. Television, a unique
medium, claiming to be neither a reality nor art, has become reality
for many of us, particularly for our children who are growing up in
front of it.

–Jerzy Kosinski

On occasion a writer may even purposely delay the presentation
of a thesis until the middle or the end of an essay. If the thesis is controversial or needs extended discussion and illustration, the writer
might present it later to make it easier for the reader to understand
and accept it. Appearing near or at the end of an essay, a thesis also
gains prominence.

Some kinds of writing do not need thesis statements. These include descriptions, narratives, and personal writing such as letters
and diaries. But any essay that seeks to explain or prove a point has a
thesis that is usually set forth in a thesis statement.

The Most Important Day

■ **Helen Keller**

Helen Keller (1880–1968) was afflicted by a disease that left her blind and deaf at the age of eighteen months. With the aid of her teacher, Anne Sullivan, she was able to overcome her severe handicaps, to graduate from Radcliffe College, and to lead a productive and challenging adult life. In the following selection from her autobiography, The Story of My Life *(1902), Keller tells of the day she first met Anne Sullivan, a day she regarded as the most important in her life. As you read, note that Keller states her thesis in the first paragraph and that the remaining paragraphs maintain unity by emphasizing the importance of the day her teacher arrived, even though they deal with the days and weeks following.*

FOR YOUR JOURNAL

Imagine what your life would be like without the use of your eyes and your ears. What would your other senses be able to tell you? Try to imagine how you would communicate with others.

The most important day I remember in all my life is the one on which my teacher, Anne Mansfield Sullivan, came to me. I am filled with wonder when I consider the immeasurable contrast between the two lives which it connects. It was the third of March, 1887, three months before I was seven years old.   1

On the afternoon of that eventful day, I stood on the porch, dumb, expectant. I guessed vaguely from my mother's signs and from the hurrying to and fro in the house that something unusual was about to happen, so I went to the door and waited on the steps. The afternoon sun penetrated the mass of honeysuckle that covered the porch and fell on my upturned face. My fingers lingered almost unconsciously on the familiar leaves and blossoms which had just come forth to greet the sweet southern spring. I did not know what the future held of marvel or surprise for me. Anger and bitterness had preyed upon me continually for weeks and a deep languor had succeeded this passionate struggle.   2

Have you ever been at sea in a dense fog, when it seemed as if a 3
tangible white darkness shut you in, and the great ship, tense and
anxious, groped her way toward the shore with plummet and sounding-
line, and you waited with beating heart for something to happen? I
was like that ship before my education began, only I was without
compass or sounding-line, and had no way of knowing how near the
harbor was. "Light! give me light!" was the wordless cry of my soul,
and the light of love shone on me in that very hour.

I felt approaching footsteps. I stretched out my hand as I sup- 4
posed to my mother. Someone took it, and I was caught up and held
close in the arms of her who had come to reveal all things to me, and,
more than all things else, to love me.

The morning after my teacher came she led me into her room and 5
gave me a doll. The little blind children at the Perkins Institution had
sent it and Laura Bridgman had dressed it; but I did not know this
until afterward. When I had played with it a little while, Miss
Sullivan slowly spelled into my hand the word "d-o-l-l." I was at
once interested in this finger play and tried to imitate it. When I
finally succeeded in making the letters correctly I was flushed with
childish pleasure and pride. Running downstairs to my mother I held
up my hand and made the letters for doll. I did not know that I was
spelling a word or even that words existed; I was simply making my
fingers go in monkeylike imitation. In the days that followed I
learned to spell in this uncomprehending way a great many words,
among them *pin, hat, cup* and a few verbs like *sit, stand,* and *walk.*
But my teacher had been with me several weeks before I understood
that everything has a name.

One day, while I was playing with my new doll, Miss Sullivan 6
put my big rag doll into my lap also, spelled "d-o-l-l" and tried to
make me understand that "d-o-l-l" applied to both. Earlier in the day
we had had a tussle over the words "m-u-g" and "w-a-t-e-r." Miss
Sullivan had tried to impress it upon me that "m-u-g" is *mug* and
that "w-a-t-e-r" is *water,* but I persisted in confounding the two. In
despair she had dropped the subject for the time, only to renew it at
the first opportunity. I became impatient at her repeated attempts
and, seizing the new doll, I dashed it upon the floor. I was keenly
delighted when I felt the fragments of the broken doll at my feet.
Neither sorrow nor regret followed my passionate outburst. I had not
loved the doll. In the still, dark world in which I lived there was no
strong sentiment or tenderness. I felt my teacher sweep the fragments
to one side of the hearth, and I had a sense of satisfaction that the

cause of my discomfort was removed. She brought me my hat, and I knew I was going out into the warm sunshine. This thought, if a wordless sensation may be called a thought, made me hop and skip with pleasure.

We walked down the path to the well-house, attracted by the fra- 7 grance of the honeysuckle with which it was covered. Someone was drawing water and my teacher placed my hand under the spout. As the cool stream gushed over one hand she spelled into the other the word *water*, first slowly, then rapidly. I stood still, my whole attention fixed upon the motions of her fingers. Suddenly I felt a misty consciousness as of something forgotten — a thrill of returning thought; and somehow the mystery of language was revealed to me. I knew then that "w-a-t-e-r" meant the wonderful cool something that was flowing over my hand. The living word awakened my soul, gave it light, hope, joy, set it free! There were barriers still, it is true, but barriers that could in time be swept away.

I left the well-house eager to learn. Everything had a name, and 8 each name gave birth to a new thought. As we returned to the house every object which I touched seemed to quiver with life. That was because I saw everything with the strange, new sight that had come to me. On entering the door I remembered the doll I had broken. I felt my way to the hearth and picked up the pieces. I tried vainly to put them together. Then my eyes filled with tears; for I realized what I had done, and for the first time I felt repentance and sorrow.

I learned a great many new words that day. I do not remember 9 what they all were; but I do know that *mother, father, sister, teacher* were among them — words that were to make the world blossom for me, "like Aaron's rod, with flowers." It would have been difficult to find a happier child than I was as I lay in my crib at the close of that eventful day and lived over the joys it had brought me, and for the first time longed for a new day to come.

QUESTIONS FOR STUDY AND DISCUSSION

1. What is Keller's thesis in this essay? What question do you think Keller is trying to answer? How does this question help focus her subject? Does her thesis answer her question?

2. What is Keller's purpose in this essay? (Glossary: *Purpose*)

3. What was Keller's state of mind before Anne Sullivan arrived to help her? To what does she compare herself? (Glossary: *Analogy*) How effective is this comparison? Explain.

4. Why was the realization that everything has a name important to Keller?

5. How was the "mystery of language" (7) revealed to Keller? What were the consequences of this new understanding of the nature of language for her?

6. Keller narrates the events of the day Sullivan arrived (2–4), the morning after she arrived (5), and one day several weeks after her arrival (6–9). Describe what happens on each day, and explain how these separate incidents support Keller's thesis.

VOCABULARY

Refer to your dictionary to define the following words as they are used in this selection. Then use each word in a sentence of your own.

dumb (2)   plummet (3)
preyed (2)   tussle (6)
languor (2)   vainly (8)
passionate (2)

CLASSROOM ACTIVITY USING THESIS

One effective way of focusing on your subject is to brainstorm a list of specific questions about it at the start. This strategy has a number of advantages. Each question narrows the general subject area, suggesting a more manageable essay. Also, simply phrasing your topic as a question gives you a starting point; your work has focus and direction from the outset. Finally, a one- or two-sentence answer to your question often provides you with a preliminary thesis statement.

To test this strategy, develop a list of five questions about the subject of "recycling paper waste on campus." To get you started, here is one possible question: Should students be required to recycle paper waste?

1. _____

2. _____

3. _____

4. _____

5. _____

SUGGESTED WRITING ASSIGNMENTS

1. Think about an important day in your own life. Using the thesis statement "The most important day of my life was _____," write an essay in which you show the significance of that day by recounting and explaining the events that took place like Keller does in her essay.

2. For many people around the world, the life of Helen Keller is a symbol of what an individual can achieve despite seemingly insurmountable disabilities. Her achievements have also inspired many who have no disabilities, leading them to believe that they can accomplish more than they ever thought possible. Consider the role of disabled people in our society, develop an appropriate thesis, and write an essay on the topic.

Anxiety: Challenge by Another Name

■ **James Lincoln Collier**

James Lincoln Collier is a freelance writer with more than six hundred articles to his credit. He was born in New York in 1928 and graduated from Hamilton College in 1950. Among his published books are many works of fiction, including novels for young adults. His nonfiction writing has often focused on American music, particularly jazz. Collier has produced biographies of Louis Armstrong, Duke Ellington, and Benny Goodman, but his best-known book is The Making of Jazz: A Comprehensive History *(1978), still regarded as the best general history of the subject. He has added* Jazz: The American Theme Song *(1995) and* Jazz: An American Saga *(1997) to his list of publications. With his son Christopher he has written a number of history books including* A Century of Immigration: 1820–1924 *(2000) and* The Civil War *(2000). As you read the following essay, pay particular attention to where Collier places his thesis. Note also how his thesis statement identifies the topic (anxiety) and makes an assertion about it (that it can have a positive impact on our lives).*

FOR YOUR JOURNAL

Many people tend to associate anxiety with stress and to think of it as a negative thing. Are there good kinds of anxiety, too? Provide an example of anxiety that has been beneficial to you or to someone you know.

Between my sophomore and junior years at college, a chance came up for me to spend the summer vacation working on a ranch in Argentina. My roommate's father was in the cattle business, and he wanted Ted to see something of it. Ted said he would go if he could take a friend, and he chose me.

The idea of spending two months on the fabled Argentine Pampas was exciting. Then I began having second thoughts. I had never been very far from New England, and I had been homesick my first few weeks at college. What would it be like in a strange country? What about the language? And besides, I had promised to teach my younger brother to sail that summer. The more I thought about it, the more the prospect daunted me. I began waking up nights in a sweat.

In the end I turned down the proposition. As soon as Ted asked 3 somebody else to go, I began kicking myself. A couple of weeks later I went home to my old summer job, unpacking cartons at the local supermarket, feeling very low. I had turned down something I wanted to do because I was scared, and had ended up feeling depressed. I stayed that way for a long time. And it didn't help when I went back to college in the fall to discover that Ted and his friend had had a terrific time.

In the long run that unhappy summer taught me a valuable les- 4 son out of which I developed a rule for myself: *do what makes you anxious; don't do what makes you depressed.*

I am not, of course, talking about severe states of anxiety or de- 5 pression, which require medical attention. What I mean is that kind of anxiety we call stage fright, butterflies in the stomach, a case of nerves—the feelings we have at a job interview, when we're giving a big party, when we have to make an important presentation at the office. And the kind of depression I am referring to is that downhearted feeling of the blues, when we don't seem to be interested in anything, when we can't get going and seem to have no energy.

I was confronted by this sort of situation toward the end of my 6 senior year. As graduation approached, I began to think about taking a crack at making my living as a writer. But one of my professors was urging me to apply to graduate school and aim at a teaching career.

I wavered. The idea of trying to live by writing was scary—a lot 7 more scary than spending a summer on the Pampas, I thought. Back and forth I went, making my decision, unmaking it. Suddenly, I realized that every time I gave up the idea of writing, that sinking feeling went through me; it gave me the blues.

The thought of graduate school wasn't what depressed me. It was 8 giving up on what deep in my gut I really wanted to do. Right then I learned another lesson. To avoid that kind of depression meant, inevitably, having to endure a certain amount of worry and concern.

The great Danish philosopher Søren Kierkegaard believed that 9 anxiety always arises when we confront the possibility of our own development. It seems to be a rule of life that you can't advance without getting that old, familiar, jittery feeling.

Even as children we discover this when we try to expand our-   10
selves by, say, learning to ride a bike or going out for the school play.
Later in life we get butterflies when we think about having that first
child, or uprooting the family from the old hometown to find a better
opportunity halfway across the country. Any time, it seems, that we
set out aggressively to get something we want, we meet up with anxiety. And it's going to be our traveling companion, at least part of the
way, into any new venture.

When I first began writing magazine articles, I was frequently re-   11
quired to interview big names—people like Richard Burton, Joan
Rivers, sex authority William Masters, baseball-great Dizzy Dean.
Before each interview I would get butterflies and my hands would
shake.

At the time, I was doing some writing about music. And one per-   12
son I particularly admired was the great composer Duke Ellington.
Onstage and on television, he seemed the very model of the confident, sophisticated man of the world. Then I learned that Ellington
still got stage fright. If the highly honored Duke Ellington, who had
appeared on the bandstand some 10,000 times over 30 years, had
anxiety attacks, who was I to think I could avoid them?

I went on doing those frightening interviews, and one day, as I   13
was getting onto a plane for Washington to interview columnist
Joseph Alsop, I suddenly realized to my astonishment that I was
looking forward to the meeting. What had happened to those butterflies?

Well, in truth, they were still there, but there were fewer of them.   14
I had benefited, I discovered, from a process psychologists call "extinction." If you put an individual in an anxiety-provoking situation
often enough, he will eventually learn that there isn't anything to be
worried about.

Which brings us to a corollary to my basic rule: *you'll never elimi-*   15
nate anxiety by avoiding the things that caused it. I remember how
my son Jeff was when I first began to teach him to swim at the lake
cottage where we spent our summer vacations. He resisted, and when
I got him into the water he sank and sputtered and wanted to quit.
But I was insistent. And by summer's end he was splashing around
like a puppy. He had "extinguished" his anxiety the only way he
could—by confronting it.

The problem, of course, is that it is one thing to urge somebody   16
else to take on those anxiety-producing challenges; it is quite another
to get ourselves to do it.

Some years ago I was offered a writing assignment that would re- 17 quire three months of travel through Europe. I had been abroad a couple of times on the usual "If it's Tuesday this must be Belgium" trips, but I hardly could claim to know my way around the continent. Moreover, my knowledge of foreign languages was limited to a little college French.

I hesitated. How would I, unable to speak the language, totally 18 unfamiliar with local geography or transportation systems, set up interviews and do research? It seemed impossible, and with considerable regret I sat down to write a letter begging off. Halfway through, a thought—which I subsequently made into another corollary to my basic rule—ran through my mind: *you can't learn if you don't try*. So I accepted the assignment.

There were some bad moments. But by the time I had finished 19 the trip I was an experienced traveler. And ever since, I have never hesitated to head for even the most exotic of places, without guides or even advanced bookings, confident that somehow I will manage.

The point is that the new, the different, is almost by definition 20 scary. But each time you try something, you learn, and as the learning piles up, the world opens to you.

I've made parachute jumps, learned to ski at 40, flown up the 21 Rhine in a balloon. And I know I'm going to go on doing such things. It's not because I'm braver or more daring than others. I'm not. But I don't let the butterflies stop me from doing what I want. Accept anxiety as another name for challenge and you can accomplish wonders.

QUESTIONS FOR STUDY AND DISCUSSION

1. What is Collier's thesis in this essay? Based on your own experiences, do you think that Collier's thesis is a valid one? Explain.

2. What is the process known to psychologists as "extinction"?

3. What caused Collier to come up with his basic rule for himself: "Do what makes you anxious; don't do what makes you depressed" (4)? (Glossary: *Cause and Effect*) How did he develop the two corollaries to his basic rule? How do the basic rule and the two corollaries prepare you for his thesis?

4. What do you think Collier's purpose was in writing this essay? (Glossary: *Purpose*) Explain.

5. Identify the figure of speech that Collier uses toward the end of paragraph 10. (Glossary: *Figure of Speech*)

6. Explain how paragraphs 17–19 function within the context of Collier's essay. (Glossary: *Illustration*)

VOCABULARY

Refer to your dictionary to define the following words as they are used in this selection. Then use each word in a sentence of your own.

daunted (2)   butterflies (5)
proposition (3)   crack (6)
anxiety (5)   venture (10)
depression (5)   corollary (15)

CLASSROOM ACTIVITY USING THESIS

A good thesis statement identifies the topic and makes an assertion about it. Evaluate each of the following sentences as a thesis statement, and explain why each one either works or doesn't work as one.

1. Americans are suffering from overwork.
2. Life is indeed precious, and I believe the death penalty helps to affirm this fact.
3. Birthday parties are loads of fun.
4. New York is a city of sounds: muted sounds and shrill sounds; shattering sounds and soothing sounds; urgent sounds and aimless sounds.
5. Everyone is talking about the level of violence in American society.
6. Neighborhoods are often assigned human characteristics, one of which is a life cycle: they have a birth, a youth, a middle age, and an old age.

SUGGESTED WRITING ASSIGNMENTS

1. Building on your own experiences and the reading you have done, write an essay in which you use as your thesis either Collier's basic rule or one of his corollaries to that basic rule.
2. Write an essay in which you use any one of the following as your thesis:

Good manners are a thing of the past.
We need rituals in our lives.
To tell a joke well is an art.
We are a drug-dependent society.
Losing weight is a breeze.

Why "Model Minority" Doesn't Fit

■ **Diane Yen-Mei Wong**

Diane Yen-Mei Wong writes about Asian American issues in a column that appears in the Hawaii Herald *and has edited* Making Waves: An Anthology of Writings by and about Asian American Women *(1989). She currently lives in Oakland, California. In the following selection, which appeared in* USA Weekend *in January 1994, she discusses the dangers of stereotypes and how personal experience has forced her to re-evaluate her own ethnic community. Wong begins her essay with an extended example in which she explains the circumstances of the murder of her best friend's mother. This example sets the context for her somewhat surprising thesis about images of Asian American communities.*

FOR YOUR JOURNAL

What images do you have of Asian American communities? On what experiences do you base your impressions? Do you think that the images you have are shared by your community at large?

I stopped by a peaceful lake on one of Seattle's rare sunny days to   1
watch a wonderfully multiracial, multiethnic parade of people walk, jog, bicycle and skate along the bike path. For them, life looked good and the whole weekend lay ahead. The irony did not escape me.

Just a few hours before, I had been inside a windowless court-   2
room listening to a judge render a final sentence of 70 years in prison to a Vietnamese-American man, Dung Hoang Le, barely out of his teens. He had fatally stabbed my best friend's mother, Mayme Lui, a petite septuagenarian Chinese-American widow. He had mutilated her body to wrench off a jade bracelet, then attempted to extort money from her family as he led them to believe she was still alive.

He needed money fast. He had just wrecked his cousin's car and   3
discovered his girlfriend was pregnant. Without a job or marketable skills, he was at a critical juncture. Rather than earn money through hard work, he chose crime. This decision changed our lives forever.

I used to see my friend's mother whenever I was visiting in town;   4
we laughed and talked and ate. Now I try to comfort the family as
they negotiate their lives around her absence. I am haunted by frequent nightmares of the terror and pain she must have felt. But this
man's act also has compelled me to rethink how I view my own community of Asian Americans.

For more than two decades, I have argued that the diverse Asian-   5
American community cannot be stereotyped. One of the most trou-
bling and persistent images is that we are a "model minority," people
who have succeeded when other people of color have not. We are held
up as proof that racial discrimination either does not exist or, if it does,
is not much of a handicap. I have argued that this stereotype negates the
existence of the large segments of our ethnic communities that live in
poverty, have little or no education, and work in sweatshops for less
than the minimum wage or in family-owned businesses for no wages.

Violence in the Asian-American community, like violence in   6
many other communities, is growing at such an alarming rate that
several cities, including Seattle, have assigned special units to investigate crimes committed by Asian-American gangs. City officials in
Seattle say that from 1988 to 1993, for example, the number of
Asian–Pacific Islander youths involved in gangs increased eightfold.

Despite this reality, too many Asian Americans and others cling   7
to the mythical model-minority image. They want to believe that
crime, especially violent crime, happens in other communities, not in
one that spawns valedictorians and scientists and espouses respect for
authority and close family ties.

The model-minority mantra, however, no matter how frequently   8
repeated, cannot protect us against the intensifying violence perpe-
trated by our own.

I have heard "experts" say that some immigrants and refugees   9
may commit crimes because of cultural unfamiliarity or a lack of so-
phistication about the American way of life. Some say there is a
heightened sense of detachment adopted by refugees dulled by the
horror of seeing so many deaths in war.

Even if true, these arguments do not explain why many other   10
people facing similar circumstances do not extort, kidnap and murder. Surely killing someone for money is not an acceptable act in any
country.

And it may get worse. As the interaction among the different   11
Asian-American ethnic groups grows, crimes increasingly will cross
ethnic lines.

A Chinese-American wedding reception becomes the target of   12
non-Chinese-American criminals whose eyes see not the ethnicity of
the newlyweds but only the jade and gold jewelry worn just for the
special occasion. Is it any wonder that some wedding parties now
include security guards?

At the sentencing, I happened to sit next to a small, elderly well-   13
to-do and prominent Chinese American. I found myself wondering
how much of her interest in the outcome was related to how unsafe
she felt now that her ethnicity no longer could protect her.

Asian Americans have been considered different from other mi-   14
norities. We are supposed to be harmless and somehow exotic, the
least offensive minority group to have around if one must have any
around at all. Tragically, it may be the rising crime rate within our
own "model-minority" community that finally proves, once and for
all, that we are more like everyone else than some of us ever thought.

QUESTIONS FOR STUDY AND DISCUSSION

1. Reread paragraphs 1–3. Why does Wong use them to begin her
   essay? (Glossary: *Beginnings and Endings*) In what way do they
   help unify the essay?

2. What is Wong's thesis? (Glossary: *Thesis*) Where is it stated?
   What does Wong gain by stating her thesis where she does?

3. Who is Wong's audience? (Glossary: *Audience*) Explain your answer.

4. Why does Wong think that the "model minority" stereotype of
   the Asian American community is harmful? Identify how she illustrates her argument. (Glossary: *Illustration*)

5. What purpose does paragraph 13 serve? How does it help Wong
   unify her essay?

6. How does paragraph 14 serve to summarize Wong's argument?
   Identify the sentence in this paragraph in which she restates her
   thesis. Is the way Wong concludes her essay effective? Why, or
   why not?

VOCABULARY

Refer to your dictionary to define the following words as they are
used in this selection. Then use each word in a sentence of your own.

render (2)   valedictorians (7)
septuagenarian (2)   espouses (7)
extort (2)   mantra (8)

CLASSROOM ACTIVITY USING THESIS

Based on your reading of Wong's essay, write at least one thesis statement for each of the following questions:

1. How has the "model minority" label hurt Asian Americans?
2. Why did the "model minority" stereotype come into being?
3. What do Asian Americans have to learn about themselves with respect to stereotyping?

SUGGESTED WRITING ASSIGNMENTS

1. Using Wong's essay as a model, explore how a personal experience changed your thinking about a particular subject. It can be about any subject you choose—how you view your peers or another group of people, an issue in current events, political beliefs, etc. Write a unified essay in which you incorporate your revised opinion or belief into the thesis statement. Make sure that each paragraph contributes to your exploration of how and why your thinking has changed.
2. Write a unified essay using the following sentence as a thesis: "Ethnic stereotypes, whether positive or negative, are harmful."

Unity

Unity is an essential quality in a well-written essay. The principle of unity requires that every element in a piece of writing—whether a paragraph or an essay—be related to the main idea. Sentences that stray from the subject, even though they might be related to it or provide additional information, can weaken an otherwise strong piece of writing. Note how the italicized segments in the following paragraph undermine its unity and divert our attention from its main idea:

> When I was growing up, one of the places I enjoyed most was the cherry tree in the backyard. *Behind the yard was an alley and then more houses.* Every summer when the cherries began to ripen, I used to spend hours high up in the tree, picking and eating the sweet, sun-warmed cherries. *My mother always worried about my falling out of the tree, but I never did.* But I had some competition for the cherries—flocks of birds that enjoyed them as much as I did and would perch all over the tree, devouring the fruit whenever I wasn't there. I used to wonder why the grown-ups never ate any of the cherries—*my father loved all kinds of fruit*—but actually, when the birds and I had finished, there weren't many left.

A well-written essay should be unified both within and between paragraphs; that is, everything in it should be related to its thesis, the main idea of the essay. The first requirement for unity is that the thesis itself be clear, either through a direct statement, called the *thesis statement,* or by implication. The second requirement is that there be no digressions, no discussion or information that is not shown to be logically related to the thesis. A unified essay stays within the limits of its thesis.

Here, for example, is a short essay called "Over-Generalizing" about the dangers of making generalizations. As you read, notice how carefully author Stuart Chase sticks to his point:

One swallow does not make a summer, nor can two or three 1
cases often support a dependable generalization. Yet all of us, including the most polished eggheads, are constantly falling into
this mental peopletrap. It is the most common, probably the most
seductive, and potentially the most dangerous, of all the fallacies.

You drive through a town and see a drunken man on the 2
sidewalk. A few blocks further on you see another. You turn to
your companion: "Nothing but drunks in this town!" Soon you
are out in the country, bowling along at fifty. A car passes you as
if you were parked. On a curve a second whizzes by. Your companion turns to you: "All the drivers in this state are crazy!" Two
thumping generalizations, each built on two cases. If we stop to
think, we usually recognize the exaggeration and the unfairness
of such generalizations. Trouble comes when we do not stop to
think—or when we build them on a prejudice.

This kind of reasoning has been around for a long time. Aris- 3
totle was aware of its dangers and called it "reasoning by example," meaning too few examples. What it boils down to is
failing to count your swallows before announcing that summer is
here. Driving from my home to New Haven the other day, a distance of about forty miles, I caught myself saying: "Every time I
look around I see a new ranch-type house going up." So on the
return trip I counted them; there were exactly five under construction. And how many times had I "looked around"? I suppose I had glanced to right and left—as one must at side roads
and so forth in driving—several hundred times.

In this fallacy we do not make the error of neglecting facts al- 4
together and rushing immediately to the level of opinion. We
start at the fact level properly enough, but *we do not stay there.*
A case of two and up we go to a rousing over-simplification
about drunks, speeders, ranch-style houses—or, more seriously,
about foreigners, African Americans, labor leaders, teen-agers.

Why do we over-generalize so often and sometimes so disas- 5
trously? One reason is that the human mind is a generalizing machine. We would not be people without this power. The old
academic crack: "All generalizations are false, including this
one," is only a play on words. We *must* generalize to communicate and to live. But we should beware of beating the gun; of not
waiting until enough facts are in to say something useful. Meanwhile it is a plain waste of time to listen to arguments based on a
few handpicked examples.

Everything in the essay relates to Chase's thesis statement, which is included in the essay's first sentence: ". . . nor can two or three cases often support a dependable generalization." Paragraphs 2 and 3 document the thesis with examples; paragraph 4 explains how over-generalizing occurs; paragraph 5 analyzes why people over-generalize; and, for a conclusion, Chase restates his thesis in different words. An essay may be longer, more complex, and more wide-ranging than this one, but to be effective it must also avoid digressions and remain close to the author's main idea.

A good way to check that your essay is indeed unified is to underline your thesis and then to explain to yourself how each paragraph in your essay is related to the thesis. If you find a paragraph that does not appear to be logically connected, you can revise it so that the relationship is clear. Similarly, it is useful to make sure that each sentence in a paragraph is related to the topic sentence.

My Name

■ **Sandra Cisneros**

Sandra Cisneros was born in Chicago in 1954. After attending the Iowa Writers' Workshop in the late 1970s, she moved to the Southwest and now lives in San Antonio, Texas. Cisneros has had numerous occupations within the fields of education and the arts and has been a visiting writer at various universities. Although she has written two well-received books of poetry, My Wicked, Wicked Ways *(1987) and* Loose Woman *(1994), she is better known for the autobiographical fiction of* The House on Mango Street *(1984) — from which the following selection was taken — and for* Woman Hollering Creek and Other Stories *(1991). In 1995 she was awarded a grant from the prestigious MacArthur Foundation. In 2000 she published* Days and Nights of Love and War *with Eduardo H. Galeano. As you read "My Name," pay particular attention to how tightly Cisneros unifies her paragraphs by intertwining the meanings of her name (originally Esperanza) and her feelings about the great-grandmother with whom she shares that name.*

FOR YOUR JOURNAL

Who chose your name, and why was it given to you? Does your name have a special meaning for the person who gave it to you? What does the sound of your name suggest to you? Are you happy with your name?

In English my name means hope. In Spanish it means too many letters. It means sadness, it means waiting. It is like the number nine. A muddy color. It is the Mexican records my father plays on Sunday mornings when he is shaving, songs like sobbing. 1

It was my great-grandmother's name and now it is mine. She was a horse woman too, born like me in the Chinese year of the horse — which is supposed to be bad luck if you're born female — but I think this is a Chinese lie because the Chinese, like the Mexicans, don't like their women strong. 2

My great-grandmother. I would've liked to have known her, a wild horse of a woman, so wild she wouldn't marry until my great-grandfather threw a sack over her head and carried her off. Just like that, as if she were a fancy chandelier. That's the way he did it. 3

And the story goes she never forgave him. She looked out the win- 4
dow all her life, the way so many women sit their sadness on an elbow.
I wonder if she made the best with what she got or was she sorry because she couldn't be all the things she wanted to be. Esperanza. I have
inherited her name, but I don't want to inherit her place by the window.

At school they say my name funny as if the syllables were made out 5
of tin and hurt the roof of your mouth. But in Spanish my name is made
out of a softer something like silver, not quite as thick as my sister's
name Magdalena which is uglier than mine. Magdalena who at least
can come home and become Nenny. But I am always Esperanza.

I would like to baptize myself under a new name, a name more 6
like the real me, the one nobody sees. Esperanza as Lisandra or Mar-
itza or Zeze the X. Yes. Something like Zeze the X will do.

QUESTIONS FOR STUDY AND DISCUSSION

1. What is Cisneros's thesis? (Glossary: *Thesis*) Where does she state her thesis?
2. Are there any digressions, discussions, or information in this essay that do not logically connect to Cisneros's thesis? Explain how each paragraph in the essay relates to her thesis.
3. What is Cisneros's purpose in writing the essay? (Glossary: *Purpose*) Explain your answer.
4. In what way do you think a name can be like the number nine? Like a muddy color? What is your impression of the author's name, based on these similes? (Glossary: *Figure of Speech*)
5. What is Cisneros's tone in the essay? (Glossary: *Tone*) How does she establish the tone? What does it tell the reader about how she feels about her name?
6. Why do you think Cisneros waits until the end of paragraph 4 to reveal her given name?
7. Why do you think Cisneros chose "Zeze the X" as a name that better represents her inner self?

VOCABULARY

Refer to your dictionary to define the following words as they are used in this selection. Then use each word in a sentence of your own.

sobbing (1)   chandelier (3)   baptize (6)

CLASSROOM ACTIVITY USING UNITY

Take a paragraph from a draft of a paper you have been working on, and test it for unity. Be prepared to read the paragraph in class and explain why it is unified, or why it is not, and what you need to do to make it unified.

SUGGESTED WRITING ASSIGNMENTS

1. If you, like Cisneros, wished to choose a different name for yourself, what would it be? Write an essay that reveals your choice of a new name and explains why you like it or why it might be particularly appropriate for you. Make sure the essay is unified and that every paragraph directly supports your name choice.

2. Choose a grandparent or other relative at least two generations older than you about whom you know an interesting story. What impact has the relative, or the stories about him or her, had on your life? Write a unified narrative essay about the relative and what is interesting about him or her.

Life under the Chief
Doublespeak Officer

■ William Lutz

William Lutz, professor of English at Rutgers University, was for many years the editor of the Quarterly Review of Doublespeak. *Born in Racine, Wisconsin, in 1940, Lutz is best known for his important works* Doublespeak: From Revenue Enhancement to Terminal Living *(1990) and* The New Doublespeak: Why No One Knows What Anyone's Saying Anymore *(1997). As chair of the National Council of Teachers of English's Committee on Public Doublespeak, Lutz has been a watchdog of public officials who use language to "mislead, distort, deceive, inflate, circumvent, and obfuscate." Each year the committee presents the Orwell Awards, recognizing the most outrageous uses of public doublespeak in the worlds of government and business. In the following essay, which first appeared as a commentary on National Public Radio's* Morning Edition, *and then, in an expanded form, in* USA Today *(October 17, 1996), Lutz argues that American business produces an extraordinarily high quantity of doublespeak.*

FOR YOUR JOURNAL

Imagine that you work for a manufacturing plant in your town and your boss has just told you that you are on the list of people who will be "dehired" or that you are part of a program of "negative employee retention." What would you think was happening to you? Would you be happy about it? What would you think of the language your boss used to describe your situation?

If there's one product American business can produce in large amounts, it's doublespeak. Doublespeak is language that only pretends to say something; it's language that hides, evades or misleads.

Doublespeak comes in many forms, from the popular buzzwords that everyone uses but no one really understands — "globalization," "competitive dynamics," "re-equitizing" and "empowerment" — to language that tries to hide meaning: "re-engineering," "synergy," "adjustment," "restructure" and "force management program."

With doublespeak, no truck driver is the worst driver, just the 3
"least-best" driver, and bribes and kickbacks are called "rebates" or
"fees for product testing." Even robbery can be magically transformed with doublespeak, as a bank in Texas did when it declared a
robbery of an ATM to be an "unauthorized transaction." Willie Sut-
ton would have loved to have heard that.

Automobile junkyards, junk and used car parts dealers have be- 4
come "auto dismantlers and recyclers" who sell "predismantled, previously owned parts." Don't want people to know you're in the
business of disposing of radioactive and chemical wastes? Then call
your company "U.S. Ecology Inc."

Wages may not be increasing, but the doublespeak of job titles 5
sure has increased. These days, your job title has to have the word
"chief" in it. How many kinds of "chiefs" are there? Try these titles
on for size: Chief Nuclear Officer, Chief Procurement Officer, Chief
Information Officer, Chief Learning Officer, Chief Transformation
Officer, Chief Cultural Officer, Chief People Officer, Chief Ethics Officer, Chief Turnaround Officer, Chief Technology Officer, and Chief
Creative Officer. After all the "operations improvement" corporations have undergone, you have to wonder who all those "chiefs" are
leading. Never before have so few been led by so many.

These days, a travel agent may be called a "travel counselor," 6
"vacation specialist," "destination counselor" or "reservation specialist." As part of their merger, Chase Manhattan Bank and Chemical Bank decided that the position of "Relationship Manager" would
be divided between executives of both banks. What is a "Relationship Manager"? Once upon a time this person was called a salesman.
And if you're late in paying your bill after buying something from
one of these "Relationship Managers," you'll be called by the "Per-
sistency Specialist," or bill collector. If you're "downsized," the
"Outplacement Consultant" or unemployment counselor will help
you with "re-employment engineering," or how to find another job.

With doublespeak, banks don't have "bad loans" or "bad 7
debts"; they have "nonperforming assets" or "nonperforming
credits" which are "rolled over" or "rescheduled." Corporations
never lose money; they just experience "negative cash flow," "deficit
enhancement," "net profit revenue deficiencies," or "negative
contributions to profits."

No one gets fired these days, and no one gets laid off. If you're 8
high enough in the corporate pecking order, you "resign for personal

reasons." (And then you're never unemployed; you're just in an "orderly transition between career changes.")

But even those far below the lofty heights of corporate power are 9 not fired or laid off. Firing workers is such big business in these days of "re-engineering," "restructuring" and "downsizing" that there are companies whose business is helping other companies fire their workers. (Think about that for a minute.) These companies provide "termination and outplacement consulting" for corporations involved in "reduction activities." In other words, they teach companies how to fire or lay off workers. During these days of "cost rationalization," companies fire or lay off workers many different ways. How do I fire thee? Let me count the ways.

Companies make "workforce adjustments," "headcount reduc- 10 tions," "census reductions," or institute a program of "negative employee retention." Corporations offer workers "vocational relocation," "career assignment and relocation," a "career change opportunity," or "voluntary termination." Workers are "dehired," "deselected," "selected out," "repositioned," "surplussed," "rightsized," "correct sized," "excessed," or "uninstalled." Some companies "initiate operations improvements," "assign candidates to a mobility pool," "implement a skills mix adjustment," or "eliminate redundancies in the human resources area."

One company denied it was laying off 500 people at its headquar- 11 ters. "We don't characterize it as a layoff," said the corporate doublespeaker (sometimes called a spin doctor). "We're managing our staff resources. Sometimes you manage them up, and sometimes you manage them down." Congratulations. You've just been managed down, you staff resource you.

An automobile company announced the closing of an entire as- 12 sembly plant and the elimination of over 8,000 jobs by announcing "a volume-related production schedule adjustment." Not to be outdone by its rival, another car company "initiated a career alternative enhancement program" that enhanced over 5,000 workers out of their jobs. By calling the permanent shutdown of a steel plant an "indefinite idling," a corporation thought that it wouldn't have to pay severance or pension benefits to the workers who were left without jobs.

Doublespeak can pay for the company, but usually not for the 13 workers who lose their jobs.

As Pogo said, "We have met the enemy, and he is us." Or maybe 14 Dilbert got it better: "Do we really get paid for writing this stuff?"

QUESTIONS FOR STUDY AND DISCUSSION

1. What is Lutz's thesis in this essay? (Glossary: *Thesis*) Where does he state his thesis?
2. Study each of Lutz's paragraphs. Explain how each paragraph helps to unify his essay by relating to his thesis.
3. Consider Lutz's use of transitions. (Glossary: *Transition*) How does he link the material in one paragraph to the material in the next?
4. As an ending for his essay, how effective is Lutz's final paragraph? (Glossary: *Beginnings and Endings*)
5. What, in your own words, is wrong with doublespeak? Is it simply sloppy, unclear language that sometimes becomes humorous in its absurdity?
6. Does Lutz offer any solutions to the problems of the widespread use and harmful effects of doublespeak in our society? Is he under any obligation as an expert in doublespeak to offer such solutions? Explain.

VOCABULARY

Refer to your dictionary to define the following words as they are used in this selection. Then use each word in a sentence of your own.

evades (1)   outplacement (6)
dismantlers (4)   rationalization (9)
procurement (5)   severance (12)
ethics (5)

CLASSROOM ACTIVITY USING UNITY

A student wrote the following paragraphs for an essay using this thesis statement:

> In order to provide a good learning environment in school, the teachers and administrators need to be strong leaders.

Unfortunately, some of the sentences disrupt the unity of the essay. Find these sentences, eliminate them, and reread the essay.

STRONG SCHOOL LEADERS

School administrators and teachers must do more than simply supply students with information and a school building. They must also provide students with an atmosphere that allows them to focus on learning within the walls of the school. Whether the walls are brick, steel, or cement, they are only walls, and they do not help to create an appropriate atmosphere. Strong leadership both inside and outside the classroom yields a school in which students are able to excel in their studies, because they know how to conduct themselves in their relationships with their teachers and fellow students.

A recent change in the administration of Eastside High School demonstrated how important strong leadership is to learning. Under the previous administration, parents and students complained that not enough emphasis was placed on studies. Most of the students lived in an impoverished neighborhood that had only one park for several thousand residents. Students were allowed to leave school at any time of the day, and little was done to curb the growing substance abuse problem. "What's the point of trying to teach algebra to students who are just going to get jobs as part-time sales clerks, anyway?" Vice Principal Iggy Norant said when questioned about his school's poor academic standards. Mr. Norant was known to students as Twiggy Iggy because of his tall, thin frame. Standardized test scores at the school lagged well behind the state average, and only 16% of the graduates attended college within two years.

Five years ago, the school board hired Mary Peña, former chair of the state educational standards committee, as principal. A cheerleader in college, Ms. Peña got her B.A. in recreation science before getting her masters in education. She immediately emphasized the importance of learning, replacing any faculty members who did not share her high expectations of the students. Among those she fired was Mr. Norant; she also replaced two social studies teachers, one math teacher, four English teachers, and a lab instructor who let students play Gameboy in lab. She also established a code of conduct, which clearly stated the rules all students had to follow. Students were allowed second chances, but those who continued to conduct themselves in a way that interfered with the other students' ability to learn were dealt with quickly and severely. "The attitude at Eastside has changed so much since Mary Peña arrived," said math teacher Jeremy Rifkin after Peña's second year. "Students come to class much more relaxed and ready to learn. I feel like I can teach again." Test scores at Eastside are now well above state averages, and 68% of the most recent graduating class went straight to college.

SUGGESTED WRITING ASSIGNMENTS

1. In his conclusion, Lutz quotes the cartoon character Pogo: "We have met the enemy, and he is us." Write an essay in which you consider the effects of doublespeak. Is it harmful to our society? Is it a form of lying? How can we measure its effects? Be sure to cite some instances of doublespeak that are not included in Lutz's essay, examples that you uncover yourself through your reading, Web browsing, or library research.

2. Lutz demonstrates in his essay that it is revealing and sometimes very important to become "language aware," to observe the language we use, that is used around us, and that is common in society in general. Write an essay in which you argue for the importance of this notion of language awareness, and explain how it can help us to understand one another on a personal level, in our academic or professional lives, or, more broadly, in the news media or in government.

The Meanings of a Word

■ **Gloria Naylor**

*American novelist and essayist Gloria Naylor was born in 1950
in New York City, where she lives today. She worked first as a
missionary for the Jehovah's Witnesses from 1967 to 1975, then
as a telephone operator until 1981. That year she graduated
from Brooklyn College of the City University of New York and
began graduate work in African American studies at Yale University. Naylor has taught writing and literature at George
Washington University, New York University, and Cornell University, in addition to publishing several novels:* The Women of
Brewster Place *(1982),* Linden Hills *(1985),* Mama Day *(1988),
and* Bailey's Cafe *(1992). The following essay first appeared in
the* New York Times *in 1986. In it Naylor examines the ways in
which words can take on meaning, depending on who uses them
and to what purpose. Notice how the paragraphs describing her
experiences with the word* nigger *relate back to a clearly stated
thesis at the end of paragraph 2.*

FOR YOUR JOURNAL

Have you ever been called a derogatory name? What was the
name, and how did you feel about it?

Language is the subject. It is the written form with which I've   1
managed to keep the wolf away from the door and, in diaries, to
keep my sanity. In spite of this, I consider the written word inferior to
the spoken, and much of the frustration experienced by novelists is
the awareness that whatever we manage to capture in even the most
transcendent passages falls far short of the richness of life. Dialogue
achieves its power in the dynamics of a fleeting moment of sight,
sound, smell, and touch.

I'm not going to enter the debate here about whether it is lan-   2
guage that shapes reality or vice versa. That battle is doomed to be
waged whenever we seek intermittent reprieve from the chicken and
egg dispute. I will simply take the position that the spoken word, like
the written word, amounts to a nonsensical arrangement of sounds or

letters without a consensus that assigns "meaning." And building from the meanings of what we hear, we order reality. Words themselves are innocuous; it is the consensus that gives them true power.

I remember the first time I heard the word *nigger*. In my third- 3 grade class, our math tests were being passed down the rows, and as I handed the papers to a little boy in back of me, I remarked that once again he had received a much lower mark than I did. He snatched his test from me and spit out that word. Had he called me a nymphomaniac or a necrophiliac, I couldn't have been more puzzled. I didn't know what a nigger was, but I knew that whatever it meant, it was something he shouldn't have called me. This was verified when I raised my hand, and in a loud voice repeated what he had said and watched the teacher scold him for using a "bad" word. I was later to go home and ask the inevitable question that every black parent must face — "Mommy, what does *nigger* mean?"

And what exactly did it mean? Thinking back, I realize that this 4 could not have been the first time the word was used in my presence. I was part of a large extended family that had migrated from the rural South after World War II and formed a close-knit network that gravitated around my maternal grandparents. Their ground-floor apartment in one of the buildings they owned in Harlem was a weekend mecca for my immediate family, along with countless aunts, uncles, and cousins who brought along assorted friends. It was a bustling and open house with assorted neighbors and tenants popping in and out to exchange bits of gossip, pick up an old quarrel, or referee the ongoing checkers game in which my grandmother cheated shamelessly. They were all there to let down their hair and put up their feet after a week of labor in the factories, laundries, and shipyards of New York.

Amid the clamor, which could reach deafening proportions — 5 two or three conversations going on simultaneously, punctuated by the sound of a baby's crying somewhere in the back rooms or out on the street — there was still a rigid set of rules about what was said and how. Older children were sent out of the living room when it was time to get into the juicy details about "you-know-who" up on the third floor who had gone and gotten herself "p-r-e-g-n-a-n-t!" But my parents, knowing that I could spell well beyond my years, always demanded that I follow the others out to play. Beyond sexual misconduct and death, everything else was considered harmless for our young ears. And so among the anecdotes of the triumphs and disappointments in the various workings of their lives, the word *nigger* was used in my presence, but it was set within contexts and inflections that caused it to register in my mind as something else.

In the singular, the word was always applied to a man who had 6
distinguished himself in some situation that brought their approval
for his strength, intelligence, or drive:

"Did Johnny *really* do that?" 7

"I'm telling you, that nigger pulled in $6,000 of overtime last 8
year. Said he got enough for a down payment on a house."

When used with a possessive adjective by a woman—"my nig- 9
ger"—it became a term of endearment for her husband or boyfriend.
But it could be more than just a term applied to a man. In their
mouths it became the pure essence of manhood—a disembodied
force that channeled their past history of struggle and present sur-
vival against the odds into a victorious statement of being: "Yeah,
that old foreman found out quick enough—you don't mess with a
nigger."

In the plural, it became a description of some group within the 10
community that had overstepped the bounds of decency as my family
defined it. Parents who neglected their children, a drunken couple
who fought in public, people who simply refused to look for work,
those with excessively dirty mouths or unkempt households were all
"trifling niggers." This particular circle could forgive hard times, unemployment, the occasional bout of depression—they had gone
through all of that themselves—but the unforgivable sin was a lack
of self-respect.

A woman could never be a "nigger" in the singular, with its con- 11
notation of confirming worth. The noun *girl* was its closest equivalent in that sense, but only when used in direct address and regardless
of the gender doing the addressing. *Girl* was a token of respect for a
woman. The one-syllable word was drawn out to sound like three in
recognition of the extra ounce of wit, nerve, or daring that the
woman had shown in the situation under discussion.

"G-i-r-l, stop. You mean you said that to his face?" 12

But if the word was used in a third-person reference or shortened 13
so that it almost snapped out of the mouth, it always involved some
element of communal disapproval. And age became an important factor in these exchanges. It was only between individuals of the same
generation, or from any older person to a younger (but never the
other way around), that *girl* would be considered a compliment.

I don't agree with the argument that use of the word *nigger* at this 14
social stratum of the black community was an internalization of

racism. The dynamics were the exact opposite: the people in my grand-mother's living room took a word that whites used to signify worth-lessness or degradation and rendered it impotent. Gathering there together, they transformed *nigger* to signify the varied and complex human beings they knew themselves to be. If the word was to disappear totally from the mouths of even the most liberal of white society, no one in that room was naive enough to believe it would disappear from white minds. Meeting the word head-on, they proved it had absolutely nothing to do with the way they were determined to live their lives.

So there must have been dozens of times that *nigger* was spoken 15 in front of me before I reached the third grade. But I didn't "hear" it until it was said by a small pair of lips that had already learned it could be a way to humiliate me. That was the word I went home and asked my mother about. And since she knew that I had to grow up in America, she took me in her lap and explained.

QUESTIONS FOR STUDY AND DISCUSSION

1. Naylor states her thesis in the last sentence of paragraph 2. How does what she says in the first two paragraphs build unity by connecting to her thesis statement? (Glossary: *Thesis*)

2. What are the two meanings of the word *nigger* as Naylor uses it in her essay? Where in the essay is the clearest definition of each use of the word presented? (Glossary: *Definition*)

3. Naylor says she must have heard the word *nigger* many times while she was growing up; yet she "heard" it for the first time when she was in the third grade. How does she explain this seeming contradiction?

4. Naylor gives a detailed narration of her family and its lifestyle in paragraphs 4 and 5. What kinds of details does she include in her brief story? (Glossary: *Narration* and *Details*) How does this narration contribute to your understanding of the word *nigger* as used by her family? Why do you suppose she offers so little in the way of a definition of the other use of the word *nigger*? Explain.

5. Would you characterize Naylor's tone as angry, objective, cyni-cal, or something else? (Glossary: *Tone*) Cite examples of her diction to support your answer. (Glossary: *Diction*)

6. What is the meaning of Naylor's last sentence? How well does it work as an ending for her essay? (Glossary: *Beginnings and Endings*)

VOCABULARY

Refer to your dictionary to define the following words as they are used in this selection. Then use each word in a sentence of your own.

transcendent (1)	anecdotes (5)
innocuous (2)	inflections (5)
consensus (2)	unkempt (10)
nymphomaniac (3)	trifling (10)
necrophiliac (3)	internalization (14)
mecca (4)	impotent (14)
clamor (5)	

CLASSROOM ACTIVITY USING UNITY

Carefully read the following five-paragraph sequence, paying special attention to how each paragraph relates to the writer's thesis. Identify the paragraph that disrupts the unity of the sequence, and explain why it doesn't belong.

Though "experts" differ as to the best technique to follow 1
when building a fire, one generally accepted method consists of first laying a generous amount of crumpled newspaper on the hearth between the andirons. Kindling wood is then spread generously over this layer of newspaper and one of the thickest logs is placed across the back of the andirons. This should be as close to the back of the fireplace as possible, but not quite touching it. A second log is then placed an inch or so in front of this, and a few additional sticks of kindling are laid across these two. A third log is then placed on top to form a sort of pyramid with air space between all logs so that flames can lick freely up between them.

Roaring fireplace fires are particularly welcome during the 2
winter months, especially after hearty outdoor activities. To avoid any mid-winter tragedies, care should be taken to have a professional inspect and clean the chimney before starting to use the fireplace in the fall. Also, be sure to clean out the fireplace after each use.

A mistake frequently made is building the fire too far for- 3
ward so that the rear wall of the fireplace does not get properly heated. A heated back wall helps increase the draft and tends to

suck smoke and flames rearward with less chance of sparks or smoke spurting out into the room.

Another common mistake often made by the inexperienced 4 fire-tender is to try to build a fire with only one or two logs, instead of using at least three. A single log is difficult to ignite properly, and even two logs do not provide an efficient bed with adequate fuel-burning capacity.

Use of too many logs, on the other hand, is also a common 5 fault and can prove hazardous. Building too big a fire can create more smoke and draft than the chimney can safely handle, increasing the possibility of sparks or smoke being thrown out into the room. For best results, the homeowner should start with three medium-size logs as described above, then add additional logs as needed if the fire is to be kept burning.

The five paragraphs on "How to Build a Fire in a Fireplace" are taken from Bernard Gladstone's book *The New York Times Complete Manual of Home Repair.*

SUGGESTED WRITING ASSIGNMENTS

1. Naylor disagrees with the notion that use of the word *nigger* in the African American community can be taken as an "internalization of racism." Reexamine her essay and discuss in what ways her definition of the word *nigger* affirms or denies her position. Draw on your own experiences, observations, and reading to support your answer.

2. Write a short essay in which you define a word, for example, *wife, macho, liberal, success,* or *marriage,* that has more than one meaning, depending on one's point of view.

Organization

In an essay, ideas and information cannot be presented all at once; they have to be arranged in some order. That order is the essay's organization.

The pattern of organization in an essay should be suited to the writer's subject and purpose. For example, if you are writing about your experience working in a fast-food restaurant and your purpose is to tell about the activities of a typical day, you might present those activities in chronological order. If, on the other hand, you wish to argue that working in a bank is an ideal summer job, you might proceed from the least rewarding to the most rewarding aspect of this job; this is called "climactic" order.

Some often-used patterns of organization are time order, space order, and logical order. Time order, or chronological order, is used to present events as they occurred. A personal narrative, a report of a campus incident, or an account of a historical event can be most naturally and easily related in chronological order. In the following paragraph, the author uses chronological order to recount a disturbing childhood memory:

> I clearly remember my sixth birthday because Dad was in the hospital with pneumonia. He was working so hard he paid very little attention to his health. As a result, he spent almost the entire summer before I entered the first grade in the hospital. Mom visited him nightly. On my birthday I was allowed to see him. I have memories of sitting happily in the lobby of the hospital talking to the nurses, telling them with a big smile that I was going to see my dad because it was my birthday. I couldn't wait to see him because children under 12 were not allowed to visit patients, so I had not seen him in a long time. When I entered the hospital room, I saw tubes inserted into his nose and needles stuck in his arm. He was very, very thin. I was frightened and wanted to cry, but I was determined to have a good visit. So I stayed for a while, and he wished me a

happy birthday. When it was time to go, I kissed him good-bye and waited until I left his room to cry.

–Grace Ming-Yee Wai

Of course, the order of events can sometimes be rearranged for special effect. For, example, an account of an auto accident may begin with the collision itself and then "flash back" in time to the events leading up to it.

The description of a process — such as framing a poster, constructing a bookcase with cinder blocks and boards, or serving a tennis ball—almost always calls for a chronological organization.

When analyzing a causally related series of events, writers often use a chronological organization to clarify for readers the exact sequence of events. In the following selection, the writer examines sequentially the series of malfunctions that led to the near disaster at the Three Mile Island nuclear facility in Harrisburg, Pennsylvania, showing clearly how each one led to the next:

On March 28, 1979, at 3:53 A.M., a pump at the Harrisburg plant failed. Because the pump failed, the reactor's heat was not drawn off in the heat exchanger and the very hot water in the primary loop overheated. The pressure in the loop increased, opening a release valve that was supposed to counteract such an event. But the valve stuck open and the primary loop system lost so much water (which ended up as a highly radioactive pool, six feet deep, on the floor of the reactor building) that it was unable to carry off all the heat generated within the reactor core. Under these circumstances, the intense heat held within the reactor could, in theory, melt its fuel rods, and the resulting "meltdown" could then carry a hugely radioactive mass through the floor of the reactor. The reactor's emergency cooling system, which is designed to prevent this disaster, was then automatically activated, but when it was, apparently, turned off too soon, some of the fuel rods overheated. This produced a bubble of hydrogen gas at the top of the reactor. (The hydrogen is dissolved in the water in order to react with oxygen that is produced when the intense reactor radiation splits water molecules into their atomic constituents. When heated, the dissolved hydrogen bubbles out of the solution.) This bubble blocked the flow of cooling water so that despite the action of the emergency cooling system the reactor core was again in danger of melting down. Another danger was that the gas might contain enough oxygen to cause an explosion that could rupture the huge containers that surround the reactor and release a deadly cloud of radioactive material into the surrounding

countryside. Working desperately, technicians were able to gradually reduce the size of the gas bubble using a special apparatus
brought in from the atomic laboratory at Oak Ridge, Tennessee, and
the danger of a catastrophic release of radioactive materials sub-
sided. But the sealed-off plant was now so radioactive that no one
could enter it for many months—or, according to some observers,
for years—without being exposed to a lethal dose of radiation.

—Barry Commoner

Space order is used when describing a person, place, or thing.
This organizational pattern begins at a particular point and moves in
some direction, such as left to right, top to bottom, east to west, outside to inside, front to back, near to far, around, or over. In describing a house, for example, a writer could move from top to bottom,
from outside to inside, or in a circle around the outside.

In the following paragraph, the subject is a baseball, and the
writer describes it from the inside out, moving from its composition-
cork nucleus to the print on its stitched cowhide cover.

It weighs just over five ounces and measures between 2.86 and
2.94 inches in diameter. It is made of a composition-cork nucleus en-
cased in two thin layers of rubber, one black and one red, surrounded by 121 yards of tightly wrapped blue-gray wool yarn,
45 yards of white wool yarn, 54 more yards of blue-gray wool yarn,
150 yards of fine cotton yarn, a coat of rubber cement, and a
cowhide (formerly horsehide) exterior, which is held together with
216 slightly raised red cotton stitches. Printed certifications, endorse-
ments, and outdoor advertising spherically attest to its authenticity.

—Roger Angell

Logical order can take many forms, depending on the writer's
purpose. Often used patterns include general to specific, most familiar to least familiar, and smallest to biggest. Perhaps the most common type of logical order is order of importance. Notice how the
writer uses this order in the following paragraph:

The Egyptians have taught us many things. They were excellent farmers. They knew all about irrigation. They built temples
which were afterwards copied by the Greeks and which served as
the earliest models for the churches in which we worship nowadays.
They invented a calendar which proved such a useful instrument for
the purpose of measuring time that it has survived with few changes

until today. But most important of all, the Egyptians learned how to preserve speech for the benefit of future generations. They invented the art of writing.

By organizing the material according to the order of increasing importance, the writer places special emphasis on the final sentence.

Logical order can take many different forms, but the exact rationale is always dependent upon the topic of the writing. For example, in writing a descriptive essay about a place you visited, you can move from the least striking to the most striking detail, so as to keep your readers interested and involved in the description. In an essay explaining how to pick individual stocks for investment, you can start with the point that readers will find least difficult to understand and move on to the most difficult (that's how teachers organize many courses). Or, in writing an essay arguing for more internships and service learning courses, you can move from your least controversial point to the most controversial, preparing your reader gradually to accept your argument.

A simple way to check the organization of an essay is to outline it once you have a draft. Does the outline represent the organizational pattern—chronological, spatial, or logical—that you set out to use? Problems in outlining will naturally indicate sections that you need to revise.

A View from the Bridge

■ **Cherokee Paul McDonald**

A fiction writer and journalist, Cherokee Paul McDonald was raised and schooled in Fort Lauderdale, Florida. In 1970, he returned home from a tour of duty in Vietnam and joined the Fort Lauderdale Police Department, where he remained until 1980, resigning with the rank of sergeant. During this time, McDonald received a degree in criminal science from Broward Community College. He left the police department to become a writer and worked a number of odd jobs before publishing his first book, The Patch, *in 1986. McDonald has said that almost all of his writing comes from his police work, and his common themes of justice, balance, and fairness reflect his life as part of the "thin blue line" (the police department). In 1991, he published* Blue Truth, *a memoir. His first novel,* Summer's Reason, *was released in 1994, and he is now working on a new novel,* Secret Songs. *"A View from the Bridge" was originally published in* Sunshine *magazine in 1990. Notice how McDonald uses dialogue to narrate the story of a chance encounter with a young fisherman.*

FOR YOUR JOURNAL

Make a list of your interests, focusing on those to which you devote a significant amount of time. Do you share any of these interests with people you know? What does a shared interest do for a relationship between two people?

I was coming up on the little bridge in the Rio Vista neighborhood 1
of Fort Lauderdale, deepening my stride and my breathing to negotiate the slight incline without altering my pace. And then, as I neared the crest, I saw the kid.

He was a lumpy little guy with baggy shorts, a faded T-shirt and 2
heavy sweat socks falling down over old sneakers.

Partially covering his shaggy blond hair was one of those blue 3
baseball caps with gold braid on the bill and a sailfish patch sewn onto the peak. Covering his eyes and part of his face was a pair of those stupid-looking '50s-style wrap-around sunglasses.

He was fumbling with a beat-up rod and reel, and he had a little 4
bait bucket by his feet. I puffed on by, glancing down into the empty
bucket as I passed.

"Hey mister! Would you help me, please?" 5

The shrill voice penetrated my jogger's concentration, and I was 6
determined to ignore it. But for some reason, I stopped.

With my hands on my hips and the sweat dripping from my nose 7
I asked, "What do you want, kid?"

"Would you please help me find my shrimp? It's my last one and 8
I've been getting bites and I know I can catch a fish if I can just find
that shrimp. He jumped outta my hand as I was getting him from the
bucket."

Exasperated, I walked slowly back to the kid, and pointed. 9

"There's the damn shrimp by your left foot. You stopped me for 10
that?"

As I said it, the kid reached down and trapped the shrimp. 11

"Thanks a lot, mister," he said. 12

I watched as the kid dropped the baited hook down into the 13
canal. Then I turned to start back down the bridge.

That's when the kid let out a "Hey! Hey!" and the prettiest tar- 14
pon I'd ever seen came almost six feet out of the water, twisting and
turning as he fell through the air.

"I got one!" the kid yelled as the fish hit the water with a loud 15
splash and took off down the canal.

I watched the line being burned off the reel at an alarming rate. 16
The kid's left hand held the crank while the extended fingers felt for
the drag setting.

"No, kid!" I shouted. "Leave the drag alone . . . just keep that 17
damn rod tip up!"

Then I glanced at the reel and saw there were just a few loops of 18
line left on the spool.

"Why don't you get yourself some decent equipment?" I said, but 19
before the kid could answer I saw the line go slack.

"Ohhh, I lost him," the kid said. I saw the flash of silver as the 20
fish turned.

"Crank, kid, crank! You didn't lose him. He's coming back to- 21
ward you. Bring in the slack!"

The kid cranked like mad, and a beautiful grin spread across his 22
face.

"He's heading in for the pilings," I said. "Keep him out of those 23
pilings!"

The kid played it perfectly. When the fish made its play for the   24
pilings, he kept just enough pressure on to force the fish out. When
the water exploded and the silver missile hurled into the air, the kid
kept the rod tip up and the line tight.

As the fish came to the surface and began a slow circle in the   25
middle of the canal, I said, "Whooee, is that a nice fish or what?"

The kid didn't say anything, so I said, "Okay, move to the   26
edge of the bridge and I'll climb down to the seawall and pull him
out."

When I reached the seawall I pulled in the leader, leaving the fish   27
lying on its side in the water.

"How's that?" I said.   28

"Hey, mister, tell me what it looks like."   29

"Look down here and check him out," I said. "He's beautiful."   30

But then I looked up into those stupid-looking sunglasses and it   31
hit me. The kid was blind.

"Could you tell me what he looks like, mister?" he said again.   32

"Well, he's just under three, uh, he's about as long as one of your   33
arms," I said. "I'd guess he goes about 15, 20 pounds. He's mostly
silver, but the silver is somehow made up of *all* the colors, if you
know what I mean." I stopped. "Do you know what I mean by colors?"

The kid nodded.   34

"Okay. He has all these big scales, like armor all over his body.   35
They're silver too, and when he moves they sparkle. He has a strong
body and a large powerful tail. He has big round eyes, bigger than a
quarter, and a lower jaw that sticks out past the upper one and is
very tough. His belly is almost white and his back is a gunmetal gray.
When he jumped he came out of the water about six feet, and his
scales caught the sun and flashed it all over the place."

By now the fish had righted itself, and I could see the bright-red   36
gills as the gill plates opened and closed. I explained this to the kid,
and then said, more to myself, "He's a beauty."

"Can you get him off the hook?" the kid asked. "I don't want to   37
kill him."

I watched as the tarpon began to slowly swim away, tired but   38
still alive.

By the time I got back up to the top of the bridge the kid had his   39
line secured and his bait bucket in one hand.

He grinned and said, "Just in time. My mom drops me off here,   40
and she'll be back to pick me up any minute."

He used the back of one hand to wipe his nose.   41

"Thanks for helping me catch that tarpon," he said, "and for   42
helping me to see it."

I looked at him, shook my head, and said, "No, my friend, thank   43
you for letting *me* see that fish."

I took off, but before I got far the kid yelled again.   44

"Hey, mister!"   45

I stopped.   46

"Someday I'm gonna catch a sailfish and a blue marlin and a   47
giant tuna and *all* those big sportfish!"

As I looked into those sunglasses I knew he probably would. I   48
wished I could be there when it happened.

QUESTIONS FOR STUDY AND DISCUSSION

1. How has McDonald organized his essay? What period of time
   would you estimate is covered in this essay?

2. What clues lead up to the revelation that the kid is blind? Why
   does it take the narrator so long to realize it?

3. Notice the way the narrator chooses and adjusts some of the
   words he uses to describe the fish to the kid in paragraphs
   33–36. Why does he do this? How does he organize his description of the fish so that the boy can visualize it better? Explain.

4. By the end of the essay, we know much more about the kid than
   the fact that he is blind, but after the initial description, McDonald characterizes him only indirectly. As the essay unfolds, what
   do we learn about the kid, and how does the author convey this
   knowledge?

5. McDonald tells much of his story through dialogue. (Glossary:
   Dialogue) What does this dialogue add to the story? What would
   have been lost had McDonald not used it?

6. Near the end of the story, why does the narrator say to the kid,
   "No, my friend, thank you for letting *me* see that fish"(43)?

7. What is the connotation of the word *view* in the title? Of the
   word *bridge*? (Glossary: *Connotation/Denotation*)

VOCABULARY

Refer to your dictionary to define the following words as they are
used in this selection. Then use each word in a sentence of your own.

negotiate (1)   tarpon (14)
exasperated (9)   pilings (23)

CLASSROOM ACTIVITY USING ORGANIZATION

Consider the ways in which you might organize a discusssion of the seven states listed below. For each state, we have provided you with some basic information: the date it entered the Union, population, land area, and number of electoral votes in a presidential election.

MAINE
March 15, 1820
1,240,209 people
30,865 square miles
4 electoral votes

MONTANA
November 8, 1889
856,047 people
145,556 square miles
3 electoral votes

ALASKA
January 3, 1959
606,276 people
570,374 square miles
3 electoral votes

ARIZONA
February 14, 1912
4,075,052 people
113,642 square miles
8 electoral votes

FLORIDA
March 3, 1845
13,952,714 people
53,937 square miles
25 electoral votes

OREGON
February 14, 1859
3,086,188 people
96,002 square miles
7 electoral votes

MISSOURI
August 10, 1821
5,277,640 people
68,898 square miles
11 electoral votes

SUGGESTED WRITING ASSIGNMENTS

1. In groups of two or three, take turns describing a specific beautiful or remarkable thing to the others as if they were blind. You may want to actually bring an object to observe while your classmates cover their eyes. Help each other find the best words to create a vivid verbal picture. Using McDonald's paragraphs 33–36 as a model, write a brief description of your object, retaining the informal style of your speaking voice.

2. Recall a time when you and one other person held a conversation that helped you see something more clearly—visually, in terms of understanding, or both. Using McDonald's narrative as a model, tell the story of that moment, re-creating the dialogue as exactly as you remember it.

Reach Out and Write Someone

■ Lynn Wenzel

Lynn Wenzel has been published in many major newspapers and magazines, including Ms., Newsweek, *the* New York Times, Newsday, *and* Down East: The Magazine of Maine. *Her book* I Hear America Singing: A Nostalgic Tour of Popular Sheet Music *appeared in 1989. Wenzel, who graduated magna cum laude from William Paterson College, makes her home in Maywood, New Jersey. In the essay below, which was first published in* Newsweek on Campus *in 1984, she organizes her ideas chronologically, yet within that larger time-order arrangement she also establishes the relative importance of her reasons for writing letters, ending with the "most important of all."*

FOR YOUR JOURNAL

When was the last time you wrote a letter to a friend? Are you, like so many others, usually tempted to pick up the telephone or to send an email instead of writing a letter when you need to communicate? Begin writing a letter to someone to whom you have something important to say. Remember that "important" does not have to mean "big news"; it may simply mean telling someone how important he or she is to you.

Everyone is talking about the breakup of the telephone company. 1
Some say it will be a disaster for poor people and a bonanza for large companies while others fear a personal phone bill so exorbitant that—horror of horrors—we will all have to start writing letters again.

It's about time. One of the many talents lost in this increasingly 2 technological age is that of putting pen to paper in order to communicate with family, friends and lovers.

Reading, and enjoying it, may not be the strong suit of our young 3 but writing has truly become a lost art. I am not talking about creative writing because this country still has its full share of fine fiction and poetry writers. There will always be those special few who need to transform experiences into short stories or poetry.

No, the skill we have lost is that of letter writing. When was the 4 last time the mailbox contained anything more than bills, political and fund-raising appeals, advertisements, catalogs, magazines or junk mail?

Once upon a time, the only way to communicate from a distance 5 was through the written word. As the country expanded and people moved west, they knew that when they left mother, father, sister, brother, it was very probably the last time they would see them again. So daughters, pioneering in Indiana or Michigan, wrote home with the news that their first son had been born dead, but the second child was healthy and growing and they also had a house and barn. By the time the letter reached east, another child might have been born, yet it was read over and over again, then smoothed out and slipped into the family Bible or keepsake box.

Letters were essential then. Imagine John Adams fomenting revo- 6 lution and forming a new government without Abigail's letters to sustain him. Think of Elizabeth Barrett and Robert Browning without their written declarations of love; of all the lovers who, parted against their will, kept hope alive through letters often passed by hand or mailed in secret.

And what of history? Much of our knowledge of events and of 7 the people who lived them is based on such commonplace communi- cation. Harry Truman's letters to Bess, Mamie and Ike's correspon- dence and Eleanor Roosevelt's letters to some of her friends all illuminate actions and hint at intent. F. Scott Fitzgerald's letters to his daughter, Scottie, which were filled with melancholy over his wife's mental illness, suggest in part the reason why his last years were so frustratingly uncreative. Without letters we would have history—dry facts and dates of wars, treaties, elections, revolutions. But the causes and effects might be left unclear.

We would also know little about women's lives. History, until re- 8 cently, neglected women's contributions to events. Much of what we now know about women in history comes from letters found, more often than not, in great-grandmother's trunk in the attic, carefully tied with ribbon, or stored, yellowed and boxed, in a carton in the archives of a "women's college." These letters have helped immensely over the past ten years to create a verifiable women's history which is now taking its rightful place alongside weighty tomes about men's contributions to the changing world.

The story of immigration often begins with a letter. Millions of 9
brave souls, carrying their worldly possessions in one bag, stepped off a
ship and into American life on the strength of a note saying, "Come.
It's better here."

To know how important the "art" of letter writing was, we have 10
only to look at the accouterments our ancestors treasured and considered necessary: inkstands of silver, gold or glass, crafted to occupy a
prominent place on the writing table; hot wax for a personal seal; the
seals themselves, sometimes ornately carved in silver; quills, and then
fountain pens. These were not luxuries but necessities.

Perhaps most important of all, letter writing required *thinking* 11
before putting pen to paper. No hurried telephone call can ever replace the thoughtful, intelligent correspondence between two people,
the patching up of a friendship, the formal request for the pleasure of
someone's company, or a personal apology. Once written and sent,
the writer can never declare, "But I never said that." Serious letter
writing demands thought, logic, organization and sincerity because
words, once written, cannot be taken back. These are qualities we must
not lose, but ones we should polish and bring to luster.

What, after all, will we lose: our lover's letters tied with an old 12
hair ribbon, written from somewhere far away; our children's first
scribbled note from summer camp; the letters friends sent us as we
scattered after college; letters we sent our parents telling them how
much they meant to us? Without letters, what will we save, laugh
about, read out loud to each other 20 years from now on a snowy afternoon in front of a fire?

Telephone bills. 13

And that is the saddest note of all. 14

QUESTIONS FOR STUDY AND DISCUSSION

1. What is Wenzel's thesis in this essay? Where is it stated? (Glossary: *Thesis*)
2. Why does Wenzel concentrate on letter writing in her essay and
   not on other kinds of writing?
3. What role has letter writing played in our understanding of history, according to Wenzel?
4. In what ways is writing a letter different from making a phone call?
   From sending an email? What can letter writing do to help us
   develop as human beings? (Glossary: *Comparison and Contrast*)

5. How has Wenzel organized her examples of the importance of letter writing? Support your answer with examples.

6. How effective do you find the beginning and ending of Wenzel's essay? Explain. (Glossary: *Beginnings and Endings*)

VOCABULARY

Refer to your dictionary to define the following words as they are used in this selection. Then use each word in a sentence of your own.

exorbitant (1)   accouterments (10)
fomenting (6)   seal (10)
tomes (8)

CLASSROOM ACTIVITY USING ORGANIZATION

Carefully read the following descriptive paragraph from *Blue Highways* by William Least Heat Moon, and identify the organizational pattern that he uses to structure his description.

> The old store, lighted only by three fifty-watt bulbs, smelled of coal and baking bread. In the middle of the rectangular room, where the oak floor sagged a little, stood an iron stove. To the right was a wooden table with an unfinished game of checkers and a stool made from an apple-tree stump. On the shelves around the walls sat earthen jugs with corncob stoppers . . . , a few canned goods, and some of the two thousand old clocks and clockworks Thurmond Watts owned. Only one was ticking; the others he just looked at. I asked how long he'd been in the store.

Based upon Least Heat Moon's description, sketch the inside of Thurmond Watts's store. Compare your sketch with those of your classmates, and discuss how the paragraph's organization influenced the relative prominence of various objects in your sketch.

SUGGESTED WRITING ASSIGNMENTS

1. Since Wenzel wrote this essay, Americans have been introduced to email. What impact, if any, has email had on your writing habits? In what ways does email respond to Wenzel's call for more letter writing? In comparison to letter writing, what are the

advantages and disadvantages of email? Write an essay in which you address one of these questions.

2. Think of a commonplace subject that people might take for granted but that you find interesting. Write an essay on that subject, using one of the following types of logical order:

least important to most important

most familiar to least familiar

smallest to biggest

oldest to newest

easiest to understand to most difficult to understand

good news to bad news

general to specific

The Corner Store

■ **Eudora Welty**

Eudora Welty is one of the most honored and respected writers at work today. She was born in 1909 in Jackson, Mississippi, where she has lived most of her life. Her published works include many short stories, now available in her Collected Stories *(1980); a collection of her essays,* The Eye of the Story *(1975); collected book reviews,* The Writer's Eye *(1994); five novels; and a memoir,* One Writer's Beginnings *(1987). Her novel* The Optimist's Daughter *won the Pulitzer Prize for fiction in 1973. Welty's description of the corner store, taken from an essay about growing up in Jackson, recalls for many readers the neighborhood store in the town or city where they grew up. As you read, pay particular attention to the effect Welty's spatial arrangement of descriptive details has on the dominant impression of the store.*

FOR YOUR JOURNAL

Write about a store you frequented as a child. Maybe it was the local supermarket, the hardware store, or the corner convenience store. Using your five senses (sight, smell, taste, touch, and hearing), describe what you remember about the place.

Our Little Store rose right up from the sidewalk; standing in a street of family houses, it alone hadn't any yard in front, any tree or flower bed. It was a plain frame building covered over with brick. Above the door, a little railed porch ran across on an upstairs level and four windows with shades were looking out. But I didn't catch on to those.

Running in out of the sun, you met what seemed total obscurity inside. There were almost tangible smells—licorice recently sucked in a child's cheek, dill pickle brine that had leaked through a paper sack in a fresh trail across the wooden floor, ammonia-loaded ice that had been hoisted from wet croker sacks and slammed into the icebox with its sweet butter at the door, and perhaps the smell of still untrapped mice.

Then through the motes of cracker dust, cornmeal dust, the Gold   3
Dust of the Gold Dust Twins that the floor had been swept out with,
the realities emerged. Shelves climbed to high reach all the way
around, set out with not too much of any one thing but a lot of
things—lard, molasses, vinegar, starch, matches, kerosene, Octagon
soap (about a year's worth of octagon-shaped coupons cut out and
saved brought a signet ring addressed to you in the mail). It was up to
you to remember what you came for, while your eye traveled from
cans of sardines to tin whistles to ice-cream salt to harmonicas to fly-
paper (over your head, batting around on a thread beneath the blades
of the ceiling fan, stuck with its testimonial catch).

Its confusion may have been in the eye of its beholder. Enchant-   4
ment is cast upon you by all those things you weren't supposed to
have need for, to lure you close to wooden tops you'd outgrown,
boys' marbles and agates in little net pouches, small rubber balls that
wouldn't bounce straight, frail, frazzly kite string, clay bubble pipes
that would snap off in your teeth, the stiffest scissors. You could contemplate those long narrow boxes of sparklers gathering dust while
you waited for it to be the Fourth of July or Christmas, and noisemak-
ers in the shape of tin frogs for somebody's birthday party you hadn't
been invited to yet, and see that they were all marvelous.

You might not have even looked for Mr. Sessions when he came   5
around his store cheese (as big as a doll's house) and in front of the
counter looking for you. When you'd finally asked him for, and received from him in its paper bag, whatever single thing it was that
you had been sent for, the nickel that was left over was yours to
spend.

Down at a child's eye level, inside those glass jars with mouths in   6
their sides through which the grocer could run his scoop or a child's
hand might be invited to reach for a choice, were wineballs, all-day
suckers, gumdrops, peppermints. Making a row under the glass of a
counter were the Tootsie Rolls, Hershey bars, Goo Goo Clusters,
Baby Ruths. And whatever was the name of those pastilles that came
stacked in a cardboard cylinder with a cardboard lid? They were thin
and dry, about the size of tiddledy-winks, and in the shape of twisted
rosettes. A kind of chocolate dust came out with them when you
shook them out in your hand. Were they chocolate? I'd say, rather,
they were brown. They didn't taste of anything at all, unless it was
wood. Their attraction was the number you got for a nickel.

Making up your mind, you circled the store around and around,   7
around the pickle barrel, around the tower of Crackerjack boxes; Mr.

Sessions had built it for us himself on top of a packing case like a house of cards.

If it seemed too hot for Crackerjacks, I might get a cold drink. 8 Mr. Sessions might have already stationed himself by the cold-drinks barrel, like a mind reader. Deep in ice water that looked black as ink, murky shapes — that would come up as Coca-Colas, Orange Crushes, and various flavors of pop — were all swimming around together. When you gave the word, Mr. Sessions plunged his bare arm in to the elbow and fished out your choice, first try. I favored a locally bottled concoction called Lake's Celery. (What else could it be called? It was made by a Mr. Lake out of celery. It was a popular drink here for years but was not known universally, as I found out when I arrived in New York and ordered one in the Astor bar.) You drank on the premises, with feet set wide apart to miss the drip, and gave him back his bottle and your nickel.

But he didn't hurry you off. A standing scales was by the door, 9 with a stack of iron weights and a brass slide on the balance arm, that would weigh you up to three hundred pounds. Mr. Sessions, whose hands were gentle and smelled of carbolic, would lift you up and set your feet on the platform, hold your loaf of bread for you, and taking his time while you stood still for him, he would make certain of what you weighed today. He could even remember what you weighed the last time, so you could subtract and announce how much you'd gained. That was goodbye.

QUESTIONS FOR STUDY AND DISCUSSION

1. Which of the three patterns of organization has Welty used in this essay: chronological, spatial, or logical? If she has used more than one, where precisely has she used each type?

2. In paragraph 2, Welty describes the smells that a person encountered when entering the corner store. Why do you think she presents these smells before giving any visual details of the inside of the store?

3. What is the dominant impression that Welty creates in her description of the corner store? (Glossary: *Dominant Impression*) How does Welty create this dominant impression?

4. What impression of Mr. Sessions does Welty create? What details contribute to this impression? (Glossary: *Details*)

5. Welty places certain pieces of information in parentheses in this essay. Why are they in parentheses? What, if anything, does this information add to our understanding of the corner store? Might this information be left out? Explain.

6. Comment on Welty's ending. Is it too abrupt? Why or why not? (Glossary: *Beginnings and Endings*)

VOCABULARY

Refer to your dictionary to define the following words as they are used in this selection. Then use each word in a sentence of your own.

frame (1)	signet (3)
tangible (2)	agates (4)
brine (2)	concoction (8)
motes (3)	scales (9)

CLASSROOM ACTIVITY USING ORGANIZATION

Yesterday, while cleaning out the center drawer of his desk, a student found the following items:

2 no. 2 pencils	2 pairs of scissors
3 rubber bands	1 book mailing bag
1 roll of adhesive tape	1 mechanical pencil
1 plastic comb	3 first-class postage stamps
25 3 × 5 cards	5 postcards
3 ballpoint pens	2 clasps
1 eraser	2 8 × 10 manila envelopes
6 paper clips	7 thumbtacks
1 nail clipper	1 bottle of correction fluid
1 highlighting marker	1 nail file
1 bottle of glue	1 toothbrush
3 business envelopes	1 felt-tip pen
6 postcard stamps	2 airmail stamps

To organize the student's drawer, into what categories would you divide these items? Explain which items you would place in each category. (Glossary: *Division and Classification*)

SUGGESTED WRITING ASSIGNMENTS

1. Using Welty's essay as a model, describe your neighborhood store or supermarket. Gather a large quantity of detailed information from memory and from an actual visit to the store if that is still possible. You may find it helpful to reread what you wrote in response to the journal prompt for this essay. Once you have gathered your information, try to select those details that will help you create a dominant impression of the store. Finally, organize your examples and illustrations according to some clear organizational pattern.

2. Write an essay on one of the following topics:

   local restaurants
   reading materials
   television shows
   ways of financing a college education
   types of summer employment

   Be sure to use an organizational pattern that is well thought out and is suited to both your material and your purpose.

Beginnings and Endings

"Begin at the beginning and go on till you come to the end: then stop," advised the King of Hearts in *Alice in Wonderland*. "Good advice, but more easily said than done," you might be tempted to reply. Certainly, no part of writing essays can be more daunting than coming up with effective beginnings and endings. In fact, many writers feel these are the most important parts of any piece of writing regardless of its length. Even before coming to your introduction, your readers will usually know something about your intentions from your title. Titles like "The Case against Euthanasia," "How to Buy a Used Car," or "What Is a Migraine Headache?" indicate both your subject and approach and prepare your readers for what is to follow.

■ Beginnings

What makes for an effective beginning? Not unlike a personal greeting, a good beginning should catch a reader's interest and then hold it. The experienced writer realizes that many readers would rather do almost anything than make a commitment to read, so the opening or "lead," as journalists refer to it, requires a lot of thought and much revising to make it right and to keep the reader's attention from straying. The inexperienced writer, on the other hand, knows that the beginning is important but tries to write it first and to perfect it before moving on to the rest of the essay. Although there are no "rules" for writing introductions, we can offer one bit of general advice: wait until the writing process is well under way or almost completed before focusing on your lead. Following this advice will keep you from spending too much time on an introduction that you will undoubtedly revise. More important, once you actually see how your essay develops, you will know better how to introduce it to your reader.

In addition to capturing your reader's attention, a good beginning usually introduces your thesis and either suggests or actually reveals the structure of the composition. Keep in mind that the best beginning is not necessarily the most catchy or the most shocking but the one most appropriate for the job you are trying to do.

There are many effective ways of beginning an essay. Consider using one of the following:

ANECDOTE

Introducing your essay with a brief narrative drawn from current news events, history, or your personal experience can be an effective way to capture your readers' interest. In the following example, Stephen L. Carter introduces an essay on the topic of integrity by recounting a surprising experience he had as a public speaker.

> A couple of years ago I began a university commencement address by telling the audience that I was going to talk about integrity. The crowd broke into applause. Applause! Just because they had heard the word "integrity": that's how starved for it they were. They had no idea how I was using the word, or what I was going to say about integrity, or, indeed, whether I was for it or against it. But they knew they liked the idea of talking about it.

ANALOGY/COMPARISON

An analogy or comparison can be useful in getting readers to contemplate a topic they might otherwise reject as unfamiliar or uninteresting. (Glossary: *Analogy*) In the following example, Pico Iyer introduces a subject few would consider particularly engrossing—the comma—with an analogy to breath. By pairing these two seemingly unrelated concepts, he both introduces and vividly illustrates the idea he will develop in his essay: that the comma is a vital element of writing.

> The gods, they say, give breath, and they take it away. But the same could be said—could it not?—of the humble comma. Add it to the present clause and, all of a sudden, the mind is, quite literally, given pause to think; take it out if you wish or forget it and the mind is deprived of a resting place. Yet still the comma gets no respect. It seems just a slip of a thing, a pedant's tick, a blip on the edge of our consciousness, a kind of printer's smudge almost. Small, we claim, is beautiful (especially in the age of the microchip), yet what is so often used, and so rarely recalled, as the comma—unless it be breath itself?

DIALOGUE/QUOTATION

While relying heavily on the ideas of others can weaken an effective introduction, opening your essay with a quotation or a brief dialogue can attract a reader's attention and can succinctly illustrate a particular attitude or point of view that you want to discuss. In the following example, Bob Greene introduces an essay on the habits of teenagers in shopping malls with a brief dialogue between two Midwestern teenagers contemplating an oceangoing raft.

> "This would be excellent, to go in the ocean with this thing," says Dave Gembutis, fifteen.
> He is looking at a $170 Sea Cruiser raft.
> "Great," says his companion, Dan Holmes, also fifteen.
> This is at Herman's World of Sporting Goods, in the middle of the Woodfield Mall in Schaumburg, Illinois.

FACTS AND STATISTICS

For the most part, you should support your argument with facts and statistics rather than letting them speak for you, but a brief and startling fact or statistic can be an effective way to engage readers in your essay.

> Charles Darwin and Abraham Lincoln were born on the same day
> —February 12, 1809. They are also linked in another curious way
> —for both must simultaneously play, and for similar reasons, the
> role of man and legend.
>
> –Stephen Jay Gould

IRONY OR HUMOR

It is often effective to introduce an essay with irony or humor. Humor, especially, signals to the reader that your essay will be entertaining to read, and irony can indicate an unexpected approach to a topic. In his essay "Shooting an Elephant," George Orwell begins by simultaneously establishing a wry tone and indicating to the reader that he, the narrator, occupies the position of outsider in the events he is about to relate.

> In Moulmein, in lower Burma, I was hated by large numbers of people—the only time in my life that I have been important enough for this to happen to me.

There are several other good ways to begin an essay; the following opening sentence leads illustrate each approach.

SHORT GENERALIZATION

It is a miracle that New York works at all.

–E. B. White

STARTLING CLAIM

It is possible to stop most drug addiction in the United States within a very short time.

–Gore Vidal

RHETORICAL QUESTIONS

Just how interconnected *is* the animal world? Is it true that if we change any part of that world we risk unduly damaging life in other, larger parts of it?

–Matthew Douglas

There are also ways of beginning an essay that should be avoided. Some of these follow:

APOLOGY

I am a college student and do not consider myself an expert on the computer industry, but I think that many computer companies make false claims about just how easy it is to learn to use a computer.

COMPLAINT

I'd rather write about a topic of my own choice than the one that is assigned, but here goes.

WEBSTER'S DICTIONARY

Webster's New Collegiate Dictionary defines the verb *to snore* as follows: "to breathe during sleep with a rough hoarse noise due to vibration of the soft palate."

PLATITUDE

America is the land of opportunity, and no one knows it better than Madonna.

REFERENCE TO TITLE

As you can see from my title, this essay is about why we should continue to experiment with human heart transplants.

■ Endings

An effective ending does more than simply indicate where the writer stopped writing. A conclusion may summarize; may inspire the reader to further thought or even action; may return to the beginning by repeating key words, phrases, or ideas; or may surprise the reader by providing a particularly convincing example to support a thesis. Indeed, there are many ways to write a conclusion, but the effectiveness of any choice must be measured by how appropriately it fits what has gone before it. You might consider concluding with a restatement of your thesis, concluding with a prediction, or concluding with a recommendation.

In an essay contrasting the traditional Hispanic understanding of the word *macho* with the meaning it has developed in mainstream American culture, Rose Del Castillo Guilbault begins her essay with a succinct, two-sentence paragraph offering her thesis:

> What is *macho?* That depends which side of the border you come from.

She concludes her essay by restating her thesis, but in a manner that reflects the detailed examination she has given the concept of *macho* in her essay:

> The impact of language in our society is undeniable. And the misuse of *macho* hints at a deeper cultural misunderstanding that extends mere word definitions.

In the following conclusion to a long chapter on weasel words, a form of deceptive advertising language, writer Paul Stevens summarizes the points that he has made, ending with a recommendation to the reader:

A weasel word is a word that's used to imply a meaning that cannot be truthfully stated. Some weasels imply meanings that are not the same as their actual definition, such as "help," "like," or "fortified." They can act as qualifiers and/or comparatives. Other weasels, such as "taste" and "flavor," have no definite meanings, and are simply subjective opinions offered by the manufacturer. A weasel of omission is one that implies a claim so strongly that it forces you to supply the bogus fact. Adjectives are weasels used to convey feelings and emotions to a greater extent than the product itself can.

In dealing with weasels, you must strip away the innuendos and try to ascertain the facts, if any. To do this, you need to ask questions such as: How? Why? How many? How much? Stick to basic definitions of words. Look them up if you have to. Then, apply the strict definition to the text of the advertisement or commercial. "Like" means similar to, but not the same as. "Virtually" means the same in essence, but not in fact.

Above all, never underestimate the devious qualities of a weasel. Weasels twist and turn and hide in dark shadows. You must come to grips with them, or advertising will rule you forever.

My advice to you is: Beware of weasels. They are nasty and untrainable, and they attack pocketbooks.

In the conclusion to her composition entitled "Title IX Just Makes Sense," student Jen Jarjosa offers an overview of her argument and concludes by predicting the outcome of the solution she advocates:

> There have undeniably been major improvements in the treatment of female college athletes since the enactment of Title IX. But most colleges and universities still don't measure up to the actual regulation standards, and many have quite a ways to go. The Title IX fight for equality is not a radical feminist movement, nor is it intended to take away the privileges of male athletes. It is, rather, a demand for fairness, for women to receive the same opportunities that men have always had. When colleges and universities stop viewing Title IX budget requirements as an inconvenience and start complying with the spirit and not merely the letter of the law, collegiate female athletes will finally reach the parity they deserve.

If you are having trouble with your conclusion — and this is not an uncommon occurrence — it may be because of problems with your essay itself. Frequently, writers do not know when to end because they are not sure about their overall purpose in the first place. For example, if you are taking a trip and your purpose is to go to Chicago, you'll know when you get there and will stop. But if you don't really know where you are going, it's very difficult to know when to stop.

It's usually a good idea in your conclusion to avoid such overworked expressions as "In conclusion," "In summary," "I hope I have shown," or "Finally." Your conclusion should also do more than simply repeat what you've said in your opening paragraph. The most satisfying essays are those in which the conclusion provides an interesting way of wrapping up ideas introduced in the beginning and developed throughout.

You might find it revealing as your course progresses to read with special attention the beginnings and endings of the essays throughout *Models for Writers*. Take special note of the varieties of beginnings and endings, the possible relationship between a beginning and an ending, and the general appropriateness of these elements to the writer's subject and purpose.

Of My Friend Hector
and My Achilles Heel

■ Michael T. Kaufman

The former writer of the "About New York" column for the
New York Times, Michael T. Kaufman was born in 1938 in
Paris and grew up in the United States. He studied at the Bronx
High School of Science, City College of New York, and Colum-
bia University. He began his career at the New York Times *as a*
reporter and feature writer, and before assuming his position as
columnist, he served as bureau chief in Ottawa and Warsaw.
The experience in Warsaw is evident in his book about Poland,
Mad Dreams, Saving Graces, *published in 1989. Kaufman is*
also a past winner of the George Polk Award for International
Reporting. In the following selection, which appeared in the New
York Times *in 1992, Kaufman uses the story of his childhood*
friend Hector Elizondo to reflect on his own "prejudice and stu-
pidity." Take note of how the two very brief sentences at the be-
ginning establish the chronological and narrative structure of
what follows.

FOR YOUR JOURNAL

Many schools "track" students by intellectual ability into such
categories as "honors," "college bound," "vocational," "reme-
dial," or "terminal." Did you go to a high school that tracked
its students? How did the tracking system work? How did you
feel about your placement? What did you think about classmates who were on tracks higher or lower than yours?

This story is about prejudice and stupidity. My own.   1
It begins in 1945 when I was a 7-year-old living on the fifth floor   2
of a tenement walkup on 107th Street between Columbus and Manhattan Avenues in New York City. The block was almost entirely
Irish and Italian, and I believe my family was the only Jewish one
around.

One day a Spanish-speaking family moved into one of the four   3
apartments on our landing. They were the first Puerto Ricans I had
met. They had a son who was about my age named Hector, and the
two of us became friends. We played with toy soldiers and I particularly remember how, using rubber bands and wood from orange
crates, we made toy pistols that shot off little squares we cut from old
linoleum.

We visited each other's home and I know that at the time I liked   4
Hector and I think he liked me. I may even have eaten my first avo-
cado at his house.

About a year after we met, my family moved to another part of   5
Manhattan's West Side and I did not see Hector again until I entered
Booker T. Washington Junior High School as an 11-year-old.

THE SPECIAL CLASS

The class I was in was called 7SP-1; the SP was for special. Earlier, I   6
recall, I had been in the IGC class, for "intellectually gifted children."
The SP class was to complete the seventh, eighth and ninth grades in
two years and almost all of us would then go to schools like Bronx
Science, Stuyvesant or Music and Art, where admission was based on
competitive exams. I knew I was in the SP class and the IGC class. I
guess I also knew that other people were not.

Hector was not. He was in some other class, maybe even 7-2, the   7
class that was held to be the next-brightest, or maybe 7-8. I remember I was happy to see him whenever we would meet, and sometimes
we played punchball during lunch period. Mostly, of course, I stayed
with my own classmates, with other Intellectually Gifted Children.

Sometimes children from other classes, those presumably not so   8
intellectually gifted, would tease and taunt us. At such times I was
particularly proud to have Hector as a friend. I assumed that he was
tougher than I and my classmates and I guess I thought that if necessary he would come to my defense.

DIFFERENT HIGH SCHOOLS

For high school, I went uptown to Bronx Science. Hector, I think,   9
went downtown to Commerce. Sometimes I would see him in River-
side Park, where I played basketball and he worked out on the parallel bars. We would acknowledge each other, but by this time the
conversations we held were perfunctory—sports, families, weather.

After I finished college, I would see him around the neighbor- 10
hood pushing a baby carriage. He was the first of my contemporaries
to marry and to have a child.

A few years later, in the 60's, married and with children of my own, 11
I was once more living on the West Side, working until late at night as a
reporter. Some nights as I took the train home I would see Hector in the
car. A few times we exchanged nods, but more often I would pretend
that I didn't see him, and maybe he also pretended he didn't see me. Usually he would be wearing a knitted watch cap, and from that I deduced
that he was probably working on the docks as a longshoreman.

I remember quite distinctly how I would sit on the train and think 12
about how strange and unfair fate had been with regard to the two of
us who had once been playmates. Just because I had become an intellectually gifted adult or whatever and he had become a longshoreman
or whatever, was that any reason for us to have been left with nothing
to say to each other? I thought it was wrong and unfair, but I also
thought that conversation would be a chore or a burden. That is pretty
much what I thought about Hector, if I thought about him at all, until
one Sunday in the mid-70's, when I read in the drama section of this
newspaper that my childhood friend, Hector Elizondo, was replacing
Peter Falk in the leading role in "The Prisoner of Second Avenue."

Since then, every time I have seen this versatile and acclaimed 13
actor in movies or on television I have blushed for my assumptions. I
have replayed the subway rides in my head and tried to fathom why
my thoughts had led me where they did.

In retrospect it seems far more logical that the man I saw on the 14
train, the man who had been my friend as a boy, was coming home
from an Off Broadway theater or perhaps from a job as a waiter
while taking acting classes. So why did I think he was a longshoreman? Was it just the cap? Could it be that his being Puerto Rican had
something to do with it? Maybe that reinforced the stereotype I
concocted, but it wasn't the root of it.

WHEN IT GOT STARTED

No, the foundation was laid when I was 11, when I was in 7SP-1 and he 15
was not, when I was in the IGC class and he was not.

I have not seen him since I recognized how I had idiotically kept 16
tracking him for years and decades after the school system had
tracked both of us. I wonder now if my experience was that unusual,
whether social categories conveyed and absorbed before puberty do

not generally tend to linger beyond middle age. And I wonder, too, that if they affected the behavior of someone like myself who had been placed on the upper track, how much more damaging it must have been for someone consigned to the lower.

I have at times thought of calling him, but kept from doing it be-   17
cause how exactly does one apologize for thoughts that were never expressed? And there was still the problem of what to say. "What have you been up to for the last 40 years?" Or "Wow, was I wrong about you!" Or maybe just, "Want to come over and help me make a linoleum gun?"

QUESTIONS FOR STUDY AND DISCUSSION

1. How do Kaufman's first two sentences affect how the reader views the rest of the essay? Did they catch your attention? Why, or why not?
2. If you are unfamiliar with the Greek myth of Hector and Achilles, look it up in a book on mythology. Why does Kaufman allude to Hector and Achilles in his title? (Glossary: *Allusion*)
3. How does Kaufman organize his essay? (Glossary: *Organization*)
4. What is Kaufman's purpose in the essay? How does his organization of the essay help him express his purpose? (Glossary: *Purpose*)
5. Why did Kaufman ignore Hector after he graduated from college? What does this tell him about society in general?
6. Why is Kaufman's ending effective? What point does he want to emphasize with the ending he uses?

VOCABULARY

Refer to your dictionary to define the following words as they are used in this selection. Then use each word in a sentence of your own.

intellectually (6)	acclaimed (13)
perfunctory (9)	concocted (14)
contemporaries (10)	

CLASSROOM ACTIVITY USING BEGINNINGS AND ENDINGS

Carefully read the following three beginnings for an essay on the world's most famous practical joker, Hugh Troy. What are the advantages and disadvantages of each? Which one would you select as an opening paragraph? Why?

Whether questioning the values of American society or simply relieving the monotony of daily life, Hugh Troy always managed to put a little of himself into each of his stunts. One day he attached a plaster hand to his shirt sleeve and took a trip through the Holland Tunnel. As he approached the tollbooth, with his toll ticket between the fingers of the artificial hand, Troy left both ticket and hand in the grasp of the stunned tollbooth attendant and sped away.

Nothing seemed unusual. In fact, it was a rather common occurrence in New York City. Five men dressed in overalls roped off a section of busy Fifth Avenue in front of the old Rockefeller residence, hung out MEN WORKING signs, and began ripping up the pavement. By the time they stopped for lunch, they had dug quite a hole in the street. This crew was different, however, from all the others that had descended upon the streets of the city. It was led by Hugh Troy — the world's greatest practical joker.

Hugh Troy was born in Ithaca, New York, where his father was a professor at Cornell University. After graduating from Cornell, Troy left for New York City, where he became a successful illustrator of children's books. When World War II broke out, he went into the army and eventually became a captain in the 21st Bomber Command, 20th Air Force, under General Curtis LeMay. After the war he made his home in Garrison, New York, for a short while before finally settling in Washington, D.C., where he lived until his death.

SUGGESTED WRITING ASSIGNMENTS

1. Kaufman's essay is a deeply personal one. Use it as a model to write an essay about a time or an action in your life that you are not proud of. What happened? Why did it happen? What would you do differently if you could? Be sure to catch the reader's attention in the beginning and to end your essay with a thought-provoking conclusion.

2. Everyone has childhood friends that we either have lost track of or don't communicate with as often as we would like. Choose an old friend whom you have lost track of and would like to see again. Write an essay about your relationship. What made your friend special to you as a child? Why did you lose touch? What does the future hold? Organize your essay chronologically.

How to Take a Job Interview

■ **Kirby W. Stanat**

Formerly a personnel recruiter and placement officer at the University of Wisconsin–Milwaukee, and presently an executive search consultant in Milwaukee, Kirby W. Stanat has helped thousands of people get jobs. His book Job Hunting Secrets and Tactics *(1977) tells readers what they need to know to get the jobs they want. In this selection, Stanat analyzes the campus interview, a process that hundreds of thousands of college students undergo each year as they seek to enter the job market. Notice how he establishes an effective and engaging context with his brief opening paragraph, and how the "snap" of his ending echoes back through the essay.*

FOR YOUR JOURNAL

While seeking summer employment or selecting a college or university to attend, you may have had the experience of being interviewed. What do you remember most about the interviewer? What kinds of questions did this person ask you? If you could take the interview over again, what would you change?

To succeed in campus job interviews, you have to know where   1
that recruiter is coming from. The simple answer is that he is coming from corporate headquarters.

That may sound obvious, but it is a significant point that too   2
many students do not consider. The recruiter is not a free spirit as he flies from Berkeley to New Haven, from Chapel Hill to Boulder. He's on an invisible leash to the office, and if he is worth his salary, he is mentally in corporate headquarters all the time he's on the road.

If you can fix that in your mind—that when you walk into that   3
bare-walled cubicle in the placement center you are walking into a branch office of Sears, Bendix or General Motors—you can avoid a lot of little mistakes and maybe some big ones.

If, for example, you assume that because the interview is on cam-   4
pus the recruiter expects you to look and act like a student, you're in for a shock. A student is somebody who drinks beer, wears blue jeans

and throws a Frisbee. No recruiter has jobs for student Frisbee whizzes.

A cool spring day in late March, Sam Davis, a good recruiter who has been on the college circuit for years, is on my campus talking to candidates. He comes out to the waiting area to meet the student who signed up for an 11 o'clock interview. I'm standing in the doorway of my office taking in the scene. 5

Sam calls the candidate: "Sidney Student." There sits Sidney. He's at a 45-degree angle, his feet are in the aisle, and he's almost lying down. He's wearing well-polished brown shoes, a tasteful pair of brown pants, a light brown shirt, and a good-looking tie. Unfortunately, he tops off this well-coordinated outfit with his Joe's Tavern Class A Softball Championship jacket, which has a big woven emblem over the heart. 6

If that isn't bad enough, in his left hand is a cigarette and in his right hand is a half-eaten apple. 7

When Sam calls his name, the kid is caught off guard. He ditches the cigarette in an ashtray, struggles to his feet, and transfers the apple from the right to the left hand. Apple juice is everywhere, so Sid wipes his hand on the seat of his pants and shakes hands with Sam. 8

Sam, who by now is close to having a stroke, gives me that what-do-I-have-here look and has the young man follow him into the interviewing room. 9

The situation deteriorates even further—into pure Laurel and Hardy. The kid is stuck with the half-eaten apple, doesn't know what to do with it, and obviously is suffering some discomfort. He carries the apple into the interviewing room with him and places it in the ashtray on the desk—right on top of Sam's freshly lit cigarette. 10

The interview lasts five minutes. . . . 11

Let us move in for a closer look at how the campus recruiter operates. 12

Let's say you have a 10 o'clock appointment with the recruiter from the XYZ Corporation. The recruiter gets rid of the candidate in front of you at about 5 minutes to 10, jots down a few notes about what he is going to do with him or her, then picks up your résumé or data sheet (which you have submitted in advance). . . . 13

Although the recruiter is still in the interview room and you are still in the lobby, your interview is under way. You're on. The recruiter will look over your sheet pretty carefully before he goes out to call you. He develops a mental picture of you. 14

He thinks, "I'm going to enjoy talking with this kid," or "This   15
one's going to be a turkey." The recruiter has already begun to make
a screening decision about you.

His first impression of you, from reading the sheet, could come   16
from your grade point. It could come from misspelled words. It could
come from poor erasures or from the fact that necessary information
is missing. By the time the recruiter has finished reading your sheet,
you've already hit the plus or minus column.

Let's assume the recruiter got a fairly good impression from your   17
sheet.

Now the recruiter goes out to the lobby to meet you. He almost   18
shuffles along, and his mind is somewhere else. Then he calls your name,
and at that instant he visibly clicks into gear. He just went to work.

As he calls your name he looks quickly around the room, waiting   19
for somebody to move. If you are sitting on the middle of your back,
with a book open and a cigarette going, and if you have to rebuild yourself to stand up, the interest will run right out of the recruiter's face.
You, not the recruiter, made the appointment for 10 o'clock, and the
recruiter expects to see a young professional come popping out of that
chair like today is a good day and you're anxious to meet him.

At this point, the recruiter does something rude. He doesn't walk   20
across the room to meet you halfway. He waits for you to come to
him. Something very important is happening. He wants to see you
move. He wants to get an impression about your posture, your stride,
and your briskness.

If you slouch over to him, sidewinderlike, he is not going to be   21
impressed. He'll figure you would probably slouch your way through
your workdays. He wants you to come at him with lots of good
things going for you. If you watch the recruiter's eyes, you can see the
inspection. He glances quickly at shoes, pants, coat, shirt; dress,
blouse, hose — the whole works.

After introducing himself, the recruiter will probably say, "Okay,   22
please follow me," and he'll lead you into his interviewing room.

When you get to the room, you may find that the recruiter will   23
open the door and gesture you in — with him blocking part of the doorway. There's enough room for you to get past him, but it's a near thing.

As you scrape past, he gives you a closeup inspection. He looks   24
at your hair; if it's greasy, that will bother him. He looks at your
collar; if it's dirty, that will bother him. He looks at your shoulders; if
they're covered with dandruff, that will bother him. If you're a man,

he looks at your chin. If you didn't get a close shave, that will irritate him. If you're a woman, he checks your makeup. If it's too heavy, he won't like it.

Then he smells you. An amazing number of people smell bad. Oc- 25 casionally a recruiter meets a student who smells like a canal horse. That student can expect an interview of about four or five minutes.

Next the recruiter inspects the back side of you. He checks your 26 hair (is it combed in front but not in back?), he checks your heels (are they run down?), your pants (are they baggy?), your slip (is it show-ing?), your stockings (do they have runs?).

Then he invites you to sit down. 27

At this point, I submit, the recruiter's decision on you is 75 to 80 28 percent made.

Think about it. The recruiter has read your résumé. He knows 29 who you are and where you are from. He knows your marital status, your major and your grade point. And he knows what you have done with your summers. He has inspected you, exchanged greetings with you and smelled you. There is very little additional hard information that he must gather on you. From now on it's mostly body chemistry.

Many recruiters have argued strenuously with me that they don't 30 make such hasty decisions. So I tried an experiment. I told several re-cruiters that I would hang around in the hall outside the interview room when they took candidates in.

I told them that as soon as they had definitely decided not to rec- 31 ommend (to department managers in their companies) the candidate they were interviewing, they should snap their fingers loud enough for me to hear. It went like this.

First candidate: 38 seconds after the candidate sat down: Snap! 32

Second candidate: 1 minute, 42 seconds: Snap! 33

Third candidate: 45 seconds: Snap! 34

One recruiter was particularly adamant, insisting that he didn't 35 rush to judgment on candidates. I asked him to participate in the snapping experiment. He went out in the lobby, picked up his first candidate of the day, and headed for an interview room.

As he passed me in the hall, he glared at me. And his fingers went 36 "Snap!"

QUESTIONS FOR STUDY AND DISCUSSION

1. Stanat's opening paragraph concisely identifies the point of view of the interviewer in a campus interview setting. Why is this such

an important piece of information? How does it serve to prepare the reader for the information that follows?

2. What are Stanat's purpose and thesis in telling the reader how the recruitment process works? (Glossary: *Purpose* and *Thesis*)

3. In paragraphs 12–29, Stanat explains how the campus recruiter works. Make a list of the steps in that process. (Glossary: *Process Analysis*)

4. Why do recruiters pay so much attention to body language when they interview job candidates?

5. What specifically have you learned from reading Stanat's essay? Do you feel that the essay is useful in preparing someone for a job interview? Explain.

6. Stanat's tone—his attitude toward his subject and audience—in this essay is informal. What in his sentence structure and diction creates this informality? (Glossary: *Diction*) Cite examples. How might the tone be made more formal for a different audience? (Glossary: *Tone*)

7. Summarize Stanat's final seven paragraphs in one sentence. Is his use of the anecdote an effective way to get his point across? (Glossary: *Anecdote*) Why, or why not?

VOCABULARY

Refer to your dictionary to define the following words as they are used in this selection. Then use each word in a sentence of your own.

cubicle (3)   résumé (13)

deteriorates (10)   adamant (35)

CLASSROOM ACTIVITY USING BEGINNINGS AND ENDINGS

Stanat introduces his finger-snapping experiment very late in his essay (paragraph 30) and uses it as an ending. Could he have ended the essay with paragraph 29? Why, or why not? Review Stanat's essay through paragraph 29, and then try your hand at writing a new conclusion to the essay.

SUGGESTED WRITING ASSIGNMENTS

1. Stanat's purpose is to offer practical advice to students interviewing for jobs. Determine a subject about which you can offer

advice to a specific audience. Using Stanat's essay as a model, present your advice in the form of an essay, being careful to provide an attention-grabbing beginning and a convincing conclusion.

2. Stanat gives us an account of the interview process from the viewpoint of the interviewer. If you have ever been interviewed and remember the experience well, write an essay on your feelings and thoughts as the interview took place. What were the circumstances of the interview? What questions were asked of you, how did you feel about them, and how comfortable was the process? How did the interview turn out? What precisely, if anything, did you learn from the experience? What advice would you give someone about to be interviewed? You may find it helpful to review the journal entry that you wrote for this selection before beginning your essay.

Intelligence

■ Isaac Asimov

Born in the Soviet Union, Isaac Asimov emigrated to the United States in 1923. His death in 1992 ended a long, prolific career as a science-fiction and nonfiction writer. Asimov was uniquely talented at making a diverse range of topics, from Shakespeare to atomic physics, not only comprehensible, but also entertaining to the general reader. Asimov earned three degrees at Columbia University and later taught biochemistry at Boston University. At the time of his death, he had published more than five hundred books. In the following essay, Asimov, an intellectually gifted man, ponders the nature of intelligence. His academic brilliance, he concedes, would mean little or nothing if likeminded intellectuals had not established the standards for intelligence in our society.

FOR YOUR JOURNAL

Our society defines the academically gifted as intelligent, but perhaps *book smart* would be a better term. IQ tests don't take into account common sense or experience, attributes that the academically gifted sometimes lack outside of a scholarly setting. Who's the smartest person you know? Is he or she academically gifted or smart in some way that would not be readily recognized as a form of intelligence?

What is intelligence, anyway? When I was in the army I received a kind of aptitude test that soldiers took and, against a norm of 100, scored 160. No one at the base had ever seen a figure like that, and for two hours they made a big fuss over me. (It didn't mean anything. The next day I was still a buck private with KP as my highest duty.)

All my life I've been registering scores like that, so that I have the complacent feeling that I'm highly intelligent, and I expect other people to think so, too. Actually, though, don't such scores simply mean that I am very good at answering the type of academic questions that are considered worthy of answers by the people who make up the intelligence tests—people with intellectual bents similar to mine?

For instance, I had an auto-repair man once, who, on these intel- 3
ligence tests, could not possibly have scored more than 80, by my estimate. I always took it for granted that I was far more intelligent
than he was. Yet, when anything went wrong with my car I hastened
to him with it, watched him anxiously as he explored its vitals, and
listened to his pronouncements as though they were divine oracles —
and he always fixed my car.

Well, then, suppose my auto-repair man devised questions for an 4
intelligence test. Or suppose a carpenter did, or a farmer, or, indeed,
almost anyone but an academician. By every one of those tests, I'd
prove myself a moron. And I'd *be* a moron, too. In a world where I
could not use my academic training and my verbal talents but had to
do something intricate or hard, working with my hands, I would do
poorly. My intelligence, then, is not absolute but is a function of the
society I live in and of the fact that a small subsection of that society
has managed to foist itself on the rest as an arbiter of such matters.

Consider my auto-repair man, again. He had a habit of telling me 5
jokes whenever he saw me. One time he raised his head from under the
automobile hood to say: "Doc, a deaf-and-dumb guy went into a hardware store to ask for some nails. He put two fingers together on the
counter and made hammering motions with the other hand. The clerk
brought him a hammer. He shook his head and pointed to the two fingers he was hammering. The clerk brought him nails. He picked out the
sizes he wanted, and left. Well doc, the next guy who came in was a
blind man. He wanted scissors. How do you suppose he asked for them?"

Indulgently, I lifted my right hand and made scissoring motions 6
with my first two fingers. Whereupon my auto-repair man laughed
raucously and said, "Why you dumb jerk, he used his *voice* and
asked for them." Then he said, smugly, "I've been trying that on all
my customers today." "Did you catch many?" I asked. "Quite a
few," he said, "but I knew for sure I'd catch *you*." "Why is that?" I
asked. "Because you're so goddamned educated, doc, I *knew* you
couldn't be very smart."

And I have an uneasy feeling he had something there. 7

QUESTIONS FOR STUDY AND DISCUSSION

1. Why does Asimov begin his essay with a rhetorical question?
(Glossary: *Rhetorical Question*) What does he emphasize by asking the question? How does the rest of his first paragraph relate
to the question?

2. What is Asimov's thesis? (Glossary: *Thesis*) Where does he state it? How do his interactions with his auto-repair man serve to illustrate the thesis?

3. Analyze how Asimov transitions from one paragraph to the next. What transitional expressions or devices does he use? (Glossary: *Transition*)

4. Asimov refers to himself as a "moron" in most fields outside academics. What does the term *moron* connote to you? (Glossary: *Connotation/Denotation*) Why do you think Asimov uses the term, rather than simply stating that he would not do well in other fields?

5. How does Asimov's conclusion, although concise and ambiguous, serve to expand upon his thesis, identified in the previous question? Why do you think he chose ambiguity instead of a strong statement?

VOCABULARY

Refer to your dictionary to define the following words as they are used in this selection. Then use each word in a sentence of your own.

aptitude (1)	foist (4)
complacent (2)	arbiter (4)
intellectual (2)	indulgently (6)
oracles (3)	raucously (6)
academician (4)	

CLASSROOM ACTIVITY USING BEGINNINGS AND ENDINGS

Asimov uses a rhetorical question to begin his essay. Pick two of the other seven methods discussed in the introduction to this chapter, and use each to write alternative opening sentences or paragraphs for Asimov's essay.

SUGGESTED WRITING ASSIGNMENTS

1. Write an essay in which you address Asimov's opening question: "What is intelligence, anyway?" Define what intelligence means to you, both in yourself and in those around you. Is intelligence a reflection of how well you can function in your environment, or can someone be simultaneously intelligent and inept? Be sure to avoid beginning your essay with a dictionary definition or a platitude, both of which may be tempting to use.

2. Think about people you know well whose "book smarts" are exceeded by another attribute or a different kind of intelligence. They need not be academically challenged—indeed, they may be gifted—but perhaps they left their studies to pursue music, art, crafts, or another field. Write an essay in which you describe one such person's situation. Has he or she benefited from a "different" intelligence? Why, or why not? Has this person's lack of academic achievement hindered him or her in any way? If so, in what ways? How has this person influenced your thinking about your studies and your career goals? Craft both your beginning and your ending to create and enhance the dominant impression you wish the reader to have about this person. You may wish to review what you wrote in your journal exercise for this selection before starting to write.

The Wounds That Can't Be Stitched Up

■ **Ruth Russell**

Ruth Russell was born in Greenfield, Massachusetts, and attends Greenfield Community College. When we selected Russell's essay for inclusion in Models for Writers, *we had no idea that she had used the sixth edition as the textbook in her college composition course. Russell said of her experience with* Models, *"The book was tremendously helpful to me in learning to write. I would do a lot of the exercises at the end of the essays, even when they were not assigned, as a way of deconstructing them, of finding out how they were written, what their essential parts were. I was really interested in improving my writing." After writing the following essay for her course, she submitted it to the "My Turn" column in* Newsweek, *where it soon appeared, without much editing by the column's editor, Pam Hammer. "Her suggestions helped to make it a little shorter and stronger," recalls Russell, who feels very proud to have made so much progress with her writing. "At one point I had entitled the piece 'Full Circle,' but I much prefer the present title. I often think how amazing it is that the incident that caused me to write the essay occurred on about the twentieth anniversary of my mother's accident."*

FOR YOUR JOURNAL

Everyone has childhood fears that are often associated with a particular event or experience, fears that can last for years. What particular fear or fears did you have as a child? Were they caused by a specific incident that you can recall? How have they affected your life as a teenager and young adult?

It was a mild December night. Christmas was only two weeks away. 1
The evening sky was overcast, but the roads were dry. All was quiet in our small town as I drove to my grandmother's house.

I heard the sirens first. Red lights and blue lights strobed in tan-   2
dem. Ambulances with their interiors lit like television screens in a
dark room flew by, escorted by police cruisers on the way to the hospital.

When I arrived at my gram's, she was on the porch steps strug-   3
gling to put on her coat. "Come on," she said breathlessly, "your
mother has been in an accident." I was 17 then, and it would take a
long time before sirens lost their power to reduce me to tears.

Twenty-three years have passed, but only recently have I realized   4
how deeply affected I was by events caused by a drunk driver so long
ago.

When the accident occurred, my youngest brother was 8. He was   5
sitting in the back seat of our family's large, sturdy sedan. The force
of the crash sent him flying headlong into the back of the front seat,
leaving him with a grossly swollen black eye. He was admitted to the
hospital for observation. He didn't talk much when I visited him that
night. He just sat in the bed, a lonely little figure in a darkened hospital room.

My sister, who was 12, was sitting in the front seat. She confided   6
to me later how much she missed the beautiful blue coat she'd been
wearing at the time. It was an early Christmas present, and it was destroyed beyond repair by the medical personnel who cut it off her
body as they worked to save her life. She had a severely fractured
skull that required immediate surgery. The resulting facial scar became for our family a permanent reminder of how close she came to
dying that night.

My mother was admitted to the intensive-care unit to be stabi-   7
lized before her multiple facial cuts could be stitched up. Dad tried to
prepare me before we went in to see her by telling me that she looked
and sounded worse than she was. One eye was temporarily held in
place by a bandage wrapped around her head. Her lower lip
hideously gaped, exposing a mouthful of broken teeth. Delirious, she
cried out for her children and apologized for an accident she neither
caused nor could have avoided. An accident that happened when her
car was hit head-on by a drunk driver speeding down the wrong side
of the road in a half-ton truck with no headlights.

My dad, my brothers, my sister and I spent Christmas at the hos-   8
pital visiting my mother. Sometimes she was so out of it from medication that she barely recognized us. We celebrated two of my brothers'
birthdays—one only days after Christmas and the other in early
January—there too.

I remember watching the police escort the drunk driver out of the   9
hospital the night of the accident. He looked about 35 years old, but
his face was so distorted by rage and alcohol that I could only guess.
A bandaged wrist was his only visible injury. He kept repeating that
he'd done nothing wrong as several officers tried to get him into the
cruiser waiting outside the emergency-room exit.

The man was jailed over the weekend and lost his license for 30   10
days for driving while intoxicated. I don't know if that was his first
alcohol-related traffic violation, but I know it wasn't the last. Now
and then I'd see his name in the court log of our local paper for another DWI, and wonder how he could still be behind the wheel.

Sometimes when I tell this story, I'd be asked in an accusatory   11
tone if my mom and siblings were wearing seat belts. I think that's a
lot like asking a rape victim how she was dressed. The answer is no.
This all happened before seat-belt-awareness campaigns began. In
fact, if they had been in a smaller car, seat belts or not, I believe my
mother and sister would have died.

Many local people who know the driver are surprised when they   12
hear about the accident, and they are quick to defend him. They tell
me he was a war hero. His parents aren't well. He's an alcoholic. Or
my favorite: "He's a good guy when he doesn't drink."

Two years ago I discovered this man had moved into my apart-   13
ment building. I felt vaguely apprehensive, but I believed the accident
was ancient history. Nothing could have prepared me for what
happened next.

It was a mild afternoon, just a few days before Christmas. I had   14
started down the back staircase of the building, on my way to visit
my son, when I recognized my neighbor's new pickup truck as it
roared down the street. The driver missed the entrance to our shared
parking lot. He reversed crookedly in the road, slammed the transmission into forward, then quickly pulled into his parking space.
Gravel and sand flew as he stomped on the brakes to halt his truck
just inches from where I stood frozen on the staircase. As he staggered from his vehicle, he looked at me and asked drunkenly, "Did I
scare you?"

QUESTIONS FOR STUDY AND DISCUSSION

1. Russell begins her essay with a somewhat generic description —
   season, weather, road conditions — of the day of her mother's

accident. Why are such details important in her memory? How does her first paragraph work with her title to draw the reader in?

2. Russell provides the reader with an image of her little brother — the least injured of the three in the car — before discussing her sister and mother. What is the image? Why is it an effective introduction to the scene at the hospital?

3. What is Russell's tone in her essay? (Glossary: *Tone*) How does she establish it? Cite specific examples from the text.

4. Russell ironically describes the platitude, "He's a good guy when he doesn't drink," as her "favorite" (12). Why is the statement ironic? (Glossary: *Irony*) Why do you think Russell emphasizes it as her favorite excuse for the man?

5. Russell's ending does not offer a neat conclusion to her situation and makes no concrete statement about her own feelings. Why does she leave the interaction between the drunk driver and herself so open-ended? How does her ending tie in with her purpose for writing the essay? (Glossary: *Purpose*)

VOCABULARY

Refer to your dictionary to define the following words as they are used in the selection. Then use each word in a sentence of your own.

confided (6) accusatory (11)
gaped (7) apprehensive (13)
distorted (9)

CLASSROOM ACTIVITY USING BEGINNINGS AND ENDINGS

Choose one of the essays you have been writing for your course, and write at least two different beginnings for it. If you are having trouble coming up with two, check to see whether or not one of the paragraphs in the body of your essay is appropriate, or consult the list of effective beginnings in the introduction to this chapter. After you have finished, have several classmates read your beginnings and select their favorite. Do any of your new beginnings suggest ways that you can improve the focus, the organization, or the ending of your essay? Explain these revision possibilities to your partners.

SUGGESTED WRITING ASSIGNMENTS

1. Russell's essay says a lot about how our society reacts to drunk drivers, but she never directly argues a point. Her experiences alone speak to the problem very clearly. Using her essay as a model, write an essay in which you present an indirect argument about a topic that is important to you, using your experiences and observations to lead the reader to the desired conclusion. Construct your beginning and ending with care so that the reader immediately understands how your experiences are relevant to the issue and is left with a strong image or statement that supports your point of view.

2. Write a short essay about an ongoing conflict or situation that you are either working to resolve or hoping will be resolved in the near future. For example, you can use a test you are studying for, an up-and-down relationship, a search for employment, and so on. Have a clear purpose in mind regarding how you want the reader to react—with anger, sympathy, amusement, and so on—and craft your essay to accomplish your goal. Pay particular attention to the conclusion, which will be open-ended but should clearly communicate your purpose to the reader.

chapter *5*

Paragraphs

Within an essay, the paragraph is the most important unit of thought. Like the essay, it has its own main idea, often stated directly in a topic sentence. Like a good essay, a good paragraph is unified: it avoids digressions and develops its main idea. Paragraphs use many of the rhetorical strategies that essays use, strategies like classification, comparison and contrast, and cause and effect. As you read the following three paragraphs, notice how each writer develops his or her topic sentence with explanations, concrete details and statistics, or vivid examples. The topic sentence in each paragraph is italicized.

I've learned from experience that good friendships are based on a delicate balance. When friends are on a par, professionally and personally, it's easier for them to root for one another. It's taken me a long time to realize that not all my "friends" wish me well. Someone who wants what you have may not be able to handle your good fortune: If you find yourself apologizing for your hard-earned raise or soft-pedaling your long-awaited promotion, it's a sure sign that the friendship is off balance. Real friends are secure enough in their own lives to share each other's successes — not begrudge them.

–Stephanie Mansfield

The problem of substance abuse is far more complex and far more pervasive than any of us really knows or is willing to admit. *Most stories of illegal drugs overshadow Americans' struggles with alcohol, tobacco, food, and nonprescription drugs — our so-called legal addictions.* In 1990, for example, 14,000 deaths were attributed to cocaine and heroin. In that same year, 390,000 deaths were attributed to tobacco and 90,000 to alcohol. It's not surprising, then, that many sociologists believe we are a nation of substance abusers — drinkers, smokers, overeaters, and pill poppers. Although the statistics are alarming, they do not begin to suggest the heavy toll of substance abuse on Americans and their families. Loved ones die, relationships are fractured, children are abandoned, job productivity falters, and the dreams of young people are extinguished.

—Alfred Rosa and Paul Eschholz

Photographs have let me know my parents before I was born, as the carefree college students they were, in love and awaiting the rest of their lives. I have seen the light blue Volkswagen van my Dad used to take surfing down the coast of California and the silver dress my Mom wore to her senior prom. Through pictures I was able to witness their wedding, which showed me that there is much in their relationship that goes beyond their children. I saw the look in their eyes as they held their first, newborn daughter, as well as the jealous expressions of my sister when I was born a few years later. There is something almost magical about viewing images of yourself and your family that you were too young to remember.

—Carrie White, student

Many writers find it helpful to think of the paragraph as a very small, compact essay. Here is a paragraph from an essay on testing:

Multiple-choice questions distort the purposes of education. Picking one answer among four is very different from thinking a question through to an answer of one's own, and far less useful in life. Recognition of vocabulary and isolated facts makes the best kind of multiple-choice questions, so these dominate the tests, rather than questions that test the use of knowledge. Because schools want their children to perform well, they are often tempted to teach the limited sorts of knowledge most useful on the tests.

This paragraph, like all well-written paragraphs, has several distinguishing characteristics: it is unified, coherent, and adequately developed. It is unified in that every sentence and every idea relate to the main idea, stated in the topic sentence, "Multiple-choice questions distort the purposes of education." It is coherent in that the sentences and ideas are arranged logically and the relationships among them are made clear by the use of effective transitions. Finally, the paragraph is adequately developed in that it presents a short but persuasive argument supporting its main idea.

How much development is "adequate" development? The answer depends on many things: how complicated or controversial the main idea is; what readers already know and believe; how much space the writer is permitted. Everyone, or nearly everyone, agrees that the earth circles around the sun; a single sentence would be enough to make that point. A writer trying to argue that affirmative action has outlived its usefulness, however, would need many sentences, indeed many paragraphs, to develop that idea convincingly.

Here is another model of an effective paragraph. As you read this paragraph about the resourcefulness of pigeons in evading attempts to control them, pay particular attention to its main idea, unity, development, and coherence.

> Pigeons (and their human friends) have proved remarkably resourceful in evading nearly all the controls, from birth-control pellets to carbide shells to pigeon apartment complexes, that pigeon-haters have devised. One of New York's leading museums once put large black rubber owls on its wide ledges to discourage the large number of pigeons that roosted there. Within the day the pigeons had gotten over their fear of owls and were back perched on the owls' heads. A few years ago San Francisco put a sticky coating on the ledges of some public buildings, but the pigeons got used to the goop and came back to roost. The city then tried trapping, using electric owls, and periodically exploding carbide shells outside a city building, hoping the noise would scare the pigeons away. It did, but not for long, and the program was abandoned. More frequent explosions probably would have distressed the humans in the area more than the birds. Philadelphia tried a feed that makes pigeons vomit, and then, they hoped, go away. A New York firm claimed it had a feed that made a pigeon's nervous system send "danger signals" to the other members of its flock.

The main idea is stated at the beginning in a topic sentence. Other sentences in the paragraph support this idea with examples. Since all the separate examples illustrate how pigeons have evaded attempts to control them, the paragraph is unified. Since there are enough examples to convince the reader of the truth of the topic statement, the paragraph is adequately developed. Finally, the regular use of transitional words and phrases like *once, within the day, a few years ago,* and *then* lends the paragraph coherence.

How long should a paragraph be? In modern essays, most paragraphs range from 50 to 250 words, but some run a full page or more, and others may be only a few words long. The best answer is that a paragraph should be long enough to develop its main idea adequately. Some writers, when they find a paragraph running very long, may break it into two or more paragraphs so that readers can pause and catch their breath. Other writers forge ahead, relying on the unity and coherence of their paragraph to keep their readers from getting lost.

Articles and essays that appear in magazines and newspapers often have relatively short paragraphs, some of only one or two sentences. Short paragraphs are a convention in journalism because of the narrow columns, which make paragraphs of average length appear very long. But often you will find that these journalistic "paragraphs" could be joined together into a few longer, more normal paragraphs. Longer, more normal paragraphs are the kind you should use in all but journalistic writing.

Simplicity

■ **William Zinsser**

William Zinsser was born in New York City in 1922. After graduating from Princeton University, he worked for the New York Herald Tribune, *first as a feature writer and later as its drama editor and film critic. Zinsser has also taught writing at Yale University and has served as general editor of the Book-of-the-Month Club. He is currently the series editor for The Writer's Craft Series, which publishes talks by writers and is cosponsored by the Book-of-the-Month Club and the New York Public Library. Zinsser's own published works cover many aspects of contemporary American culture, but he is best known as the author of lucid and accessible books about writing, including* Writing with a Word Processor *(1983),* Writing to Learn *(1988), and* On Writing Well *(Sixth Edition, 1998), a perennial favorite for college writing courses as well as the general population. In the following piece, he reminds us, as did Henry David Thoreau before him, to "simplify, simplify." As you read each paragraph, notice the clarity with which Zinsser presents its main idea, and note how he develops that idea with adequate and logically related supporting information. You should also note that he follows his own advice about simplicity.*

FOR YOUR JOURNAL

Sometimes we get so caught up in what's going on around us that we start to feel frantic, and we lose sight of what is really important or meaningful to us. At such times it's a good idea to take stock of what we are doing and to simplify our lives by dropping activities that are no longer rewarding. Write about a time when you've felt the need to simplify your life.

Clutter is the disease of American writing. We are a society strangling in unnecessary words, circular constructions, pompous frills, and meaningless jargon.

Who can understand the clotted language of everyday American commerce: the memo, the corporation report, the business letter, the notice from the bank explaining its latest "simplified" statement? What member of an insurance or medical plan can decipher the brochure explaining his costs and benefits? What father or mother can put together a child's toy from the instructions on the box? Our national tendency is to inflate and thereby sound important. The airline pilot who announces that he is presently anticipating experiencing considerable precipitation wouldn't think of saying it may rain. The sentence is too simple — there must be something wrong with it.

But the secret of good writing is to strip every sentence to its 3 cleanest components. Every word that serves no function, every long word that could be a short word, every adverb that carries the same meaning that's already in the verb, every passive construction that leaves the reader unsure of who is doing what — these are the thousand and one adulterants that weaken the strength of a sentence. And they usually occur in proportion to education and rank.

During the 1960s the president of my university wrote a letter to 4 mollify the alumni after a spell of campus unrest. "You are probably aware," he began, "that we have been experiencing very considerable potentially explosive expressions of dissatisfaction on issues only partially related." He meant the students had been hassling them about different things. I was far more upset by the president's English than by the students' potentially explosive expressions of dissatisfaction. I would have preferred the presidential approach taken by Franklin D. Roosevelt when he tried to convert into English his own government's memos, such as this blackout order of 1942:

> Such preparations shall be made as will completely obscure all Federal buildings and non-Federal buildings occupied by the Federal government during an air raid for any period of time from visibility by reason of internal or external illumination.

"Tell them," Roosevelt said, "that in buildings where they have 5 to keep the work going to put something across the windows."

Simplify, simplify. Thoreau said it, as we are so often reminded, 6 and no American writer more consistently practiced what he preached. Open *Walden* to any page and you will find a man saying in a plain and orderly way what is on his mind:

> I went to the woods because I wished to live deliberately, to front only the essential facts of life, and see if I could not learn what it had to teach, and not, when I came to die, discover that I had not lived.

How can the rest of us achieve such enviable freedom from clut- 7
ter? The answer is to clear our heads of clutter. Clear thinking becomes clear writing; one can't exist without the other. It's impossible
for a muddy thinker to write good English. He may get away with it
for a paragraph or two, but soon the reader will be lost, and there's
no sin so grave, for the reader will not easily be lured back.

Who is this elusive creature, the reader? The reader is someone 8
with an attention span of about 30 seconds — a person assailed by
other forces competing for attention. At one time those forces were
relatively few: newspapers, magazines, radio, spouse, children, pets.
Today they also include a "home entertainment center" (television,
VCR, tapes, CDs), e-mail, the Internet, the cellular phone, the fax
machine, a fitness program, a pool, a lawn, and that most potent of
competitors, sleep. The man or woman snoozing in a chair with a
magazine or a book is a person who was being given too much unnecessary trouble by the writer.

It won't do to say that the reader is too dumb or too lazy to keep 9
pace with the train of thought. If the reader is lost, it's usually because the writer hasn't been careful enough. The carelessness can take
any number of forms. Perhaps a sentence is so excessively cluttered
that the reader, hacking through the verbiage, simply doesn't know
what it means. Perhaps a sentence has been so shoddily constructed
that the reader could read it in several ways. Perhaps the writer has
switched pronouns in midsentence, or has switched tenses, so the
reader loses track of who is talking or when the action took place.
Perhaps Sentence B is not a logical sequel to Sentence A; the writer, in
whose head the connection is clear, hasn't bothered to provide the
missing link. Perhaps the writer has used a word incorrectly by not
taking the trouble to look it up. He or she may think "sanguine" and
"sanguinary" mean the same thing, but the difference is a bloody big
one. The reader can only infer (speaking of big differences) what the
writer is trying to imply.

Faced with such obstacles, readers are at first tenacious. They 10
blame themselves — they obviously missed something, and they go
back over the mystifying sentence, or over the whole paragraph, piecing it out like an ancient rune, making guesses and moving on. But
they won't do this for long. The writer is making them work too
hard, and they will look for one who is better at the craft.

Writers must therefore constantly ask: what am I trying to say? 11
Surprisingly often they don't know. Then they must look at what

they have written and ask: have I said it? Is it clear to someone encountering the subject for the first time? If it's not, some fuzz has worked its way into the machinery. The clear writer is someone clearheaded enough to see this stuff for what it is: fuzz.

I don't mean that some people are born clearheaded and are there- 12 fore natural writers, whereas others are naturally fuzzy and will never write well. Thinking clearly is a conscious act that writers must force upon themselves, as if they were working on any other project that requires logic: making a shopping list or doing an algebra problem. Good writing doesn't come naturally, though most people obviously think it does. Professional writers are constantly bearded by people who say they'd like to "try a little writing sometime" — meaning when they retire from their real profession, like insurance or real estate, which is hard. Or they say, "I could write a book about that." I doubt it.

Writing is hard work. A clear sentence is no accident. Very few 13 sentences come out right the first time, or even the third time. Remember this in moments of despair. If you find that writing is hard, it's because it *is* hard.

QUESTIONS FOR STUDY AND DISCUSSION

1. What exactly does Zinsser mean by "clutter" (1)? How does Zinsser believe we can free ourselves of clutter?
2. Identify the main idea in each of Zinsser's thirteen paragraphs. How is each paragraph related to Zinsser's topic and purpose?
3. In what ways do paragraphs 4–6 serve to illustrate the main idea of paragraph 3? (Glossary: *Illustration*)
4. In paragraph 11, Zinsser says that writers must constantly ask themselves some questions. What are these questions, and why are they important?
5. How do Zinsser's first and last paragraphs serve to introduce and conclude his essay? (Glossary: *Beginnings and Endings*)
6. What is the relationship between thinking and writing for Zinsser?

VOCABULARY

Refer to your dictionary to define the following words as they are used in this selection. Then use each word in a sentence of your own.

pompous (1)   enviable (7)
decipher (2)   tenacious (10)
adulterants (3)   bearded (12)
mollify (4)

CLASSROOM ACTIVITY USING PARAGRAPHS

Below you will find a passage from Zinsser's final manuscript of this chapter from the first editon of *On Writing Well*. Zinsser has included these manuscript pages showing his editing for clutter in every edition of his book because he believes they are instructive. He says, "Although they look like a first draft, they had already been rewritten and retyped—like almost every other page—four or five times. With each rewrite I try to make what I have written tighter, stronger, and more precise, eliminating every element that's not doing useful work. Then I go over it once more, reading it aloud, and am always amazed at how much clutter can still be cut. (In later editions I eliminated the sexist pronoun 'he' denoting 'the writer' and 'the reader.')"

Carefully study these manuscript pages and Zinsser's editing, and be prepared to discuss how the changes enhance his paragraphs' unity, coherence, and logical development.

---

is too dumb or too lazy to keep pace with the ~~writer's~~ train of thought. My sympathies are ~~entirely~~ with him. ~~He's not so dumb.~~ If the reader is lost, it is generally because the writer ~~of the article~~ has not been careful enough to keep him on the ~~proper~~ path.

This carelessness can take any number of ~~different~~ forms. Perhaps a sentence is so excessively ~~long and~~ cluttered that the reader, hacking his way through ~~all~~ the verbiage, simply doesn't know what *it* ~~the writer~~ means. Perhaps a sentence has been so shoddily constructed that the reader could read it in any of *several* ~~two or three different~~ ways. ~~He thinks he knows what the writer is trying to say, but he's not sure.~~ Perhaps the writer has switched pronouns in mid-sentence, or ~~perhaps he~~ has switched tenses, so the reader loses track of who is talking ~~to whom~~ or ~~exactly~~ when the action took place. Perhaps Sentence B is not a logical sequel to Sentence A -- the writer, in whose head the connection is ~~perfectly~~ clear, has not ~~given enough thought to providing~~ *bothered to provide* the missing link. Perhaps the writer has used an important word incorrectly by not taking the trouble to look it up~~, and make sure.~~ He may think that "sanguine" and "sanguinary" mean the same thing, but ~~I can assure you that~~ (the difference is a bloody big one~~, to the reader.~~ *The reader* ~~He~~ can only ~~try to~~ infer ~~xxxx~~ (speaking of big differences) what the writer is trying to imply.

Faced with ~~such a variety of~~ *these* obstacles, the reader is at first a remarkably tenacious bird. He ~~tends to~~ blame*s* himself, ~~he~~ *He* obviously missed something, ~~he thinks,~~ and he goes back over the mystifying sentence, or over the whole paragraph, piecing it out like an ancient rune, making guesses and moving on. But he won't do this for long. ~~He will soon run out of patience.~~ (The writer is making him work too hard, ~~-- harder than he should have to work --~~ (and the reader will look for ~~a writer~~ *one* who is better at his craft.

The writer must therefore constantly ask himself: What am I trying to say? ~~in this sentence?~~ Surprisingly often, he doesn't know. ~~And~~ Then he must look at what he has ~~just~~ written and ask: Have I said it? Is it clear to someone ~~who is coming upon~~ *encountering* the subject for the first time? If it's not~~, clear,~~ it is because some fuzz has worked its way into the machinery. The clear writer is a person ~~who is~~ clear-headed enough to see this stuff for what it is: fuzz.

I don't mean ~~to suggest~~ that some people are born clear-headed and are therefore natural writers, whereas

~~other people~~ **others** are naturally fuzzy and will ~~therefore~~ never write well. Thinking clearly is ~~an entirely~~ **a** conscious act that the writer must ~~keep forcing~~ **force** upon himself, just as if he were ~~starting out~~ **embarking** on any other ~~kind of~~ project that ~~calls for~~ **requires** logic: adding up a laundry list or doing an algebra problem ~~or playing chess~~. Good writing doesn't ~~just~~ come naturally, though most people obviously think ~~it's as easy as walking~~ **it does.** The professional

SUGGESTED WRITING ASSIGNMENTS

1. If what Zinsser writes about clutter is an accurate assessment, we should easily be able to find numerous examples of clutter all around us. During the next few days, make a point of looking for clutter in the written materials you come across. Choose one example that you find—an article, an essay, a form letter, or a chapter from a textbook, for example—and write an extended analysis explaining how it might have been written more simply. Develop your paragraphs well, make sure they are coherent, and try not to "clutter" your own writing.

2. Using some of the ideas you explored in your journal entry for this selection, write a brief essay analyzing your need to simplify some aspect of your life. For example, are you involved in too many extracurricular activities, taking too many courses, working too many hours at an off-campus job, or not making sensible choices with regard to your social life?

"I Just Wanna Be Average"

■ **Mike Rose**

Born in Altoona, Pennsylvania, to Italian American parents, Mike Rose moved to California in the early 1950s. A graduate of Loyola University in Los Angeles, Rose is now a professor at the UCLA Graduate School of Education and Information Studies. He has written a number of books and articles on language and literacy. His best-known book, Lives on the Boundary: The Struggles and Achievements of America's Underprepared, *was recognized by the National Council of Teachers of English with its highest award in 1989. More recently he published* Possible Lives: The Promise of Public Education *(1995). In the following selection from* Lives on the Boundary, *Rose explains how his high school English teacher, Jack MacFarland, picked him up out of the doldrums of "scholastic indifference." As you read, notice that although his paragraphs are fairly lengthy, Rose never digresses from the main point of each.*

FOR YOUR JOURNAL

Often our desire to get more out of school and to go on to college can be traced back to the influence of a single teacher. Which teacher turned you on to learning? Describe what that person did to stimulate change in you.

Jack MacFarland couldn't have come into my life at a better time. 1 My father was dead, and I had logged up too many years of scholastic indifference. Mr. MacFarland had a master's degree from Columbia and decided, at twenty-six, to find a little school and teach his heart out. He never took any credentialing courses, couldn't bear to, he said, so he had to find employment in a private system. He ended up at Our Lady of Mercy teaching five sections of senior English. He was a beatnik who was born too late. His teeth were stained, he tucked his sorry tie in between the third and fourth buttons of his shirt, and his pants were chronically wrinkled. At first, we couldn't believe this guy, thought he slept in his car. But within no time, he had us so startled with work that we didn't much worry about where he slept or if he slept at all. We wrote three or four essays a month. We read a book every two to three weeks, starting with the *Iliad* and ending up with Hemingway. He gave us a quiz on the reading every other day. He brought a prep school curriculum to Mercy High.

MacFarland's lectures were crafted, and as he delivered them he 2 would pace the room jiggling a piece of chalk in his cupped hand, using it to scribble on the board the names of all the writers and philosophers and plays and novels he was weaving into his discussion. He asked questions often, raised everything from Zeno's paradox to the repeated last line of Frost's "Stopping by Woods on a Snowy Evening." He slowly and carefully built up our knowledge of Western intellectual history—with facts, with connections, with speculations. We learned about Greek philosophy, about Dante, the Elizabethan world view, the Age of Reason, existentialism. He analyzed poems with us, had us reading sections from John Ciardi's *How Does a Poem Mean?*, making a potentially difficult book accessible with his own explanations. We gave oral reports on poems Ciardi didn't cover. We imitated the styles of Conrad, Hemingway, and *Time* magazine. We wrote and talked, wrote and talked. The man immersed us in language.

Even MacFarland's barbs were literary. If Jim Fitzsimmons, hung 3 over and irritable, tried to smart-ass him, he'd rejoin with a flourish that would spark the indomitable Skip Madison—who'd lost his front teeth in a hapless tackle—to flick his tongue through the gap and opine, "good chop," drawing out the single "o" in stinging indictment. Jack MacFarland, this tobacco-stained intellectual, brandished linguistic weapons of a kind I hadn't encountered before. Here was this *egghead,* for God's sake, keeping some pretty difficult people in line. And from what I heard, Mike Dweetz and Steve Fusco and all the notorious Voc. Ed. crowd settled down as well when MacFarland took the podium. Though a lot of guys groused in the schoolyard, it just seemed that giving trouble to this particular teacher was a silly thing to do. Tomfoolery, not to mention assault, had no place in the world he was trying to create for us, and instinctively everyone knew that. If nothing else, we all recognized MacFarland's considerable intelligence and respected the hours he put into his work. It came to this: The troublemaker would look foolish rather than daring. Even Jim Fitzsimmons was reading *On the Road* and turning his incipient alcoholism to literary ends.

There were some lives that were already beyond Jack MacFarland's ministrations, but mine was not. I started reading again as I 4 hadn't since elementary school. I would go into our gloomy little bed-room or sit at the dinner table while, on the television, Danny McShane was paralyzing Mr. Moto with the atomic drop, and work slowly back through *Heart of Darkness,* trying to catch the words in Conrad's sentences. I certainly was not MacFarland's best student; most of the other guys in College Prep, even my fellow slackers, had better backgrounds than I did. But I worked very hard, for MacFarland had hooked me. He tapped my old interest in reading and creating stories. He gave me a way to feel special by using my mind. And he provided a role model that wasn't shaped on physical prowess alone, and something inside me that I wasn't quite aware of responded to that. Jack MacFarland established a literacy club, to borrow a phrase of Frank Smith's, and invited me—invited all of us—to join.

There's been a good deal of research and speculation suggesting   5 that the acknowledgment of school performance with extrinsic re-wards—smiling faces, stars, numbers, grades—diminishes the intrin-sic satisfaction children experience by engaging in reading or writing or problem solving. While it's certainly true that we've created an educational system that encourages our best and brightest to become cynical grade collectors and, in general, have developed an obsession with evaluation and assessment, I must tell you that venal though it may have been, I loved getting good grades from MacFarland. I now know how subjective grades can be, but then they came tucked in the back of essays like bits of scientific data, some sort of spectroscopic readout that said, objectively and publicly, that I had made some-thing of value. I suppose I'd been mediocre for too long and enjoyed a public redefinition. And I suppose the workings of my mind, such as they were, had been private for too long. My linguistic play moved into the world; like the intergalactic stories I told years before on Frank's berry-splattered truck bed, these papers with their circled, red B-pluses and A-minuses linked my mind to something outside it. I carried them around like a club emblem.

One day in the December of my senior year, Mr. MacFarland   6 asked me where I was going to go to college. I hadn't thought much about it. Many of the students I teach today spent their last year in high school with a physics text in one hand and the Stanford catalog in the other, but I wasn't even aware of what "entrance require-ments" were. My folks would say that they wanted me to go to col-lege and be a doctor, but I don't know how seriously I ever took that; it seemed a sweet thing to say, a bit of supportive family chatter, like telling a gangly daughter she's graceful. The reality of higher education wasn't in my scheme of things: No one in the family had gone to college; only two of my uncles had completed high school. I figured I'd get a night job and go to the local junior college because I knew that Snyder and Company were going there to play ball. But I hadn't even prepared for that. When I finally said, "I don't know," MacFarland looked down at me—I was seated in his office—and said, "Listen, you can write."

My grades stank. I had A's in biology and a handful of B's in a few English and social science classes. All the rest were C's—or worse. MacFarland said I would do well in his class and laid down the law about doing well in the others. Still, the record for my first three years wouldn't have been acceptable to any four-year school. To nobody's surprise, I was turned down flat by USC and UCLA. But Jack MacFarland was on the case. He had received his bachelor's degree from Loyola University, so he made calls to old professors and talked to somebody in admissions and wrote me a strong letter. Loyola finally accepted me as a probationary student. I would be on trial for the first year, and if I did okay, I would be granted regular status. MacFarland also intervened to get me a loan, for I could never have afforded a private college without it. Four more years of religion classes and four more years of boys at one school, girls at another. But at least I was going to college. Amazing. 7

QUESTIONS FOR STUDY AND DISCUSSION

1. Why do you think Rose chose the title "I Just Wanna Be Average"? (Glossary: *Title*) How does it relate to the essay?

2. Describe Jack MacFarland. How does his appearance contrast with his ability as a teacher?

3. Rose's paragraphs are long and full of information, but they are very coherent. Summarize the topic of each of the seven paragraphs in separate sentences.

4. How has Rose organized paragraph 2? How does Rose prepare the reader for the concluding sentence: "The man [McFarland] immersed us in language"?

5. Analyze the transitions between paragraphs 2 and 3 and between 3 and 4. (Glossary: *Transition*) What techniques does Rose use to smoothly introduce the reader to different aspects of his relationship with Jack MacFarland?

6. Rose introduces the reader to some of his classmates, quickly establishes their personalities, and names them in full: Jim Fitzsimmons, Skip Madison, Mike Dweetz. Why does he do this? How does it help him describe MacFarland?

7. Why does Rose have difficulty getting into college? How does he finally make it?

VOCABULARY

Refer to your dictionary to define the following words as they are used in this selection. Then use each word in a sentence of your own.

beatnik (1)	linguistic (3)
curriculum (1)	incipient (3)
paradox (2)	ministrations (4)
existentialism (2)	extrinsic (5)
rejoin (3)	spectroscopic (5)
indomitable (3)	gangly (6)

CLASSROOM ACTIVITY USING PARAGRAPHS

Write a unified, coherent, and adequately developed paragraph using one of the following topic sentences. Be sure to select details that clearly demonstrate or support the general statement you chose.

1. It was the noisiest place I had ever visited.
2. I was terribly frightened.
3. Signs of the sanitation strike were evident everywhere.
4. It was the best meal I've ever eaten.
5. Even though we lost, our team earned an "A" for effort.

SUGGESTED WRITING ASSIGNMENTS

1. Pick a good teacher whom you have had. Identify what about him or her was of importance and how he or she influenced your life. Write an essay about the teacher using Rose's essay as a model. Make sure that each paragraph accomplishes a specific purpose and that each paragraph is coherent enough to be readily summarized.

2. Write an essay about the process you went through to get into college. Did you visit different schools? Did your parents

pressure you to go? Had you always wanted to go to college, or did you make the decision in high school, like Rose? Did any particular teacher help you? Make sure that you develop your paragraphs fully and that you have effective transitions between paragraphs.

One Good Turn: How Machine-Made Screws Brought the World Together

■ Witold Rybczynski

An architectural historian and professor of urban studies, Witold Rybczynski graduated from McGill University with a degree in architecture in 1966. He received his masters in architecture from McGill in 1973. Rybczynski has written widely on design, building, and architecture. His books include Home: A Short History of an Idea *(1987),* Most Beautiful House in the World *(1990),* Looking Around: A Journey through Architecture *(1993), and* City Life: Urban Expectations in a New World *(1996). His most recent endeavor is the acclaimed biography of landscape architect Frederick Law Olmsted,* A Clearing in the Distance: Frederick Law Olmsted and America in the Nineteenth Century *(1999). In the following essay, which first appeared in the* New York Times Magazine *in 1999, Rybczynski draws on his personal experience building his own house as well as his knowledge of architectural history to tell the story of the ordinary machine-made screw and its impact on humankind. As you read, pay particular attention to Rybczynski's focused, well-developed, and crafted paragraphs.*

FOR YOUR JOURNAL

What's been your experience using the equipment associated with an activity you do—gardening and lawn tools for yard work, kitchen tools and utensils for cooking, carpentry tools for building, or tools associated with arts and crafts? What kinds of tools do you use? Do you have a preference for hand tools or power tools? Why?

S‌ome years ago my wife and I built a house. I mean really built   1
it—ourselves, from the ground up. Electricity being unavailable,
we used hand tools. I did not have a large toolbox. It contained

different-size saws, a mallet and chisels, a plane, several hammers (for friends conscripted into our work force) and, for correcting major mistakes, a heavy sledge. In addition I had a number of tools for measuring: a tape, a square, a spirit level and a plumb line. That was all we needed.

One of the rewards of building something yourself is the pleasure 2 of using tools. Hand tools are really extensions of the human body, for they have evolved over centuries — millenniums — of trial and error. Power tools are more convenient, of course, but they lack precisely this sense of refinement. Using a clumsy nailing gun is work, but swinging a claw hammer is satisfying work.

Had a medieval carpenter come along — untutored neophytes, we 3 could have used his help — he would have found most of my tools familiar. Indeed, even an ancient Roman carpenter would have found few surprises in my toolbox. He would recognize my plane, a version of his *plana;* he might admire my retractable tape measure, an improvement on his bronze folding *regula.* He would be puzzled by my brace and bit, a medieval invention, but being familiar with the Egyptian bow drill, he would readily infer its purpose. No doubt he would be impressed by my hard steel nails, so much superior to his hand-forged spikes.

Saws, hammers (and nails), chisels, drills and squares all date 4 from the Bronze and early Iron Ages. Many types of modern tools originated even earlier, in the Neolithic period, about 8,000 years ago. In fact, there is only one tool in my toolbox that would puzzle a Roman and a medieval carpenter: my screwdriver. They would understand the principle of screws; after all, Archimedes invented the screw in the third century B.C. Ancient screws were large wood contraptions, used for raising water. One of the earliest devices that used a screw to apply pressure was a Roman clothes press; presses were also used to make olive oil and wine. The Middle Ages applied the same principle to the printing press and to that fiendish torturing device, the thumbscrew. Yet the ordinary screw as a small fixing device was unknown.

Wood screws originated sometime in the sixteenth century. The 5 first screwdrivers were called turn-screws, flat-bladed bits that could be attached to a carpenter's brace. The inventor of the handheld screwdriver remains unknown, but the familiar tool does not appear in carpenters' toolboxes until after 1800. There was not a great call for screwdrivers, because screws were expensive. They had to be painstakingly made by hand and were used in luxury articles like clocks. It was only after 1850 that wood screws were available in large quantities.

Inexpensive screws are quintessentially modern. Their mass pro-   6
duction requires a high degree of precision and standardization. The wood screw also represents an entirely new method of attachment, more durable than nails—which can pop out if the wood dries out or expands. (This makes screws particularly useful in shipbuilding.) The tapered, gimlet-pointed wood screw—like its cousin the bolt—squeezes the two joined pieces together. The more you tighten the screw—or the nut—the greater the squeeze. In modern steel buildings, for example, high-tension bolts are tightened so hard that it is the friction between the two pieces of steel—not the bolt itself—that gives strength to the joint. On a more mundane level, screws enable a vast array of convenient attachments in the home: door hinges, drawer pulls, shelf hangers, towel bars. Perhaps that is why if you rummage around most people's kitchen drawers you will most likely find at least one screwdriver.

Wood screws are stronger and more durable than nails, pegs or   7
staples. But the aristocrat of screws is the precision screw. This was first made roughly—by hand—and later on screw-cutting lathes, which is a chicken-and-egg story, since it was the screw that made machine lathes possible. The machined screw represented a technological breakthrough of epic proportions. Screws enabled the minute adjustment of a variety of precision instruments like clocks, microscopes, telescopes, sextants, theodolites and marine chronometers.

It is not an exaggeration to say that accurately threaded screws   8
changed the world. Without screws, entire fields of science would have languished, navigation would have remained primitive and naval warfare as well as routine maritime commerce in the eighteenth and nineteenth centuries would not have been possible. Without screws there would have been no machine tools, hence no industrial products and no Industrial Revolution. Think of that the next time you pick up a screwdriver to pry open a can of paint.

QUESTIONS FOR STUDY AND DISCUSSION

1. After talking about the house that he and his wife built and giving a brief history of hand tools, Rybczynski first introduces his topic in the middle of paragraph 4 when he mentions the screwdriver. In what ways do the first three and a half paragraphs serve as an effective introduction to the topic of screws? Explain.

2. What for Rybczynski is the pleasure of using hand tools? How do they differ from other tools?

3. Rybczynski claims, "It is not an exaggeration to say that accurately threaded screws changed the world" (8). How does he support this claim?

4. How does Rybczynski make the transition between paragraphs 4 and 5, between paragraphs 5 and 6, and between paragraphs 7 and 8? (Glossary: *Transition*)

5. Explain how Rybczynski uses examples to develop his paragraphs. (Glossary: *Example*) Which examples do you find most effective? Why?

6. How does Rybczynski's diction help to establish him as an authority on the subject of hand tools in general and wood screws and machine-made screws in particular? (Glossary: *Diction*)

VOCABULARY

Refer to your dictionary to define the following words as they are used in this selection. Then use each word in a sentence of your own.

conscripted (1)	infer (3)
untutored (3)	quintessentially (6)
neophytes (3)	mundane (6)
retractable (3)	epic (7)

CLASSROOM ACTIVITY USING PARAGRAPHS

Rearrange the following sentences to create an effective paragraph. Be ready to explain why you chose the order that you did.

1. PGA golfer Fred Divot learned the hard way what overtraining could do.

2. Divot's case is typical, and most researchers believe that too much repetition makes it difficult for the athlete to reduce left-hemisphere brain activity.

3. Athletes who overtrain find it very difficult to get in the flow.

4. "Two weeks later, all I could think about was mechanics, and I couldn't hit a fairway to save my life!"

5. Athletes think about mechanics (left hemisphere) rather than feel (right hemisphere), and they lose the ability to achieve peak performance.

6. "I was playing well, so I thought with a bit more practice, I could start winning on tour," Divot recalls.

SUGGESTED WRITING ASSIGNMENTS

1. In an age of automation, when everything is faster, easier, and more convenient, Rybczynski celebrates the pleasure of doing things by hand. Do you enjoy baking bread from scratch, shoveling snow with a shovel, or paddling a canoe, or do you prefer a bread machine, a snowblower, or a power boat? Write an essay in which you defend your preference for using old-fashioned tools or techniques to accomplish a task or for using modern, high-powered tools. You might start by reading what you wrote in response to the journal prompt for this selection. Be sure to illustrate your essay with well-chosen examples.

2. Using Rybczynski's essay as a model, write about a tool or an appliance that you frequently use, such as a toothbrush, a computer mouse, a pencil, or an electric saw. You may find it helpful to consider the following questions before you start writing: Under what circumstances do you use this tool or appliance? Why do you enjoy using it? What do you know of its history? What impact has it had on your life or on the lives of others?

Transitions

Transitions are words and phrases that are used to signal the relationships among ideas in an essay and to join the various parts of an essay together. Writers use transitions to relate ideas within sentences, between sentences, and between paragraphs. Perhaps the most common type of transition is the so-called transitional expression. Following is a list of transitional expressions categorized according to their functions.

ADDITION: and, again, too, also, in addition, further, furthermore, moreover, besides

CAUSE AND EFFECT: therefore, consequently, thus, accordingly, as a result, hence, then, so

COMPARISON: similarly, likewise, by comparison

CONCESSION: to be sure, granted, of course, it is true, to tell the truth, certainly, with the exception of, although this may be true, even though, naturally

CONTRAST: but, however, in contrast, on the contrary, on the other hand, yet, nevertheless, after all, in spite of

EXAMPLE: for example, for instance

PLACE: elsewhere, here, above, below, farther on, there, beyond, nearby, opposite to, around

RESTATEMENT: that is, as I have said, in other words, in simpler terms, to put it differently, simply stated

SEQUENCE: first, second, third, next, finally

SUMMARY: in conclusion, to conclude, to summarize, in brief, in short

TIME: afterward, later, earlier, subsequently, at the same time, simultaneously, immediately, this time, until now, before, meanwhile, shortly, soon, currently, when, lately, in the meantime, formerly

Besides transitional expressions, there are two other important ways to make transitions: by using pronoun reference and by repeating key words and phrases. This paragraph begins with the phrase "Besides transitional expressions": the phrase contains the transitional word *besides* and also repeats an earlier idea. Thus the reader knows that this discussion is moving toward a new but related idea. Repetition can also give a word or idea emphasis: "Foreigners look to America as a land of freedom. Freedom, however, is not something all Americans enjoy."

Pronoun reference avoids monotonous repetition of nouns and phrases. Without pronouns, these two sentences are wordy and tiring to read: "Jim went to the concert, where he heard Beethoven's Ninth Symphony. Afterward, Jim bought a recording of the Ninth Symphony." A more graceful and readable passage results if two pronouns are substituted in the second sentence: "Afterward, he bought a recording of it." The second version has another advantage in that it is now more tightly related to the first sentence. The transition between the two sentences is smoother.

In the following example, notice how Rachel Carson uses transitional expressions, repetition of words and ideas, and pronoun reference:

Under primitive agricultural conditions the farmer had few insect problems. *These* arose with the intensification of agriculture—the devotion of immense acreages to a single crop. *Such a system* set the stage for explosive increases in specific insect populations. Single-crop farming does not take advantage of the principles by which nature works; *it* is agriculture as an engineer might conceive it to be. Nature has introduced great variety into the landscape, but man has displayed a passion for simplifying *it*. *Thus he* undoes the built-in checks and balances by which nature holds the species within bounds. One important natural *check* is a limit on the amount of suitable habitat for each species. *Obviously then,* an insect that lives on wheat can build up its population to much higher levels on a farm devoted to wheat than on one in which wheat is intermingled with other crops to which the insect is not adapted.

The same thing happens in other situations. A generation or more ago, the towns of large areas of

Margin annotations:

- repeated key idea
- pronoun reference
- repeated key word
- repeated key idea
- pronoun reference
- pronoun reference
- transitional expression; pronoun reference transitional expression

the United States lined their streets with the noble
elm tree. *Now* the beauty *they* hopefully created is
threatened with complete destruction as disease
sweeps through the elms, carried by a beetle that
would have only limited chance to build up large
populations and to spread from tree to tree if the
elms were only occasional trees in a richly diversified planting.

*transi-
tional ex-
pression;
pronoun
reference*

Carson's transitions in this passage enhance its *coherence* — that
quality of good writing that results when all sentences and paragraphs of an essay are effectively and naturally connected.

Why I Want to Have a Family

■ **Lisa Brown**

When she wrote the following essay, Lisa Brown was a junior majoring in American studies at the University of Texas. In the essay, which was published as a "My Turn" column in the October 1984 issue of Newsweek on Campus, *she uses a variety of transitional devices to put together a coherent argument—that many women in their drive to succeed have overlooked the potential for fulfillment inherent in good relationships and family life. As you read, pay particular attention to the way Brown begins many of her sentences by establishing a clear and direct relationship to the sentences immediately preceding.*

FOR YOUR JOURNAL

How do you feel about the idea of becoming a parent someday? What aspects of having children appeal to you most? Appeal to you least? In what ways will your career choice affect your decision to have a family? If you are already a parent, what led to your decision to have a child? How has being a parent affected your working or academic life?

For years the theory of higher education operated something like 1
this: men went to college to get rich, and women went to college
to marry rich men. It was a wonderful little setup, almost mathematical in its precision. To disturb it would have been to rock an American institution.

During the '60s, though, this theory lost much of its luster. As 2
the nation began to recognize the idiocy of relegating women to a secondary role, women soon joined men in what once were male-only pursuits. This rebellious decade pushed women toward independence, showed them their potential and compelled them to take charge of their lives. Many women took the opportunity and ran with it. Since then feminine autonomy has been the rule, not the exception, at least among college women.

That's the good news. The bad news is that the invisible push has 3
turned into a shove. Some women are downright obsessive about

success, to the point of becoming insular monuments to selfishness and fierce bravado, the condescending sort that hawks: "I don't need *anybody*. So there." These women dismiss children and marriage as unbearably outdated and potentially harmful to their up-and-coming careers. This notion of independence smacks of egocentrism. What do these women fear? Why can't they slow down long enough to remember that relationships and a family life are not inherently awful things?

Granted that for centuries women were on the receiving end of some shabby treatment. Now, in an attempt to liberate college women from the constraints that forced them almost exclusively into teaching or nursing as a career outside the home — always subject to the primary career of motherhood — some women have gone too far. Any notion of motherhood seems to be regarded as an unpleasant reminder of the past, when homemakers were imprisoned by husbands, tots and household chores. In short, many women consider motherhood a time-consuming obstacle to the great joy of working outside the home.

The rise of feminism isn't the only answer. Growing up has something to do with it, too. Most people find themselves in a bind as they hit their late 20s: they consider the ideals they grew up with and find that these don't necessarily mix with the ones they've acquired. The easiest thing to do, it sometimes seems, is to throw out the precepts their parents taught. Growing up, my friends and I were enchanted by the idea of starting new traditions. We didn't want self-worth to be contingent upon whether there was a man or child around the house to make us feel wanted.

I began to reconsider my values after my sister and a friend had babies. I was entertained by their pregnancies and fascinated by the births; I was also thankful that I wasn't the one who had to change the diapers every day. I was a doting aunt only when I wanted to be. As my sister's and friend's lives changed, though, my attitude changed. I saw their days flip-flop between frustration and joy. Though these two women lost the freedom to run off to the beach or to a bar, they gained something else — an abstract happiness that reveals itself when they talk about Jessica's or Amanda's latest escapade or vocabulary addition. Still in their 20s, they shuffle work and motherhood with the skill of poker players. I admire them, and I marvel at their kids. Spending time with the Jessicas and Amandas of the world teaches us patience and sensitivity and gives us a clue into

4

5

6

our own pasts. Children are also reminders that there is a future and that we must work to ensure its quality.

Now I feel challenged by the idea of becoming a parent. I want to decorate a nursery and design Halloween costumes; I want to answer my children's questions and help them learn to read. I want to be unselfish. But I've spent most of my life working in the opposite direction: toward independence, no emotional or financial strings attached. When I told a friend—one who likes kids but never, ever wants them—that I'd decided to accommodate motherhood, she accused me of undermining my career, my future, my life. "If that's all you want, then why are you even in college?" she asked.

The answer's simple: I want to be a smart mommy. I have solid career plans and look forward to working. I make a distinction between wanting kids and wanting nothing but kids. And I've accepted that I'll have to give up a few years of full-time work to allow time for being pregnant and buying Pampers. As for undermining my life, I'm proud of my decision because I think it's evidence that the women's movement is working. While liberating women from the traditional childbearing role, the movement has given respectability to motherhood by recognizing that it's not a brainless task like dishwashing. At the same time, women who choose not to have children are not treated as oddities. That certainly wasn't the case even 15 years ago. While the graying, middle-aged bachelor was respected, the female equivalent—tagged a spinster—was automatically suspect.

Today, women have choices: about careers, their bodies, children. I am grateful that women are no longer forced into motherhood as a function of their biology; it's senseless to assume that having a uterus qualifies anyone to be a good parent. By the same token, it is ridiculous for women to abandon all maternal desire because it might jeopardize personal success. Some women make the decision to go childless without ever analyzing their true needs or desires. They forget that motherhood can add to personal fulfillment.

I wish those fiercely independent women wouldn't look down upon those of us who, for whatever reason, choose to forgo much of the excitement that runs in tandem with being single, liberated and educated. Excitement also fills a family life; it just comes in different ways.

I'm not in college because I'll learn how to make tastier pot roast. I'm a student because I want to make sense of the world and of myself. By doing so, I think I'll be better prepared to be a mother to the new lives that I might bring into the world. I'll also be a better me. It's a package deal I don't want to turn down.

QUESTIONS FOR STUDY AND DISCUSSION

1. Identify Brown's use of transitions in paragraphs 2, 3, 4, 6, 8, and 9. How do these transitions help you follow her point?
2. The subject matter of Brown's concluding paragraph is not closely related to that of paragraphs 9 and 10. What transitional techniques does she use to relate her final paragraph to the rest of her essay?
3. What is Brown arguing for in this essay? What does she say prompted a change in her attitude? (Glossary: *Attitude*)
4. Against what group is Brown arguing? What does she find wrong with the beliefs of that group? (Glossary: *Argumentation*)
5. What reasons does she provide for wanting to have a family?
6. What are the implications of Brown's last two sentences in paragraph 6: "Spending time with the Jessicas and Amandas of the world teaches us patience and sensitivity and gives us a clue into our own pasts. Children are also reminders that there is a future and that we must work to ensure its quality"?
7. For what audience do you think this essay is intended? Do you think men would be as interested as women in the author's viewpoint? Explain. (Glossary: *Audience*)

VOCABULARY

Refer to your dictionary to define the following words as they are used in this selection. Then use each word in a sentence of your own.

relegating (2)   precepts (5)
autonomy (2)   contingent (5)
insular (3)   doting (6)
bravado (3)   tandem (10)

CLASSROOM ACTIVITY USING TRANSITIONS

The following sentences, which make up the first paragraph of E. B. White's essay "Once More to the Lake," have been rearranged. Place the sentences in what seems to you to be a coherent sequence by relying on language signals like transitions, repeated words, pronouns, and temporal references. Be prepared to explain your reasons for the placement of each sentence.

1. I have since become a salt-water man, but sometimes in summer there are days when the restlessness of the tides and the fearful cold of the sea water and the incessant wind which blows across the afternoon and into the evening make me wish for the placidity of a lake in the woods.

2. We all got ringworm from some kittens and had to rub Pond's Extract on our arms and legs night and morning, and my father rolled over in a canoe with all his clothes on; but outside of that the vacation was a success and from then on none of us ever thought there was any place in the world like that lake in Maine.

3. A few weeks ago this feeling got so strong I bought myself a couple of bass hooks and a spinner and returned to the lake where we used to go for a week's fishing and to revisit old haunts.

4. One summer, along about 1904, my father rented a camp on a lake in Maine and took us all there for the month of August.

5. We returned summer after summer — always on August 1st for one month.

SUGGESTED WRITING ASSIGNMENTS

1. Write an essay in which you argue any one of the following positions with regard to the women's movement: it has gone too far; it is out of control; it is misdirected; it hasn't gone far enough or done enough; it needs to reach more women and men; it should lower its sights. Or argue a position of your own different from the above. Whichever position you argue, be sure that you provide sufficient evidence including quotations from Brown's essay to support your point of view.

2. Complete the following statement and write an argument in support of it:

   The purpose of a college education is to _____
   _____.

How I Got Smart

■ **Steve Brody**

Steve Brody is a retired high school English teacher who enjoys writing about the lighter side of teaching. He was born in Chicago in 1915 and received his bachelor's degree in English from Columbia University. In addition to his articles in educational publications, Brody has published many newspaper articles on travel and a humorous book about golf, How to Break Ninety before You Reach It *(1979). As you read his account of how love made him smart, notice the way he uses transitional words and expressions to unify his essay and to make it a seamless whole.*

FOR YOUR JOURNAL

Motivation is a difficult topic about which to generalize. What motivates one person to act often will not work on another person. How do you get motivated to work, to join extracurricular activities, or to take care of yourself? Are you able to motivate yourself, or do you need to have someone else give you a push?

A common misconception among youngsters attending school is that their teachers were child prodigies. Who else but a bookworm, prowling the libraries and disdaining the normal youngster's propensity for play rather than study, would grow up to be a teacher anyway?

I tried desperately to explain to my students that the image they had of me as an ardent devotee of books and homework during my adolescence was a bit out of focus. Au contraire! I hated compulsory education with a passion. I could never quite accept the notion of having to go to school while the fish were biting.

Consequently, my grades were somewhat bearish. That's how my father, who dabbled in the stock market, described them. Presenting my report card for my father to sign was like serving him a subpoena. At midterm and other sensitive periods, my father kept a low profile.

But in my sophomore year, something beautiful and exciting happened. Cupid aimed his arrow and struck me squarely in the heart. All at once, I enjoyed going to school, if only to gaze at the lovely face beneath the raven tresses in English II. My princess sat near the pencil sharpener, and that year I ground up enough pencils to fuel a campfire.

Alas, Debbie was far beyond my wildest dreams. We were sepa- 5 rated not only by five rows of desks, but by about 50 I.Q. points. She was the top student in English II, the apple of Mrs. Larrivee's eye. I envisioned how eagerly Debbie's father awaited her report card.

Occasionally, Debbie would catch me staring at her, and she 6 would flash a smile — an angelic smile that radiated enlighten-ment and quickened my heartbeat. It was a smile that signaled hope and made me temporarily forget the intellectual gulf that sepa-rated us.

I schemed desperately to bridge that gulf. And one day, as I was 7 passing the supermarket, an idea came to me.

A sign in the window announced that the store was offering the 8 first volume of a set of encyclopedias at the introductory price of 29 cents. The remaining volumes would cost $2.49 each, but it was no time to be cynical.

I purchased Volume I — Aardvark to Asteroid — and began my 9 venture into the world of knowledge. I would henceforth become a seeker of facts. I would become chief egghead in English II and sweep the princess off her feet with a surge of erudition. I had it all planned.

My first opportunity came one day in the cafeteria line. I looked 10 behind me and there she was.

"Hi," she said. 11

After a pause, I wet my lips and said, "Know where anchovies 12 come from?"

She seemed surprised. "No, I don't." 13

I breathed a sigh of relief. "The anchovy lives in salt water and is 14 rarely found in fresh water." I had to talk fast, so that I could get all the facts in before we reached the cash register. "Fishermen catch an-chovies in the Mediterranean Sea and along the Atlantic coast near Spain and Portugal."

"How fascinating," said Debbie. 15

"The anchovy is closely related to the herring. It is thin and sil- 16 very in color. It has a long snout and a very large mouth."

"Incredible." 17

"Anchovies are good in salads, mixed with eggs, and are often 18 used as appetizers before dinner, but they are salty and cannot be di-gested too rapidly."

Debbie shook her head in disbelief. It was obvious that I had 19
made quite an impression.

A few days later, during a fire drill, I sidled up to her and asked, 20
"Ever been to the Aleutian Islands?"

"Never have," she replied. 21

"Might be a nice place to visit, but I certainly wouldn't want to 22
live there," I said.

"Why not?" said Debbie, playing right into my hands. 23

"Well, the climate is forbidding. There are no trees on any of the 24
100 or more islands in the group. The ground is rocky and very little
plant life can grow on it."

"I don't think I'd even care to visit," she said. 25

The fire drill was over and we began to file into the building, so I 26
had to step it up to get the natives in. "The Aleuts are short and
sturdy and have dark skin and black hair. They subsist on fish, and
they trap blue fox, seal and otter for their valuable fur."

Debbie's hazel eyes widened in amazement. She was undoubtedly 27
beginning to realize that she wasn't dealing with an ordinary
lunkhead. She was gaining new and valuable insights instead of engaging in the routine small talk one would expect from most sopho-
mores.

Luck was on my side, too. One day I was browsing through the 28
library during my study period. I spotted Debbie sitting at a table, absorbed in a crossword puzzle. She was frowning, apparently stumped
on a word. I leaned over and asked if I could help.

"Four-letter word for Oriental female servant," Debbie said. 29

"Try *amah*," I said, quick as a flash. 30

Debbie filled in the blanks, then turned to stare at me in amazement. 31
"I don't believe it," she said. "I just don't believe it."

And so it went, that glorious, amorous, joyous sophomore year. 32
Debbie seemed to relish our little conversations and hung on my
every word. Naturally, the more I read, the more my confidence
grew. I expatiated freely on such topics as adenoids, air brakes, and
arthritis.

In the classroom, too, I was gradually making my presence felt. 33
Among my classmates, I was developing a reputation as a wheeler-dealer
in data. One day, during a discussion of Coleridge's "The Ancient
Mariner," we came across the word *albatross*.

"Can anyone tell us what an albatross is?" asked Mrs. Larrivee. 34

My hand shot up. "The albatross is a large bird that lives mostly 35
in the ocean regions below the equator, but may be found in the

north Pacific as well. The albatross measures as long as four feet and has the greatest wingspread of any bird. It feeds on the surface of the ocean, where it catches shellfish. The albatross is a very voracious eater. When it is full it has trouble getting into the air again."

There was a long silence in the room. Mrs. Larrivee couldn't   36
quite believe what she had just heard. I sneaked a peek at Debbie and gave her a big wink. She beamed proudly and winked back.

It was a great feeling, having Debbie and Mrs. Larrivee and my   37
peers according me respect and paying attention when I spoke.

My grades edged upward and my father no longer tried to avoid me   38
when I brought home my report card. I continued reading the encyclopedia diligently, packing more and more into my brain.

What I failed to perceive was that Debbie all this while was going   39
steady with a junior from a neighboring school—a hockey player with a C+ average. The revelation hit me hard, and for a while I felt like disgorging and forgetting everything I had learned. I had saved enough money to buy Volume II—Asthma to Bullfinch—but was strongly tempted to invest in a hockey stick instead.

How could she lead me on like that—smiling and concurring   40
and giving me the impression that I was important?

I felt not only hurt, but betrayed. Like Agamemnon, but with less   41
dire consequences, thank God.

In time I recovered from my wounds. The next year Debbie   42
moved from the neighborhood and transferred to another school. Soon she became no more than a fleeting memory.

Although the original incentive was gone, I continued poring   43
over the encyclopedias, as well as an increasing number of other books. Having savored the heady wine of knowledge, I could not now alter my course. For:

> "A little knowledge is a dangerous thing:
>   Drink deep, or taste not the Pierian spring."

So wrote Alexander Pope, Volume XIV, Paprika to Pterodactyl.   44

QUESTIONS FOR STUDY AND DISCUSSION

1. How are paragraphs 2 and 3, 3 and 4, 5 and 6, 31 and 32, and 43 and 44 linked?
2. Brody uses dialogue to tell his story in paragraphs 10–35. What

does the dialogue add to his story? What would have been lost had he simply told his readers what happened? (Glossary: *Dialogue*)

3. Why didn't Brody stop reading the encyclopedia when he discovered that Debbie had a steady boyfriend?

4. If you find Brody's narrative humorous, try to explain the sources of his humor. For example, what humor resides in the choice of examples Brody uses?

5. Brody refers to Coleridge's "The Ancient Mariner" in paragraph 33 and to Agamemnon in paragraph 41, and he quotes Alexander Pope in paragraph 43. Use an encyclopedia to explain Brody's allusions. (Glossary: *Allusion*)

6. Comment on the effectiveness of the beginning and ending of Brody's essay. (Glossary: *Beginnings and Endings*)

7. Brody could have told his story using far less dialogue than he did. What, in your opinion, would have been gained or lost had he done so? (Glossary: *Dialogue*)

VOCABULARY

Refer to your dictionary to define the following words as they are used in this selection. Then use each word in a sentence of your own.

misconception (1)	forbidding (24)
prodigies (1)	subsist (26)
devotee (2)	amorous (32)
bearish (3)	expatiated (32)
dabbled (3)	adenoids (32)
surge (9)	voracious (35)
erudition (9)	disgorging (39)
snout (16)	savored (43)
sidled (20)	

CLASSROOM ACTIVITY USING TRANSITIONS

In *The New York Times Complete Manual of Home Repair,* Bernard Gladstone gives directions for applying blacktop sealer to a driveway. His directions appear below in scrambled order. First read all of Gladstone's sentences carefully. Next, arrange the sentences in what seems to you to be the logical sequence. Finally, identify places where Gladstone has used transitional expressions, the repetition of words and ideas, and pronoun reference to give coherence to his paragraph.

1. A long-handled pushbroom or roofing brush is used to spread the coating evenly over the entire area.
2. Care should be taken to make certain the entire surface is uniformly wet, though puddles should be swept away if water collects in low spots.
3. Greasy areas and oil slicks should be scraped up, then scrubbed thoroughly with a detergent solution.
4. With most brands there are just three steps to follow.
5. In most cases one coat of sealer will be sufficient.
6. The application of blacktop sealer is best done on a day when the weather is dry and warm, preferably while the sun is shining on the surface.
7. This should not be applied until the first coat is completely dry.
8. First sweep the surface absolutely clean to remove all dust, dirt and foreign material.
9. To simplify spreading and to assure a good bond, the surface of the driveway should be wet down thoroughly by sprinkling with a hose.
10. However, for surfaces in poor condition a second coat may be required.
11. The blacktop sealer is next stirred thoroughly and poured on while the surface is still damp.
12. The sealer should be allowed to dry overnight (or longer if recommended by the manufacturer) before normal traffic is resumed.

SUGGESTED WRITING ASSIGNMENTS

1. One serious thought that arises as a result of reading Brody's essay is that perhaps we learn best when we are sufficiently motivated to do so. And once we are motivated, the desire to learn seems to feed on itself: "Having savored the heady wine of knowledge, I could not now alter my course" (43). Write an essay in which you explore this same subject using your own experiences.

2. Relationships can influence our lives either positively or negatively. Even the appearance of a relationship can have an effect, as we saw in Brody's infatuation with Debbie during his sophomore year in high school. By trying to impress Debbie with his knowledge, Brody got hooked on learning and chose a career in education. Write a brief essay in which you explore the effects that a relationship had on your life.

Becoming a Writer

■ **Russell Baker**

Russell Baker has had a long and distinguished career as a news-paper reporter and columnist. He was born in Virginia and at-tended Johns Hopkins University. In 1947, he got his first newspaper job with the Baltimore Sun, *then moved to the* New York Times *in 1954, where he wrote the "Observer" column from 1962 to 1998. His columns have been collected in numer-ous books over the years. In 1979, he was awarded the Pulitzer Prize, journalism's highest award, as well as the George Polk Award for commentary. Baker's memoir,* Growing Up, *also re-ceived a Pulitzer in 1983. His autobiographical follow-up,* The Good Times, *appeared in 1989. Baker published an anthology entitled* Russell Baker's Book of American Humor *in 1993 and hosts the series* ExxonMobil Masterpiece Theater *on PBS. An-other essay by Baker appears on pages 369–71. As you read Baker's account of how he discovered his abilities as a writer, note how effectively he uses repetition of key words and ideas to achieve coherence and to emphasize his emotional responses to the events he describes.*

FOR YOUR JOURNAL

Life is full of moments that change us, for better or worse, in major and minor ways. We decide what hobbies we like and dis-like, whom we want to date and, perhaps, eventually marry, what we want to study in school, what career we eventually pur-sue. Identify an event that changed your life or helped you make an important decision. How did it clarify your situation? How might your life be different if the event had never happened?

The notion of becoming a writer had flickered off and on in my 1 head . . . but it wasn't until my third year in high school that the possibility took hold. Until then I'd been bored by everything associ-ated with English courses. I found English grammar dull and baffling. I hated the assignments to turn out "compositions," and went at them like heavy labor, turning out laden, lackluster paragraphs that were agonies for teachers to read and for me to write. The classics thrust on me to read seemed as deadening as chloroform.

When our class was assigned to Mr. Fleagle for third-year English I anticipated another grim year in that dreariest of subjects. Mr. Fleagle was notorious among City students for dullness and inability to inspire. He was said to be stuffy, dull, and hopelessly out of date. To me he looked to be sixty or seventy and prim to a fault. He wore primly severe eyeglasses, his wavy hair was primly cut and primly combed. He wore prim vested suits with neckties blocked primly against the collar buttons of his primly starched white shirts. He had a primly pointed jaw, a primly straight nose, and a prim manner of speaking that was so correct, so gentlemanly, that he seemed a comic antique.

I anticipated a listless, unfruitful year with Mr. Fleagle and for a long time was not disappointed. We read *Macbeth*. Mr. Fleagle loved *Macbeth* and wanted us to love it too, but he lacked the gift of infecting others with his own passion. He tried to convey the murderous ferocity of Lady Macbeth one day by reading aloud the passage that concludes

> . . . I have given suck, and know
> How tender 'tis to love the babe that milks me.
> I would, while it was smiling in my face,
> Have plucked my nipple from his boneless gums . . .

The idea of prim Mr. Fleagle plucking his nipple from boneless gums was too much for the class. We burst into gasps of irrepressible snickering. Mr. Fleagle stopped.

"There is nothing funny, boys, about giving suck to a babe. It is the—the very essence of motherhood, don't you see."

He constantly sprinkled his sentences with "don't you see." It wasn't a question but an exclamation of mild surprise at our ignorance. "Your pronoun needs an antecedent, don't you see," he would say, very primly. "The purpose of the Porter's scene, boys, is to provide comic relief from the horror, don't you see."

Late in the year we tackled the informal essay. "The essay, don't you see, is the. . . ." My mind went numb. Of all forms of writing, none seemed so boring as the essay. Naturally we would have to write informal essays. Mr. Fleagle distributed a homework sheet offering us a choice of topics. None was quite so simpleminded as "What I Did on My Summer Vacation," but most seemed to be almost as dull. I took the list home and dawdled until the night before the essay was due. Sprawled on the sofa, I finally faced up to the grim task, took the list out of my notebook, and scanned it. The topic on which my eye stopped was "The Art of Eating Spaghetti."

This title produced an extraordinary sequence of mental images. 7 Surging up from the depths of memory came a vivid recollection of a night in Belleville when all of us were seated around the supper table—Uncle Allen, my mother, Uncle Charlie, Doris, Uncle Hal— and Aunt Pat served spaghetti for supper. Spaghetti was an exotic treat in those days. Neither Doris nor I had ever eaten spaghetti, and none of the adults had enough experience to be good at it. All the good humor of Uncle Allen's house reawoke in my mind as I recalled the laughing arguments we had that night about the socially respectable method for moving spaghetti from plate to mouth.

Suddenly I wanted to write about that, about the warmth and 8 good feeling of it, but I wanted to put it down simply for my own joy, not for Mr. Fleagle. It was a moment I wanted to recapture and hold for myself. I wanted to relive the pleasure of an evening at New Street. To write it as I wanted, however, would violate all the rules of formal composition I'd learned in school, and Mr. Fleagle would surely give it a failing grade. Never mind. I would write something else for Mr. Fleagle after I had written this thing for myself.

When I finished it the night was half gone and there was no time 9 left to compose a proper, respectable essay for Mr. Fleagle. There was no choice next morning but to turn in my private reminiscence of Belleville. Two days passed before Mr. Fleagle returned the graded papers, and he returned everyone's but mine. I was bracing myself for a command to report to Mr. Fleagle immediately after school for discipline when I saw him lift my paper from his desk and rap for the class's attention.

"Now, boys," he said, "I want to read you an essay. This is titled 10 'The Art of Eating Spaghetti.'"

And he started to read. My words! He was reading *my words* out 11 loud to the entire class. What's more, the entire class was listening. Listening attentively. Then somebody laughed, then the entire class was laughing, and not in contempt and ridicule, but with openhearted enjoyment. Even Mr. Fleagle stopped two or three times to repress a small prim smile.

I did my best to avoid showing pleasure, but what I was feeling 12 was pure ecstasy at this startling demonstration that my words had the power to make people laugh. In the eleventh grade, at the eleventh hour as it were, I had discovered a calling. It was the happiest moment of my entire school career. When Mr. Fleagle finished he put the final seal on my happiness by saying, "Now that, boys, is an essay, don't you see. It's—don't you see—it's of the very essence of the essay, don't you see. Congratulations, Mr. Baker."

For the first time, light shone on a possibility. It wasn't a very   13
heartening possibility, to be sure. Writing couldn't lead to a job after high school, and it was hardly honest work, but Mr. Fleagle had opened a door for me. After that I ranked Mr. Fleagle among the finest teachers in the school.

QUESTIONS FOR STUDY AND DISCUSSION

1. Baker makes good use of transitional expressions, repetition of words and ideas, and pronoun reference in paragraphs 1 and 2. Carefully reread the paragraphs, and identify where he employs these techniques, using the analysis of Carson's essay in the introduction to this chapter as a model.

2. Examine the transitions Baker uses between paragraphs from paragraph 4 to the end of the essay. Explain how these transitions work to make the paragraphs flow smoothly from one to another.

3. How does Baker describe his English teacher, Mr. Fleagle, in the second paragraph? (Glossary: *Description*) Why does he repeat the word *prim* throughout the paragraph? Why is the vivid description important to the essay as a whole? (Glossary: *Dominant Impression*)

4. Baker gives Mr. Fleagle an identifiable voice. What is ironic about what Mr. Fleagle says? (Glossary: *Irony*) In what way does this irony contribute to Baker's purpose in writing the essay? (Glossary: *Purpose*)

5. What does Baker write about in his informal essay for Mr. Fleagle? Why does he write about this subject? Why doesn't he want to turn the essay in?

6. Baker's passage about Mr. Fleagle's choosing to read his essay to the class is critical to the impact of "Becoming a Writer." Baker writes in paragraph 11: "And he started to read. My words! He was reading *my words* out loud to the entire class." Why do you think Baker repeats himself? Why is his wording more effective than a simple "And he started to read my essay to the class" would be?

7. What door had Mr. Fleagle opened for Baker? Why is Baker reluctant to pursue the opportunity that Mr. Fleagle provided to him?

VOCABULARY

Refer to your dictionary to define the following words as they are used in this selection. Then use each word in a sentence of your own.

laden (1)   antecedent (5)
chloroform (1)   reminiscence (9)
irrepressible (3)

CLASSROOM ACTIVITY USING TRANSITIONS

Read the following three paragraphs. Provide transitions between paragraphs so that the narrative flows smoothly.

> In the late 1950s, I got lost on a camping trip in the Canadian wilderness. My only thought was to head south, towards warmth and civilization. My perilous journey was exhausting—the cold sapped my strength, and there were few places to find shelter and rest.
>
> There I found friendly faces and a warm fire. As I built my strength, I tried to communicate with the villagers, but they did not understand me. I came to the conclusion that I could stay in the village and wait—perhaps forever—for help to come, or I could strike out on my own again.
>
> I heard a gurgling sound. It was running water. Running water! Spring was here at last. Perhaps I would survive after all. I picked up my pack, squared my shoulders, and marched, the afternoon sun a beautiful sight, still ahead, but starting to drift to my right.

SUGGESTED WRITING ASSIGNMENTS

1. Using as a model Baker's effort to write about eating spaghetti, write something from your own experience that you would like to record for yourself, not necessarily for the teacher. Don't worry about writing a formal essay; simply use language with which you are comfortable to convey why the event or experience is important to you.

2. Write an essay in which you describe how your perception of someone important in your life changed. How did you feel about the person at first? How do you feel now? What brought about the change? What impact did the transition have on you? Make sure your essay is coherent and flows well—use transitional expressions to help the reader follow the story of *your* transition.

Effective Sentences

Each of the following paragraphs describes the city of Vancouver. Although the content of both paragraphs is essentially the same, the first paragraph is written in sentences of nearly the same length and pattern, and the second paragraph in sentences of varying length and pattern.

UNVARIED SENTENCES

Water surrounds Vancouver on three sides. The snow-crowned Coast Mountains ring the city on the northeast. Vancouver has a floating quality of natural loveliness. There is a curved beach at English Bay. This beach is in the shape of a half moon. Residential high rises stand behind the beach. They are in pale tones of beige, blue, and ice-cream pink. Turn-of-the-century houses of painted wood frown upward at the glitter of office towers. Any urban glare is softened by folds of green lawns, flowers, fountains, and trees. Such landscaping appears to be unplanned. It links Vancouver to her ultimate treasure of greenness. That treasure is thousand-acre Stanley Park. Surrounding stretches of water dominate. They have image-evoking names like False Creek and Lost Lagoon. Sailboats and pleasure craft skim blithely across Burrard Inlet. Foreign freighters are out in English Bay. They await their turn to take on cargoes of grain.

VARIED SENTENCES

Surrounded by water on three sides and ringed to the northeast by the snow-crowned Coast Mountains, Vancouver has a floating quality of natural loveliness. At English Bay, the half-moon curve of beach is backed by high rises in pale tones of beige, blue, and ice-cream pink. Turn-of-the-century houses of painted wood frown up-ward at the glitter of office towers. Yet any urban glare is quickly softened by folds of green lawns, flowers, fountains, and trees that in

a seemingly unplanned fashion link Vancouver to her ultimate treasure of greenness—thousand-acre Stanley Park. And always it is the
surrounding stretches of water that dominate, with their image-
evoking names like False Creek and Lost Lagoon. Sailboats and
pleasure craft skim blithely across Burrard Inlet, while out in English
Bay foreign freighters await their turn to take on cargoes of grain.

The difference between these two paragraphs is dramatic. The first is
monotonous because of the sameness of the sentences and because
the ideas are not related to one another in a meaningful way. The second paragraph is much more interesting and readable; its sentences
vary in length and are structured to clarify the relationships among
the ideas. Sentence variety, an important aspect of all good writing,
should not be used for its own sake, but rather to express ideas precisely and to emphasize the most important ideas within each sentence. Sentence variety includes the use of subordination, the periodic
and loose sentence, the dramatically short sentence, the active and
passive voice, and coordination.

SUBORDINATION

Subordination, the process of giving one idea less emphasis than another in a sentence, is one of the most important characteristics of an
effective sentence and a mature prose style. Writers subordinate ideas
by introducing them either with subordinating conjunctions *(because,
if, as though, while, when, after, in order that)* or with relative pronouns *(that, which, who, whomever, what).* Subordination not only
deemphasizes some ideas, but also highlights others that the writer
feels are more important.

Of course, there is nothing about an idea—*any* idea—that automatically makes it primary or secondary in importance. The writer
decides what to emphasize, and he or she may choose to emphasize
the less profound or noteworthy of two ideas. Consider, for example, the following sentence: "Melissa was reading a detective story
while the national election results were televised." Everyone, including the author of the sentence, knows that the national election is a
more noteworthy event than Melissa's reading of the detective story.
But the sentence concerns Melissa, not the election, and so the fact
that she was reading is stated in the main clause, while the election
news is subordinated in a dependent clause.

Generally, writers place the ideas they consider important in main clauses, and other ideas go into dependent clauses. For example:

> When she was thirty years old, she made her first solo flight across the Atlantic.

> When she made her first solo flight across the Atlantic, she was thirty years old.

PERIODIC AND LOOSE SENTENCES

The first sentence emphasizes the solo flight; in the second, the emphasis is on the pilot's age.

Another way to achieve emphasis is to place the most important words, phrases, and clauses at the beginning or end of a sentence. The ending is the most emphatic part of a sentence; the beginning is less emphatic; and the middle is the least emphatic of all. The two sentences about the pilot put the main clause at the end, achieving special emphasis. The same thing occurs in a much longer kind of sentence, called a *periodic sentence,* in which the main idea is placed at the end, closest to the period. Here is an example from John Updike:

> On the afternoon of the first day of spring, when the gutters were still heaped high with Monday's snow but the sky itself had been swept clean, we put on our galoshes and walked up the sunny side of Fifth Avenue to Central Park.

By holding the main clause back, Updike keeps his readers in suspense and so puts the most emphasis possible on his main idea.

A *loose sentence,* on the other hand, states its main idea at the beginning and then adds details in subsequent phrases and clauses. Rewritten as a loose sentence, Updike's sentence might read like this:

> We put on our galoshes and walked up the sunny side of Fifth Avenue to Central Park on the afternoon of the first day of spring, when the gutters were still heaped high with Monday's snow but the sky itself had been swept clean.

The main idea still gets plenty of emphasis, since it is contained in a main clause at the beginning of the sentence. A loose sentence resembles the way people talk: it flows naturally and is easy to understand.

DRAMATICALLY SHORT SENTENCES

Another way to create emphasis is to use a *dramatically short sentence*. Especially following a long and involved sentence, a short declarative sentence helps drive a point home. Here are two examples, the first from student Danielle Kuykendall and the second from David Wise:

> The qualities that Barbie promotes (slimness, youth, and beauty) allow no tolerance of gray hair, wrinkles, sloping posture, or failing eyesight and hearing. Barbie's perfect body is eternal.

> The executive suite on the thirty-fifth floor of the Columbia Broadcasting System skyscraper in Manhattan is a tasteful blend of dark wood paneling, expensive abstract paintings, thick carpets, and pleasing colors. It has the quiet look of power.

ACTIVE AND PASSIVE VOICE

Finally, since the subject of a sentence is automatically emphasized, writers may choose to use the *active voice* when they want to emphasize the doer of an action and the *passive voice* when they want to downplay or omit the doer completely. Here are two examples:

> High winds pushed our sailboat onto the rocks, where the force of the waves tore it to pieces.

> Our sailboat was pushed by high winds onto the rocks, where it was torn to pieces by the force of the waves.

The first sentence emphasizes the natural forces that destroyed the boat, while the second sentence focuses attention on the boat itself. The passive voice may be useful in placing emphasis, but it has important disadvantages. As the examples show, and as the terms suggest, active-voice verbs are more vigorous and vivid than the same verbs in the passive voice. Then, too, some writers use the passive voice to hide or evade responsibility. "It has been decided" conceals who did the deciding, whereas "I have decided" makes all clear. So the passive voice should be used only when necessary—as it is in this sentence.

COORDINATION

Often, a writer wants to place equal emphasis on several facts or ideas. One way to do this is to give each its own sentence. For example, consider these three sentences about golfer Nancy Lopez.

Nancy Lopez selected her club. She lined up her shot. She chipped the ball to within a foot of the pin.

But a long series of short, simple sentences quickly becomes tedious. Many writers would combine these three sentences by using *coordination*. The coordinating conjunctions *and, but, or, nor, for, so,* and *yet* connect words, phrases, and clauses of equal importance:

Nancy Lopez selected her club, lined up her shot, *and* chipped the ball to within a foot of the pin.

By coordinating three sentences into one, the writer not only makes the same words easier to read, but also shows that Lopez's three actions are equally important parts of a single process.

PARALLELISM

When parts of a sentence are not only coordinated but also grammatically the same, they are *parallel*. Parallelism in a sentence is created by balancing a word with a word, a phrase with a phrase, or a clause with a clause. Here is a humorous example from the beginning of Mark Twain's *Adventures of Huckleberry Finn:*

Persons attempting to find a motive in this narrative will be prosecuted; persons attempting to find a moral in it will be banished; persons attempting to find a plot in it will be shot.

Parallelism is also often found in speeches. For example, in the last sentence of the Gettysburg Address Lincoln proclaims his hope that "government of the people, by the people, for the people, shall not perish from the earth."

Hitting Pay Dirt

■ **Annie Dillard**

Annie Dillard was born in 1945 in Pennsylvania and attended Hollins College in Virginia. Although she is known primarily as an essayist for such works as Pilgrim at Tinker Creek *(1974), which won a Pulitzer Prize,* Teaching a Stone to Talk *(1982), and* For the Time Being *(2000), she has demonstrated an impressive versatility in her publications:* Tickets for a Prayer Wheel *(1974), poetry;* Holy the Firm *(1977), a prose narrative;* Living by Fiction *(1982), literary theory;* An American Childhood *(1987), autobiography; and* The Living *(1992), a novel. In* The Writing Life *(1989), Dillard explores the processes of writing itself. As you read the selection below, taken from* An American Childhood, *pay particular attention to the way Dillard's active verbs give her sentences strength and emphasis. There is also a good example of parallel sentence structure in paragraph 5.*

FOR YOUR JOURNAL

What was your favorite possession in your preteen years? How did you get it? Why was it special to you?

After I read *The Field Book of Ponds and Streams* several times, I 1
longed for a microscope. Everybody needed a microscope. Detectives used microscopes, both for the FBI and at Scotland Yard. Although usually I had to save my tiny allowance for things I wanted, that year for Christmas my parents gave me a microscope kit.

In a dark basement corner, on a white enamel table, I set up the 2
microscope kit. I supplied a chair, a lamp, a batch of jars, a candle, and a pile of library books. The microscope kit supplied a blunt black three-speed microscope, a booklet, a scalpel, a dropper, an ingenious device for cutting thin segments of fragile tissue, a pile of clean slides and cover slips, and a dandy array of corked test tubes.

One of the test tubes contained "hay infusion." Hay infusion was 3
a wee brown chip of grass blade. You added water to it, and after a week it became a jungle in a drop, full of one-celled animals. This did

not work for me. All I saw in the microscope after a week was a wet chip of dried grass, much enlarged.

Another test tube contained "diatomaceous earth." This was, I 4 believed, an actual pinch of the white cliffs of Dover. On my palm it was an airy, friable chalk. The booklet said it was composed of the siliceous bodies of diatoms—one-celled creatures that lived in, as it were, small glass jewelry boxes with fitted lids. Diatoms, I read, come in a variety of transparent geometrical shapes. Broken and dead and dug out of geological deposits, they made chalk, and a fine abrasive used in silver polish and toothpaste. What I saw in the microscope must have been the fine abrasive—grit enlarged. It was years before I saw a recognizable, whole diatom. The kit's diatomaceous earth was a bust.

All that winter I played with the microscope. I prepared slides 5 from things at hand, as the books suggested. I looked at the transparent membrane inside an onion's skin and saw the cell. I looked at a section of cork and saw the cells, and at scrapings from the inside of my cheek, ditto. I looked at my blood and saw not much; I looked at my urine and saw a long iridescent crystal, for the drop had dried.

All this was very well, but I wanted to see the wildlife I had read 6 about. I wanted especially to see the famous amoeba, who had eluded me. He was supposed to live in the hay infusion, but I hadn't found him there. He lived outside in warm ponds and streams, too, but I lived in Pittsburgh, and it had been a cold winter.

Finally late that spring I saw an amoeba. The week before, I had 7 gathered puddle water from Frick Park; it had been festering in a jar in the basement. This June night after dinner I figured I had waited long enough. In the basement at my microscope table I spread a scummy drop of Frick Park puddle water on a slide, peeked in, and lo, there was the famous amoeba. He was as blobby and grainy as his picture; I would have known him anywhere.

Before I had watched him at all, I ran upstairs. My parents were 8 still at the table, drinking coffee. They, too, could see the famous amoeba. I told them, bursting, that he was all set up, that they should hurry before his water dried. It was the chance of a lifetime.

Father had stretched out his long legs and was tilting back in his 9 chair. Mother sat with her knees crossed, in blue slacks, smoking a Chesterfield. The dessert dishes were still on the table. My sisters were nowhere in evidence. It was a warm evening; the big dining-room windows gave onto blooming rhododendrons.

Mother regarded me warmly. She gave me to understand that she   10
was glad I had found what I had been looking for, but that she and
Father were happy to sit with their coffee, and would not be coming
down.

She did not say, but I understood at once, that they had their   11
pursuits (coffee?) and I had mine. She did not say, but I began to understand then, that you do what you do out of your private passion
for the thing itself.

I had essentially been handed my own life. In subsequent years   12
my parents would praise my drawings and poems, and supply me
with books, art supplies, and sports equipment, and listen to my
troubles and enthusiasms, and supervise my hours, and discuss and
inform, but they would not get involved with my detective work, nor
hear about my reading, nor inquire about my homework or term papers or exams, nor visit the salamanders I caught, nor listen to me
play the piano, nor attend my field hockey games, nor fuss over my
insect collection with me, or my poetry collection or stamp collection
or rock collection. My days and nights were my own to plan and fill.

When I left the dining room that evening and started down the   13
dark basement stairs, I had a life. I sat down to my wonderful
amoeba, and there he was, rolling his grains more slowly now, extending an arc of his edge for a foot and drawing himself along by
that foot, and absorbing it again and rolling on. I gave him some
more pond water.

I had hit pay dirt. For all I knew, there were paramecia, too, in   14
that pond water, or daphniae, or stentors, or any of the many other
creatures I had read about and never seen: volvox, the spherical algal
colony; euglena with its one red eye; the elusive, glassy diatom;
hydra, rotifers, water bears, worms. Anything was possible. The sky
was the limit.

QUESTIONS FOR STUDY AND DISCUSSION

1. In her second sentence, Dillard says, "Everybody needed a microscope." This confident yet naive statement indicates that she is
   writing from the point of view of herself as a child. (Glossary:
   Point of View) Why does she write her essay from this point of
   view?

2. Analyze the sentences in the first four paragraphs. How would you describe Dillard's use of sentence variety? Identify her very short sentences—those with eight or fewer words. What does each contribute to the essay?

3. Why does the microscope appeal to Dillard? How does she react to her early disappointments?

4. Is Dillard's diction appropriate for the essay's content and point of view? (Glossary: *Diction*) Defend your answer with specific examples from the essay.

5. Reread paragraph 12, noting Dillard's sentence constructions. In what way does their construction reinforce Dillard's content? Explain.

6. Three of the four sentences in Dillard's concluding paragraph are five words or less. What impact do these short sentences have on readers? Explain.

VOCABULARY

Refer to your dictionary to define the following words as they are used in this selection. Then use each word in a sentence of your own.

infusion (3)   iridescent (5)

friable (4)   festering (7)

siliceous (4)

CLASSROOM ACTIVITY USING EFFECTIVE SENTENCES

Rewrite the following paragraph, presenting the information in any order you choose. Use sentence variety and subordination, as discussed in the chapter introduction, to make the paragraph more interesting to read.

When Billy saw the crime, he was in a grocery store buying hot dog buns for the barbecue he had scheduled for the next weekend. The crime was a burglary, and the criminal was someone you would never expect to see commit a crime. His basketball shoes squeaked as he ran away, and he looked no more than fifteen years old with a fresh, eager face that was the picture of innocence. Billy watched the youth steal a purse right off a woman's shoulder, and the bright sun reflected off the thief's forehead as he ran away, although the weather was quite chilly and had been for a week. The policeman who caught the thief tripped him and handcuffed him as Billy paid for the hot dog buns, got in his car, and drove away.

SUGGESTED WRITING ASSIGNMENTS

1. Dillard learned an important life lesson from her parents' reaction to her news of the amoeba. How would you describe that lesson? Use your description as the basis for a brief essay in which you discuss the role of parents in fostering children's creativity and desire for knowledge. Pay close attention to your sentences, and use them to emphasize the most important parts of your discussion.

2. Write a brief essay using one of the following sentences to focus and control the descriptive details you select. Place the sentence in the essay wherever it will have the greatest emphasis.

The music stopped.

It was broken glass.

I started to sweat.

She had convinced me.

It was my turn to step forward.

Now I understood.

Salvation

■ Langston Hughes

*Born in Joplin, Missouri, Langston Hughes (1902–1967) be-
came an important figure in the African American cultural
movement of the 1920s known as the Harlem Renaissance. He
wrote poetry, fiction, and plays and contributed columns to the*
New York Post *and an African American weekly, the* Chicago
Defender. *He is best known for* The Weary Blues *(1926) and
other books of poetry that express his racial pride, his familiar-
ity with African American traditions, and his understanding of
blues and jazz rhythms. In the following selection from his autobiography,* The Big Sea *(1940), note how Hughes varies the
length and types of sentences he uses for the sake of emphasis.
The impact of the dramatically short sentence in paragraph 12,
for instance, derives from the variety of sentences preceding it.*

FOR YOUR JOURNAL

What role does religion play in your family? Do you consider
yourself a religious person? Have you ever felt pressure from
others to participate in religious activities? How did that make
you feel?

I was saved from sin when I was going on thirteen. But not really   1
saved. It happened like this. There was a big revival at my Auntie
Reed's church. Every night for weeks there had been much preaching,
singing, praying, and shouting, and some very hardened sinners had
been brought to Christ, and the membership of the church had grown
by leaps and bounds. Then just before the revival ended, they held a
special meeting for children, "to bring the young lambs to the fold."
My aunt spoke of it for days ahead. That night I was escorted to the
front row and placed on the mourners' bench with all the other
young sinners, who had not yet been brought to Jesus.

My aunt told me that when you were saved you saw a light, and   2
something happened to you inside! And Jesus came into your life!
And God was with you from then on! She said you could see and
hear and feel Jesus in your soul. I believed her. I had heard a great

165

many old people say the same thing and it seemed to me they ought to know. So I sat there calmly in the hot, crowded church, waiting for Jesus to come to me.

The preacher preached a wonderful rhythmical sermon, all   3
moans and shouts and lonely cries and dire pictures of hell, and then he sang a song about the ninety and nine safe in the fold, but one little lamb was left out in the cold. Then he said: "Won't you come? Won't you come to Jesus? Young lambs, won't you come?" And he held out his arms to all us young sinners there on the mourners' bench. And the little girls cried. And some of them jumped up and went to Jesus right away. But most of us just sat there.

A great many old people came and knelt around us and prayed,   4
old women with jet-black faces and braided hair, old men with work-gnarled hands. And the church sang a song about the lower lights are burning, some poor sinners to be saved. And the whole building rocked with prayer and song.

Still I kept waiting to *see* Jesus.   5

Finally all the young people had gone to the altar and were saved,   6
but one boy and me. He was a rounder's son named Westley. Westley and I were surrounded by sisters and deacons praying. It was very hot in the church, and getting late now. Finally Westley said to me in a whisper: "God damn! I'm tired o' sitting here. Let's get up and be saved." So he got up and was saved.

Then I was left all alone on the mourners' bench. My aunt came   7
and knelt at my knees and cried, while prayers and songs swirled all around me in the little church. The whole congregation prayed for me alone, in a mighty wail of moans and voices. And I kept waiting serenely for Jesus, waiting, waiting — but he didn't come. I wanted to see him, but nothing happened to me. Nothing! I wanted something to happen to me, but nothing happened.

I heard the songs and the minister saying: "Why don't you come?   8
My dear child, why don't you come to Jesus? Jesus is waiting for you. He wants you. Why don't you come? Sister Reed, what is this child's name?"

"Langston," my aunt sobbed.   9

"Langston, why don't you come? Why don't you come and be   10
saved? Oh, Lamb of God! Why don't you come?"

Now it was really getting late. I began to be ashamed of myself,   11
holding everything up so long. I began to wonder what God thought about Westley, who certainly hadn't seen Jesus either, but who was now sitting proudly on the platform, swinging his knickerbockered

legs and grinning down at me, surrounded by deacons and old women on their knees praying. God had not struck Westley dead for taking his name in vain or for lying in the temple. So I decided that maybe to save further trouble, I'd better lie, too, and say that Jesus had come, and get up and be saved.

So I got up.   12

Suddenly the whole room broke into a sea of shouting, as they   13
saw me rise. Waves of rejoicing swept the place. Women leaped in the air. My aunt threw her arms around me. The minister took me by the hand and led me to the platform.

When things quieted down, in a hushed silence, punctuated by a   14
few ecstatic "Amens," all the new young lambs were blessed in the name of God. Then joyous singing filled the room.

That night, for the last time in my life but one—for I was a big boy   15
twelve years old—I cried. I cried, in bed alone, and couldn't stop. I buried my head under the quilts, but my aunt heard me. She woke up and told my uncle I was crying because the Holy Ghost had come into my life, and because I had seen Jesus. But I was really crying because I couldn't bear to tell her that I had lied, that I had deceived everybody in the church, that I hadn't seen Jesus, and that now I didn't believe there was a Jesus any more, since he didn't come to help me.

QUESTIONS FOR STUDY AND DISCUSSION

1. What is salvation? Is it important to young Langston Hughes that he be saved? Why does he expect to be saved at the revival meeting?

2. Hughes varies the length and structure of his sentences through-out the essay. How does this variety capture and reinforce the rhythms and drama of the evening's events? Explain.

3. What would be gained or lost if the essay began with the first two sentences combined as follows: "I was saved from sin when I was going on thirteen, but I was not really saved"?

4. Identify the coordinating conjunctions in paragraph 3. Rewrite the paragraph without them. Compare your paragraph with the original, and explain what Hughes gains by using coordinating conjunctions. (Glossary: *Coordination*)

5. Identify the subordinating conjunctions in paragraph 15. What is it about the ideas in this last paragraph that makes it necessary for Hughes to use these subordinating conjunctions? (Glossary: *Subordination*)

6. How does Hughes's choice of words, or diction, help to establish a realistic atmosphere for a religious revival meeting? (Glossary: *Diction*)

7. Why does young Langston cry on the night of his being "saved"? Why is the story of his being saved so ironic? (Glossary: *Irony*)

VOCABULARY

Refer to your dictionary to define the following words as they are used in this selection. Then use each word in a sentence of your own.

dire (3)   punctuated (14)
gnarled (4)   ecstatic (14)
vain (11)

CLASSROOM ACTIVITY USING EFFECTIVE SENTENCES

Using coordination or subordination, rewrite each set of short sentences as a single sentence.

> FOR EXAMPLE: This snow is good for Colorado's economy. Tourists are now flocking to ski resorts.
>
> REVISED: This snow is good for Colorado's economy because tourists are now flocking to ski resorts.

1. I can take the 6:30 express train. I can catch the 7:00 bus.

2. Miriam worked on her research paper. She interviewed five people for the paper. She worked all weekend. She was tired.

3. Juan's new job kept him busy every day. He did not have time to work out at the gym for over a month.

4. The Statue of Liberty welcomes newcomers to America. It was a gift of the French government. It was completely restored for the nation's two hundredth birthday. It is over 120 years old.

5. Carla is tall. She is strong. She is a team player. She was the starting center on the basketball team.

6. Betsy loves Bach's music. She also likes Scott Joplin.

SUGGESTED WRITING ASSIGNMENTS

1. Like the young Langston Hughes, we sometimes find ourselves in situations in which, for the sake of conformity, we do things we

do not believe in. Consider one such experience you have had, and write an essay about it. What is it about human nature that makes us occasionally act in ways that contradict our inner feelings? As you write, pay particular attention to your sentence variety.

2. Reread the introduction to this chapter. Then review one of the essays that you have written, paying particular attention to sentence structure. Recast sentences as necessary in order to make your writing more interesting and effective.

The Good Daughter

■ **Caroline Hwang**

Freelance writer and editor Caroline Hwang was born in Milwaukee, Wisconsin. After graduating from the University of Pennsylvania in 1991, she entered the world of popular magazines, holding editorial positions at Glamour, Mademoiselle, *and* Redbook. *She is currently living in New York City and pursuing her dream; she's writing a novel and is enrolled in the Master of Fine Arts program at New York University. In the following essay, which first appeared in* Newsweek *in 1998, Hwang illuminates the difficulty of growing up the daughter of Korean immigrant parents. Notice how Hwang uses sentence variety for emphasis and dramatic effect in recounting how she has been torn between her parents' dreams for her and her own dreams.*

FOR YOUR JOURNAL

What is your cultural identity? Do you consider yourself an American, or do you identify with another culture? How comfortable do you feel with this identity? Explain why you feel as you do.

The moment I walked into the dry-cleaning store, I knew the woman   1
behind the counter was from Korea, like my parents. To show her
that we shared a heritage, and possibly get a fellow countryman's discount, I tilted my head forward, in shy imitation of a traditional bow.

"Name?" she asked, not noticing my attempted obeisance.   2
"Hwang," I answered.   3
"Hwang? Are you Chinese?"   4
Her question caught me off-guard. I was used to hearing such   5
queries from non-Asians who think Asians all look alike, but never
from one of my own people. Of course, the only Koreans I knew
were my parents and their friends, people who've never asked me
where I came from, since they knew better than I.

I ransacked my mind for the Korean words that would tell her   6
who I was. It's always struck me as funny (in a mirthless sort of way)
that I can more readily say "I am Korean" in Spanish, German and
even Latin than I can in the language of my ancestry. In the end, I
told her in English.

The dry-cleaning woman squinted as though trying to see past 7
the glare of my strangeness, repeating my surname under her breath.
"Oh, *Fxuang*," she said, doubling over with laughter. "You don't
know how to speak your name."

I flinched. Perhaps I was particularly sensitive at the time, having 8
just dropped out of graduate school. I had torn up my map for the future, the one that said not only where I was going but who I was. My
sense of identity was already disintegrating.

When I got home, I called my parents to ask why they had never 9
bothered to correct me. "Big deal," my mother said, sounding more flippant than I knew she intended. (Like many people who learn English in
a classroom, she uses idioms that don't always fit the occasion.) "So
what if you can't pronounce your name? You are American," she said.

Though I didn't challenge her explanation, it left me unsatisfied. 10
The fact is, my cultural identity is hardly that clear-cut.

My parents immigrated to this country 30 years ago, two years 11
before I was born. They told me often, while I was growing up, that,
if I wanted to, I could be president someday, that here my grasp
would be as long as my reach.

To ensure that I reaped all the advantages of this country, my 12
parents saw to it that I became fully assimilated. So, like any American of my generation, I whiled away my youth strolling malls and
talking on the phone, rhapsodizing over Andrew McCarthy's blue
eyes or analyzing the meaning of a certain upperclassman's offer of a
ride to the Homecoming football game.

To my parents, I am all American, and the sacrifices they made in 13
leaving Korea—including my mispronounced name—pale in comparison to the opportunities those sacrifices gave me. They do not see
that I straddle two cultures, nor that I feel displaced in the only country I know. I identify with Americans, but Americans do not identify
with me. I've never known what it's like to belong to a community—
neither one at large, nor of an extended family. I know more about
Europe than the continent my ancestors unmistakably come from. I
sometimes wonder, as I did that day in the dry cleaner's, if I would be
a happier person had my parents stayed in Korea.

I first began to consider this thought around the time I decided to 14
go to graduate school. It had been a compromise: my parents wanted
me to go to law school; I wanted to skip the starched-collar track and
be a writer—the hungrier the better. But after 20-some years of following their wishes and meeting all of their expectations, I couldn't
bring myself to disobey or disappoint. A writing career is riskier than

law, I remember thinking. If I'm a failure and my life is a washout, then what does that make my parents' lives?

I know that many of my friends had to choose between pleasing ⁣15 their parents and being true to themselves. But for the children of immigrants, the choice seems more complicated, a happy outcome impossible. By making the biggest move of their lives for me, my parents indentured me to the largest debt imaginable—I owe them the fulfillment of their hopes for me.

It tore me up inside to suppress my dream, but I went to school ⁣16 for a Ph.D. in English literature, thinking I had found the perfect compromise. I would be able to write at least about books while pursuing a graduate degree. Predictably, it didn't work out. How could I labor for five years in a program I had no passion for? When I finally left school, my parents were disappointed, but since it wasn't what they wanted me to do, they weren't devastated. I, on the other hand, felt I was staring at the bottom of the abyss. I had seen the flaw in my life of halfwayness, in my planned life of compromises.

I hadn't thought about my love life, but I had a vague plan to make ⁣17 concessions there, too. Though they raised me as an American, my parents expect me to marry someone Korean and give them grandchildren who look like them. This didn't seem like such a huge request when I was 14, but now I don't know what I'm going to do. I've never been in love with someone I dated, or dated someone I loved. (Since I can't bring myself even to entertain the thought of marrying the non-Korean men I'm attracted to, I've been dating only those I know I can stay clear-headed about.) And as I near that age when the question of marriage stalks every relationship, I can't help but wonder if my parents expectations are responsible for the lack of passion in my life.

My parents didn't want their daughter to be Korean, but they ⁣18 don't want her fully American, either. Children of immigrants are living paradoxes. We are the first generation and the last. We are in this country for its opportunities, yet filial duty binds us. When my parents boarded the plane, they knew they were embarking on a rough trip. I don't think they imagined the rocks in the path of their daughter who can't even pronounce her own name.

QUESTIONS FOR STUDY AND DISCUSSION

1. What is Hwang's thesis, and where is it most clearly stated? (Glossary: *Thesis*)

2. Hwang begins her essay by recounting an unsettling incident in a dry-cleaning store. How effective did you find this opening? (Glossary: *Beginnings and Endings*) What contribution does dialogue make to her telling of this story? Where else does she use dialogue in her essay? (Glossary: *Dialogue*)
3. Hwang starts paragraphs 5 and 8 with short sentences. How does each of these sentences enhance the drama between Hwang and the Korean woman at the dry cleaners?
4. Analyze the sentences in paragraph 13. In what ways does the structure of these sentences reinforce Hwang's uncertainty about her own identity? Explain.
5. What does Hwang mean when she says, "Children of immigrants are living paradoxes. We are the first generation and the last" (18).

VOCABULARY

Refer to your dictionary to define the following words as they are used in this selection. Then use each word in a sentence of your own.

obeisance (2)	rhapsodizing (12)
ransacked (6)	concessions (17)
flippant (9)	paradoxes (18)
assimilated (12)	filial (18)

CLASSROOM ACTIVITY USING EFFECTIVE SENTENCES

Rewrite the following sets of sentences to combine short, simple sentences and to reduce repetition wherever possible.

> FOR EXAMPLE: Angelo's team won the championship. He pitched a two-hitter. He struck out ten batters. He hit a home run.
>
> REVISED: Angelo's team won the championship because he pitched a two-hitter, struck out ten batters, and hit a home run.

1. Bonnie wore shorts. The shorts were red. The shorts had pockets.
2. The deer hunter awoke at 5:00 A.M. He ate a quick breakfast. The breakfast consisted of coffee, juice, and cereal. He was in the woods before the sun came up.
3. My grandparents played golf every weekend for years. Last year

they stopped playing. They miss the game now.

4. Fly over any major city. Look out the airplane's window. You will be appalled at the number of tall smokestacks you will see.

5. It did not rain for over three months. Most crops in the region failed. Some farmers were on the brink of declaring bankruptcy.

6. Every weekday I go to work. I exercise. I shower and relax. I eat a light, low-fat dinner.

SUGGESTED WRITING ASSIGNMENTS

1. Hwang reveals that her passion is to become a writer. In deciding to go to graduate school for a Ph.D. in English, she thought that she had "found the perfect compromise" between her dream to be a writer and her parents' dream for her to become a lawyer. Write an essay describing your own dream, if you have one, and explain what you will need to do to fulfill it. Does your family support you in this pursuit?

2. Choose a country that you have studied, visited, or at least read about. Compare who you are now with who you think you would be if you had been born in that country. How would you be different? Why?

38 Who Saw Murder Didn't Call Police

■ **Martin Gansberg**

Martin Gansberg (1920–1995) was born in Brooklyn, New York, and graduated from St. John's University. A long-time reporter, Gansberg wrote the following essay for the New York Times *two weeks after the early morning events he so poignantly narrates. Once you've finished reading the essay, you will understand why it has been so often reprinted and why the name Kitty Genovese is still invoked whenever questions of public apathy arise. Gansberg uses dialogue effectively to emphasize his point. Pay particular attention to how he constructs the sentences that incorporate dialogue and to how subordination and coordination often determine where quoted material appears.*

FOR YOUR JOURNAL

Have you ever witnessed an accident or a crime? How did you react to the situation—did you come forward and testify, or did you choose not to get involved? Why do you think you reacted the way you did? How do you feel about your behavior?

For more than half an hour 38 respectable, law-abiding citizens in 1 Queens watched a killer stalk and stab a woman in three separate attacks in Kew Gardens.

Twice their chatter and the sudden glow of their bedroom lights 2 interrupted him and frightened him off. Each time he returned, sought her out, and stabbed her again. Not one person telephoned the police during the assault; one witness called after the woman was dead.

That was two weeks ago today. 3

Still shocked is Assistant Chief Inspector Frederick M. Lussen, in 4 charge of the borough's detectives and a veteran of 25 years of homicide investigations. He can give a matter-of-fact recitation on many murders. But the Kew Gardens slaying baffles him—not because it is a murder, but because the "good people" failed to call the police.

"As we have reconstructed the crime," he said, "the assailant had ⁵ three chances to kill this woman during a 35-minute period. He returned twice to complete the job. If we had been called when he first attacked, the woman might not be dead now."

This is what the police say happened beginning at 3:20 A.M. in ⁶ the staid, middle-class, tree-lined Austin Street area:

Twenty-eight-year-old Catherine Genovese, who was called Kitty ⁷ by almost everyone in the neighborhood, was returning home from her job as manager of a bar in Hollis. She parked her red Fiat in a lot adjacent to the Kew Gardens Long Island Rail Road Station, facing Mowbray Place. Like many residents of the neighborhood, she had parked there day after day since her arrival from Connecticut a year ago, although the railroad frowns on the practice.

She turned off the lights of her car, locked the door, and started ⁸ to walk the 100 feet to the entrance of her apartment at 82-70 Austin Street, which is in a Tudor building, with stores in the first floor and apartments on the second.

The entrance to the apartment is in the rear of the building because ⁹ the front is rented to retail stores. At night the quiet neighborhood is shrouded in the slumbering darkness that marks most residential areas.

Miss Genovese noticed a man at the far end of the lot, near a ¹⁰ seven-story apartment house at 82-40 Austin Street. She halted. Then, nervously, she headed up Austin Street toward Lefferts Boulevard, where there is a call box to the 102nd Police Precinct in nearby Richmond Hill.

She got as far as a street light in front of a bookstore before the ¹¹ man grabbed her. She screamed. Lights went on in the 10-story apartment house at 82-67 Austin Street, which faces the bookstore. Windows slid open and voices punctuated the early-morning stillness.

Miss Genovese screamed: "Oh, my God, he stabbed me! Please ¹² help me! Please help me!"

From one of the upper windows in the apartment house, a man ¹³ called down: "Let that girl alone!"

The assailant looked up at him, shrugged, and walked down ¹⁴ Austin Street toward a white sedan parked a short distance away. Miss Genovese struggled to her feet.

Lights went out. The killer returned to Miss Genovese, now try- ¹⁵ ing to make her way around the side of the building by the parking lot to get to her apartment. The assailant stabbed her again.

"I'm dying!" she shrieked. "I'm dying!" ¹⁶

Windows were opened again, and lights went on in many apart- 17
ments. The assailant got into his car and drove away. Miss Genovese
staggered to her feet. A city bus, O-10, the Lefferts Boulevard line to
Kennedy International Airport, passed. It was 3:35 A.M.

The assailant returned. By then, Miss Genovese had crawled to 18
the back of the building, where the freshly painted brown doors to
the apartment house held out hope for safety. The killer tried the first
door; she wasn't there. At the second door, 82-62 Austin Street, he
saw her slumped on the floor at the foot of the stairs. He stabbed her
a third time—fatally.

It was 3:50 by the time the police received their first call, from a 19
man who was a neighbor of Miss Genovese. In two minutes they
were at the scene. The neighbor, a 70-year-old woman, and another
woman were the only persons on the street. Nobody else came forward.

The man explained that he had called the police after much delib- 20
eration. He had phoned a friend in Nassau County for advice and
then he had crossed the roof of the building to the apartment of the
elderly woman to get her to make the call.

"I didn't want to get involved," he sheepishly told the police. 21

Six days later, the police arrested Winston Moseley, a 29-year- 22
old business-machine operator, and charged him with homicide.
Moseley had no previous record. He is married, has two children and
owns a home at 133-19 Sutter Avenue, South Ozone Park, Queens.
On Wednesday, a court committed him to Kings County Hospital for
psychiatric observation.

When questioned by the police, Moseley also said that he had 23
slain Mrs. Annie May Johnson, 24, of 146-12 133d Avenue, Jamaica,
on Feb. 29 and Barbara Kralik, 15, of 174-17 140th Avenue, Spring-
field Gardens, last July. In the Kralik case, the police are holding
Alvin L. Mitchell, who is said to have confessed to that slaying.

The police stressed how simple it would have been to have gotten 24
in touch with them. "A phone call," said one of the detectives,
"would have done it." The police may be reached by dialing "O" for
operator or SPring 7-3100.

Today witnesses from the neighborhood, which is made up of 25
one-family homes in the $35,000 to $60,000 range with the exception of the two apartment houses near the railroad station, find it difficult to explain why they didn't call the police.

A housewife, knowingly if quite casually, said, "We thought it 26
was a lovers' quarrel." A husband and wife both said, "Frankly, we

were afraid." They seemed aware of the fact that events might have been different. A distraught woman, wiping her hands in her apron, said, "I didn't want my husband to get involved."

One couple, now willing to talk about that night, said they heard the 27 first screams. The husband looked thoughtfully at the bookstore where the killer first grabbed Miss Genovese.

"We went to the window to see what was happening," he said, 28 "but the light from our bedroom made it difficult to see the street." The wife, still apprehensive, added: "I put out the light and we were able to see better."

Asked why they hadn't called the police, she shrugged and 29 replied: "I don't know."

A man peeked out from a slight opening in the doorway to his 30 apartment and rattled off an account of the killer's second attack. Why hadn't he called the police at the time? "I was tired," he said without emotion. "I went back to bed."

It was 4:25 A.M. when the ambulance arrived to take the body of 31 Miss Genovese. It drove off. "Then," a solemn police detective said, "the people came out."

QUESTIONS FOR STUDY AND DISCUSSION

1. What is the author's purpose in this selection? What are the advantages or disadvantages in using narration to accomplish this purpose? Explain. (Glossary: *Purpose*)

2. Where does the narrative actually begin? What is the function of the material that precedes the beginning of the narrative proper? (Glossary: *Narration*)

3. Analyze Gansberg's sentences in paragraphs 7–9. How does he use subordination to highlight what he believes is essential information?

4. Gansberg uses a number of two- and three-word sentences in his narrative. Identify several of these sentences, and explain how they serve to punctuate and to add drama to this story. Which short sentences have the greatest impact on you? Explain why.

5. Gansberg uses dialogue throughout his essay. How many people does he quote? What does he accomplish by using dialogue? (Glossary: *Dialogue*)

6. How would you describe Gansberg's tone? Is the tone appropriate for the story Gansberg narrates? Explain. (Glossary: *Tone*)

7. Reflect on Gansberg's ending. What would be lost or gained by adding a paragraph that analyzed the meaning of the narrative for the reader? (Glossary: *Beginnings and Endings*)

VOCABULARY

Refer to your dictionary to define the following words as they are used in this selection. Then use each word in a sentence of your own.

stalk (1)   shrouded (9)
recitation (4)   sheepishly (21)
assailant (5)   apprehensive (28)
staid (6)

CLASSROOM ACTIVITY USING EFFECTIVE SENTENCES

Repetition can be an effective writing device to emphasize important points and to enhance coherence. Unless it is handled carefully, however, it can often result in a tedious piece of writing. Rewrite the following paragraph, either eliminating repetition or reworking the repetitions to improve coherence and to emphasize important information.

Day care centers should be available to all women who work and have no one to care for their children. Day care centers should not be available only to women who are raising their children alone or to families whose income is below the poverty level. All women who work should have available to them care for their children that is reliable, responsible, convenient, and that does not cost an exorbitant amount. Women who work need and must demand more day care centers. No woman should be prevented from working because of the lack of convenient and reliable facilities for child care.

SUGGESTED WRITING ASSIGNMENTS

1. Gansberg's essay is about public apathy and fear. What reasons did Kitty Genovese's neighbors give for not calling the police when they first heard her calls for help? How do these reasons reflect on human nature, particularly as it manifests itself in contemporary American society? Modeling your essay after Gansberg's, narrate another event or series of events you know about that demonstrates either public involvement or public apathy.

2. It is common when using narration to tell about firsthand experience and to tell the story in the first person. It is good practice, however, to try writing a narration about something you don't know about firsthand but must learn about, much as a newspaper reporter gathers information for a story. For several days, be attentive to events occurring around you—in your neighborhood, school, community, region—events that would be appropriate for a narrative essay. Interview the principal characters involved in your story, take detailed notes, and then write your narration.

p a r t ■ *t w o*

The Language
of the Essay

chapter **8**

Diction and Tone

■ Diction

Diction refers to a writer's choice and use of words. Good diction is precise and appropriate—the words mean exactly what the writer intends, and the words are well suited to the writer's subject, purpose, and intended audience.

For careful writers it is not enough merely to come close to saying what they want to say; they select words that convey their exact meaning. Perhaps Mark Twain put this best when he said, "The difference between the right word and the almost right word is the difference between lightning and the lightning bug." Inaccurate, imprecise, or inappropriate diction not only fails to convey the writer's intended meaning but also may cause confusion and misunderstanding for the reader.

CONNOTATION AND DENOTATION

Both *connotation* and *denotation* refer to the meanings of words. Denotation is the dictionary meaning of a word, the literal meaning. Connotative meanings are the associations or emotional overtones that words have acquired gradually. For example, the word *home* denotes a place where someone lives, but it connotes warmth, security, family, comfort, affection, and other more private thoughts and images. The word *residence* also denotes a place where someone lives, but its connotations are colder and more formal.

Many words in English have synonyms, words with very similar denotations—for example, *mob, crowd, multitude,* and *bunch.* Deciding which to use depends largely on the connotations that each synonym has and the context in which the word is to be used. For example, you might say, "There was a crowd at the lecture," but not

"There was a mob at the lecture." Good writers are sensitive to both the denotations and the connotations of words.

ABSTRACT AND CONCRETE WORDS

Abstract words name ideas, conditions, emotions — things nobody can touch, see, or hear. Some abstract words are *love, wisdom, cowardice, beauty, fear,* and *liberty.* People often disagree about abstract things. You may find a forest beautiful, while someone else might find it frightening, and neither of you would be wrong. Beauty and fear are abstract ideas; they exist in your mind, not in the forest along with the trees and the owls. Concrete words refer to things we can touch, see, hear, smell, and taste, such as *sandpaper, soda, birch trees, smog, cow, sailboat, rocking chair,* and *pancake.* If you disagree with someone on a concrete issue — say, you claim that the forest is mostly birch trees, while the other person says it is mostly pine — only one of you can be right, and both of you can be wrong; the kinds of trees that grow in the forest is a concrete fact, not an abstract idea.

Good writing balances ideas and facts, and it also balances abstract and concrete diction. If the writing is too abstract, with too few concrete facts and details, it will be unconvincing and tiresome. If the writing is too concrete, devoid of abstract ideas and emotions, it can seem pointless and dry.

GENERAL AND SPECIFIC WORDS

General and *specific* do not necessarily refer to opposites. The same word can often be either general or specific, depending on the context: *dessert* is more specific than *food,* but more general than *chocolate cream pie.* Being very specific is like being concrete: *chocolate cream pie* is something you can see and taste. Being general, on the other hand, is like being abstract. *Food, dessert,* and even *pie* are large classes of things that bring only very general tastes or images to mind.

Good writing moves back and forth from the general to the specific. Without specific words, generalities can be unconvincing and even confusing: the writer's idea of "good food" may be very different from the reader's. But writing that does not relate specifics to each other by generalization often lacks focus and direction.

CLICHÉS

Some words, phrases, and expressions have become trite through overuse. Let's assume your roommate has just returned from an evening out. You ask her, "How was the concert?" She responds, "The concert was okay, but they had us *packed in* there *like sardines.* How was your evening?" And you reply, "Well, I finished my term paper, but the noise here is enough to *drive me crazy.* The dorm is a real *zoo.*" At one time the italicized expressions were vivid and colorful, but through constant use they have grown stale and ineffective. Experienced writers always try to avoid such clichés as *believe it or not, doomed to failure, hit the spot, let's face it, sneaking suspicion, step in the right direction,* and *went to great lengths.* They strive to use fresh language.

JARGON

Jargon, or technical language, is the special vocabulary of a trade or profession. Writers who use jargon do so with an awareness of their audience. If their audience is a group of coworkers or professionals, jargon may be used freely. If the audience is more general, jargon should be used sparingly and carefully so that readers can understand it. Jargon becomes inappropriate when it is overused, used out of context, or used pretentiously. For example, computer terms like *input, output,* and *feedback* are sometimes used in place of *contribution, result,* and *response* in other fields, especially in business. If you think about it, the terms suggest that people are machines, receiving and processing information according to a program imposed by someone else.

FORMAL AND INFORMAL DICTION

Diction is appropriate when it suits the occasion for which it is intended. If the situation is informal—a friendly letter, for example—the writing may be colloquial; that is, its words may be chosen to suggest the way people talk with each other. If, on the other hand, the situation is formal—a term paper or a research report, for example—then the words should reflect this formality. Informal writing tends to be characterized by slang, contractions, references to the reader, and concrete nouns. Formal writing tends to be impersonal, abstract, and free of contractions and references to the reader.

Formal writing and informal writing are, of course, the extremes. Most writing falls between these two extremes and is a blend of those formal and informal elements that best fit the context.

■ Tone

Tone is the attitude a writer takes toward the subject and the audience. The tone may be friendly or hostile, serious or humorous, intimate or distant, enthusiastic or skeptical.

As you read the following paragraphs, notice how each writer has created a different tone and how that tone is supported by the diction—the writer's particular choice and use of words.

NOSTALGIC

When I was six years old, I thought I knew a lot. How to jump rope, how to skip a rock across a pond, and how to color and stay between the lines—these were all things I took great pride in. Nothing was difficult, and my days were carefree. That is, until the summer when everything became complicated and I suddenly realized I didn't know that much.

–Heather C. Blue, student

ANGRY

Cans. Beer cans. Glinting on the verges of a million miles of roadways, lying in scrub, grass, dirt, leaves, sand, mud, but never hidden. Piels, Rheingold, Ballantine, Schaefer, Schlitz, shining in the sun or picked by moon or the beams of headlights at night; washed by rain or flattened by wheels, but never dulled, never buried, never destroyed. Here is the mark of savages, the testament of wasters, the stain of prosperity.

–Marya Mannes, "Wasteland"

HUMOROUS

In perpetrating a revolution, there are two requirements: someone or something to revolt against and someone to actually show up and do the revolting. Dress is usually casual and both parties may be flexible about time and place but if either faction fails to attend the whole enterprise is likely to come off badly. In the Chinese

Revolution of 1650 neither party showed up and the deposit on the hall was forfeited.

–Woody Allen, "A Brief, Yet Helpful Guide to Civil Disobedience"

RESIGNED

I make my living humping cargo for Seaboard World Airlines, one of the big international airlines at Kennedy Airport. They handle strictly all cargo. I was once told that one of the Rockefellers is the major stockholder for the airline, but I don't really think about that too much. I don't get paid to think. The big thing is to beat that race with the time clock every morning of your life so the airline will be happy. The worst thing a man could ever do is to make suggestions about building a better airline. They pay people $40,000 a year to come up with better ideas. It doesn't matter that these ideas never work; it's just that they get nervous when a guy from South Brooklyn or Ozone Park acts like he has a brain.

–Patrick Fenton, "Confessions of a Working Stiff"

IRONIC

Once upon a time there was a small, beautiful, green and graceful country called Vietnam. It needed to be saved. (In later years no one could remember exactly what it needed to be saved from, but that is another story.) For many years Vietnam was in the process of being saved by France, but the French eventually tired of their labors and left. Then America took on the job. America was well equipped for country-saving. It was the richest and most powerful nation on earth. It had, for example, nuclear explosives on hand and ready to use equal to six tons of TNT for every man, woman, and child in the world. It had huge and very efficient factories, brilliant and dedicated scientists, and most (but not everybody) would agree, it had good intentions. Sadly, America had one fatal flaw — its inhabitants were in love with technology and thought it could do no wrong. A visitor to America during the time of this story would probably have guessed its outcome after seeing how its inhabitants were treating their own country. The air was mostly foul, the water putrid, and most of the land was either covered with concrete or garbage. But Americans were never much on introspection, and they didn't foresee the result of their loving embrace on the small country. They set out to save Vietnam with the same enthusiasm and determination their forefathers had displayed in conquering the frontier.

–The Sierra Club, "A Fable for Our Times"

The diction and tone of an essay are subtle forces, but they exert a tremendous influence on readers. They are instrumental in determining how we will feel while reading the essay and what attitude we will have toward its argument or the points that it makes. Of course, readers react in a variety of ways. An essay written informally but with a largely angry tone may make one reader defensive and unsympathetic; another may feel that the author is being unusually honest and courageous and may admire these qualities and feel moved by them. Either way, the diction and tone of the piece have made a strong emotional impression. As you read the essays in this chapter and throughout this book, see if you can analyze how the diction and tone are shaping your reactions.

On Being 17, Bright, and Unable to Read

■ **David Raymond**

When the following article appeared in the New York Times *in 1976, David Raymond was a high school student in Connecticut. In 1981, Raymond graduated from Curry College outside of Boston, one of the few colleges with learning-disability programs at the time. He and his family now live in Fairfield, Connecticut, where he works as a builder. In his essay, he poignantly discusses the great difficulties he had with reading because of his dyslexia and the many problems he experienced in school as a result. As you read, pay particular attention to the natural quality of the words he uses to convey his ideas, and how that naturalness of diction contributes to the essay's informal yet sincere tone.*

FOR YOUR JOURNAL

One of the fundamental skills that we are supposed to learn in school is how to read. How would you rate yourself as a reader? Would you like to be able to read better? How important is reading in your everyday life?

One day a substitute teacher picked me to read aloud from the 1
textbook. When I told her "No, thank you," she came unhinged. She thought I was acting smart, and told me so. I kept calm, and that got her madder and madder. We must have spent 10 minutes trying to solve the problem, and finally she got so red in the face I thought she'd blow up. She told me she'd see me after class.

Maybe someone like me was a new thing for that teacher. But 2
she wasn't new to me. I've been through scenes like that all my life. You see, even though I'm 17 and a junior in high school, I can't read because I have dyslexia. I'm told I read "at a fourth-grade level," but from where I sit, that's not reading. You can't know what that means unless you've been there. It's not easy to tell how it feels when you

can't read your homework assignments or the newspaper or a menu in a restaurant or even notes from your own friends.

My family began to suspect I was having problems almost from   3
the first day I started school. My father says my early years in school were the worst years of his life. They weren't so good for me, either. As I look back on it now, I can't find the words to express how bad it really was. I wanted to die. I'd come home from school screaming, "I'm dumb. I'm dumb—I wish I were dead!"

I guess I couldn't read anything at all then—not even my own   4
name—and they tell me I didn't talk as good as other kids. But what I remember about those days is that I couldn't throw a ball where it was supposed to go, I couldn't learn to swim, and I wouldn't learn to ride a bike, because no matter what anyone told me, I knew I'd fail.

Sometimes my teachers would try to be encouraging. When I   5
couldn't read the words on the board they'd say, "Come on, David, you know that word." Only I didn't. And it was embarrassing. I just felt dumb. And dumb was how the kids treated me. They'd make fun of me every chance they got, asking me to spell "cat" or something like that. Even if I knew how to spell it, I wouldn't; they'd only give me another word. Anyway, it was awful, because more than anything I wanted friends. On my birthday when I blew out the candles I didn't wish I could learn to read; what I wished for was that the kids would like me.

With the bad reports coming from school, and with me moaning   6
about wanting to die and how everybody hated me, my parents began looking for help. That's when the testing started. The school tested me, the child-guidance center tested me, private psychiatrists tested me. Everybody knew something was wrong—especially me.

It didn't help much when they stuck a fancy name onto it. I   7
couldn't pronounce it then—I was only in second grade—and I was ashamed to talk about it. Now it rolls off my tongue, because I've been living with it for a lot of years—dyslexia.

All through elementary school it wasn't easy. I was always hav-   8
ing to do things that were "different," things the other kids didn't have to do. I had to go to a child psychiatrist, for instance.

One summer my family forced me to go to a camp for children   9
with reading problems. I hated the idea, but the camp turned out pretty good, and I had a good time. I met a lot of kids who couldn't read and somehow that helped. The director of the camp said I had a higher I.Q. than 90 percent of the population. I didn't believe him.

About the worst thing I had to do in fifth and sixth grade was go   10
to a special education class in another school in our town. A bus
picked me up, and I didn't like that at all. The bus also picked up
emotionally disturbed kids and retarded kids. It was like going to a
school for the retarded. I always worried that someone I knew would
see me on that bus. It was a relief to go to the regular junior high
school.

Life began to change a little for me then, because I began to feel   11
better about myself. I found the teachers cared; they had meetings
about me and I worked harder for them for a while. I began to work
on the potter's wheel, making vases and pots that the teachers said
were pretty good. Also, I got a letter for being on the track team. I
could always run pretty fast.

At high school the teachers are good and everyone is trying to   12
help me. I've gotten honors some marking periods and I've won a letter on the cross-country team. Next quarter I think the school might
hold a show of my pottery. I've got some friends. But there are still
some embarrassing times. For instance, every time there is writing in
the class, I get up and go to the special education room. Kids ask me
where I go all the time. Sometimes I say, "to Mars."

Homework is a real problem. During free periods in school I go   13
into the special ed room and staff members read assignments to me.
When I get home my mother reads to me. Sometimes she reads an assignment into a tape recorder, and then I go into my room and listen
to it. If we have a novel or something like that to read, she reads it
out loud to me. Then I sit down with her and we do the assignment.
She'll write, while I talk my answers to her. Lately I've taken to dic-
tating into a tape recorder, and then someone—my father, a private
tutor or my mother—types up what I've dictated. Whatever homework I do takes someone else's time, too. That makes me feel bad.

We had a big meeting in school the other day—eight of us, four   14
from the guidance department, my private tutor, my parents and me.
The subject was me. I said I wanted to go to college, and they told
me about colleges that have facilities and staff to handle people like
me. That's nice to hear.

As for what happens after college, I don't know and I'm worried   15
about that. How can I make a living if I can't read? Who will hire me?
How will I fill out the application form? The only thing that gives me
any courage is the fact that I've learned about well-known people who
couldn't read or had other problems and still made it. Like Albert

192 ■ DICTION AND TONE

Einstein, who didn't talk until he was 4 and flunked math. Like Leonardo da Vinci, who everyone seems to think had dyslexia.

I've told this story because maybe some teacher will read it and 16 go easy on a kid in the classroom who has what I've got. Or, maybe some parent will stop nagging his kid, and stop calling him lazy. Maybe he's not lazy or dumb. Maybe he just can't read and doesn't know what's wrong. Maybe he's scared, like I was.

QUESTIONS FOR STUDY AND DISCUSSION

1. Raymond uses many colloquial and idiomatic expressions, such as "she got so red in the face I thought she'd blow up" and "she came unhinged" (1). Identify other examples of such diction, and tell how they affect your reaction to the essay. (Glossary: *Colloquial Expression*)

2. In the context of the essay, comment on the appropriateness of each of the following possible choices of diction. Which word is better in each case? Why?
   a. *selected* for *picked* (1)
   b. *experience* for *thing* (2)
   c. *speak as well* for *talk as good* (4)
   d. *negative* for *bad* (6)
   e. *important* for *big* (14)
   f. *failed* for *flunked* (15)
   g. *frightened* for *scared* (16)

3. How would you describe Raymond's tone in this essay?

4. What is dyslexia? Is it essential for an understanding of the essay that we know more about dyslexia than Raymond tells us? Explain.

5. What does Raymond say his purpose is in telling his story? (Glossary: *Purpose*)

6. What does Raymond's story tell us about the importance of our early childhood experiences, especially within our educational system?

VOCABULARY

Refer to your dictionary to define the following words as they are used in this selection. Then use each word in a sentence of your own.

dyslexia (2)   psychiatrists (6)

CLASSROOM ACTIVITY USING DICTION AND TONE

Many menus use connotative language to persuade customers that they are about to have an exceptional eating experience. Phrases like the following are commonplace: "skillfully seasoned and basted with lime juice," "festive red cranberry sauce," "a bed of crisp baby vegetables," and "freshly ground coffee." Imagine that you are creating a menu. Use connotative language to describe the following basic foods. Try to make them sound as attractive and inviting as possible.

a. tomato juice   f. potatoes

b. onion soup   g. salad

c. ground beef   h. bread and butter

d. chicken   i. teas

e. peas   j. cake

SUGGESTED WRITING ASSIGNMENTS

1. Imagine that you are away at school. Recently you were caught in a speed trap—you were going 70 miles per hour in a 55-mile-per-hour zone—and have just lost your license; you will not be able to go home this coming weekend, as you had planned. Write two letters in which you explain why you will not be able to go home, one to your parents and the other to your best friend. Your audience is different in each case, so be sure to choose your diction accordingly. Try to imitate Raymond's informal yet serious tone in one of your letters.

2. Select an essay you have already completed for this course. Who was your intended audience for this essay? Rewrite the essay with a different audience in mind. For example, if your intended audience was originally your teacher and you wrote in a formal, serious tone, rewrite your essay for your sister, altering your tone accordingly. You might also choose as your intended audience your classmates, your religious leader, or the state environmental board. Reshape your essay as necessary.

La Vida Loca *(The Crazy Life): Two Generations of Gang Members*

■ **Luis J. Rodriguez**

Luis Rodriguez managed to walk away from his vida loca *in the gangs of Los Angeles. Since then he has published several volumes of poetry, including* Poems across the Pavement *(1991),* The Concrete River *(1991), and* Trochemoche: Poems by Luis Rodriguez *(1998). He is also the author of* Always Running: Gang Days in L.A. *(1993) and has produced a video entitled* The Breeding of Impotence: Perspectives on the Crisis in Our Communities and Schools *(1993). In the following selection, Rodriguez uses vivid language to describe his gang experiences and the anguish he feels when he sees his son repeating some of his own mistakes. As you read, take note of how he supports general statements with specific and startlingly concrete descriptive details.*

FOR YOUR JOURNAL

Membership in street gangs has grown rapidly in recent years, especially in America's large cities. Have you had any experience with street gangs? Were there gangs in your high school or hometown, or have you only read about them or seen them on television or in the movies? Why do you think people join gangs?

L ate winter, Chicago, 1991: The once-white snow that fell in 1 December has turned into a dark scum, an admixture of salt, car oil and decay; icicles hang from rooftops and window sills like the whiskers of old men. The bone-chilling temperatures force my family to stay inside a one-and-a-half bedroom apartment in a three-flat building in Humboldt Park. My third wife, Trini, our child Ruben and my 15-year-old son Ramiro from a previous marriage huddle around the television set. Tensions build up like a fever.

One evening, words of anger bounce back and forth between the 2 walls of our gray-stone flat. Two-year-old Ruben, confused and afraid, crawls up to my leg and hugs it. Trini and I had jumped on Ramiro's case for coming in late following weeks of trouble: Ramiro had joined the Insane Campbell Boys, a group of Puerto Rican and Mexican youth allied with the Spanish Cobras and Dragons.

Within moments, Ramiro runs out of the house, entering the 3 freezing Chicago night. I go after him, sprinting down the gangway leading to a debris-strewn alley. I see Ramiro's fleeing figure, his breath rising in quickly dissipating clouds.

I follow him toward Division Street, the neighborhood's main 4 drag. People yell out of windows and doorways: "*Que pasa, hombre?*"[1] This is not an unfamiliar sight—a father or mother chasing some child down the street.

Watching my son's escape, it is as though he enters the waters of 5 a distant time, back to my youth, back to when I ran, to when I jumped over fences, fleeing *vato locos,*[2] the police or my own shadow, in some drug-induced hysteria.

As Ramiro speeds off, I see my body enter the mouth of dark- 6 ness, my breath cut the frigid flesh of night—my voice crack open the night sky.

We are a second-generation gang family. I was involved in gangs 7 in Los Angeles in the late 1960s and early 1970s. When I was 2 years old, in 1956, my family emigrated from Mexico to Watts. I spent my teen years in a barrio called Las Lomas, east of Los Angeles.

I was arrested on charges ranging from theft, assaulting an officer 8 to attempted murder. As a teenager, I did some time. I began using drugs at age 12—including pills, weed and heroin. I had a near-death experience at 16 from sniffing toxic spray. After being kicked out of three high schools, I dropped out at 15.

By the time I turned 18, some 25 friends had been killed by rival 9 gangs, the police, overdoses, car crashes and suicides.

Three years ago, I brought Ramiro to Chicago to escape the vio- 10 lence. If I barely survived all this, it appeared unlikely my son would make it. But in Chicago, we found kindred conditions.

I had to cut Ramiro's bloodline to the street before it became too 11 late. I had to begin the long, intense struggle to save his life from the gathering storm of street violence—some 20 years after I had sneaked out of the 'hood in the dark of night and removed myself from the death fires of *La Vida Loca.*

---

[1] "What's happening, man?"
[2] crazy guys

What to do with those whom society cannot accommodate? 12
Criminalize them. Outlaw their actions and creations. Declare them
the enemy, then wage war. Emphasize the differences—the shade of
skin, the accent or manner of clothes. Like the scapegoat of the Bible,
place society's ills on them, then "stone them" in absolution. It's
convenient, it's logical.

It doesn't work. 13

Gangs are not alien powers. They begin as unstructured groupings, 14
our children who desire the same as any young person. Respect. A sense
of belonging. Protection. This is no different than the YMCA, Little
League or the Boy Scouts. It wasn't any more than what I wanted.

When I entered 109th Street School in Watts, I spoke perfect 15
Spanish. But teachers punished me for speaking it on the playground.
I peed in my pants a few times because I was unable to say in English
that I had to go. One teacher banished me to a corner, to build blocks
for a year. I learned to be silent within the walls of my body.

The older boys who lived on 103rd Street would take my money 16
or food. They chased me through alleys and side streets. Fear compelled my actions.

The police, I learned years later, had a strategy: They picked up 17
as many 7-year-old boys as they could—for loitering, throwing dirt
clods, curfew—whatever. By the time a boy turned 13, and had been
popped for something like stealing, he had accumulated a detention
record, and was bound for "juvey."

One felt besieged, under intense scrutiny. If you spoke out, dared 18
to resist, you were given a "jacket" of troublemaker; I'd tried many
times to take it off, but somebody always put it back on.

Soon after my family moved to South San Gabriel, a local group, 19
Thee Mystics, rampaged through the school. They carried bats,
chains, pipes and homemade zip guns. They terrorized teachers and
students alike. I was 12.

I froze as the head stomping came dangerously my way. But I 20
was intrigued. I wanted this power. I wanted to be able to bring a
whole school to its knees. All my school life until then had been
poised against me. I was broken and shy. I wanted what Thee Mystics had. I wanted to hurt somebody.

Police sirens broke the spell. Thee Mystics scattered in all direc- 21
tions. But they had done their damage. They had left their mark on
the school—and on me.

Gangs flourish when there's a lack of social recreation, decent 22
education or employment. Today, many young people will never

know what it is to work. They can only satisfy their needs through collective strength—against the police, who hold the power of life and death, against poverty, against idleness, against their impotence in society.

Without definitive solutions, it's easy to throw blame. George   23
Bush and Dan Quayle, for example, say the lack of family values is behind our problems.

But "family" is a farce among the propertyless and disenfran-   24
chised. Too many families are wrenched apart, as even children are forced to supplement meager incomes. At age 9, my mother walked me to the door and, in effect, told me: Now go forth and work.

People can't just consume; they have to sell something, including   25
their ability to work. If so-called legitimate work is unavailable, people will do the next best thing—sell sex or dope.

You'll find people who don't care about whom they hurt, but no-   26
body I know *wants* to sell death to their children, their neighbors, friends. If there was a viable, productive alternative, they would stop.

At 18, I had grown tired. I felt like a war veteran with a kind of   27
post-traumatic syndrome. I had seen too many dead across the pavement; I'd walk the aisles in the church wakes as if in a daze; I'd often watched my mother's weary face in hospital corridors, outside of courtrooms and cells, refusing, finally, to have anything to do with me.

In addition, I had fallen through the cracks of two languages;   28
unable to communicate well in any.

I wanted the pain to end, the self-consuming hate to wither in the   29
sunlight. With the help of those who saw potential in me, perhaps for some poetry, I got out: No more heroin, spray or pills; no more jails; no more trying to hurt somebody until I stopped hurting—which never seemed to pass.

There is an aspect of suicide in gang involvement for those whose   30
options have been cut off. They stand on street corners, flash hand signs and invite the bullets. It's life as stance, as bravado. They say "You can't touch this," but "Come kill me" is the inner cry. It's either *la torcida*[3] or death, a warrior's path, where even self-preservation doesn't make a play. If they murder, the targets are the ones who look like them, walk like them, those closest to who they are—the mirror reflection. They murder and they are killing themselves, over and over.

---

[3] deceit

Ramiro stayed away for two weeks the day he ran off. When he   31
returned, we entered him into a psychotherapy hospital. After three
months, he was back home. Since then, I've had to pull everyone into
the battle for my son. I've spent hours with teachers. I've involved
therapists, social workers, the police.

We all have some responsibility: Schools, the law, parents. But at   32
the same time, there are factors beyond our control. It's not a simple
matter of "good" or "bad" values, or even of choices. If we all had a
choice, I'm convinced nobody would choose *la vida loca,* the "insane
nation" — to gangbang. But it's going to take collective action and a
plan.

Recently, Ramiro got up at a Chicago poetry event and read a   33
piece about being physically abused by a stepfather. It stopped everyone cold. He later read the poem at Chicago's Poetry Festival. Its
title: "Running Away."

The best way to deal with your children is to help construct the   34
conditions for free and healthy development of all, but it's also true
you can't be for all children if you can't be for your own.

There's a small but intense fire burning in my son. Ramiro has just   35
turned 17; he's made it thus far, but it's day by day. Now I tell him: You
have an innate value outside of your job, outside the "jacket" imposed
on you since birth. Draw on your expressive powers.

Stop running.   36

QUESTIONS FOR STUDY AND DISCUSSION

1. Identify several words in the first paragraph that Rodriguez uses
   to describe the conditions that led to Ramiro's running away.
   What do they add to the selection? Why didn't Rodriguez simply
   say that it was cold and his family was getting cabin fever?

2. Reread paragraphs 27–29. What is the tone of the paragraphs?
   How does Rodriguez's choice of words contribute to his tone?

3. Why had Rodriguez brought Ramiro to Chicago? How did the
   move relate to his own gang experiences?

4. What do gangs offer their members? How did Rodriguez's experiences make him susceptible to the lure of gang life?

5. What does "You can't touch this" often mean for gang members? Why are gang murders often a reflection of gang members'
   suicidal tendencies?

6. What does Rodriguez suggest as ways to solve the problem of gang violence? Is his ending optimistic? (Glossary: *Beginnings and Endings*) Why, or why not?

VOCABULARY

Refer to your dictionary to define the following words as they are used in this selection. Then use each word in a sentence of your own.

admixture (1)   impotence (22)
dissipating (3)   disenfranchised (24)
kindred (10)   innate (35)
absolution (12)

CLASSROOM ACTIVITY USING DICTION AND TONE

Good writers rely on strong verbs — verbs that contribute significantly to what is being said. Because they must repeatedly describe similar situations, sportswriters, for example, are acutely aware of the need for strong action verbs. It is not enough for them to say that a team wins or loses; they must describe the type of win or loss more precisely. As a result, such verbs as *beats, buries, edges, shocks,* and *trounces* are common in the headlines on the sports page. Each of these verbs, in addition to describing the act of winning, makes a statement about the quality of the victory. Like sportswriters, all of us write about actions that are performed daily. If we were restricted only to the verbs *eat, drink, sleep,* and *work* for each of these activities, for example, our writing would be repetitious and monotonous. List as many verbs as you can that you could use in place of these four. What connotative differences do you find in your lists of alternatives? What is the importance of these connotative differences for you as a writer?

SUGGESTED WRITING ASSIGNMENTS

1. Imagine that you are Luis Rodriguez and that you are writing your son a letter to convince him not to participate in a gang. Use information from the essay to back up your argument, and make sure that your diction and tone are appropriate for a father writing to a son with whom he has a strained relationship.

2. Write an essay about a group that you joined as a teenager. It can be a sports team, a school club, scouts, a band, a church group, a gang—any group that made you feel like a member. Why did you first join the group? How did you feel being a member of the group? Was it ultimately a positive or negative experience? Why? Make sure your diction and tone communicate the feelings you had toward the group.

The Fourth of July

■ **Audre Lorde**

Audre Lorde (1934–1992) was a professor of English at Hunter College in New York City. Born in New York, she studied at Hunter and at Columbia University. Her published works in-clude several volumes of poetry, such as Undersong: Chosen Poems Old and New *(1982), which was revised in 1992; essay collections like* Sister Outsider *(1984) and* Burst of Light *(1988); and an autobiography,* Zami: A New Spelling of My Name *(1982). Her book of poems* The Arithmetics of Distance *ap-peared posthumously in 1993. The following selection from* Zami *eloquently communicates the tragedy of racism. Take spe-cial note of Lorde's tone as you read, particularly the way it in-tensifies as the essay continues and how it culminates in the anger of the final paragraph.*

FOR YOUR JOURNAL

Think about the Fourth of July or some other national holiday like Memorial Day or Thanksgiving. Perhaps you celebrate Cinco de Mayo or Bastille Day. What are your memories of celebrating that holiday? What meaning does the holiday have for you?

The first time I went to Washington, D.C., was on the edge of the 1 summer when I was supposed to stop being a child. At least that's what they said to us all at graduation from the eighth grade. My sister Phyllis graduated at the same time from high school. I don't know what she was supposed to stop being. But as graduation pres-ents for us both, the whole family took a Fourth of July trip to Wash-ington, D.C., the fabled and famous capital of our country.

It was the first time I'd ever been on a railroad train during the 2 day. When I was little, and we used to go to the Connecticut shore, we always went at night on the milk train, because it was cheaper.

Preparations were in the air around our house before school was 3 even over. We packed for a week. There were two very large suitcases that my father carried, and a box filled with food. In fact, my first trip to Washington was a mobile feast; I started eating as soon as we were comfortably ensconced in our seats, and did not stop until somewhere after Philadelphia. I remember it was Philadelphia because I was disappointed not to have passed by the Liberty Bell.

My mother had roasted two chickens and cut them up into 4 dainty bite-size pieces. She packed slices of brown bread and butter and green pepper and carrot sticks. There were little violently yellow iced cakes with scalloped edges called "marigolds," that came from Cushman's Bakery. There was a spice bun and rock-cakes from Newton's, the West Indian bakery across Lenox Avenue from St. Mark's School, and iced tea in a wrapped mayonnaise jar. There were sweet pickles for us and dill pickles for my father, and peaches with the fuzz still on them, individually wrapped to keep them from bruising. And, for neatness, there were piles of napkins and a little tin box with a washcloth dampened with rosewater and glycerine for wiping sticky mouths.

I wanted to eat in the dining car because I had read all about 5 them, but my mother reminded me for the umpteenth time that dining car food always cost too much money and besides, you never could tell whose hands had been playing all over that food, nor where those same hands had been just before. My mother never mentioned that Black people were not allowed into railroad dining cars headed south in 1947. As usual, whatever my mother did not like and could not change, she ignored. Perhaps it would go away, deprived of her attention.

I learned later that Phyllis's high school senior class trip had been 6 to Washington, but the nuns had given her back her deposit in private, explaining to her that the class, all of whom were white, except Phyllis, would be staying in a hotel where Phyllis "would not be happy," meaning, Daddy explained to her, also in private, that they did not rent rooms to Negroes. "We will take you to Washington, ourselves," my father had avowed, "and not just for an overnight in some measly fleabag hotel."

American racism was a new and crushing reality that my parents 7 had to deal with every day of their lives once they came to this country. They handled it as a private woe. My mother and father believed that they could best protect their children from the realities of race in america and the fact of american racism by never giving them name, much less discussing their nature. We were told we must never trust white people, but *why* was never explained, nor the nature of their ill will. Like so many other vital pieces of information in my childhood,

I was supposed to know without being told. It always seemed like a very strange injunction coming from my mother, who looked so much like one of those people we were never supposed to trust. But something always warned me not to ask my mother why she wasn't white, and why Auntie Lillah and Auntie Etta weren't, even though they were all that same problematic color so different from my father and me, even from my sisters, who were somewhere in-between.

In Washington, D.C., we had one large room with two double 8
beds and an extra cot for me. It was a back-street hotel that belonged to a friend of my father's who was in real estate, and I spent the whole next day after Mass squinting up at the Lincoln Memorial where Marian Anderson had sung after the D.A.R. refused to allow her to sing in their auditorium because she was Black. Or because she was "Colored," my father said as he told us the story. Except that what he probably said was "Negro," because for his times, my father was quite progressive.

I was squinting because I was in that silent agony that character- 9
ized all of my childhood summers, from the time school let out in June to the end of July, brought about by my dilated and vulnerable eyes exposed to the summer brightness.

I viewed Julys through an agonizing corolla of dazzling whiteness 10
and I always hated the Fourth of July, even before I came to realize the travesty such a celebration was for Black people in this country.

My parents did not approve of sunglasses, nor of their expense. 11

I spent the afternoon squinting up at monuments to freedom and 12
past presidencies and democracy, and wondering why the light and heat were both so much stronger in Washington, D.C., than back home in New York City. Even the pavement on the streets was a shade lighter in color than back home.

Late that Washington afternoon my family and I walked back 13
down Pennsylvania Avenue. We were a proper caravan, mother bright and father brown, the three of us girls step-standards in-between. Moved by our historical surroundings and the heat of early evening, my father decreed yet another treat. He had a great sense of history, a flair for the quietly dramatic and the sense of specialness of an occasion and a trip.

"Shall we stop and have a little something to cool off, Lin?" 14

Two blocks away from our hotel, the family stopped for a dish of 15
vanilla ice cream at a Breyer's ice cream and soda fountain. Indoors, the soda fountain was dim and fan-cooled, deliciously relieving to my scorched eyes.

Corded and crisp and pinafored, the five of us seated ourselves 16
one by one at the counter. There was I between my mother and father, and my two sisters on the other side of my mother. We settled
ourselves along the white mottled marble counter, and when the
waitress spoke at first no one understood what she was saying, and
so the five of us just sat there.

The waitress moved along the line of us closer to my father and 17
spoke again. "I said I kin give you to take out, but you can't eat here.
Sorry." Then she dropped her eyes looking very embarrassed, and
suddenly we heard what it was she was saying all at the same time,
loud and clear.

Straight-backed and indignant, one by one, my family and I got 18
down from the counter stools and turned around and marched out of
the store, quiet and outraged, as if we had never been Black before.
No one would answer my emphatic questions with anything other
than a guilty silence. "But we hadn't done anything!" This wasn't
right or fair! Hadn't I written poems about Bataan and freedom and
democracy for all?

My parents wouldn't speak of this injustice, not because they had 19
contributed to it, but because they felt they should have anticipated it
and avoided it. This made me even angrier. My fury was not going to
be acknowledged by a like fury. Even my two sisters copied my parents' pretense that nothing unusual and anti-american had occurred. I
was left to write my angry letter to the president of the united states
all by myself, although my father did promise I could type it out on
the office typewriter next week, after I showed it to him in my copy-
book diary.

The waitress was white, and the counter was white, and the ice 20
cream I never ate in Washington, D.C., that summer I left childhood
was white, and the white heat and the white pavement and the white
stone monuments of my first Washington summer made me sick to
my stomach for the whole rest of that trip and it wasn't much of a
graduation present after all.

QUESTIONS FOR STUDY AND DISCUSSION

1. Lorde's essay is not long or hyperbolic, but it is a very effective
   indictment of racism. Identify some of the words Lorde uses to
   communicate her outrage when she writes of the racism that she
   and her family faced. How does her choice of words contribute
   to her message?

2. What is the tone of Lorde's essay? Identify passages to support your answer.

3. Lorde takes great care in describing the food her family took on the train with them to Washington (4). What is Lorde's purpose in describing the food? (Glossary: *Purpose*)

4. Why did Lorde dislike the Fourth of July as a child? Why does she dislike it as an adult?

5. Do you see any irony in Lorde's title? (Glossary: *Irony*) In what way? Do you think it is an appropriate title for her essay?

6. Why do you think Lorde's family deals with racism by ignoring it? In what way is Lorde different?

VOCABULARY

Refer to your dictionary to define the following words as they are used in this selection. Then use each word in a sentence of your own.

ensconced (3)	travesty (10)
measly (6)	pinafored (16)
injunction (7)	emphatic (18)
corolla (10)	

CLASSROOM ACTIVITY USING DICTION AND TONE

Writers create and control tone in their writing in part through the words they choose. For example, words like *laugh, cheery, dance,* and *melody* help to create a tone of celebration. Make a list of the words that come to mind for each of the following tones:

humorous	tentative
angry	triumphant
authoritative	

Compare your lists of words with those of others in the class. What generalizations can you make about the connotations associated with each of these tones?

SUGGESTED WRITING ASSIGNMENTS

1. When read with the ideals of the American Revolution and the Constitution in mind, Lorde's essay is strongly ironic. What does

the Fourth of July mean to you? Why? How do your feelings relate to the stated ideals of our forebears? Choose your words
carefully, and use specific personal experiences to support your
general statements.

2. Imagine that you are Audre Lorde in 1947. Write a letter to
President Harry Truman in which you protest the reception you
received in the nation's capital on the Fourth of July. Do not
overstate your case. Show the president in what way you and
your family were treated unfairly rather than merely stating that
you were discriminated against, and carefully choose words that
will help President Truman see the irony of your experience.

The Dance within My Heart

■ Pat Mora

*Poet, essayist, and children's book author Pat Mora was born in
El Paso, Texas, in 1942. After receiving degrees from Texas
Western College and the University of Texas at El Paso (UTEP),
she worked as a teacher and administrator and served as director of the University Museum at UTEP. Mora is also host of a
radio show, "Voices: The Mexican-American Perspective," at a
National Public Radio affiliate in El Paso. Her published works
include books of poems such as* Chants *(1984) and* Borders
(1986); a collection of essays, Nepantla: Essays from the Land
in the Middle *(1993); the children's story,* Pablo's Tree *(1994);
and a family memoir,* House of Houses *(1997). As you read the
following essay, pay particular attention to the way Mora moves
back and forth between abstract concepts like* strength, inventiveness, beauty, *and* grandeur, *and more concrete and detailed
depictions of what she means by those terms.*

FOR YOUR JOURNAL

Of the museums you have visited, which succeeded best in capturing your attention? Why? Describe the exhibit or exhibits
that had the greatest impact on you.

For a Southwesterner, early spring in the Midwest is a time for ju-   1
bilation. Another winter survived. Why, then, on a soft spring
Saturday would I choose to leave the dogwoods and daffodils and
spend my day inside museums?

Certainly, I didn't spend my youth enduring trips through solemn   2
rooms, being introduced to "culture." There was only one small art
museum in my hometown, and I'm not sure how comfortable my
parents would have felt there. My father worked evenings and weekends to support the four of us and to give us what he and my mother
hadn't had, a youth without financial worries. And my mother not
only helped him in his optical business but was our willing chauffeur
in addition to assisting the grandmother and aunt who lived with us,
our extended Mexican American family.

But as an adult I began to visit those echoing buildings. A fellow-   3
ship allowed trips to modest and grand museums in New York, Paris,
Washington, Mexico, Hawaii, and the Dominican Republic. And
much to my surprise, I even found myself directing a small university
museum for a time, having the opportunity to convince people of all
ages and backgrounds that indeed the museum was theirs. I was
hooked for life.

For me, museums are pleasure havens. When I enter, my breath-   4
ing changes just as it does when I visit aquariums, zoos, botanical
gardens. These latter sites offer a startling array of living species. Unless we have become totally desensitized to nature's grandeur, to its
infinite variations, arboretums and nature centers inspire us to treat
our planet with more care, to be more attentive to the life around us,
no matter how minute. I stand entranced by the spriteliness of glass
shrimp, the plushness of the jaguar, the haughtiness of birds of para-
dise in bloom. Parrots make me laugh, fins spin my blood, ferns hush
my doubts. I leave refreshed.

When they were younger, my children could far more easily un-   5
derstand my desire to visit displays of living creatures than they could
my penchant for natural history and art museums, for gazing at bas-
kets and pottery, at sculpture and flashing neon. It sounded like work
walking through room after room, up and down stairs, being relatively quiet, not eating, reading small cards of text, staring at "weird"
objects. This is fun?

But museums remind me of the strength and inventiveness of the   6
human imagination through time. They remind me that offering
beauty to a community is a human habit, a needed reminder in a society with little time for observing, listening, appreciating. I gaze at
African masks crusted with cowrie shells, at drums and carvings of
old, wrinkled wood, at the serenity of Buddha. I watch my fellow
visitors, drawn to cases both by the beauty and craft but also as a
kind of testimony to humans who once sat under our sun and moon
and with rough hands graced our world.

I walk on to see the sturdy pre-Columbian female figures from   7
Nayarit, Mexico, women of broad dimensions who occupy space
rather than shrink as we sometimes do. I see pan pipes and bone
flutes from Peru, 180 B.C., back then, high in the Andes, hear a man
transforming his breath into music.

Room after room I watch light and shadow play on sandstone,   8
silver, wood, bronze, earthenware, copper, ivory, hemp, oil, acrylic,
watercolor, straw, gold. I study toenails on a headless marble statue,

watch light stroke the soft curves, wish I could touch her outstretched Roman hand. The next room, or turning a corner, can yield surprise, the halls and rooms a pleasure maze. I stand in Chagall's blue light, see his glass bird poised to fly from room to room.

I ignore the careful museum maps, enjoying the unexpected, the 9 independence of viewing at will, the private pleasure of letting myself abandon order and logic room to room. Purposeless wandering? Not really, for I now know I come not only for the intellectual and sensory stimulation but for comfort. I come to be with humans I admire, with those who produced these drums and breathing dancers, who through the ages added beauty to this world. Their work gives me hope, reminds me that art is not a luxury: it nourishes our parched spirits. It is essential.

I think again of how privileged I am to be in these quiet rooms, 10 not having to wait for a free day, having time to spend wandering these galleries rather than having to care for someone else's children while mine are alone, or having to iron clothes that I will never wear.

And certainly free days and increased public programming — the 11 democratization of museums — are an improvement from past eras, an acknowledgment, although sometimes grudging, that not only the "washed and worthy" deserve entrance. Museums are slowly changing, realizing that artifacts and art belong to all people, not some people. Museums are even becoming a bit embarrassed about how they acquired what they own, about why they arrogantly ushered certain groups past their polished doors. The faces viewing with me have been more varied in recent years.

I walk on. I, who can barely sew a button, study an array of quilts, 12 glad that such women's art is now displayed, think of the careful fingers — stitch, stitch, stitch — and probably careful voices that produced these works. The text of a bronze of Shiva says that her dance takes place within her heart. I study her and think of that dance, of the private nature of that spring of emotion. I watch a group of teenage girls walk by and wonder if they can hear or feel their private dance in a world that equates noise and brutality with entertainment.

The contemporary art halls most baffled my children when they 13 were young. "Why, I could do that!" they would scoff staring at a Jackson Pollock. I smile secretly when my youngest, now taller than I am, asks, "Where are our favorite rooms?" meaning, yes, those rooms with massive canvases, with paint everywhere, the rooms that loosen me up inside, that provide escape from the confines of the predictable.

I walk outside glad to breathe in sky and wind but also brimming   14
with all I saw and felt, hearing the dance within my heart.

QUESTIONS FOR STUDY AND DISCUSSION

1. What word or words would you use to describe the prevailing tone of Mora's essay? How is this tone achieved? Identify a paragraph that you feel exemplifies it.

2. Throughout the essay, Mora cites many examples of museum exhibits that have attracted her. To describe them she chooses descriptive words rich in connotation. For example, in paragraph 4 she employs the phrase "the plushness of the jaguar." Plushness *denotes* furry softness; it *connotes* luxury, richness, majesty. In the same paragraph appears the phrase "the spriteliness of glass shrimp." In a dictionary, look up *sprightliness* and *sprite*. What connotations arise from combining these two words? Find other examples of words or phrases with connotations that add depth to the meaning of the essay.

3. Mora offers a number of reasons to explain her love of museums. What are they? Notice the order in which these reasons are presented. Why does she write about exhibits of living things first, before moving on to human art and artifacts?

4. "Museums are slowly changing," Mora says in paragraph 11. Why and in what ways are they changing? Why does she take a positive view of the changes?

5. At the conclusion of the opening paragraph, Mora leads the reader into the essay with a rhetorical question instead of the more usual thesis statement. (Glossary: *Rhetorical Question*) Is this an effective organizational strategy? Why, or why not? Where in the essay is the thesis located? Is it implied or stated directly?

6. What is the meaning of the title? (Glossary: *Title*) How does the title serve both to introduce and to reinforce the central idea of the essay?

VOCABULARY

Refer to your dictionary to define the following words as they are used in this selection. Then use each word in a sentence of your own.

havens (4) penchant (5)

grandeur (4) cowrie (6)

arboretums (4) parched (9)

CLASSROOM ACTIVITY USING DICTION AND TONE

Writers use different sorts of diction to communicate with different audiences of readers. (Glossary: *Audience*) Recall a fairground activity or amusement park ride that you have enjoyed. Write a paragraph in which you describe this ride or activity to an older relative. Then rewrite the paragraph to appeal to a ten-year-old.

SUGGESTED WRITING ASSIGNMENTS

1. What sort of public places do you like to visit? Perhaps you enjoy visiting libraries, county fairs, cathedrals, movie theaters, or sports arenas. Write an essay in which you describe the characteristics of a public place you enjoy visiting, and explain the reasons it pleases you. Like Mora, be sure to include sensory details that evoke a vivid impression of this pleasurable setting for the reader.

2. Mora says that "art is not a luxury" (9). Do you agree or disagree with her opinion? Write an essay using one of these thesis statements: "Art is a luxury" or "Art is not a luxury." Each paragraph in the body of the essay should contain a topic sentence that clearly states one of your reasons. Make sure your tone is appropriate and consistent with your attitude toward the subject.

Figurative Language

Figurative language is language used in an imaginative rather than a literal sense. Although it is most often associated with poetry, figurative language is used widely in our daily speech and in our writing. Prose writers have long known that figurative language not only brings freshness and color to writing, but also helps to clarify ideas. For example, when asked by his teacher to explain the concept of brainstorming, one student replied, "Well, brainstorming is like having a tornado in your head." This figurative language helps others imagine the whirl of ideas in this young writer's head as he brainstorms a topic for writing.

Two of the most commonly used figures of speech are the simile and the metaphor. A *simile* is an explicit comparison between two essentially different ideas or things that uses the words *like* or *as* to link them.

> Canada geese sweep across the hills and valleys like a formation of strategic bombers.
>
> –Benjamin B. Bachman

> I walked toward her and hailed her as a visitor to the moon might salute a survivor of a previous expedition.
>
> –John Updike

A *metaphor,* on the other hand, makes an implicit comparison between dissimilar ideas or things without using *like* or *as.*

> She was very old and small and she walked slowly in the dark pine shadows, moving a little from side to side in her steps, with the balanced heaviness and lightness of a pendulum in a grandfather clock.
>
> –Eudora Welty

> Charm is the ultimate weapon, the supreme seduction, against
> which there are few defenses.
>
> —Laurie Lee

To take full advantage of the richness of a particular comparison,
writers sometimes use several sentences or even a whole paragraph to
develop a metaphor. Such a comparison is called an *extended
metaphor.*

> The point is that you have to strip down your writing before
> you can build it back up. You must know what the essential tools
> are and what job they were designed to do. If I may belabor the
> metaphor on carpentry, it is first necessary to be able to saw wood
> neatly and to drive nails. Later you can bevel the edges or add ele-
> gant finials, if that is your taste. But you can never forget that you
> are practicing a craft that is based on certain principles. If the nails
> are weak, your house will collapse. If your verbs are weak and your
> syntax is rickety, your sentences will fall apart.
>
> —William Zinsser

Another frequently used figure of speech is *personification.* In *personification,* the writer attributes human qualities to animals or inanimate objects.

> Blond October comes striding over the hills wearing a crimson shirt
> and faded green trousers.
>
> —Hal Borland

> Indeed, haste can be the assassin of elegance.
>
> —T. H. White

In the preceding examples, the writers have, through the use of
figurative language, both enlivened their prose and emphasized their
ideas. Each has vividly communicated an idea or the essence of an object by comparing it to something concrete and familiar. In each case,
too, the figurative language grows out of the writer's thinking, reflecting the way he or she sees the material. Be similarly honest in
your use of figurative language, and keep in mind that figurative language should never be used merely to "dress up" writing; above all, it
should help you develop your ideas and clarify your meaning for the
reader.

The Barrio

■ **Robert Ramirez**

Robert Ramirez has worked as a cameraman, reporter, anchor-
man, and producer for the news team at KGBT-TV in Edin-
burg, Texas, and in the Latin American division of the Northern
Trust Bank in Chicago. In the following essay, Ramirez uses
figurative language, particularly metaphors, to awaken the
reader's senses to the sights, smells, and sounds that are the
essense of the barrio.

FOR YOUR JOURNAL

Where did you grow up? What do you remember most about
your childhood neighborhood? How did it feel as a young person to live in this world? Do you still call this neighborhood
"home"? Explain.

The train, its metal wheels squealing as they spin along the silvery   1
tracks, rolls slower now. Through the gaps between the cars
blinks a streetlamp, and this pulsing light on a barrio streetcorner
beats slower, like a weary heartbeat, until the train shudders to a
halt, the light goes out, and the barrio is deep asleep.

Throughout Aztlán (the Nahuatl term meaning "land to the   2
north"), trains grumble along the edges of a sleeping people. From
Lower California, through the blistering Southwest, down the Rio
Grande to the muddy Gulf, the darkness and mystery of dreams en-
gulf communities fenced off by railroads, canals, and expressways.
Paradoxical communities, isolated from the rest of the town by concrete columned monuments of progress, and yet stranded in the past.
They are surrounded by change. It eludes their reach, in their own
backyards, and the people, unable and unwilling to see the future, or
even touch the present, perpetuate the past.

Leaning from the expressway or jolting across the tracks, one en-   3
ters a different physical world permeated by a different attitude. The
physical dimensions are impressive. It is a large section of town
which extends for fifteen blocks north and south along the tracks,
and then advances eastward, thinning into nothingness beyond the

city limits. Within the invisible (yet sensible) walls of the barrio are many, many people living in too few houses. The homes, however, are much more numerous than on the outside.

Members of the barrio describe the entire area as their home. It is   4
a home, but it is more than this. The barrio is a refuge from the harshness and the coldness of the Anglo world. It is a forced refuge. The leprous people are isolated from the rest of the community and contained in their section of town. The stoical pariahs of the barrio accept their fate, and from the angry seeds of rejection grow the flowers of closeness between outcasts, not the thorns of bitterness and the mad desire to flee. There is no want to escape, for the feeling of the barrio is known only to its inhabitants, and the material needs of life can also be found here.

The *tortillería* [tortilla factory] fires up its machinery three times   5
a day, producing steaming, round, flat slices of barrio bread. In the winter, the warmth of the tortilla factory is a wool *sarape* [blanket] in the chilly morning hours, but in the summer, it unbearably toasts every noontime customer.

The *panadería* [bakery] sends its sweet messenger aroma down   6
the dimly lit street, announcing the arrival of fresh, hot sugary *pan dulce* [sweet rolls].

The small corner grocery serves the meal-to-meal needs of cus-   7
tomers, and the owner, a part of the neighborhood, willingly gives credit to people unable to pay cash for foodstuffs.

The barbershop is a living room with hydraulic chairs, radio, and   8
television, where old friends meet and speak of life as their salted hair falls aimlessly about them.

The pool hall is a junior level country club where *'chucos* [young   9
men], strangers in their own land, get together to shoot pool and rap, while veterans, unaware of the cracking, popping balls on the green felt, complacently play dominoes beneath rudely hung *Playboy* foldouts.

The *cantina* [canteen or snackbar] is the night spot of the barrio.   10
It is the country club and the den where the rites of puberty are enacted. Here the young become men. It is in the taverns that a young dude shows his *machismo* through the quantity of beer he can hold, the stories of *rucas* [women] he has had, and his willingness and ability to defend his image against hardened and scarred old lions.

No, there is no frantic wish to flee. It would be absurd to leave   11
the familiar and nervously step into the strange and cold Anglo community when the needs of the Chicano can be met in the barrio.

The barrio is closeness. From the family living unit, familial rela- 12
tionships stretch out to immediate neighbors, down the block,
around the corner, and to all parts of the barrio. The feeling of family, a rare and treasurable sentiment, pervades and accounts for the
inability of the people to leave. The barrio is this attitude manifested
on the countenances of the people, on the faces of their homes, and in
the gaiety of their gardens.

The color-splashed homes arrest your eyes, arouse your curiosity, 13
and make you wonder what life scenes are being played out in them.
The flimsy, brightly colored, wood-frame houses ignore no neon-
brilliant color. Houses trimmed in orange, chartreuse, lime-green, yellow, and mixtures of these and other hues beckon the beholder to
reflect on the peculiarity of each home. Passing through this land is
refreshing like Brubeck,[1] not narcoticizing like revolting rows of
similar houses, which neither offend nor please.

In the evenings, the porches and front yards are occupied with 14
men calmly talking over the noise of children playing baseball in the
unpaved extension of the living room, while the women cook supper
or gossip with female neighbors as they water the *jardines* [gardens].
The gardens mutely echo the expressive verses of the colorful houses.
The denseness of multicolored plants and trees gives the house the
appearance of an oasis or a tropical island hideaway, sheltered from
the rest of the world.

Fences are common in the barrio, but they are fences and not the 15
walls of the Anglo community. On the western side of town, the high
wooden fences between houses are thick, impenetrable walls, built to
keep the neighbors at bay. In the barrio, the fences may be rusty, wire
contraptions or thick green shrubs. In either case you can see through
them and feel no sense of intrusion when you cross them.

Many lower-income families of the barrio manage to maintain a 16
comfortable standard of living through the communal action of family members who contribute their wages to the head of the family.
Economic need creates interdependence and closeness. Small bare-
footed boys sell papers on cool, dark Sunday mornings, deny themselves pleasantries, and give their earnings to *mamá*. The older the
child, the greater the responsibility to help the head of the household
provide for the rest of the family.

There are those, too, who for a number of reasons have not 17
achieved a relative sense of financial security. Perhaps it results from

[1] Dave Brubeck, pianist, composer, and conductor of "cool" modern jazz

too many children too soon, but it is the homes of these people and their situation that numbs rather than charms. Their houses, aged and bent, oozing children, are fissures in the horn of plenty. Their wooden homes may have brick-pattern asbestos tile on the outer walls, but the tile is not convincing.

Unable to pay city taxes or incapable of influencing the city to   18
live up to its duty to serve all the citizens, the poorer barrio families remain trapped in the nineteenth century and survive as best they can. The backyards have well-worn paths to the outhouses, which sit near the alley. Running water is considered a luxury in some parts of the barrio. Decent drainage is usually unknown, and when it rains, the water stands for days, an incubator of health hazards and an avoidable nuisance. Streets, costly to pave, remain rough, rocky trails. Tires do not last long, and the constant rattling and shaking grind away a car's life and spread dust through screen windows.

The houses and their *jardines,* the jollity of the people in an ad-   19
verse world, the brightly feathered alarm clock pecking away at supper and cautiously eyeing the children playing nearby, produce a mystifying sensation at finding the noble savage alive in the twentieth century. It is easy to look at the positive qualities of life in the barrio, and look at them with a distantly envious feeling. One wishes to experience the feelings of the barrio and not the hardships. Remembering the illness, the hunger, the feeling of time running out on you, the walls, both real and imagined, reflecting on living in the past, one finds his envy becoming more elusive, until it has vanished altogether.

Back now beyond the tracks, the train creaks and groans, the   20
cars jostle each other down the track, and as the light begins its pulsing, the barrio, with all its meanings, greets a new dawn with yawns and restless stretchings.

QUESTIONS FOR STUDY AND DISCUSSION

1. What is the barrio? Where is it? What does Ramirez mean when he says, "There is no want to escape, for the feeling of the barrio is known only to its inhabitants, and the material needs of life can also be found here" (4)?

2. Ramirez uses Spanish phrases throughout his essay. Why do you suppose he uses them? What is their effect on the reader? He also uses the words *home, refuge, family,* and *closeness.* What do they connote in the context of this essay? (Glossary:

Connotation/Denotation) In what ways, if any, are they essential to the writer's purpose? (Glossary: *Purpose*)

3. Identify several of the metaphors and similes that Ramirez uses in his essay, and explain why they are particularly appropriate.

4. In paragraph 6, Ramirez uses personification when he calls the aroma of freshly baked sweet rolls a "messenger" who announces the arrival of the baked goods. Cite other words or phrases that Ramirez uses to give human characteristics to the barrio.

5. Explain Ramirez's use of the imagery of walls and fences to describe a sense of cultural isolation. What might this imagery be symbolic of? (Glossary: *Symbol*)

6. Ramirez begins his essay with a relatively positive picture of the barrio, but ends on a more disheartening note. Why has he organized his essay this way? What might the effect have been if he had reversed these images? (Glossary: *Beginnings and Endings*)

VOCABULARY

Refer to your dictionary to define the following words as they are used in this selection. Then use each word in a sentence of your own.

paradoxical (2)   Chicano (11)
eludes (2)   countenances (12)
permeated (3)   fissures (17)
stoical (4)   adverse (19)
pariahs (4)   elusive (19)
complacently (9)

CLASSROOM ACTIVITY USING FIGURATIVE LANGUAGE

Create a metaphor or simile that would be helpful in describing each item in the following list. The first one has been completed for you to illustrate the process.

1. a skyscraper: The skyscraper sparkled like a huge glass needle.
2. the sound of an explosion
3. an intelligent student
4. a crowded bus
5. a slow-moving car

6. a pillow
7. a narrow alley
8. greasy french fries
9. hot sun
10. a dull knife

Compare your metaphors and similes with those written by other members of your class. Which metaphors and similes for each item on the list seem to work best? Why? Do any seem tired or clichéd?

SUGGESTED WRITING ASSIGNMENTS

1. In paragraph 19 of his essay, Ramirez says, "One wishes to experience the feelings of the barrio and not the hardships." Explore his meaning in light of what you have just read and of other experience or knowledge you may have of "ghetto" living. In what way can it be said that the hardships of such living are a necessary part of its "feelings"? How might barrio life change, for better or for worse, if the city were to "live up to its duty to serve all the citizens" (18)?
2. Write a brief essay in which you describe your own neighborhood. You may find it helpful to review what you wrote in response to the journal prompt for this selection.

A Hanging

■ **George Orwell**

Although probably best known for his novels Animal Farm *(1945) and* 1984 *(1949), George Orwell (1903–1950) was also a renowned essayist on language and politics. Two of his most famous essays, "Shooting an Elephant" and "Politics and the English Language," are among the most frequently reprinted. Orwell was born in Bengal, India, and educated in England. He traveled a great deal during his life and spent five years serving with the British colonial police in Burma. The following essay is a product of that experience. In it, Orwell relies consistently on similes to help convey and emphasize his attitude about the events he describes, events in which he is both an observer and a participant.*

FOR YOUR JOURNAL

Throughout history, people have gone out of their way to witness events in which someone was certain to be killed, such as fights between gladiators, jousting tournaments, and public executions. Why do you think such events fascinate people?

It was in Burma, a sodden morning of the rains. A sickly light, like yellow tinfoil, was slanting over the high walls into the jail yard. We were waiting outside the condemned cells, a row of sheds fronted with double bars, like small animal cages. Each cell measured about ten feet by ten and was quite bare within except for a plank bed and a pot of drinking water. In some of them brown silent men were squatting at the inner bars, with their blankets draped round them. These were the condemned men, due to be hanged within the next week or two.

One prisoner had been brought out of his cell. He was a Hindu, a puny wisp of a man, with a shaven head and vague liquid eyes. He had a thick, sprouting moustache, absurdly too big for his body, rather like the moustache of a comic man in the films. Six tall Indian warders were guarding him and getting him ready for the gallows. Two of them stood by with rifles with fixed bayonets, while the others handcuffed him, passed a chain through his handcuffs and fixed it to their belts, and lashed his arms tight to his sides. They crowded very close about him, with their hands always on him in a careful, caressing grip, as though all the while feeling him to make sure he was there. It was like men handling a fish which is still alive and may jump back into the water. But he stood quite unresisting, yielding his arms limply to the ropes, as though he hardly noticed what was happening.

Eight o'clock struck and a bugle call, desolately thin in the wet   3
air, floated from the distant barracks. The superintendent of the jail, who was standing apart from the rest of us, moodily prodding the gravel with his stick, raised his head at the sound. He was an army doctor, with a grey toothbrush moustache and a gruff voice. "For God's sake hurry up, Francis," he said irritably. "The man ought to have been dead by this time. Aren't you ready yet?"

Francis, the head jailer, a fat Dravidian in a white drill suit and   4
gold spectacles, waved his black hand. "Yes sir, yes sir," he bubbled. "All iss satisfactorily prepared. The hangman iss waiting. We shall proceed."

"Well, quick march, then. The prisoners can't get their breakfast   5
till this job's over."

We set out for the gallows. Two warders marched on either side   6
of the prisoner, with their files at the slope; two others marched close against him, gripping him by arm and shoulder, as though at once pushing and supporting him. The rest of us, magistrates and the like, followed behind. Suddenly, when we had gone ten yards, the procession stopped short without any order or warning. A dreadful thing had happened — a dog, come goodness knows whence, had appeared in the yard. It came bounding among us with a loud volley of barks, and leapt round us wagging its whole body, wild with glee at finding so many human beings together. It was a large woolly dog, half Airedale, half pariah. For a moment it pranced round us, and then, before anyone could stop it, it had made a dash for the prisoner, and jumping up tried to lick his face. Everyone stood aghast, too taken aback even to grab at the dog.

"Who let that bloody brute in here?" said the superintendent angrily. "Catch it, someone!"   7

A warder, detached from the escort, charged clumsily after the   8
dog, but it danced and gambolled just out of his reach, taking everything as part of the game. A young Eurasian jailer picked up a handful of gravel and tried to stone the dog away, but it dodged the stones

and came after us again. Its yaps echoed from the jail walls. The prisoner, in the grasp of the two warders, looked on incuriously, as though this was another formality of the hanging. It was several minutes before someone managed to catch the dog. Then we put my handkerchief through its collar and moved off once more, with the dog still straining and whimpering.

It was about forty yards to the gallows. I watched the bare 9 brown back of the prisoner marching in front of me. He walked clumsily with his bound arms, but quite steadily, with that bobbing gait of the Indian who never straightens his knees. At each step his muscles slid neatly into place, the lock of hair on his scalp danced up and down, his feet printed themselves on the wet gravel. And once, in spite of the men who gripped him by each shoulder, he stepped slightly aside to avoid a puddle on the path.

It is curious, but till that moment I had never realised what it 10 means to destroy a healthy, conscious man. When I saw the prisoner step aside to avoid the puddle, I saw the mystery, the unspeakable wrongness, of cutting a life short when it is in full tide. This man was not dying, he was alive just as we were alive. All the organs of his body were working—bowels digesting food, skin renewing itself, nails growing, tissues forming—all toiling away in solemn foolery. His nails would still be growing when he stood on the drop, when he was falling through the air with a tenth of a second to live. His eyes saw the yellow gravel and the grey walls, and his brain still remembered, foresaw, reasoned—reasoned even about puddles. He and we were a party of men walking together, seeing, hearing, feeling, understanding the same world; and in two minutes, with a sudden snap, one of us would be gone—one mind less, one world less.

The gallows stood in a small yard, separate from the main 11 grounds of the prison, and overgrown with tall prickly weeds. It was a brick erection like three sides of a shed, with planking on top, and above that two beams and a crossbar with the rope dangling. The hangman, a grey-haired convict in the white uniform of the prison, was waiting beside his machine. He greeted us with a servile crouch as we entered. At a word from Francis the two warders, gripping the prisoner more closely than ever, half led, half pushed him to the gallows and helped him clumsily up the ladder. Then the hangman climbed up and fixed the rope round the prisoner's neck.

We stood waiting, five yards away. The warders had formed in a 12 rough circle round the gallows. And then, when the noose was fixed, the prisoner began crying out to his god. It was a high, reiterated cry of "Ram! Ram! Ram! Ram!," not urgent and fearful like a prayer or a cry for help, but steady, rhythmical, almost like the tolling of a bell. The dog answered the sound with a whine. The hangman, still standing on the gallows, produced a small cotton bag like a flour bag and drew it down over the prisoner's face. But the sound, muffled by the cloth, still persisted, over and over again: "Ram! Ram! Ram! Ram! Ram!"

The hangman climbed down and stood ready, holding the lever. 13 Minutes seemed to pass. The steady, muffled crying from the prisoner went on and on, "Ram! Ram! Ram!" never faltering for an instant. The superintendent, his head on his chest, was slowly poking the ground with his stick; perhaps he was counting the cries, allowing the prisoner a fixed number—fifty, perhaps, or a hundred. Everyone had changed colour. The Indians had gone grey like bad coffee, and one or two of the bayonets were wavering. We looked at the lashed, hooded man on the drop, and listened to his cries—each cry another second of life; the same thought was in all our minds: oh, kill him quickly, get it over, stop that abominable noise!

Suddenly the superintendent made up his mind. Throwing up his 14 head he made a swift motion with his stick. "Chalo!" he shouted almost fiercely.

There was a clanking noise, and then dead silence. The prisoner 15 had vanished, and the rope was twisting on itself. I let go of the dog, and it galloped immediately to the back of the gallows; but when it got there it stopped short, barked, and then retreated into the corner of the yard, where it stood among the weeds, looking timorously out at us. We went round the gallows to inspect the prisoner's body. He was dangling with his toes pointed straight downwards, very slowly revolving, as dead as a stone.

The superintendent reached out with his stick and poked the bare 16 body; it oscillated, slightly. "*He's* all right, "said the superintendent. He backed out from under the gallows, and blew out a deep breath. The moody look had gone out of his face quite suddenly. He glanced at his wristwatch. "Eight minutes past eight. Well, that's all for this morning, thank God."

The warders unfixed bayonets and marched away. The dog, 17 sobered and conscious of having misbehaved itself, slipped after them. We walked out of the gallows yard, past the condemned cells with their waiting prisoners, into the big central yard of the prison.

The convicts, under the command of warders armed with lathis,[1] were already receiving their breakfast. They squatted in long rows, each man holding a tin pannikin, while two warders with buckets marched round ladling out rice; it seemed quite a homely, jolly scene, after the hanging. An enormous relief had come upon us now that the job was done. One felt an impulse to sing, to break into a run, to snigger. All at once everyone began chattering gaily.

The Eurasian boy walking beside me nodded towards the way we had come, with a knowing smile: "Do you know, sir, our friend (he meant the dead man), when he heard his appeal had been dismissed, he pissed on the floor of his cell. From fright.—Kindly take one of my cigarettes, sir. Do you not admire my new silver case, sir? From the boxwallah,[2] two rupees eight annas. Classy European style."   18

Several people laughed—at what, nobody seemed certain.   19

Francis was walking by the superintendent, talking garrulously: "Well, sir, all hass passed off with the utmost satisfactoriness. It wass all finished—flick! like that. It iss not always so—oah, no! I have known cases where the doctor wass obliged to go beneath the gallows and pull the prisoner's legs to ensure decease. Most disagreeable!"   20

"Wriggling about, eh? That's bad," said the superintendent.   21

"Ach, sir, it iss worse when they become refractory! One man, I recall, clung to the bars of hiss cage when we went to take him out. You will scarcely credit, sir, that it took six warders to dislodge him, three pulling at each leg. We reasoned with him. 'My dear fellow,' we said, 'think of all the pain and trouble you are causing to us!' But no, he would not listen! Ach, he wass very troublesome!"   22

I found that I was laughing quite loudly. Everyone was laughing. Even the superintendent grinned in a tolerant way. "You'd better all come out and have a drink," he said quite genially. "I've got a bottle of whisky in the car. We could do with it."   23

We went through the big double gates of the prison, into the road. "Pulling at his legs!" exclaimed a Burmese magistrate suddenly, and burst into a loud chuckling. We all began laughing again. At that moment Francis's anecdote seemed extraordinarily funny. We all had a drink together, native and European alike, quite amicably. The dead man was a hundred yards away.   24

---

[1] A wooden or metal baton
[2] A trader or peddler

QUESTIONS FOR STUDY AND DISCUSSION

1. In paragraph 6, why is the appearance of the dog "a dreadful thing"? From whose point of view is it dreadful? Why?
2. The role of the narrator of this essay (Glossary: *Narration*) is never clearly defined, nor is the nature of the prisoner's transgression. Why does Orwell deliberately withhold this information?
3. In paragraphs 9 and 10, the prisoner steps aside to avoid a puddle, and Orwell considers the implications of this action. What understanding does he reach? In paragraph 10, what is the meaning of the phrase "one mind less, one world less"?
4. In paragraph 22, what is ironic about Francis's story of the "troublesome" prisoner? (Glossary: *Irony*)
5. Throughout this essay, Orwell uses figurative language, primarily similes, to bring a foreign experience closer to the reader's understanding. Find and explain three or four similes that clarify the event for a modern American reader.
6. Orwell goes to some pains to identify the multicultural nature of the group participating in the hanging scene: Hindu, Dravidian, Eurasian, European, Burmese. Why is the variety of backgrounds of the participants important to the central idea of the essay? Even the dog is "half Airedale, half pariah." What is a pariah, and why is its inclusion appropriate?
7. What word or words would you use to describe the mood of the group that observed the hanging before the event? Afterward? Cite specific details to support your word choice. Why are the moods so extreme?

VOCABULARY

Refer to your dictionary to define the following words as they are used in this selection. Then use each word in a sentence of your own.

magistrates (6)	timorously (15)
volley (6)	oscillated (16)
gambolled (8)	garrulously (20)
erection (11)	refractory (22)
servile (11)	genially (23)
abominable (13)	amicably (24)

CLASSROOM ACTIVITY USING FIGURATIVE LANGUAGE

Think of a time when you were one of a group of people assembled to do something most or all of you didn't really want to do. People in such a situation behave in various ways, showing their discomfort. One might stare steadily at the ground, for example. A writer describing the scene could use a metaphor to make it more vivid for the reader: "With his gaze he drilled a hole in the ground between his feet."

Other people in an uncomfortable situation might fidget, lace their fingers together, breathe rapidly, squirm, or tap an object, such as a pen or a key. Create a simile or a metaphor to describe each of these behaviors.

SUGGESTED WRITING ASSIGNMENTS

1. Are the men who carry out the hanging in Orwell's essay cruel? Are they justified in their actions, following orders from others better able to judge? Or should they question their assigned role as executioners? Who has the right to take the life of another? Write an essay in which you either condemn or support Orwell's role in the hanging of the Hindu. Was it appropriate for him to have participated, even as a spectator? What, if anything, should or could he have done when he "saw the mystery, the unspeakable wrongness, of cutting a life short when it is in full tide" (10)?

2. Recall and narrate an event in your life when you or someone you know underwent some sort of punishment. You may have been a participant or a spectator in the event. How did you react when you learned what the punishment was to be? When it was administered? After it was over? Use figurative language to make vivid the scene during which the punishment was imposed.

The Flight of the Eagles

■ N. Scott Momaday

Celebrated writer and educator N. Scott Momaday is a Kiowa Indian. He has based much of his writing on his Native American ancestry, particularly on his childhood experiences with his Kiowa grandmother. In 1969, he won the Pulitzer Prize for his novel House Made of Dawn *(1968). His other works include* The Way to Rainy Mountain *(1969),* Angle of Geese and Other Poems *(1974),* The Gourd Dancer *(1976), and* In the Bear's House *(1999). In the following selection, taken from* House Made of Dawn, *Momaday closely observes the mating flight of a pair of golden eagles. Notice how his sensitive choice of verbs enables him to capture the beautiful and graceful movements of these birds.*

FOR YOUR JOURNAL

Recall an encounter with nature. What made this encounter memorable? What words would you use to capture the action in this encounter? Briefly describe the encounter so that a reader can experience it as you did.

They were golden eagles, a male and a female, in their mating flight. They were cavorting, spinning and spiraling on the cold, clear columns of air, and they were beautiful. They swooped and hovered, leaning on the air, and swung close together, feinting and screaming with delight. The female was full-grown, and the span of her broad wings was greater than any man's height. There was a fine flourish to her motion; she was deceptively, incredibly fast, and her pivots and wheels were wide and full-blown. But her great weight was streamlined and perfectly controlled. She carried a rattlesnake; it hung shining from her feet, limp and curving out in the trail of her flight. Suddenly her wings and tail fanned, catching full on the wind, and for an instant she was still, widespread and spectral in the blue, while her mate flared past and away, turning around in the distance to look for her. Then she began to beat upward at an angle from the rim until she was small in the sky, and she let go of the snake. It fell slowly, writhing and rolling, floating out like a bit of silver thread against the wide backdrop of the land. She held still above, buoyed up on the cold current, her crop and hackles gleaming like copper in the sun. The male swerved and sailed. He was younger than she and a little more than half as large. He was quicker, tighter in his moves. He let the carrion drift by; then suddenly he gathered himself and swooped, sliding down in a blur of motion to the strike. He hit the snake in the head, with not the slightest deflection of his course or speed, cracking its long body like a whip. Then he rolled and swung upward in a great pendulum arc, riding out his momentum. At the top of his glide he let go of the snake in turn, but the female did not go for it. Instead she soared out over the plain, nearly out of sight, like a mote receding into the haze of the far mountain. The male followed.

QUESTIONS FOR STUDY AND DISCUSSION

1. Identify the figurative language that Momaday uses in this selection, and describe how each example functions in the essay.
2. What are the differences between the two eagles as Momaday describes them?
3. In describing the mating flight of the golden eagles, Momaday has tried to capture their actions accurately. Identify the strong verbs that he uses, and discuss how these verbs enhance his description. (Glossary: *Verb*)
4. Comment on the denotative and connotative meanings of the italicized words and phrases in the following excerpts:

   a. on the *cold, clear* columns of air

   b. feinting and screaming with *delight*

   c. a *fine flourish* to her motion

   d. her *pivots* and *wheels* were wide and full-blown

   e. her *crop* and *hackles* gleaming
5. Identify several examples of Momaday's use of concrete and specific diction. What effect does this diction have on you? (Glossary: *Diction*)

VOCABULARY

Refer to your dictionary to define the following words as they are used in this selection. Then use each word in a sentence of your own.

cavorting

feinting

spectral

CLASSROOM ACTIVITY USING FIGURATIVE LANGUAGE

Carefully read the following descriptions of October. Identify the figures of speech that each writer uses. Did you find one description more effective than the other? Why, or why not? Compare your reactions with those of others in the class.

THE FADING SEASON

October's lyrics are spilled in scarlet syllables on shadowed paths that bend with the wind as they wander through field and forest to heights where foliate hills commune with azure skies in the last golden moments of the autumns of our days.

Where a wisp of the wind tingles with the cidery essences of vagrant apples, fluttering leaflets bear bittersweet messages of another season's passing and warnings of harsh moments yet to be. Caught for a breath of a moment in the fingers of slim sunbeams, they glisten and gleam in a saffron splendor before they settle gently into the dappled pattern on the forest floor.

Walk slowly in October and you can savor the scents of cedar and pine, the musky odor of the earth before it dozes off for another winter, and the crackling leaves beneath your feet will snap and echo in the silences that only woods contain. Stop for a moment and you will sense scurryings in the underbrush where squirrels dash to and fro in a frenetic race to hoard as much as they can before winter sets in. A whirr of sudden wings will tell you that you have invaded the partridge's exclusive territory.

In the dusk of an October day when the sun's last crimson embers have slipped behind the hills, the crisp chill in the air signals fall's coming surrender to the approaching winter's legions.

—Burlington Free Press

OCTOBER

Blond October comes striding over the hills wearing a crimson shirt and faded green trousers. His morning breath is the mist in the valleys, and at evening there are stars in his eyes, a waxing moon over his shoulder, and the cool whisper of a valley breeze in his voice. He comes this way to light the fires of autumn in the maple groves, to put a final polish on the late winesaps, to whistle a farewell to summer and set the foxes to barking and tell the owls that now they can ask their eternal questions.

October might be called a god of travel, if we were to fashion a new mythology; for now come the perfect days to get out and wander the hills and valleys of these latitudes. The scene changes from day to day, as though all the color in the spectrum were being spilled across the landscape—radiant blue of the sky and the lakes and ponds reflecting it, green of every tone in the conifers and in the reluctant oaks, yellows verging from the sun simmer to moon orange in the elms, the beeches, the maples, and reds that range to purplish browns, sumac and dogwood and maple and oak and sour gum and sassafras and viburnum. There is the indigo of fox grapes, if you know where to find them.

October is colorful, it is exuberant, it is full of lively spirit. Spring fever can't hold a candle to October fever, when it comes to inner restlessness. The birds are on the wing, the leaves are footloose and eager for a breeze, the horizon is a challenge that amounts to an insidious summons. Listen closely and you can hear October, that fellow in the crimson shirt, whistling a soft melody that is as old as autumn upon this earth.

–Hal Borland, *New York Times*

SUGGESTED WRITING ASSIGNMENTS

1. Select one of the following activities as the subject for a brief descriptive essay. Use figurative language, as Momaday has done, and describe the action accurately and vividly.

   the movements of a dancer

   the actions of a kite

   the antics of a pet

   a traffic jam

   a violent storm

2. Accounts of natural events often rely on scientific data and are frequently presented in the third person. Carefully observe some natural event (fire, hurricane, birth of an animal, bird migration, etc.), and note significant details and facts about that occurrence. Then, using very carefully chosen diction, write an account of the event.

part ■ *three*

Types
of Essays

Illustration

Illustration is the use of examples — facts, opinions, samples, and anecdotes or stories — to make ideas more concrete and to make generalizations more specific and detailed. Examples enable writers not just to tell, but also to show what they mean. The more specific the example, the more effective it is. For instance, in an essay about recently developed alternative sources of energy, a writer might offer an example of how a local architecture firm designed a home heated by solar collectors instead of a conventional oil, gas, or electric system.

In an essay, a writer uses examples to clarify or support the thesis; in a paragraph, to clarify or support the main idea. Sometimes a single striking example suffices; sometimes a whole series of related examples is necessary. The following paragraph presents a single extended example — an anecdote that illustrates Edward T. Hall's point about cultural differences:

> Whenever there is a great cultural distance between two people, there are bound to be problems arising from differences in behavior and expectations. An example is the American couple who consulted a psychiatrist about their marital problems. The husband was from New England and had been brought up by reserved parents who taught him to control his emotions and to respect the need for privacy. His wife was from an Italian family and had been brought up in close contact with all the members of her large family, who were extremely warm, volatile and demonstrative. When the husband came home after a hard day at the office, dragging his feet and longing for peace and quiet, his wife would rush to him and smother him. Clasping his hands, rubbing his brow, crooning over his weary head, she never left him alone. But when the wife was upset or anxious about her day, the husband's response was to withdraw completely and leave her alone. No comforting, no affectionate embrace, no attention — just solitude. The woman became convinced her husband didn't love her and, in desperation, she

consulted a psychiatrist. Their problem wasn't basically psychological but cultural.

–Edward T. Hall

This single example is effective because it is *representative*—that is, essentially similar to other such problems Hall might have described and familiar to many readers. Hall tells the story with enough detail that readers can understand the couple's feelings and so better understand the point he is trying to make.

In contrast, Edwin Way Teale supports his topic sentence about country superstitions with ten examples:

In the folklore of the country, numerous superstitions relate to winter weather. Back-country farmers examine their corn husks— the thicker the husk, the colder the winter. They watch the acorn crop—the more acorns, the more severe the season. They observe where white-faced hornets place their paper nests—the higher they are, the deeper will be the snow. They examine the size and shape and color of the spleens of butchered hogs for clues to the severity of the season. They keep track of the blooming of dogwood in the spring—the more abundant the blooms, the more bitter the cold in January. When chipmunks carry their tails high and squirrels have heavier fur and mice come into country houses early in the fall, the superstitious gird themselves for a long, hard winter. Without any scientific basis, a wider-than-usual black band on a woolly-bear caterpillar is accepted as a sign that winter will arrive early and stay late. Even the way a cat sits beside the stove carries its message to the credulous. According to a belief once widely held in the Ozarks, a cat sitting with its tail to the fire indicates very cold weather is on the way.

–Edwin Way Teale

Teale uses numerous examples because he is writing about various superstitions. Also, putting all those strange beliefs side by side in a kind of catalog makes the paragraph fun to read as well as convincing and informative.

To use illustration effectively, begin by thinking of ideas and generalizations about your topic that you can make clearer and more persuasive by illustrating them with facts, anecdotes, or specific details. You should focus primarily on your main point, the central generalization that you will develop in your essay. Also be alert for other statements or references that may gain from illustration. Points that are already clear and uncontroversial, that your readers will understand and immediately agree with, can stand on their own as you pass along quickly to your next idea; belaboring the obvious wastes your time and energy, as well as your readers'. Often, however, you will find that examples add clarity, color, and weight to what you say.

Consider the following generalization:

> Americans are a pain-conscious people who would rather get rid of pain than seek and cure its root causes.

This assertion is broad and general; it raises the following questions: How so? What does this mean exactly? Why does the writer think so? The statement could be the topic sentence of a paragraph or perhaps even the thesis of an essay or of an entire book. As a writer, you could make the generalization stronger and more meaningful through illustration. You might support this statement by citing specific situations or specific cases in which Americans have gone to the drugstore instead of to a doctor, as well as by supplying sales figures per capita of painkillers in the United States as compared with other countries.

Illustration is so useful and versatile a strategy that it is found in all kinds of writing. It is essential, for example, in writing a successful argument essay. When freshman Hilda Alvarado wrote an essay arguing that non-English-speaking students starting school in the United States should be taught English as a second language, she supported her argument with the following illustration, drawn from her own experience as a Spanish-speaking child in an English-only school:

> Without the use of Spanish, unable to communicate with the teacher or students, for six long weeks we guessed at everything we did. When we lined up to go anywhere, neither my sister nor I knew what to expect. Once, the teacher took the class on a bathroom break, and I mistakenly thought we were on our way to the cafeteria for lunch. Before we left, I grabbed our lunch money, and one of the girls in line began sneering and pointing. Somehow she figured out my mistake before I did. When I realized why she was laughing, I became embarrassed and threw the money into my sister's desk as we walked out of the classroom.

Alvarado could have summarized her point in the preceding paragraph in fewer words:

Not only are non-English-speaking students in English-only schools unable to understand the information they are supposed to be learning, but they are subject to frequent embarrassment and teasing from their classmates.

By offering an illustration, however, Alvarado makes her point more vividly and effectively.

A Crime of Compassion

■ Barbara Huttmann

Barbara Huttmann received her nursing degree in 1976. After obtaining a master's degree in nursing administration, she co-founded a health-care consulting firm for hospitals, nursing organizations, and consumers. Her interest in patients' rights is clearly evident in her two books, The Patient's Advocate *and* Code Blue. *In the following essay, which first appeared in* Newsweek *in 1983, Huttmann narrates the final months of the life of Mac, one of her favorite patients. By using emotional and graphic detail, Huttmann hopes the example of Mac will convince her audience of the need for new legislation that would permit terminally ill patients to choose to die rather than suffer great pain and indignity. As you read about Mac, consider the degree to which his experience seems representative of what patients often endure because medical technology is now able to keep them alive longer than they would be able to survive on their own.*

FOR YOUR JOURNAL

For most people, being sick is at best an unpleasant experience. Reflect on an illness you have had, whether you were sick with a simple common cold or with an affliction that required you to be hospitalized for a time. What were your concerns, your fears? For what were you most thankful?

"Murderer," a man shouted. "God help patients who get *you* for a nurse."   1

"What gives you the right to play God?" another one asked.   2

It was the Phil Donahue show where the guest is a fatted calf and   3
the audience a 200-strong flock of vultures hungering to pick at the bones. I had told them about Mac, one of my favorite cancer patients. "We resuscitated him 52 times in just one month. I refused to resuscitate him again. I simply sat there and held his hand while he died."

There wasn't time to explain that Mac was a young, witty, macho cop who walked into the hospital with 32 pounds of attack equipment, looking as if he could single-handedly protect the whole city, if not the entire state. "Can't get rid of this cough," he said. Otherwise, he felt great. 4

Before the day was over, tests confirmed that he had lung cancer. And before the year was over, I loved him, his wife, Maura, and their three kids as if they were my own. All the nurses loved him. And we all battled his disease for six months without ever giving death a thought. Six months isn't such a long time in the whole scheme of things, but it was long enough to see him lose his youth, his wit, his macho, his hair, his bowel and bladder control, his sense of taste and smell, and his ability to do the slightest thing for himself. It was also long enough to watch Maura's transformation from a young woman into a haggard, beaten old lady. 5

When Mac had wasted away to a 60-pound skeleton kept alive by liquid food we poured down a tube, IV solutions we dripped into his veins, and oxygen we piped to a mask on his face, he begged us: "Mercy . . . for God's sake, please just let me go." 6

The first time he stopped breathing, the nurse pushed the button that calls a "code blue" throughout the hospital and sends a team rushing to resuscitate the patient. Each time he stopped breathing, sometimes two or three times in one day, the code team came again. The doctors and technicians worked their miracles and walked away. The nurses stayed to wipe the saliva that drooled from his mouth, irrigate the big craters of bedsores that covered his hips, suction the lung fluids that threatened to drown him, clean the feces that burned his skin like lye, pour the liquid food down the tube attached to his stomach, put pillows between his knees to ease the bone-on-bone pain, turn him every hour to keep the bedsores from getting worse, and change his gown and linen every two hours to keep him from being soaked in perspiration. 7

At night I went home and tried to scrub away the smell of decaying flesh that seemed woven into the fabric of my uniform. It was in my hair, the upholstery of my car—there was no washing it away. And every night I prayed that Mac would die, that his agonized eyes would never again plead with me to let him die. 8

Every morning I asked his doctor for a "no-code" order. Without that order, we had to resuscitate every patient who stopped breathing. His doctor was one of several who believe we must extend life as long as we have the means and knowledge to do it. To not do it is to be liable 9 for negligence, at least in the eyes of many people, including some nurses. I thought about what it would be like to stand before a judge, accused of murder, if Mac stopped breathing and I didn't call a code.

And after the fifty-second code, when Mac was still lucid enough   10
to beg for death again, and Maura was crumbled in my arms again, and when no amount of pain medication stilled his moaning and agony, I wondered about a spiritual judge. Was all this misery and suffering supposed to be building character or infusing us all with the sense of humility that comes from impotence?

Had we, the whole medical community, become so arrogant that   11
we believed in the illusion of salvation through science? Had we become so self-righteous that we thought meddling in God's work was our duty, our moral imperative and our legal obligation? Did we really believe that we had the right to force "life" on a suffering man who had begged for the right to die?

Such questions haunted me more than ever early one morning   12
when Maura went home to change her clothes and I was bathing Mac. He had been still for so long, I thought he at last had the blessed relief of coma. Then he opened his eyes and moaned, "Pain . . . no more . . . Barbara . . . do something . . . God, let me go."

The desperation in his eyes and voice riddled me with guilt. "I'll   13
stop," I told him as I injected the pain medication.

I sat on the bed and held Mac's hands in mine. He pressed his   14
bony fingers against my hand and muttered, "Thanks." Then there was one soft sigh and I felt his hands go cold in mine. "Mac?" I whispered, as I waited for his chest to rise and fall again.

A clutch of panic banded my chest, drew my finger to the code   15
button, urged me to do something, anything . . . but sit there alone with death. I kept one finger on the button, without pressing it, as a waxen pallor slowly transformed his face from person to empty shell. Nothing I've ever done in my 47 years has taken so much effort as it took *not* to press that code button.

Eventually, when I was as sure as I could be that the code team   16
would fail to bring him back, I entered the legal twilight zone and pushed the button. The team tried. And while they were trying, Maura walked into the room and shrieked, "No . . . don't let them do this to him . . . for God's sake . . . please, no more."

Cradling her in my arms was like cradling myself, Mac, and all   17
those patients and nurses who had been in this place before, who do the best they can in a death-denying society.

So a TV audience accused me of murder. Perhaps I am guilty. If a   18
doctor had written a no-code order, which is the only *legal* alternative, would he have felt any less guilty? Until there is legislation making it a criminal act to code a patient who has requested the right to
die, we will all of us risk the same fate as Mac. For whatever reason,
we developed the means to prolong life, and now we are forced to use
it. We do not have the right to die.

QUESTIONS FOR STUDY AND DISCUSSION

1. Why did people in the audience of the *Phil Donahue Show* call
   Huttmann a "murderer"? Is there any sense in which their accusation is justified? In what ways do you think Huttmann might
   agree with them?

2. In paragraph 15, Huttmann says, "Nothing I've ever done in my
   47 years has taken so much effort as it took *not* to press that
   code button." How effectively does she describe her struggle
   against pressing the button? What steps led to her ultimate decision not to press the code button?

3. What, according to Huttmann, is the "only legal alternative"
   to her action? What does she find hypocritical about that
   choice?

4. Huttmann makes a powerfully emotional appeal for a patient's
   right to die. Some readers might even find some of her story
   shocking or offensive. Cite examples of some of the graphic
   scenes Huttmann describes and discuss their impact on you as a
   reader. (Glossary: *Example*) Did they help persuade you to
   Huttmann's point of view or did you find them overly un-
   nerving? What would have been gained or lost had she left them
   out?

5. The story in Huttmann's example covers a period of six months.
   In paragraphs 4–6, she describes the first five months of Mac's
   illness; in paragraphs 7–10, the sixth month; and in paragraphs
   12–17, the final morning. What important point about narration
   does her use of time in this sequence demonstrate?

6. Huttmann concludes her essay with the statement, "We do not
   have the right to die." What does she mean by this? In your
   opinion, is she exaggerating or simply stating the facts? Does her
   example of Mac adequately illustrate Huttmann's concluding
   point?

VOCABULARY

Refer to your dictionary to define the following words as they are used in this selection. Then use each word in a sentence of your own.

resuscitate (3)   imperative (11)

irrigate (7)   waxen (15)

lucid (10)   pallor (15)

CLASSROOM ACTIVITY USING ILLUSTRATION

Barbara Huttmann illustrates her thesis by using the single example of Mac's experience in the hospital. For each of the following potential thesis statements, what single example might be used to best illustrate each one:

Seat belts save lives. (*Possible answer:* The example of an automobile accident in which a relative's life was saved because she was wearing her seat belt.)

Friends can be very handy.

Having good study skills can improve a student's grades.

Loud music can damage your hearing.

Reading the directions for a new product you have just purchased can save time and aggravation.

Humor can often make a bad situation more tolerable.

American manufacturers can make their products safer.

SUGGESTED WRITING ASSIGNMENTS

1. Write a letter to the editor of *Newsweek* in which you respond to Huttmann's essay. Would you be for or against legislation that would give terminally ill patients the right to die? Give examples from your personal experience or from your reading to support your opinion.

2. Using one of the following sentences as your thesis statement, write an essay giving examples from personal experience or from reading to support your opinion.

   Consumers have more power than they realize.

   Most products do/do not measure up to the claims of their advertisements.

Religion is/is not alive and well in America.

Our government works far better than its critics claim.

Being able to write well is more than a basic skill.

The seasons for professional sports are too long.

Today's college students are serious minded when it comes to academics.

Be Specific

■ **Natalie Goldberg**

Natalie Goldberg has made a specialty of writing about writing. Her first and best-known work, Writing Down the Bones: Freeing the Writer Within, *was published in 1986. Goldberg's advice to would-be writers is, on the one hand, practical and pithy; on the other, it is almost mystical in its call to know and appreciate the world. "Be Specific," the excerpt that appears below, is representative of the work as a whole. Amid widespread acclaim for the book, one critic commented, "Goldberg teaches us not only how to write better, but how to live better."* Writing Down the Bones *was followed by three more successful books about writing:* Wild Mind: Living the Writer's Life *(1990),* Living Color *(1996), and* Thunder and Lightning: Cracking Open the Writer's Craft *(2000). Altogether, more than half a million copies of Goldberg's books are now in print. Goldberg has also written fiction; her first novel,* Banana Rose, *was published in 1994. Notice the way in which Goldberg demonstrates her advice to be specific in the following selection.*

FOR YOUR JOURNAL

Suppose someone says to you, "I walked in the woods." What do you envision? Write down what you see in your mind's eye. Now suppose someone says, "I walked in the redwood forest." Again, write what you see. How are the two descriptions different, and why?

B e specific. Don't say "fruit." Tell what kind of fruit—"It is a pomegranate." Give things the dignity of their names. Just as with human beings, it is rude to say, "Hey, girl, get in line." That "girl" has a name. (As a matter of fact, if she's at least twenty years old, she's a woman, not a "girl" at all.) Things, too, have names. It is much better to say "the geranium in the window" than "the flower in the window." "Geranium"—that one word gives us a much more specific picture. It penetrates more deeply into the beingness of that

1

flower. It immediately gives us the scene by the window—red petals, green circular leaves, all straining toward sunlight.

About ten years ago I decided I had to learn the names of plants 2
and flowers in my environment. I bought a book on them and walked down the tree-lined streets of Boulder, examining leaf, bark, and seed, trying to match them up with their descriptions and names in the book. Maple, elm, oak, locust. I usually tried to cheat by asking people working in their yards the names of the flowers and trees growing there. I was amazed how few people had any idea of the names of the live beings inhabiting their little plot of land.

When we know the name of something, it brings us closer to the 3
ground. It takes the blur out of our mind; it connects us to the earth. If I walk down the street and see "dogwood," "forsythia," I feel more friendly toward the environment. I am noticing what is around me and can name it. It makes me more awake.

If you read the poems of William Carlos Williams, you will see 4
how specific he is about plants, trees, flowers—chicory, daisy, locust, poplar, quince, primrose, black-eyed Susan, lilacs—each has its own integrity. Williams says, "Write what's in front of your nose." It's good for us to know what is in front of our nose. Not just "daisy," but how the flower is in the season we are looking at it— "The days-eye hugging the earth/in August . . . brownedged,/green and pointed scales/armor his yellow.* Continue to hone your awareness: to the name, to the month, to the day, and finally to the moment.

Williams also says: "No idea, but in things." Study what is "in 5
front of your nose." By saying "geranium" instead of "flower," you are penetrating more deeply into the present and being there. The closer we can get to what's in front of our nose, the more it can teach us everything. "To see the World in a Grain of Sand, and a heaven in a Wild Flower . . .**

In writing groups and classes too, it is good to quickly learn the 6
names of all the other group members. It helps to ground you in the group and make you more attentive to each other's work.

Learn the names of everything: birds, cheese, tractors, cars, 7
buildings. A writer is all at once everything—an architect, French cook, farmer—and at the same time, a writer is none of these things.

---

* William Carlos Williams, "Daisy," in *The Collected Earlier Poems* (New York: New Directions, 1938).
** William Blake, "The Auguries of Innocence."

QUESTIONS FOR STUDY AND DISCUSSION

1. How does Goldberg "specifically" follow the advice she gives writers in this essay?

2. How does Goldberg use specifics to illustrate her point? She makes several lists of the names of things. What purpose do these lists serve? (Glossary: *Purpose*)

3. Throughout the essay, Goldberg instructs the reader to be specific and to be aware of the physical world. Of what besides names is the reader advised to be aware? Why?

4. In paragraphs 3, 5, and 6, Goldberg cites a number of advantages to be gained by knowing the names of things. What are these advantages? Do they ring true to you?

5. Goldberg says that to name an object gives it dignity (paragraph 1) and integrity (paragraph 4). What does she mean in each case?

6. What specific audience is Goldberg addressing in this essay? (Glossary: *Audience*) How do you know?

VOCABULARY

Refer to your dictionary to define the following words as they are used in this selection. Then use each word in a sentence of your own.

pomegranate (1)

integrity (4)

CLASSROOM ACTIVITY USING ILLUSTRATION

A useful exercise in learning to be specific is to see the words we use for people, places, things, and ideas as being positioned somewhere on a "ladder of abstraction." In the following chart, notice how the words progress from more general to more specific.

More General	*General*	*Specific*	*More Specific*
organism	plant	flower	Alstrumaria
vehicle	car	Chevrolet	'58 Chevrolet Impala

Try to fill in the missing parts of the following ladder of abstraction:

More General	General	Specific	More Specific
Writing instrument	_____	fountain pen	Waterman fountain pen
_____	sandwich	corned beef sandwich	Reuben
American	_____	Navaho	Laguna Pueblo
book	reference book	dictionary	_____
school	high school	technical high school	_____
medicine	oral medicine	gel capsule	_____

SUGGESTED WRITING ASSIGNMENTS

1. Natalie Goldberg likes William Carlos Williams's statement, "No idea, but in things." Using this line as both a title and a thesis, write your own argument for the use of the specific over the general in a certain field—news reporting, poetry, or airport traffic control, for example. Be sure to support your argument with examples.

2. Write a brief essay advising your readers of something they should do. Title your essay, as Goldberg does, with a directive ("Be Specific"). Tell your readers how they can improve their lives by taking your advice, and give strong examples of the behavior you are recommending.

The Case for Short Words

■ Richard Lederer

Richard Lederer has been a prolific and popular writer about language. A former high school English teacher, he is the vice president of S.P.E.L.L. (the Society for the Preservation of English Literature and Language). Lederer has written numerous books about how Americans use language, including Anguished English *(1987),* The Play of Words *(1990),* The Miracle of Language *(1991),* More Anguished English *(1993),* Adventures of a Verbivore *(1994), and his most recent,* Fractured English *(1996). In addition to writing books, Lederer pens a weekly column called "Looking at Language" for newspapers and magazines all over the United States. He is also the Grammar Grappler for* Writer's Digest *and the language commentator for* National Public Radio. *In the essay below, pay particular attention to the different ways Lederer uses examples to illustrate. The title and first four paragraphs serve as an extended example of his point about small words, while later in the essay he incorporates examples from his students' writing to illustrate that point more deliberately.*

FOR YOUR JOURNAL

We all carry with us a vocabulary of short, simple-looking words that possess a special personal meaning. For example, to some the word *rose* represents not just a flower, but a whole array of gardens, ceremonies, and romantic occasions. What little words have special meaning for you? What images do they bring to mind?

When you speak and write, there is no law that says you have to 1
use big words. Short words are as good as long ones, and short, old words—like *sun* and *grass* and *home*—are best of all. A lot of small words, more than you might think, can meet your needs with a strength, grace, and charm that large words do not have.

Big words can make the way dark for those who read what you 2
write and hear what you say. Small words cast their clear light on big

things — night and day, love and hate, war and peace, and life and death. Big words at times seem strange to the eye and the ear and the mind and the heart. Small words are the ones we seem to have known from the time we were born, like the hearth fire that warms the home.

Short words are bright like sparks that glow in the night, prompt   3
like the dawn that greets the day, sharp like the blade of a knife, hot like salt tears that scald the cheek, quick like moths that flit from flame to flame, and terse like the dart and sting of a bee.

Here is a sound rule: Use small, old words where you can. If a   4
long word says just what you want to say, do not fear to use it. But know that our tongue is rich in crisp, brisk, swift, short words. Make them the spine and the heart of what you speak and write. Short words are like fast friends. They will not let you down.

The title of this chapter and the four paragraphs that you have   5
just read are wrought entirely of words of one syllable. In setting myself this task, I did not feel especially cabined, cribbed, or confined. In fact, the structure helped me to focus on the power of the message I was trying to put across.

One study shows that twenty words account for twenty-five per-   6
cent of all spoken English words, and all twenty are monosyllabic. In order of frequency they are: *I, you, the, a, to, is, it, that, of, and, in, what, he, this, have, do, she, not, on,* and *they.* Other studies indicate that the fifty most common words in written English are each made of a single syllable.

For centuries our finest poets and orators have recognized and   7
employed the power of small words to make a straight point between two minds. A great many of our proverbs punch home their points with pithy monosyllables: "Where there's a will, there's a way," "A stitch in time saves nine," "Spare the rod and spoil the child," "A bird in the hand is worth two in the bush."

Nobody used the short word more skillfully than William Shake-   8
speare, whose dying King Lear laments:

> And my poor fool is hang'd! No, no, no life!
> Why should a dog, a horse, a rat have life,
> And thou no breath at all? . . .
> Do you see this? Look on her, look, her lips.
> Look there, look there!

Shakespeare's contemporaries made the King James Bible a cen-   9
terpiece of short words — "And God said, Let there be light: and

there was light. And God saw the light, that it was good." The descendants of such mighty lines live on in the twentieth century. When asked to explain his policy to Parliament, Winston Churchill responded with these ringing monosyllables: "I will say: it is to wage war, by sea, land, and air, with all our might and with all the strength that God can give us." In his "Death of the Hired Man" Robert Frost observes that "Home is the place where, when you have to go there, / They have to take you in." And William H. Johnson uses ten two-letter words to explain his secret of success: "If it is to be, / It is up to me."

You don't have to be a great author, statesman, or philosopher   10
to tap the energy and eloquence of small words. Each winter I ask my ninth graders at St. Paul's School to write a composition composed entirely of one-syllable words. My students greet my request with obligatory moans and groans, but, when they return to class with their essays, most feel that, with the pressure to produce high-sounding polysyllables relieved, they have created some of their most powerful and luminous prose. Here are submissions from two of my ninth graders:

> What can you say to a boy who has left home? You can say that he has done wrong, but he does not care. He has left home so that he will not have to deal with what you say. He wants to go as far as he can. He will do what he wants to do.
>
> This boy does not want to be forced to go to church, to comb his hair, or to be on time. A good time for this boy does not lie in your reach, for what you have he does not want. He dreams of ripped jeans, shorts with no starch, and old socks.
>
> So now this boy is on a bus to a place he dreams of, a place with no rules. This boy now walks a strange street, his long hair blown back by the wind. He wears no coat or tie, just jeans and an old shirt. He hates your world, and he has left it.
>
> –Charles Shaffer

> For a long time we cruised by the coast and at last came to a wide bay past the curve of a hill, at the end of which lay a small town. Our long boat ride at an end, we all stretched and stood up to watch as the boat nosed its way in.
>
> The town climbed up the hill that rose from the shore, a space in front of it left bare for the port. Each house was a clean white with sky blue or grey trim; in front of each one was a small yard, edged by a white stone wall strewn with green vines.

As the town basked in the heat of noon, not a thing stirred in the streets or by the shore. The sun beat down on the sea, the land, and the back of our necks, so that, in spite of the breeze that made the vines sway, we all wished we could hide from the glare in a cool, white house. But, as there was no one to help dock the boat, we had to stand and wait.

At last the head of the crew leaped from the side and strode to a large house on the right. He shoved the door wide, poked his head through the gloom, and roared with a fierce voice. Five or six men came out, and soon the port was loud with the clank of chains and creak of planks as the men caught ropes thrown by the crew, pulled them taut, and tied them to posts. Then they set up a rough plank so we could cross from the deck to the shore. We all made for the large house while the crew watched, glad to be rid of us.

–Celia Wren

You too can tap into the vitality and vigor of compact expres-   11
sion. Take a suggestion from the highway department. At the boundaries of your speech and prose place a sign that reads "Caution: Small
Words at Work."

QUESTIONS FOR STUDY AND DISCUSSION

1. Lederer says in paragraph 1 that "short, old words—like *sun* and *grass* and *home*—are best of all." What are the attributes of these words that make them "best"? Why are short old words superior to short newer words? (Glossary: *Connotation/ Denotation*)

2. In this essay, written to encourage the use of short words, Lederer himself employs many polysyllabic words, especially in paragraphs 5–9. What is his purpose in doing so?

3. Lederer quotes a wide variety of passages to illustrate the effectiveness of short words. For example, he quotes from famous, universally familiar old sources such as Shakespeare and the King James Bible, and from unknown contemporary sources such as his own ninth-grade students. How does the variety of his illustrations serve to inform his readers? (Glossary: *Exposition*) How does each example gain impact from the inclusion of the others?

4. To make clear to the reader why short words are effective, Lederer relies heavily on metaphor and simile, especially in the first four paragraphs. (Glossary: *Figure of Speech*) Choose at

least one metaphor and one simile from these paragraphs, and explain the comparison implicit in each.

5. In paragraph 10, Lederer refers to the relief his students feel when released from "the pressure to produce high-sounding polysyllables." Where does this pressure come from? How does it relate to the central purpose of this essay?

6. How does the final paragraph serve to close the essay effectively? (Glossary: *Beginnings and Endings*)

7. This essay abounds with examples of striking sentences and passages consisting entirely of words of one syllable. Choose four of the single-sentence examples or a section of several sentences from one of the longer examples and rewrite them, using only words of two or more syllables. Notice how the effect differs from the original.

VOCABULARY

Refer to your dictionary to define the following words as they are used in this selection. Then use each word in a sentence of your own.

cabined (5)	eloquence (10)
cribbed (5)	obligatory (10)
monosyllabic (6)	vitality (11)
proverbs (7)	

CLASSROOM ACTIVITY USING ILLUSTRATION

In your opinion, what is the finest sort of present to give or receive? Why? Define the ideal gift. Illustrate by describing one or more of the best gifts you have received or given, making it clear how each fits the ideal.

SUGGESTED WRITING ASSIGNMENTS

1. Follow the assignment Lederer gives his own students: "Write a composition composed entirely of one-syllable words." Make your piece about the length of his student examples or of his own four-paragraph opening.

2. A chief strength of Lederer's essay is his use of a broad variety of examples to illustrate his thesis that short words are the most effective. Choose a subject about which you are knowledgeable,

and find as wide a range of examples as you can to illustrate its appeal. For example, if you are enthusiastic about water, you could explore the relative attractions of puddles, ponds, lakes, and oceans; if a music lover, you might consider why Bach and/or the Beatles became popular far beyond the boundaries of the musical tastes of their eras.

Don't Let Stereotypes Warp Your Judgments

■ Robert L. Heilbroner

Economist Robert L. Heilbroner was educated at Harvard and at the New School for Social Research, where he is Norman Thomas Professor of Economics Emeritus. His many books over the past few decades include The Future as History *(1960),* A Primer of Government Spending: Between Capitalism and Socialism *(1970),* An Inquiry into the Human Prospect *(1974), and* Visions of the Future *(1995). "Don't Let Stereotypes Warp Your Judgments" first appeared in* Reader's Digest *and is particularly timely for people seeking understanding and respect for all in a culturally diverse, pluralistic society. In the essay, Heilbroner relies on the authority of questionnaires, university studies, and the findings of criminologists to bolster his own opinions. He also uses quotes from people known for their observations about human behavior to support and illustrate his statements about stereotypes and prejudice.*

FOR YOUR JOURNAL

"Stereotypes are a kind of gossip about the world, a gossip that makes us prejudge people before we ever lay eyes on them," writes Robert L. Heilbroner (5). Do you find yourself relying on stereotypes? What are they? Are they helpful to you in any way?

Is a girl called Gloria apt to be better-looking than one called 1
Bertha? Are criminals more likely to be dark than blond? Can you tell a good deal about someone's personality from hearing his voice briefly over the phone? Can a person's nationality be pretty accurately guessed from his photograph? Does the fact that someone wears glasses imply that he is intelligent?

The answer to all these questions is obviously, "No." 2

Yet, from all the evidence at hand, most of us believe these 3
things. Ask any college boy if he'd rather take his chances with a Gloria or a Bertha, or ask a college girl if she'd rather blind-date a

Richard or a Cuthbert. In fact, you don't have to ask: college students in questionnaires have revealed that names conjure up the same images in their minds as they do in yours — and for as little reason.

Look into the favorite suspects of persons who report "suspicious characters" and you will find a large percentage of them to be "swarthy" or "dark and foreign-looking" — despite the testimony of criminologists that criminals do *not* tend to be dark, foreign or "wild-eyed." Delve into the main asset of a telephone stock swindler and you will find it to be a marvelously confidence-inspiring telephone "personality." And whereas we all think we know what an Italian or a Swede looks like, it is the sad fact that when a group of Nebraska students sought to match faces and nationalities of 15 European countries, they were scored wrong in 93 percent of their identifications. Finally, for all the fact that horn-rimmed glasses have now become the standard television sign of an "intellectual," optometrists know that the main thing that distinguishes people with glasses is just bad eyes. 4

Stereotypes are a kind of gossip about the world, a gossip that makes us prejudge people before we ever lay eyes on them. Hence it is not surprising that stereotypes have something to do with the dark world of prejudice. Explore most prejudices (note that the word means prejudgment) and you will find a cruel stereotype at the core of each one. 5

For it is the extraordinary fact that once we have typecast the world, we tend to see people in terms of our standardized pictures. In another demonstration of the power of stereotypes to affect our vision, a number of Columbia and Barnard students were shown 30 photographs of pretty but unidentified girls, and asked to rate each in terms of "general liking," "intelligence," "beauty" and so on. Two months later, the same group were shown the same photographs, this time with fictitious Irish, Italian, Jewish and "American" names attached to the pictures. Right away the ratings changed. Faces which were now seen as representing a national group went down in looks and still farther down in likability, while the "American" girls suddenly looked decidedly prettier and nicer. 6

Why is it that we stereotype the world in such irrational and harmful fashion? In part, we begin to type-cast people in our childhood years. Early in life, as every parent whose child has watched a TV Western knows, we learn to spot the Good Guys from the Bad Guys. Some years ago, a social psychologist showed very clearly how powerful these stereotypes of childhood vision are. He secretly asked 7 the most popular youngsters in an elementary school to make errors in their morning gym exercises. Afterwards, he asked the class if anyone had noticed any mistakes during gym period. Oh, yes, said the children. But it was the *unpopular* members of the class—the "bad guys"—they remembered as being out of step.

We not only grow up with standardized pictures forming inside   8 of us, but as grown-ups we are constantly having them thrust upon us. Some of them, like the half-joking, half-serious stereotypes of mothers-in-law, or country yokels, or psychiatrists, are dinned into us by the stock jokes we hear and repeat. In fact, without such stereotypes, there would be a lot fewer jokes. Still other stereotypes are perpetuated by the advertisements we read, the movies we see, the books we read.

And finally, we tend to stereotype because it helps us make sense   9 out of a highly confusing world, a world which William James once described as "one great, blooming, buzzing confusion." It is a curious fact that if we don't *know* what we're looking at, we are often quite literally unable to *see* what we're looking at. People who recover their sight after a lifetime of blindness actually cannot at first tell a triangle from a square. A visitor to a factory sees only noisy chaos where the superintendent sees a perfectly synchronized flow of work. As Walter Lippmann has said, "For the most part we do not first see, and then define; we define first, and then we see."

Stereotypes are one way in which we "define" the world in order   10 to see it. They classify the infinite variety of human beings into a convenient handful of "types" towards whom we learn to act in stereotyped fashion. Life would be a wearing process if we had to start from scratch with each and every human contact. Stereotypes economize on our mental effort by covering up the blooming, buzzing confusion with big recognizable cut-outs. They save us the "trouble" of finding out what the world is like— they give it its accustomed look.

Thus the trouble is that stereotypes make us mentally lazy. As   11 S. I. Hayakawa, the authority on semantics, has written: "The danger of stereotypes lies not in their existence, but in the fact that they become for all people some of the time, and for some people all the time, *substitutes for observation.*" Worse yet, stereotypes get in the way of our judgment, even when we do observe the world. Someone who has formed rigid preconceptions of all Latins as "excitable," or all teenagers as "wild," doesn't alter his point of view when he meets a calm and deliberate Genoese, or a serious-minded high school student. He brushes them aside as "exceptions that prove the rule."

And, of course, if he meets someone true to type, he stands triumphantly vindicated. "They're all like that," he proclaims, having encountered an excited Latin, an ill-behaved adolescent.

Hence, quite aside from the injustice which stereotypes do to others, they impoverish ourselves. A person who lumps the world into simple categories, who type-casts all labor leaders as "racketeers," all businessmen as "reactionaries," all Harvard men as "snobs," and all Frenchmen as "sexy," is in danger of becoming a stereotype himself. He loses his capacity to be himself—which is to say, to see the world in his own absolutely unique, inimitable and independent fashion. 12

Instead, he votes for the man who fits his standardized picture of what a candidate "should" look like or sound like, buys the goods that someone in his "situation" in life "should" own, lives the life that others define for him. The mark of the stereotyped person is that he never surprises us, that we do indeed have him "typed." And no one fits this strait-jacket so perfectly as someone whose opinions about *other people* are fixed and inflexible. 13

Impoverishing as they are, stereotypes are not easy to get rid of. The world we type-cast may be no better than a Grade B movie, but at least we know what to expect of our stock characters. When we let them act for themselves in the strangely unpredictable way that people do act, who knows but that many of our fondest convictions will be proved wrong? 14

Nor do we suddenly drop our standardized pictures for a blinding vision of the Truth. Sharp swings of ideas about people often just substitute one stereotype for another. The true process of change is a slow one that adds bits and pieces of reality to the pictures in our heads, until gradually they take on some of the blurriness of life itself. Little by little, we learn not that Jews and Negroes and Catholics and Puerto Ricans are "just like everybody else"—for that, too, is a stereotype—but that each and every one of them is unique, special, different and individual. Often we do not even know that we have let a stereotype lapse until we hear someone saying, "all so-and-so's are like such-and-such," and we hear ourselves saying, "Well—maybe." 15

Can we speed the process along? Of course we can. 16

First, we can become *aware* of the standardized pictures in our heads, in other people's heads, in the world around us. 17

Second, we can become suspicious of all judgments that we allow exceptions to "prove." There is no more chastening thought than that in the vast intellectual adventure of science, it takes but one tiny exception to topple a whole edifice of ideas. 18

Third, we can learn to be chary of generalizations about people. 19
As F. Scott Fitzgerald once wrote: "Begin with an individual, and before you know it you have created a type; begin with a type, and you
find you have created — nothing."

Most of the time, when we type-cast the world, we are not in fact 20
generalizing about people at all. We are only revealing the embarrassing facts about the pictures that hang in the gallery of stereotypes in
our own heads.

QUESTIONS FOR STUDY AND DISCUSSION

1. What is Heilbroner's main point, or thesis, in this essay? (Glossary: *Thesis*)

2. Study paragraphs 6, 8, and 15. Each paragraph illustrates Heilbroner's thesis. How? What does each paragraph contribute to
   support the thesis?

3. Transitional devices indicate relationships between paragraphs
   and thus help to unify the essay. Identify three transitions in this
   essay. Explain how they help to unify the essay. (Glossary: *Transition*)

4. What are the reasons Heilbroner gives for why we stereotype individuals? What are some of the dangers of stereotypes, according to Heilbroner? How does he say we can rid ourselves of
   stereotypes?

5. Heilbroner uses the word *picture* in his discussion of stereotypes.
   Why is this an appropriate word in this discussion? (Glossary:
   Diction)

VOCABULARY

Refer to your dictionary to define the following words as they are
used in this selection. Then use each word in a sentence of your own.

irrational (7)   impoverish (12)
perpetuated (8)   chastening (18)
infinite (10)   edifice (18)
preconceptions (11)   chary (19)
vindicated (11)

CLASSROOM ACTIVITY USING ILLUSTRATION

To present a good example you need to provide details, and to collect telling details you must be observant. To test your powers of observation, try listing the features or qualities of an ordinary object—a soft drink can, a Styrofoam coffee cup, a ballpoint pen—something everyone in the class has access to. Compare your list of characteristics with those of other members of the class. Discuss whether having a label for something—soft drink can, coffee cup, or ballpoint pen—is a help or a hindrance in describing it.

SUGGESTED WRITING ASSIGNMENTS

1. Write an essay in which you attempt to convince your readers that it is not in their best interests to perform a particular act—for example, smoke, take stimulants to stay awake, go on a crash diet, or make snap judgments. In writing your essay, follow Heilbroner's lead: first identify the issue; then explain why it is a problem; and, finally, offer a solution or some advice. Remember to unify the various parts of your essay and to include illustrations.

2. Have you ever been stereotyped—as a student, or a member of a particular class, ethnic, national, or racial group? Write a unified essay that examines how stereotyping has affected you, how it has perhaps changed you, and how you regard the process.

Narration

To *narrate* is to tell a story or to recount a series of events. Whenever you relate an incident or use an anecdote to make a point, you use narration. In its broadest sense, narration is any account of any event or series of events. We all love to hear stories; some people believe that sharing stories is a part of what defines us as human beings. Good stories are interesting, sometimes suspenseful—we need to know "how things turn out"—and always instructive because they give us insights into the human condition. Although most often associated with fiction, narration is effective and useful in all kinds of writing. For example, in "How I Got Smart" (142–45), retired high school English teacher Steve Brody narrates the humorous story of how an infatuation with a classmate, Debbie, motivated him to hit the books. In "As They Say, Drugs Kill" (427–30), writer Laura Rowley recounts a particularly poignant experience to argue against substance abuse.

Good narration has five essential features: a clear context; well-chosen and thoughtfully emphasized details; a logical, often chronological organization; an appropriate and consistent point of view; and a meaningful point or purpose. Consider, for example, the following story, entitled "Is Your Jar Full?"

One day, an expert in time management was speaking to a group of business students and, to drive home a point, used an illustration those students will never forget. As he stood in front of the group of high-powered overachievers he said, "Okay, time for a quiz" and he pulled out a one-gallon mason jar and set it on the table in front of him. He also produced about a dozen fist-sized rocks and carefully placed them, one at a time, into the jar. When the jar was filled to the top and no more rocks would fit inside, he asked, "Is this jar full?"

Everyone in the class yelled, "Yes."

The time management expert replied, "Really?" He reached under the table and pulled out a bucket of gravel. He dumped some gravel in and shook the jar causing pieces of gravel to work themselves down into the spaces between the big rocks. He then asked the group once more, "Is the jar full?" By this time the class was on to him.

"Probably not," one of them answered.

"Good!" he replied. He reached under the table and brought out a bucket of sand. He started dumping the sand in the jar and it went into all of the spaces left between the rocks and the gravel. Once more he asked the question, "Is this jar full?"

"No!" the class shouted.

Once again he said, "Good." Then he grabbed a pitcher of water and began to pour it in until the jar was filled to the brim. Then he looked at the class and asked, "What is the point of this illustration?"

One eager beaver raised his hand and said, "The point is, no matter how full your schedule is, if you try really hard you can always fit some more things in it!"

"No," the speaker replied, "that's not the point. The truth this illustration teaches us is: If you don't put the big rocks in first, you'll never get them in at all. What are the 'big rocks' in your life—time with your loved ones, your faith, your education, your dreams, a worthy cause, teaching or mentoring others? Remember to put these BIG ROCKS in first or you'll never get them in at all."

So, tonight, or in the morning, when you are reflecting on this short story, ask yourself this question: What are the "big rocks" in my life? Then, put those in your jar first.

This story contains all the elements of good narration. The writer begins by establishing a clear context for her narrative, telling when, where, and to whom the action happened. She has chosen details well, including enough detail so that we know what is happening but not so much that we become overwhelmed, confused, or bored. The writer organizes her narration logically, with a beginning that sets the scene, a middle that relates the exchange between the time-management expert and the students, and an end that makes her point, all arranged chronologically. She tells the story from the third-person point of view. Finally, she reveals the point of her narration: people need to think about what's important in their lives and put these activities first.

The writer could have told her story from the first-person point of view. In this point of view, the narrator is a participant in the action and uses the pronoun *I*. In the following example, Willie Morris tells a story of how the comfortably well-off respond coolly to the tragedies of the ghetto. We experience the event directly through the writer's eyes and ears, as if we too had been on the scene of the action.

> One afternoon in late August, as the summer's sun streamed into the [railroad] car and made little jumping shadows on the windows, I sat gazing out at the tenement-dwellers, who were themselves looking out of their windows from the gray crumbling buildings along the tracks of upper Manhattan. As we crossed into the Bronx, the train unexpectedly slowed down for a few miles. Suddenly from out of my window I saw a large crowd near the tracks, held back by two policemen. Then, on the other side from my window, I saw a sight I would never be able to forget: a little boy almost severed in halves, lying at an incredible angle near the track. The ground was covered with blood, and the boy's eyes were opened wide, strained and disbelieving in his sudden oblivion. A policeman stood next to him, his arms folded, staring straight ahead at the windows of our train. In the orange glow of late afternoon the policemen, the crowd, the corpse of the boy were for a brief moment immobile, motionless, a small tableau to violence and death in the city. Behind me, in the next row of seats, there was a game of bridge. I heard one of the four men say as he looked out at the sight, "God, that's horrible." Another said, in a whisper, "Terrible, terrible." There was a momentary silence, punctuated only by the clicking of the wheels on the track. Then, after the pause, I heard the first man say: "Two hearts."
>
> –Willie Morris

As you begin to write your own narration, take time to ask yourself why you are telling your story. Your purpose in writing will influence which events and details you include and which you leave out. You should include enough detail about the action and its context so that your readers can understand what's going on. You should not get so carried away with details that your readers become confused or bored by an excess of information, however. In good storytelling, deciding what to leave out is as important as deciding what to include.

Be sure to give some thought to the organization of your narrative. While chronological organization is natural in narration because it is a reconstruction of the original order of events, it is not always the most interesting. To add interest to your storytelling, try using a technique common in the movies and theater called *flashback*. Begin your narration midway through the story with an important or exciting event and then use flashback to fill in what happened earlier.

Shame

■ Dick Gregory

Dick Gregory, a well-known comedian and nutrition expert, has long been active in the civil-rights movement. During the 1960s, Gregory was also an outspoken critic of America's involvement in Vietnam. In the following episode from his autobiography Nigger *(1964), he narrates the story of a childhood experience that taught him the meaning of shame. Through his use of realistic dialogue and vivid details, he dramatically re-creates the experience for readers. Notice also how he uses the first three paragraphs to establish a context for the events that follow.*

FOR YOUR JOURNAL

We all learn many things in school beyond the lessons we study formally. Some of the extracurricular truths we learn stay with us for the rest of our lives. Write about something you learned in school that you still find very useful—something that has made life easier or more understandable for you.

I never learned hate at home, or shame. I had to go to school for 1 that. I was about seven years old when I got my first big lesson. I was in love with a little girl named Helene Tucker, a light-complexioned little girl with pigtails and nice manners. She was always clean and she was smart in school. I think I went to school then mostly to look at her. I brushed my hair and even got me a little old handkerchief. It was a lady's handkerchief, but I didn't want Helene to see me wipe my nose on my hand. The pipes were frozen again, there was no water in the house, but I washed my socks and shirt every night. I'd get a pot, and go over to Mister Ben's grocery store, and stick my pot down into his soda machine. Scoop out some chopped ice. By evening the ice melted to water for washing. I got sick a lot that winter because the fire would go out at night before the clothes were dry. In the morning I'd put them on, wet or dry, because they were the only clothes I had.

Everybody's got a Helene Tucker, a symbol of everything you 2 want. I loved her for her goodness, her cleanness, her popularity.

She'd walk down my street and my brothers and sisters would yell, "Here comes Helene," and I'd rub my tennis sneakers on the back of my pants and wish my hair wasn't so nappy and the white folks' shirt fit me better. I'd run out on the street. If I knew my place and didn't come too close, she'd wink at me and say hello. That was a good feeling. Sometimes I'd follow her all the way home, and shovel the snow off her walk and try to make friends with her Momma and her aunts. I'd drop money on her stoop late at night on my way back from shining shoes in the taverns. And she had a Daddy, and he had a good job. He was a paper hanger.

I guess I would have gotten over Helene by summertime, but 3
something happened in that classroom that made her face hang in front of me for the next twenty-two years. When I played the drums in high school it was for Helene and when I broke track records in college it was for Helene and when I started standing behind microphones and heard applause I wished Helene could hear it, too. It wasn't until I was twenty-nine years old and married and making money that I finally got her out of my system. Helene was sitting in that classroom when I learned to be ashamed of myself.

It was on a Thursday. I was sitting in the back of the room, in a 4
seat with a chalk circle drawn around it. The idiot's seat, the troublemaker's seat.

The teacher thought I was stupid. Couldn't spell, couldn't read, 5
couldn't do arithmetic. Just stupid. Teachers were never interested in finding out that you couldn't concentrate because you were so hungry, because you hadn't had any breakfast. All you could think about was noontime, would it ever come? Maybe you could sneak into the cloakroom and steal a bite of some kid's lunch out of a coat pocket. A bite of something. Paste. You can't really make a meal of paste, or put it on bread for a sandwich, but sometimes I'd scoop a few spoonfuls out of the paste jar in the back of the room. Pregnant people get strange tastes. I was pregnant with poverty. Pregnant with dirt and pregnant with smells that made people turn away, pregnant with cold and pregnant with shoes that were never bought for me, pregnant with five other people in my bed and no Daddy in the next room, and pregnant with hunger. Paste doesn't taste too bad when you're hungry.

The teacher thought I was a troublemaker. All she saw from the 6
front of the room was a little black boy who squirmed in his idiot's seat and made noises and poked the kids around him. I guess she couldn't see a kid who made noises because he wanted someone to know he was there.

It was on a Thursday, the day before the Negro payday. The   7
eagle always flew on Friday. The teacher was asking each student
how much his father would give to the Community Chest. On Friday
night, each kid would get the money from his father, and on Monday
he would bring it to the school. I decided I was going to buy me a
Daddy right then. I had money in my pocket from shining shoes and
selling papers, and whatever Helene Tucker pledged for her Daddy I
was going to top it. And I'd hand the money right in. I wasn't going
to wait until Monday to buy me a Daddy.

I was shaking, scared to death. The teacher opened her book and   8
started calling out names alphabetically.

"Helene Tucker?"   9

"My daddy said he'd give two dollars and fifty cents."   10

"That's very nice, Helene. Very, very nice indeed."   11

That made me feel pretty good. It wouldn't take too much to top   12
that. I had almost three dollars in dimes and quarters in my pocket. I
stuck my hand in my pocket and held onto the money, waiting for
her to call my name. But the teacher closed her book after she called
everybody else in the class.

I stood up and raised my hand.   13

"What is it now?"   14

"You forgot me."   15

She turned toward the blackboard. "I don't have time to be play-   16
ing with you, Richard."

"My Daddy said he'd . . ."   17

"Sit down, Richard, you're disturbing the class."   18

"My Daddy said he'd give . . . fifteen dollars."   19

She turned around and looked mad. "We are collecting this   20
money for you and your kind, Richard Gregory. If your Daddy can
give fifteen dollars you have no business being on relief."

"I got it right now, I got it right now, my Daddy gave it to me to   21
turn in today, my Daddy said . . ."

"And furthermore," she said, looking right at me, her nostrils   22
getting big and her lips getting thin and her eyes opening wide, "we
know you don't have a Daddy."

Helene Tucker turned around, her eyes full of tears. She felt sorry   23
for me. Then I couldn't see her too well because I was crying, too.

"Sit down, Richard."   24

And I always thought the teacher kind of liked me. She always   25
picked me to wash the blackboard on Friday, after school. That was

a big thrill, it made me feel important. If I didn't wash it, come Monday the school might not function right.

"Where are you going, Richard?"   26

I walked out of school that day, and for a long time I didn't go   27
back very often. There was shame there.

Now there was shame everywhere. It seemed like the whole   28
world had been inside that classroom, everyone had heard what the teacher had said, everyone had turned around and felt sorry for me. There was shame in going to the Worthy Boys Annual Christmas Dinner for you and your kind, because everybody knew what a worthy boy was. Why couldn't they just call it the Boys Annual Dinner; why'd they have to give it a name? There was shame in wearing the brown and orange and white plaid mackinaw the welfare gave to three thousand boys. Why'd it have to be the same for everybody so when you walked down the street the people could see you were on relief? It was a nice warm mackinaw and it had a hood, and my Momma beat me and called me a little rat when she found out I stuffed it in the bottom of a pail full of garbage way over on Cottage Street. There was shame in running over to Mister Ben's at the end of the day and asking for his rotten peaches, there was shame in asking Mrs. Simmons for a spoonful of sugar, there was shame in running out to meet the relief truck. I hated that truck, full of food for you and your kind. I ran into the house and hid when it came. And then I started to sneak through alleys, to take the long way home so the people going into White's Eat Shop wouldn't see me. Yeah, the whole world heard the teacher that day, we all know you don't have a Daddy.

QUESTIONS FOR STUDY AND DISCUSSION

1. What does Gregory mean by "shame"? What precisely was he ashamed of, and what in particular did he learn from the incident? (Glossary: *Definition*)

2. How do the first three paragraphs of the essay help to establish a context for the narrative that follows?

3. Why do you think Gregory narrates this episode from the first-person point of view? What would be gained or lost if he instead wrote it from the third-person point of view? (Glossary: *Point of View*)

4. What is the teacher's attitude toward Gregory? Consider her own words and actions as well as Gregory's opinion in arriving at your answer.

5. What role does money play in Gregory's narrative? How does money relate to his sense of shame?

6. Specific details can enhance the reader's understanding and appreciation of a narrative. (Glossary: *Details*) Gregory's description of Helene Tucker's manners or the plaid of his mackinaw, for example, makes his account vivid and interesting. Cite several other specific details he gives, and consider how the narrative would be different without them.

7. Effective narration often depends on establishing an accurate sense of the chronology of the events discussed as well as carefully adhering to this chronology even if one chooses to reorder the events. Make a list of the chronological references Dick Gregory makes in his essay. Compare your list with those made by others in your class.

VOCABULARY

Refer to your dictionary to define the following words as they are used in this selection. Then use each word in a sentence of your own.

nappy (2)   mackinaw (28)

CLASSROOM ACTIVITY USING NARRATION

Gregory tells his story from the first-person point of view. Rewrite his first paragraph in the third person. In a class discussion, compare notes on what you did to change the point of view. What problems did you have? How did you solve them? Which version do you like better? Why?

SUGGESTED WRITING ASSIGNMENTS

1. Using Gregory's essay as a model, write an essay narrating an experience that made you especially afraid, angry, surprised, embarrassed, or proud. Include sufficient detail so that your readers will know exactly what happened.

2. Most of us have had frustrating experiences with mechanical objects that seem to have perverse minds of their own. Write a brief narrative recounting one such experience with a vending machine, television set, computer, pay telephone, or any other such object. Be sure to establish a clear context for your narrative.

The Dare

■ **Roger Hoffmann**

Born in 1948, Roger Hoffmann is a freelance writer and the author of The Complete Software Marketplace *(1984). In "The Dare," first published in the* New York Times Magazine *in 1986, Hoffmann recounts how in his youth he accepted a friend's challenge to dive under a moving freight train and to roll out on the other side. As an adult, Hoffmann appreciates the act for what it was—a crazy, dangerous childhood stunt. But he also remembers what the episode meant to him as a seventh-grader trying to prove himself to his peers. As you read the essay, pay particular attention to how Hoffman incorporates both of these perspectives into his point of view concerning "I-dare-you's."*

FOR YOUR JOURNAL

When we are growing up, most of us want more than anything to be a part of a group. Was being part of a group something you cherished as a youngster? Or did you have a desire to be independent, to be your own person? Why do you think young people in particular worry about the issue of independence versus belonging?

The secret to diving under a moving freight train and rolling out   1
the other side with all your parts attached lies in picking the right spot between the tracks to hit with your back. Ideally, you want soft dirt or pea gravel, clear of glass shards and railroad spikes that could cause you instinctively, and fatally, to sit up. Today, at thirty-eight, I couldn't be threatened or baited enough to attempt that dive. But as a seventh grader struggling to make the cut in a tough Atlanta grammar school, all it took was a dare.

I coasted through my first years of school as a fussed-over smart   2
kid, the teacher's pet who finished his work first and then strutted around the room tutoring other students. By the seventh grade, I had more A's than friends. Even my old cronies, Dwayne and O.T., made it clear I'd never be one of the guys in junior high if I didn't dirty up

my act. They challenged me to break the rules, and I did. The I-dare-you's escalated: shoplifting, sugaring teachers' gas tanks, dropping lighted matches into public mailboxes. Each guerrilla act won me the approval I never got for just being smart.

Walking home by the railroad tracks after school, we started   3
playing chicken with oncoming trains. O.T., who was failing that year, always won. One afternoon he charged a boxcar from the side, stopping just short of throwing himself between the wheels. I was stunned. After the train disappeared, we debated whether someone could dive under a moving car, stay put for a 10-count, then scramble out the other side. I thought it could be done and said so. O.T. immediately stepped in front of me and smiled. Not by me, I added quickly, I certainly didn't mean that I could do it. "A smart guy like you," he said, his smile evaporating, "you could figure it out easy." And then, squeezing each word for effect, "I . . . DARE . . . you." I'd just turned twelve. The monkey clawing my back was Teacher's Pet. And I'd been dared.

As an adult, I've been on both ends of life's implicit business and   4
social I-dare-you's, although adults don't use those words. We provoke with body language, tone of voice, ambiguous phrases. I dare you to: argue with the boss, tell Fred what you think of him, send the wine back. Only rarely are the risks physical. How we respond to dares when we are young may have something to do with which of the truly hazardous male inner dares — attacking mountains, tempting bulls at Pamplona — we embrace or ignore as men.

For two weeks, I scouted trains and tracks. I studied moving box-   5
cars close up, memorizing how they squatted on their axles, never getting used to the squeal or the way the air fell hot from the sides. I created an imaginary, friendly train and ran next to it. I mastered a shallow, head-first dive with a simple half-twist. I'd land on my back, count to ten, imagine wheels and, locking both hands on the rail to my left, heave myself over and out. Even under pure sky, though, I had to fight to keep my eyes open and my shoulders between the rails.

The next Saturday, O.T., Dwayne and three eighth graders met   6
me below the hill that backed up to the lumberyard. The track followed a slow bend there and opened to a straight, slightly uphill climb for a solid third of a mile. My run started two hundred yards after the bend. The train would have its tongue hanging out.

The other boys huddled off to one side, a circle on another   7
planet, and watched quietly as I double-knotted my shoelaces. My

hands trembled. O.T. broke the circle and came over to me. He kept his hands hidden in the pockets of his jacket. We looked at each other. BB's of sweat appeared beneath his nose. I stuffed my wallet in one of his pockets, rubbing it against his knuckles on the way in, and slid my house key, wired to a red-and-white fishing bobber, into the other. We backed away from each other, and he turned and ran to join the four already climbing up the hill.

I watched them all the way to the top. They clustered together as   8
if I were taking their picture. Their silhouette resembled a round-shouldered tombstone. They waved down to me, and I dropped them from my mind and sat down on the rail. Immediately, I jumped back. The steel was vibrating.

The train sounded like a cow going short of breath. I pulled my   9
shirttail out and looked down at my spot, then up the incline of track ahead of me. Suddenly the air went hot, and the engine was by me. I hadn't pictured it moving that fast. A man's bare head leaned out and stared at me. I waved to him with my left hand and turned into the train, burying my face in the incredible noise. When I looked up, the head was gone.

I started running alongside the boxcars. Quickly, I found their   10
pace, held it, and then eased off, concentrating on each thick wheel that cut past me. I slowed another notch. Over my shoulder, I picked my car as it came off the bend, locking in the image of the white mountain goat painted on its side. I waited, leaning forward like the anchor in a 440-relay, wishing the baton up the track behind me. Then the big goat fired by me, and I was flying and then tucking my shoulder as I dipped under the train.

A heavy blanket of red dust settled over me. I felt bolted to the   11
earth. Sheet-metal bellies thundered and shook above my face. Count to ten, a voice said, watch the axles and look to your left for daylight. But I couldn't count, and I couldn't find left if my life depended on it, which it did. The colors overhead went from brown to red to black to red again. Finally, I ripped my hands free, forced them to the rail, and, in one convulsive jerk, threw myself into the blue light.

I lay there face down until there was no more noise, and I could   12
feel the sun against the back of my neck. I sat up. The last ribbon of train was slipping away in the distance. Across the tracks, O.T. was leading a cavalry charge down the hill, five very small, galloping boys, their fists whirling above them. I pulled my knees to my chest. My corduroy pants puckered wet across my thighs. I didn't care.

QUESTIONS FOR STUDY AND DISCUSSION

1. Why did Hoffmann accept O.T.'s dare when he was twelve years old? Would he accept the same dare today? Why, or why not?

2. How does paragraph 4 function in the context of Hoffmann's narrative?

3. How has Hoffmann organized his essay? (Glossary: *Organization*) What period of time is covered in paragraphs 2–5? In paragraphs 6–12? What conclusions about narrative time can you draw from what Hoffmann has done?

4. What were Hoffmann's feelings on the day of his dive under the moving freight train? Do you think he was afraid? How do you know?

5. Identify four figures of speech that Hoffmann uses in his essay. (Glossary: *Figure of Speech*) What does each figure add to his narrative?

6. Hoffmann tells his story in the first person: the narrator is the principal actor. What would have been gained or lost had Hoffmann used either O.T. or Dwayne to tell the story as third person observers? Explain. (Glossary: *Point of View*)

VOCABULARY

Refer to your dictionary to define the following words as they are used in this selection. Then use each word in a sentence of your own.

shards (1)	evaporating (3)
baited (1)	implicit (4)
cronies (2)	ambiguous (4)
escalated (2)	convulsive (11)
guerrilla (2)	

CLASSROOM ACTIVITY USING NARRATION

At the heart of Hoffmann's narrative in paragraphs 10 and 11 is a very detailed depiction of the precise movements he made as he threw himself under the train and swung himself out to the other side of the tracks. Using these paragraphs as a model, spend 10 or 15 minutes trying to depict a simple sequence of movements. You might try, for example, to capture a movement in gymnastics, a classic ballet step, a turn at bat in baseball, a skateboarding stunt, or any action of your own choosing. Share your narration with classmates to see how successful you have been.

SUGGESTED WRITING ASSIGNMENTS

1. Can you remember any dares that you made or accepted while growing up? What were the consequences of these dares? Did you and your peers find dares a way to test or prove yourselves? Using Hoffmann's essay as a model, write a narrative essay about a dare that you made, accepted, or simply witnessed.

2. Each of us can tell of an experience, like the one narrated by Hoffmann, that has been unusually significant for us. Think about your past, identify one experience that has been especially important for you, and write an essay about it. In preparing to write your narrative, you may find it helpful to ask such questions as: Why is the experience important for me? What details are necessary in order for me to re-create the experience in an interesting and engaging way? How can my narrative of the experience be most effectively organized? Over what period of time did the experience occur? What point of view will work best? What did I learn from this experience?

Momma, the Dentist, and Me

■ **Maya Angelou**

Maya Angelou is best known as the author of I Know Why the Caged Bird Sings *(1970), the first book in a series that constitutes her autobiography, and for "On the Pulse of the Morning," a characteristically optimistic poem on the need for personal and national renewal that she read at President Clinton's inauguration on January 20, 1993. Starting with her beginnings in St. Louis in 1928, Angelou's autobiography presents a life of joyful triumph over hardships that test her courage and threaten her spirit. The most recent chapter in that life story,* Wouldn't Take Nothing for My Journey Now, *appeared in 1993. Angelou is also a successful and respected poet. Her several volumes of poetry were collected in* Complete Collected Poems of Maya Angelou *in 1994. Trained as a dancer, Angelou also acted in the television series* Roots, *and at the request of Martin Luther King Jr., served as a coordinator of the Southern Christian Leadership Conference. In the following excerpt from* I Know Why the Caged Bird Sings, *Angelou narrates what happened, and what might have happened, when her grandmother, the "Momma" of the story, took her to the local dentist. As you read, consider how vital first-person narration is to the essay's success, particularly as you gauge the effect of the italicized paragraphs.*

FOR YOUR JOURNAL

When you were growing up, were you ever present when one or both of your parents were arguing with another adult about a matter concerning you? What were the circumstances? Perhaps, for example, you saw your parents criticizing a babysitter for letting you stay up past your bedtime or arguing with school officials about the school's dress code or a class activity that they found objectionable. Narrate the events that brought about the controversy, and show how it was resolved. Were you embarrassed by your parents' actions or happy that they stood up for you?

The angel of the candy counter had found me out at last, and was ex-   1
acting excruciating penance for all the stolen Milky Ways,
Mounds, Mr. Goodbars and Hersheys with Almonds. I had two cavi-
ties that were rotten to the gums. The pain was beyond the bailiwick of
crushed aspirins or oil of cloves. Only one thing could help me, so I
prayed earnestly that I'd be allowed to sit under the house and have the
building collapse on my left jaw. Since there was no Negro dentist in
Stamps, nor doctor either, for that matter, Momma had dealt with previous toothaches by pulling them out (a string tied to the tooth with the
other end looped over her fist), pain killers and prayer. In this particular instance the medicine had proved ineffective; there wasn't enough
enamel left to hook a string on, and the prayers were being ignored because the Balancing Angel was blocking their passage.

I lived a few days and nights in blinding pain, not so much toying   2
with as seriously considering the idea of jumping in the well, and
Momma decided I had to be taken to a dentist. The nearest Negro
dentist was in Texarkana, twenty-five miles away, and I was certain
that I'd be dead long before we reached half the distance. Momma
said we'd go to Dr. Lincoln, right in Stamps, and he'd take care of
me. She said he owed her a favor.

I knew there were a number of whitefolks in town that owed her   3
favors. Bailey and I had seen the books which showed how she had
lent money to Blacks and whites alike during the Depression, and
most still owed her. But I couldn't aptly remember seeing Dr. Lincoln's name, nor had I ever heard of a Negro's going to him as a patient. However, Momma said we were going, and put water on the
stove for our baths. I had never been to a doctor, so she told me that
after the bath (which would make my mouth feel better) I had to put
on freshly starched and ironed underclothes from inside out. The
ache failed to respond to the bath, and I knew then that the pain was
more serious than that which anyone had ever suffered.

Before we left the Store, she ordered me to brush my teeth and   4
then wash my mouth with Listerine. The idea of even opening my
clamped jaws increased the pain, but upon her explanation that when
you go to a doctor you have to clean yourself all over, but most especially the part that's to be examined, I screwed up my courage and
unlocked my teeth. The cool air in my mouth and the jarring of my
molars dislodged what little remained of my reason. I had frozen to
the pain, my family nearly had to tie me down to take the toothbrush
away. It was no small effort to get me started on the road to the
dentist. Momma spoke to all the passers-by, but didn't stop to chat.

She explained over her shoulder that we were going to the doctor and she'd "pass the time of day" on our way home.

Until we reached the pond the pain was my world, an aura that 5 haloed me for three feet around. Crossing the bridge into whitefolks' country, pieces of sanity pushed themselves forward. I had to stop moaning and start walking straight. The white towel, which was drawn under my chin and tied over my head, had to be arranged. If one was dying, it had to be done in style if the dying took place in whitefolks' part of town.

On the other side of the bridge the ache seemed to lessen as if a 6 whitebreeze blew off the whitefolks and cushioned everything in their neighborhood—including my jaw. The gravel road was smoother, the stones smaller and the tree branches hung down around the path and nearly covered us. If the pain didn't diminish then, the familiar yet strange sights hypnotized me into believing that it had.

But my head continued to throb with the measured insistence of 7 a bass drum, and how could a toothache pass the calaboose, hear the songs of the prisoners, their blues and laughter, and not be changed? How could one or two or even a mouthful of angry tooth roots meet a wagonload of powhitetrash children, endure their idiotic snobbery and not feel less important?

Behind the building which housed the dentist's office ran a small 8 path used by servants and those tradespeople who catered to the butcher and Stamps' one restaurant. Momma and I followed that lane to the backstairs of Dentist Lincoln's office. The sun was bright and gave the day a hard reality as we climbed up the steps to the second floor.

Momma knocked on the back door and a young white girl 9 opened it to show surprise at seeing us there. Momma said she wanted to see Dentist Lincoln and to tell him Annie was there. The girl closed the door firmly. Now the humiliation of hearing Momma describe herself as if she had no last name to the young white girl was equal to the physical pain. It seemed terribly unfair to have a toothache and a headache and have to bear at the same time the heavy burden of Blackness.

It was always possible that the teeth would quiet down and 10 maybe drop out of their own accord. Momma said we would wait. We leaned in the harsh sunlight on the shaky railings of the dentist's back porch for over an hour.

He opened the door and looked at Momma. "Well, Annie, what 11 can I do for you?"

He didn't see the towel around my jaw or notice my swollen face.   12

Momma said, "Dentist Lincoln. It's my grandbaby here. She got   13
two rotten teeth that's giving her a fit."

She waited for him to acknowledge the truth of her statement.   14
He made no comment, orally or facially.

"She had this toothache purt' near four days now, and today I   15
said, 'Young lady, you going to the Dentist.'"

"Annie?"   16

"Yes, sir, Dentist Lincoln."   17

He was choosing words the way people hunt for shells. "Annie,   18
you know I don't treat nigra, colored people."

"I know, Dentist Lincoln. But this here is just my little grand-   19
baby, and she ain't gone be no trouble to you . . ."

"Annie, everybody has a policy. In this world you have to have a   20
policy. Now, my policy is I don't treat colored people."

The sun had baked the oil out of Momma's skin and melted the   21
Vaseline in her hair. She shone greasily as she leaned out of the dentist's shadow.

"Seem like to me, Dentist Lincoln, you might look after her, she   22
ain't nothing but a little mite. And seems like maybe you owe me a
favor or two."

He reddened slightly. "Favor or no favor. The money has all   23
been repaid to you and that's the end of it. Sorry, Annie." He had his
hand on the doorknob. "Sorry." His voice was a bit kinder on the
second "Sorry," as if he really was.

Momma said, "I wouldn't press on you like this for myself but I   24
can't take No. Not for my grandbaby. When you come to borrow my
money you didn't have to beg. You asked me, and I lent it. Now, it
wasn't my policy. I ain't no moneylender, but you stood to lose this
building and I tried to help you out."

"It's been paid, and raising your voice won't make me change my   25
mind. My policy . . ." He let go of the door and stepped nearer Momma.
The three of us were crowded on the small landing. "Annie, my policy
is I'd rather stick my hand in a dog's mouth than in a nigger's."

He had never once looked at me. He turned his back and went   26
through the door into the cool beyond. Momma backed up inside
herself for a few minutes. I forgot everything except her face which
was almost a new one to me. She leaned over and took the doorknob,
and in her everyday soft voice she said, "Sister, go on downstairs.
Wait for me. I'll be there directly."

Under the most common of circumstances I knew it did no good 27
to argue with Momma. So I walked down the steep stairs, afraid to
look back and afraid not to do so. I turned as the door slammed, and
she was gone.

Momma walked in that room as if she owned it. She shoved that 28
silly nurse aside with one hand and strode into the dentist's office. He
was sitting in his chair, sharpening his mean instruments and putting
extra sting into his medicines. Her eyes were blazing like live coals
and her arms had doubled themselves in length. He looked up at her
just before she caught him by the collar of his white jacket.

"Stand up when you see a lady, you contemptuous scoundrel." 29
Her tongue had thinned and the words rolled off well enunciated.
Enunciated and sharp like little claps of thunder.

The dentist had no choice but to stand at R.O.T.C. attention. His 30
head dropped after a minute and his voice was humble. "Yes, ma'am,
Mrs. Henderson."

"You knave, do you think you acted like a gentleman, speaking 31
to me like that in front of my granddaughter?" She didn't shake him,
although she had the power. She simply held him upright.

"No, ma'am, Mrs. Henderson." 32

"No, ma'am, Mrs. Henderson, what?" Then she did give him the 33
tiniest of shakes, but because of her strength the action set his head
and arms to shaking loose on the ends of his body. He stuttered much
worse than Uncle Willie. "No, ma'am, Mrs. Henderson, I'm sorry."

With just an edge of her disgust showing, Momma slung him 34
back in his dentist's chair. "Sorry is as sorry does, and you're about
the sorriest dentist I ever laid my eyes on." (She could afford to slip
into the vernacular because she had such eloquent command of En-
glish.)

"I didn't ask you to apologize in front of Marguerite, because I 35
don't want her to know my power, but I order you, now and here-
with. Leave Stamps by sundown."

"Mrs. Henderson, I can't get my equipment . . ." He was shaking 36
terribly now.

"Now, that brings me to my second order. You will never again 37
practice dentistry. Never! When you get settled in your next place,
you will be a vegetarian caring for dogs with the mange, cats with the
cholera and cows with the epizootic. Is that clear?"

The saliva ran down his chin and his eyes filled with tears. "Yes, 38
ma'am. Thank you for not killing me. Thank you, Mrs. Henderson."

Momma pulled herself back from being ten feet tall with eight- 39
foot arms and said, "You're welcome for nothing, you varlet, I
wouldn't waste a killing on the likes of you."

On her way out she waved her handkerchief at the nurse and 40
turned her into a crocus sack of chicken feed.

Momma looked tired when she came down the stairs, but who 41
wouldn't be tired if they had gone through what she had. She came
close to me and adjusted the towel under my jaw (I had forgotten the
toothache; I only knew that she made her hands gentle in order not to
awaken the pain). She took my hand. Her voice never changed.
"Come on, Sister."

I reckoned we were going home where she would concoct a brew 42
to eliminate the pain and maybe give me new teeth too. New teeth
that would grow overnight out of my gums. She led me toward the
drugstore, which was in the opposite direction from the Store. "I'm
taking you to Dentist Baker in Texarkana."

I was glad after all that I had bathed and put on Mum and Cash- 43
mere Bouquet talcum powder. It was a wonderful surprise. My
toothache had quieted to solemn pain, Momma had obliterated the
evil white man, and we were going on a trip to Texarkana, just the
two of us.

On the Greyhound she took an inside seat in the back, and I sat 44
beside her. I was so proud of being her granddaughter and sure that
some of her magic must have come down to me. She asked if I was
scared. I only shook my head and leaned over on her cool brown
upper arm. There was no chance that a dentist, especially a Negro
dentist, would dare hurt me then. Not with Momma there. The trip
was uneventful, except that she put her arm around me, which was
very unusual for Momma to do.

The dentist showed me the medicine and the needle before he 45
deadened my gums, but if he hadn't I wouldn't have worried.
Momma stood right behind him. Her arms were folded and she
checked on everything he did. The teeth were extracted and she
bought me an ice cream cone from the side window of a drug
counter. The trip back to Stamps was quiet, except that I had to spit
into a very small empty snuff can which she had gotten for me and it
was difficult with the bus humping and jerking on our country roads.

At home, I was given a warm salt solution, and when I washed 46
out my mouth I showed Bailey the empty holes, where the clotted
blood sat like filling in a pie crust. He said I was quite brave, and that

was my cue to reveal our confrontation with the peckerwood dentist and Momma's incredible powers.

I had to admit that I didn't hear the conversation, but what else 47 could she have said than what I said she said? What else done? He agreed with my analysis in a lukewarm way, and I happily (after all, I'd been sick) flounced into the Store. Momma was preparing our evening meal and Uncle Willie leaned on the door sill. She gave her version.

"Dentist Lincoln got right uppity. Said he'd rather put his hand 48 in a dog's mouth. And when I reminded him of the favor, he brushed it off like a piece of lint. Well, I sent Sister downstairs and went inside. I hadn't never been in his office before, but I found the door to where he takes out teeth, and him and the nurse was in there thick as thieves. I just stood there till he caught sight of me." Crash bang the pots on the stove. "He jumped just like he was sitting on a pin. He said, 'Annie, I done tole you, I ain't gonna mess around in no niggah's mouth.' I said, 'Somebody's got to do it then,' and he said, 'Take her to Texarkana to the colored dentist' and that's when I said, 'If you paid me my money I could afford to take her.' He said, 'It's all been paid.' I tole him everything but the interest been paid. He said, ''Twasn't no interest.' I said, ''Tis now. I'll take ten dollars as payment in full.' You know, Willie, it wasn't no right thing to do, 'cause I lent that money without thinking about it.

"He tole that little snippety nurse of his'n to give me ten dollars 49 and make me sign a 'paid in full' receipt. She gave it to me and I signed the papers. Even though by rights he was paid up before, I figger, he gonna be that kind of nasty, he gonna have to pay for it."

Momma and her son laughed and laughed over the white man's 50 evilness and her retributive sin.

I preferred, much preferred, my version. 51

QUESTIONS FOR STUDY AND DISCUSSION

1. What is Angelou's purpose in narrating the story she tells? (Glossary: *Purpose*)
2. Compare and contrast the content and style of the interaction between Momma and the dentist that is given in italics with the one given at the end of the narrative. (Glossary: *Comparison and Contrast*)

3. Angelou tells her story chronologically and in the first person. What are the advantages of the first-person narrative? (Glossary: *Point of View*)

4. Identify three similes that Angelou uses in her narrative. Explain how each simile serves her purpose. (Glossary: *Figure of Speech*)

5. Why do you suppose Angelou says she prefers her own version of the episode to that of her grandmother?

6. This story is a story of pain and not just the pain of a toothache. How does Angelou describe the pain of the toothache? What other pain does Angelou tell of in this autobiographical narrative?

VOCABULARY

Refer to your dictionary to define the following words as they are used in this selection. Then use each word in a sentence of your own.

bailiwick (1)	varlet (39)
calaboose (7)	concoct (42)
mite (22)	snippety (49)
vernacular (34)	retributive (50)

CLASSROOM ACTIVITY USING NARRATION

One of Angelou's themes in "Momma, the Dentist, and Me" is that cruelty, whether racial, social, professional, or personal, is very difficult to endure and leaves a lasting impression on a person. As a way of practicing chronological order, consider a situation in which an unthinking or insensitive person made you feel inferior. Rather than write a draft of an essay at this point, simply list the sequence of events that occurred, in chronological order. Once you have completed this step, consider whether there is a more dramatic order you might use if you were actually to write an essay.

SUGGESTED WRITING ASSIGNMENTS

1. Using Angelou's essay as a model, give two versions of an actual event — one the way you thought or wished it had happened, and the other the way events actually took place. You may want to refer to your journal entry for this reading.

2. Every person who tells a story does so by putting his or her signature on it in some way—by the sequencing of events, the amount and type of details used, and the tone the teller of the story employs. If you and a relative or friend experienced the same interesting sequence of events, try telling the story of those events from your unique perspective. Once you have done so, try telling the story from what you imagine the other person's perspective to be. Perhaps you even heard the other person actually tell the story. What is the same in both versions? How do the renditions differ?

The Story of an Hour

■ Kate Chopin

Kate Chopin (1851–1904) was born in St. Louis, of Creole Irish descent. After her marriage she lived in Louisiana, where she acquired the intimate knowledge of Creole Cajun culture that provided the impetus for much of her work and earned her a reputation as a writer who captured the ambience of the bayou region. When her first novel, The Awakening *(1899), was published, however, it generated scorn and outrage for its explicit depiction of a southern woman's sexual awakening. Only recently has Chopin been recognized for her literary talent and originality. Besides* The Awakening, *her works include two collections of short fiction,* Bayou Folk *(1894) and* A Night in Acadie *(1897). In 1969,* The Complete Works of Kate Chopin *was published by Louisiana State University Press. As you read the selection below, try to gauge how your reactions to Mrs. Mallard are influenced by Chopin's use of third-person narration.*

FOR YOUR JOURNAL

How do you react to the idea of marriage—committing to someone for life? What are the advantages of such a union? What are the disadvantages?

K nowing that Mrs. Mallard was afflicted with a heart trouble, great care was taken to break to her as gently as possible the news of her husband's death. 1

It was her sister Josephine who told her, in broken sentences; veiled hints that revealed in half concealing. Her husband's friend Richards was there, too, near her. It was he who had been in the newspaper office when intelligence of the railroad disaster was received, with Brently Mallard's name leading the list of "killed." He had only taken the time to assure himself of its truth by a second telegram, and had hastened to forestall any less careful, less tender friend in bearing the sad message. 2

She did not hear the story as many women have heard the same, with a paralyzed inability to accept its significance. She wept at once, 3 with sudden, wild abandonment, in her sister's arms. When the storm of grief had spent itself she went away to her room alone. She would have no one follow her.

There stood, facing the open window, a comfortable, roomy 4 armchair. Into this she sank, pressed down by a physical exhaustion that haunted her body and seemed to reach into her soul.

She could see in the open square before her house the tops of 5 trees that were all aquiver with the new spring life. The delicious breath of rain was in the air. In the street below a peddler was crying his wares. The notes of a distant song which someone was singing reached her faintly, and countless sparrows were twittering in the eaves.

There were patches of blue sky showing here and there through 6 the clouds that had met and piled one above the other in the west facing her window.

She sat with her head thrown back upon the cushion of the chair, 7 quite motionless, except when a sob came up into her throat and shook her, as a child who has cried itself to sleep continues to sob in its dreams.

She was young, with a fair, calm face, whose lines bespoke re- 8 pression and even a certain strength. But now there was a dull stare in her eyes, whose gaze was fixed away off yonder on one of those patches of blue sky. It was not a glance of reflection, but rather indicated a suspension of intelligent thought.

There was something coming to her and she was waiting for it, 9 fearfully. What was it? She did not know; it was too subtle and elusive to name. But she felt it, creeping out of the sky, reaching toward her through the sounds, the scents, the color that filled the air.

Now her bosom rose and fell tumultuously. She was beginning to 10 recognize this thing that was approaching to possess her, and she was striving to beat it back with her will—as powerless as her two white slender hands would have been.

When she abandoned herself a little whispered word escaped her 11 slightly parted lips. She said it over and over under her breath: "free, free, free!" The vacant stare and the look of terror that had followed it went from her eyes. They stayed keen and bright. Her pulses beat fast, and the coursing blood warmed and relaxed every inch of her body.

She did not stop to ask if it were or were not a monstrous joy 12 that held her. A clear and exalted perception enabled her to dismiss the suggestion as trivial.

She knew that she would weep again when she saw the kind, ten- 13
der hands folded in death; the face that had never looked save with
love upon her, fixed and gray and dead. But she saw beyond that bitter moment a long procession of years to come that would belong to
her absolutely. And she opened and spread her arms out to them in
welcome.

There would be no one to live for her during those coming years; 14
she would live for herself. There would be no powerful will bending
hers in that blind persistence with which men and women believe
they have a right to impose a private will upon a fellow-creature. A
kind intention or a cruel intention made the act seem no less a crime
as she looked upon it in that brief moment of illumination.

And yet she had loved him—sometimes. Often she had not. 15
What did it matter! What could love, the unsolved mystery, count for
in face of this possession of self-assertion which she suddenly recognized as the strongest impulse of her being!

"Free! Body and soul free!" she kept whispering. 16

Josephine was kneeling before the closed door with her lips to the 17
keyhole, imploring for admission. "Louise, open the door! I beg;
open the door—you will make yourself ill. What are you doing,
Louise? For heaven's sake open the door."

"Go away. I am not making myself ill." No; she was drinking in 18
a very elixir of life through that open window.

Her fancy was running riot along those days ahead of her. Spring 19
days, and summer days, and all sorts of days that would be her own.
She breathed a quick prayer that life might be long. It was only yesterday she had thought with a shudder that life might be long.

She arose at length and opened the door to her sister's importuni- 20
ties. There was a feverish triumph in her eyes, and she carried herself
unwittingly like a goddess of Victory. She clasped her sister's waist,
and together they descended the stairs. Richards stood waiting for
them at the bottom.

Some one was opening the front door with a latchkey. It was 21
Brently Mallard who entered, a little travel-stained, composedly carrying his grip-sack and umbrella. He had been far from the scene of
the accident, and did not even know there had been one. He stood
amazed at Josephine's piercing cry; at Richards' quick motion to
screen him from the view of his wife.

But Richards was too late. 22

When the doctors came they said she had died of heart disease— 23
of joy that kills.

QUESTIONS FOR STUDY AND DISCUSSION

1. What assumptions do Mrs. Mallard's relatives and friends make about her feelings toward her husband? How would you describe her true feelings?

2. Reread paragraphs 5–9. What is Chopin's purpose in this section of the story? (Glossary: *Purpose*) Do these paragraphs add to the story's effectiveness? Why, or why not?

3. Why does Mrs. Mallard fight her feeling of freedom, however briefly?

4. All of the events of this story take place in an hour. Would the story be as poignant if they had taken place over the course of a day, or even several days? Explain. Why do you suppose the author selected the time frame as a title for her story? (Glossary: *Title*)

5. Chopin could have written an essay detailing the oppression of women in marriage, but she chose instead to write a fictional narrative. This allows her to show readers the type of situation that can arise in an outwardly happy marriage, rather than tell them about it. Why else do you think she chose to write a fictional narrative? What other advantages does it give her over nonfiction?

6. Why do you suppose Chopin chose to narrate her story in the third person?

VOCABULARY

Refer to your dictionary to define the following words as they are used in this selection. Then use each word in a sentence of your own.

afflicted (1)	exalted (12)
aquiver (5)	imploring (17)
bespoke (8)	elixir (18)
tumultuously (10)	importunities (20)

CLASSROOM ACTIVITY USING NARRATION

Using cues in the following sentences, rearrange them into chronological order.

1. The sky was gray and gloomy for as far as she could see, and sleet hissed off the glass.

2. "Oh, hi, I'm glad you called," she said happily, but her smile dimmed when she looked outside.

3. As Betty crossed the room, the phone rang, startling her.

4. "No, the weather's awful, so I don't think I'll get out to visit you today," she sighed.

5. "Hello," she said, and she wandered over to the window, dragging the phone cord behind her.

Write five sentences of your own that cover a progression of events. Try to include dialogue. Then scramble them and see if a classmate can put them back into the correct order.

SUGGESTED WRITING ASSIGNMENTS

1. Using Chopin's story as a model, write a short piece of narrative fiction in which your main character reacts to a specific, dramatic event. Portray the character's emotional response, as well as how the character perceives his or her surroundings—what does the character see, hear, touch? How are these senses affected by the situation?

2. Write a narrative essay in which you describe your reaction to a piece of news that you once received—good or bad—that provoked a strong emotional response. What were your emotions? What did you do in the couple of hours after you received the news? How did your perceptions of the world around you change? What made the experience memorable?

---

chapter **12**

Description

To describe is to create a verbal picture. A person, a place, a thing—even an idea or a state of mind—can be made vividly concrete through description. Here, for example, is Thomas Mann's brief description of a delicatessen:

> It was a narrow room, with a rather high ceiling, and crowded from floor to ceiling with goodies. There were rows and rows of hams and sausages of all shapes and colors—white, yellow, red, and black; fat and lean and round and long—rows of canned preserves, cocoa and tea, bright translucent glass bottles of honey, marmalade, and jam; round bottles and slender bottles, filled with liqueurs and punch—all these things crowded every inch of the shelves from top to bottom.

Writing any description requires, first of all, that the writer gather many details about a subject, relying not only on what the eyes see but on the other sense impressions—touch, taste, smell, hearing—as well. From this catalog of details the writer selects those that will most effectively create a *dominant impression*—the single quality, mood, or atmosphere that the writer wishes to emphasize. Consider, for example, the details that Mary McCarthy uses to evoke the dominant impression in the following passage from *Memories of a Catholic Girlhood*, and contrast them with those in the subsequent example, by student Dan Bubany:

> Whenever we children came to stay at my grandmother's house, we were put to sleep in the sewing room, a bleak, shabby, utilitarian rectangle, more office than bedroom, more attic than office, that played to the hierarchy of chambers the role of poor relation. It was a room without pride: the old sewing machine, some cast-off chairs, a shadeless lamp, rolls of wrapping paper, piles of cardboard boxes that might someday come in handy, papers of

pins, and remnants of a material united with the iron folding cots put out for our use and the bare floor boards to give an impression of intense and ruthless temporality. Thin white spreads, of the kind used in hospitals and charity institutions, and naked blinds at the windows reminded us of our orphaned condition and of the ephemeral character of our visit; there was nothing here to encourage us to consider this our home.

> For this particular Thursday game against Stanford, Fleming wears white gloves, a maroon sport coat with brass buttons, and gray slacks. Shiny silver-framed bifocals match the whistle pressed between the lips on his slightly wrinkled face, and he wears freshly polished black shoes so glossy that they reflect the grass he stands on. He is not fat, but his coat neatly conceals a small, round pot belly.

The dominant impression that McCarthy creates is one of clutter, bleakness, and shabbiness. There is nothing in the sewing room that suggests permanence or warmth. Bubany, on the other hand, creates a dominant impression of a neat, kindly man.

Writers must also carefully plan the order in which to present their descriptive details. The pattern of organization must fit the subject of the description logically and naturally and must also be easy to follow. For example, visual details can be arranged spatially—from left to right, top to bottom, near to far, or in any other logical order. Other patterns include smallest to largest, softest to loudest, least significant to most significant, most unusual to least unusual. McCarthy, for example, suggests a jumble of junk not only by her choice of details but by the apparently random order in which she presents them.

How much detail is enough? There is no fixed answer. A good description includes enough vivid details to create a dominant impression and to bring a scene to life, but not so many that readers are distracted, confused, or bored. In an essay that is purely descriptive, there is room for much detail. Usually, however, writers use description to create the setting for a story, to illustrate ideas, to help clarify a definition or a comparison, or to make the complexities of a process more understandable. Such descriptions should be kept short and should include just enough detail to make them clear and helpful.

Subway Station

■ Gilbert Highet

*Gilbert Highet (1906–1978) was born in Scotland and became a
naturalized U.S. citizen in 1951. A prolific writer and translator,
Highet was for many years a professor of classics at Columbia
University, as well as a popular radio essayist. The following selection is from his book* Talents and Geniuses (1957). *Take note
of Highet's keen eye for detail as you read. Concrete and vivid
images help him re-create the unseemly world of a subway
station.*

FOR YOUR JOURNAL

Try to remember what it is like to be in a subway station, airport,
or bus station. What are the sights, sounds, and smells you recall?
What do you remember most about any of these crowded, transient places? What was your overall impression of the place?

Standing in a subway station, I began to appreciate the place—almost to enjoy it. First of all, I looked at the lighting: a row of
meager electric bulbs, unscreened, yellow, and coated with filth,
stretched toward the black mouth of the tunnel, as though it were a
bolt hole in an abandoned coal mine. Then I lingered, with zest, on
the walls and ceiling: lavatory tiles which had been white about fifty
years ago, and were now encrusted with soot, coated with the remains of a dirty liquid which might be either atmospheric humidity
mingled with smog or the result of a perfunctory attempt to clean
them with cold water; and, above them, gloomy vaulting from which
dingy paint was peeling off like scabs from an old wound, sick black
paint leaving a leprous white undersurface. Beneath my feet, the floor
was a nauseating dark brown with black stains upon it which might
be stale oil or dry chewing gum or some worse defilement; it looked
like the hallway of a condemned slum building. Then my eye traveled
to the tracks, where two lines of glittering steel—the only positively
clean objects in the whole place—ran out of darkness into darkness
above an unspeakable mass of congealed oil, puddles of dubious
liquid, and a mishmash of old cigarette packets, mutilated and filthy

newspapers, and the débris that filtered down from the street above through a barred grating in the roof. As I looked up toward the sunlight, I could see more débris sifting slowly downward, and making an abominable pattern in the slanting beam of dirt-laden sunlight. I was going on to relish more features of this unique scene: such as the advertisement posters on the walls — here a text from the Bible, there a half-naked girl, here a woman wearing a hat consisting of a hen sitting on a nest full of eggs, and there a pair of girl's legs walking up the keys of a cash register — all scribbled over with unknown names and well-known obscenities in black crayon and red lipstick; but then my train came in at last, I boarded it, and began to read. The experience was over for the time.

QUESTIONS FOR STUDY AND DISCUSSION

1. What dominant impression does Highet create in his description? (Glossary: *Dominant Impression*) Make a list of the details that help Highet create his dominant impression.

2. Why do you think Highet observes the subway station with "zest" and "relish"? What does he find appealing about the experience?

3. What similes and metaphors can you find in Highet's description? How do they help to make the description vivid? (Glossary: *Figure of Speech*)

4. What mix of advertisements does Highet observe? Based on Highet's description of what they depict, their current appearance, and the atmosphere of their surroundings, suggest what product each poster might be advertising. Explain your suggestions.

5. Highet has an eye for detail that is usually displayed by those who are seeing something for the first time. Do you think it is his first time in a subway station, or is he a regular rider who is taking time out to "relish" his physical surroundings? What in the essay leads you to your conclusion?

VOCABULARY

Refer to your dictionary to define the following words as they are used in this selection. Then use each word in a sentence of your own.

perfunctory   dubious
leprous   abominable
defilement

CLASSROOM ACTIVITY USING DESCRIPTION

Make a long list of the objects and people in your classroom as well as the physical features of the classroom—desks, windows, blackboard, students, professor, dirty walls, burned-out lightbulb, a clock that is always ten minutes fast, and so on. Determine a dominant impression that you would like to create in describing the classroom. Now choose from your list those items that would best illustrate the dominant impression you have chosen. Your instructor may wish to have students compare their responses.

SUGGESTED WRITING ASSIGNMENTS

1. Using Highet's essay as a model, write an extended one-paragraph description of a room in your house or apartment where you do not spend much time. Spend some time observing the details in the room. Before you write, decide on the dominant impression you wish to communicate to the reader.

2. Write a short essay in which you describe one of the following places or another place of your choice. Arrange the details of your description from top to bottom, left to right, near to far, or according to some other spatial organization.

a closet	a barbershop or beauty salon
a pizza parlor	a bookstore
a locker room	a campus dining hall

The Sounds of the City

■ James Tuite

James Tuite had a long career at the New York Times, *where he once served as sports editor. As a freelance writer he has contributed to all of the major sports magazines and has written* Snowmobiles and Snowmobiling *(1973) and* How to Enjoy Sports on TV *(1976). The following selection is a model of how a place can be described by using a sense other than sight. Tuite describes New York City by its sounds, which for him comprise the very life of the city.*

FOR YOUR JOURNAL

Sit in a relatively busy place—your dormitory lounge, a campus eatery, a science laboratory, a classroom as it begins to fill with students for your next class. Close your eyes, and try to take in all the sounds you hear for approximately 20 seconds. Record in your journal what you have heard. Then listen again for another 20 seconds and record again. Repeat this process five or six times. Finally, make a journal entry describing the place you chose, using only the sounds that you have heard.

N ew York is a city of sounds: muted sounds and shrill sounds; 1
shattering sounds and soothing sounds; urgent sounds and aim- less sounds. The cliff dwellers of Manhattan—who would be racked by the silence of the lonely woods—do not hear these sounds be- cause they are constant and eternally urban.

The visitor to the city can hear them, though, just as some ani- 2
mals can hear a high-pitched whistle inaudible to humans. To the ca- sual caller to Manhattan, lying restive and sleepless in a hotel twenty or thirty floors above the street, they tell a story as fascinating as life itself. And back of the sounds broods the silence.

Night in midtown is the noise of tinseled honky-tonk and vio- 3
lence. Thin strains of music, usually the firm beat of rock 'n' roll or the frenzied outbursts of the discotheque, rise from ground level. This is the cacophony, the discordance of youth, and it comes on strongest when nights are hot and young blood restless.

Somewhere in the canyons below there is shrill laughter or raucous shouting. A bottle shatters against concrete. The whine of a police siren slices through the night, moving ever closer, until an eerie Doppler effect[1] brings it to a guttural halt.   4

There are few sounds so exciting in Manhattan as those of fire apparatus dashing through the night. At the outset there is the tentative hint of the first-due company bullying his way through midtown traffic. Now a fire whistle from the opposite direction affirms that trouble is, indeed, afoot. In seconds, other sirens converging from other streets help the skytop listener focus on the scene of excitement.   5

But he can only hear and not see, and imagination takes flight. Are the flames and smoke gushing from windows not far away? Are victims trapped there, crying out for help? Is it a conflagration, or only a trash-basket fire? Or, perhaps, it is merely a false alarm.   6

The questions go unanswered and the urgency of the moment dissolves. Now the mind and the ear detect the snarling, arrogant bickering of automobile horns. People in a hurry. Taxicabs blaring, insisting on their checkered priority.   7

Even the taxi horns dwindle down to a precocious few in the gray and pink moments of dawn. Suddenly there is another sound, a morning sound that taunts the memory for recognition. The growl of a predatory monster? No, just garbage trucks that have begun a day of scavenging.   8

Trash cans rattle outside restaurants. Metallic jaws on sanitation trucks gulp and masticate the residue of daily living, then digest it with a satisfied groan of gears. The sounds of the new day are businesslike. The growl of buses, so scattered and distant at night, becomes a demanding part of the traffic bedlam. An occasional jet or helicopter injects an exclamation point from an unexpected quarter. When the wind is right, the vibrant bellow of an ocean liner can be heard.   9

The sounds of the day are as jarring as the glare of a sun that outlines the canyons of midtown in drab relief. A pneumatic drill frays countless nerves with its rat-a-tat-tat, for dig they must to perpetuate the city's dizzy motion. After each screech of brakes there is a moment of suspension, of waiting for the thud or crash that never seems to follow.   10

---

[1] The drop in pitch that occurs as a source of sound quickly passes by a listener

The whistles of traffic policemen and hotel doormen chirp from 11
all sides, like birds calling for their mates across a frenzied aviary.
And all of these sounds are adult sounds, for childish laughter has no
place in these canyons.

Night falls again, the cycle is complete, but there is no surcease 12
from sound. For the beautiful dreamers, perhaps, the "sounds of the
rude world heard in the day, lulled by the moonlight have all passed
away," but this is not so in the city.

Too many New Yorkers accept the sounds about them as bland 13
parts of everyday existence. They seldom stop to listen to the sounds,
to think about them, to be appalled or enchanted by them. In the big
city, sounds are life.

QUESTIONS FOR STUDY AND DISCUSSION

1. In your opinion, what is Tuite's main purpose in describing the
   sounds of New York City? (Glossary: *Purpose*)

2. What dominant impression of New York City does Tuite create
   in his essay? (Glossary: *Dominant Impression*)

3. Tuite describes "raucous shouting" (4) and the "screech of
   brakes" (10). Make a list of the various sounds that he describes
   in his essay. How do the varied adjectives and verbs Tuite uses to
   capture the essence of each sound enhance his description? (Glossary: *Diction*)

4. According to Tuite, why are visitors to New York City more sensitive to or aware of the multitude of sounds than the "cliff
   dwellers of Manhattan" (1)? What does he believe that New
   Yorkers have missed when they fail to take notice of these
   sounds?

5. Locate several metaphors and similes in the essay. What picture
   of the city does each give you? (Glossary: *Figure of Speech*)

6. How does Tuite organize his essay? Do you think the organization is effective? (Glossary: *Organization*)

VOCABULARY

Refer to your dictionary to define the following words as they are
used in this selection. Then use each word in a sentence of your own.

muted (1)   precocious (8)

inaudible (2)   taunts (8)

restive (2)   vibrant (9)

raucous (4)   perpetuate (10)

tentative (5)

CLASSROOM ACTIVITY USING DESCRIPTION

Write five sentences describing the place you would most like to go. What details about the place do you want to include? Choose your words carefully so that you create the dominant impression that you have of that place—beautiful, dangerous, serene, fun, relaxing, etc.

SUGGESTED WRITING ASSIGNMENTS

1. As Tuite has done, write a short composition describing a city you know well. Try to include as many sights, sounds, and smells as you can in your description. Your goal should be to create a single dominant impression of the city.

2. Describe a familiar inanimate object in a way that brings out its character and makes it interesting to the reader. First, determine your purpose in describing the object. Suppose, for example, your family has had the same dining table for as long as you can remember. Think of what that table has been a part of over the years—the birthday parties, the fights, the holiday meals, the long hours of studying and doing homework. A description of such a table would give your reader a sense of the history of your family. Next, make an exhaustive list of the object's physical features, and include in your descriptive essay the features that contribute to a dominant impression and support your purpose in writing the essay.

Unforgettable Miss Bessie

■ **Carl T. Rowan**

In addition to being a popular syndicated newspaper columnist, Carl T. Rowan is a former ambassador to Finland and director of the U.S. Information Agency. Born in 1925 in Ravenscroft, Tennessee, he received degrees from Oberlin College and the University of Minnesota. He worked as a columnist for the Min-neapolis Tribune *and the* Chicago Sun-Times *before moving to Washington, D.C., where he lives today. In 1991, Rowan published* Breaking Barriers: A Memoir. *His most recent book,* The Coming Race War in America, *appeared in 1996. In the following essay, he describes a high school teacher whose lessons went far beyond the subjects she taught. After reading the details Rowan presents about Miss Bessie's background, behavior, and appearance, determine what kind of dominant impression of Miss Bessie he leaves you with.*

FOR YOUR JOURNAL

Perhaps you have at some time taught a friend or younger brother or sister how to do something—tie a shoe, hit a ball, read, solve a puzzle, drive a car—but you never thought of yourself as a teacher. Did you enjoy the experience of sharing what you know with someone else? Would you consider becoming a teacher someday?

She was only about five feet tall and probably never weighed more   1
than 110 pounds, but Miss Bessie was a towering presence in the classroom. She was the only woman tough enough to make me read *Beowulf* and think for a few foolish days that I liked it. From 1938 to 1942, when I attended Bernard High School in McMinnville, Tenn., she taught me English, history, civics—and a lot more than I realized.

I shall never forget the day she scolded me into reading *Beowulf*.   2
"But Miss Bessie," I complained, "I ain't much interested in it."   3
Her large brown eyes became daggerish slits. "Boy," she said,   4
"how dare you say 'ain't' to me! I've taught you better than that."

296

"Miss Bessie," I pleaded, "I'm trying to make first-string end on   5
the football team, and if I go around saying 'it isn't' and 'they aren't,'
the guys are gonna laugh me off the squad."

"Boy," she responded, "you'll play football because you have   6
guts. But do you know what *really* takes guts? Refusing to lower
your standards to those of the crowd. It takes guts to say you've got
to live and be somebody fifty years after all the football games are
over."

I started saying "it isn't" and "they aren't," and I still made first-   7
string end—and class valedictorian—without losing my buddies' respect.

During her remarkable 44-year career, Mrs. Bessie Taylor   8
Gwynn taught hundreds of economically deprived black youngsters—including my mother, my brother, my sisters and me. I remember her now with gratitude and affection—especially in this era
when Americans are so wrought-up about a "rising tide of medioc-
rity" in public education and the problems of finding competent, caring teachers. Miss Bessie was an example of an informed, dedicated
teacher, a blessing to children and an asset to the nation.

Born in 1895, in poverty, she grew up in Athens, Ala., where   9
there was no public school for blacks. She attended Trinity School, a
private institution for blacks run by the American Missionary Association, and in 1911 graduated from the Normal School (a "super"
high school) at Fisk University in Nashville. Mrs. Gwynn, the essence
of pride and privacy, never talked about her years in Athens; only in
the months before her death did she reveal that she had never attended Fisk University itself because she could not afford the four-
year course.

At Normal School she learned a lot about Shakespeare, but most   10
of all about the profound importance of education—especially, for a
people trying to move up from slavery. "What you put in your head,
boy," she once said, "can never be pulled out by the Ku Klux Klan,
the Congress or anybody."

Miss Bessie's bearing of dignity told anyone who met her that she   11
was "educated" in the best sense of the word. There was never a discipline problem in her classes. We didn't dare mess with a woman
who knew about the Battle of Hastings, the Magna Carta and the Bill
of Rights—and who could also play the piano.

This frail-looking woman could make sense of Shakespeare,   12
Milton, Voltaire, and bring to life Booker T. Washington and

W. E. B. Du Bois. Believing that it was important to know who the officials were that spent taxpayers' money and made public policy, she made us memorize the names of everyone on the Supreme Court and in the President's Cabinet. It could be embarrassing to be unprepared when Miss Bessie said, "Get up and tell the class who Frances Perkins is and what you think about her."

Miss Bessie knew that my family, like so many others during the Depression, couldn't afford to subscribe to a newspaper. She knew we didn't even own a radio. Still, she prodded me to "look out for your future and find some way to keep up with what's going on in the world." So I became a delivery boy for the Chattanooga *Times*. I rarely made a dollar a week, but I got to read a newspaper every day. 13

Miss Bessie noticed things that had nothing to do with schoolwork, but were vital to a youngster's development. Once a few classmates made fun of my frayed, hand-me-down overcoat, calling me "Strings." As I was leaving school, Miss Bessie patted me on the back of that old overcoat and said, "Carl, never fret about what you *don't* have. Just make the most of what you *do* have—a brain." 14

Among the things that I did not have was electricity in the little frame house that my father had built for $400 with his World War I bonus. But because of her inspiration, I spent many hours squinting beside a kerosene lamp reading Shakespeare and Thoreau, Samuel Pepys and William Cullen Bryant. 15

No one in my family had ever graduated from high school, so there was no tradition of commitment to learning for me to lean on. Like millions of youngsters in today's ghettos and barrios, I needed the push and stimulation of a teacher who truly cared. Miss Bessie gave plenty of both, as she immersed me in a wonderful world of similes, metaphors and even onomatopoeia. She led me to believe that I could write sonnets as well as Shakespeare, or iambic-pentameter verse to put Alexander Pope to shame. 16

In those days the McMinnville school system was rigidly "Jim Crow," and poor black children had to struggle to put anything in their heads. Our high school was only slightly larger than the once-typical little red schoolhouse, and its library was outrageously inadequate—so small, I like to say, that if two students were in it and one wanted to turn a page, the other one had to step outside. 17

Negroes, as we were called then, were not allowed in the town library, except to mop floors or dust tables. But through one of those secret Old South arrangements between whites of conscience and blacks of stature, Miss Bessie kept getting books smuggled out of the 18 white library. That is how she introduced me to the Brontës, Byron, Coleridge, Keats and Tennyson. "If you don't read, you can't write, and if you can't write, you might as well stop dreaming," Miss Bessie once told me.

So I read whatever Miss Bessie told me to, and tried to remember 19
the things she insisted that I store away. Forty-five years later, I can still recite her "truths to live by," such as Henry Wadsworth Longfellow's lines from "The Ladder of St. Augustine":

> The heights by great men reached and kept
> Were not attained by sudden flight.
> But they, while their companions slept,
> Were toiling upward in the night.

Years later, her inspiration, prodding, anger, cajoling and almost 20
osmotic infusion of learning finally led to that lovely day when Miss Bessie dropped me a note saying, "I'm so proud to read your column in the Nashville *Tennessean*."

Miss Bessie was a spry 80 when I went back to McMinnville and 21
visited her in a senior citizens' apartment building. Pointing out proudly that her building was racially integrated, she reached for two glasses and a pint of bourbon. I was momentarily shocked, because it would have been scandalous in the 1930s and '40s for word to get out that a teacher drank, and nobody had ever raised a rumor that Miss Bessie did.

I felt a new sense of equality as she lifted her glass to mine. Then 22
she revealed a softness and compassion that I had never known as a student.

"I've never forgotten that examination day," she said, "when 23
Buster Martin held up seven fingers, obviously asking you for help with question number seven, 'Name a common carrier.' I can still picture you looking at your exam paper and humming a few bars of 'Chattanooga Choo Choo.' I was so tickled, I couldn't punish either of you."

Miss Bessie was telling me, with bourbon-laced grace, that I 24
never fooled her for a moment.

When Miss Bessie died in 1980, at age 85, hundreds of her for- 25
mer students mourned. They knew the measure of a great teacher: love and motivation. Her wisdom and influence had rippled out across generations.

Some of her students who might normally have been doomed to 26
poverty went on to become doctors, dentists and college professors.

Many, guided by Miss Bessie's example, became public-school teachers.

"The memory of Miss Bessie and how she conducted her class- 27 room did more for me than anything I learned in college," recalls Gladys Wood of Knoxville, Tenn., a highly respected English teacher who spent 43 years in the state's school system. "So many times, when I faced a difficult classroom problem, I asked myself, *How would Miss Bessie deal with this?* And I'd remember that she would handle it with laughter and love."

No child can get all the necessary support at home, and millions 28 of poor children get *no* support at all. This is what makes a wise, educated, warm-hearted teacher like Miss Bessie so vital to the minds, hearts and souls of this country's children.

QUESTIONS FOR STUDY AND DISCUSSION

1. Throughout the essay Rowan offers details of Miss Bessie's physical appearance. (Glossary: *Details*) What specific details does he give, and in what context does he give them? Did Miss Bessie's physical characteristics match the quality of her character? Explain.

2. How would you sum up the character of Miss Bessie? Make a list of the key words that Rowan uses that you feel best describe her.

3. At what point in the essay does Rowan give us the details of Miss Bessie's background? Why do you suppose he delays giving us this important information? (Glossary: *Beginnings and Endings*)

4. How does dialogue serve Rowan's purpose? (Glossary: *Dialogue*)

5. Does Miss Bessie's drinking influence your opinion of her? Explain. Why do you think Rowan included this part of her behavior in his essay?

6. In his opening paragraph Rowan states that Miss Bessie "taught me English, history, civics—and a lot more than I realized." What did she teach her students beyond the traditional public school curriculum?

VOCABULARY

Refer to your dictionary to define the following words as they are used in this selection. Then use each word in a sentence of your own.

civics (1)   cajoling (20)
barrios (16)   osmotic (20)
conscience (18)   measure (25)

CLASSROOM ACTIVITY USING DESCRIPTION

The verbs you use in writing a description can themselves convey much descriptive information. Take, for example, the verb *think*. This word actually tells us little more than the general sense of "mental activity." Using more precise and descriptive alternatives — *ponder, conceive, imagine, picture, muse, consider, contemplate, cogitate, ruminate, meditate* — could easily enhance your descriptive powers and enliven your writing. For each of the following verbs, make a list of at least six descriptive alternatives:

go   throw   exercise
see   take   study
say   drink

SUGGESTED WRITING ASSIGNMENTS

1. In paragraph 18, Rowan writes the following: "'If you don't read, you can't write, and if you can't write, you might as well stop dreaming,' Miss Bessie once told me." Write an essay in which you explore this theme (which, in essence, is also the theme of *Models for Writers*).

2. Think of all the teachers you have had, and write a description of the one who has had the greatest influence on you. Remember to give some consideration to the balance you want to achieve between physical attributes and personality traits.

Grocer's Daughter

■ **Marianne Wiggins**

Marianne Wiggins was born in 1947 in Lancaster, Pennsylvania. She is the author of several novels and collections of short stories, most of which depict women who challenge traditional roles assigned to them by society. Her most recent novel, Almost Heaven, *was published in 1999. "Grocer's Daughter," which appeared in her book* Bet They'll Miss Us When We're Gone *(1991), is both a tribute to and a description of her father; it also reveals important aspects of her own childhood. You may detect an apparently haphazard organizational pattern in Wiggins's presentation of details and her arrangement of paragraphs, but consider how the essay's structure may be appropriate to her purpose.*

FOR YOUR JOURNAL

Think about an important person, place, or object in your life. What are its manifestations or traits — what do your sight, hearing, taste, touch, and smell reveal about the subject? Consider whether such sense impressions tell the whole story of that person, place, or object. Is there more to know? If so, what might it be and how do you think you might be able to reveal it in writing?

I am shameless in the way I love my father. 1

Like little girls who ride big horses, big girls who hold their fa- 2 thers in devotion are talked about in overtones of sexual pathology. Love is always judged. No one's love is like another's. What I feel is mine, alone. If my heart is in my mouth, and if I speak it, judgment comes. Surviving judgment, like admitting love, takes courage. Here is what John Wiggins taught me:

The moon at crescent is God's fingernail.

When your shelves look empty, stack your canned goods toward the front.

Keep your feet off other people's furniture.

Don't lean your belly on the scale weighing out the produce, or the devil will tip it his way when your time comes.

Take anybody's check.

Go nowhere in a hurry.

Sing.

Take your hat off inside churches and in the rain, when the spirit moves you.

Don't wax cucumbers.

Don't sleep late on Sundays.

Start each week with gratitude and six clean aprons.

    He was born in Pennsylvania, died in the woods and never, to my   3 knowledge, saw an island. He sunburned easily. He wore a yellow pencil stub behind his ear for jotting orders. He was so accustomed to jotting grocery orders on a pad for a clerk to read, he lost his longhand. The supermarkets in the suburbs squeezed him out. We moved a lot. Each time we moved, the house got smaller, things we didn't need got sold. We didn't need his army helmet or the cardboard notebooks, black and white, in which he'd learned to write. One can't save everything. One trims the fat, one trims the lettuce: produce, when it comes in crates from Florida, needs trimming. For years I saved the only letter he'd written in his lifetime to me. He'd printed it, of course, so there'd be no misunderstanding in the way a pen can curve a word. I lost that letter in my latest move. It's said three moves are like a single fire in their power to destroy one's camp. We moved nine times before I was eighteen. I search in vain, sometimes, for anything my father might have touched.

    He always liked a good laugh; his jokes weren't always funny.   4 He concocted odd pranks. He scared my mother half to death one year, when they were first married, by burglarizing their apartment. He rigged a water bucket on his sister's bedroom door the night of her first date: that was 1939, when cotton dresses took half an hour's pressing and a girl might spend an afternoon wrapping dark hair on a curling iron. To my mother, who gets dizzy looking in round mirrors, he wrote love letters that germinated from the center of the page and spiraled out. Those days, he still wrote in script. I think I could identify his longhand, if need be. Handwriting speaks. I think I could remember his.

    I remember what his footsteps sounded like: heavier on one leg   5 than the other, made the change rattle in his pocket. He always carried change, most grocers did, because the kids would come in to buy cookies from the bin with pennies and their pennies crowded up the cash drawer. Year in, year out, he wore pleated pants in dark colors. He had three good suits—one gray, one black, one brown. I see him in them in the photographs. The gray one took a lot of coaxing from my mother and wasn't often worn. Every year for Christmas he received:

six new pairs of black socks
six new undershirts
six pairs of boxer shorts
two new sweater vests
six white shirts
six aprons
one subdued pastel shirt from me
one knit tie from my sister

6 The year I knew there was no Santa Claus was the year he fell asleep beneath the Christmas tree assembling my sister's tricycle.

7 His favorite pie was something only Grandma Wiggins made: butterscotch custard. Even when my sister and I were kids and loved sweet things, its sweetness made our teeth hurt. I never knew his favorite color. I think he must have had a favorite song, I never knew it, he was always singing, had a song for each occasion, favored "Someone's in the Kitchen with Dinah" while he was washing dishes and "Oh Promise Me" while he was driving in the car. Sometimes, early in the mornings, he'd sing "Buckle Down, Winsocki." I used to think Winsocki was as funny-sounding a name as that of his favorite politician, Wendell Wilkie. He liked FDR, hated Truman, voted for Dwight Eisenhower. By 1960, I was old enough to reason through my parents' pig Latin and moderately schooled in spelling, so everything they had to say in front of me, they couldn't code. My father was Republican, my mother fell for Kennedy's charisma. "Who did you vote for, John?" my mother asked him that November.

8 "Mary," my father answered, needing to be secret. "What do you think that curtain in the voting booth is for—?"

9 "What the hell," he told me later. "If I'd voted like I wanted to, your mother and me, we would have canceled one another out. What's the point of voting like you want to when you know that you'll be canceled out?"

I wonder if he ever dreamed that he could change things. He taught   10
me how to pitch softball. We played croquet in the front yard. He
taught me how to spot a plant called preacher-in-the-pulpit along the
country roads. He taught me harmony to "Jingle Bells." He taught me
how to drive a car. He unscrewed the training wheels and taught me
how to ride a bike. He told me strange, portenting things: if I ate too
much bread, I'd get dandruff. He read *Reader's Digest, Coronet* and
Pageant and didn't believe in evolution. There were times I didn't like
him. He left abruptly. He left me much unfinished business.

He visited New York City four times in his lifetime. He was in   11
Times Square, a tourist, on V-J Day. Somehow, I'm glad for him, as a
believer is for a novitiate, that he was there: Celebration needs a
crowd. He thought not badly of large cities, after that; but he never
lived in one.

He never sailed, his life was landlocked. I think he clammed   12
once, with my uncle, at Virginia Beach. I cannot say for certain that
he knew his body's way in water. Water was not an element he knew,
except as rain on crops. He was a farmer's son. Without the farmer's
land, his legacy was vending farmer's goods. I planted a garden last
week, north of where he lived and died, on an island where all roads
lead to water. "Now, when you plant a small plot," he once said,
"plant what you and yours can eat, or plant what makes you happy,
like a sunflower, and offer your surplus to the ones who want. Don't
waste. For God's sake, don't waste."

I wish that he could see the things I've sown. Diluted in me is   13
John Wiggins, as today's rain will be in summer's harvest. I wish that
I could see him once again, hear his footfalls on the gravel driveway,
heavy on one foot: These dried leavings aren't complete in their re-
membrance, like the trimmings swept from green growth on the grocer's floor, they crumble on my fingertips and fly piecemeal to the
wind. I do not do my father justice, that was his charge. I've borne
his name, in and out of marriage, a name that is my own, sometimes I
wish his strain would leave me, sometimes I'd like to choke it to full
bloom. I'd like to turn to him today and say, "I love you: too late:
I'm sorry: you did the best you could: you were my father: I learned
from you: you were an honest man."

I cultivate a tiny garden, "plot" reminds me of a cemetery. I plant   14
only what my family guarantees to eat. The rest I give to those who
want. Had you known him, I'd like to think you would have bought
your groceries from John Wiggins. He always had a pleasant word.
He could tell you how to plan a meal for twenty people, give you

produce wholesale, trim your cut of meat before he weighed it, profit wasn't Daddy's motive, life was. Life defeated him. He taught me how to pack a grocery bag, I worked there weekends, canned goods on the bottom, perishables on top. Someone puts tomatoes on the bottom of my bag these days, I repack it. I was taught respect of certain order. One sees one's father's face, as one grows older, in the most peculiar places. I see Daddy in each bud. I see his stance on corners. I, myself, wear grocer's aprons, when I cook. My mother always said there was no cleaning that damned blood from those white aprons. My father left a stain: I miss him. I write longhand, and in ink.

QUESTIONS FOR STUDY AND DISCUSSION

1. How does Wiggins's first sentence influence the rest of the essay? How effective do you find Wiggins's last sentence as a conclusion for her essay? Explain. (Glossary: *Beginnings and Endings*)

2. What does the list of things that John Wiggins taught his daughter tell you about him?

3. Discuss Wiggins's writing style in "Grocer's Daughter." (Glossary: *Style*) Is it effective for you? Why, or why not?

4. Why did the Wiggins family move so often?

5. Wiggins says of her father, "I wonder if he ever dreamed that he could change things" (10). How did he change things for his daughter?

6. Wiggins never states how or when her father died. Why do you think she explores the impact of his death, rather than describing its occurrence? How and when do you think John Wiggins died? Defend your answer with excerpts from the essay.

VOCABULARY

Refer to your dictionary to define the following words as they are used in this selection. Then use each word in a sentence of your own.

pathology (2) portenting (10)
concocted (4) novitiate (11)
germinated (4) piecemeal (13)
charisma (7)

CLASSROOM ACTIVITY USING DESCRIPTION

Important advice for writing well is to show rather than tell. Let's assume that your task is to reveal a person's character. What activities might you show the person doing to give your readers the correct impression of his or her character? For example, to indicate that the person is concerned about current events without coming out and saying so, you might show him or her reading the morning newspaper or watching the evening news. Or you might show a character's degree of formality by including that person's typical greeting: *Hi, how are ya?* versus *I am very pleased to meet you.* In other words, the things a person says and does are often important indicators of personality. Choose one of the following traits, and make a list of at least six ways to show rather than tell how a particular person possesses that trait.

simple but good	politically involved
reckless	irresponsible
sensitive to the arts	independent
a sports lover	quick-witted
thoughtful	public spirited

SUGGESTED WRITING ASSIGNMENTS

1. In her essay, Wiggins reveals something of herself—her tastes, her values, her intelligence. Write an essay in which you argue that every writer, to some degree, reveals something of himself or herself in writing about any subject. Choose whatever examples you wish to make your point. You might, for instance, decide to use Carl T. Rowan and his essay on Miss Bessie as your primary example. Finally, you might wish to emphasize the significance of the self-revealing qualities of writing.

2. Describe a close relative of yours, such as a parent or sibling. Be sure to establish a purpose and a dominant impression for your description. Your audience will not know your subject—what are the little things that make up his or her character and make him or her special?

Process Analysis

When you give someone directions to your home, tell how to make ice cream, or explain how a president is elected, you are using *process analysis.*

Process analysis usually arranges a series of events in order and relates them to one another, as narration and cause and effect do, but process analysis has a different emphasis. Whereas narration tells mainly *what* happens and cause and effect focuses on *why* it happens, process analysis tries to explain—in detail—*how* it happens.

There are two types of process analysis: directional and informational. The *directional* type provides instructions on how to do something. These instructions can be as brief as the directions for making instant coffee printed on the label or as complex as the directions in a manual for assembling a new gas grill. The purpose of directional process analysis is simple: to give the reader directions to follow that will lead to the desired results.

Consider Florence H. Pettit's directions for sharpening a knife:

> If you have never done any whittling or wood carving before, the first skill to learn is how to sharpen your knife. You may be surprised to learn that even a brand-new knife needs sharpening. Knives are never sold honed (finely sharpened), although some gouges and chisels are. It is essential to learn the firm stroke on the stone that will keep your blades sharp. The sharpening stone must be fixed in place on the table, so that it will not move around. You can do this by placing a piece of rubber inner tube or a thin piece of foam rubber under it. Or you can tack four strips of wood, if you have a rough worktable, to frame the stone and hold it in place. Put a generous puddle of oil on the stone—this will soon disappear into the surface of a new stone, and you will need to keep adding more oil. Press the knife blade flat against the stone in the puddle of oil, using your index finger. Whichever way the cutting edge of the knife faces is the side of the blade that should get a little more

pressure. Move the blade around three or four times in a narrow oval about the size of your fingernail, going *counterclockwise* when the sharp edge is facing right. Now turn the blade over in the same spot on the stone, press hard, and move it around the small oval *clockwise,* with more pressure on the cutting edge that faces left. Repeat the ovals, flipping the knife blade over six or seven times, and applying lighter pressure to the blade the last two times. Wipe the blade clean with a piece of rag or tissue and rub it flat on the piece of leather strop at least twice on each side. Stroke *away* from the cutting edge to remove the little burr of metal that may be left on the blade.

After first establishing her context and purpose, Pettit presents step-by-step directions for sharpening a knife, selecting details that a novice would understand.

The *informational* type of process analysis, on the other hand, tells how something works, how something is made, or how something occurs. You would use informational process analysis if you wanted to explain how the human heart functions, how an atomic bomb works, how hailstones are formed, how you selected the college you are attending, or how the polio vaccine was developed. Rather than giving specific directions, informational process analysis explains and informs.

In the following illustration by Nigel Holmes on page 310, Jim Collins uses informational process analysis to explain a basic legislative procedure: how a bill becomes a law.

Clarity is crucial for successful process analysis. The most effective way to explain a process is to divide it into steps and to present those steps in a clear (usually chronological) sequence. Transitional words and phrases such as *first, next, after,* and *before* help to connect steps to one another. Naturally, you must be sure that no step is omitted or given out of order. Also, you may sometimes have to explain *why* a certain step is necessary, especially if it is not obvious. With intricate, abstract, or particularly difficult steps, you might use analogy or comparison to clarify the steps for your reader.

Illustration by Nigel Holmes

How to Write a Personal Letter

■ **Garrison Keillor**

Writer and broadcaster Garrison Keillor was born in Anoka, Minnesota, in 1942. After graduating from the University of Minnesota, he became a successful writer of humorous stories, many of which appeared in the New Yorker. *He is perhaps best known for his radio program,* A Prairie Home Companion, *which is broadcast on National Public Radio. Keillor has written many books, including* Lake Wobegon Days *(1985),* Leaving Home: A Collection of Lake Wobegon Stories *(1987), and* Me: By Jimmy (Big Boy) Valente *(1999). He has also produced a wide selection of audiocassettes featuring his stories and radio shows. In this selection, written as part of a popular and highly successful advertising campaign for the International Paper Company, the sage of Lake Wobegon offers some sound and practical directions for writing personal letters.*

FOR YOUR JOURNAL

How do you feel when you receive a letter from a relative or friend? Do you feel the same way about telephone calls or email messages? To you, what does a letter say about the person who wrote it?

We shy persons need to write a letter now and then, or else we'll dry up and blow away. It's true. And I speak as one who loves to reach for the phone and talk. The telephone is to shyness what Hawaii is to February; it's a way out of the woods. *And yet:* a letter is better.

Such a sweet gift—a piece of handmade writing, in an envelope that is not a bill, sitting in our friend's path when she trudges home from a long day spent among wahoos and savages, a day our words will help repair. They don't need to be immortal, just sincere. She can read them twice and again tomorrow: *You're someone I care about, Corinne, and think of often, and every time I do, you make me smile.*

We need to write, otherwise nobody will know who we are. They will have only a vague impression of us as A Nice Person, because, frankly, we don't shine at conversation, we lack the confidence to thrust our faces forward and say, "Hi, I'm Heather Hooten, let me tell you about my week." Mostly we say "Uh-huh" and "Oh really." People smile and look over our shoulder, looking for someone else to talk to.

So a shy person sits down and writes a letter. To be known by another person—to meet and talk freely on the page—to be close despite distance. To escape from anonymity and be our own sweet selves and express the music of our souls.

We want our dear Aunt Eleanor to know that we have fallen in love, that we quit our job, that we're moving to New York, and we want to say a few things that might not get said in casual conversation: *Thank you for what you've meant to me. I am very happy right now.*

The first step in writing letters is to get over the guilt of *not* writing. You don't "owe" anybody a letter. Letters are a gift. The burning shame you feel when you see unanswered mail makes it harder to pick up a pen and makes for a cheerless letter when you finally do. *I feel bad about not writing, but I've been so busy,* etc. Skip this. Few letters are obligatory, and they are *Thanks for the wonderful gift* and *I am terribly sorry to hear about George's death.* Write these promptly if you want to keep your friends. Don't worry about the others, except love letters, of course. When your true love writes *Dear Light of My Life, Joy of My Heart,* some response is called for.

Some of the best letters are tossed off in a burst of inspiration, so keep your writing stuff in one place where you can sit down for a few minutes and—*Dear Roy, I am in the middle of an essay but thought I'd drop you a line. Hi to your sweetie too*—dash off a note to a pal. Envelopes, stamps, address book, everything in a drawer so you can write fast when the pen is hot.

A blank white 8 × 11 sheet can look as big as Montana if the pen's not so hot—try a smaller page and write boldly. Get a pen that makes a sensuous line, get a comfortable typewriter, a friendly word processor—whichever feels easy to the hand.

Sit for a few minutes with the blank sheet of paper in front of you, and let your friend come in mind. Remember the last time you saw each other and how your friend looked and what you said and what perhaps was unsaid between you; when your friend becomes real to you, start to write.

Write the salutation—*Dear You*—and take a deep breath and plunge in. A simple declarative sentence will do, followed by another and another. As if you were talking to us. Don't think about grammar, don't think about style, just give us your news. Where did you go, who did you see, what did they say, what do you think?

If you don't know where to begin, start with the present: *I'm sitting at the kitchen table on a rainy Saturday morning. Everyone is gone and the house is quiet.* Let the letter drift along. The toughest letter to crank out is one that is meant to impress, as we all know from writing job applications; if it's hard work to slip off a letter to a friend, maybe you're trying too hard to be terrific. A letter is only a report to someone who already likes you for reasons other than your brilliance. Take it easy. 11

Don't worry about form. It's not a term paper. When you come to the end of one episode, just start a new paragraph. You can go from a few lines about the sad state of rock 'n' roll to the fight with your mother to your fond memories of Mexico to the kitchen sink and what's in it. The more you write, the easier it gets, and when you have a True True Friend to write to, a soul sibling, then it's like driving a car; you just press on the gas. 12

Don't tear up the page and start over when you write a bad line — try to write your way out of it. Make mistakes and plunge on. Let the letter cook along and let yourself be bold. Outrage, confusion, love — whatever is in your mind, let it find a way to the page. Writing is a means of discovery, always, and when you come to the end and write *Yours ever* or *Hugs and Kisses,* you'll know something you didn't when you wrote *Dear Pal.* 13

Probably your friend will put your letter away, and it'll be read again a few years from now — and it will improve with age. 14

And forty years from now, your friend's grandkids will dig it out of the attic and read it, a sweet and precious relic of the [late twentieth century] that gives them a sudden clear glimpse of the world we old-timers knew. You will have then created an object of art. Your simple lines about where you went, who you saw, what they said, will speak to those children and they will feel in their hearts the humanity of our times. 15

You can't pick up a phone and call the future and tell them about our times. You have to pick up a piece of paper. 16

QUESTIONS FOR STUDY AND DISCUSSION

1. Keillor calls a personal letter a "gift" (2). Why do you suppose he thinks of a letter in this way?

2. What advice does Keillor have for people before they start writing? In what ways is this advice part of his process analysis? Why does he suggest small stationery instead of 8 × 11 sheets of paper?

3. Is Keillor's process analysis directional or informational? What led you to this conclusion?

4. Keillor suggests that before starting to write a friend, you think about that friend for a while until he or she becomes real for you. At that point you're ready to write. What should happen next in the process?

5. What do you think Keillor means when he says, "We need to write, otherwise nobody will know who we are" (3)?

6. Instead of taking us step-by-step through a personal letter in paragraphs 12–14, Keillor anticipates the problems that a letter writer is likely to encounter and offers his own advice. What are the most common problems? What solutions does Keillor offer? (Glossary: *Examples*) How has he organized his advice? (Glossary: *Organization*)

7. By the time you have come to the end of a letter, what, according to Keillor, should have happened? Why?

VOCABULARY

Refer to your dictionary to define the following words as they are used in this selection. Then use each word in a sentence of your own.

trudges (2)   crank (11)
wahoos (2)   episode (12)
anonymity (4)   relic (15)
sensuous (8)

CLASSROOM ACTIVITY USING PROCESS ANALYSIS

Most do-it-yourself jobs require that you follow a set process to achieve the best results. Make a list of the steps involved in doing one of the following household activities:

cleaning windows
repotting a plant
doing laundry
baking chocolate chip cookies

changing a flat tire
unclogging a drain

SUGGESTED WRITING ASSIGNMENTS

1. What does Keillor see as the advantages of a letter over a telephone call? Can you think of times when a telephone call or email is preferable? Write an essay in which you agree or disagree with Keillor's position on the importance of personal letters. Before starting to write, you may find it helpful to review what you wrote in your journal for this selection.

2. Write an essay in which you give directions or advice for finding a summer job or part-time employment during the school year. In what ways is looking for such jobs different from looking for permanent positions? You can use Keillor's essay as a model for your own.

The Beekeeper

■ **Sue Hubbell**

Essayist and nature writer Sue Hubbell was born in Kalamazoo, Michigan. After graduating from Swarthmore College, she moved to the Missouri Ozarks and took up beekeeping, an activity she pursued for twenty-five years. Hubbell recounts her experiences with bees in A Book of Bees: And How to Keep Them *(1988). Her other books on country living and the natural world include* A Country Year: Living the Questions *(1986),* Broadsides from the Other Orders: A Book of Bugs *(1993),* Far-Flung Hubbell: Essays from the American Road *(1995), and* Waiting for Aphrodite: Journeys into the Time before Bones *(1999). Today Hubbell lives on the coast of Maine. In the following selection from* A Book of Bees, *Hubbell carefully explains the process of getting a person prepared to work with bees.*

FOR YOUR JOURNAL

Each of us has little routines or rituals that we follow to get ready to do something. For example, before sitting down to write, one author routinely makes a fresh cup of coffee, cuts up a piece of fruit for a snack, sharpens two pencils, locates a pad of paper for notes, cleans his computer table, and loads paper in his printer. Some athletes and entertainers eat the same foods, wear the same clothes, or talk with the same people before each game or performance. Briefly describe one of your routines or rituals.

The time to harvest honey is summer's end, when it is hot. The temper of the bees requires that we wear protective clothing: a full set of overalls, a zippered bee veil and leather gloves. Even a very strong young man works up a sweat wrapped in a bee suit in the heat, hustling 60-pound supers while being harassed by angry bees. It is a hard job, harder even than haying, but jobs are scarce here and I've always been able to hire help.

This year David, the son of a friend of mine, is working for me. He is big and strong and used to labor, but he was nervous about

1

2

bees. After we had made the job arrangement I set about desensitizing him to bee stings. I put a piece of ice on his arm to numb it and then, holding a bee carefully by its head, I put it on the numbed spot and let it sting him. A bee stinger is barbed and stays in the flesh, pulling loose from the body of the bee as it struggles to free itself. The bulbous poison sac at the top of the stinger continues to pulsate after the bee has left, pumping the venom and forcing the stinger deeper into the flesh.

That first day I wanted David to have only a partial dose of   3
venom, so after a minute I scraped the stinger out. A few people are seriously sensitive to bee venom; each sting they receive can cause a more severe reaction than the one before — reactions ranging from hives, breathing difficulties, accelerated heart beat and choking to anaphylactic shock and death. I didn't think David would be allergic in that way, but I wanted to make sure.

We sat down and had a cup of coffee and I watched him. The   4
spot where the stinger went in grew red and began to swell. That was a normal reaction, and so was the itching that he felt later on.

The next day I coaxed a bee into stinging him again, repeating   5
the procedure, but I left the stinger in place for 10 minutes, until the venom sac was empty. Again the spot was red, swollen and itchy but had disappeared in 24 hours. By that time David was ready to catch a bee himself and administer his own sting. He also decided that the ice cube was a bother and gave it up. I told him to keep to one sting a day until he had no redness or swelling and then to increase to two stings. He was ready for them the next day. The greater amount of venom caused redness and swelling for a few days, but soon his body could tolerate it without reaction and he increased the number of stings once again.

Today he told me he was up to six stings. His arms look as   6
though they have track marks on them, but the fresh stings are having little effect. I'll keep him at it until he can tolerate 10 a day with no reaction and then I'll not worry about taking him out to the bee yard.

QUESTIONS FOR STUDY AND DISCUSSION

1. What are the steps in the process of desensitizing a person to bee venom? Is Hubbell's process analysis directional or informational? Explain.

2. Initially, Hubbell gives David only a partial dose of bee venom. Why is she so cautious with David at first?

3. What happens to the area on David's arm where the stinger went in? Why do you suppose Hubbell describes David's reaction in detail? (Glossary: *Description*)

4. At the end of paragraph 5, Hubbell has David increasing the number of stings from two a day to three. She starts paragraph 6 by announcing that David is up to six stings a day. Why do you suppose that she doesn't mention the four-a-day and five-a-day steps? What would she gain or lose had she added them? Explain.

5. Because every individual reacts to bee stings differently, Hubbell doesn't tell us how long the whole desensitizing process takes. Based on the information that Hubbell gives, how long would you estimate it took David to become desensitized? Explain how you arrived at your estimate.

VOCABULARY

Refer to your dictionary to define the following words as they are used in this selection. Then use each word in a sentence of your own.

barbed (2)   coaxed (5)
bulbous (2)   tolerate (6)
anaphylactic (3)

CLASSROOM ACTIVITY USING PROCESS ANALYSIS

Carefully read the directions for constructing an Astro Tube—a cylindrical airfoil made out of a sheet of heavy writing paper—that appear on page 319. Now construct your own Astro Tube, and fly it. How helpful did you find the illustrations that accompany the verbal directions?

SUGGESTED WRITING ASSIGNMENTS

1. Have you or someone you know ever been treated for allergies? Make a list of the individual steps in the treatment process. Using Hubbell's essay as a model, write an essay in which you describe the process involved in making a person less sensitive to certain allergens.

2. Write a directional process analysis for a "simple" task that could easily be executed incorrectly and that might even cause a mishap or accident if not explained correctly. Consider analyzing one of the following tasks: changing a tire, cutting your own hair, driving a standard transmission vehicle, downloading a document from the Internet, setting an alarm clock, packing for a camping trip, or loading film into a camera.

Making an Astro Tube

Start with an 8.5-inch by 11-inch sheet of heavy writing paper. (Never use newspaper in making paper models because it isn't strongly bonded and can't hold a crease.) Follow these numbered steps, corresponding to the illustrations.
1. With the long side of the sheet toward you, fold up one third of the paper.
2. Fold the doubled section in half.
3. Fold the section in half once more and crease well.
4. Unfold preceding crease.
5. Curve the ends together to form a tube, as shown in the illustration.

6. Insert the right end inside the left end between the single outer layer and the doubled layers. Overlap the ends about an inch and a half. (This makes a tube for right-handers, to be used with an underhand throw. For an overhand tube, or an underhand version to be thrown by a lefty, reverse the directions, and insert the left end inside the right end at this step.)
7. Hold the tube at the seam with one hand, where shown by the dot in the illustration, and turn the rim inward along the crease made in step 3. Start turning in at the seam and roll the rim under, moving around the circumference in a circular manner. Then

round out the rim.
8. Fold the fin to the left, as shown, then raise it so that it's perpendicular to the tube. Be careful not to tear the paper at the front.
9. Hold the tube from above, near the rim. Hold it between the thumb and fingers. The rim end should be forward, with the fin on the bottom. Throw the tube underhanded, with a motion like throwing a bowling ball, letting it spin off the fingers as it is released. The tube will float through the air, spinning as it goes. Indoor flights of 30 feet or more are easy. With practice you can achieve remarkable accuracy.

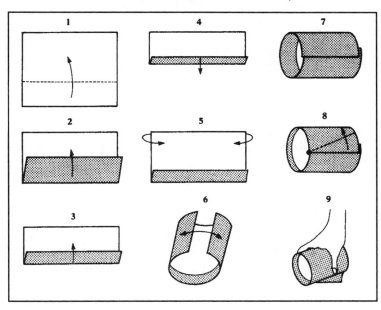

Why Leaves Turn Color in the Fall

■ **Diane Ackerman**

Born in Waukegan, Illinois, in 1948, Diane Ackerman received degrees from Pennsylvania State University and Cornell University. She has written several books of poetry, a prose memoir, a play, and several collections of essays, including The Moon by Whale Light, and Other Adventures among Bats, Penguins, Crocodilians, and Whales *(1991);* A Natural History of Love *(1994);* The Rarest of the Rare: Vanishing Animals, Timeless Worlds *(1995);* The Curious Naturalist *(1998); and* Deep Play *(1999). Ackerman has worked as a writer-in-residence at several major universities, has directed the Writers' Program at Washington University in St. Louis, and has been a staff writer at the* New Yorker. *Currently she lives in upstate New York. Every October, residents of the northeastern United States are dazzled by a spectacular color show that sets them to wondering, "Where do the colors come from?" In the following selection, from Ackerman's acclaimed* A Natural History of the Senses *(1990), she lets us in on one of nature's secrets. Notice the way Ackerman shares her enthusiasm for the natural world as she explains the process by which autumn leaves assume their brilliant colors.*

FOR YOUR JOURNAL

What is your favorite season? What about this season makes it your favorite—the weather, the activities and memories, the time of year, or a combination of these and other factors?

The stealth of autumn catches one unaware. Was that a goldfinch 1 perching in the early September woods, or just the first turning leaf? A red-winged blackbird or a sugar maple closing up shop for the winter? Keen-eyed as leopards, we stand still and squint hard, looking for signs of movement. Early-morning frost sits heavily on the grass, and turns barbed wire into a string of stars. On a distant hill, a small square of yellow appears to be a lighted stage. At last the truth dawns on us: Fall is staggering in, right on schedule, with its baggage of chilly nights, macabre holidays, and spectacular, heart-stoppingly beautiful leaves. Soon the leaves will start cringing on the trees, and roll up in clenched fists before they actually fall off. Dry seedpods will rattle like tiny gourds. But first there will be weeks of gushing color so bright, so pastel, so confettilike, that people will travel up and down the East Coast just to stare at it — a whole season of leaves.

Where do the colors come from? Sunlight rules most living things 2 with its golden edicts. When the days begin to shorten, soon after the summer solstice on June 21, a tree reconsiders its leaves. All summer it feeds them so they can process sunlight, but in the dog days of summer the tree begins pulling nutrients back into its trunk and roots, pares down, and gradually chokes off its leaves. A corky layer of cells forms at the leaves' slender petioles, then scars over. Undernourished, the leaves stop producing the pigment chlorophyll, and photosynthesis ceases. Animals can migrate, hibernate, or store food to prepare for winter. But where can a tree go? It survives by dropping its leaves, and by the end of autumn only a few fragile threads of fluid-carrying xylem hold leaves to their stems.

A turning leaf stays partly green at first, then reveals splotches of 3 yellow and red as the chlorophyll gradually breaks down. Dark green seems to stay longest in the veins, outlining and defining them. During the summer, chlorophyll dissolves in the heat and light, but it is also being steadily replaced. In the fall, on the other hand, no new pigment is produced, and so we notice the other colors that were always there, right in the leaf, although chlorophyll's shocking green hid them from view. With their camouflage gone, we see these colors for the first time all year, and marvel, but they were always there, hidden like a vivid secret beneath the hot glowing greens of summer.

The most spectacular range of fall foliage occurs in the northeast- 4 ern United States and in eastern China, where the leaves are robustly colored, thanks in part to a rich climate. European maples don't achieve the same flaming reds as their American relatives, which thrive on cold nights and sunny days. In Europe, the warm, humid weather turns the leaves brown or mildly yellow. Anthocyanin, the pigment that gives apples their red and turns leaves red or red-violet, is produced by sugars that remain in the leaf after the supply of nutrients dwindles. Unlike the carotenoids, which color carrots, squash, and corn, and turn leaves orange and yellow, anthocyanin varies

from year to year, depending on the temperature and amount of sunlight. The fiercest colors occur in years when the fall sunlight is
strongest and the nights are cool and dry (a state of grace scientists
find vexing to forecast). This is also why leaves appear dizzyingly
bright and clear on a sunny fall day: The anthocyanin flashes like a
marquee.

Not all leaves turn the same colors. Elms, weeping willows, and   5
the ancient ginkgo all grow radiant yellow, along with hickories,
aspens, bottlebrush buckeyes, cottonweeds, and tall, keening poplars.
Basswood turns bronze, birches bright gold. Water-loving maples put
on a symphonic display of scarlets. Sumacs turn red, too, as do flowering dogwoods, black gums, and sweet gums. Though some oaks
yellow, most turn a pinkish brown. The farmlands also change color,
as tepees of cornstalks and bales of shredded-wheat-textured hay
stand drying in the fields. In some spots, one slope of a hill may be
green and the other already in bright color, because the hillside facing
south gets more sun and heat than the northern one.

An odd feature of the colors is that they don't seem to have any   6
special purpose. We are predisposed to respond to their beauty, of
course. They shimmer with the colors of sunset, spring flowers, the
tawny buff of a colt's pretty rump, the shuddering pink of a blush.
Animals and flowers color for a reason — adaptation to their environment — but there is no adaptive reason for leaves to color so beauti-
fully in the fall any more than there is for the sky or ocean to be blue.
It's just one of the haphazard marvels the planet bestows every year.
We find the sizzling colors thrilling, and in a sense they dupe us. Colored like living things, they signal death and disintegration. In time,
they will become fragile and, like the body, return to dust. They are
as we hope our own fate will be when we die: Not to vanish, just to
sublime from one beautiful state into another. Though leaves lose
their green life, they bloom with urgent colors, as the woods grow
mummified day by day, and Nature becomes more carnal, mute, and
radiant.

We call the season "fall," from the Old English *feallan*, to fall,   7
which leads back through time to the Indo-European *phol*, which
also means to fall. So the word and the idea are both extremely ancient, and haven't really changed since the first of our kind needed a
name for fall's leafy abundance. As we say the word, we're reminded
of that other Fall, in the garden of Eden, when fig leaves never with-
ered and scales fell from our eyes. Fall is the time when leaves fall

from the trees, just as spring is when flowers spring up, summer is when we simmer, and winter is when we whine from the cold.

Children love to play in piles of leaves, hurling them into the air   8
like confetti, leaping into soft unruly mattresses of them. For children, leaf fall is just one of the odder figments of Nature, like hailstones or snowflakes. Walk down a lane overhung with trees in the never-never land of autumn, and you will forget about time and death, lost in the sheer delicious spill of color. Adam and Eve concealed their nakedness with leaves, remember? Leaves have always hidden our awkward secrets.

But how do the colored leaves fall? As a leaf ages, the growth hor-   9
mone, auxin, fades, and cells at the base of the petiole divide. Two or three rows of small cells, lying at right angles to the axis of the petiole, react with water, then come apart, leaving the petioles hanging on by only a few threads of xylem. A light breeze, and the leaves are airborne. They glide and swoop, rocking in invisible cradles. They are all wing and may flutter from yard to yard on small whirlwinds or updrafts, swiveling as they go. Firmly tethered to earth, we love to see things rise up and fly—soap bubbles, balloons, birds, fall leaves. They remind us that the end of a season is capricious, as is the end of life. We especially like the way leaves rock, careen, and swoop as they fall. Everyone knows the motion. Pilots sometimes do a maneuver called a "falling leaf," in which the plane loses altitude quickly and on purpose, by slipping first to the right, then to the left. The machine weighs a ton or more, but in one pilot's mind it is a weightless thing, a falling leaf. She has seen the motion before, in the Vermont woods where she played as a child. Below her the trees radiate gold, copper, and red. Leaves are falling, although she can't see them fall, as she falls, swooping down for a closer view.

At last the leaves leave. But first they turn color and thrill us for   10
weeks on end. Then they crunch and crackle underfoot. They *shush,* as children drag their small feet through leaves heaped along the curb. Dark, slimy mats of leaves cling to one's heels after a rain. A damp, stuccolike mortar of semidecayed leaves protects the tender shoots with a roof until spring, and makes a rich humus. An occasional bulge or ripple in the leafy mounds signals a shrew or a field mouse tunneling out of sight. Sometimes one finds in fossil stones the imprint of a leaf, long since disintegrated, whose outlines remind us how detailed, vibrant, and alive are the things of this earth that perish.

QUESTIONS FOR STUDY AND DISCUSSION

1. According to Ackerman, exactly what causes leaves to change color? What particular conditions cause the brightest colors in autumn leaves?
2. Briefly summarize the steps of the process by which leaves change color in autumn.
3. Not only does Ackerman describe the process by which leaves change color, she includes other information as well. For example, she uses cause-and-effect analysis to explain what causes leaves to be particularly bright some years, to explain why trees turn color at different rates, and to explain why leaves lose their grip and fall from the trees. (Glossary: *Cause and Effect*) Did you find this information useful? What, if anything, did it add to your appreciation of her process analysis?
4. How has Ackerman organized her essay? (Glossary: *Organization*) Explain why this organization seems most appropriate for her subject.
5. Identify several figures of speech—simile, metaphor, and personification—that Ackerman uses, and explain how each functions in the context of her essay. (Glossary: *Figure of Speech*)
6. Reread Ackerman's concluding sentence. What does she mean? Why do you suppose she has chosen to end her essay in this way? In what ways, if any, is it a particularly appropriate ending for her essay? (Glossary: *Beginnings and Endings*)

VOCABULARY

Refer to your dictionary to define the following words as they are used in this selection. Then use each word in a sentence of your own.

stealth (1)
clenched (1)
gushing (1)
camouflage (3)

tawny (6)
figments (8)
stuccolike (10)
vibrant (10)

CLASSROOM ACTIVITY USING PROCESS ANALYSIS

To give another person clear directions about how to do something, you need to have a thorough understanding of the process yourself.

Analyze one of the following activities by listing any materials you might need and the steps you would follow in completing it:

studying for an exam

determining miles per gallon for an automobile

finding a person's name and address (or email address) on the Internet

beginning an exercise program

getting from where your writing class meets to where you normally have lunch

installing new software on your computer

writing an essay

buying a compact disk player on the Internet

adding or dropping a class from your course schedule

SUGGESTED WRITING ASSIGNMENTS

1. Our world is filled with hundreds of natural processes—for example, the cycle of the moon, the "rising" and "setting" of the sun, the germination of a seed, the movement of the tides, the formation of a tornado, the transformation of a caterpillar into a butterfly or moth, and the flowering of a tree. Using Ackerman's essay as a model, write an informational process analysis explaining one such natural process.

2. Select one of the tasks listed in the "Classroom Activity," and write a brief essay in which you give directions for successfully performing the task.

On Dumpster Diving

■ **Lars Eighner**

Born in Texas in 1948, Lars Eighner attended the University of Texas at Austin. After graduation, he launched a career writing essays and fiction. A volume of his short stories, Bayou Boy and Other Stories, *was published in 1985. Eighner became homeless in 1988 when he left his job as an attendant at a mental hospital. The following piece, which appeared in the* Utne Reader, *is an abridged version of an essay that first appeared in* Three-penny Review. *The piece eventually became part of Eighner's startling account of the three years he spent as a homeless person,* Travels with Lizbeth *(1993). Since then he has written two novels,* Pawn to Queen Four *(1995) and* Whispered in the Dark *(1996), and a collection of essays,* Gay Cosmos *(1995). Eighner uses a number of rhetorical strategies in "On Dumpster Diving," but pay particular attention to the importance of process analysis in the success of the essay overall as he delineates the "stages a person goes through in learning to scavenge."*

FOR YOUR JOURNAL

Some people believe that acquiring material objects is what life is all about and that the measure of their own "worth" is in the inventory of their possessions. Comment on the role that material objects play in your life and on whether your view of their importance has changed as you have grown older.

I began Dumpster diving about a year before I became homeless. 1
I prefer the term *scavenging*. I have heard people, evidently 2 meaning to be polite, use the word *foraging*, but I prefer to reserve that word for gathering nuts and berries and such, which I also do, according to the season and opportunity.

I like the frankness of the word *scavenging*. I live from the refuse 3 of others. I am a scavenger. I think it a sound and honorable niche, although if I could I would naturally prefer to live the comfortable consumer life, perhaps — and only perhaps — as a slightly less wasteful consumer owing to what I have learned as a scavenger.

Except for jeans, all my clothes come from Dumpsters. Boom   4
boxes, candles, bedding, toilet paper, medicine, books, a typewriter, a
virgin male love doll, coins sometimes amounting to many dollars: all
came from Dumpsters. And, yes, I eat from Dumpsters, too.

There is a predictable series of stages that a person goes through   5
in learning to scavenge. At first the new scavenger is filled with disgust and self-loathing. He is ashamed of being seen.

This stage passes with experience. The scavenger finds a pair of   6
running shoes that fit and look and smell brand-new. He finds a
pocket calculator in perfect working order. He finds pristine ice
cream, still frozen, more than he can eat or keep. He begins to understand: people do throw away perfectly good stuff, a lot of perfectly
good stuff.

At this stage he may become lost and never recover. All the   7
Dumpster divers I have known come to the point of trying to acquire
everything they touch. Why not take it, they reason, it is all free. This
is, of course, hopeless, and most divers come to realize that they must
restrict themselves to items of relatively immediate utility.

The finding of objects is becoming something of an urban art.   8
Even respectable, employed people will sometimes find something
tempting sticking out of a Dumpster or standing beside one. Quite a
number of people, not all of them of the bohemian type, are willing
to brag that they found this or that piece in the trash.

But eating from Dumpsters is the thing that separates the dilet-   9
tanti from the professionals. Eating safely involves three principles:
using the senses and common sense to evaluate the condition of the
found materials; knowing the Dumpsters of a given area and checking them regularly; and seeking always to answer the question "Why
was this discarded?"

Yet perfectly good food can be found in Dumpsters. Canned   10
goods, for example, turn up fairly often in the Dumpsters I frequent. I
also have few qualms about dry foods such as crackers, cookies, cereal, chips, and pasta if they are free of visible contaminants and still
dry and crisp. Raw fruits and vegetables with intact skins seem perfectly safe to me, excluding, of course, the obviously rotten. Many
are discarded for minor imperfections that can be pared away.

A typical discard is a half jar of peanut butter—though nonor-   11
ganic peanut butter does not require refrigeration and is unlikely
to spoil in any reasonable time. One of my favorite finds is yo-
gurt—often discarded, still sealed, when the expiration date has
passed—because it will keep for several days, even in warm weather.

No matter how careful I am I still get dysentery at least once a 12 month, oftener in warm weather. I do not want to paint too romantic a picture. Dumpster diving has serious drawbacks as a way of life.

I find from the experience of scavenging two rather deep lessons. 13 The first is to take what I can use and let the rest go. I have come to think that there is no value in the abstract. A thing I cannot use or make useful, perhaps by trading, has no value, however fine or rare it may be.

The second lesson is the transience of material being. I do not 14 suppose that ideas are immortal, but certainly they are longer-lived than material objects.

The things I find in Dumpsters, the love letters and rag dolls of so 15 many lives, remind me of this lesson. Now I hardly pick up a thing without envisioning the time I will cast it away. This, I think, is a healthy state of mind. Almost everything I have now has already been cast out at least once, proving that what I own is valueless to someone.

I find that my desire to grab for the gaudy bauble has been largely 16 sated. I think this is an attitude I share with the very wealthy — we both know there is plenty more where whatever we have came from. Between us are the rat-race millions who have confounded their selves with the objects they grasp and who nightly scavenge the cable channels for they know not what.

I am sorry for them.   17

QUESTIONS FOR STUDY AND DISCUSSION

1. What is "Dumpster diving"? Why does Eighner prefer the word *scavenging* to *foraging* or *Dumpster diving?* What do these three terms mean to him? What does his discussion of these terms at the beginning of his essay tell you about Eighner himself?

2. What stages do beginning Dumpster divers go through before they become what Eighner terms "professionals"? What examples does Eighner use to illustrate the passage through these stages? What "separates the dilettanti from the professionals" (9) of Dumpster divers?

3. Summarize the various steps in Eighner's explanation of the process of Dumpster diving. Why do you think Eighner did not title the essay "How to Dumpster Dive"?

4. What are the two lessons Eighner learns from scavenging? Why are they important to him? In what ways has scavenging benefited Eighner? In what ways has it harmed him?

5. Eighner's essay deals with both the immediate, physical aspects of Dumpster diving, such as what can be found in a typical Dumpster and the physical price one pays for eating out of them, and the larger, abstract issues that Dumpster diving raises, such as materialism and the transience of material objects. (Glossary: *Concrete/Abstract*) Why do you suppose he describes the concrete details before he discusses the abstract issues? What does he achieve by using both types of elements?

6. Writers often use process analysis in conjunction with another strategy—especially argument—to try to improve the way a process is carried out or to comment on issues exposed by the process analysis. In this essay, for example, Eighner uses a full process analysis to present his views on American values and materialism. In what ways does Eighner's process analysis support his opinions about our society?

VOCABULARY

Refer to your dictionary to define the following words as they are used in this selection. Then use each word in a sentence of your own.

refuse (3)	qualms (10)
niche (3)	transience (14)
pristine (6)	sated (16)
bohemian (8)	

CLASSROOM ACTIVITY USING PROCESS ANALYSIS

In her best-selling Italian memoir *Under the Tuscan Sun,* Frances Mayes shares a number of her favorite recipes, including this one for Lemon Cake. Carefully read her directions as you imagine yourself making this cake. Did you find her recipe interesting to read? How clear did you find her directions? Were there any parts of the recipe where you felt you needed clarification? Is it necessary to be familiar with the world of baking to read or appreciate Mayes's recipe? Explain.

LEMON CAKE

A family import, this Southern cake is one I've made a hundred times. Thin slices seem at home here with summer strawberries and cherries or winter pears. . . .

Cream together 1 cup of sweet butter and 2 cups of sugar. Beat in 3 eggs, one at a time. The mixture should be light. Mix together 3 cups of flour, 1 teaspoon of baking powder, 1/4 teaspoon of salt, and incorporate this with the butter mixture alternately with 1 cup buttermilk. (In Italy, I use one cup of cream since buttermilk is not available.) Begin and end with the flour mixture. Add 3 tablespoons of lemon juice and the grated zest of the lemon. Bake in a nonstick tube pan at 300° for 50 minutes. Test for doneness with a toothpick. The cake can be glazed with 1/4 cup of soft butter into which 1-1/2 cups of powdered sugar and 3 tablespoons of lemon juice have been beaten. Decorate with tiny curls of lemon rind.

SUGGESTED WRITING ASSIGNMENTS

1. How important are material objects to you? Eighner emphasizes the transience of material objects and thinks that all of us delude ourselves with the objects we strive to acquire. Is there anything wrong with desiring material goods? Write an essay in which you react to Eighner's position on materialism.

2. Write a process analysis in which you explain the steps you usually follow when deciding to make a purchase of some importance or expense to you. Hint: it's best to analyze your process with a specific product or products in mind. Do you compare brands, store prices, and so on? What are your priorities — must the item be stylish, durable, offer good overall value, give high performance?

Definition

Definition allows you to communicate precisely what you want to say. At the most basic level, you will frequently need to define key words. Your reader needs to know just what you mean when you use unfamiliar words, such as *accoutrement,* or words that are open to various interpretations, such as *liberal,* or words that, while generally familiar, are used in a particular sense. Failure to define important terms, or to define them accurately, confuses readers and hampers communication.

There are three basic ways to define a word; each is useful in its own way. The first method is to give a *synonym,* a word that has nearly the same meaning as the word you wish to define: *face* for *countenance, nervousness* for *anxiety.* No two words ever have *exactly* the same meaning, but you can nevertheless pair an unfamiliar word with a familiar one and thereby clarify your meaning.

Another way to define a word quickly, often within a single sentence, is to give a *formal definition;* that is, to place the term to be defined in a general class and then to distinguish it from other members of that class by describing its particular characteristics. For example:

Word	*Class*	*Characteristics*
A *watch*	is a *mechanical device*	*for telling time* and is usually *carried* or *worn.*
Semantics	is an *area of linguistics*	*concerned with the study of the meaning of words.*

The third method is known as *extended definition.* While some extended definitions require only a single paragraph, more often than not you will need several paragraphs or even an entire essay to define a new or difficult term or to rescue a controversial word from misconceptions and associations that may obscure its meaning.

In an essay-length extended definition, you provide your readers with far more information than you would in a synonym or a formal definition. You are, in most cases, exploring the meaning of your topic, whether it be a single word, a concept, or an object. In many cases, you must consider what your readers already know, or think they know, about your topic. Are there popular misconceptions that need to be done away with? Are there aspects of the topic that are seldom considered? Have particular experiences helped you understand the topic? You can use synonyms or formal definitions to help you define your topic, but you must convince your readers to accept your particular understanding of it.

Consider the following four-paragraph sequence in which Jerald M. Jellison and John H. Harvey provide an extended definition of *freedom,* an important but elusive concept.

> Choosing between negative alternatives often seems like no choice at all. Take the case of a woman trying to decide whether to stay married to her inconsiderate, incompetent husband, or get a divorce. She doesn't want to stay with him, but she feels divorce is a sign of failure and will stigmatize her socially. Or think of the decision faced by many young men [over thirty] years ago, when they were forced to choose between leaving their country and family or being sent to Vietnam.

> When we face decisions involving only alternatives we see as negatives, we feel so little freedom that we twist and turn searching for another choice with some positive characteristics.

> Freedom is a popular word. Individuals talk about how they feel free with one person and not with another, or how their bosses encourage or discourage freedom on the job. We hear about civil wars and revolutions being fought for greater freedom, with both sides righteously making the claim. The feeling of freedom is so important that people say they're ready to die for it, and supposedly have.

> Still, most people have trouble coming up with a precise definition of freedom. They give answers describing specific situations — "Freedom means doing what I want to do, not what the Government wants me to do," or "Freedom means not having my mother tell me when to come home from a party" — rather than a general definition covering many situations. The idea they seem to be expressing is that freedom is associated with making decisions, and that other people sometimes limit the number of alternatives from which they can select.

One controversial term that illustrates the need for extended definition is *obscene*. What is obscene? Books that are banned in one school system are considered perfectly acceptable in another. Movies that are shown in one town cannot be shown in a neighboring town. Clearly, the meaning of *obscene* has been clouded by contrasting personal opinions as well as by conflicting social norms. Therefore, if you use the term *obscene* (and especially if you tackle the issue of obscenity itself), you must be careful to define clearly and thoroughly what you mean by that term—that is, you have to give an extended definition. There are a number of methods you might use to develop such a definition. You could define *obscene* by explaining what it does not mean. You could also make your meaning clear by narrating an experience, by comparing and contrasting it to related terms such as *pornographic* or *exotic*, by citing specific examples, or by classifying the various types of obscenity.

A Jerk

■ Sydney J. Harris

For more than forty years, Sydney J. Harris (1917–1986) wrote a syndicated column for the Chicago Daily News *and the* Chicago Sun-Times *entitled "Strictly Personal," in which he considered virtually every aspect of contemporary American life. In the following essay from his book* Last Things First *(1961), Harris defines the term* jerk *by differentiating it from other similar slang terms. His essay is basically an extended definition but culminates in a formal definition in the final paragraph.*

FOR YOUR JOURNAL

Do you think that others see you as you see yourself? How do you know? What accounts for how others see you? Are we known by anything more than the total of our actions?

I don't know whether history repeats itself, but biography certainly   1
does. The other day, Michael came in and asked me what a "jerk" was—the same question Carolyn put to me a dozen years ago.

At that time, I fluffed her off with some inane answer, such as "A   2
jerk isn't a very nice person," but both of us knew it was an unsatisfactory reply. When she went to bed, I began trying to work up a suitable definition.

It is a marvelously apt word, of course. Until it was coined, not   3
more than 25 years ago, there was really no single word in English to describe the kind of person who is a jerk—"boob" and "simp" were too old hat, and besides they really didn't fit, for they could be lovable, and a jerk never is.

Thinking it over, I decided that a jerk is basically a person with-   4
out insight. He is not necessarily a fool or a dope, because some extremely clever persons can be jerks. In fact, it has little to do with intelligence as we commonly think of it; it is, rather, a kind of subtle but persuasive aroma emanating from the inner part of the personality.

I know a college president who can be described only as a jerk.   5
He is not an unintelligent man, nor unlearned, nor even unschooled

in the social amenities. Yet he is a jerk *cum laude,* because of a fatal flaw in his nature—he is totally incapable of looking into the mirror of his soul and shuddering at what he sees there.

A jerk, then, is a man (or woman) who is utterly unable to see himself as he appears to others. He has no grace, he is tactless without meaning to be, he is a bore even to his best friends, he is an egotist without charm. All of us are egotists to some extent, but most of us—unlike the jerk—are perfectly and horribly aware of it when we make asses of ourselves. The jerk never knows. 6

QUESTIONS FOR STUDY AND DISCUSSION

1. What, according to Harris, is a jerk?
2. Jerks, boobs, simps, fools, and dopes are all in the same class. How does Harris differentiate a jerk from a boob or a simp on the one hand, and from a fool or a dope on the other? (Glossary: *Division and Classification*)
3. What does Harris see as the relationship between intelligence and/or cleverness and the idea of a jerk?
4. In paragraph 5, Harris presents the example of the college president. How does this example support his definition? (Glossary: *Example*)
5. In the first two paragraphs, Harris tells how both his son and his daughter asked him what *jerk* means. How does this brief anecdote serve to introduce Harris's essay? (Glossary: *Beginnings and Endings*) Do you think it works well? Explain.

VOCABULARY

Refer to your dictionary to define the following words as they are used in this selection. Then use each word in a sentence of your own.

inane (2)	emanating (4)
apt (3)	amenities (5)
coined (3)	tactless (6)

CLASSROOM ACTIVITY USING DEFINITION

Try formally defining (p. 331) one of the following terms by putting it in a class and then differentiating it from other words in that class:

potato chips tenor saxophone
love   physical therapy
sociology

SUGGESTED WRITING ASSIGNMENTS

1. Usng Harris's essay as a model, write one or two paragraphs in which you give your own definition of *jerk*. How do you suppose Harris would react to your definition?

2. Every generation develops its own slang, which generally enlivens the speech and writing of those who use it. Ironically, however, no generation can arrive at a consensus definition of even its most popular slang terms—for example, *dweeb, lame, nimrod, airhead, fly*. Select a slang term that you use frequently, and write an essay in which you define the term. Read your definition aloud in class. Do the other members of your class agree with your definition?

The Company Man

■ **Ellen Goodman**

Ellen Goodman was born in Boston in 1941. After graduating cum laude *from* Radcliffe College *in 1963, she worked as a reporter and researcher for* Newsweek. *In 1967, she began working at the* Boston Globe *and, since 1974, has been a full-time columnist. Her regular column, "At Large," is syndicated by the* Washington Post's Writer's Group *and appears in nearly four hundred newspapers across the country. In addition, her writing has appeared in* McCall's, Harper's Bazaar, *and* Family Circle, *and her commentaries have been broadcast on radio and television. Several collections of Goodman's columns have been published as books, including* Close to Home *(1979),* At Large *(1981),* Keeping in Touch *(1985), and* Value Judgments *(1995). Her most recent book is* I Know Just What You Mean: The Power of Friendship in Women's Lives *(2000). In "The Company Man," taken from* Close to Home, *Goodman defines the* workaholic *by offering a poignant case-in-point example.*

FOR YOUR JOURNAL

While many jobs have regular hours, some, like journalism, medicine, high-level management, and jobs in new media, are less predictable and may require far more time. In contemplating your career goals, do you anticipate a greater emphasis on your work life or your home life? How much time beyond the standard forty hours per week are you willing to sacrifice to advance your career? Has this issue influenced your choice of career in any way, or do you anticipate that it will? Explain.

He worked himself to death, finally and precisely, at 3:00 A.M. 1
Sunday morning.

The obituary didn't say that, of course. It said that he died of a 2
coronary thrombosis—I think that was it—but everyone among his friends and acquaintances knew it instantly. He was a perfect Type A, a workaholic, a classic, they said to each other and shook their heads—and thought for five or ten minutes about the way they lived.

This man who worked himself to death finally and precisely at   3
3:00 A.M. Sunday morning—on his day off—was fifty-one years old
and a vice-president. He was, however, one of six vice-presidents,
and one of three who might conceivably—if the president died or retired soon enough—have moved to the top spot. Phil knew that.

He worked six days a week, five of them until eight or nine at   4
night, during a time when his own company had begun the four-
day week for everyone but the executives. He worked like the Important People. He had no outside "extracurricular interests," unless, of
course, you think about a monthly golf game that way. To Phil, it
was work. He always ate egg salad sandwiches at his desk. He was,
of course, overweight, by 20 or 25 pounds. He thought it was okay,
though, because he didn't smoke.

On Saturdays, Phil wore a sports jacket to the office instead of a   5
suit, because it was the weekend.

He had a lot of people working for him, maybe sixty, and most   6
of them liked him most of the time. Three of them will be seriously
considered for his job. The obituary didn't mention that.

But it did list his "survivors" quite accurately. He is survived by   7
his wife, Helen, forty-eight years old, a good woman of no particular
marketable skills, who worked in an office before marrying and
mothering. She had, according to her daughter, given up trying to
compete with his work years ago, when the children were small. A
company friend said, "I know how much you will miss him." And
she answered, "I already have."

"Missing him all these years," she must have given up part of   8
herself which had cared too much for the man. She would be "well
taken care of."

His "dearly beloved" eldest of the "dearly beloved" children is a   9
hard-working executive in a manufacturing firm down South. In the
day and a half before the funeral, he went around the neighborhood
researching his father, asking the neighbors what he was like. They
were embarrassed.

His second child is a girl, who is twenty-four and newly married.   10
She lives near her mother and they are close, but whenever she was
alone with her father, in a car driving somewhere, they had nothing
to say to each other.

The youngest is twenty, a boy, a high-school graduate who has   11
spent the last couple of years, like a lot of his friends, doing enough
odd jobs to stay in grass and food. He was the one who tried to grab
at his father, and tried to mean enough to him to keep the man at

home. He was his father's favorite. Over the last two years, Phil stayed up nights worrying about the boy.

The boy once said, "My father and I only board here."   12

At the funeral, the sixty-year-old company president told the   13
forty-eight-year-old widow that the fifty-one-year-old deceased had meant much to the company and would be missed and would be hard to replace. The widow didn't look him in the eye. She was afraid he would read her bitterness and, after all, she would need him to straighten out the finances — the stock options and all that.

Phil was overweight and nervous and worked too hard. If he   14
wasn't at the office, he was worried about it. Phil was a Type A, a heart-attack natural. You could have picked him out in a minute from a lineup.

So when he finally worked himself to death, at precisely 3:00   15
A.M. Sunday morning, no one was really surprised.

By 5:00 P.M. the afternoon of the funeral, the company president   16
had begun, discreetly of course, with care and taste, to make inquiries about his replacement. One of three men. He asked around: "Who's been working the hardest?"

QUESTIONS FOR STUDY AND DISCUSSION

1. After reading Goodman's essay, how would you define a *company man*? As you define the term, consider what such a man is not, as well as what he is. Is *company man* synonymous with *workaholic*? Why, or why not?

2. In paragraph 4, Goodman says that Phil worked like "the Important People." How would you define that term in the context in which it is used in the essay?

3. What is Goodman's purpose in this essay? (Glossary: *Purpose*) Explain your answer.

4. Do you think Goodman's unemotional tone is appropriate for her purpose? (Glossary: *Tone*) Why, or why not?

5. Describe Phil's relationship with each of his children. What does each relationship indicate about the impact of Phil's work habits on his family?

6. Goodman repeats the day and time that Phil worked himself to death. Why are those facts important enough to bear repetition? What about them is ironic?

VOCABULARY

Refer to your dictionary to define the following words as they are used in this selection. Then use each word in a sentence of your own.

obituary (2)
extracurricular (4)
discreetly (16)

CLASSROOM ACTIVITY USING DEFINITION

The connotation of the term *workaholic* depends on the context. For Phil's employers—and at his workplace in general—the term obviously had a positive connotation. For those who knew Phil outside the workplace, it had a negative one. Choose one of the terms below, and provide two definitions, one positive and one negative, that could apply to the term in different contexts.

go-getter
party animal
overachiever
mover and shaker

SUGGESTED WRITING ASSIGNMENTS

1. A procrastinator—a person who continually puts off responsibilities—is very different from a workaholic. Write an essay, modeled on Goodman's, using an extended example to define this interesting personality type.

2. One issue that Goodman does not raise is how a person becomes a workaholic. Write an essay in which you speculate about how someone might develop workaholism. How does a desirable trait like hard work begin to adversely affect someone? How might workaholism be avoided?

Who Wins? Who Cares?

■ **Mariah Burton Nelson**

Athlete, author, and motivational speaker Mariah Burton Nelson was born and raised in Blue Bell, Pennsylvania. She was a star basketball player at Stanford and, following her graduation in 1978, played professionally both in Europe and with the WBL, the first women's professional basketball league in the United States. She was inducted into the National Women in Sports Hall of Fame in 1996. After leaving professional sports to earn a master's degree in public health from San Jose State University in 1983, Nelson pursued a career in writing, focusing on sports, competition, and gender issues. Her articles have appeared in the Washington Post, New York Times, Cosmopolitan, Shape, USA Today, *and many other publications. She is also the author of several books, the latest being* The Unburdened Heart: Five Keys to Forgiveness and Freedom *(2000). The following article, in which Nelson assesses what competition means to women—and what it can and should mean to everyone—first appeared in* Women's Sports and Fitness *magazine.*

FOR YOUR JOURNAL

Would you describe yourself as competitive? If so, at what do you like to compete? How important is winning and losing to you? If not, do you avoid competitive activities, or can you still enjoy them? Explain what it is about competition that you do not like or that you choose to ignore.

C ompetition can damage self-esteem, create anxiety and lead to cheating and hurt feelings. But so can romantic love. No one suggests we do away with love; rather, we must perfect our understanding of what love means. 1

So too with competition. "To compete" is derived from the Latin *competere*, meaning "to seek together." Women seem to understand this. Maybe it's because we sat on the sidelines for so long, watching. Maybe it's because we were raised to be kind and nurturing. I'm not sure why it is. But I've noticed that it's not women who greet each 2

other with a ritualistic, "Who won?"; not women who memorize
scores and statistics; not women who pride themselves on "killer instincts." Passionate though we are, women don't take competition
that seriously. Or rather, we take competition seriously, but we don't
take winning and losing seriously. We've always been more interested
in playing.

In fact, since the early part of this century, women have devised   3
ways to make sport specifically inclusive and cooperative. Physical
educators of the 1920s taught sportswomanship as well as sport
skills, emphasizing health, vigor, high moral conduct, participation,
respect for other players and friendship. So intent were these women
on dodging the pitfalls of men's sports that many shied away from
competition altogether.

Nowadays, many women compete wholeheartedly. But we don't   4
buy into the "Super Bull" mentality that the game is everything. Like
Martina Navratilova and Chris Evert, former "rivals" whose rapport
has come to symbolize a classically female approach to competition,
many women find ways to remain close while also reaching for victory. We understand that trying to win is not tantamount to trying to
belittle; that winning is not wonderful if the process of play isn't
challenging, fair or fun; and that losing, though at times disappoint-
ing, does not connote failure. For women, if sports are power plays,
they're not about power over (power as dominance) but power to
(power as competence). Sports are not about domination and defeat
but caring and cooperation.

"The playing of a game has to do with your feelings, your emo-   5
tions, how you care about the people you're involved with," says
University of Iowa basketball coach C. Vivian Stringer.

Pam Shriver has said of Steffi Graf, "I hope in the next couple of   6
years that I get to be friends with her because it's just easier. It's more
fun. I don't think it affects the competitive side of things."

Friendship has been a major theme of my sporting life as well,   7
along with physical competence, achievement and joy. Though I've
competed in seven sports from the high school to the professional
level, I have few memories of victories or losses. I don't think winning
taught me to be a gracious winner. I don't think losing readied me for
more serious losses in life. Rather, my nearly 30 years of competition
have taught me how to *play,* with empathy, humor and honesty. If
another player challenges me to row harder, swim faster or make
more clever moves toward the basket, the games take on a special

thrill. But the final score is nearly irrelevant. Chris Evert once said the joy of winning "lasts about an hour."

I'm choosy about whom I compete with, and how. I don't partici- 8
pate in games in which "losers" are no longer allowed to play. Monopoly, poker, musical chairs, and single-elimination tournaments are a few examples. If playing is the point, then exclusion never makes sense. I also eschew competitions that pit women against men; they only serve to antagonize and polarize. I no longer injure myself in the name of victory. Nor, as a coach, will I allow players to get that carried away.

Some women, scarred by childhood exclusion, shamed by early 9
"defeats," or sickened by abuses such as cheating and steroid use, still avoid competition. They're right to be wary. Although these things are more visible in men's sports, female athletes and coaches can also succumb to the "winning is the only thing" myth, committing myriad ethical and personal offenses, from recruiting violations to bulimia, in the name of victory.

But once one understands the spirit of the game, it's not a matter 10
of *believing* that winning and losing aren't important, it's a matter of noticing that they're not. Women seem to notice. Most women can play soccer, golf, or run competitively and enjoy themselves, regardless of outcome. They can play on a "losing" team but leave the court with little or no sense of loss. They can win without feeling superior.

I think it's the responsibility of these women — and the men who 11
remain unblinded by the seductive glow of victory — to share this vision with young players. Children, it seems to me, naturally enjoy comparing their skills: "How far can you throw the ball? Farther than I can? How did you do it? Will you show me?" It's only when adults ascribe undue importance to victory that losing becomes devastating and children get hurt.

Adults must show children that what matters is how one plays 12
the game. It's important that we not just parrot that cliché, but demonstrate our commitment to fair, participatory competition by paying equal attention to skilled and unskilled children; by allowing all children to participate fully in games, regardless of the score; and by caring more about process than results. This way, children can fully comprehend what they seem to intuit: that competition can be a way to get to know other people, to be challenged, and to have fun in a close and caring environment. To seek together.

Some of my best friends are the women and men who share a 13
court or pool or field with me. Together we take risks, make

mistakes, laugh, push ourselves and revel in the grace and beauty of sports. Who wins? Who cares? We're playing *with*, not *against* each other, using each other's accomplishments to inspire.

At its best, competition is not divisive but unifying, not hateful 14 but loving. Like other expressions of love, it should not be avoided simply because it has been misunderstood.

QUESTIONS FOR STUDY AND DISCUSSION

1. Nelson's discussion of the Latin root for *to compete* in paragraph 2 provides the foundation for her extended definition of the term. Using the whole essay, provide a concise two-sentence summary of Nelson's definition for *to compete*.

2. Nelson identifies her definition of *to compete* as a feminine one—a definition that is quite different from the prevailing masculine definition. How would Nelson define *to compete* from a masculine point of view? What aspects of the masculine definition does she find disagreeable?

3. Nelson begins her essay by identifying some of the negative consequences associated with competition and by comparing them with those of romantic love. Why do you think she begins her essay, which carries a positive overall message, with negative associations? (Glossary: *Beginnings and Endings*) Do you find her comparison of competition with romantic love effective? Why, or why not?

4. According to Nelson, why do some women dislike or avoid competition?

5. The athletes Nelson uses to illustrate her points about competition are all tennis players—Chris Evert, Martina Navratilova, Pam Shriver. (Glossary: *Example*) Why do you think Nelson focuses on tennis in her essay?

6. "It's not whether you win or lose, it's how you play the game," the cliché Nelson invokes in paragraph 12, could serve as a reasonably good summary of Nelson's message. Why do you think she uses the cliché? What connotations does this cliché carry for you? (Glossary: *Connotation/Denotation*) How does Nelson propose that coaches and parents should go beyond the cliché to teach children about the proper meaning of competition?

VOCABULARY

Refer to your dictionary to define the following words as they are used in this selection. Then use each word in a sentence of your own.

ritualistic (2) myriad (9)

tantamount (4) bulimia (9)

empathy (7) parrot (12)

eschew (8) intuit (12)

polarize (8)

CLASSROOM ACTIVITY USING DEFINITION

Definitions are often dependent upon context. In Nelson's essay, the context is gender. In her view, men and women usually define *competition* in very different ways. Discuss with your classmates other words or terms whose definitions might differ between men and women. Choose two or three words, and write definitions for them from your perspective. Discuss your definitions with your classmates. What gender differences, if any, are apparent in the definitions?

SUGGESTED WRITING ASSIGNMENTS

1. In her essay, Nelson writes about "the process of play," and she identifies that process as more important in the end than winning or losing. Write a short essay in which you define *play*. To you, what is play? How important is it in your life? How is it limited by the other demands on your time? How might your definition differ from those of other people?

2. What do you like best about your favorite sport? For example, it could be sportsmanship, exertion, technique, victory, precision, or another aspect of the sport that helps make it compelling for you. Write an essay in which you present a particular game, practice, or workout that illustrates why you like the sport and what it is about it that makes it appealing to you. (If you don't play sports, choose a favorite hobby.)

Division and Classification

A writer practices division by separating a class of things or ideas into categories following a clear principle or basis. In the following paragraph, journalist Robert MacNeil establishes categories of speech according to the level of formality:

> It fascinates me how differently we all speak in different circumstances. We have levels of formality, as in our clothing. There are very formal occasions, often requiring written English: the job application or the letter to the editor — the darksuit, serious-tie language, with everything pressed and the lint brushed off. There is our less formal out-in-the-world language — a more comfortable suit, but still respectable. There is language for close friends in the evenings, on weekends — bluejeans-and-sweat-shirt language, when it's good to get the tie off. There is family language, even more relaxed, full of grammatical short cuts, family slang, echoes of old jokes that have become intimate shorthand — the language of pyjamas and uncombed hair. Finally, there is the language with no clothes on; the talk of couples — murmurs, sighs, grunts — language at its least self-conscious, open, vulnerable, and primitive.

With classification, on the other hand, a writer groups individual objects or ideas into already established categories. Division and classification can operate separately but often accompany one another. Here, for example, is a passage about levers in which the writer first discusses generally how levers work. In the second paragraph, the writer uses division to establish three categories of levers and then uses classification to group individual levers into those categories:

> Every lever has one fixed point called the "fulcrum" and is acted upon by two forces — the "effort" (exertion of hand muscles) and the "weight" (object's resistance). Levers work according to a simple formula: the effort (how hard you push or pull) multiplied by its distance from the fulcrum (effort arm) equals the weight

multiplied by its distance from the fulcrum (weight arm). Thus two pounds of effort exerted at a distance of four feet from the fulcrum will raise eight pounds located one foot from the fulcrum.

There are three types of levers, conventionally called "first kind," "second kind," and "third kind." Levers of the first kind have the fulcrum located between the effort and the weight. Examples are a pump handle, an oar, a crowbar, a weighing balance, a pair of scissors, and a pair of pliers. Levers of the second kind have the weight in the middle and magnify the effort. Examples are the handcar crank and doors. Levers of the third kind, such as a power shovel or a baseball batter's forearm, have the effort in the middle and always magnify the distance.

In writing, division and classification are affected directly by the writer's practical purpose. That purpose—what the writer wants to explain or prove—determines the class of things or ideas being divided and classified. For instance, a writer might divide television programs according to their audiences—adults, families, or children—and then classify individual programs into each of these categories to show how much emphasis the television stations place on reaching each audience. A different purpose would require different categories. A writer concerned about the prevalence of violence in television programming would first divide television programs into those that include fights and murders and those that do not, and would then classify a large sample of programs into those categories. Other writers with different purposes might divide television programs differently—by the day and time of broadcast, for example, or by the number of women featured in prominent roles—and then classify individual programs accordingly.

Another example may help clarify how division and classification work hand in hand in writing. Suppose a sociologist wants to determine whether the socioeconomic status of the people in a particular neighborhood has any influence on their voting behavior. Having decided on her purpose, the sociologist chooses as her subject the fifteen families living on Maple Street. Her goal then becomes to group these families in a way that will be relevant to her purpose. She immediately knows that she wants to divide the neighborhood in two ways: (1) according to socioeconomic status (low-income earners, middle-income earners, and high-income earners) and (2) according to voting behavior (voters and nonvoters). However, her process of division won't be complete until she can classify individual families into her various groupings.

In confidential interviews with each family, the sociologist learns first its income and then whether any member of the household has voted in a state or federal election during the last four years. Based on this information, she begins to classify each family according to her established categories and at the same time to divide the neighborhood into the subclasses crucial to her study. Her work leads her to construct a diagram of her divisions and classifications.

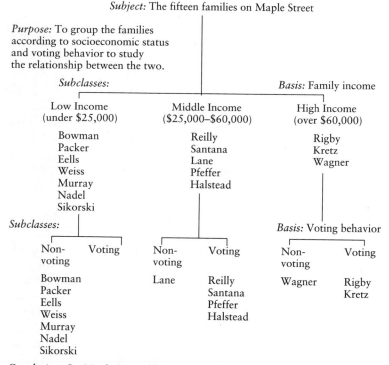

Subject: The fifteen families on Maple Street

Purpose: To group the families according to socioeconomic status and voting behavior to study the relationship between the two.

Subclasses: *Basis:* Family income

Low Income (under $25,000)	Middle Income ($25,000–$60,000)	High Income (over $60,000)
Bowman	Reilly	Rigby
Packer	Santana	Kretz
Eells	Lane	Wagner
Weiss	Pfeffer	
Murray	Halstead	
Nadel		
Sikorski		

Subclasses: *Basis:* Voting behavior

Non-voting	Voting	Non-voting	Voting	Non-voting	Voting
Bowman		Lane	Reilly	Wagner	Rigby
Packer			Santana		Kretz
Eells			Pfeffer		
Weiss			Halstead		
Murray					
Nadel					
Sikorski					

Conclusion: On Maple Street, there seems to be a relationship between socioeconomic status and voting behavior: the low-income families are nonvoters.

This diagram allows the sociologist to visualize her division and classification system and its essential components: subject; basis or principle of division; subclasses or categories; and conclusion. It is clear that her ultimate conclusion depends on her ability to work back and forth between the potential divisions or subclasses and the actual families to be classified.

The following guidelines can help you in using division and classification in your writing:

1. *Identify a clear purpose, and be sure that your principle of division is appropriate to that purpose.* If, for example, you wished to examine the common characteristics of four-year athletic scholarship recipients at your college or university, you might consider the following principles of division: program of study, sport, place of origin, or sex. In this case it would not be useful to divide students on the basis of their favorite type of music because that seems irrelevant to your purpose.

2. *Divide your subject into categories that are mutually exclusive.* An item can belong to only one category. For example, it would be unsatisfactory to divide students as men, women, and athletes.

3. *Make your division and classification complete.* Your categories should account for all items in a subject class. In dividing students on the basis of geographic origin, for example, it would be inappropriate to consider only the United States, for such a division would not account for foreign students. Then, for your classification to be complete, every student must be placed in one of the established categories.

4. *Be sure to state clearly the conclusion that your division and classification lead you to draw.* For example, after conducting your division and classification of athletic scholarship recipients, you might conclude that the majority of male athletes with athletic scholarships come from the western United States.

The Ways of Meeting Oppression

■ **Martin Luther King Jr.**

Martin Luther King Jr. (1929–1968) was the leading spokesman for the rights of African Americans during the 1950s and 1960s before he was assassinated in 1968. He established the Southern Christian Leadership Conference, organized many civil-rights demonstrations, and opposed the Vietnam War and the draft. In 1964, he was awarded the Nobel Prize for Peace. In the following essay, taken from his book Strive toward Freedom *(1958), King classifies the three ways oppressed people throughout history have reacted to their oppressors. As you read, pay particular attention to how King's discussions within the categories of classification lead him to the conclusion he presents in paragraph 8.*

FOR YOUR JOURNAL

Someone once said, "Violence is the last resort of the incompetent." What are your thoughts on the reasons for violent behavior on either a personal or a national level? Is violence ever justified? If so, under what circumstances?

Oppressed people deal with their oppression in three characteris-   1
tic ways. One way is acquiescence: the oppressed resign themselves to their doom. They tacitly adjust themselves to oppression, and thereby become conditioned to it. In every movement toward freedom some of the oppressed prefer to remain oppressed. Almost 2800 years ago Moses set out to lead the children of Israel from the slavery of Egypt to the freedom of the promised land. He soon discovered that slaves do not always welcome their deliverers. They become accustomed to being slaves. They would rather bear those ills they have, as Shakespeare pointed out, than flee to others that they know not of. They prefer the "fleshpots of Egypt" to the ordeals of emancipation.

There is such a thing as the freedom of exhaustion. Some people   2
are so worn down by the yoke of oppression that they give up. A few
years ago in the slum areas of Atlanta, a Negro guitarist used to sing
almost daily: "Been down so long that down don't bother me." This
is the type of negative freedom and resignation that often engulfs the
life of the oppressed.

But this is not the way out. To accept passively an unjust system is to   3
cooperate with that system; thereby the oppressed become as evil as the
oppressor. Noncooperation with evil is as much a moral obligation as is
cooperation with good. The oppressed must never allow the conscience
of the oppressor to slumber. Religion reminds every man that he is his
brother's keeper. To accept injustice or segregation passively is to say to
the oppressor that his actions are morally right. It is a way of allowing his
conscience to fall asleep. At this moment the oppressed fails to be his
brother's keeper. So acquiescence — while often the easier way — is not
the moral way. It is the way of the coward. The Negro cannot win the respect of his oppressor by acquiescing; he merely increases the oppressor's
arrogance and contempt. Acquiescence is interpreted as proof of the
Negro's inferiority. The Negro cannot win the respect of the white
people of the South or the peoples of the world if he is willing to sell the
future of his children for his personal and immediate comfort and safety.

A second way that oppressed people sometimes deal with oppres-   4
sion is to resort to physical violence and corroding hatred. Violence
often brings about momentary results. Nations have frequently won
their independence in battle. But in spite of temporary victories, violence never brings permanent peace. It solves no social problem; it
merely creates new and more complicated ones.

Violence as a way of achieving racial justice is both impractical   5
and immoral. It is impractical because it is a descending spiral ending
in destruction for all. The old law of an eye for an eye leaves
everybody blind. It is immoral because it seeks to humiliate the
opponent rather than win his understanding; it seeks to annihilate
rather than to convert. Violence is immoral because it thrives on
hatred rather than love. It destroys community and makes brotherhood impossible. It leaves society in monologue rather than dialogue.
Violence ends by defeating itself. It creates bitterness in the survivors and brutality in the destroyers. A voice echoes through time
saying to every potential Peter, "Put up your sword."* History is

---

*The apostle Peter had drawn his sword to defend Christ from arrest. The voice was
Christ's, who surrendered himself for trial and crucifixion (John 18:11).

cluttered with the wreckage of nations that failed to follow this command.

If the American Negro and other victims of oppression succumb 6 to the temptation of using violence in the struggle for freedom, future generations will be the recipients of a desolate night of bitterness, and our chief legacy to them will be an endless reign of meaningless chaos. Violence is not the way.

The third way open to oppressed people in their quest for free- 7 dom is the way of nonviolent resistance. Like the synthesis in Hegelian philosophy, the principle of nonviolent resistance seeks to reconcile the truths of two opposites—acquiescence and violence— while avoiding the extremes and immoralities of both. The nonviolent resister agrees with the person who acquiesces that one should not be physically aggressive toward his opponent; but he balances the equation by agreeing with the person of violence that evil must be resisted. He avoids the nonresistance of the former and the violent resistance of the latter. With nonviolent resistance, no individual or group need submit to any wrong, nor need anyone resort to violence in order to right a wrong.

It seems to me that this is the method that must guide the actions 8 of the Negro in the present crisis in race relations. Through nonviolent resistance the Negro will be able to rise to the noble height of opposing the unjust system while loving the perpetrators of the system. The Negro must work passionately and unrelentingly for full stature as a citizen, but he must not use inferior methods to gain it. He must never come to terms with falsehood, malice, hate, or destruction.

Nonviolent resistance makes it possible for the Negro to remain 9 in the South and struggle for his rights. The Negro's problem will not be solved by running away. He cannot listen to the glib suggestion of those who would urge him to migrate en masse to other sections of the country. By grasping his great opportunity in the South he can make a lasting contribution to the moral strength of the nation and set a sublime example of courage for generations yet unborn.

By nonviolent resistance, the Negro can also enlist all men of good 10 will in his struggle for equality. The problem is not a purely racial one, with Negroes set against whites. In the end, it is not a struggle between people at all, but a tension between justice and injustice. Nonviolent resistance is not aimed against oppressors but against oppression. Under its banner consciences, not racial groups, are enlisted.

QUESTIONS FOR STUDY AND DISCUSSION

1. What is King's purpose in writing this essay? How does classifying the three types of resistance to oppression serve this purpose? (Glossary: *Purpose*)
2. What principle of division does King use in this essay?
3. Why do you suppose King discusses acquiescence, violence, and nonviolent resistance in that order? (Glossary: *Organization*)
4. Why, according to King, do slaves not always welcome their deliverers?
5. What does King mean in paragraph 2 by the "freedom of exhaustion"?
6. King states that he favors nonviolent resistance over the other two ways of meeting oppression. What are the disadvantages that King sees in meeting oppression with acquiescence or with violence? Look closely at the words he uses to describe nonviolent resistance and those he uses to describe acquiescence and violence. How does his choice of words contribute to his argument? Show examples. (Glossary: *Connotation/Denotation*)

VOCABULARY

Refer to your dictionary to define the following words as they are used in this selection. Then use each word in a sentence of your own.

acquiescence (1) desolate (6)
tacitly (1) synthesis (7)
corroding (4) sublime (9)
annihilate (5)

CLASSROOM ACTIVITY USING DIVISION AND CLASSIFICATION

Examine the following lists of hobbies, books, and buildings. Determine at least three principles that could be used to divide the items listed in each group. Finally, classify the items in each group according to one of the principles you have established.

HOBBIES
watching sports on TV
stamp collecting

scuba diving
surfing the Web
hiking
dancing
running

BOOKS
The Adventures of Huckleberry Finn
Guinness Book of World Records
The Joy of Cooking
American Heritage Dictionary (College Edition)
To Kill a Mockingbird
Gone with the Wind

BUILDINGS
World Trade Center
White House
The Alamo
Taj Mahal
Library of Congress
Buckingham Palace

SUGGESTED WRITING ASSIGNMENTS

1. Using King's essay as a model, write an essay about a current social or personal problem, using division and classification to discuss various possible solutions. You might discuss something
personal, such as the problem of giving up smoking, or a pressing social issue, such as gun control or gay marriage. Whatever
your topic, use an appropriate principle of division to establish
categories that suit the purpose of your discussion.

2. Consider any one of the following topics for an essay of classification. You may find it helpful to review the guidelines for using
division and classification on page 349.

movies	country music
college courses	newspapers
sports fans	pets
teenage lifestyles	students

The Three Faces of Stress

■ **Sarah Federman**

Sarah Federman, a freelance writer now living in San Francisco, was born in New York City in 1976. She graduated from the University of Pennsylvania in 1998, where she majored in intellectual history. A strong interest in alternative medicine led her to her current work as a researcher at the Institute for Health and Healing at California Pacific Medical Center. Federman wrote "The Three Faces of Stress" expressly for a non-scientific general audience. She first became curious about stress as an undergraduate when she started to become aware of how stress was affecting her own body and her sense of wellness. As she relates in this essay, it is essential to identify and understand the three main types of stress in our lives before we can effectively deal with them and the symptoms they produce.

FOR YOUR JOURNAL

What are the stresses in your life, and what do you do to relieve them? Are there any stresses in your life over which you have no control?

M y roommate, Megan, pushes open the front door, throws her 1
keys on the counter, and flops down on the couch.
"Hey, Megan, how are you?" I yell from the kitchen. 2
"I don't know what's wrong with me. I sleep all the time, but I'm 3
still tired. No matter what I do, I just don't feel well."
"What did the doctor say?" 4
"She said it sounds like chronic fatigue syndrome." 5
"Do you think it might be caused by stress?" I ask. 6
"Nah, stress doesn't affect me very much. I like keeping busy and 7
running around. This must be something else."
Like most Americans, Megan does not recognize the numerous 8
factors in her life that cause her stress. When she gets run down or
catches a cold, she feels helpless and victimized by her body's reactions. Hundreds of articles have been written about coping with the
effects of stress, offering great tips on how to relax, slow down, take

a deep breath, and shut off the body's immune-suppressing response. But surprisingly little has been written about the three types of stresses—physical stress, chemical stress, and emotional stress—which, according to practitioners of traditional Chinese medicine, lead to all internal disease. Our ability to recognize and reduce these three types of stresses not only helps us avoid disease, but can also alleviate fatigue, sluggishness, moodiness, headaches, irritability, allergies, and nausea. Relieving such symptoms can improve the quality of our lives, but before we can begin to deal with the symptoms of our stresses, we need to be able to identify the stresses themselves.

Many people have difficulty recognizing the three main types of   9
stresses, lumping all the unpleasant aspects of their lives into one broad category. I recently asked three of my friends, all struggling with the pressures of post-college life, how they define and experience stress. Jill, twenty-six, says, "Stress is when your eyes narrow together and a little crease forms. Stress is not knowing what to do with your life. Stress is everything that isn't relaxing." Anne, twenty-three, says that her shoulders get sore whenever she faces an inability to pay her rent or when she anticipates separation from her family and close friends. Jen, twenty-five, says, "Lately stress has been finding meaning. Actually, I think that has always been a source of stress for me, that what I am doing isn't meaningful."

All of the stresses my friends identified—confusion about life   10
choices, separation from family and friends, and financial concerns—fall under the category of emotional stress. This seems to be the type of stress that people can most readily identify in their lives. By underestimating the impact of physical and chemical stresses, however, people who enjoy intensity or have learned not to overreact to emotional stress are often surprised to find that they, too, are experiencing considerable stress.

Three of my friends, Megan, Howie, and Jim, lead highly stress-   11
ful lives, and each is, to some degree, unhappy as a result. An examination of the particular stresses on each friend reveals that much could be done to alleviate their discomfort and unhappiness.

MEGAN

My exhausted roommate, Megan, seemed surprised and perhaps a   12
little annoyed when I suggested that stress might be the source of her chronic fatigue. A windsurfer, skier, mountain climber, and corporate powerhouse, Megan exposes herself to far more stressors than she re-

alizes. Despite a four-hour commute each day and a fifty-hour work-week, she spends weekends skiing in zero-degree temperatures or pursuing other strenuous activities.

Megan knows her sports put a lot of physical stress on her body; 13 no one can dispute that the 50-degree water in the San Francisco Bay can be taxing on even the most passionate windsurfer. Every several weeks she hobbles home with a physical wound, whether it be a bruised thigh from a hard fall on an icy mountain, a twisted knee from a game of tennis, or a swollen ankle from marathon training. By neglecting to stretch adequately before or after exercising, she adds to her physical stress.

The chemical stress in Megan's life comes mostly from her diet 14 and from time spent in the city. Despite living in California, a state where fresh organic vegetables are available year-round, she continues to buy frozen vegetables grown with pesticides and frozen chicken raised with growth hormones. She also has a sweet tooth. She sometimes bakes and snacks on cookies late at night, and the sudden rush of sugar that follows can prevent her from sleeping. Other hidden chemical stresses in her life include car exhaust, the new coat of paint in her bedroom, and the nail polish she ingests when she bites her nails.

As a talented athlete and an accomplished, passionate business- 15 woman, Megan has attracted lots of friends and finds herself invited to countless parties. Despite this attention, Megan's hectic lifestyle prevents her from keeping up with old friends, which means that she suffers the emotional stress of not being able to relax with or confide in someone she knows well and can trust.

Eager to do it all, Megan finds herself in constant motion, 16 putting herself under far more stress than she realizes. While she can't easily avoid some stressors, such as car exhaust, she can take her fatigue as an opportunity to evaluate her lifestyle choices, choosing, for example, to spend some weekends at home with friends rather than making a long car trip to a ski area. By slowing down, eating healthier foods, and spending more time with friends, she might have more energy to do the sports and work she loves.

HOWIE

Like Megan, Howie enjoys working and playing hard. Lately, how- 17 ever, he has found himself irritable at work, impatient with his daughter, nauseated by simple foods, and unable to fall asleep before

1 A.M. A writer for a daily newspaper, he often works twelve-hour days, dividing his time between interviewing bystanders at the city's endless art festivals and cultural celebrations and spending five to six hours a day at his computer. Happy to be able to live his lifelong dream of working as a reporter, he accepts his poorly lit office with its awkwardly positioned computer and uncomfortable swivel chair. To improve his physical fitness, Howie decided to train for the California AIDS Ride. To prepare for this 570-mile trip from San Francisco to Los Angeles, he pedals 45 to 70 miles each weekend.

Howie admits that working for a daily paper can be emotionally draining — he struggles to turn in high-quality work, only to find that his editor has cut crucial portions of his articles — but the drain on his personal life is more severe. His relationship with his daughter, his personal writing, and meals with friends had always been great sources of pleasure for him and an opportunity for renewal. Because his job demands so much personal interaction, he now feels too tired to pay attention to his daughter or to spend time with friends. He spends much of his free time alone, either biking or eating, and rarely does he feel inspired to work on his short stories. The resultant emotional stress is considerable. 18

While Howie's intention to stay in shape is laudable, the combined effect of his work and athletic training puts a phenomenal amount of physical stress on his body. Both activities, biking and writing, have him hunched over for hours. With no back support from the old swivel chair and with the low handlebars on his bike, Howie unknowingly compresses his spine. This compression diminishes his body's ability to release tension and communicate signals to his brain. He also spends many hours each week squinting. The low light in his office makes his small laptop screen hard to see, and his refusal to buy a new pair of sunglasses for bike riding means that he squints for four or five hours at a time. As a result, he starts to get headaches and finds himself irritable, rather than refreshed, after a long workout. 19

By adhering to a balanced training diet and biking far from city traffic, Howie avoids a great deal of chemical stress. Still, he has a few habits that contribute to his moodiness, nausea, and fretful sleep. Rather than using ice or taking a hot bath after a strenuous bike ride, he relaxes by drinking a few beers and swallowing two aspirin. He also waits for his morning bus at one of the city's largest intersections, rather than the quieter stop a few blocks up the street. 20

An enthusiastic and committed activist and athlete, Howie has unintentionally developed a toxic lifestyle that affects not only his 21 physical health, but also his ability to connect with coworkers, express his love for his daughter, and develop his own writing. Even the best attempts to "get healthy" can backfire when they are not informed by a good understanding of stressors and their compounding effect on the body.

JIM

After losing his mother to cancer and his grandmother to heart disease,   22
Jim started to worry that his lifestyle would exacerbate any genetic predisposition to health problems that he might have. A forty-three-year-old business manager, Jim had spent fifteen years working in a small office in San Jose, California, and eating pizza or Chinese food for lunch. The loss of his mother and grandmother inspired Jim to lose twenty-five pounds. To reach his target weight of 175, he drank diet soda instead of regular soda, chewed sugar-free gum to avoid snacking, substituted vegetables for the meat on his pizza, and stopped ordering fried food from the Chinese restaurant. In good weather, he would take a brisk twenty-five-minute walk after work.

By reaching his target weight, Jim took a good deal of physical   23
stress off his heart. His evening walks not only helped him fit into his old jeans, but also enabled him to release some of each day's emotional stresses. Unfortunately, Jim's new health plan actually increased the chemical stresses on his body.

While diet soda may have less sugar and fewer calories than regu-   24
lar soda, it contains unhealthy sweeteners and dyes. Some doctors still consider sweeteners like saccharine to be unsafe, even though saccharine was taken off the Food and Drug Administration's list of known carcinogens. The dyes, made from energetic molecules, can interact with and damage DNA, possibly leading to cancer. Chewing gum may prevent snacking, but the added sorbitol stresses the gastrointestinal tract, promotes ulcerative colitis, and can cause diarrhea. Jim made a good decision when he stopped eating fried Chinese food, but he should ask that his food be prepared without monosodium glutamate (MSG). Added to many Chinese dishes to enhance flavor, MSG also adds extra sodium and causes many allergic reactions, from racing heartbeats to throbbing headaches. The cheese on Jim's pizza may contain bovine growth hormone, and the vegetables can contain pesticide residue.

Despite the chemical stresses of his new diet, Jim felt great physi-   25
cally after losing the weight. But his wife noticed that Jim still did not

seem quite himself. She asked him about this, and he admitted that he was experiencing a strange sense of sadness and emptiness. Together they explored why this might be and discovered that Jim emotionally connected the loss of his mother and grandmother to his weight loss. Jim began to understand that in letting go of the weight, he was, in a sense, finally able to grieve for their loss and let them go as well. Identifying and sharing this emotional stress enabled Jim to enjoy his new life without a sense of guilt.

We tend to think that only major lifestyle choices and events like 26 the diagnosis of a major illness or an acrimonious divorce have a major impact on our lives. Megan, Howie, and Jim serve as examples that this is not necessarily the case. The minor stresses we encounter—physical, emotional, and chemical—can have a significant cumulative impact on our lives, and the quality of our personal, professional, and emotional lives depends on our ability to maintain a healthy balance. While we cannot avoid every bump, scrape, deadline, or genetic predisposition, we have a phenomenal ability to heal ourselves. The next time you feel overwhelmed by "stress," pain, or discomfort, try listing all of the possible emotional, chemical, and physical stresses you might be experiencing. Then, decide which ones can be eliminated. Reducing these stresses will help you move toward greater balance and control over your own experience.

QUESTIONS FOR STUDY AND DISCUSSION

1. What, according to Federman, are the three types of stresses? Illustrate each type with an example from your own experience. Do you find the three types of stress difficult to distinguish? Explain.
2. Why does Federman believe that it is important for people to be able to identify and understand the three types of stresses? Why is it sometimes difficult to identify these stresses?
3. Federman asks three friends for their definitions of stress (9). What point do their thoughts on stress help Federman make? Explain.
4. Federman uses the experiences of Megan, Howie, and Jim as the main examples in the body of her essay. How does she use division and classification to organize the information within each example? How does paragraph 11 function in the context of her essay?

5. What do you learn from Federman's first ten paragraphs? Do they make an effective introduction to her essay? (Glossary: *Beginnings and Endings*) Why, or why not?

6. What does Federman suggest readers do the next time they are feeling overwhelmed by stress?

VOCABULARY

Refer to your dictionary to define the following words as they are used in this selection. Then use each word in a sentence of your own.

symptoms (8)   phenomenal (19)
chronic (12)   predisposition (22)
pesticides (14)   carcinogens (24)
laudable (19)   enhance (24)

CLASSROOM ACTIVITY USING DIVISION AND CLASSIFICATION

Divide each item in the following list into at least three different categories, and be prepared to discuss your principles of division. Also provide several examples that might be classified into each category. For example, pets can be divided into the categories mammals (cat, hamster, guinea pig), birds (parrot, finch, parakeet), reptiles (snake, chameleon, iguana), fish (guppy, goldfish, angelfish), and insects (ant, spider, bee).

computers   colleges
fast-food restaurants   soft drinks
professional sports   checking accounts
newspapers   mall stores

SUGGESTED WRITING ASSIGNMENTS

1. College is a time of stress for many students. Write an essay discussing the specific emotional, physical, and chemical stresses experienced by students at your school. In what ways do the stresses of college students differ from those of the recent graduates Federman discusses? You may find it helpful to read what you wrote in response to the journal prompt for this essay before you start.

2. Write an essay that divides and classifies the students at your college or university. Be sure to use principles of division that will lead to interesting insights into your school.

Friends, Good Friends—and Such Good Friends

■ Judith Viorst

Judith Viorst was born in Newark, New Jersey, in 1931 and attended Rutgers University. She has published several volumes of light verse and collections of prose, as well as many articles in popular magazines. Her numerous children's books include the perennial favorite Alexander and the Terrible, Horrible, No Good, Very Bad Day *(1972). Her recent books for adults include* Necessary Losses: The Loves, Illusions, Dependencies, and Impossible Expectations That All of Us Have to Give Up in Order to Grow *(1997),* Imperfect Control: Our Lifelong Struggles with Power and Surrender *(1998), and* Suddenly 60: And Other Shocks of Late-Life *(2000). The following selection appeared in her regular column in* Redbook. *In it she analyzes and classifies the various types of friends that a person can have. As you read, assess the validity of Viorst's analysis by trying to place your own friends into her categories. Determine also whether the categories themselves are mutually exclusive.*

FOR YOUR JOURNAL

Think about your friends. Do you regard them all in the same light? Would you group them in any way? On what basis would you group them?

Women are friends, I once would have said, when they totally love   1
and support and trust each other, and bare to each other the secrets of their souls, and run—no questions asked—to help each other, and tell harsh truths to each other (no, you can't wear that dress unless you lose ten pounds first) when harsh truths must be told.

Women are friends, I once would have said, when they share the   2
same affection for Ingmar Bergman, plus train rides, cats, warm rain, charades, Camus, and hate with equal ardor Newark and Brussels sprouts and Lawrence Welk and camping.

In other words, I once would have said that a friend is a friend all   3
the way, but now I believe that's a narrow point of view. For the friend-

ships I have and the friendships I see are conducted at many levels of intensity, serve many different functions, meet different needs and range from those as all-the-way as the friendship of the soul sisters mentioned above to that of the most nonchalant and casual playmates.

Consider these varieties of friendship: 4

1. Convenience friends. These are women with whom, if our paths 5
weren't crossing all the time, we'd have no particular reason to be
friends: a next-door neighbor, a woman in our car pool, the mother of
one of our children's closest friends or maybe some mommy with whom
we serve juice and cookies each week at the Glenwood Co-op Nursery.

Convenience friends are convenient indeed. They'll lend us their 6
cups and silverware for a party. They'll drive our kids to soccer when
we're sick. They'll take us to pick up our car when we need a lift to
the garage. They'll even take our cats when we go on vacation. As we
will for them.

But we don't, with convenience friends, ever come too close or 7
tell too much; we maintain our public face and emotional distance.
"Which means," says Elaine, "that I'll talk about being overweight
but not about being depressed. Which means I'll admit being mad but
not blind with rage. Which means that I might say that we're pinched
this month but never that I'm worried sick over money."

But which doesn't mean that there isn't sufficient value to be 8
found in these friendships of mutual aid, in convenience friends.

2. Special-interest friends. These friendships aren't intimate, and 9
they needn't involve kids or silverware or cats. Their value lies in
some interest jointly shared. And so we may have an office friend or a
yoga friend or a tennis friend or a friend from the Women's Democratic Club.

"I've got one woman friend," says Joyce, "who likes, as I do, to 10
take psychology courses. Which makes it nice for me — and nice for
her. It's fun to go with someone you know and it's fun to discuss
what you've learned, driving back from the classes." And for the
most part, she says, that's all they discuss.

"I'd say that what we're doing is *doing* together, not being to- 11
gether," Suzanne says of her Tuesday-doubles friends. "It's mainly a
tennis relationship, but we play together well. And I guess we all need
to have a couple of playmates."

I agree. 12

My playmate is a shopping friend, a woman of marvelous taste, a 13
woman who knows exactly *where* to buy *what,* and furthermore is a
woman who always knows beyond a doubt what one ought to be

buying. I don't have the time to keep up with what's new in eyeshadow, hemlines and shoes and whether the smock look is in or finished already. But since (oh, shame!) I care a lot about eyeshadow, hemlines and shoes, and since I don't *want* to wear smocks if the smock look is finished, I'm very glad to have a shopping friend.

3. Historical friends. We all have a friend who knew us when . . .   14
maybe way back in Miss Meltzer's second grade, when our family lived in that three-room flat in Brooklyn, when our dad was out of work for seven months, when our brother Allie got in that fight where they had to call the police, when our sister married the endodontist from Yonkers and when, the morning after we lost our virginity, she was the first, the only, friend we told.

The years have gone by and we've gone separate ways and we've   15
little in common now, but we're still an intimate part of each other's past. And so whenever we go to Detroit we always go to visit this friend of our girlhood. Who knows how we looked before our teeth were straightened. Who knows how we talked before our voice got un-Brooklyned. Who knows what we ate before we learned about artichokes. And who, by her presence, puts us in touch with an earlier part of ourself, a part of ourself it's important never to lose.

"What this friend means to me and what I mean to her," says   16
Grace, "is having a sister without sibling rivalry. We know the texture of each other's lives. She remembers my grandmother's cabbage soup. I remember the way her uncle played the piano. There's simply no other friend who remembers those things."

4. Crossroads friends. Like historical friends, our crossroads   17
friends are important for *what was* — for the friendship we shared at a crucial, now past, time of life. A time, perhaps, when we roomed in college together; or worked as eager young singles in the Big City together; or went together, as my friend Elizabeth and I did, through pregnancy, birth and that scary first year of new motherhood.

Crossroads friends forge powerful links, links strong enough to   18
endure with not much more contact than once-a-year letters at Christmas. And out of respect for those crossroad years, for those dramas and dreams we once shared, we will always be friends.

5. Cross-generational friends. Historical friends and crossroads   19
friends seem to maintain a special kind of intimacy — dormant but always ready to be revived — and though we may rarely meet, whenever we do connect, it's personal and intense. Another kind of intimacy exists in the friendships that form across generations in what one woman calls her daughter–mother and her mother–daughter relationships.

Evelyn's friend is her mother's age—"but I share so much more 20
than I ever could with my mother"—a woman she talks to of music,
of books and of life. "What I get from her is the benefit of her experience. What she gets—and enjoys—from me is a youthful perspective. It's a pleasure for both of us."

I have in my own life a precious friend, a woman of 65 who has 21
lived very hard, who is wise, who listens well; who has been where I am
and can help me understand it; and who represents not only an ultimate
ideal mother to me but also the person I'd like to be when I grow up.

In our daughter role we tend to do more than our share of self- 22
revelation; in our mother role we tend to receive what's revealed. It's
another kind of pleasure—playing wise mother to a questing
younger person. It's another very lovely kind of friendship.

6. Part-of-a-couple friends. Some of the women we call our friends 23
we never see alone—we see them as part of a couple at couples' parties.
And though we share interests in many things and respect each other's
views, we aren't moved to deepen the relationship. Whatever the reason, a lack of time or—and this is more likely—a lack of chemistry,
our friendship remains in the context of a group. But the fact that our
feeling on seeing each other is always, "I'm *so* glad she's here" and the
fact that we spend half the evening talking together says that this too,
in its own way, counts as a friendship.

(Other part-of-a-couple friends are the friends that came with the 24
marriage, and some of these are friends we could live without. But
sometimes, alas, she married our husband's best friend; and sometimes, alas, she *is* our husband's best friend. And so we find ourself
dealing with her, somewhat against our will, in a spirit of what I'll
call *reluctant* friendship.)

7. Men who are friends. I wanted to write just of women friends, 25
but the women I've talked to won't let me—they say I must mention
man–woman friendships too. For these friendships can be just as
close and as dear as those that we form with women. Listen to Lucy's
description of one such friendship:

"We've found we have things to talk about that are different 26
from what he talks about with my husband and different from what I
talk about with his wife. So sometimes we call on the phone or meet
for lunch. There are similar intellectual interests—we always pass on
to each other the books that we love—but there's also something
tender and caring too."

In a couple of crises, Lucy says, "he offered himself for talking 27
and for helping. And when someone died in his family he wanted me

there. The sexual, flirty part of our friendship is very small, but *some*—just enough to make it fun and different." She thinks—and I agree—that the sexual part, though small, is always *some*, is always there when a man and a woman are friends.

It's only in the past few years that I've made friends with men, in the   28
sense of a friendship that's *mine*, not just part of two couples. And achieving with them the ease and the trust I've found with women friends has value indeed. Under the dryer at home last week, putting on mascara and rouge, I comfortably sat and talked with a fellow named Peter. Peter, I finally decided, could handle the shock of me minus mascara under the dryer. Because we care for each other. Because we're friends.

8. There are medium friends, and pretty good friends, and very   29
good friends indeed, and these friendships are defined by their level of intimacy. And what we'll reveal at each of these levels of intimacy is calibrated with care. We might tell a medium friend, for example, that yesterday we had a fight with our husband. And we might tell a pretty good friend that this fight with our husband made us so mad that we slept on the couch. And we might tell a very good friend that the reason we got so mad in that fight that we slept on the couch had something to do with that girl that works in his office. But it's only to our very best friends that we're willing to tell all, to tell what's going on with that girl in his office.

The best of friends, I still believe, totally love and support and   30
trust each other, and bare to each other the secrets of their souls, and run—no questions asked—to help each other, and tell harsh truths to each other when they must be told.

But we needn't agree about everything (only 12-year-old girl   31
friends agree about *everything*) to tolerate each other's point of view. To accept without judgment. To give and to take without ever keeping score. And to *be* there, as I am for them and as they are for me, to comfort our sorrows, to celebrate our joys.

QUESTIONS FOR STUDY AND DISCUSSION

1. In her opening paragraph, Viorst explains how she once would have defined friendship. Why does she now think differently?

2. What is Viorst's purpose in this essay? Why is division and classification an appropriate strategy for her to use? (Glossary: *Purpose*)

3. Into what categories does Viorst divide her friends?

4. What principles of division does Viorst use to establish her categories of friends? Where does she state these principles?
5. Discuss the ways in which Viorst makes her categories distinct and memorable.
6. What is Viorst's tone in this essay? (Glossary: *Tone*) In what ways is this tone appropriate for both her audience and her subject matter? Explain.

VOCABULARY

Refer to your dictionary to define the following words as they are used in this selection. Then use each word in a sentence of your own.

ardor (2)	forge (18)
nonchalant (3)	dormant (19)
sibling (16)	perspective (20)

CLASSROOM ACTIVITY USING DIVISION AND CLASSIFICATION

The drawing on the following page is a basic exercise in classification. By determining the features that the figures have in common, establish the general class to which they all belong. Next, establish subclasses by determining the distinctive features that distinguish one subclass from another. Finally, place each figure in an appropriate subclass within your classification system. You may wish to compare your classification system with those developed by other members of your class and to discuss any differences that exist.

SUGGESTED WRITING ASSIGNMENTS

1. Review the categories of friends that Viorst establishes in her essay. Do Viorst's categories apply to your friends? What new categories would you create? Write an essay in which you explain the types of friends in your life.
2. Music can be classified into many different types, such as jazz, country, pop, rock, hard rock, alternative, classical, big band, and so on. Each of these large classifications has a lot of variety within it. Write an essay in which you identify your favorite type of music, then identify at least three subclassifications of the music. Explain the characteristics of each of your categories, using at least two artists to illustrate each.

The Plot against People

■ **Russell Baker**

Russell Baker has had a long and distinguished career as a newspaper reporter and columnist. He was born in Virginia and attended Johns Hopkins University. In 1947, he got his first newspaper job with the Baltimore Sun, *then moved to the* New York Times *in 1954, where he wrote the "Observer" column from 1962 to 1998. His columns have been collected in numerous books over the years. In 1979, he was awarded the Pulitzer Prize, journalism's highest award, as well as the George Polk award for commentary. Baker's memoir* Growing Up *also received a Pulitzer in 1983. His autobiographical follow-up,* The Good Times, *appeared in 1989. Baker published an anthology entitled* Russell Baker's Book of American Humor *in 1993 and hosts the series* ExxonMobil Masterpiece Theater *on PBS. Another essay by Baker appears on pages 149–52.*

FOR YOUR JOURNAL

How do you usually react when your car won't start or your printer won't work? How do you deal with your frustration in such situations?

1 Inanimate objects are classified scientifically into three major categories—those that break down, those that get lost, and those that don't work.

2 The goal of all inanimate objects is to resist man and ultimately to defeat him, and the three major classifications are based on the method each object uses to achieve its purpose. As a general rule, any object capable of breaking down at the moment when it is most needed will do so. The automobile is typical of the category.

3 With the cunning peculiar to its breed, the automobile never breaks down while entering a filling station which has a large staff of idle mechanics. It waits until it reaches a downtown intersection in the middle of the rush hour, or until it is fully loaded with family and luggage on the Ohio Turnpike. Thus it creates maximum inconve-

nience, frustration, and irritability, thereby reducing its owner's life-span.

Washing machines, garbage disposals, lawn mowers, furnaces, 4
TV sets, tape recorders, slide projectors—all are in league with the
automobile to take their turn at breaking down whenever life threatens to flow smoothly for their enemies.

Many inanimate objects, of course, find it extremely difficult to 5
break down. Pliers, for example, and gloves and keys are almost totally incapable of breaking down. Therefore, they have had to evolve
a different technique for resisting man.

They get lost. Science has still not solved the mystery of how they 6
do it, and no man has ever caught one of them in the act. The most
plausible theory is that they have developed a secret method of loco-
motion which they are able to conceal from human eyes.

It is not uncommon for a pair of pliers to climb all the way from 7
the cellar to the attic in its single-minded determination to raise its
owner's blood pressure. Keys have been known to burrow three feet
under mattresses. Women's purses, despite their great weight, frequently travel through six or seven rooms to find hiding space under
a couch.

Scientists have been struck by the fact that things that break 8
down virtually never get lost, while things that get lost hardly ever
break down. A furnace, for example, will invariably break down at
the depth of the first winter cold wave, but it will never get lost. A
woman's purse hardly ever breaks down; it almost invariably chooses
to get lost.

Some persons believe this constitutes evidence that inanimate ob- 9
jects are not entirely hostile to man. After all, they point out, a furnace could infuriate a man even more thoroughly by getting lost than
by breaking down, just as a glove could upset him far more by breaking down than by getting lost.

Not everyone agrees, however, that this indicates a conciliatory 10
attitude. Many say it merely proves that furnaces, gloves, and pliers
are incredibly stupid.

The third class of objects—those that don't work—is the most curi- 11
ous of all. These include such objects as barometers, car clocks . . . flash-
lights, and toy-train locomotives. It is inaccurate, of course, to say that
they *never* work. They work once, usually for the first few hours after
being brought home, and then quit. Thereafter, they never work again.

In fact, it is widely assumed that they are built for the purpose of 12
not working. Some people have reached advanced ages without ever

seeing some of these objects—barometers, for example—in working order.

Science is utterly baffled by the entire category. There are many   13 theories about it. The most interesting holds that the things that don't work have attained the highest state possible for an inanimate object, the state to which things that break down and things that get lost can still only aspire.

They have truly defeated man by conditioning him never to ex-   14 pect anything of them. When his [car clock won't keep time] or his flashlight fails to illuminate, it does not raise his blood pressure. Objects that don't work have given man the only peace he receives from inanimate society.

QUESTIONS FOR STUDY AND DISCUSSION

1. Into what three broad categories does Baker classify inanimate objects? How do you suppose he arrived at these particular categories? In what other ways might inanimate objects be classified?

2. How does Baker organize his essay? Why do you think he waits until the conclusion to discuss objects "that don't work"? (Glossary: *Organization*)

3. How does paragraph 5 act as a transition? How does Baker use this transition to strengthen his classification? (Glossary: *Transition*)

4. Throughout his essay, Baker personifies inanimate objects. What is the effect of his doing so? Identify several specific examples of personification. (Glossary: *Figure of Speech*) Explain the meaning of Baker's title. Why does he use the word *plot*?

5. How does Baker use exemplification in paragraphs 6 and 7? Besides paragraph 7, where else does Baker offer examples? For what purposes does he use them? (Glossary: *Example*)

6. How does Baker make it clear at the beginning of the essay that his approach to the subject is humorous? How does he succeed in being more than simply silly? Point to several passages to illustrate your answer.

VOCABULARY

Refer to your dictionary to define the following words as they are used in this selection. Then use each word in a sentence of your own.

cunning (3)   conciliatory (10)
league (4)   baffled (13)
plausible (6)

CLASSROOM ACTIVITY USING DIVISION AND CLASSIFICATION

Visit a local supermarket, and from the many department or product areas (frozen foods, dairy products, cereals, soft drinks, meats, produce) select one for an exercise in classification. First, establish the general class of products in the area you have selected by determining the features that the products have in common. Next, establish subclasses by determining the features that distinguish one subclass from another. Finally, place the products from your selected area in appropriate subclasses within your classification system.

SUGGESTED WRITING ASSIGNMENTS

1. Using Baker's essay as a model, create a system of classification for one of the following topics. Then write an essay like Baker's classifying objects within that system.
   a. cars
   b. friends
   c. recreational activities
   d. sports
   e. drivers
   f. students
   g. music
   h. pet peeves

2. Most of us have had frustrating experiences with mechanical objects that seem to have perverse minds of their own. Write a narrative recounting one such experience—with a vending machine, a television set, an automobile, a computer, a pay telephone, or any other such object. Be sure to establish a clear context for your essay. (Glossary: *Narration*)

chapter **16**

Comparison and Contrast

A *comparison* points out the ways that two or more people, places, or things are alike. A *contrast* points out how they differ. The subjects of a comparison or contrast should be in the same class or general category; if they have nothing in common, there is no good reason for setting them side by side.

The function of any comparison or contrast is to clarify and explain. The writer's purpose may be simply to inform, or to make readers aware of similarities or differences that are interesting and significant in themselves. Or the writer may explain something unfamiliar by comparing it with something very familiar, perhaps explaining squash by comparing it with tennis. Finally, the writer can point out the superiority of one thing by contrasting it with another—for example, showing that one product is the best by contrasting it with all its competitors.

As a writer, you have two main options for organizing a comparison or contrast: the subject-by-subject pattern or the point-by-point pattern. For a short essay comparing and contrasting the Atlanta Braves and the Seattle Mariners, you would probably follow the *subject-by-subject* pattern of organization. With this pattern you first discuss the points you wish to make about one team, and then go on to discuss the corresponding points for the other team. An outline of your essay might look like this:

I. Atlanta Braves
   A. Pitching
   B. Fielding
   C. Hitting
II. Seattle Mariners
   A. Pitching
   B. Fielding
   C. Hitting

The subject-by-subject pattern presents a unified discussion of each team by placing the emphasis on the teams and not on the three points of comparison. Since these points are relatively few, readers should easily remember what was said about the Braves' pitching when you later discuss the Mariners' pitching and should be able to make the appropriate connections between them.

For a somewhat longer essay comparing and contrasting solar energy and wind energy, however, you should consider the *point-by-point* pattern of organization. With this pattern, your essay is organized according to the various points of comparison. Discussion alternates between solar and wind energy for each point of comparison. An outline of your essay might look like this:

I. Installation Expenses	IV. Convenience
A. Solar	A. Solar
B. Wind	B. Wind
II. Efficiency	V. Maintenance
A. Solar	A. Solar
B. Wind	B. Wind
III. Operating Costs	VI. Safety
A. Solar	A. Solar
B. Wind	B. Wind

The point-by-point pattern allows the writer to make immediate comparisons between solar and wind energy, thus enabling readers to consider each of the similarities and differences separately.

Each organizational pattern has its advantages. In general, the subject-by-subject pattern is useful in short essays where there are few points to be considered, whereas the point-by-point pattern is preferable in long essays where there are numerous points under consideration.

A good essay of comparison and contrast tells readers something significant that they do not already know. That is, it must do more than merely point out the obvious. As a rule, therefore, writers tend to draw contrasts between things that are usually perceived as being similar or comparisons between things usually perceived as different. In fact, comparison and contrast often go together. For example, an essay about Minneapolis and St. Paul might begin by showing how much they are alike but end with a series of contrasts revealing how much they differ. A consumer magazine might report the contrasting claims made by six car manufacturers and then go on to demonstrate that the cars all actually do much the same thing in the same way.

Analogy is a special form of comparison. When a subject is unobservable, complex, or abstract—when it is so generally unfamiliar that readers may have trouble understanding it—*analogy* can be most effective. By pointing out certain similarities between a difficult subject and a more familiar or concrete subject, writers can help their readers achieve a firmer grasp of the difficult subject. Unlike a true comparison, though, which analyzes items that belong to the same class—breeds of dogs or types of engines—analogy pairs things from different classes, things that have nothing in common except through the imagination of the writer. In addition, whereas comparison seeks to illuminate specific features of both subjects, the primary purpose of analogy is to clarify the one subject that is complex or unfamiliar. For example, an exploration of the similarities (and differences) between short stories and novels—two forms of fiction—would constitute a logical comparison; short stories and novels belong to the same class (fiction), and your purpose is to reveal something about both. If, however, your purpose is to explain the craft of fiction writing, you might note its similarities to the craft of carpentry. Then, you would be drawing an analogy, because the two subjects clearly belong to different classes. Carpentry is the more concrete subject and the one more people will have direct experience with. If you use your imagination, you will easily see many ways the tangible work of the carpenter can be used to help readers understand the more abstract work of the novelist. Depending on its purpose, an analogy can be made in several paragraphs to clarify a particular aspect of the larger topic being discussed, as in the example below, or it can provide the organizational strategy for an entire essay.

> It has long struck me that the familiar metaphor of "climbing the ladder" for describing the ascent to success or fulfillment in any field is inappropriate and misleading. There are no ladders that lead to success, although there may be some escalators for those lucky enough to follow in a family's fortunes.
>
> A ladder proceeds vertically, rung by rung, with each rung evenly spaced, and with the whole apparatus leaning against a relatively flat and even surface. A child can climb a ladder as easily as an adult, and perhaps with a surer footing.
>
> Making the ascent in one's vocation or profession is far less like ladder climbing than mountain climbing, and here the analogy

is a very real one. Going up a mountain requires a variety of skills, and includes a diversity of dangers, that are in no way involved in mounting a ladder.

Young people starting out should be told this, both to dampen their expectations and to allay their disappointments. A mountain is rough and precipitous, with uncertain footing and a predictable number of falls and scrapes, and sometimes one has to take the long way around to reach the shortest distance.

–Sydney J. Harris

Two Ways of Seeing a River

■ **Mark Twain**

*Samuel L. Clemens (1835–1910), who wrote under the pen name
of Mark Twain, was born in Florida, Missouri, and raised in
Hannibal, Missouri. He wrote the novels* Tom Sawyer *(1876),*
The Prince and the Pauper *(1882),* Huckleberry Finn *(1884),
and* A Connecticut Yankee in King Arthur's Court *(1889), as
well as many other works of fiction and nonfiction. One of
America's most popular writers, Twain is generally regarded as
the most important practitioner of the realistic school of writing, a style that emphasizes observable details. The following
passage is taken from* Life on the Mississippi *(1883), Twain's
study of the great river and his account of his early experiences
learning to be a river steamboat pilot. As you read the passage,
notice how Twain makes use of figurative language in describing two quite different ways of seeing the Mississippi River.*

FOR YOUR JOURNAL

As we age and gain experience, our interpretation of the same
memory—or how we view the same scene—can change. For
example, the way we view our own appearance changes all the
time, and photos from our childhood or teenage years may surprise us in the decades that follow. Perhaps something we found
amusing in our younger days may make us feel uncomfortable
or embarrassed now, or the house we grew up in later seems
smaller or less appealing. Write about a memory that has
changed for you over the years. How does your interpretation of
it now contrast with how you experienced it at the time?

Now when I had mastered the language of this water and had come   1
to know every trifling feature that bordered the great river as fa-
miliarly as I knew the letters of the alphabet, I had made a valuable acquisition. But I had lost something, too. I had lost something which
could never be restored to me while I lived. All the grace, the beauty, the
poetry, had gone out of the majestic river! I still kept in mind a certain
wonderful sunset which I witnessed when steamboating was new to

me. A broad expanse of the river was turned to blood; in the middle distance the red hue brightened into gold, through which a solitary log came floating, black and conspicuous; in one place a long, slanting mark lay sparkling upon the water; in another the surface was broken by boiling, tumbling rings that were as many-tinted as an opal; where the ruddy flush was faintest was a smooth spot that was covered with graceful circles and radiating lines, ever so delicately traced; the shore on our left was densely wooded, and the somber shadow that fell from this forest was broken in one place by a long, ruffled trail that shone like silver; and high above the forest wall a clean-stemmed dead tree waved a single leafy bough that glowed like a flame in the unobstructed splendor that was flowing from the sun. There were graceful curves, reflected images, woody heights, soft distances, and over the whole scene, far and near, the dissolving lights drifted steadily, enriching it every passing moment with new marvels of coloring.

I stood like one bewitched. I drank it in, in a speechless rapture. 2 The world was new to me and I had never seen anything like this at home. But as I have said, a day came when I began to cease from noting the glories and the charms which the moon and the sun and the twilight wrought upon the river's face; another day came when I ceased altogether to note them. Then, if that sunset scene had been repeated, I should have looked upon it without rapture and should have commented upon it inwardly after this fashion: "This sun means that we are going to have wind tomorrow; that floating log means that the river is rising, small thanks to it; that slanting mark on the water refers to a bluff reef which is going to kill somebody's steamboat one of these nights, if it keeps on stretching out like that; those tumbling 'boils' show a dissolving bar and a changing channel there; the lines and circles in the slick water over yonder are a warning that that troublesome place is shoaling up dangerously; that silver streak in the shadow of the forest is the 'break' from a new snag and he has located himself in the very best place he could have found to fish for steamboats; that tall dead tree, with a single living branch, is not going to last long, and then how is a body ever going to get through this blind place at night without the friendly old landmark?"

No, the romance and beauty were all gone from the river. All the 3 value any feature of it had for me now was the amount of usefulness it could furnish toward compassing the safe piloting of a steamboat. Since those days, I have pitied doctors from my heart. What does the lovely flush in a beauty's cheek mean to a doctor but a "break" that ripples above some deadly disease? Are not all her visible charms sown thick with what are to him the signs and symbols of hidden decay? Does he ever see her beauty at all, or doesn't he simply view her professionally and comment upon her unwholesome condition all to himself? And doesn't he sometimes wonder whether he has gained most or lost most by learning his trade?

QUESTIONS FOR STUDY AND DISCUSSION

1. What method of organization does Twain use in this selection? What alternative methods might he have used? What would have been gained or lost? (Glossary: *Organization*)
2. Explain the analogy that Twain uses in paragraph 3. What is his purpose in using this analogy? (Glossary: *Analogy*)
3. Explain this sentence of Twain's: "All the grace, the beauty, the poetry, had gone out of the majestic river!" (1). What is "the poetry"? Why was it lost for him?
4. Twain uses a number of similes and metaphors in this selection. Identify three of each, and explain what Twain is comparing in each case. What do these figures of speech add to Twain's writing? (Glossary: *Figure of Speech*)
5. Now that he has learned the trade of steamboating, does Twain feel he has "gained most or lost most" (3)? What has he gained, and what has he lost?

VOCABULARY

Refer to your dictionary to define the following words as they are used in this selection. Then use each word in a sentence of your own.

acquisition (1)   rapture (2)
hue (1)   romance (3)
opal (1)

CLASSROOM ACTIVITY USING COMPARISON AND CONTRAST

Compare two places that have the same purpose. For example, compare your college cafeteria with your dining room at home, or the classroom you are in now with another one on campus. Draw up a list of descriptive adjectives for each, and discuss them with your classmates. What do you like about each place? What do you dislike?

What do you learn from comparing them? How important are your surroundings to you?

SUGGESTED WRITING ASSIGNMENTS

1. Twain's essay contrasts the perception of one person before and after acquiring a particular body of knowledge. Of course, different people usually do perceive the same scene or event differently, even if they are experiencing it simultaneously. To use an example from Twain's writing, a poet and a doctor might perceive a rosy-cheeked young woman in entirely different ways. Write a comparison and contrast essay in which you show how two people with different experience might perceive the same subject. It can be a case of profound difference, such as a musician and an electrician at the same pyrotechnic rock music concert, or more subtle, such as a novelist and a screenwriter seeing the same lovers' quarrel in a restaurant. Add a short postscript in which you explain your choice of subject-by-subject comparison or point-by-point comparison in your essay.

2. Learning how to drive a car may not be as involved as learning how to pilot a steamboat on the Mississippi River, but it still has a tremendous impact on how we function and on how we perceive our surroundings. Write an essay about a short trip you took as a passenger and as a driver. Compare and contrast your perceptions and actions. What is most important to you as a passenger? What is most important to you as a driver? How do your perceptions shift between the two roles? What changes in what you notice around you and in the way you notice it?

Grammy Rewards

■ **Deborah Dalfonso**

Deborah Dalfonso first published the following piece in Parenting *magazine. As you read it, note that she uses a point-by-point pattern of contrasts in the first six paragraphs to help clarify and emphasize the idea she explores in the final three.*

FOR YOUR JOURNAL

Did any of your grandparents have a large influence in your life as you grew up? What interaction did you have with them? How did they influence you?

O ur daughter, Jill, has two grandmothers who are as different as 1
chalk and cheese. One taught her to count cards and make her face blank when she bluffed at blackjack. The other taught her where to place salad forks. When Jill was three, this grandmother taught her not to touch anything until invited to do so. The other one taught her to slide down carpeted stairs on a cookie sheet.

Both grandmothers are widows. One lives in a trailer park in 2
Florida from October until May, then moves to an old lake-front camp in Maine for the summer. The camp is a leaning structure filled with furniture impervious to wet swimsuits. Raccoons sleep on the deck every night.

The other grandmother resides in a town house at the Best Ad- 3
dress in the City—a regal-looking brick building boasting a security system and plants tended by florists.

One grandmother plays the lottery and bingo. The other plays 4
bridge with monogrammed playing cards. One grandmother wears primary colors, favoring fluorescents when she has a tan; the other wears suits, largely taupe or black.

One grandmother would be delighted to learn that many people 5
think of her as eccentric. The other hopes that people will refer to her as "correct." This grandmother, when startled, says "Oh, my word," her strongest expletive. The other one says "hot damn," or worse.

During Hurricane Bob, one of Jill's grandmothers bought her a 6
duckling-yellow slicker and took her to the beach to watch the surf.

382 ■ COMPARISON AND CONTRAST

She believes the ocean throws off positive ions, excellent for growth and peace of mind. While they were experiencing the elements, Jill's other grandmother called to make sure we were safe in the cellar.

"Are there many ways to live?" my puzzled six-year-old asked me. 7

"Yes," I said gently, "and you may choose which feels right for 8
you." And, I promised myself, I will let her make her own choice.

Two grandmothers, two different worlds. Both want for Jill no 9
less than the lion's share. One will be her anchor; the other, her
mainsail.

QUESTIONS FOR STUDY AND DISCUSSION

1. Why do you think Dalfonso chose to use a point-by-point organization?

2. Dalfonso uses an unusual turn of phrase when she introduces
   Jill's grandmothers as being "as different as chalk and cheese."
   (Glossary: *Figure of Speech*) Which of Jill's grandmothers might
   one classify as chalk and which one as cheese? Explain your
   choice.

3. It is quite apparent after the first paragraph which grandmother
   is which in Dalfonso's essay, yet she never identifies them other
   than by "one" and "the other." What point does Dalfonso make
   by doing this? How does it add to the effectiveness of the essay?

4. What is Dalfonso's purpose for writing the essay? (Glossary:
   Purpose) How does Jill's response to the extremes her two
   grandmothers represent help Dalfonso present her purpose?

5. Why do you think Dalfonso uses metaphors to represent the
   grandmothers' projected influence in Jill's life? Is Dalfonso's use
   of metaphors an effective way to conclude her essay? (Glossary:
   Beginnings and Endings) Why, or why not?

VOCABULARY

Refer to your dictionary to define the following words as they are
used in this selection. Then use each word in a sentence of your own.

impervious (2)   expletive (5)
regal (3)   ions (6)
taupe (4)

CLASSROOM ACTIVITY USING COMPARISON AND CONTRAST

Dalfonso writes an effective essay by contrasting the responses of two very different people to the same situations. To do so in such a short essay, she needed to focus on the situations that brought out the differences between the two grandmothers and at the same time revealed as much as possible about what each was like as an individual. Think of two friends or relatives whom you know well who have different personalities. Write a sentence about how each reacted or would react to four situations. Select the situations carefully, so that you capture the personality of each person. For example, the following situations would probably provoke strong and varied reactions:

learning to snorkel	going out to a Halloween party
having a picnic	choosing a pet

SUGGESTED WRITING ASSIGNMENTS

1. In what ways are your grandparents similar to your parents when it comes to hobbies, conversation topics, cooking, discipline, and so on? How do they differ? Using Dalfonso's essay as a model, write a comparison and contrast essay about your parents and/or grandparents. You may find it helpful to reread what you wrote in response to the journal prompt for this article before starting to write. Discuss how you interact with your grandparents as compared with your parents.

2. Select one of the following topics for an essay of comparison and contrast:

two cities	two actors
two friends	two teachers
two ways to heat a home	two brands of pizza
two fast-food restaurants	two books by the same author

A Case of "Severe Bias"

■ **Patricia Raybon**

A resident of Denver, Colorado, Patricia Raybon is a practicing journalist as well as an associate professor of journalism at the University of Colorado School of Journalism and Mass Communication in Boulder. She was born in 1941, graduated from Ohio State University in 1971, and earned her master's degree from the University of Colorado in 1977. She has worked as a reporter and editor, and her writing has appeared in such publications as the New York Times, *the* Wall Street Journal, USA Today, *and the* Washington Post. *Her book* My First White Friend: Confessions on Race, Love, and Forgiveness *was published in 1996. The following essay, which first appeared in* Newsweek *in 1989, reflects two of Raybon's main interests — race and the media. Here, Raybon highlights the differences she sees between the portrayal of African Americans by the media and the reality of their lives as she knows it. Notice how her use of contrast demonstrates the superiority of one view over another, in this case the superiority of the more accurate and truthful representation of African Americans.*

FOR YOUR JOURNAL

We live in a complex, complicated society, one that is so vast and diverse that it is perhaps never really possible to know who we are as Americans. Naturally, we rely on both our own experiences and media information for our sense of ourselves. How much value do you place on your own experiences, and how much do you rely on the media in building a sense of who we are as a people?

This is who I am not. I am not a crack addict. I am not a welfare   1
mother. I am not illiterate. I am not a prostitute. I have never been in jail. My children are not in gangs. My husband doesn't beat me. My home is not a tenement. None of these things defines who I am, nor do they describe the other black people I've known and worked with and loved and befriended over these forty years of my life.

Nor does it describe most of black America, period. 2

Yet in the eyes of the American news media, this is what black 3
America is: poor, criminal, addicted, and dysfunctional. Indeed,
media coverage of black America is so one-sided, so imbalanced that
the most victimized and hurting segment of the black community — a
small segment, at best — is presented not as the exception but as the
norm. It is an insidious practice, all the uglier for its blatancy.

In recent months, I have observed a steady offering of media re- 4
ports on crack babies, gang warfare, violent youth, poverty, and
homelessness — and in most cases, the people featured in the photos
and stories were black. At the same time, articles that discuss other
aspects of American life — from home buying to medicine to technology to nutrition — rarely, if ever, show blacks playing a positive role,
or for that matter, any role at all.

Day after day, week after week, this message — that black America 5
is dysfunctional and unwhole — gets transmitted across the American
landscape. Sadly, as a result, America never learns the truth about what
is actually a wonderful, vibrant, creative community of people.

Most black Americans are *not* poor. Most black teenagers are 6
not crack addicts. Most black mothers are *not* on welfare. Indeed, in
sheer numbers, more *white* Americans are poor and on welfare than
are black. Yet one never would deduce that by watching television or
reading American newspapers and magazines.

Why do the American media insist on playing this myopic, inaccu- 7
rate picture game? In this game, white America is always whole and
lovely and healthy, while black America is usually sick and pathetic and
deficient. Rarely, indeed, is black America ever depicted in the media as
functional and self-sufficient. The free press, indeed, as the main inter-
preter of American culture and American experience, holds the mirror
on American reality — so much so that what the media say is *is,* even if
it's not that way at all. The media are guilty of a severe bias and the
problem screams out for correction. It is worse than simply lazy journalism, which is bad enough; it is inaccurate journalism.

For black Americans like myself, this isn't just an issue of vanity — 8
of wanting to be seen in a good light. Nor is it a matter of closing one's
eyes to the very real problems of the urban underclass — which undeni-
ably is disproportionately black. To be sure, problems besetting the
black underclass deserve the utmost attention of the media, as well as
the understanding and concern of the rest of American society.

But if their problems consistently are presented as the *only* reality 9
for blacks, any other experience known in the black community

ceases to have validity, or to be real. In this scenario, millions of
blacks are relegated to a sort of twilight zone, where who we are and
what we are isn't based on fact but on image and perception. That's
what it feels like to be a black American whose lifestyle is outside of
the aberrant behavior that the media present as the norm.

For many of us, life is a curious series of encounters with white   10
people who want to know why we are "different" from other blacks —
when, in fact, most of us are only "different" from the now common
negative images of black life. So pervasive are these images that they
aren't just perceived as the norm, they're *accepted* as the norm.

I am reminded, for example, of the controversial Spike Lee film   11
Do the Right Thing and the criticism by some movie reviewers that
the film's ghetto neighborhood isn't populated by addicts and drug
pushers — and thus is not a true depiction.

In fact, millions of black Americans live in neighborhoods where   12
the most common sights are children playing and couples walking
their dogs. In my own inner-city neighborhood in Denver — an area
that the local press consistently describes as "gang territory" — I have
yet to see a recognizable "gang" member or any "gang" activity
(drug dealing or drive-by shootings), nor have I been the victim of
"gang violence."

Yet to students of American culture — in the case of Spike Lee's   13
film, the movie reviewers — a black, inner-city neighborhood can
only be one thing to be real: drug-infested and dysfunctioning. Is this
my ego talking? In part, yes. For the millions of black people like myself — ordinary, hard-working, law-abiding, tax-paying Americans —
the media's blindness to the fact that we even exist, let alone to our
contributions to American society, is a bitter cup to drink. And as
self-reliant as most black Americans are — because we've had to be
self-reliant — even the strongest among us still crave affirmation.

I want that. I want it for my children. I want it for all the beauti-   14
ful, healthy, funny, smart black Americans I have known and loved
over the years.

And I want it for the rest of America, too.   15

I want America to know us — all of us — for who we really are.   16
To see us in all of our complexity, our subtleness, our artfulness, our
enterprise, our specialness, our loveliness, our American-ness. That is
the real portrait of black America — that we're strong people, surviving people, capable people. That may be the best-kept secret in
America. If so, it's time to let the truth be known.

QUESTIONS FOR STUDY AND DISCUSSION

1. What do you think is the purpose of Raybon's comparison and contrast technique? (Glossary: *Purpose*) What does she want? What do you think she wants us to think and/or do as a result of reading her essay?

2. What is the basic contrast that Raybon establishes in her first paragraph? What examples does she use to establish the contrast that she sees? Can you think of any other examples? (Glossary: *Example*)

3. Why do you think Raybon feels it is necessary to define herself by contrast in her opening paragraph? Why doesn't she simply say who she is in a positive manner?

4. How are paragraphs 1 and 6 stylistically similar? Why do you think Raybon wrote them in the way she did? (Glossary: *Style*)

5. What is Raybon's thesis in this essay? (Glossary: *Thesis*) Where does she present it? Does she support her thesis accurately in your view? Why, or why not?

6. How would you describe Raybon's tone in this essay? (Glossary: *Tone*) What in the style of the essay led you to your response?

VOCABULARY

Refer to your dictionary to define the following words as they are used in this selection. Then use each word in a sentence of your own.

tenement (1)   scenario (9)
dysfunctional (3)   aberrant (9)
insidious (3)   pervasive (10)
myopic (7)   subtleness (16)
besetting (8)   enterprise (16)

CLASSROOM ACTIVITY USING COMPARISON AND CONTRAST

In preparation for writing a comparison and contrast essay on two world leaders (or popular singers, actors, or subjects of your own choosing), write out answers to the following questions:

Who could I compare and contrast?
What is my purpose?

Should I emphasize similarities or differences?

What specific points should I discuss?

What organizational pattern will best suit my purposes: subject-by-subject or point-by-point?

SUGGESTED WRITING ASSIGNMENTS

1. Write an essay in which you compare and/or contrast the issues and argumentative strategies used by Patricia Raybon with those of Joanmarie Kalter in "Exposing Media Myths: TV Doesn't Affect You as Much as You Think," on pp. 438–43.

2. Using one of the following "before and after" situations, write a short essay of comparison and contrast:

before and after a diet

before and after urban renewal

before and after a visit to the dentist

before and after a physical workout

A Battle of Cultures

■ K. Connie Kang

K. Connie Kang was born in Korea in 1942 but grew up in Japan and the United States. After graduating from the School of Journalism at the University of Missouri, Kang went on to earn a master of science degree from the Medill School of Journalism at Northwestern University. During more than three decades in journalism, this award-winning newspaperwoman has worked as a reporter, editor, foreign correspondent, columnist, and editorial writer for the San Francisco Examiner, *the* San Francisco Chronicle, *and* United Press International. *Currently, she is a reporter for the* Los Angeles Times. *Kang's career began in June 1964, when there was only a handful of Asians in the metropolitan newsrooms in the United States. Always mindful of her Asian heritage, she wrote about Asians and the issues affecting their communities long before they were considered newsworthy. In 1995, she published* Home Was the Land of Morning Calm: A Saga of a Korean American Family. *The following essay, which first appeared in* Asian Week *in May 1990, reminds us that we need both "cultural insight" and understanding if we are to "make democracy work" in a multicultural society. Notice how Kang uses comparison and contrast when presenting aspects of Korean and African American cultures in order to demonstrate her point.*

FOR YOUR JOURNAL

People of different ethnic, racial, and cultural backgrounds sometimes find it difficult to achieve a common ground of understanding. What suggestions do you have for what we can do, either personally or through our institutions, to increase understanding? Rather than composing an answer, make a list of several suggestions that you would like to contribute to a classroom discussion.

 volatile inner-city drama is taking place in New York where blacks have been boycotting Korean groceries for four months.

1

The recent attack on three Vietnamese men by a group of blacks   2
who mistook them for Koreans has brought this long-simmering tension between two minority groups to the world's attention. Korean
newspapers from San Francisco to Seoul have been running front-
page stories. Non-Asian commentators around the country, whose
knowledge of Korea may not be much more than images from the
Korean War and the ridiculous television series "M.A.S.H.," are
making all sorts of comments.

As I see it, the problem in the Flatbush area of Brooklyn started   3
with cultural misunderstanding and was compounded by a lack of
bilingual and bicultural community leaders to intervene quickly.

Frictions between Korean store owners in New York and blacks   4
had been building for years. Korean merchants have been complain-
ing about thefts. On the other hand, their black customers have been
accusing immigrant store owners of making money in their neighborhoods without putting anything back into the community. They have
also complained about store owners being brusque. Over the past
eight years, there have been sporadic boycotts but none has lasted as
long as the current one, which stemmed from an accusation by a
black customer in January that she had been attacked by a store employee. In defense, the store owner has said the employee caught the
woman stealing.

The attack on the Vietnamese on May 13 wasn't the first time   5
one group of Asians has been mistaken for another in America. But
the publicity surrounding the case has made this unfortunate situation a case study in inter-ethnic tension.

What's missing in this inner-city drama is cultural insight.   6

What struck me more than anything was a recent remark by a   7
black resident: "The Koreans are a very, very rude people. They don't
understand you have to smile."

I wondered whether her reaction would have been the same, had   8
she known that Koreans don't smile at Koreans either without a reason.
To a Korean, a smile is not a facial expression he can turn on and off
mechanically. Koreans have a word for it—"mu-ttuk-ttuk-hada"
(stiff). In other words, the Korean demeanor is "myu-po-jung"—lack
of expression.

It would be an easy thing for blacks who are naturally friendly   9
and gregarious to misunderstand Korean ways.

As a Korean American I've experienced this many times. When-   10
ever I'm in Korea, which is often, I'm chided for smiling too much.
"Why do you smile so easily? You act like a Westerner," people tell

me. My inclination is to retort: "Why do you always have to look like you've got indigestion?" But I restrain myself because I know better.

In our culture, a smile is reserved for people we know and for a 11 proper occasion. Herein lies a big problem when newcomers from Korea begin doing business in America's poor inner-city neighborhoods.

Culturally and socially, many newcomers from Korea, like other 12 Asian immigrants, are ill-equipped to run businesses in America's inner cities. But because they are denied entry into mainstream job markets, they pool resources and open mom-and-pop operations in the only places where they can afford it. They work 14 and 15 hours a day, seven days a week, dreaming of the day when their children will graduate from prestigious schools and make their sacrifices worthwhile.

From the other side, inner-city African Americans must wonder 13 how these new immigrants find the money to run their own businesses, when they themselves can't even get a small loan from a bank. Their hope of getting out of the poverty cycle is grim, yet they see newcomers living in better neighborhoods and driving new cars.

"They ask me, 'Where do you people get the money to buy a 14 business?'" Bong-jae Jang, owner of one of the grocery stores being boycotted, told me. "How can I explain to my neighbors in my poor English the concept of our family system, the idea of 'kye' (uniquely Korean private money-lending system), our way of life?"

I think a little learning is in order on both sides. Korean immi- 15 grants, like other newcomers, need orientation before they leave their country as well as when they arrive in the United States. It's also important for Korean immigrants, like other Asians who live in the United States, to realize that they are indebted to blacks for the social gains won by their civil rights struggle. They face less discrimination today because blacks have paved the way. Instead of looking down on their culture, it would be constructive to learn their history, literature, music and values and see our African American brothers and sisters in their full humanity.

I think it is also important to remind ourselves that while the 16 Confucian culture has taught us how to be good parents, sons and daughters and how to behave with people we know, it has not prepared us for living in a democracy. The Confucian ethos lacks the value of social conscience, which makes democracy work.

It isn't enough that we think of educating our children and send 17 them to the best schools. We need to think of other peoples' children, too. Most of all, we need to be more tolerant of other peoples' cultures. We need to celebrate our similarities as well as our differences.

Jang, the grocer, told me this experience has been painful but he 18 has learned an important lesson. "We Koreans must learn to participate in this society," he said. "When this is over, I'm going to reach out. I want to give part-time work to black youths."

He also told me that he has been keeping a journal. "I'm not a 19 writer but I've been keeping a journal," he said. "I want to write about this experience someday. It may help someone."

By reaching out, we can make a difference. The Korean grocer's 20 lesson is a reminder to us all that making democracy work in a multicultural society is difficult but we have no choice but to strive for it.

QUESTIONS FOR STUDY AND DISCUSSION

1. What is the "battle of cultures" named in the title? (Glossary: *Title*) How are the contrasts between the cultures helping to cause the "battle," according to Kang? What specific differences does she identify in her comparison and contrast analysis of the situation?

2. What is Kang's thesis? (Glossary: *Thesis*) How does her use of comparison and contrast help her argue her thesis?

3. Why are the Korean grocery stores being boycotted by African American customers? (Glossary: *Cause and Effect*)

4. Why are most Asian immigrants ill-equipped to run businesses in the inner cities of the United States, according to Kang? Why are they indebted to African Americans?

5. How does Kang's point of view contribute to the effectiveness of the essay? (Glossary: *Point of View*)

6. What is it about their culture that makes it difficult for Koreans to adapt to life in a multicultural society?

VOCABULARY

Refer to your dictionary to define the following words as they are used in this selection. Then use each word in a sentence of your own.

volatile (1)	intervene (3)
boycotting (1)	brusque (4)
bilingual (3)	sporadic (4)

gregarious (9)   ethos (16)
inclination (10)

CLASSROOM ACTIVITY USING COMPARISON AND CONTRAST

Review the discussion of analogy in the introduction to this chapter, and then create an analogy to explain your relationship with one of your parents or with a relative.

SUGGESTED WRITING ASSIGNMENTS

1. Choose an ethnic group other than your own that lives in or near your home community. Using Kang's essay as a model, compare and/or contrast its culture with your own. What could you do to understand the other culture better? How would you describe relations between the two groups?

2. Choose a country that you have studied, visited, or at least read about. Compare who you are now with who you think you would be if you had been born and raised in that country. How do you think you would be different? Why?

Cause and Effect

Every time you try to answer a question that asks *why,* you engage in the process of *causal analysis*—you attempt to determine a *cause* or series of causes for a particular *effect.* When you try to answer a question that asks *what if,* you attempt to determine what *effect* will result from a particular *cause.* You will have frequent opportunity to use cause-and-effect analysis in the writing that you will do in college. For example, in history you might be asked to determine the causes for the breakup of the former Soviet Union; in political science you might be asked to determine the critical issues in the 2000 presidential election; in sociology you might be asked to analyze the effects that the AIDS epidemic has had on sexual-behavior patterns among Americans; and in economics you might be asked to predict what will happen to our country if we enact large tax cuts.

Fascinated by the effects that private real estate development was having on his neighborhood, student Kevin Cunningham decided to find out what was happening in the older sections of cities across the country. Here are two paragraphs from his essay of causal analysis.

One of three fates awaits the aging neighborhood. Decay may continue until the neighborhood becomes a slum. It may face urban renewal, with old buildings being razed and ugly new apartment houses taking their place. Or it may undergo redevelopment, in which government encourages the upgrading of existing housing stock by offering low-interest loans or outright grants; thus, the original character of the neighborhood may be retained or restored, allowing the city to keep part of its identity.

An example of redevelopment at its best is Hoboken, New Jersey. In the early 1970s Hoboken was a dying city, with rundown housing and many abandoned buildings. However, low-interest loans enabled some younger residents to refurbish their homes, and soon the area began to show signs of renewed vigor. Even outsiders moved in and rebuilt some of the abandoned houses. Today, whole blocks have been restored, and neighborhood life is active again. The city does well, too, because property values are higher and so are property taxes.

In the first paragraph, Cunningham describes three possible effects (or fates) of a city's aging. In his second paragraph, he singles out one effect, redevelopment, and discusses in detail the impact it has had upon Hoboken.

Determining causes and effects is usually thought-provoking and quite complex. One reason for this is that there are two types of causes: *immediate causes,* which are readily apparent because they are closest to the effect, and *ultimate causes,* which, being somewhat removed, are not as apparent and may perhaps even be hidden. Furthermore, ultimate causes may bring about effects which themselves become immediate causes, thus creating a *causal chain.* Consider the following causal chain: Sally, a computer salesperson, prepared extensively for a meeting with an important client (ultimate cause), impressed the client (immediate cause), and made a very large sale (effect). The chain did not stop there: the large sale caused her to be promoted by her employer (effect). For a detailed example of a causal chain, read Barry Commoner's analysis of the near disaster at the Three Mile Island nuclear facility (pp. 66–67).

A second reason why causal analysis can be so complex is that an effect may have any number of possible or actual causes, and a cause may have any number of possible or actual effects. An upset stomach may be caused by eating spoiled food, but it may also be caused by overeating, flu, allergy, nervousness, pregnancy, or any combination of factors. Similarly, the high cost of electricity may have multiple effects: higher profits for utility companies, fewer sales of electrical appliances, higher prices for other products, and the development of alternative sources of energy.

Sound reasoning and logic, while present in all good writing, are central to any causal analysis. Writers of believable causal analysis examine their material objectively and develop their essays carefully. They examine methodically all causes and effects and evaluate them. They are convinced by their own examination of the material but are not afraid to admit other possible causes and effects. Above all, they do not let their own prejudices interfere with the logic of their analyses and presentations.

Because people are accustomed to thinking of causes with their effects, they sometimes commit an error in logic known as the "after this, therefore because of this" fallacy (in Latin, *post hoc, ergo propter hoc*). This fallacy leads people to believe that because one event occurred after another event, the first event somehow caused the second; that is, they sometimes make causal connections that are not proven. For example, if students began to perform better after a free breakfast program was instituted at their school, one could not assume that the improvement was caused by the breakfast program. There could, of course, be any number of other causes for this effect, and a responsible writer would analyze and consider them all before suggesting the cause.

The Effects of the Telephone

■ John Brooks

John Brooks (1920–1993) wrote for the New Yorker *for forty years. Although he published respected novels like* The Big Wheel *(1949) and* The Man Who Broke Things *(1958), he was best known for his nonfiction. His book on corporate culture in the 1980s,* The Takeover Game, *was a best-seller. Brooks was also a trustee of* The New York Public Library *for fifteen years. In the following essay, he identifies the telephone as the ultimate cause of numerous changes in society over a period of decades. After reading his analysis, see if you can identify some of the more immediate cause-and-effect relationships that would constitute causal chains leading from the telephone as ultimate cause to the effects he discusses.*

FOR YOUR JOURNAL

The twentieth century saw technology advance at a dizzying speed. Many new products or services have become integrated into our culture so thoroughly that it is now hard to envision what life was like sixty years ago, before television, or even twenty years ago, before personal computers. Many of these advances are dependent on services that were not around just one hundred years ago. Think about the last time your electricity or phone service went out. How did you feel? How dependent *are* we on our utilities?

What has the telephone done to us, or for us, in the hundred years 1 of its existence? A few effects suggest themselves at once. It has saved lives by getting rapid word of illness, injury, or famine from remote places. By joining with the elevator to make possible the multistory residence or office building, it has made possible—for better or worse—the modern city. By bringing about a quantum leap in the speed and ease with which information moves from place to place, it has greatly accelerated the rate of scientific and technological change and growth in industry. Beyond doubt it has crippled if not killed the ancient art of letter writing. It has made living alone possible for persons with normal social impulses; by so doing, it has played a role in one of the greatest social changes of this century, the breakup of the multigenerational household. It has made the waging of war chillingly more efficient than formerly. Perhaps (though not provably) it has prevented wars that might have arisen out of international misunderstanding caused by written communication. Or perhaps — again not provably — by magnifying and extending irrational personal conflicts based on voice contact, it has caused wars. Certainly it has extended the scope of human conflicts, since it impartially disseminates the useful knowledge of scientists and the babble of bores, the affection of the affectionate and the malice of the malicious.

But the question remains unanswered. The obvious effects just   2
cited seem inadequate, mechanistic; they only scratch the surface. Perhaps the crucial effects are evanescent and unmeasurable. Use of the telephone involves personal risk because it involves exposure; for some, to be "hung up on" is among the worst of fears; others dream of a ringing telephone and wake up with a pounding heart. The telephone's actual ring — more, perhaps, than any other sound in our daily lives — evokes hope, relief, fear, anxiety, joy, according to our expectations. The telephone is our nerve-end to society.

In some ways it is in itself a thing of paradox. In one sense a   3
metaphor for the times it helped create, in another sense the telephone is their polar opposite. It is small and gentle — relying on low voltages and miniature parts — in times of hugeness and violence. It is basically simple in times of complexity. It is so nearly human, re-creating voices so faithfully that friends or lovers need not identify themselves by name even when talking across oceans, that to ask its effects on human life may seem hardly more fruitful than to ask the effect of the hand or the foot. The Canadian philosopher Marshall McLuhan — one of the few who have addressed themselves to these questions — was perhaps not far from the mark when he spoke of the telephone as creating "a kind of extra-sensory perception."

QUESTIONS FOR STUDY AND DISCUSSION

1. Brooks opens his essay with a rhetorical question. (Glossary: *Rhetorical Question*) Why is the question difficult, if not impossible, to answer fully?

2. Brooks says that telephones and elevators made modern cities possible (1), but he does little to illustrate this statement.

(Glossary: *Illustration*) How did these two inventions pave the way for the development of modern cities? Provide an example of how this influence might have worked.

3. Brooks characterizes the effects of the personal use of the telephone as the "crucial" effects. Why do they make charting the overall effects of the telephone so difficult?

4. Brooks says that the telephone is "a metaphor for the times it helped create" (3). (Glossary: *Figure of Speech*) What does he mean? What aspect of modern society does the telephone represent?

5. Brooks describes the telephone as being "nearly human" and equates its effects on human life to those of hands and feet (3). What do you think he means by this? Do you agree with his assessment? Why, or why not?

VOCABULARY

Refer to your dictionary to define the following words as they are used in this selection. Then use each word in a sentence of your own.

quantum (1)   evanescent (2)
impartially (1)   paradox (3)
disseminates (1)   polar (3)
mechanistic (2)

CLASSROOM ACTIVITY USING CAUSE AND EFFECT

In preparation for writing a cause-and-effect essay, list two effects on society and two effects on personal behavior for one of the following items: television, cell phones, email, microwave ovens, DVD technology, the Internet, or an item of your choice. For example, a car could be said to have the following effects:

SOCIETY

development of an infrastructure based on asphalt roads
expansion of the size and influence of the petroleum and insurance industries

PERSONAL BEHAVIOR

convenient transportation
freedom and independence

400 ■ CAUSE AND EFFECT

SUGGESTED WRITING ASSIGNMENTS

1. Using Brooks's essay as a model, write an essay on the effects of computers on society. Computers have an enormous impact on society as a whole as well as on the way we live our daily lives. For example, telecommuting, in which an employee works at home and communicates with coworkers via phone, modem, and fax, could eliminate the need for much of the workforce to live near cities. What other effects do you see? Which do you think are the most important to society? Which are the most important to you personally? Be sure to explain your reasoning.

2. There is often more than one cause for an event. List at least six possible causes for one of the following:

   an upset victory in a game or competition

   your excellent performance on an exam

   an injury you suffered

   changing your major

   a quarrel you had with a friend

   Examine your list, and identify the causes that seem most probable. Which of these are immediate causes, and which are ultimate causes? Using this material, write a short cause-and-effect essay on one of the topics.

I Refuse to Live in Fear

■ **Diana Bletter**

Diana Bletter is an American living in Israel. She was born in New York in 1957 and received a degree in comparative literature from Cornell University in 1978. A freelance writer since her graduation, with the exception of a year she spent on staff with the National Lampoon, *Bletter's many articles have appeared in well-known periodicals like the* International Herald Tribune *and* Newsday. *She is also the author of* The Invisible Thread: A Portrait of Jewish American Women, *which was nominated for a national Jewish book award in 1989. Bletter and Samia Zina, the friend she mentions in her essay, helped organize Dove of Peace, a friendship group for Arab and Jewish women. The following selection was first published in the November 1996 issue of* Mademoiselle. *As you finish reading it, consider how Bletter's final paragraph offers an ironic twist to what might be a more expected cause-and-effect relationship between terrorism and fear.*

FOR YOUR JOURNAL

Think about how you reacted to the news of the Oklahoma City bombing or the heightened security surrounding the millennium celebration. Have those events altered the way you look at your surroundings? If so, how? Do you feel safe from the threat of terrorism?

For most of my life, I thought a shoe box was just a shoe box. Until 1
the afternoon I discovered that it could also be considered a lethal weapon.

This is what happened: I had just gone shopping for shoes—one 2
of my favorite pastimes—in the small Mediterranean town of Nahariyya in northern Israel, where I've lived for the last five years. I sat down on a bench to change into my new purchase. I was so busy admiring my feet that I left the shoe box (with my old shoes) on the bench. Fifteen minutes later, I suddenly remembered it and turned

401

back. When I approached the street, I saw crowds of people, barricades and at least five policemen.

"What happened?" I asked.　　3

"Everyone's been evacuated. Someone reported a suspicious object on a bench down the street."　　4

"Oh, no!" I shouted. "My shoes!"　　5

Had I arrived even a few seconds later, a special bomb squad—complete with robot—would have imploded my shoe box to deactivate what could have been a bomb hidden inside. The policeman shook his finger at me. "This is the Middle East!" he said angrily. "You can't be careless like that!"　　6

REALITY BITES, HARD

Moving to Israel from America's tranquil suburbia has taught me about living with the threat of terrorism, something we Americans—after the bomb at Atlanta's Olympic Games and the explosion of TWA Flight 800—are finally being forced to think about on our own turf. The brutal fact of a terrorist attack is that it shatters the innocent peace of our days, the happy logic of our lives. It inalterably changes the way we live.　　7

I can no longer daydream as I walk down a street—now I know that, to stay alive, I have to remain aware of who and what surrounds me. As my fiancé always tells me, "Your eyes are your best friends!" and I use them to keep track of emergency exits, the closest windows, the nearest heavy object that could be used in self-defense.　　8

I used to be a reflexive litter-grabber—in my hometown, I never hesitated to pick up a coffee cup from the sidewalk and toss it in a nearby garbage can. In Israel, I've learned not to touch litter and to stay away from garbage cans—on several occasions, bombs have been placed in them. If I see a knapsack, shopping bag or—yes—a shoe box left unattended, I now do three things: One, ask passersby if they forgot the package; two, get away from it as fast as I can; and three, report it to the police.　　9

NECESSARY INCONVENIENCES

Living in a country where terrorism is always a possibility means that at every entrance to a public place, guards search every bag. I forgot this the first time I walked into Nahariyya's lone department store; a guard stopped me to look through my pocketbook. "How could I have shoplifted?" I asked. "I haven't set foot in the store." Then I re-　　10 membered that in America, people worry about what someone might sneak *out* of a store; in Israel, people worry what weapons or bombs someone might sneak *in* to a store.

The first few days after a terrorist attack seem very quiet. Since 11 all of Israel is only the size of New Jersey, everybody usually knows someone who was hurt or killed. The nation slips into mourning: People avoid going out, attending parties, sitting in cafés.

Gradually, though, daily life returns to normal. Israelis (and now, 12 Americans) have to prove again and again to potential terrorists that we're not giving in to our fears. If we voluntarily restrict our movements and our lives, terrorists have vanquished us.

During the latest hostilities in Lebanon (whose border is about 13 seven miles from Nahariyya), Samia Zina, my dear friend—and a Muslim Arab—dreamed about me, one of those vivid dreams that seems prophetic when you wake. She dreamed that the fighting had forced her to flee her home, and that I'd hidden her and her children in my house (and I certainly would have, had the nightmare been a reality). The next day, Samia popped by to tell me her dream and give me the two stuffed chickens she'd been moved to cook for me.

"Thank you," I said, astonished by the food and the dream. "But 14 I know you would have hidden me, too."

Terrorists attempt to divide people by fear, but in our community 15 they've brought so-called enemies together: Even Arabs and Jews watch out for each other in public places, knowing that terrorists target everyone. By resisting the temptation to become paranoid and isolated, by sticking up for one another, we remain undefeated.

QUESTIONS FOR STUDY AND DISCUSSION

1. Bletter's shoe box story illustrates the effects of a forgetful act on daily life in a society threatened by terrorism. What connotation does an unattended shoe box carry with it in Israel? (Glossary: *Connotation/Denotation*) How does it differ from a shoe box in the United States? (Glossary: *Comparison and Contrast*)

2. Bletter quotes the policeman's response to her carelessness. (Glossary: *Dialogue*) How does his reprimand underscore the serious effects of Bletter's act? Why is it important for the reader to "hear" what he said?

3. Why is daydreaming a dangerous activity in public places in Israel? What pieces of information are vital to perceive in one's surroundings?

4. What does Samia Zina's dream symbolize to Bletter? (Glossary: *Symbol*) Why is her relationship with Zina important to the effectiveness of the essay?

5. How is terrorism defeated? What is the cause-and-effect relationship between terrorism and the way Bletter says one should live one's life?

6. What is Bletter's tone in her essay? (Glossary: *Tone*) Explain your answer.

VOCABULARY

Refer to your dictionary to define the following words as they are used in this selection. Then use each word in a sentence of your own.

imploded (6)	prophetic (13)
suburbia (7)	paranoid (15)
vanquished (12)	

CLASSROOM ACTIVITY USING CAUSE AND EFFECT

Determining causes and effects can be thought-provoking and quite complex. Establishing a causal chain of events often brings clarity and understanding to issues like pollution and environmental stewardship:

Ultimate cause	Industrial smokestack emissions
Immediate cause	Smog and acid rain damage
Effect	Clean air legislation
Effect	Improved air quality and forest growth

Develop a causal chain for each of the following cause-and-effect pairs:

terrorism/fear
giving a speech/anxiety
party/excitement
vacation/relaxation

Then mix two of the pairs. For example, develop a causal chain for vacation/anxiety. Be prepared to discuss your answers with the class.

SUGGESTED WRITING ASSIGNMENTS

1. According to Bletter, terrorism succeeds only if it frightens and divides the general public. It is therefore important to show terrorists that "we're not giving in to our fears" (12). Terrorism is an extreme example, but we all face events and situations in our lives that cause fear, and we must learn to control or moderate our fear to succeed or, at times, even to function. Using Bletter's essay as a model, write a cause-and-effect essay in which you present something that frightens you, how and why it frightens you, and how you control the involuntary effect—fear.

2. Write a cause-and-effect essay that explores some of the effects of your choice of where to live on how you live your life. Is your area urban or rural? Is crime a problem or not? How easy is it to get around? Do you like where you live?

Why We Crave Horror Movies

■ **Stephen King**

Stephen King's name is synonymous with horror stories. A 1970 graduate of the University of Maine, King worked as a janitor in a knitting mill, a laundry worker, and a high school English teacher before he struck it big with his writing. Many consider King to be the most successful writer of modern horror fiction today. To date, he has written thirty-five novels, seven collections of short stories and novellas, and ten screenplays. His books have sold well over 250 million copies worldwide, and many of his novels have been made into popular motion pictures, including Stand by Me, Misery, *and* The Green Mile. *His books, starting with* Carrie *in 1974, include* Salem's Lot *(1975),* The Shining *(1977),* The Dead Zone *(1979),* Christine *(1983),* Pet Sematary *(1983),* The Dark Half *(1989),* Bag of Bones *(1998), and* The Girl Who Loved Tom Gordon *(1999). Each year King and his wife, novelist Tabitha King, donate at least 10 percent of their pretaxable income to charitable organizations, many of them local. The widespread popularity of horror books and films attests to the fact that many people share King's fascination with the macabre. In the following selection, King analyzes the reasons we flock to good horror movies.*

FOR YOUR JOURNAL

What movies have you seen recently? Do you prefer watching any particular kind of movie—comedy, drama, science fiction, or horror, for example—more than others? How do you explain your preference?

I think that we're all mentally ill; those of us outside the asylums only   1
hide it a little better—and maybe not all that much better, after all.
We've all known people who talk to themselves, people who sometimes
squinch their faces into horrible grimaces when they believe no one is
watching, people who have some hysterical fear—of snakes, the dark,
the tight place, the long drop . . . and, of course, those final worms and
grubs that are waiting so patiently underground.

When we pay our four or five bucks and seat ourselves at tenth-   2
row center in a theater showing a horror movie, we are daring the
nightmare.

Why? Some of the reasons are simple and obvious. To show that   3
we can, that we are not afraid, that we can ride this roller coaster.
Which is not to say that a really good horror movie may not surprise
a scream out of us at some point, the way we may scream when a
roller coaster twists through a complete 360 or plows through a lake
at the bottom of the drop. And horror movies, like roller coasters,
have always been the special province of the young; by the time one
turns 40 or 50, one's appetite for double twists or 360-degree loops
may be considerably depleted.

We also go to re-establish our feelings of essential normality; the   4
horror movie is innately conservative, even reactionary. Freda Jackson
as the horrible melting woman in *Die, Monster, Die!* confirms for us
that no matter how far we may be removed from the beauty of a Robert
Redford or a Diana Ross, we are still light-years from true ugliness.

And we go to have fun.   5

Ah, but this is where the ground starts to slope away, isn't it? Be-   6
cause this is a very peculiar sort of fun, indeed. The fun comes from seeing others menaced—sometimes killed. One critic has suggested that if
pro football has become the voyeur's version of combat, then the horror film has become the modern version of the public lynching.

It is true that the mythic, "fairy-tale" horror film intends to take   7
away the shades of gray. . . . It urges us to put away our more civilized and adult penchant for analysis and to become children again,
seeing things in pure blacks and whites. It may be that horror movies
provide psychic relief on this level because this invitation to lapse into
simplicity, irrationality and even outright madness is extended so
rarely. We are told we may allow our emotions a free rein . . . or no
rein at all.

If we are all insane, then sanity becomes a matter of degree. If your   8
insanity leads you to carve up women like Jack the Ripper or the Cleve-
land Torso Murderer, we clap you away in the funny farm (but neither
of those two amateur-night surgeons was ever caught, heh-heh-heh); if,
on the other hand, your insanity leads you only to talk to yourself when
you're under stress or to pick your nose on your morning bus, then you
are left alone to go about your business . . . though it is doubtful that
you will ever be invited to the best parties.

The potential lyncher is in almost all of us (excluding saints, past   9
and present; but then, most saints have been crazy in their own

ways), and every now and then, he has to be let loose to scream and roll around in the grass. Our emotions and our fears form their own body, and we recognize that it demands its own exercise to maintain proper muscle tone. Certain of these emotional muscles are accepted—even exalted—in civilized society; they are, of course, the emotions that tend to maintain the status quo of civilization itself. Love, friendship, loyalty, kindness—these are all the emotions that we applaud, emotions that have been immortalized in the couplets of Hallmark cards and in the verses (I don't dare call it poetry) of Leonard Nimoy.

When we exhibit these emotions, society showers us with positive reinforcement; we learn this even before we get out of diapers. When, as children, we hug our rotten little puke of a sister and give her a kiss, all the aunts and uncles smile and twit and cry, "Isn't he the sweetest little thing?" Such coveted treats as chocolate-covered graham crackers often follow. But if we deliberately slam the rotten little puke of a sister's fingers in the door, sanctions follow—angry remonstrance from parents, aunts and uncles; instead of a chocolate-covered graham cracker, a spanking. 10

But anticivilization emotions don't go away, and they demand periodic exercise. We have such "sick" jokes as, "What's the difference between a truckload of bowling balls and a truckload of dead babies? (You can't unload a truckload of bowling balls with a pitchfork. . . . a joke, by the way, that I heard originally from a ten-year-old). Such a joke may surprise a laugh or a grin out of us even as we recoil, a possibility that confirms the thesis: if we share a brotherhood of man, then we also share an insanity of man. None of which is intended as a defense of either the sick joke or insanity but merely as an explanation of why the best horror films, like the best fairy tales, manage to be reactionary, anarchistic, and revolutionary all at the same time. 11

The mythic horror movie, like the sick joke, has a dirty job to do. It deliberately appeals to all that is worst in us. It is morbidity unchained, our most base instincts let free, our nastiest fantasies realized . . . and it all happens, fittingly enough, in the dark. For those reasons, good liberals often shy away from horror films. For myself, I like to see the most aggressive of them—*Dawn of the Dead,* for instance—as lifting a trap door in the civilized forebrain and throwing a basket of raw meat to the hungry alligators swimming around in that subterranean river beneath. 12

Why bother? Because it keeps them from getting out, man. It 13
keeps them down there and me up here. It was Lennon and McCartney who said that all you need is love, and I would agree with that.

As long as you keep the gators fed. 14

QUESTIONS FOR STUDY AND DISCUSSION

1. What, according to King, causes people to crave horror movies? What other reasons can you add to King's list?

2. Identify the analogy King uses in paragraph 3, and explain how it works. (Glossary: *Analogy*)

3. What does King mean when he says, "The horror movie is innately conservative, even reactionary" (4)?

4. What emotions does society applaud? Why? Which ones does King label "anticivilization" emotions?

5. In what ways is a horror movie like a sick joke? What is the "dirty job" or effect that the two have in common (12)?

6. King starts his essay with the attention-grabbing sentence "I think that we're all mentally ill." How does he develop this idea of insanity in his essay? What does King mean when he says, "The potential lyncher is in almost all of us" (9)? How does King's last line relate to the theme of mental illness?

7. What is King's tone in this essay? (Glossary: *Tone*) Point to particular words or sentences that led you to this conclusion.

VOCABULARY

Refer to your dictionary to define the following words as they are used in this selection. Then use each word in a sentence of your own.

grimaces (1)	puke (10)
hysterical (1)	sanctions (10)
voyeur's (6)	remonstrance (10)
penchant (7)	recoil (11)
rein (7)	anarchistic (11)
exalted (9)	morbidity (12)
status quo (9)	subterranean (12)

CLASSROOM ACTIVITY USING CAUSE AND EFFECT

William V. Haney has developed the following test to determine your ability to analyze accurately evidence that is presented to you. After completing Haney's test, discuss your answers with other members of your class.

THE UNCRITICAL INFERENCE TEST

DIRECTIONS

1. You will read a brief story. Assume that all of the information presented in the story is definitely accurate and true. Read the story carefully. You may refer back to the story whenever you wish.
2. You will then read statements about the story. Answer them in numerical order. *Do not go back* to fill in answers or to change answers. This will only distort your test score.
3. After you read each statement carefully, determine whether the statement is:
   a. "T" — meaning: On the basis of the information presented in the story the statement is *definitely true.*
   b. "F" — meaning: On the basis of the information presented in the story the statement is *definitely false.*
   c. "?" — The statement *may* be true (or false) but on the basis of the information presented in the story you cannot be definitely certain. (If any part of the statement is doubtful, mark the statement "?".)
4. Indicate your answer by circling either "T" or "F" or "?" opposite the statement.

THE STORY

Babe Smith has been killed. Police have rounded up six suspects, all of whom are known gangsters. All of them are known to have been near the scene of the killing at the approximate time that it occurred. All had substantial motives for wanting Smith killed. However, one of these suspected gangsters, Slinky Sam, has positively been cleared of guilt.

STATEMENTS ABOUT THE STORY

1. Slinky Sam is known to have been near the scene
   of the killing of Babe Smith.   T   F   ?

2. All six of the rounded-up gangsters were known to have been near the scene of the murder.   T   F   ?

3. Only Slinky Sam has been cleared of guilt.   T   F   ?

4. All six of the rounded-up suspects were near the scene of Smith's killing at the approximate time that it took place.   T   F   ?

5. The police do not know who killed Smith.   T   F   ?

6. All six suspects are known to have been near the scene of the foul deed.   T   F   ?

7. Smith's murderer did not confess of his own free will.   T   F   ?

8. Slinky Sam was not cleared of guilt   T   F   ?

9. It is known that the six suspects were in the vicinity of the cold-blooded assassination.   T   F   ?

SUGGESTED WRITING ASSIGNMENTS

1. Write an essay in which you analyze, in light of King's remarks about the causes of our cravings for horror movies, a horror movie you've seen. In what ways did the movie satisfy your "anti-civilization" emotions? How did you feel before going to the theater? How did you feel when leaving?

2. Write an essay in which you analyze the most significant reasons or causes for your going to college. You may wish to discuss such matters as your high school experiences, people and events that influenced your decision, and your goals in college as well as in later life.

How Not to Lose Friends over Money

■ Lois Duncan

Lois Duncan is a versatile writer with more than five hundred periodical articles to her credit, in addition to books of both fiction and nonfiction. Young adults know her primarily for her novels of mystery, suspense, and the supernatural. A successful movie version of her 1973 novel, I Know What You Did Last Summer, *was released in 1997. She has also written books for young children, including some books of poetry. Adult readers, particularly women, recognize her as a columnist for* Woman's Day. *In 1982 she published* Chapters: My Growth as a Writer. *Duncan was born in 1934 in Philadelphia, received her Bachelor of Arts degree from the University of New Mexico, and currently lives in Albuquerque. In the essay below, she identifies a cause-and-effect relationship in her first few paragraphs that serves as the underlying rationale for each of the solutions she goes on to discuss. Notice, however, that each of these solutions introduces its own stated or implied cause-and-effect relationship as well.*

FOR YOUR JOURNAL

One of Shakespeare's best-known quotes is "Neither a borrower nor a lender be." How do you feel about lending money to friends? Have money issues ever caused tension between you and a friend?

When I was in the third grade, a girl named Olivia borrowed money from me to buy a Coke. She never paid it back. I was too embarrassed to ask for it. I didn't want my friend to think I didn't trust her.

One day Olivia was absent from school. She had moved to Philadelphia, and my money had gone with her. I was outraged!

Many years later, I am still outraged. I wake in the night with the feel of Olivia's throat in my hands! Surpassing my fury, however, is contempt for my eight-year-old self because I did not stand up to that pigtailed shyster and demand what was mine.

I'd like to say that the experience taught me a lesson. But the sad 4
truth is I still have problems with friends and money. Almost everyone I know has similar difficulties. The stickiest situations seem to be
those in which the amounts are so small that it doesn't seem worth
the risk of alienating a friend to make a fuss. At the same time, we all
resent being treated unfairly, and our buried hostility often threatens
the very friendship we are struggling so hard to preserve.

As Dr. Sidney Rosenblum, professor of psychology and psychia- 5
try at the University of New Mexico, explains, "Money is important
not just for what it can buy, but for what it may symbolize—power,
social status, even love. When a friend takes advantage of us financially, it is hard to be objective. Subconsciously, we get the message
that we are not important enough to that person to merit fair treatment."

What seems fair to one person, however, often seems totally un- 6
fair to another. A candid discussion may help, but differences in values cannot always be resolved. In some cases, you simply have to
decide how much a friendship is worth—and act accordingly. But
most of these problems can be handled successfully—sometimes with
surprising ease.

I consulted psychologists and counselors on this issue, but found 7
that some of the best advice came from women who had learned to
cope through trial and error. Here are their solutions to ten common
money problems that come between friends:

1. *A companion suggests splitting a restaurant tab in half when* 8
her share is much larger than yours. Randy and Sally get together for
a long, gossipy lunch at least once a month. Randy, who is perenni-
ally on a diet, always orders a salad and coffee, while skinny Sally
goes for broke with veal scallopini and a lavish dessert. Many times,
she also has a glass or two of wine. When the bill arrives, Sally always says, "Let's just split it, OK?" Although Randy's meal usually
cost about a third of Sally's, she's reluctant to appear cheap.

"I used to tell myself that such inequities even out in the long 9
run," Randy says, "but they *don't*. The person who orders the most
expensive dish on the menu one day is usually the one who does it the
next time too."

Her solution is a pocket calculator. "Before Sally can suggest 10
going halfsies," she says, "I offer to do the accounting. I tell her I love
to use this nifty gadget my husband gave me for my birthday. Then I
do a quick calculation and plunk down cash to cover my share; Sally

pays the rest. She's never complained so maybe she just hates to do arithmetic."

2. *You become involved in an unequal gift exchange.* Nobody ex- 11
pects the presents she receives to cost exactly the same as those she gives, but a wide disparity is embarrassing for both parties. Some women avoid this problem by getting friends to agree on a maximum amount in advance. This can only work, however, when the gift exchange is an established tradition.

"The most distressing situations occur when you're taken by sur- 12
prise," says Reneé, a schoolteacher. "The day school let out for Christmas, a colleague stopped me to say she had a little gift for me in her car. I had nothing for her, so I rushed out and bought a pair of lovely earrings on my lunch hour. Her present turned out to be a dime-store joke gift. She thanked me profusely for the earrings, but it was obvious that she was embarrassed—and so was I."

If this were to happen again, Reneé says she'd open the package 13
before deciding on an appropriate form of reciprocation. "I might not give a present at all," she says. "Instead, I could invite her over for eggnog during the holidays or ask her to be my guest at a Christmas program. Every gesture of friendship doesn't have to be repaid in kind."

Many other women agreed. Said one: "I think people should give 14
what they want to and can afford—without worrying over-much about equality of cost. When you're hung up on monetary value, you're not *giving,* you're *trading.* If you're going to do that, you might just as well exchange checks for equal amounts."

3. *A passenger in your car neglects to pay her share of expenses.* 15
"When Amy and I took a long trip in my car," says Phyllis, "I just as-sumed we'd each pay half. Amy did her part as she saw it, paying for every other tank of gas. But when the radiator hose burst in Salt Lake City, I paid for the replacement. When the fuel pump went out in Chicago, I paid for repairs. The cost of a tune-up and oil change before the trip and the car wash when we got back—I absorbed them all."

Phyllis realizes that she was partly to blame for not discussing fi- 16
nances in advance, but will not make the same mistake again. "When I use my own car for business," she says, "I get reimbursed twenty cents a mile. So the next time I furnish transportation for a pleasure trip, I'll make it clear from the start that I expect my companion to contribute ten cents a mile."

A more common problem arises when one person provides regu- 17
lar chauffeur service for a friend who never chips in for gas. "I don't

think most nondrivers mean to take advantage," one woman said; "they just don't realize how much it costs to operate a car. One day I pulled into a self-service station and asked my friend to finish filling the tank while I dashed to the ladies' room. By the time I got back, she was staring in horror at the price gauge and fishing for her wallet."

4. *You are given a check that bounces.* When Roberta went out   18 to dinner and the theater with a friend from out of town, she paid both bills with her credit card. Lisa then paid for her share of the evening's expenses by giving Roberta a check — one that later bounced.

"It was very awkward," Roberta recalls. "I considered absorbing the   19 whole cost of the evening myself just to avoid embarrassing Lisa. I knew, though, that if I did that I'd always feel resentful. Our friend-ship would be bound to suffer — and Lisa wouldn't even know why."

Roberta handled the situation by sending Lisa the bounced check,   20 along with a lighthearted note saying, "If your bank is like mine, they botched up your account. Shall we try again?" Lisa responded with a note of apology and another check — one that cleared — and the inci-dent was never referred to by either woman again.

5. *A friend invites you to participate in an activity that costs*   21 *more than you can afford — or want — to spend.* "When my college roommate asked me to be matron-of-honor at her wedding, I was flat-tered," Louise recalls. "My immediate response was, 'I'd love to!' After I hung up, however, I began to realize how much expense was involved. The dress had to be specially made, with new shoes dyed to match — and the wedding was halfway across the country. My hus-band and I were saving to go to Europe and couldn't afford to do both."

Louise decided to be honest. "I called her back and explained the   22 situation," she says. "My roommate was hurt, of course, and I felt bad about that. But I'd have felt even worse if I'd sacrificed the trip I'd been looking forward to for so long."

Not everyone I polled agreed with this approach. All thought   23 Louise had been right to turn down the invitation, but some felt she could have done it more kindly. "She might have said that previous plans made it impossible for her to attend the wedding," one woman suggested. "She didn't have to explain that the plans were for a trip to Europe. In Louise's place, I'd have tried to spare my friend's feel-ings by not mentioning that this milestone in her life was not nearly as important to me as it was to her."

6. *You are asked to contribute toward a gift for someone you* 24
don't know well or don't like. "Every week it seems," says Eileen,
"I'm asked to make a contribution toward another gift or a party to
celebrate somebody's new baby, birthday or retirement. I resent fork-
ing over money for people I hardly know, but how do you get out of
it when everybody else is doing it?"

The simplest solution: just say no. "It doesn't sound that bad if 25
you do it regretfully," one woman suggests. "'I wish I could contribute,' I'd say, 'but it just isn't possible.'"

Another friend handles this problem differently. "If the honored 26
person is somebody I'd be buying for anyway," she explains, "I donate the amount I'd have spent myself. If it's someone I know only
slightly, I give a few coins as a token. What I *don't* do is apologize for
my contribution — or let myself be pressured into giving more than I feel
is really appropriate."

7. *A friend is able to spend far more — or far less — than you can.* 27
We don't choose friends on the basis of how much money they have,
of course, but vast differences can be disturbing to both sides. Erin,
for example, is single and earns a very good salary. Her friend Pat, a
divorced mother of three, is struggling to make ends meet.

"We're both theater buffs," Erin explains. "And I'd gladly pay 28
for two tickets just to have Pat's company at plays and concerts. But
she won't go anywhere unless she can pay her own way. I hate to go
alone, so we both stay home. It all seems so silly."

Pat sees the situation differently. "After an unhappy marriage to 29
a domineering man," she says, "it's very important to me to carry my
own weight. I'm not comfortable in any relationship where all I do is
take."

The impasse was finally broken when Erin moved recently. Pat's 30
children were with their father so she took a picnic lunch to her
friend's new place, then spent the day helping her unpack and get
settled. "I was so grateful," Erin says, "that I persuaded Pat to let me
return the favor in my own way — with season tickets to our little
theater group. I think she is beginning to recognize that she contributes as much to our friendship as I do."

8. *Social pressure forces you to overspend.* "When you're out 31
with a group, weird things can happen to common sense," says Valerie. "For example, my husband and I often meet after work on Fri-
days at a club we belong to. We always run into people we know
there, and inevitably somebody snatches the bar tab and says, 'I'll get

this round; you can get the next one.' That seems fair on the surface, but a single beer is my husband's limit and I drink club soda. More often than not, we find ourselves hosting a round of double martinis for casual acquaintances."

After several such occasions, Valerie and her husband agreed to refuse to be shoved into "picking up a round" again. "Now when a second batch of drinks is ordered, we just insist, 'No more for us, thanks,'" Valerie says. "We don't make excuses or offer prolonged explanations. If the person who paid for the first round gets upset, that's *his* problem. *Ours* is solved!" 32

9. A friend asks personal questions about your finances. "Some people don't seem to mind being asked how much they earn or what they spend for their clothes, but I am offended by such questions," says Heather. "To my way of thinking, our finances are nobody else's business. Yet when we were first married, a nosy acquaintance asked what my husband's salary was and I was so startled I actually *told* her!" 33

In the years since, Heather has developed techniques for putting money snoops in their place. "It's a state secret," she tells them, or "I can't remember what I paid." Today, if someone is crass enough to ask about her husband's salary, she responds with questions of her own: "Why do you care about that? Are you planning to apply for his job?" 34

10. A companion borrows money and "forgets" to repay it. Large loans are seldom the issue; they're usually treated as business transactions, with the terms spelled out on paper. But many women suffer in silence over problems like Carol's. "My friend Ginny is always short of cash," she says. "I hate to recall how often I've 'loaned' her a dollar or two for a drink or a movie. Each loan is so small I'd feel really cheap making a big deal out of it; still, I *do* resent the fact that she never pays me back." 35

Carol admits to being "too inhibited or something" to demand repayment, but she has resolved to stop giving money to Ginny. "The last time she asked for five dollars to pay for her dry cleaning, I just told her I couldn't spare it." 36

Another woman suggests a gutsier response. "When somebody cops out on repaying a loan, I turn the tables by requesting one myself," she says. "'I left home without my wallet,' I'll say. 'Can you lend me enough to cover lunch?' Then, when the money is safely in hand, I am struck by a sudden realization. 'Why, this is exactly the 37 amount I loaned you last week! How convenient! Now you won't have to repay me!'" She says it works like a charm.

Then, there's the *really* gutsy solution in which we simply ask, 38 straight out, in no-nonsense language, for what is rightfully ours. This, I've come to realize, is what I should have done with Olivia. If I were to run into her today, I like to think I'd have the strength of character to step right up and say, "Olivia, I have an overwhelming desire for a soda. How about giving me the cash I loaned you forty years ago?"

If she did hand it over, I think I might forgive her and renew our 39 friendship—despite the fact that you can no longer buy a Coke with a dime!

QUESTIONS FOR STUDY AND DISCUSSION

1. Duncan's anecdote about Olivia and the Coke seems trivial, yet she says she is still outraged many years later. (Glossary: *Anecdote*) How do the anecdote and Duncan's response to it serve to spotlight the effect money can have on personal relationships?

2. Why is money such a volatile topic between friends? Why do you think Duncan's best sources were laypeople, not psychologists and counselors? What does Duncan gain by using concrete examples provided by friends instead of abstract theories provided by experts in the field? (Glossary: *Concrete/Abstract* and *Illustration*)

3. In her seventh point, Duncan presents an ultimate cause (Pat is getting over an unhappy marriage and is struggling with self-esteem and finances), leading to an immediate cause (Pat resents Erin's attempts to pay for her theater tickets), leading to the effect that both stay home from the theater. Summarize the cause-and-effect relationship of four of Duncan's other "common money problems." What are the causes of the problems? What are the effects?

4. How does Duncan organize her essay? (Glossary: *Organization*) Do you think that her organization is an effective way to present her information? Why, or why not?

5. In three of her ten scenarios Duncan presents multiple strategies (causes) for achieving the desired result (effect). Are such choices a help or a hindrance? Why do you think she presented the different viewpoints?

6. Duncan concludes with her solution to the annoying situation presented at the beginning of her essay. Is presenting this solution an effective technique for ending her essay? (Glossary: *Beginnings and Endings*) Why, or why not?

VOCABULARY

Refer to your dictionary to define the following words as they are used in this selection. Then use each word in a sentence of your own.

inequities (9)   milestone (23)
disparity (11)   impasse (30)
reciprocation (13)   crass (34)

CLASSROOM ACTIVITY USING CAUSE AND EFFECT

Develop a causal chain in which you examine the ramifications of a past action of yours. Identify each part of the chain. For example, you decided you wanted to do well in a course (ultimate cause), so you got started on a research project early (immediate cause), which enabled you to write several drafts of your paper (immediate cause), which earned you an A for the project (effect), which earned you an excellent grade in the class (effect), which enabled you to take the advanced seminar you wanted (effect).

SUGGESTED WRITING ASSIGNMENTS

1. Friendship is a complex give-and-take relationship that changes and evolves over time. Duncan focuses on money, but changes are caused by a variety of issues and situations. Write an essay about a sudden change you had in a close friendship. What do you think was the ultimate cause? What was the immediate cause? What were the effects? What is your current relationship with this person?

2. Write an essay in which you establish the cause-and-effect relationship that exists in one of the following pairs:

winter and depression   health and happiness
poverty and crime   old age and wisdom
wealth and power   good looks and popularity

Argument

The word *argument* probably brings to mind a verbal disagreement of the sort that everyone has at least witnessed, if not participated in directly. Such disputes are occasionally satisfying; you can take pleasure in knowing you have converted someone to your point of view. More often, though, verbal arguments are inconclusive, frustrating you when you realize that you have failed to make your position understood, or enraging you when you feel that your opponent has been stubborn and unreasonable. Such dissatisfaction is inevitable because verbal arguments generally arise spontaneously and so cannot be thoughtfully planned or researched; it is difficult to come up with appropriate evidence on the spur of the moment or to find the language that will make a point hard to deny. Indeed, it is often not until later, in retrospect, that the convincing piece of evidence, the forcefully phrased assertion, finally comes to mind.

Written arguments share common goals with spoken ones: they attempt to convince a reader to agree with a particular point of view, to make a particular decision, and/or to pursue a particular course of action. Written arguments, however, involve the presentation of well-chosen evidence and the artful control of language. Writers of arguments have no one around to dispute their words directly, so they must imagine their probable audience to predict the sorts of objections that may be raised. Written arguments, therefore, must be much more carefully planned—the writer must settle in advance on a specific, sufficiently detailed thesis or proposition. There is a greater need for organization, for choosing the most effective types of evidence from all that is available, for determining the strategies of rhetoric, language, and style that will best suit the argument's subject, its purpose, and its thesis, as well as ensure its effect on the intended audience. In the end, however, such work can be far more satisfying than spontaneous oral argument.

Most people who specialize in the study of arguments identify two essential categories: persuasion and logic. *Persuasive appeals* are directed at readers' emotions, at their subconscious, even at their biases and prejudices. These appeals involve diction, slanting, figurative language, analogy, rhythmic patterns of speech, and the establishment of a tone that will encourage a positive response. It is important to understand, as well, that persuasion very often attempts to get the audience to take action. Examples of persuasive argument are found in the exaggerated claims of advertisers and the speechmaking of political and social activists.

Logical appeals, on the other hand, are directed primarily at the audience's intellectual faculties, understanding, and knowledge. Such appeals depend on the reasoned movement from assertion to evidence to conclusion and on an almost mathematical system of proof and counterproof. Logical argument, unlike persuasion, does not normally impel its audience to action. Logical argument is commonly found in scientific or philosophical articles, in legal decisions, and in technical proposals.

Most arguments, however, are neither purely persuasive nor purely logical. A well-written newspaper editorial, for example, will present a logical arrangement of assertions and evidence, but it will also employ striking diction and other persuasive patterns of language to reinforce its effectiveness. Thus, the kinds of appeals a writer emphasizes depend on the nature of the topic, the thesis or proposition of the argument, the writer's purpose, the various kinds of support (for example, evidence, opinions, examples, facts, statistics) offered, and a thoughtful consideration of the audience. Knowing the differences between persuasive and logical appeals is essential in learning both to read and to write arguments.

True arguments make assertions about which there is a legitimate and recognized difference of opinion. It is unlikely that anyone will ever need to convince a reader that falling in love is a beautiful and intense experience, that crime rates should be reduced, or that computers are changing the world; most everyone would agree with such assertions. But not everyone would agree that women experience love more intensely than men, that reinstating the death penalty will reduce the incidence of crime, or that computers are changing the world for the worse; these assertions are arguable and admit of differing perspectives. Similarly, a leading heart specialist might argue in a popular magazine that too many doctors are advising patients to have pacemakers implanted when the devices are not necessary; the editorial writer for a small-town newspaper could write urging that a local agency supplying food to poor families be given a larger percentage of the tax budget; in a long and complex book, a foreign-policy specialist might attempt to prove that the current administration exhibits no consistent policy in its relationship with other countries and that the Department of State needs to be overhauled. No matter what its forum or its structure, an argument has as its chief purpose the detailed setting forth of a particular point of view and the rebuttal of any opposing views.

Argumentation frequently utilizes the other rhetorical strategies. In your efforts to argue convincingly, you may find it necessary to define, to compare and contrast, to analyze causes and effects, to classify, to describe, or to narrate. Nevertheless, it is the writer's attempt to convince, not explain, that is of primary importance in an argumentative essay. In this respect, it is helpful to keep in mind that there are two basic patterns of thinking and presenting our thoughts that are followed in argumentation: induction and deduction.

Inductive reasoning, the more common type of reasoning, moves from a set of specific examples to a general statement. In doing so, the writer makes what is known as an *inductive leap* from the evidence to the generalization. For example, after examining enrollment statistics, we can conclude that students do not like to take courses offered early in the morning or late in the afternoon.

Deductive reasoning, on the other hand, moves from a general statement to a specific conclusion. It works on the model of the *syllogism,* a simple three-part argument that consists of a major premise, a minor premise, and a conclusion, as in the following example:

a. All women are mortal. *(Major premise)*
b. Jeanne is a woman. *(Minor premise)*
c. Jeanne is mortal. *(Conclusion)*

Obviously, a syllogism will fail to work if either of the premises is untrue.

a. All living creatures are mammals. *(Major premise)*
b. A butterfly is a living creature. *(Minor premise)*
c. A butterfly is a mammal. *(Conclusion)*

The problem is immediately apparent. The major premise is obviously false: many living creatures are not mammals, and a butterfly happens to be one of the non-mammals. Consequently, the conclusion is invalid.

Writing an argument is a challenging assignment but one that can be very rewarding. By nature, an argument must be carefully reasoned and thoughtfully structured to have maximum effect. Allow yourself, therefore, enough time to think about your thesis, to gather the evidence you need, and to draft, revise, edit, and proofread your essay. Fuzzy thinking, confused expression, and poor organization will be immediately evident to your reader and will diminish your chances for completing the assignment successfully. The following steps will remind you of some key features of arguments and will help you sequence your activities as you research and write.

I. DETERMINE THE THESIS OR PROPOSITION

Begin by deciding on a topic that interests you and about which there is some significant difference of opinion or about which you have a number of questions. Find out what's in the news about your topic, what people are saying about it, what authors and instructors are emphasizing as important intellectual arguments. As you pursue your research, consider what assertion or assertions you can make about the topic you choose. The more specific this thesis or proposition, the more directed your research can become and the more focused your ultimate argument will be. Don't hesitate along the way to modify or even reject an initial thesis as your continued research warrants.

A thesis can be placed anywhere in an argument, but it is probably best while learning to write arguments to place the statement of your controlling idea somewhere near the beginning of your composition. Explain the importance of the thesis, and make clear to your reader that you share a common concern or interest in this issue. You may wish to state your central assertion directly in your first or second paragraph so that your reader will have no doubt or confusion about your position. You may also wish to lead off with a particularly striking piece of evidence to capture your reader's interest.

2. TAKE ACCOUNT OF YOUR AUDIENCE

In no other type of writing is the question of audience more important than in argumentation. The tone you establish, the type of diction you choose, the kinds of evidence you select to buttress your assertions, and indeed the organizational pattern you follow can influence your audience to trust you and believe your assertions. If you judge the nature of your audience accurately, respect its knowledge of the subject, and correctly envision whether it is likely to be hostile, neutral, complacent, or receptive, you will be able to tailor the various aspects of your argument appropriately.

3. GATHER THE NECESSARY SUPPORTING EVIDENCE

For each point of your argument, be sure to provide appropriate and sufficient evidence: verifiable facts and statistics, illustrative examples and narratives, or quotations from authorities. Don't overwhelm your reader with evidence, but don't skimp either; it is important to demonstrate your command of the topic and control of the thesis by choosing carefully among all the evidence at your disposal.

4. SETTLE ON AN ORGANIZATIONAL PATTERN

Once you think you have sufficient evidence to make your assertion convincing, consider how best to organize your argument. To some extent, your organization will depend on your method of reasoning: inductive, deductive, or a combination of the two. For example, is it necessary to establish a major premise before moving on to discuss a minor premise? Should most of your evidence precede your direct statement of an assertion, or follow it? Will induction work better with the particular audience you have targeted? As you present your primary points, you may find it effective to move from least important to most important or from least familiar to most familiar. A scratch outline can help; but often a writer's most crucial revisions in an argument involve rearranging its components into a sharper, more coherent order. Very often it is difficult to tell what that order should be until the revision stage of the writing process.

5. CONSIDER REFUTATIONS TO YOUR ARGUMENT

As you proceed with your argument, you may wish to take into account well-known and significant opposing arguments. To ignore opposing views would be to suggest to your readers any one of the following: You don't know about the opposing views; you know about them and are obviously and unfairly weighting the arguments in your favor; or you know about them and have no reasonable answers for them. Grant the validity of opposing arguments or refute them, but respect your reader's intelligence by addressing the objections to your assertion. Your readers will in turn respect you for doing so.

6. AVOID FAULTY REASONING

Have someone read your argument for errors in judgment and for faulty reasoning. Sometimes others can see easily what you can't see because you are so intimately tied to your assertion. Review the following list of errors in reasoning, making sure that you have not committed any of them.

OVERSIMPLIFICATION:
A foolishly simple solution to what is clearly a complex problem: *We have a balance-of-trade deficit because foreigners make better products than we do.*

HASTY GENERALIZATION:
In inductive reasoning, a generalization that is based on too little evidence or on evidence that is not representative: *My grandparents eat bran flakes for breakfast, just as most older folks do.*

POST HOC ERGO PROPTER HOC:
"After this, therefore because of this." Confusing chance or coincidence with causation. The fact that one event comes after another does not necessarily mean that the first event caused the second: *I went to the hockey game last night. The next thing I knew I had a cold.*

BEGGING THE QUESTION:
Assuming in a premise something that needs to be proven: *Parking fines work because they keep people from parking illegally.*

FALSE ANALOGY:
Making a misleading analogy between logically unconnected ideas: *If we can clone mammals, we should be able to find a cure for cancer.*

EITHER/OR THINKING:
Seeing only two alternatives when there may in fact be other possibilities: *Either you love your job or you hate it.*

NON SEQUITUR:
"It does not follow." An inference or conclusion that is not clearly related to the established premises or evidence: *She is very sincere. She must know what she's talking about.*

7. CONCLUDE FORCEFULLY

In the conclusion of your essay, be sure to restate your position in new language, at least briefly. Besides persuading your reader to accept your point of view, you may also want to encourage some specific course of action. Above all, your conclusion should not introduce new information that may surprise your reader; it should seem to follow naturally, almost seamlessly, from the series of points that you have carefully established in the body of the essay. Don't overstate your case, but at the same time don't qualify your conclusion with the use of too many words or phrases like *I think, in my opinion, maybe, sometimes,* and *probably.* These words can make you sound indecisive and fuzzy-headed rather than rational and sensible.

As They Say, Drugs Kill

■ **Laura Rowley**

*Laura Rowley was born in Oak Lawn, Illinois, in 1965 and gradu-
ated from the University of Illinois at Urbana–Champaign in 1987
with a degree in journalism. While in college, Rowley was the city
editor of the* Daily Illini. *After graduation she worked at the*
United Nations Chronicle *in New York City. Rowley now works
as a freelance writer and hopes someday to travel and work in
Africa under the auspices of either the United Nations or the
Peace Corps. In the following essay, which first appeared in*
Newsweek on Campus *in 1987, Rowley argues against substance
abuse by recounting a particularly poignant experience. Although
her narrative appeals primarily to readers' emotions, she nonetheless attempts to persuade without preaching.*

FOR YOUR JOURNAL

What is your best argument against the use of drugs? If you
could tell a story that argues against drugs and that would persuade young people not to use them, what would that story be?
It might be a personal story, a story about friends who were
unlucky in their use of drugs, or a story that you read about or
saw portrayed in the movies or on television.

The fastest way to end a party is to have someone die in the 1
middle of it.

At a party last fall I watched a 22-year-old die of cardiac arrest 2
after he had used drugs. It was a painful, undignified way to die. And
I would like to think that anyone who shared the experience would
feel his or her ambivalence about substance abuse dissolving.

This victim won't be singled out like Len Bias* as a bitter ex- 3
ample for "troubled youth." He was just another ordinary guy celebrating with friends at a private house party, the kind where they roll

---

*College basketball star who died of a drug overdose after signing a contract with the
Boston Celtics.

in the keg first thing in the morning and get stupefied while watching the football games on cable all afternoon. The living room was littered with beer cans from last night's party — along with dirty socks and the stuffing from the secondhand couch.

And there were drugs, as at so many other college parties. The 4 drug of choice this evening was psilocybin, hallucinogenic mushrooms. If you're cool you call them "'shrooms."

This wasn't a crowd huddled in the corner of a darkened room 5 with a single red bulb, shooting needles in their arms. People played darts, made jokes, passed around a joint and listened to the Grateful Dead on the stereo.

Suddenly, a thin, tall, brown-haired young man began to gasp. 6 His eyes rolled back in his head, and he hit the floor face first with a crash. Someone laughed, not appreciating the violence of his fall, thinking the afternoon's festivities had finally caught up with another guest. The laugh lasted only a second, as the brown-haired guest began to convulse and choke. The sound of the stereo and laughter evaporated. Bystanders shouted frantic suggestions:

"It's an epileptic fit, put something in his mouth!" 7

"Roll him over on his stomach!" 8

"Call an ambulance; God, somebody breathe into his mouth." 9

A girl kneeling next to him began to sob his name, and he seemed 10 to moan.

"Wait, he's semicoherent." Four people grabbed for the tele- 11 phone, to find no dial tone, and ran to use a neighbor's. One slammed the dead phone against the wall in frustration — and miraculously produced a dial tone.

But the body was now motionless on the kitchen floor. "He has a 12 pulse, he has a pulse."

"But he's not breathing!" 13

"Well, get away — give him some f——ing air!" The three or 14 four guests gathered around his body unbuttoned his shirt.

"Wait — is he OK? Should I call the damn ambulance?" 15

A chorus of frightened voices shouted, "Yes, yes!" 16

"Come on, come on, breathe again. Breathe!" 17

Over muffled sobs came a sudden grating, desperate breath that 18 passed through bloody lips and echoed through the kitchen and living room.

"He's had this reaction before — when he did acid at a concert 19 last spring. But he recovered in 15 seconds . . . ," one friend confided.

The rest of the guests looked uncomfortably at the floor or paced   20
purposelessly around the room. One or two whispered, "Oh, my God,"
over and over, like a prayer. A friend stood next to me, eyes fixed on the
kitchen floor. He mumbled, just audibly, "I've seen this before. My dad
died of a heart attack. He had the same look. . . ." I touched his shoulder and leaned against a wall, repeating reassurances to myself. People
don't die at parties. People don't die at parties.

Eventually, no more horrible, gnashing sounds tore their way   21
from the victim's lungs. I pushed my hands deep in my jeans pockets
wondering how much it costs to pump a stomach and how someone
could be so careless if he had had this reaction with another drug.
What would he tell his parents about the hospital bill?

Two uniformed paramedics finally arrived, lifted him onto a   22
stretcher and quickly rolled him out. His face was grayish blue, his
mouth hung open, rimmed with blood, and his eyes were rolled back
with a yellowish color on the rims.

The paramedics could be seen moving rhythmically forward and   23
back through the small windows of the ambulance, whose lights
threw a red wash over the stunned watchers on the porch. The paramedics' hands were massaging his chest when someone said, "Did
you tell them he took psilocybin? Did you tell them?"

"No, I . . ."   24

"My God, so tell them—do you want him to die?" Two people   25
ran to tell the paramedics the student had eaten mushrooms five minutes before the attack.

It seemed irreverent to talk as the ambulance pulled away. My   26
friend, who still saw his father's image, muttered, "That guy's dead."
I put my arms around him half to comfort him, half to stop him from
saying things I couldn't believe.

The next day, when I called someone who lived in the house, I   27
found that my friend was right.

My hands began to shake and my eyes filled with tears for some-   28
one I didn't know. Weeks later the pain has dulled, but I still can't
unravel the knot of emotion that has moved from my stomach to my
head. When I told one friend what happened, she shook her head and
spoke of the stupidity of filling your body with chemical substances.
People who would do drugs after seeing that didn't value their lives
too highly, she said.

But others refused to read any universal lessons from the inci-   29
dent. Many of those I spoke to about the event considered him the

victim of a freak accident, randomly struck down by drugs as a pedestrian might be hit by a speeding taxi. They speculated that the student must have had special physical problems; what happened to him could not happen to them.

Couldn't it? Now when I hear people discussing drugs I'm 30 haunted by the image of him lying on the floor, his body straining to rid itself of substances he chose to take. Painful, undignified, unnecessary — like a wartime casualty. But in war, at least, lessons are supposed to be learned, so that old mistakes are not repeated. If this death cannot make people think and change, that will be an even greater tragedy.

QUESTIONS FOR STUDY AND DISCUSSION

1. Rowley uses an extended narrative example to develop her argument. How does she use dialogue, diction choices, and appropriate details to make her argument more compelling? (Glossary: *Narration; Dialogue; Diction;* and *Details*)

2. Rowley does not argue her point until the last sentence of the essay, but the purpose of her essay is clear. (Glossary: *Purpose*) What does she want us to believe? What does she want us to do? How does her anecdote serve as the foundation for her argument? (Glossary: *Anecdote*)

3. What does Rowley gain by sharing this powerful experience with her readers? How did Rowley's friends react when she told them her story?

4. Why do you think Rowley chose not to name the young man who died? In what ways is this young man different from Len Bias, the talented basketball player who died of a drug overdose?

5. What in Rowley's tone — her attitude toward her subject and audience — particularly contributes to the persuasiveness of the essay? (Glossary: *Tone*) Cite examples from the selection that support your conclusion.

6. How did Rowley's opening paragraph affect you? What would have been lost had she combined the first two paragraphs? (Glossary: *Beginnings and Endings*)

7. For what audience do you suppose Rowley wrote this essay? (Glossary: *Audience*) In your opinion, would most readers be convinced by what Rowley says about drugs? Are you convinced? Why, or why not?

VOCABULARY

Refer to your dictionary to define the following words as they are used in this selection. Then use each word in a sentence of your own.

ambivalence (2)	gnashing (21)
stupefied (3)	irreverent (26)
convulse (6)	unravel (28)
semicoherent (11)	speculated (29)
audibly (20)	tragedy (30)

CLASSROOM ACTIVITY USING ARGUMENT

Choose one of the following position statements for an exercise in argumentation:

1. More parking spaces should be provided on campus for students.
2. English should be declared the official language of the United States.
3. Performance standards in our schools should be raised.
4. The Food and Drug Administration takes too long to decide whether new drugs will be made available to consumers.
5. Job placement is not the responsibility of colleges and universities.

Make a list of the types of information and evidence you would need to write an argumentative essay on the topic you chose. Indicate where and how you might obtain this information.

SUGGESTED WRITING ASSIGNMENTS

1. Write an essay in which you argue against either drinking or smoking. What would drinkers and smokers claim are the benefits of their habits? What are the key arguments against these types of substance abuse? Like Rowley, use examples from your personal experience or from your reading to document your essay.

2. Write a persuasive essay in which you support or refute the following proposition: "Television advertising is in large part responsible for Americans' belief that over-the-counter drugs are cure-alls." Does such advertising, in fact, promote drug dependence or abuse?

3. What is the most effective way to bring about social change and to influence societal attitudes? Concentrating on the sorts of changes you have witnessed over the last ten years, write an essay in which you describe how best to influence public opinion.

Against the Great Divide

■ **Brian Jarvis**

*When the following essay was published as a "My Turn" col-
umn in* Newsweek *in May 1993, Brian Jarvis was a high school
junior in St. Louis. He graduated from Claremont College in
California and is working on a novel about his high school experiences. Jarvis organizes the first part of his essay inductively,
using a series of examples that lead to a generalization at the beginning of paragraph 9. After that, he explores the potential for
remedying the voluntary segregation at his high school that he
describes so concretely in his first eight paragraphs.*

FOR YOUR JOURNAL

Think of the four or five people you consider to be your closest
friends. Are any of them of a different ethnic background than
yours? If so, do you find that the differences create any challenges, either from inside or outside the relationship? If not, why
not? Do you give the matter much thought?

I always notice one thing when I walk through the commons at my   1
high school: the whites are on one side of the room and the blacks
are on the other. When I enter the room, I think I'm at an African na-
tionalist meeting. The atmosphere is lively, the clothes are colorful,
the voices are loud, the students are up and about, the language is different and there's not a white face to be seen. But the moment I cross
the invisible line to the other side, I feel I've moved to another country. There are three times as many people, the voices are softer, the
clothes more subdued. Everyone's sitting or lying down, and one has
as much chance of seeing a black student as a Martian.

The commons is a gathering spot where students relax on   2
benches and talk with friends. They also buy candy and soda, watch
TV and make phone calls. It's a place where all sorts of things happen. But you'll never find a white student and a black student talking
to each other.

After three years, I still feel uncomfortable when I have to walk   3
through the "black" side to get to class. It's not that any black

students threaten or harass me. They just quietly ignore me and look in the other direction, and I do the same. But there's one who sometimes catches my eye, and I can't help feeling awkward when I see him. He was a close friend from childhood.

Ten years ago, we played catch in our backyards, went bike riding and slept over at one another's houses. By the fifth grade, we went to movies and amusement parks, and bunked together at the same summer camps. We met while playing on the same Little League team, though we attended different grade schools. We're both juniors now at the same high school. We usually don't say anything when we see each other, except maybe a polite "Hi" or "Hey." I can't remember the last time we talked on the phone, much less got together outside of school.

Since entering high school, we haven't shared a single class or sport. He plays football, a black-dominated sport, while I play tennis, which is, with rare exception, an all-white team. It's as if fate has kept us apart; though, more likely, it's peer pressure.

In the lunchroom, I sit with my white friends and my childhood friend sits with his black ones. It's the same when we walk through the hallways or sit in the library. If Michael Jackson thinks, "It don't matter if you're black or white," he should visit my high school.

I wonder if proponents of desegregation realized that even if schools were integrated, students would choose to remain apart. It wasn't until 1983 that St. Louis's voluntary city–suburban desegregation program was approved. Today, my school has 25 percent black students. While this has given many young people the chance for a better education, it hasn't brought the two races closer together.

In high school, I've become friends with Vietnamese-Americans, Korean-Americans, Iranian-Americans, Indian-Americans, Russian-Americans and exchange students from France and Sweden. The only group that remains at a distance is the African-Americans. I've had only a handful of black students in all my classes and only one black teacher (from Haiti).

CRUCIAL COURSE

In its effort to put students through as many academic classes as possible and prepare them for college, my school seems to have overlooked one crucial course: teaching black and white students how to get along, which in my opinion, would be more valuable than all the others. It's not that there haven't been efforts to improve race relations. Last fall, a group of black and white students established a program called Students Organized Against Racism. But at a recent meeting, SOAR members decided that the separation of blacks and whites was largely voluntary and there was little they could do about it. Another youth group tried to help by moving the soda machine from the "white" side of the commons to the "black" side, so that white students would have to cross the line to get a Coke. But all that's happened is that students buy their sodas, then return to their own territory.

Last summer, at a youth camp called Miniwanca in Michigan, I did see black and white teens get along. I don't mean just tolerate one another. I mean play sports together, dance together, walk on the beach together and become friends. The students came from all races and backgrounds, as well as from overseas. Camp organizers purposely placed me in a cabin and activity group that included whites, blacks, Southerners, Northerners and foreigners, none of whom I'd met before. 10

For 10 days, I became great friends with a group of strangers, at least half of whom were black. One wouldn't know that racism existed at that idyllic place, where we told stories around campfires, acted in plays and shared our deepest thoughts about AIDS, parents, abortion and dating. Everyone got along so well there that it was depressing for me to return to high school. But at the same time, it made me hopeful. If black and white teenagers could be friends at leadership camp, couldn't they mix in school as well? 11

Schools need to make it a real priority to involve whites and blacks together as much as possible. This would mean more multicultural activities, mandatory classes that teach black history and discussions of today's racial controversies. Teachers should mix whites and blacks more in study groups so they *have* to work together in and out of school. (Students won't do it on their own.) And most important, all students should get a chance to attend a camp like Miniwanca. Maybe the Clinton administration could find a way to help finance other camps like it. 12

As it is now, black and white teenagers just don't know one another. I think a lot about my friend from childhood—what he does on weekends, what he thinks about college, what he wants to do with his life. I have no answers, and it saddens me. 13

QUESTIONS FOR STUDY AND DISCUSSION

1. To argue his thesis, Jarvis uses personal experiences as his evidence. How convincing do you find his evidence? What would be gained—or lost—by using data from outside sources? (Glossary: *Evidence*)

2. Jarvis's camp experience gave him hope, but it was an artificial setting—he even calls it an "idyllic place" (11)—with a select group of young people. Do you think it is an effective piece of supporting evidence in his argument? Why, or why not?

3. Why do Jarvis and his childhood friend interact so little now that they are in high school? Why is this specific situation an effective way to illustrate the overall situation Jarvis presents? (Glossary: *Illustration*)

4. Why do the African Americans and whites remain at a distance from one another? Why have the efforts to bring them closer together failed at Jarvis's high school?

5. What do you think of Jarvis's suggestion about having a course that would teach whites and blacks how to get along? How much impact do you think such a course would have in his high school? Explain your answer.

6. Who is Jarvis hoping to reach in his essay? (Glossary: *Audience*) Which sentences in the essay led you to your conclusion?

VOCABULARY

Refer to your dictionary to define the following words as they are used in this selection. Then use each word in a sentence of your own.

commons (1)   idyllic (11)
proponents (7)   multicultural (12)
desegregation (7)

CLASSROOM ACTIVITY USING ARGUMENT

Write a paragraph that argues that people should compliment one another more. Use one of the following quotes as evidence to support your argument:

"Compliments are the high point of a person's day," said self-help author Melodie Bronson. "Without compliments anyone's life is sure to be much more difficult."

"Compliments have been proven to lower blood pressure and increase endorphin production in the brain," said Dr. Ruth West of the Holistic Medicine Committee. "A compliment a day may lengthen your life span by as much as a year."

"Compliments are a special way people communicate with each other," said Bill Goodbody, therapist at the Good Feeling Institute. "Ninety percent of our patients report happier relationships or marriages after they begin compliment therapy."

Explain your choice. How did you integrate the quotation into your paragraph?

SUGGESTED WRITING ASSIGNMENTS

1. Write an essay in which you argue either for or against Jarvis's contention that interaction between black and white teenagers needs to be mandatory and that a class could bring the two groups closer together. Would such measures be enough to overcome the apparently voluntary segregation at his high school? Does your own experience with this issue give you any insights into how to break down the barrier between the black and white "countries"?

2. In the past twenty-five years, a great deal of effort has gone into the attempt to desegregate public schools so that all ethnic groups, both genders, and as diverse a collection of backgrounds as possible are represented. Whether desegregation is enforced, as in court-ordered busing, or pursued voluntarily, as in the current quest for diversity on campuses around the country, it has yielded increasingly heterogeneous student bodies. Write an essay in which you argue that diversity is an ideal that should be aggressively pursued or that schools that offer voluntary segregation and a more homogeneous student body have something to offer. How much does a diverse school population increase students' understanding and appreciation of different ethnic groups and backgrounds?

Exposing Media Myths: TV Doesn't Affect You as Much as You Think

■ Joanmarie Kalter

Joanmarie Kalter has written extensively about television news and about the press in the Third World. After graduating from Cornell University in 1972 and working as a freelance writer for a number of years, Kalter received her master's degree from the Columbia Graduate School of Journalism in 1981. She joined TV Guide *as a staff writer in 1984, but returned to freelancing in 1989. Her articles have appeared in numerous and diverse periodicals, including the* New York Times, *the* Christian Science Monitor, *the* Bulletin of Atomic Scientists, *and* Africa Report. *In the following selection, note how Kalter uses her evidence to chip away at some "false truths" about television news. The rhetorical mode of cause and effect also plays a significant role in Kalter's argument as she reveals the serious implications of the myths she exposes.*

FOR YOUR JOURNAL

Reflect on your sense of the importance of television news. Do you watch a news program regularly? Do you find it valuable? How much of what you see and hear do you remember, and for how long?

Once upon a time, there was a new invention—television. It became so popular, so quickly, that more American homes now have a TV set (98 percent) than an indoor toilet (97 percent). Around this new invention, then, an industry rapidly grew, and around this industry, a whole mythology. It has become a virtual truism, often heard and often repeated, that TV—and TV news, in particular—has an unparalleled influence on our lives. 1

Over the past 20 years, however, communications scholars have been quietly examining such truisms and have discovered, sometimes to their surprise, that many are not so true at all. *TV Guide* asked 2 more than a dozen leading researchers for their findings and found an eye-opening collection of mythbusters. Indeed, they suggest that an entire body of political strategy and debate has been built upon false premises. . . .

Myth No. 1: Two-thirds of the American people receive most of 3 their news from TV. This little canard is at the heart of our story. It can be traced to the now-famous Roper polls, in which Americans are queried: "I'd like to ask you where you usually get most of your news about what's going on in the world today. . . ." In 1959, when the poll was first conducted, 51 percent answered "television," with a steady increase ever since. The latest results show that 66 percent say they get most of their news from TV; only about a third credit newspapers.

Trouble is, that innocent poll question is downright impossible to 4 answer. Just consider: it asks you to sort through the issues in your mind, pinpoint what and where you learned about each, tag it, and come up with a final score. Not too many of us can do it, especially since we get our news from a variety of sources. Even pollster Burns Roper concedes, "Memories do get fuzzy."

Scholars have found, however, that when they ask a less general, 5 more specific question — Did you read a newspaper yesterday? Did you watch a TV news show yesterday? — the results are quite different. Dr. John Robinson, professor of sociology at the University of Maryland, found that on a typical day 67 percent read a newspaper, while 52 percent see a local or national TV newscast. Dr. Robert Stevenson, professor of journalism at the University of North Carolina, analyzed detailed diaries of TV use, and further found that only 18 percent watch network news on an average day, and only 13 percent pay full attention to it. Says Robinson, "TV is part of our overall mix, but in no way is it our number one source of news."

Yet it's a myth with disturbing consequences. Indeed, it is so 6 widespread, says Dr. Mark Levy, associate professor of journalism at the University of Maryland, that it shapes — or misshapes — our political process. In the words of Michael Deaver, White House deputy chief of staff during President Reagan's first term, "The majority of the people get their news from television, so . . . we construct events and craft photos that are designed for 30 seconds to a minute so that it can fit into that 'bite' on the evening news." And thus the myth, says Levy, "distorts the very dialogue of democracy, which cannot be responsibly conducted in 30-second bites."

Myth No. 2: TV news sets the public agenda. It was first said 7 succinctly in 1963, and has long been accepted: while the mass media may not tell us what to think, they definitely tell us what to think about. And on some issues, the impact of TV is indisputable: the Ethiopian famine, the Challenger explosion. Yet for the more routine story, new research has challenged that myth, suggesting TV's influence may be surprisingly more limited.

For one thing, TV news most often reacts to newspapers in framing issues of public concern. Dr. David Weaver, professor of journalism at Indiana University, found that newspapers led TV through the 1976 campaign. Given the brevity of broadcasts, of course, that's understandable. "TV has no page 36," explains Dr. Maxwell McCombs, professor of communications at the University of Texas. "So TV journalists have to wait until an issue has already achieved substantial public interest." TV, then, does not so much set the public agenda as spotlight it.

Even among those issues spotlighted, viewers do make independent judgments. It seems the old "hypodermic" notions no longer hold, says Dr. Doris Graber, political science professor at the University of Illinois. "We're not sponges for this stuff, and while TV may provide the raw material, people do select."

Indeed, even TV entertainment is less influential than once was thought. According to Robinson, studies found no difference in racial attitudes among those who saw *Roots* and those who didn't. Ditto "The Day After" on nuclear war, and *Amerika* on the Soviets. As for news, Graber notes that the public took a long time to share the media's concern about Watergate, and even now are lagging the media on Iran-Contragate. And finally, there are many issues on which the press must belatedly catch up with the public. Which brings us to . . .

Myth No. 3: TV news changed public opinion about the war in Vietnam. Contrary to this most common of beliefs, research shows just the opposite. Lawrence Lichty, professor of radio/television/film at Northwestern University, analyzed network war coverage and found that it did not become relatively critical until 1967. By then, however, a majority of Americans already thought U.S. involvement in Vietnam was a mistake. And they thought so not because of TV coverage, but because of the number of young Americans dying.

Yet this fable about the "living-room war" is so accepted it has become "fact": that gory TV pictures of bloody battles undermined public support for the war; that, in a 1968 TV-news special, Walter Cronkite mistakenly presented the Tet offensive as a defeat for the U.S.; and that, because President Johnson so believed in the power of TV, he concluded then that his war effort was lost.

In fact, Lichty found few "gory" pictures. "TV presented a distant 13
view," he says, with less than five percent of TV's war reports showing
heavy combat. Nor, as we now know, was a rapt audience watching at
home in their living rooms. As for Cronkite's report on the Tet offensive, the CBS anchor said on the evening news, "First and simplest, the
Vietcong suffered a military defeat." And, in his now-famous TV special, Cronkite concluded, "we are mired in a stalemate," and should
"negotiate." By that time, Lichty says, "public opinion had been on a
downward trend for a year and a half. A majority of Americans
agreed." And so Johnson's concern, it seems, was not that Cronkite
would influence public opinion, but rather that he reflected it.

Indeed, Professor John Mueller of the University of Rochester 14
has compared the curve of public opinion on the war in Vietnam,
covered by TV, with that of the war in Korea, hardly covered. He
found the two curves strikingly similar: in both cases, public support
dropped as the number of American deaths rose.

Disturbingly, the misconception about TV's influence in Vietnam 15
has had broad consequences, for it has framed an important debate
ever since. Can a democratic society, with a free flow of dramatic TV
footage, retain the public will to fight a war? Many argue no. And
this has been the rationale more recently for censoring the Western
press in the Falklands and Grenada. Yet it is, says Lichty, a policy
based on a myth.

Myth No. 4: TV today is the most effective medium in communi- 16
cating news. Most of us think of TV fare as simple, direct, easy to understand—with the combination of words and pictures making it all
the more powerful. But recent research shows that TV news, as distinct from entertainment, is often very confusing. In study after study,
Robinson and Levy have found that viewers understand only about a
third of network news stories.

Why is TV news so tough to understand? Dr. Dan Drew, profes- 17
sor of journalism at Indiana University, suggests that the verbal and
visual often conflict. Unlike TV entertainment, in which the two are
composed together, TV-news footage is gathered first, and the story
it illustrates often diverges. We may see fighting across the Green
Line in Beirut—for a story about peace talks. We may see "file
footage" of Anglican envoy Terry Waite walking down the street—
for a story on his disappearance. As viewers try to make sense of the
visual, they lose the gist of the verbal. "The myth," says Levy, "is
that since we are a visual medium, we must always have pictures. . . .
But that's a disaster, a recipe for poor communication."

Journalists also are much more familiar with the world of public   18
affairs, says Levy, and rely on its technical jargon: from "leading economic indicators" to "the Druse militia." Their stories, say researchers, are overillustrated, with most pictures on the screen for
less than 20 seconds. They assume, mistakenly, that viewers pay
complete attention, and so they often do not repeat the main theme.
Yet while understanding TV news takes concentration, watching TV
is full of distractions. In one study, researchers mounted cameras on
top of sets and recorded the amount of time viewers also read, talked,
walked in and out of the room. They concluded that viewers actually
watch only 55 percent of what's on.

The audience does recall the extraordinary, such as a man on the   19
moon, and better comprehends human-interest stories. But since most
news is not covered night after night, tomorrow's broadcast tends to
wash away today's. "People don't remember much from TV news,"
says Graber. "It's like the ocean washing over traces that have been
very faintly formed."

Today's TV news is carefully watched by politicians, who keep a   20
sharp eye on how they're covered. But while it may provide theater
for a handful, this research increasingly shows it's lost on the American public. And sadly, then, hard-working TV journalists may be
missing an opportunity to inform.

Yet TV remains a medium with great potential. And studies show   21
that it does extend the awareness of the poor and ill-educated, who
cannot afford additional sources. What's more, research suggests that
the clarity of TV news can be improved—without compromising
journalistic standards. "We have been glitzed by the glamour of TV,
all these gee-whiz gimmicks," says Robinson. "And we have lost
sight of one of the oldest and most durable findings of communications research. . . . The most important element is the writer, who sits
at a typewriter and tries to tell the story in a simple and organized
way. That's the crucial link."

Research also shows that viewers want a broadcast they can un-   22
derstand. The success of *60 Minutes* proves there's an audience still
hungry for sophisticated factual information. "When someone does
this for news, they'll grab the ratings," says Levy. "Nobody loses!"
Ironically, no corporation would launch an ad campaign without extensive testing on how best to reach its audience. But many broadcast
journalists, working under intense pressure, remain unaware of the
problems. "There's a lot we have to learn about how people comprehend," says William Rubens, NBC research vice-president. "But no,

it hasn't been the thrust of our research." According to Robinson and Levy, this requires the attention of those in charge, a collective corporate will. With the networks under a financial squeeze, their news audiences having recently declined some 15 percent, "This may be the time for them to rethink their broadcasts," says Levy.

And if they do, they may just live . . . happily ever after.   23

QUESTIONS FOR STUDY AND DISCUSSION

1. Kalter begins by discussing television — and her title implies that the article is about television in general — but the focus of her article is television news. (Glossary: *Focus*) In what ways does narrowing her focus help her argue her point?

2. How does Kalter organize her argument in paragraphs 16–20? (Glossary: *Organization*) What does each paragraph accomplish? (Glossary: *Paragraph*)

3. Kalter uses the term *myth* to describe assumptions about TV news. Look up the definition of *myth* in your dictionary. How does the use of this term help Kalter influence her audience? (Glossary: *Audience*)

4. How can general survey questions lead to inaccurate data? How have the Roper polls contributed to the myths about television news?

5. According to Kalter, why is it a myth that TV news changed public opinion about the Vietnam War? (Glossary: *Cause and Effect*) What are the broad consequences of this myth?

6. In what ways does TV remain a "medium with great potential" (21)? How can TV news be changed to make it more effective? Why hasn't it been changed in the past?

VOCABULARY

Refer to your dictionary to define the following words as they are used in this selection. Then use each word in a sentence of your own.

truism (1)	rapt (13)
canard (3)	rationale (15)
succinctly (7)	gist (17)
brevity (8)	glitzed (21)

CLASSROOM ACTIVITY USING ARGUMENT

The effectiveness of a writer's argument depends in large part on the writer's awareness of audience. For example, if a writer wished to argue for the use of technology to solve environmental problems, that argument would normally have to be more convincing (i.e., more factual, better reasoned) for an environmentalist than for an industrialist because environmentalists might tend to distrust technology.

Review each of the essays you have read thus far in this chapter. In your opinion, for what primary audience was each essay intended? What types of evidence did you use in determining your answer?

SUGGESTED WRITING ASSIGNMENTS

1. How much do you think television—and television news in particular—has affected you? Write an argumentative essay in which you either agree or disagree with Kalter's position, based on your personal experiences.

2. How would you change television news to make it more effective for you? Write a letter to the head of a network news show in which you argue for your proposed changes in the format of the show.

In Praise of the F Word

■ Mary Sherry

Mary Sherry was born in Bay City, Michigan, and received her B.A. from Rosary College in River Forest, Illinois. She owns her own research and publishing company specializing in information for economic and development organizations. Sherry also teaches in adult-literacy programs and has written essays on educational problems for various newspapers, including the Wall Street Journal *and* Newsday. *In the following essay, reprinted from* Newsweek, *Sherry takes a provocative stance—that the threat of flunking is a "positive teaching tool." She believes students would all be better off if they had a "healthy fear of failure," and she marshals a series of logical appeals to both clarify and support her argument.*

FOR YOUR JOURNAL

Comment on what you see as the relationship between learning and grades. Do teachers and students pay too much attention to grades at the expense of learning? Or are grades not seen as important enough?

Tens of thousands of 18-year-olds will graduate this year and be   1
handed meaningless diplomas. These diplomas won't look any different from those awarded their luckier classmates. Their validity will be questioned only when their employers discover that these graduates are semiliterate.

Eventually a fortunate few will find their way into educational-   2
repair shops—adult-literacy programs, such as the one where I teach basic grammar and writing. There, high-school graduates and high-school dropouts pursuing graduate-equivalency certificates will learn the skills they should have learned in school. They will also discover they have been cheated by our educational system.

445

As I teach, I learn a lot about our schools. Early in each session I   3
ask my students to write about an unpleasant experience they had in
school. No writers' block here! "I wish someone would have made
me stop doing drugs and made me study." "I liked to party and no
one seemed to care." "I was a good kid and didn't cause any trouble,
so they just passed me along even though I didn't read well and
couldn't write." And so on.

I am your basic do-gooder, and prior to teaching this class I   4
blamed the poor academic skills our kids have today on drugs, divorce and other impediments to concentration necessary for doing
well in school. But, as I rediscover each time I walk into the classroom, before a teacher can expect students to concentrate, he has to
get their attention, no matter what distractions may be at hand.
There are many ways to do this, and they have much to do with
teaching style. However, if style alone won't do it, there is another
way to show who holds the winning hand in the classroom. That is to
reveal the trump card of failure.

I will never forget a teacher who played that card to get the atten-   5
tion of one of my children. Our youngest, a world-class charmer, did
little to develop his intellectual talents but always got by. Until Mrs.
Stifter.

Our son was a high-school senior when he had her for English. "He   6
sits in the back of the room talking to his friends," she told me. "Why
don't you move him to the front row?" I urged, believing the embarrassment would get him to settle down. Mrs. Stifter looked at me steely-
eyed over her glasses. "I don't move seniors," she said. "I flunk them."
I was flustered. Our son's academic life flashed before my eyes. No
teacher had ever threatened him with that before. I regained my com-
posure and managed to say that I thought she was right. By the time I
got home I was feeling pretty good about this. It was a radical approach
for these times, but, well, why not? "She's going to flunk you," I told
my son. I did not discuss it any further. Suddenly English became a priority in his life. He finished out the semester with an A.

I know one example doesn't make a case, but at night I see a pa-   7
rade of students who are angry and resentful for having been passed
along until they could no longer even pretend to keep up. Of average
intelligence or better, they eventually quit school, concluding they
were too dumb to finish. "I should have been held back" is a comment I hear frequently. Even sadder are those students who are high-
school graduates who say to me after a few weeks of class, "I don't
know how I ever got a high-school diploma."

Passing students who have not mastered the work cheats them   8
and the employers who expect graduates to have basic skills. We
excuse this dishonest behavior by saying kids can't learn if they come
from terrible environments. No one seems to stop to think that—no
matter what environments they come from—most kids don't put
school first on their list unless they perceive something is at stake.
They'd rather be sailing.

Many students I see at night could give expert testimony on un-   9
employment, chemical dependency, abusive relationships. In spite of
these difficulties, they have decided to make education a priority.
They are motivated by the desire for a better job or the need to hang
on to the one they've got. They have a healthy fear of failure.

People of all ages can rise above their problems, but they need to   10
have a reason to do so. Young people generally don't have the maturity
to value education in the same way my adult students value it. But fear
of failure, whether economic or academic, can motivate both.

Flunking as a regular policy has just as much merit today as it   11
did two generations ago. We must review the threat of flunking and
see it as it really is—a positive teaching tool. It is an expression of
confidence by both teachers and parents that the students have the
ability to learn the material presented to them. However, making it
work again would take a dedicated, caring conspiracy between teachers and parents. It would mean facing the tough reality that passing
kids who haven't learned the material—while it might save them
grief for the short term—dooms them to long-term illiteracy. It
would mean that teachers would have to follow through on their
threats, and parents would have to stand behind them, knowing their
children's best interests are indeed at stake. This means no more
doing Scott's assignments for him because he might fail. No more
passing Jodi because she's such a nice kid.

This is a policy that worked in the past and can work today. A wise   12
teacher, with the support of his parents, gave our son the opportunity
to succeed—or fail. It's time we return this choice to all students.

QUESTIONS FOR STUDY AND DISCUSSION

1. What is Sherry's thesis? (Glossary: *Thesis*) What evidence does
   she use to support her argument?
2. Sherry uses dismissive terms to characterize objections to flunking: *cheats* and *excuses*. In your opinion, does she do enough to
   acknowledge the other side of the argument? Why, or why not?

3. What is the "F word" discussed in the essay? Does referring to it as the "F word" increase the effectiveness of the essay? Why?
4. Who is Sherry's audience? (Glossary: *Audience*) Is it receptive to the "F word"? Explain your answer.
5. What does Sherry accomplish in paragraph 3?
6. In what way is Sherry qualified to comment on the potential benefits of flunking students? Do you think her induction is accurate?
7. Why does Sherry think flunking is a valuable tool for educators and for students?

VOCABULARY

Refer to your dictionary to define the following words as they are used in this selection. Then use each word in a sentence of your own.

validity (1)   trump (4)
semiliterate (1)   testimony (9)
impediments (4)

CLASSROOM ACTIVITY USING ARGUMENT

A first-year composition student, Marco Schmidt, is preparing to write an essay in which he will argue that music should be a required course for all public high school students. He has compiled the following pieces of evidence:

Informal interviews with four classmates. Three of the classmates stated that they would have enjoyed and benefited from taking a music course in high school, and the fourth stated that she would not have been interested in taking music.

An article from a professional journal for teachers comparing the study habits of students who were involved in music and those who were not. The author, a psychologist, found that students who play an instrument or sing regularly have better study habits than students who do not.

A brief article from a national news magazine praising an inner-city high school's experimental curriculum, in which music classes play a prominent part.

The personal Web site of a high school music teacher who posts information about the successes and achievements of her former students.

Discuss these pieces of evidence with your classmates. Which are most convincing? Which provide the least support for Marco's argument? Why? What other types of evidence might Marco find to support his argument?

SUGGESTED WRITING ASSIGNMENTS

1. Write an essay in which you argue against Sherry's thesis. In what ways is flunking bad for students? Are there techniques more positive than a "fear of failure" that can be used to motivate students?

2. Think of something that involves short-term pain or sacrifice, but can be beneficial in the long run. For example, exercising requires exertion, but it may help prevent health problems. Studying and writing papers when you'd rather be having fun or even sleeping may seem painful, but a college degree leads to personal growth and development. Even if the benefits are obvious, imagine a skeptical audience, and write an argument in favor of the short-term sacrifice over the long-term consequences of avoiding it.

The Right to Fail

■ **William Zinsser**

William Zinsser was born in New York City in 1922. After graduating from Princeton University, he worked for the New York Herald Tribune, first as a feature writer and later as its drama and film critic. He also taught writing at Yale University and served as the general editor of the Book-of-the-Month Club. He is currently the series editor for The Writer's Craft Series, publications of talks given by writers sponsored by the Book-of-the-Month Club and The New York Public Library. Zinsser's own published works cover many aspects of contemporary American culture, but he is best known as the author of lucid and accessible books about writing, including Writing with a Word Processor *(1983),* Writing to Learn *(1988), and* On Writing Well *(1976), a perennial favorite for college-writing courses as well as the general public. Zinsser now teaches at the New School for Social Research in New York. In the following essay, he argues the benefits of failing or dropping out and uses numerous examples to illustrate his points. As you read, consider the degree to which these examples serve as compelling evidence for the validity of Zinsser's point of view.*

FOR YOUR JOURNAL

Think about a time when, despite your best efforts, you could be said to have failed at something. Perhaps it was a loss in sports, a poor performance on a test in school, or even a vocational or educational path that you tried but were not able to see through. How did it feel to fail? Were you able to learn from the experience? How long did it take you to put the failure behind you?

I like "dropout" as an addition to the American language because 1
it's brief and it's clear. What I don't like is that we use it almost
entirely as a dirty word.

We only apply it to people under twenty-one. Yet an adult who 2
spends his days and nights watching mindless TV programs is more

of a dropout than an eighteen-year-old who quits college, with its frequently mindless courses, to become, say, a VISTA volunteer. For the young, dropping out is often a way of dropping in.

To hold this opinion, however, is little short of treason in America. A boy or girl who leaves college is branded a failure—and the right to fail is one of the few freedoms that this country does not grant its citizens. The American dream is a dream of "getting ahead," painted in strokes of gold wherever we look. Our advertisements and TV commercials are a hymn to material success, our magazine articles a toast to people who made it to the top. Smoke the right cigarette or drive the right car—so the ads imply—and girls will be swooning into your deodorized arms or caressing your expensive lapels. Happiness goes to the man who has the sweet smell of achievement. He is our national idol, and everybody else is our national fink. 3

I want to put in a word for the fink, especially the teen-age fink, because if we give him time to get through his finkdom—if we release him from the pressure of attaining certain goals by a certain age—he has a good chance of becoming our national idol, a Jefferson or a Thoreau, a Buckminster Fuller or an Adlai Stevenson, a man with a mind of his own. We need mavericks and dissenters and dreamers far more than we need junior vice-presidents, but we paralyze them by insisting that every step be a step up to the next rung of the ladder. Yet in the fluid years of youth, the only way for boys and girls to find their proper road is often to take a hundred side trips, poking out in different directions, faltering, drawing back, and starting again. 4

"But what if we fail?" they ask, whispering the dreadful word across the Generation Gap to their parents, who are back home at the Establishment, nursing their "middle-class values" and cultivating their "goal-oriented society." The parents whisper back: "Don't!" 5

What they should say is "Don't be afraid to fail!" Failure isn't fatal. Countless people have had a bout with it and come out stronger as a result. Many have even come out famous. History is strewn with eminent dropouts, "loners" who followed their own trail, not worrying about its odd twists and turns because they had faith in their own sense of direction. To read their biographies is always exhilarating, not only because they beat the system, but because their system was better than the one that they beat. 6

Luckily, such rebels still turn up often enough to prove that individualism, though badly threatened, is not extinct. Much has been 7 written, for instance, about the fitful scholastic career of Thomas P. F. Hoving, New York's former Parks Commissioner and now director of the Metropolitan Museum of Art. Hoving was a dropout's dropout, entering and leaving schools as if they were motels, often at the request of the management. Still, he must have learned something during those unorthodox years, for he dropped in again at the top of his profession.

His case reminds me of another boyhood—that of Holden 8 Caulfield in J. D. Salinger's *The Catcher in the Rye,* the most popular literary hero of the postwar period. There is nothing accidental about the grip that this dropout continues to hold on the affections of an entire American generation. Nobody else, real or invented, has made such an engaging shambles of our "goal-oriented society," so gratified our secret belief that the "phonies" are in power and the good guys up the creek. Whether Holden has also reached the top of his chosen field today is one of those speculations that delight fanciers of good fiction. I speculate that he has. Holden Caulfield, incidentally, is now thirty-six.

I'm not urging everyone to go out and fail just for the sheer ther- 9 apy of it, or to quit college just to coddle some vague discontent. Obviously it's better to succeed than to flop, and in general a long education is more helpful than a short one. (Thanks to my own education, for example, I can tell George Eliot from T. S. Eliot. I can handle the pluperfect tense in French, and I know that Caesar beat the Helvetii because he had enough frumentum.) I only mean that failure isn't bad in itself, or success automatically good.

Fred Zinnemann, who has directed some of Hollywood's most 10 honored movies, was asked by a reporter, when *A Man for All Seasons* won every prize, about his previous film *Behold a Pale Horse,* which was a box-office disaster. "I don't feel any obligation to be successful," Zinnemann replied. "Success can be dangerous—you feel you know it all. I've learned a great deal from my failures." A similar point was made by Richard Brooks about his ambitious money loser, *Lord Jim.* Recalling the three years of his life that went into it, talking almost with elation about the troubles that befell his unit in Cambodia, Brooks told me that he learned more about his craft from this considerable failure than from his many earlier hits.

It's a point, of course, that applies throughout the arts. Writers, 11 playwrights, painters and composers work in the expectation of periodic defeat, but they wouldn't keep going back into the arena if they thought it was the end of the world. It isn't the end of the world. For an artist—and perhaps for anybody—it is the only way to grow.

Today's younger generation seems to know that this is true, 12 seems willing to take the risks in life that artists take in art. "Society," needless to say, still has the upper hand—it sets the goals and condemns as a failure everybody who won't play. But the dropouts and the hippies are not as afraid of failure as their parents and grandparents. This could mean, as their elders might say, that they are just plumb lazy, secure in the comforts of an affluent state. It could also mean, however, that they just don't buy the old standards of success and are rapidly writing new ones.

Recently it was announced, for instance, that more than two 13 hundred thousand Americans have inquired about service in VISTA (the domestic Peace Corps) and that, according to a Gallup survey, "more than three million American college students would serve VISTA in some capacity if given the opportunity." This is hardly the road to riches or to an executive suite. Yet I have met many of these young volunteers, and they are not pining for traditional success. On the contrary, they appear more fulfilled than the average vice-president with a swimming pool.

Who is to say, then, if there is any right path to the top, or even 14 to say what the top consists of? Obviously the colleges don't have more than a partial answer—otherwise the young would not be so disaffected with an education that they consider vapid. Obviously business does not have the answer—otherwise the young would not be so scornful of its call to be an organization man.

The fact is, nobody has the answer, and the dawning awareness 15 of this fact seems to me one of the best things happening in America today. Success and failure are again becoming individual visions, as they were when the country was younger, not rigid categories. Maybe we are learning again to cherish this right of every person to succeed on his own terms and to fail as often as necessary along the way.

QUESTIONS FOR STUDY AND DISCUSSION

1. What does Zinsser argue? (Glossary: *Thesis*) Does he state his thesis outright? If so, where? If not, how does he present it to the reader?

2. Zinsser defines young adulthood as "the fluid years of youth" (4). What does his use of the word *fluid* convey to you? How

does he use this definition to strengthen his argument regarding the nature of failure?

3. Zinsser wrote "The Right to Fail" more than twenty years ago. His reasoning and his argument remain sound, but at times his diction places him in a different era. (Glossary: *Diction*) Find the words that you perceive as being dated. What would their modern equivalents be?

4. Look up *fink* in the dictionary. Why do you think Zinsser chose this word to characterize those who do not have the "sweet smell of achievement" (3)? In what way are those who are willing to risk failure — as defined by society — "finks"?

5. Zinsser argues that many people who are considered very successful have "failed" at various times in their careers. Why does Zinsser use movie directors to illustrate his point? (Glossary: *Illustration*) What makes them good examples?

6. Why does Zinsser use VISTA volunteers to represent those who are not pursuing society's definition of success? In what way might one say they are "dropping in," not dropping out?

VOCABULARY

Refer to your dictionary to define the following words as they are used in this selection. Then use each word in a sentence of your own.

dissenters (4)	coddle (9)
strewn (6)	affluent (12)
eminent (6)	vapid (14)

CLASSROOM ACTIVITY USING ARGUMENT

Deductive reasoning works on the model of the syllogism. After reviewing the material on syllogisms in the introduction to this chapter (pp. 422–23), analyze the following syllogisms. Which work well, and which do not?

1. All of my CDs have blue lettering on them.
   I saw the new Youssou N'Dour CD the other day.
   The new Youssou N'Dour CD has blue lettering on it.

2. I have never lost a tennis match.
   I played a tennis match yesterday.
   I won my tennis match yesterday.

3. Surfers all want to catch the perfect wave.
   Jenny is a surfer.
   Jenny wants to catch the perfect wave.
4. Writers enjoy reading books.
   Bill enjoys reading books.
   Bill is a writer.
5. Cotton candy is an incredibly sticky kind of candy.
   Amy ate some incredibly sticky candy.
   Amy ate cotton candy.

Write two effective syllogisms of your own.

SUGGESTED WRITING ASSIGNMENTS

1. Based on your own experience, argue for or against the following statement: "You learn more from failure than you do from success." If you agree with this statement, do you think that you need to fail in order to eventually achieve more than you would have otherwise? If you disagree, what do you think success teaches you? How do you get strong and adaptable if all you encounter for a long time is success? How do your views compare with those of Zinsser and Sherry?

2. Zinsser's article is critical of the tyranny of the American dream of "getting ahead." Write an essay in which you discuss Americans' materialistic tendencies. When did we lose our ability to tell the difference between what we need and what we want? How would our quality of life improve if we could be content with fewer possessions? What changes would you propose to reduce the conspicuous-consumption mentality of our society?

Cruel and Unusual

■ Sherwin B. Nuland

Surgeon and medical ethicist Sherwin B. Nuland was born and raised in New York and graduated from Bronx High School in 1948. He went on to do undergraduate work at New York University, then obtained his M.D. at Yale Medical School. He has taught at Yale since 1962, during which time he has also become a prolific author. His book How We Die: Reflections on Life's Final Chapter *(1994) received the National Book Award and was a finalist for the Pulitzer Prize. Other published works include* The Wisdom of the Body *(1997),* The Mysteries Within: A Surgeon Reflects on Medical Myths *(2000), and articles for the* New Yorker, National Geographic, Time, Life, *and other magazines. In the following selection, published in 1999, Nuland examines the medical and ethical consequences of using the electric chair as a tool for execution.*

FOR YOUR JOURNAL

The cliché "nothing is certain but death and taxes" is one of the few contexts in which the inevitability of death can be mentioned in a casual or humorous manner in our society. The reality of our own death causes discomfort, anxiety, and confusion. How do you view death, or do you try not to think about it at all? Does it frighten you? If so, how? If not, from what source do you find reassurance or comfort?

A swift and painless death is a mercy that few of us will be   1
granted. Disease and aging do not often complete their lethal work without laying down lengthy and devastating barrages. Even the so-called "sudden death" of major injury is all too commonly accompanied by seconds or even minutes of anguish. But of all trauma victims, the murdered are most likely to end their lives in some form of agony and terror.

And so, some find it paradoxical that when murderers are to be   2
executed, our society often tries to provide them with the painless
death that only a small number of us will have been granted by nature or fortune. This paradox stands out anew with the announce-
ment that the Supreme Court will soon decide whether Florida's use
of the electric chair constitutes cruel and unusual punishment. Electrocution is the only method of capital punishment in Florida, Alabama, Georgia and Nebraska. It is a choice given to the condemned
in Ohio, South Carolina and Virginia. What is specifically feared by
those on death row, according to court papers, is that they will undergo "physical violence, disfigurement and torment" during the
process of dying.

If the court decides that murderers deserve a quietus of which   3
they have deprived others, then the electric chair should unquestion-
ably be abolished as a method of execution.

Even when it functions exactly as it should, the electric chair is a   4
brutal killer. It depends on three jolts of electricity—some 2,000
volts each, traveling from head to foot for anywhere from 8 seconds
to 20 seconds. When performance is optimal, a very small circumference of burnt skin will be produced at points of entrance and exit,
but not much else will be visible. For this to happen, the electrodes
and their attachments must be perfectly placed, resistance must be
minimal and all parts of the electrical apparatus—like the generator,
switches and wiring—must be in excellent working order.

Technical failures in any part of this complex apparatus can re-   5
sult in a failure of the entire system. This explains the botched executions we occasionally read about: the sparking, the smoke and flame
and the need for repeated shocks in a subject who may still be at least
partially conscious.

If the electrical system does work perfectly, what then? What is   6
the mechanism of death? Ideally, passage of current through the head
and into the trunk should instantly cause unconsciousness, although
it simultaneously stimulates acute contractions of virtually every
muscle in the body. If the condemned is at all conscious, such contractions are exquisitely painful.

Death may be caused in any of several ways. By passing through   7
the cardiac center in the brain's medulla, the current arrests the heart.
By passing through the respiratory center, it stops breathing and asphyxiates the subject. By passing through the heart, it distorts normal
ventricular rhythm into an ineffective wormlike wriggling called fib-
rillation, which has the same effect as cardiac arrest.

All of these mechanisms take more than two minutes to cause   8
brain death, the legal definition of the end of life. Should the initial
shock not render the subject fully unconscious, he remains aware of
what is happening, particularly if he is being asphyxiated, a situation
appallingly obvious at autopsy.

Compared to the effectiveness and ease of executions carried out   9
by lethal injection, electrocution is a barbaric way to kill someone.
Unless revenge is what our society wants—and some would indeed
say that such a goal is justifiable—the court's path is clear: the electric chair should be forbidden. The answer is as simple as that.

QUESTIONS FOR STUDY AND DISCUSSION

1. Why do you think Nuland prefaces his argument about the electric chair with the "paradox," as he calls it (2), of providing
   murderers with a quiet death? Does it detract from his argument,
   which is his ultimate condemnation of the electric chair as a device for execution? Explain your answer.

2. Nuland describes the mechanism of death in the electric chair in
   gruesome detail. He only briefly mentions lethal injection, however, and asks the reader to accept that it is a far more "effective" alternative without providing any information to support
   his statement. Would his argument against the electric chair have
   been strengthened if he had provided a stronger contrast with
   lethal injection? (Glossary: *Comparison and Contrast*) Why, or
   why not?

3. Analyze Nuland's choice of words in paragraphs 4–8. (Glossary:
   Diction) What words does he use to strengthen the impression he
   wishes to convey about what the condemned experience in the
   electric chair?

4. How does the electric chair cause death? Why might the cause or
   causes of death constitute "cruel and unusual punishment"?

5. Nuland's conclusion is very concise, but the caveat "Unless revenge is what our society wants—and some would indeed say
   that such a goal is justifiable" (9) strengthens the impression
   that Nuland himself is unclear as to whether society should
   seek revenge. Based on your reading of the essay, where do
   you think Nuland stands on capital punishment and the means
   of execution? Defend your answer with references from the
   essay.

VOCABULARY

Refer to your dictionary to define the following words as they are used in this selection. Then use each word in a sentence of your own.

trauma (1)
paradoxical (2)
quietus (3)

botched (5)
asphyxiates (7)
ventricular (7)

CLASSROOM ACTIVITY USING ARGUMENT

Read the following passages. What type of logical fallacy does each represent? See page 425.

1. He'll be an excellent windsurfer. He won several skateboarding competitions when he was a student.
2. Ever since 1985, the year people in the United States started to eat more fish, the average height of ten-year-olds has increased each year.
3. Stressful jobs with long hours are the reason the divorce rate is going up.
4. This breed of dog is very loyal, so it's a good choice for people with small apartments.
5. The Internet is growing at a phenomenal rate. Other methods of communication will soon become obsolete.

SUGGESTED WRITING ASSIGNMENTS

1. The revenge mentality regarding punishment for criminals, often summarized as "an eye for an eye," is generally not advocated in today's society. Nonetheless, that criminals must be punished in some way for their crimes is seldom questioned, and candidates for political office often run on platforms that pronounce them "tough on crime." What, then, is the happy medium for capital crimes that provoke debate regarding the death penalty? What is your position on the death penalty? Did you find yourself agreeing or disagreeing with Nuland's argument against the use of the electric chair? Write an argument paper in which you present what you consider the best way to punish people convicted of capital crimes.
2. Our society is struggling with the issue of violence in the news and entertainment media and the effect it may have on children

and young adults. News reports of the Columbine tragedy, for example, often referred to the fascination the perpetrators felt for "first-person shooter" video games. We know that violence sells—it is now pervasive in movies, on TV, in video games— yet direct evidence that violent images lead to violent behavior remains difficult to obtain. Write an argument paper in which you consider the issue based on your experience and that of your friends. Do you enjoy violent action movies and "shoot 'em up" video games? Do you feel they glorify violence or numb you to it in any way? Argue what, if anything, should be done to limit violent images in the media, especially in material designed to reach children. Are the current rating systems enough? Should they be applied more strictly to shows and games that contain certain kinds of violence?

When Justice Lets Us Down

■ **Jim Dwyer, Peter Neufeld, and Barry Scheck**

Two-time Pulitzer Prize–winning journalist Jim Dwyer gradu-
ated from the Columbia Graduate School of Journalism in
1980. After working for three different newspapers in New Jer-
sey, he joined Newsday *in New York City in 1984. He is cur-*
rently a columnist for the New York Daily News. *Dwyer met*
defense lawyers Peter Neufeld and Barry Scheck while covering
a trial for his column. Neufeld and Scheck were public defenders
in the South Bronx in 1988 when they worked on a case in
which they concluded that DNA testing would have easily es-
tablished the innocence of an accused man but had been ignored
as a tool for justice. That experience led them to found the Inno-
cence Project in 1992, which has since used DNA evidence to
exonerate thirty-seven people convicted of crimes they did not
commit. Neufeld, who has a private practice in Manhattan, and
Scheck, currently a professor at the Benjamin N. Cardozo Law
School, teamed with Dwyer to write Actual Innocence, *a book*
that details the work of the Innocence Project and calls for in-
creased use of DNA testing to establish guilt or innocence. The
following selection, published in Newsweek *on February 14,*
2000, is adapted from the book.

FOR YOUR JOURNAL

What is your opinion of the death penalty? What beliefs or experiences have contributed to the formation of your opinion?

The warden was seated at the head of a long table when Ron   1
Williamson was led into the office and told to sit down. Once,
Williamson had been a professional baseball player, the hero jock
who married the beauty queen in his small Oklahoma town. Now, on
an August morning in 1994, at 41, the athlete had passed directly
from his prime to a state beyond age. His hair had gone stringy and
white; his face had shrunk to a skeletal mask wrapped in pasty, tone-
less skin.

The warden said he had a duty to carry out, and he read from a   2
piece of paper: You have been sentenced to die by lethal injection,
and such sentence will be carried out at 12:30 A.M., the 24th of September, 1994. The prison had received no stay of execution, the warden said, so Williamson would be brought to the holding area next to
the death chamber until the 24th.

He was led back to a cell, screaming from that moment on, night   3
and day, even after they moved him into another unit with double
doors to muffle the noise. On Sept. 17, Williamson was shifted into
the special cell for prisoners with less than a week to live. By then, the
screaming had torn his throat to ribbons, but everyone knew his
raspy, desperate litany: "I did not rape or kill Debra Sue Carter! I am
an innocent man!" In Norman, Okla., a public defender named Janet
Chesley frantically scrambled a team to move the case into federal
court, assembling a mass of papers and fresh arguments. With just
five days to go, they won a stay.

One year later, U.S. district court Judge Frank Seay would rule   4
that Williamson's trial had been a constitutional shambles. His conviction and death sentence—ratified by every state court in Oklahoma—had been plagued by unreliable informants, prosecutorial
misconduct, an inept defense lawyer, bogus scientific evidence and a
witness who himself was a likely suspect, the federal judge said. He
vacated the conviction.

Last April, before Williamson could be tried again, DNA tests   5
arranged by the Innocence Project at the Benjamin N. Cardozo Law
School in New York proved that he was actually innocent. Across the
country, the Ron Williamson story has happened over and over.
Since 1976, Illinois has executed 12 people—and freed 13 from
death row as innocent. Last week Illinois Governor George Ryan declared a moratorium on executions. The next day a California judge
threw out the convictions of nine people after prosecutors said they
were among at least 32 framed by a group of corrupt police officers
within the Los Angeles Police Department. New innocence cases,
based on DNA tests, are on the horizon in California, Texas, Florida
and Louisiana.

A rare moment of enlightenment is at hand. In the last decade,   6
DNA tests have provided stone-cold proof that 69 people were sent
to prison and death row in North America for crimes they did not
commit. The number has been rising at a rate of more than one a
month. What matters most is not how the wrongly convicted got out
of jail, but how they got into it. "How do you prevent another

innocent man or woman from paying the ultimate penalty for a crime he or she did not commit?" asked Governor Ryan, a Republican and death-penalty supporter. "Today I cannot answer that question."

In 22 states, the fabric of false guilt has been laid bare, and the same vivid threads bind a wealthy Oklahoma businessman and a Maryland fisherman; a Marine corporal in California and a boiler repairman in Virginia; a Chicago drifter and a Louisiana construction worker; a Missouri schoolteacher and the Oklahoma ballplayer. Sometimes, it turns out, eyewitnesses make mistakes. Snitches tell lies. Confessions are coerced or fabricated. Racism trumps the truth. Lab tests are rigged. Defense lawyers sleep. Cops lie.

DNA testing can't solve these problems but it reveals their existence. Many can be fixed with simple reforms. To simply ignore them means that more criminals go free, and the innocent will suffer. Clyde Charles learned the crushing weight of the status quo: he was freed just before Christmas, after 19 years of his life were squandered in Louisiana's Angola prison. The last nine years were spent fighting for the DNA lab work that cleared him in a matter of hours. In 48 states, prisoners don't have statutory rights to tests that could prove their innocence, and too often authorities stubbornly resist. In more than half its exonerations, the Innocence Project was forced into fierce litigation simply to get the DNA tests.

"Our procedure," wrote Justice Learned Hand in 1923, "has always been haunted by the ghost of the innocent man convicted. It is an unreal dream." Nearly 75 years later, Judge Seay in Oklahoma wrote an epilogue to the writ of habeas corpus for Ron Williamson: "God help us, if ever in this great country we turn our heads while people who have not had fair trials are executed. That almost happened in this case." For all the gigabytes of crime statistics kept in the United States, no account is taken of the innocent person, wrongly convicted, ultimately exonerated. No one has the job of figuring out what went wrong, or who did wrong. The moment has come to do so.

QUESTIONS FOR STUDY AND DISCUSSION

1. The authors begin their argument piece with an anecdote rather than data or a preliminary statement of their point of view. (Glossary: *Beginnings and Endings*) Why is the anecdote an effective way to introduce their argument? What does the Williamson case illustrate about the death penalty? (Glossary: *Illustration*)

2. Reread the quotation from Governor George Ryan in paragraph 6. Identify two ways in which the quotation strengthens the authors' argument.

3. According to the authors, "A rare moment of enlightenment is at hand" (6). Who is being "enlightened," and what about?

4. Identify the figurative language used in paragraph 7. (Glossary: *Figure of Speech*) Why do the authors include it in what is otherwise a prosaic piece of writing? What image does it bring to mind?

5. What problems with the justice system can DNA testing reveal? Why do you think that it is so difficult to obtain DNA testing when it can so quickly provide clear-cut evidence of a convicted person's innocence?

VOCABULARY

Refer to your dictionary to define the following words as they are used in this selection. Then use each word in a sentence of your own.

stay (2)	vivid (7)
litany (3)	coerced (7)
inept (4)	statutory (8)
moratorium (5)	exonerations (8)

CLASSROOM ACTIVITY USING ARGUMENT

Choose one of the following controversial subjects, and think about how you would write an argument for or against it. Write three sentences that summarize three important points, two based on logic and one based on persuasion/emotion. Then write one sentence that acknowledges the opposing point of view. For example, if you were to argue for stricter enforcement of a leash law and waste pickup ordinance for dog owners in your town, you might write:

logic Dogs allowed to run free can be a menace to joggers and local wildlife.

logic Dog waste poses a health risk, particularly in areas where children play.

emotion How would you feel if you hit an unleashed dog with your car?

counterargument Dogs need fresh air and exercise, too.

Gun control
Tobacco restrictions
Cutting taxes and cutting social programs
Paying college athletes
Assisted suicide for terminally ill people
Widespread legalization of gambling (i.e., video poker machines)

SUGGESTED WRITING ASSIGNMENTS

1. Think about a specific event that helped form or strengthen an opinion you have on an issue. It can be from your own experience or something that you observed, read about, or watched in a movie or on television. For example, you may have decided not to eat meat after seeing a documentary about slaughterhouses. Or you may feel that your school's pre-exam study period is too short after doing poorly on a difficult test for which you could not find enough time to study. Using "When Justice Lets Us Down" as a model, write an argument paper in which you use the event or situation as an anecdote to help present your point of view. Try to convey to the reader what it was about the event or situation that had such a powerful influence on you.

2. Using your journal entry as a starting point, write an argument essay in which you either support or oppose the death penalty. In your essay, be sure to address possible objections to your point of view. For example, if you support the death penalty, how can the execution of innocent people be prevented? If you oppose it, what is the harshest penalty society can mete out? What should we do with people who are conclusively convicted of heinous crimes?

Cyberghetto: Blacks Are Falling through the Net

■ Frederick L. McKissack

Frederick L. McKissack and his wife, Pat, have collaborated on more than fifty books, most for young readers, focusing on African American topics. He does background research, while his wife does most of the writing. Several of their books have won awards over the years, including Christmas in the Big House, Christmas in the Quarters, *which won the* Coretta Scott King *and the* Boston Globe Horn Book *awards. This writing team lives outside of St. Louis, Missouri. In the following selection, McKissack argues that minorities are being left out of current technological advancements spearheaded by the Internet. Without access to the business opportunities and information that are at the fingertips of those who are on-line, McKissack contends, the financial gap between the wealthy and the poor in our society can only widen.*

FOR YOUR JOURNAL

How much time did you spend on computers during your grade school years (kindergarten through eighth grade)? Do you think it was too much, not enough, or about enough time? What effect do you think increased computer time would have had on you? How has your computer skill—or lack thereof—shaped your later education and your career goals?

I left journalism last year and started working for an Internet development firm because I was scared. While many of my crypto-Luddite friends ("I find e-mail so impersonal") have decided that the Web is the work of the devil and is being monitored by the NSA, CIA, FBI, and the IRS, I began to have horrible dreams that 16-year-

1

old punks were going to take over publishing in the next century because they knew how to write good computer code. I'd have to answer to some kid with two earrings who'll make fun of me because I have one earring and didn't study computer science in my spare time.

You laugh, but one of the best web developers in the country is a   2
teenager who has written a very sound book on web design and programming. He's still in his prime learning years, and he's got a staff.

What should worry me more is that I am one of the few African   3
Americans in this country who has a computer at home, uses one at work, and can use a lot of different kinds of software on multiple platforms. According to those in the know, I'm going to remain part of that very small group for quite some time.

The journal *Science* published a study . . . which found that, in   4
households with annual incomes below $40,000, whites were six times more likely than blacks to have used the World Wide Web in the last week. Low-income white households were twice as likely to have a home computer as low-income black homes. Even as computers become more central to our society, minorities are falling through the Net.

The situation is actually considerably worse than the editors of   5
Science made it seem. Some 18 percent of African American households don't even have phones, as Philip Bereano, a professor of technical communications at the University of Washington, pointed out in a letter to the *New York Times*. Since the researchers who published their study in *Science* relied on a telephone survey to gather their data, Bereano explains, the study was skewed—it only included people who had at least caught up to the 20th century.

About 30 percent of American homes have computers, with the   6
bulk of those users being predominantly white, upper-middle-class households. Minorities are much worse off: Only about 15 percent have a terminal at home.

The gulf between technological haves and have-nots is the differ-   7
ence between living the good life and surviving in what some technologists and social critics term a "cyberghetto." Professor Michio Kaku, a professor of theoretical physics at City University of New York, wrote in his book *Visions: How Science Will Revolutionize the Twenty-first Century*, of the emergence of "information ghettos."

"The fact is, each time society made an abrupt leap to a new level   8
of production, there were losers and winners," Kaku wrote. "It may well be that the computer revolution will exacerbate the existing fault lines of society."

The term "cyberghetto" suggests that minorities have barely 9
passable equipment to participate in tech culture. But most minorities
aren't even doing that well.

Before everybody goes "duh," just think what this means down the 10
line. Government officials are using the Web more often to disseminate
information. Political parties are holding major on-line events. And
companies are using the Web for making job announcements and collecting resumes. Classes, especially continuing-education classes, are
being offered more and more on the Web. In politics, commerce, and
education, the Web is leaving minorities behind.

The disparity between the techno-rich and techno-poor comes to 11
a head with this statistic: A person who is able to use a computer at
work earns 15 percent more than someone in the same position who
lacks computer skills.

"The equitable distribution of technology has always been the 12
real moral issue about computers," Jon Katz, who writes the "Rants
and Raves" column for *Wired* on-line, wrote in a recent e-mail. "The
poor can't afford them. Thus they will be shut out of the booming hi-
tech job market and forced to do the culture's menial jobs."

This technological gap, not Internet pornography, should be the 13
public's main concern with the Web.

"Politicians and journalists have suggested frightening parents 14
into limiting children's access to the Internet, but the fact is they have
profoundly screwed the poor, who need access to this technology if
they are to compete and prosper," Katz said. "I think the culture
avoids the complex and expensive issues by focusing on the silly ones.
In 25 years, when the underclass wakes up to discover it is doing all
the muscle jobs while everybody else is in neat, clean offices with
high-paying jobs, they'll go berserk. We don't want to spend the
money to avoid this problem, so we worry about Johnny going to the
Playboy web site. It's sick."

In his 1996 State of the Union address, President Clinton chal- 15
lenged Congress to hook up schools to the Internet.

"We are working with the telecommunications industry, educa- 16
tors, and parents to connect . . . every classroom and every library in
the entire United States by the year 2000," Clinton said. "I ask Congress to support this educational technology initiative so that we can
make sure the national partnership succeeds."

The national average is approximately 10 students for every one 17
computer in the public schools. According to a study by the consulting firm McKinsey & Co., the President's plan — a ratio of one

computer to every five students—would cost approximately $11 billion per year over the next 10 years.

Some government and business leaders, worried about a technologically illiterate work force in the 21st century, recognize the need for increased spending. "AT&T and the Commerce Department have suggested wiring up schools at a 4:1 ratio for $6 or $7 billion," says Katz.

But according to the U.S. Department of Education, only 1.3 percent of elementary and secondary education expenditures are allocated to technology. That figure would have to be increased to 3.9 percent. Given the tightness of urban school district budgets, a tripling of expenditures seems unlikely.

Then there's the question of whether computers in the schools are even desirable. Writer Todd Oppenheimer, in a July 1997 article for *Atlantic Monthly* entitled "The Computer Delusion," argued that there is no hard evidence that computers in the classroom enhance learning. In fact, he took the opposite tack: that computers are partially responsible for the decline of education.

Proponents of computers in the classroom struck back. "On the issue of whether or not technology can benefit education, the good news is that it is not—nor should be—an all-or-nothing proposition," writes Wendy Richard Bollentin, editor of *OnTheInternet* magazine, in an essay for *Educom Review.*

There is an unreal quality about this debate, though, since computer literacy is an indispensable part of the education process for many affluent, white schoolchildren.

Consumers are seeing a decline in prices for home computers. Several PC manufacturers have already introduced sub-$1,000 systems, and there is talk of $600 systems appearing on the market by the fall. Oracle has spent a great deal of money on Network Computers, cheap hardware where software and files are located on large networks. The price is in the sub-$300 range. And, of course, there is WebTV, which allows you to browse on a regular home television set with special hardware.

Despite the trend to more "affordable" computers, a Markle Foundation-Bellcore Labs study shows that this may not be enough to help minorities merge onto the Information Superhighway. There is "evidence of a digital divide," the study said, with "Internet users being generally wealthier and more highly educated, and blacks and Hispanics disproportionately unaware of the Internet."

So, what now?

"For every black family to become empowered, they need to have 26 computers," journalist Tony Brown told the *Detroit News*. "There is no way the black community is going to catch up with white society under the current system. But with a computer, you can take any person from poverty to the middle class."

This is the general line for enlightened blacks and community 27 leaders. But having a computer won't bridge the racial and economic divide. Even if there is a 1:1 ratio of students to computers in urban schools, will students' interest be piqued when they don't have access to computers at home? One out of every 49 computer-science professors in the United States is black. Will this inhibit black students from learning how to use them? And even if every black student had a computer at home and at school, would that obliterate all racial obstacles to success?

Empowerment is not just a question of being able to find your 28 way around the Web. But depriving minorities of access to the technology won't help matters any. We need to make sure the glass ceiling isn't replaced by a silicon ceiling.

QUESTIONS FOR STUDY AND DISCUSSION

1. Before he begins actively to make his argument, McKissack refers to the future power of "16-year-old punks" (1) and the current power of a teenage Web developer. (Glossary: *Beginnings and Endings*) Why does he begin in this way? How does the information subsequently strengthen McKissack's argument?

2. What is McKissack's thesis? (Glossary: *Thesis*) Why is he particularly qualified to argue his point?

3. What does the term *cyberghetto* mean? Why is it potentially misleading?

4. How has Internet pornography served as a diversion from what Jon Katz, as quoted by McKissack, views as the main problem regarding the Web?

5. What evidence does McKissack provide to show that the dropping prices for computers and specialized Web accessing devices do not translate into increased Internet use by minorities? (Glossary: *Evidence*)

6. Summarize McKissack's answer to his own question, "So, what now?" What solutions, if any, does he offer to the problem of the "cyberghetto"?

VOCABULARY

Refer to your dictionary to define the following words as they are used in this selection. Then use each word in a sentence of your own.

Luddite (1)   menial (12)

exacerbate (8)   allocated (19)

disseminate (10)   affluent (22)

CLASSROOM ACTIVITY USING ARGUMENT

You may want to try to complete this activity over several class periods.

Find an editorial in your local newspaper or in a national paper that presents a view of an issue that you disagree with. Bring the editorial to class and reread it, study it for a few minutes, and then write a brief letter to the editor of the newspaper arguing against its position. Your letter should be brief; short letters have a better chance of being published than long ones.

During a subsequent class you may want to form groups of two to three students to share your letters and comment on the effectiveness of each other's arguments. Revise your letter, if necessary, and consider sending it to the newspaper for possible publication.

SUGGESTED WRITING ASSIGNMENTS

1. McKissack argues that minorities have far less access to computers and to the Internet than affluent whites do, but he presents no explicit remedy for the situation. If readers accept his argument that there is an information gap, what should be done about it? What is the best course of action to encourage the use of technology by minorities? Does the answer lie in schools, in government subsidies (as Gary T. Dempsey argues against on pp. 473–75), in private education efforts, or in other means? Write an argument paper in which you present one possible way to start to bridge the gap and argue its merits versus both the status quo and other possible strategies.

2. African Americans were systematically denied access to many of our society's opportunities and benefits until relatively recently. Not surprisingly, the reality of prejudice and diminished opportunity has persisted for African Americans and other minorities,

even though activism and legislation have created a theoretically level playing field. Efforts to create equality in fact, not just in theory, have proved to be extremely controversial, however. Busing, affirmative action, and other programs met with initial resistance and have been controversial in terms of their validity and effectiveness. Choose a program, such as busing or affirmative action, that was designed to increase opportunities for African Americans and other minorities, and research its history and the conflicts surrounding it. Write a paper in which you argue either for or against its implementation and the benefits of its results. If you argue for the abolition of a particular program, discuss how the situation that the program attempted to address could be improved. How can minorities be given a truly fair opportunity to enjoy all that our society has to offer? Would a government program with a different strategy work? Or should nongovernmental organizations or programs be allowed to address the problem?

The Myth of an Emerging Information Underclass

■ **Gary T. Dempsey**

Gary T. Dempsey is currently a researcher and foreign policy analyst for the Cato Institute, an organization that promotes "public policy based on individual liberty, limited government, free markets, and peace." Dempsey graduated from Rutgers University with a degree in international relations in 1991 and obtained a master's degree in government from the College of William and Mary in 1995. He now specializes in U.S. security issues, with an emphasis on the Balkans. He has traveled extensively through the former Yugoslavia, including Kosovo during the conflict there in 1998, and served three times as an international elections supervisor in Bosnia-Herzegovina. His commentary on the Balkans has appeared on the CBS Evening News, *on the* NewsHour with Jim Lehrer, *and in many op-ed pieces in newspapers around the country. The following selection, written in November 1997, addresses a topic closer to home: Internet access. Given the Cato Institute's mission statement, it is not surprising that he questions the validity of concerns about an emerging "information underclass" and argues against any government subsidies for Internet access.*

FOR YOUR JOURNAL

How important is the Internet to you? How much do you use it for work or study? How much do you use it for entertainment? What would you miss most if you no longer had access to it?

Since 1993, the Clinton administration has argued that people 1
without Internet access will be at a serious social and economic disadvantage. Subsidies, one executive white paper claims, are required to bring Internet access to lower-income households. Otherwise, we risk becoming "a society of information 'haves' and 'have-nots.'" Similarly, advocacy groups like the Alliance for Public Technology and the Center for Media Education fear that without

Internet subsidies an "information underclass" will emerge in the digital age.

Yet proponents of Internet subsidies make two false assumptions: 2
1) The fact that people do not log on does not necessarily imply that they cannot afford to do so. They may simply have other priorities.
2) Access to an Internet connection does not necessarily imply that someone is "information rich." Just as living next door to a public library doesn't by itself make a person more knowledgeable, there is nothing automatically informative about being wired.

Moreover, there are several reasons to doubt the likelihood that 3 an information underclass will emerge in the absence of government-mandated Internet subsidies.

First, the number of low-income households with Internet access 4 continues to grow each year. In the last quarter of 1996, for instance, a survey by Wirthlin Worldwide found that Internet use by people earning less than $15,000 a year may have increased by as much as 160 percent. A recent *Business Week* poll found that as many as 18 percent of today's Internet-using households earn less than $25,000 a year. Such trends have led Novell's Eric Schmidt to predict, "At the current rate of growth every man, woman, and child on the earth will be connected to the Internet by 2007."

Second, researchers at Carnegie Mellon University have found 5 that people use the Internet primarily for amusement. That suggests that entertainment, not information services, will drive the Internet's commercial development. As an entertainment technology, the Internet will likely penetrate households just as VCRs (88 percent of households) and color televisions (98 percent of households) have done.

Third, recent technological innovations like cable modems and 6 wireless local multipoint distribution systems (LMDS) will expand the availability and lower the cost of Internet access. Cable is now available to 97 percent of U.S. homes, according to the National Cable Television Association, and several companies are currently developing cable modems that will allow users 24-hour access to the Internet at speeds unmatched by telephone lines. Transmitting a five-megabyte file over a typical telephone modem takes approximately 22 minutes. To send the same package of data through a cable modem will take four seconds.

Cellular technology is also advancing. Wireless LMDS, for example, will allow simultaneous, high-speed interactive voice, video and Internet services without the expense of laying costly new wires. 7

What both cable and LMDS technologies will provide is Internet access that is diversified, faster and, with competition, cheaper.

Fourth, charitable organizations can offer low-cost or free Internet access as part of their programs. That is precisely what the Plugged In organization does. The East Palo Alto–based non-profit is committed to extending network access to low-income people. The group also offers more than 30 classes designed to give community members basic Internet and computer skills. 8

Private companies around the country are also stepping forward and offering free Internet access. DIGEX Inc. donates Internet access to the Robert Taylor housing project in Chicago, Illinois, and Imperium Internet donates Internet access to the Eternal Light Church's public computer lab in urban Canton, Ohio, to give two examples. 9

Finally, one obvious reason lower-income households lag in Internet access is that they do not have computers to begin with. But that is changing. By 1995, one-fifth of computer-owning households earned less than $30,000 a year, 30 percent more households than the previous year, according to a survey by Computer Intelligence Infocorp. One reason for the rapid growth of computer ownership among lower-income households is the ever-increasing supply of used computers. Fifteen to 19 million used business computers go on the market each year, according to the Gartner Marketing Group, plus an estimated 1 million used government computers. It's not surprising, then, that 29 percent of all first-time buyers in 1995 bought their computers used, up from 19 percent in 1994. 10

Added to the growing pool of hardware will be new, low-cost, network computers designed especially for Internet use. Such "information appliances," as they are sometimes called, are now being introduced into the marketplace. Oracle advertises a $299 version, and Hewlett-Packard and Sun Microsystems plan to introduce sub-$500 models. 11

What all of this suggests is that an information underclass is far from inevitable. Rather, information technology is on course to spread everywhere without government-mandated subsidies. The voluntary institutions of civil society—markets and charitable giving—are doing it on their own. 12

QUESTIONS FOR STUDY AND DISCUSSION

1. Dempsey argues that one reason no "information underclass" will emerge is that Internet use among low-income people is

growing so quickly. Does his argument include any logical fallacies? If so, what are they? If not, how would you counter his argument?

2. Dempsey's argument has two central components: first, that proponents of government-subsidized Internet access are making false assumptions regarding the importance of Internet access, and second, that low-income people will have adequate Internet access without government assistance. Which component do you find most important to Dempsey's overall argument? Given your answer, do you find Dempsey's organization effective? (Glossary: *Organization*) Why, or why not?

3. What analogy does Dempsey use to show that easy access to information will not necessarily lead to its use? (Glossary: *Analogy*) Is the analogy an effective tool with which to present the argument? Why, or why not?

4. Why does Dempsey argue that wider availability of LMDSs will make the Internet more accessible? What assumptions does he make in presenting his argument?

5. Define the title word *underclass* in the context of Dempsey's essay. (Glossary: *Definition*) What does the term connote to you beyond its definition? (Glossary: *Connotation/Denotation*)

VOCABULARY

Refer to your dictionary to define the following words as they are used in this selection. Then use each word in a sentence of your own.

advocacy (1)

proponents (2)

diversified (7)

inevitable (12)

CLASSROOM ACTIVITY USING ARGUMENT

The Internet is a powerful tool, and as such it has the potential to be both hugely beneficial and incredibly harmful, depending on who uses it and how. Imagine you are assigned to write two argument essays, one on the Internet's benefits and another on its dangers. List three points you would make in each argument paper. Discuss your answers with your classmates.

SUGGESTED WRITING ASSIGNMENTS

1. Dempsey's essay was written in late 1997, so it is now possible to assess his predictions regarding the increased accessibility of the Internet for everyone. Write an argument essay in which you agree with his contention that the barriers to Internet access have been adequately reduced—making government subsidies redundant—or in which you disagree, arguing instead that lower-income people still need assistance in accessing this powerful tool. How much more accessible has the Internet become for all consumers since 1997? How many of Dempsey's predictions are accurate, and how many are not?

2. Politicians, industry insiders, and security experts have wrestled with the issue of free speech on the Internet for years. Free speech is a basic right for Americans, but some forms of speech—how to build bombs, for example, or why to hate members of ethnic groups different from your own—have traditionally been closely monitored and limited. With the advent of the Internet, it has become difficult to monitor the more controversial forms of free speech. Write an argument paper in which you determine what, if any, restrictions should be placed upon Internet content. If you argue for restrictions, how can they be enforced without limiting important freedoms? If you think no restrictions are necessary, how do you account for the potential negative effects of dangerous or hate-filled content available on the Internet?

Writing a Research Paper

The research paper is an important part of a college education—and for good reason. In writing a research paper, you acquire a number of indispensable skills that you can adapt to other college assignments and to situations after graduation.

The real value of writing a research paper, however, goes beyond acquiring basic skills; it is a unique hands-on learning experience. The purpose of a research paper is not to present a collection of quotations that show you can report what others have said about your topic. Rather, your goal is to analyze, evaluate, and synthesize the materials you research—and thereby learn how to do so with any topic. You learn how to view the results of research from your own perspective and to arrive at an informed opinion of a topic.

Writing a researched essay is not very different from the other writing you will be doing in your college writing course. You will find yourself drawing heavily on what you have learned from the four student papers in the Introduction to this text. First you determine what you want to write about. Then you decide on a purpose, consider your audience, develop a thesis, collect your evidence, write a first draft, revise and edit, and prepare a final copy. What differentiates the research paper from other kinds of papers is your use of outside sources and how you acknowledge them.

In this appendix, you will learn how to locate and use print and Internet sources; how to evaluate these sources; how to take useful notes; how to summarize, paraphrase, and quote your sources; how to integrate your notes into your paper; how to acknowledge your sources; and how to avoid plagiarism. You will also find extensive guidelines for documenting your essay in MLA (Modern Language Association) style. MLA guidelines are widely accepted by English and foreign-language scholars and teachers, and we encourage their use. Before you begin work on your research paper, your instructor will let you know which style you should follow.

Your library research will involve working with print as well as electronic sources. In both cases, however, the process is essentially the same: your aim is to select the most appropriate sources for your research from the many that are available on your topic.

■ Using Print Sources

In most cases, you should use print sources (books, newspapers, journals, periodicals, encyclopedias, pamphlets, brochures, and government publications) as your primary tools for research. Print sources, unlike many Internet sources, are often reviewed by experts in the field before they are published, are generally overseen by a reputable publishing company or organization, and are examined by editors and fact checkers for accuracy and reliability. Unless you are instructed otherwise, you should try to use print sources in your research.

To find print sources, search through your library's reference works, card catalog, periodical indexes, and other databases to generate a preliminary listing of books, magazine and newspaper articles, public documents and reports, and other sources that may be helpful in exploring your topic. At this early stage, it is better to err on the side of listing too many sources. Then, later on, you will not have to relocate sources you discarded too hastily.

PREVIEW PRINT SOURCES

Although you want to be thorough in your research, you will soon realize that you do not have enough time to read every source you encounter. Rather, you must preview your sources to decide what you will read, what you will skim, and what you will simply eliminate.

Questions for Previewing Print Sources
1. Is the book or article directly related to your research topic?
2. Is the book or article obviously outdated (for example, a source on language-related brain research that is from the 1970s)?
3. Have you checked tables of contents and indexes in books to locate material that may be important and relevant to your topic?
4. If an article appears to be what you are looking for, have you read the abstract (a summary of the main points of the article, which appears in some journals) or the opening and concluding paragraphs?

5. Is it necessary to read the entire article quickly to be sure that it is relevant?

DEVELOP A WORKING BIBLIOGRAPHY

It is important to develop a working bibliography of the books, articles, and other materials that you think are relevant to your topic. Compiling a working bibliography lets you know at a glance which works you have consulted and the shape your research is taking. A working bibliography also guides you to other materials you may wish to consider. Naturally, you will want to capture early on all the information you need for each work so that you do not have to return to the library at a later time to retrieve publication data for your final bibliography or list of works cited. Accuracy and completeness are, of course, essential at this final stage of the research.

For each work that you think might be helpful, make a separate bibliography card, using a 4 × 6 index card. As your collection of cards grows, alphabetize them by the authors' last names. By using a separate card for each book or article, you can continually edit your working bibliography, dropping sources that are not helpful for one reason or another and adding new ones. You will also use the cards to compile your final list of works cited.

For books, record the following information:

- All authors; any editors or translators
- Title and subtitle
- Edition (if not the first)
- Publication data: city, publishing company, and year
- Call number

For periodical articles, record the following information:

- All authors
- Title and subtitle
- Title of journal, magazine, or newspaper
- Volume and issue numbers
- Year and page numbers

Using correct bibliographic form ensures that your entries are complete, reduces the chance of introducing careless errors, and saves time when you are ready to prepare your final list of works cited.

You will find MLA-style guidelines for the list of works cited on pages 494–99.

EVALUATE PRINT SOURCES

Before beginning to take notes, you should read your sources and evaluate them for their relevance and reliability in helping you explore your topic. Examine your sources for the writers' main ideas. Pay particular attention to abstracts or introductions, tables of contents, section headings, and indexes. Also, look for information about the authors themselves—information that will help you determine their authority and perspective on the issues.

Questions for Evaluating Print Sources

1. Is your source focused on your particular research topic?
2. Is your source too abstract, too general, or too technical for your needs?
3. Does your source build on current thinking and existing research in the field?
4. Does your source promote a particular view, or is it meant to provide balanced coverage of the topic? What biases, if any, does your source exhibit?
5. Is the author of your source an authority on the topic? Do other writers mention the author of your source in their work?

■ Using Internet Sources

You will find that Internet sources can be informative and valuable additions to your research. The Internet is especially useful in providing recent data, stories, and reports. For example, you might find a just-published article from a university laboratory or a news story in your local newspaper's online archives. Generally, however, Internet sources should be used along with print sources and not as a replacement for them. Whereas print sources are generally published under the guidance of a publisher or an organization, practically anyone with access to a computer and a modem can put text and pictures onto the Internet; there is often no governing body that checks for content or accuracy. The Internet offers a vast number of useful and carefully maintained resources, but it also contains much unreliable information. It is your responsibility to evaluate whether a given Internet source should be trusted.

Your Internet research will probably produce many more sources than you can reasonably use. By carefully previewing Web sites and other Internet sources, developing a working bibliography of potentially useful ones, and evaluating them for their reliability, you will ensure that you are making the best use of Internet sources in researching your topic.

If you do not know how to access the Internet, or if you need more instruction on conducting Internet searches, you should go to your on-campus computer center for more information or consult one of the many books written for Internet beginners. You can also access the links to Internet information offered by Bedford/St. Martin's at <http://www.bedfordstmartins.com/hacker/resdoc>.

PREVIEW INTERNET SOURCES

The key to successful Internet research is being able to identify the sites that will help you the most. Answering the following questions will help you weed out sources that hold no promise.

Questions for Previewing Internet Sources

1. Scan the Web site. Do the contents and links appear to be related to your research topic?
2. Can you identify the author of the site? Are the author's credentials available, and are they appropriate to the content of the site?
3. Has the site been updated within the last six months? It is not always necessary to use updated information, especially if your topic is not a current one and the information about it is fairly stable. Information about the most recent update is usually provided at the bottom of the homepage of the Web site.

If you answer "no" to any of these questions, you should consider eliminating the source from further consideration.

DEVELOP A WORKING BIBLIOGRAPHY

Just as for print sources, you must maintain accurate records for the Internet sources you use. Here is what you need for each source:

- All authors or sponsoring agents
- Title and subtitle of the document
- Title of complete work (if applicable)
- Document date (or date "last modified")
- Date you accessed the site
- Publishing data for print version (if available)
- Address of the site, uniform resource locator (URL), or network path

EVALUATE INTERNET SOURCES

Because the quality of sources on the Internet varies tremendously, it is important to evaluate the information you find there. Answering the following questions will help you evaluate the sites you have included in your working bibliography.

Questions for Evaluating Web Sites

1. *What type of Web site is it?*

   a. Who sponsors the site? A corporation? An individual? The URL indicates the sponsor of the site. Some common domain names are:

   .com   Business/commercial
   .edu   Educational institution
   .gov   Government
   .mil   Military
   .net   Various types of networks
   .org   Nonprofit organization

2. *Who is the authority or author?*

   a. What individual or company is responsible for the site?

   b. Can you verify if the site is official, actually sanctioned by an organization or company?

   c. What are the author's or company's qualifications for writing on this subject?

   d. Is there a way to verify the legitimacy of this individual or company? Are there links to a homepage or résumé?

3. *What is the site's purpose and audience?*

   a. What appears to be the author's or sponsor's purpose or motivation?

    b. Who is the intended audience?

4. *Is the site objective?*

    a. Are advertising, opinion, and factual information clearly distinguished?

    b. What biases, if any, can you detect?

5. *How accurate is the site?*

    a. Is important information documented through links so that it can be verified or corroborated by other sources?

    b. Is the text well written and free of careless errors in spelling and grammar?

6. *Is the coverage thorough and current?*

    a. Is there any indication that the site is still under construction?

    b. For sources with print equivalents, is the Web version more or less extensive than the print version?

    c. How detailed is the site's treatment of its subject matter?

    d. Is there any indication of the currency of the information (the date of the last update or a statement regarding frequency of updates)?

You can also find sources on the Internet itself that offer useful guidelines for evaluating electronic sources. One excellent set of guidelines has been created by reference librarians at the Wolfgram Memorial Library at Widener University; see <http://www2.swidener .edu/Wolfgram-Memorial-Library/webeval.htm>. Also see Jan Alexander and Marsha Ann Tote's book *Web Wisdom* published by Lawrence Erlbaum Associates in 1999.

■ Taking Notes

As you gather and sort your source materials, you'll want to record the information that you consider most pertinent to your topic. As you read, take notes. You're looking for ideas, facts, opinions, statistics, examples, and other evidence that you think will be useful as you write your paper. As you work through books and articles, look for recurring themes and notice where writers are in agreement and where they differ. Try to remember that the effectiveness of your paper is largely determined by the quality—not necessarily the quantity—of your notes. You will want to analyze, evaluate, and synthesize the information you collect to use it for your own purpose.

Now for some practical advice on taking notes: First, be systematic in your note taking. As a rule, write one note on a card and include the author's full name, the complete title of the source, and a page number indicating the origin of the note. Use cards of uniform size, preferably 4 × 6 cards because they are large enough to accommodate even a long note on a single card and yet small enough to be easily handled and conveniently carried. Following this system will also help you when you get to the planning and writing stage because you will be able to sequence your notes according to the plan you have envisioned for your paper. Furthermore, should you decide to alter your organizational plan, you can easily reorder your cards to reflect your revisions. You can, of course, do note taking on your computer as well, which makes it easy for you to reorder your notes. An added advantage of the computer is that the Copy and Paste features let you move notes and their citations directly into your essay.

Second, try not to take too many notes. One good way to control your note taking is to ask yourself, "How exactly does this material help prove or disprove my thesis?" Try to envision where in your paper you could use the information. If it does not seem relevant to your thesis, don't bother to take a note.

Once you decide to take a note, you must decide whether to summarize, paraphrase, or quote directly. The approach you take should be determined by the content of the passage and the way you plan to use it in your paper.

SUMMARY

When you *summarize* material from one of your sources, you capture in condensed form the essential idea of a passage, article, or entire chapter. Summaries are particularly useful when you are working with lengthy, detailed arguments or long passages of narrative or descriptive background information in which the details are not germane to the overall thrust of your paper. You simply want to capture the essence of the passage because you are confident that your readers will readily understand the point being made or do not need to be convinced about its validity. Because you are distilling information, a summary is always shorter than the original; often a chapter or more can be reduced to a paragraph, or several paragraphs to a sentence or two. Remember, in writing a summary you should use your own words.

Consider the following long descriptive paragraph in which Diane Ackerman classifies trees by the color their leaves turn in the fall.

> Not all leaves turn the same colors. Elms, weeping willows, and the ancient ginkgo all grow radiant yellow, along with hickories, aspens, bottlebrush buckeyes, cottonweeds, and tall, keening poplars. Basswood turns bronze, birches bright gold. Water-loving maples put on a symphonic display of scarlets. Sumacs turn red, too, as do flowering dogwoods, black gums, and sweet gums. Though some oaks yellow, most turn a pinkish brown. The farmlands also change color, as tepees of cornstalks and bales of shredded-wheat-textured hay stand drying in the fields. In some spots, one slope of a hill may be green and the other already in bright color, because the hillside facing south gets more sun and heat than the northern one.
>
> DIANE ACKERMAN "Why Leaves Turn Color in the Fall," page 322

A student wishing to capture the gist of Ackerman's point without repeating her detailed account wrote the following summary:

Summary Note Card

```
Leaf color

Ackerman notes that the leaves of different
types of trees predictably turn certain col-
ors in the fall.

            Diane Ackerman, "Why Leaves Turn
                Color in the Fall," 322
```

PARAPHRASE

When you *paraphrase* material from a source, you restate the information in your own words instead of quoting directly. Unlike a summary, which gives a brief overview of the essential information in the original, a paraphrase seeks to maintain the same level of detail as the original to aid readers in understanding or believing the information presented. A paraphrase presents the original information in approximately the same number of words, but in your own wording. To put it another way, your paraphrase should closely parallel the presentation of ideas in the original, but it should not use the same words or sentence structure as the original. Even though you are using your own words in a paraphrase, it's important to remember that you are borrowing ideas and therefore must acknowledge the source of these ideas with a citation.

How would you paraphrase the following passage from "The Ways of Meeting Oppression" by Martin Luther King Jr., which appears on pages 350–54 of this text?

> If the American Negro and other victims of oppression succumb to the temptation of using violence in the struggle for freedom, future generations will be the recipients of a desolate night of bitterness, and our chief legacy to them will be an endless reign of meaningless chaos. Violence is not the way.

The following note card illustrates how a student paraphrased the passage:

Paraphrase Note Card

```
African Americans and other oppressed
peoples must not resort to taking up arms
against their oppressors because to do so
would lead the country into an era of tur-
moil and confusion. Armed confrontation will
not yield the desired results.

                    Martin Luther King Jr.,
        "The Ways of Meeting Oppression," 352
```

In most cases it is best to summarize or paraphrase material—which by definition means using your own words—instead of quoting verbatim (word for word). Capturing an idea in your own words ensures that you have thought about and understood what your source is saying.

DIRECT QUOTATION

To quote a source directly, copy onto your note card the exact words of your source, putting all quoted material in quotation marks. When you make a quotation note card, check the passage carefully for accuracy, including punctuation and capitalization. Be selective about what you choose to quote; reserve direct quotation for important ideas stated memorably, for especially clear explanations by authorities, and for arguments by proponents of a particular position in their own words.

Consider, for example, the following passage from William Zinsser's "Simplicity," on page 116 in this text, emphasizing the importance—and the current rarity—of clear, concise writing:

Direct Quotation Note Card

"Clutter is the disease of American writing. We are a society strangling in unnecessary words, circular constructions, pompous frills, and meaningless jargon."

William Zinsser, "Simplicity," 116

On occasion you'll find a long, useful passage with some memorable wording in it. Avoid the temptation to quote the whole passage; instead, try combining summary or paraphrase with direct quotation. Consider the following paragraph from Lynn Wenzel's essay "Reach Out and Write Someone," which appears on pages 75–79 of this text.

Once upon a time, the only way to communicate from a distance was through the written word. As the country expanded and people moved west, they knew that when they left mother, father, sister, brother, it was probably the last time they would see them again. So daughters, pioneering in Indiana or Michigan, wrote home with the news that their first son had been born dead, but the second child was healthy and growing and they also had a house and barn. By the time the letter reached east, another child might have been born, yet it was read over and over again, then smoothed out and slipped into the family Bible or keepsake box.

Notice how the student who took the following note was careful to put quotation marks around all the words that were borrowed directly.

Quotation and Summary Note Card

In our early history when our country was
expanding, letters home were the only means
of communicating with the folks back east
that they might never see again. "So daughters, pioneering in Indiana or Michigan,
wrote home with the news that their first
son had been born dead, but the second child
was healthy and growing and they also had a
house and barn. By the time the letter
reached east, another child might have been
born, yet it was read over and over again,
then smoothed out and slipped into the family Bible or keepsake box."

Lynn Wenzel, "Reach Out and Write
Someone," 76

NOTES FROM INTERNET SOURCES

Working from the computer screen or from a printout, you can take notes just as you would from print sources. You will need to decide whether to summarize, paraphrase, or quote directly the information you wish to borrow. Use the same 4 × 6 index-card system that you use with print sources. The medium of the Internet, however, has an added advantage. An easy and accurate technique for capturing passages of text from the Internet is to copy the material into a separate computer file on your hard drive or diskette. In Netscape, for example, you can use your mouse to highlight the portion of the text you want to save and then use the Copy and Paste features to add it to your file of research notes. You can also use the same commands to capture the bibliographic information you will need later.

▌ Integrating Borrowed Material into Your Text

Being familiar with the material in your notes will help you decide how to integrate it into your drafts. Though it is not necessary to use all of your notes, or to use them all at once in your first draft, you do need to know which ones support your thesis, extend your ideas, offer better wording of your ideas, and reveal the opinions of noted authorities. Occasionally you will want to use notes that include ideas contrary to your own so that you can rebut them in your own argument. Once you have analyzed all of your notes, you may even alter your thesis slightly in light of the information and ideas you have found.

Whenever you want to use borrowed material, be it a summary, paraphrase, or quotation, it's best to introduce the material with a *signal phrase*—a phrase that alerts the reader that borrowed information is to follow. A signal phrase usually consists of the author's name and a verb. Well-chosen signal phrases help you integrate quotations, paraphrases, and summaries into the flow of your paper. Besides, signal phrases let your reader know who is speaking and, in the case of summaries and paraphrases, exactly where your ideas end and someone else's begin. Never confuse your reader with a quotation that appears suddenly without introduction. Unannounced quotations leave your reader wondering how the quoted material relates to the point you are trying to make. Look at the following example. The quotation is from Pat Mora's essay "The Dance within My Heart," which appears on pages 207–10 in this text.

UNANNOUNCED QUOTATION

> Millions of Americans visit our country's museums each year, but not all of them really appreciate or understand what they see there. For many, however, museum artifacts offer special insights into human creativity. Visitors are "drawn to cases both by the beauty and craft but also as a kind of testimony to humans who once sat under our sun and moon and with rough hands graced our world" (Mora 208).

In the following rewrite, the student writer has integrated the quotation into the text not only by means of a signal phrase, but in a number of other ways as well. By giving the name of the speaker, referring to the speaker's credentials, and noting that the speaker "empathizes with visitors," the writer provides more context so that the reader can better understand how the quotation fits into the discussion.

INTEGRATED QUOTATION

> Millions of Americans visit our country's museums each year, but not all of them really appreciate or understand what they see

there. For many, however, museum artifacts offer special insights into human creativity. Pat Mora, director of the Museum at the University of Texas at El Paso, empathizes with visitors who are "drawn to cases both by the beauty and craft but also as a kind of testimony to humans who once sat under our sun and moon and with rough hands graced our world" (208).

How well you integrate a quote, paraphrase, or summary into your paper depends partly on varying your signal phrases and, in particular, on choosing a verb for the signal phrase that accurately conveys the tone and intent of the writer you are citing. If a writer is arguing, use the verb *argues* (or *asserts, claims,* or *contends*); if a writer is contesting a particular position or fact, use the verb *contests* (or *denies, disputes, refutes,* or *rejects*). In using verbs that are specific to the situation in your paper, you bring your readers into the intellectual debate and avoid the monotony of such all-purpose verbs as *says* or *writes*. Following are just a few examples of how you can vary signal phrases to add precision to your paper:

Robert L. Heilbroner asserts that . . .

To summarize Judith Viorst's observations on friends, . . .

A clinical professor of surgery at Yale, Sherwin B. Nuland, demonstrates . . .

Lois Duncan explains . . .

George Orwell rejects the widely held belief that . . .

Frederick L. McKissack exposes the myth that . . .

Other verbs that you should keep in mind when constructing signal phrases include the following:

acknowledges	declares	points out
adds	endorses	reasons
admits	grants	reports
believes	implies	responds
compares	insists	suggests
confirms		

■ Documenting Sources

Whenever you summarize, paraphrase, or quote a person's thoughts and ideas, and whenever you use facts or statistics that are not commonly known or believed, you must properly acknowledge the source of your information. If you do not properly acknowledge ideas and information created by someone else, you are guilty of *plagiarism,* of using someone else's material but making it look as if it were your own. You must document the source of your information whenever you do the following:

- quote a source word-for-word
- refer to information and ideas from another source that you present in your own words as either a paraphrase or a summary
- cite statistics, tables, charts, or graphs

You do not need to document these types of information:

- your own observations, experiences, and ideas
- factual information available in a number of reference works (known as "common knowledge")
- proverbs, sayings, and familiar quotations

A reference to the source of your borrowed information is called a *citation.* There are many systems for making citations, and your citations must consistently follow one of these systems. As noted earlier, the documentation style recommended by the Modern Language Association (MLA) is commonly used in English and the humanities and is the style used throughout this book. Another common system is the American Psychological Association (APA) style, which is generally used in the social sciences. Your instructor will usually tell you which style to use. For more information on documentation styles, consult the appropriate manual or handbook. For MLA style, consult the *MLA Handbook for Writers of Research Papers,* 5th ed. (New York: MLA, 1999). You may also check MLA guidelines on the Internet at <http://www.mla.org>.

There are two components of documentation: *in-text citations* are placed in the body of your paper; the *list of works cited* provides complete publication data for your in-text citations and is placed at the end of your paper. Both are necessary for complete documentation.

IN-TEXT CITATIONS

In-text citations, also known as *parenthetical citations,* give the reader citation information immediately, at the point at which it is most meaningful. Rather than having to turn to a footnote or an endnote, the reader sees the citation as a part of the writer's text.

Most in-text citations consist of only the author's last name and a page reference. Usually the author's name is given in an introductory or signal phrase at the beginning of the borrowed material, and the page reference is given in parentheses at the end. If the author's name is not given at the beginning, put it in parentheses along with the page reference. The parenthetical reference signals the end of the borrowed material and directs your readers to the list of works cited should they want to pursue a particular source. Treat electronic sources as you do print sources, keeping in mind that some electronic sources use paragraph numbers instead of page numbers. Consider the following examples of in-text citations, which are from a student paper.

IN-TEXT CITATIONS (MLA STYLE)

Citation with author's name in the signal phrase

Educators today are debating whether a flunking grade has any place in today's educational arena. In other words, is there some good that comes out of the threat of a flunking grade or even the grade of F itself? Educator Mary Sherry argues that the threat of flunking can be "a positive teaching tool" and that students with a "healthy fear of failure" (447) are motivated. On the other hand, students should not be overly afraid to fail. As one popular writer and university professor reminds us, "Failure isn't fatal. Countless people have had a bout with it and come out stronger as a result" (Zinsser 451).

Citation with author's name in parentheses

The following shows how the preceding in-text citations should appear in the list of works cited at the end of the essay.

LIST OF WORKS CITED (MLA STYLE)

Sherry, Mary. "In Praise of the F Word." <u>Models for Writers</u>. Ed. Alfred Rosa and Paul Eschholz. 7th ed. Boston: Bedford, 2001. 445–47.

Zinsser, William. "The Right to Fail." <u>Models for Writers</u>. Ed. Alfred Rosa and Paul Eschholz. 7th ed. Boston: Bedford, 2001. 450–53.

LIST OF WORKS CITED

In this section, you will find general MLA guidelines for creating a works cited list followed by sample entries that cover the citation situations you will encounter most often. Make sure that you follow the formats as they appear on the following pages.

General Guidelines

- Begin the list on a new page following the last page of text.
- Organize the list alphabetically by author's last name. If the entry has no author name, alphabetize the first major word of the title.
- Double-space within and between entries.
- Begin each entry at the left margin. If the entry is longer than one line, indent the second and subsequent lines five spaces or one-half inch.
- Do not number entries.

Books

BOOKS BY ONE AUTHOR

List the author's last name first, followed by a comma and the first name. Underline the title. Follow with the city of publication and a shortened version of the publisher's name—for example, *Houghton* for *Houghton Mifflin,* or *Cambridge UP* for *Cambridge University Press.* End with the date of publication.

Pinker, Steven. The Language Instinct: How the Mind
Creates Language. New York: Morrow, 1994.

BOOKS BY TWO OR THREE AUTHORS

List the first author (following order on title page) in the same way as for a single-author book; list subsequent authors, first name first, in the order in which they appear on the title page.

Young Bear, Severt, and R. D. Theisz. Standing in the
Light: A Lokata Way of Seeing. Lincoln: U of Nebraska P, 1994.

BOOK BY FOUR OR MORE AUTHORS

List the first author in the same way as for a single-author book, followed by a comma and the abbreviation *et al.* ("and others").

Morris, Desmond, et al. Gesture Maps. London: Cape,
1978.

TWO OR MORE BOOKS BY THE SAME AUTHOR

List two or more books by the same author in alphabetical order by title. List the first book by the author's name. After the first book, in place of the author's name substitute three unspaced hyphens followed by a period.

Lederer, Richard. Anguished English. Charleston: Wyrick, 1987.

---.Crazy English. New York: Pocket Books, 1990.

REVISED EDITION

Hassan, Ihab. The Dismemberment of Orpheus: Toward a Postmodern Literature. 2nd ed. Madison: U of Wisconsin P, 1982.

EDITED BOOK

Douglass, Frederick. Narrative of the Life of Frederick Douglass, an American Slave, Written by Himself. Ed. Benjamin Quarles. Cambridge: Belknap, 1960.

TRANSLATION

Ueda, Akinari. Tales of Moonlight and Rain: Japanese Gothic Tales. Trans. Kengi Hamada. New York: Columbia UP, 1972.

ANTHOLOGY

Rosa, Alfred, and Paul Eschholz, eds. Language: Readings in Culture and Language. 5th ed. New York: St. Martin's, 1998.

WORK IN AN ANTHOLOGY

Lutz, William. "Types of Doublespeak." Subjects/Strategies. Ed. Paul Eschholz and Alfred Rosa. 8th ed. Boston: Bedford, 1999. 366-70.

SECTION OR CHAPTER IN A BOOK

Carver, Raymond. "Why Don't You Dance?" What We Talk About When We Talk About Love. New York: Knopf, 1981.

Periodicals

ARTICLE IN A JOURNAL WITH CONTINUOUS PAGINATION THROUGHOUT

Some journals paginate issues continuously, by volume; that is, the page numbers in one issue pick up where the previous issue left off. For these journals, follow the volume number by the date of publication in parentheses.

Gazzaniga, Michael S. "Right Hemisphere Language Fol-
    lowing Brain Bisection: A Twenty-year Perspective."
    American Psychologist 38 (1983): 528-49.

ARTICLE IN A JOURNAL WITH SEPARATE PAGINATION IN EACH ISSUE

Some journals paginate by issue; each issue begins with page 1.
For these journals, follow the volume number with a period and the
issue number. Then give the date of publication in parentheses.

Douglas, Ann. "The Failure of the New York Intellectu-
    als." Raritan 17.4 (1998): 1-23.

ARTICLE IN A WEEKLY OR BIWEEKLY MAGAZINE

Delbanco, Andrew. "On Alfred Kazin (1915-1998)." New
    York Review of Books 16 July 1998: 22.

ARTICLE IN A NEWSPAPER

If an article in a newspaper or magazine appears discontinu-
ously — that is, if it starts on one page and skips one or more pages before continuing — include only the first page followed by a plus sign.

Faison, Seth. "President Arrives in Shanghai: Focuses
    on Talk with Citizens." New York Times 30 June 1998,
    late ed.: A1+.

EDITORIAL OR LETTER TO THE EDITOR

"The Court Vetoes Line Item." Editorial. New York Times
    26 June 1998, late ed.: A32.

Gitter, Elizabeth. Letter. New York Times 28 June 1998,
    late ed., sec. 4: 16.

Internet Sources

When listing sources from the Internet or the World Wide Web, give
the title of the project or database and underline it. Also include the editor, if available. Give the date of publication or date of latest update, if
available, the name of any sponsoring institution, and the date you accessed the source. The uniform resource locator, or URL, which is the
address of the source, appears in angle brackets at the end of the entry.

SCHOLARLY PROJECT

Project Gutenberg. Ed. Michael Hart. 1998. 15 June 1999
    <http://promo.net/pg>.

PROFESSIONAL SITE

MLA on the Web. Modern Language Association. 6 May
    1998. 15 July 1999 <http://www.mla.org>.

PERSONAL SITE

Rosa, Alfred. English 104: Language Awareness. 15 July
    1999 <http://www.uvm.edu/~arosa/1041a.htm>.

BOOK

Whitman, Walt. Leaves of Grass. 1900. Project Bartleby.
    Ed. Steven van Leeuwen. Feb. 1994. Columbia U. 30
    Jan. 1998 <http://www.columbia.edu/acis/bartleby/
    whitman>.

POEM

Blake, William, "London." The William Blake Page. Ed.
    Richard Record. 25 Feb. 1998 <http://members.aa.net/
    ~urizen/experience/soe.html>.

ARTICLE IN A JOURNAL

Kallen, Evelyn. "Hate on the Net: A Question of
    Rights/A Question of Power." Electronic Journal of
    Sociology 3.2 (1997). 1 July 1999 <http://www.soci-
    ology.org/vol003.002/kallen.article.1997.html>.

ARTICLE IN A NEWSPAPER

Broder, David S. "Quayle to Pull Out of GOP Race."
    Washington Post 27 Sept. 1999. 27 Sept. 1999
    <http://washington.com/wp-srv/politics/campaign/
    wh2000/stories/quayle/092799.html>.

Other Sources

TELEVISION OR RADIO PROGRAM

The American Experience: Chicago 1968. Writ. Chana
    Gazit. Narr. W. S. Merwin. PBS. WNET, New York, 13
    Nov. 1997.

MOVIE, VIDEOTAPE, RECORD, OR SLIDE PROGRAM

<u>The X Files</u>. Dir. Rob Bowman. Perf. David Duchovny, Gillian Anderson, Martin Landau, Blythe Danner, and Armin Mueller-Stahl. Twentieth Century Fox, 1998.

PERSONAL INTERVIEW

Alameno, Joseph. Personal interview. 15 Apr. 1998.

LECTURE

Losambe, Lokangaka. Lecture. English 104. U of Vermont Department of English, Burlington. 8 Apr. 1998.

■ A Note on Plagiarism

The importance of honesty and accuracy in doing research can't be stressed enough. Any material borrowed word for word must be placed within quotation marks and be properly cited; any idea, explanation, or argument you have paraphrased or summarized must be documented, and it must be clear where the borrowed material begins and ends. In short, to use someone else's ideas, whether in their original form or in an altered form, without proper acknowledgment is to be guilty of plagiarism. And plagiarism is plagiarism even if it is accidental. A little attention and effort at the note-taking stage can help you eliminate the possibility of inadvertent plagiarism. Check all direct quotations against the wording of the original, and double-check your paraphrases to be sure that you have not used the writer's wording or sentence structure. It is easy to forget to put quotation marks around material taken verbatim or to use a writer's sentence structure and most of his or her words—and record it as a paraphrase. In working closely with the ideas and words of others, intellectual honesty demands that you distinguish between what you borrow—and therefore acknowledge in a citation—and what is your own.

■ An Annotated Student Research Paper

Jake Jamieson's writing assignment was to write an argument, and he was free to choose his own topic. After considering a number of possible topics and doing some preliminary research on several of them, he turned to the material he was studying in another of his courses, which focused on the study of the English language. In that course, he had become intrigued with the English-only movement. As he said, "I chose this topic to do my paper on because it is an aspect of speech that I had previously explored, and my interest was piqued when I heard my instructor talking about the issues, on both sides, involved in the argument. I had done research before on aspects of free speech and people who are attempting to restrict it, but I had never really looked into this issue. After doing some reading on the subject, I realized that it absolutely intrigued me, from the prospect of banning languages other than English right down to the question of funding for bilingualism."

Jake began by brainstorming about his topic. He made lists of ideas, facts, issues, arguments, and opposing arguments. Once he was confident that he had amassed enough information to begin writing, he made a rough outline of an organizational pattern he felt he could work from. Keeping this pattern in mind, Jake wrote a first draft of his essay. Then he went back and examined it carefully, assessing how it could be improved.

After he reread his first draft, he realized that his organization pattern could be clearer and that his examples needed to be sharper and more to the point. He also struck upon the idea of asking a series of rhetorical questions in the eighth paragraph, and he took particular delight in being able to use them in this paper: "I have always enjoyed these kinds of rhetorical questions, and I was excited when I got a chance to sneak them into this paper, lampooning the air of superiority and unwillingness to accept difference that seem to fill the English-only viewpoint." Most importantly, Jake scoured his sources for the most appropriate and memorable quotations to include in his paper, all the while being careful to keep accurate notes on where he found them.

The final draft of Jake's paper illustrates that he has learned how the parts of a well-researched and well-written paper fit together and how to make the revisions that emulate some of the qualities of the model essays he has read and studied. The following is the final draft of Jake's paper.

The English-Only Movement: Can America
Proscribe Language with a Clear Conscience?
Jake Jamieson

A common conception among many people in
this country is that the United States is a giant
cultural "melting pot." For these people, the
melting pot is a place where people from other
places come together and bathe in the warm
waters of assimilation. For many others, however, the melting pot analogy doesn't work. They
see the melting pot as a giant cauldron into
which immigrants are placed; here their cultures,
values, and backgrounds are boiled away in the
scalding waters of discrimination. One major
point of contention in this debate is language:
Should immigrants be pushed toward learning English or encouraged to retain their native
tongues?

Announces melting pot debate

Asks question to be answered in paper

Those who argue that the melting pot analogy
is valid believe that people who come to America
do so willingly and should be expected to become
a part of its culture instead of hanging on to
their past. For them, the expectation that people
who come to this country celebrate this country's
holidays, dress as we do, embrace our values, and
most importantly speak our language is not unreasonable. They believe that assimilation offers
the only way for everyone in this country to live
together in harmony and the only way to dissipate
the tensions that inevitably arise when cultures
clash. A major problem with this argument, however, is that no one seems to be able to agree on
what exactly constitutes "our way" of doing
things.

Not everyone in America is of the same religious persuasion or has the exact same set of values, and different people affect vastly different styles of dress. There are so many sets of variables that it would be hard to defend the argument that there is only one culture in the United States. What seems to be the most widespread constant in our country is that much of the population speaks English, and a major movement is being staged in favor of making English the official language. Making English America's official language would, according to William F. Buckley, involve making it the only language in which government business can be conducted on any level, from federal dealings right down to the local level (16). Many reasons are given to support the notion that making English the official language is a good idea and that it is exactly what this country needs, especially in the face of growing multilingualism. Indeed, one Los Angeles school recently documented sixty different languages spoken in the homes of its students (National Education Association, par. 4).

Defines English as the official language

Uses in-text MLA citation format, including introductory signal phrase and parenthetical page number

Supporters of English-only contend that all government communication must be in English. Because communication is absolutely necessary for a democracy to survive, they believe that the only way to insure the existence of our nation is to make sure a common language exists. Making English official would insure that all government business from ballots to official forms to judicial hearings would have to be conducted in English. According to former senator and presidential candidate Bob Dole, "Promoting English as our national language is not an act of

Introduces English-only position

hostility but a welcoming act of inclusion." He goes on to state that while immigrants are encouraged to continue speaking their native languages, "thousands of children [are] failing to learn the language, English, that is the ticket to the 'American Dream'" (qtd. in Donegan 52).

For those who do not subscribe to this way of thinking, however, this type of legislation is anything but the "welcoming act of inclusion" that it is described to be. For them, anyone attempting to regulate language is treading dangerously close to the First Amendment and must have a hidden agenda of some type. Why, it is asked, make a language official when it is already firmly entrenched and widely used in this country and, according to United States General Accounting Office statistics, 99.96 percent of all federal documents are already in English without legislation to mandate it (Underwood, par. 2)? According to author James Crawford, the answer is quite plain: discrimination. He states that "it is certainly more respectable to discriminate by language than by race." He points out that "most people are not sensitive to language discrimination in this nation, so it is easy to argue that you're doing someone a favor by making them speak English" (51). English-only legislation has been described as bigoted, anti-immigrant, mean-spirited, and steeped in nativism by those who oppose it, and some go so far as to say that this type of legislation will not foster better communication as is the claim, but will instead encourage a "fear of being subsumed by a growing 'foreignness' in our midst" (Mujica and Underwood 65).

Introduces anti-English-only position

Uses example to question English-only position that speaking Spanish in the home is abusive

For example, when a judge in Texas ruled that a mother was abusing her five-year-old girl by speaking to her only in Spanish, an uproar ensued. This ruling was accompanied by the statement that by talking to her in a language other than English, she was "abusing that child and [. . .] relegating her to the position of house maid." This statement was condemned by the National Association for Bilingual Education (NABE) for "labeling the Spanish language as abuse." The judge, Samuel C. Kiser, subsequently apologized to the housekeepers of the nation, adding that he held them "in the highest esteem," but stood firm on his ruling (Donegan 51). One might notice that he went out of his way to apologize to the housekeepers he might have offended but saw no need to apologize to the hundreds of thousands of Spanish speakers whose language had just been belittled in a nationally publicized case.

Argues against the English-only idea of multilingualism as irrational

This tendency of official-English proponents to put down other languages is one that shows up again and again, even though it is maintained that they have nothing against other languages or the people who speak them. If there is no malice toward other languages, why is the use of any language other than English tantamount to lunacy according to an almost constant barrage of literature and editorial opinions? In a recent publication of the "New Year's Resolutions" of various conservative organizations, a group called U.S. English, Inc., stated that the U.S. government was not doing its job of convincing immigrants that they "must learn English to succeed in this country." Instead, according to this publication, "in a bewildering display of irrationality, the U.S. government makes it possible to vote, file a tax return, get married, obtain a driver's license, and become a U.S. citizen in many languages" (Moore 46).

Now, according to this mindset, not only is speaking any language other than English abusive, but it is also irrational and bewildering. What is this world coming to when people want to speak and make transactions in their native language? Why do they refuse to change and become more like us? Why can immigrants not see that speaking English is right and anything else is wrong? These and many other questions are implied by official-English proponents as they discuss the issue.

Asks rhetorical questions

Conservative attorney David Price wrote that official-English legislation is a good idea because many English-speaking Americans prefer "out of pride and convenience to speak their native language on the job" (13). Not only does this statement imply that the pride and convenience of non-English-speaking Americans is unimportant, but that their native tongues are not as important as English. The scariest prospect of all is that this opinion is quickly gaining popularity all around the country.

Points to growing popularity of English-only position

As of early 1996, six official-English bills and one amendment to the Constitution have been proposed in the House and Senate. There are twenty-two states, including Alabama, California, and Arizona, that have made English their official language, and more are debating it every day (Donegan 92). An especially disturbing fact about this debate is that official-English laws always seem to be linked to other anti-immigrant legislation, such as proposals to "limit immigration

Presents status report of English-only legislation

and restrict government benefits to immigrants"
("English-Only Law Faces Test" 1).

Although official-English proponents maintain that their bid for language legislation is
in the best interest of immigrants, the facts
tend to show otherwise. A decision has to be made
in this country about what kind of message we
will send to the rest of the world. Do we plan to
allow everyone in this country the freedom of
speech that we profess to cherish, or will we decide to reserve it only for those who speak the
same language as we do? Will we hold firm to our
belief that everyone is deserving of life, liberty, and the pursuit of happiness in this country? Or will we show the world that we believe in
these things only when they pertain to ourselves
and people like us?

Concludes that English-only legislation is not in our best interest

Works Cited

Follows MLA citation guidelines

Buckley, William F. "Se Hable Ingles: English as
    the Official American Language." National
    Review 9 Oct. 1995: 70-71.
Donegan, Craig. "Debate over Bilingualism: Should
    English Be the Nation's Official Language?"
    CQ Researcher 19 Jan. 1996: 51-71.
"English-Only Law Faces Test." Burlington Free
    Press 26 Mar. 1996: 1.
Moore, Stephen, et al. "New Year's Resolutions."
    National Review 29 Jan. 1996: 46-48.
Mujica, Mauro, and Robert Underwood. "Should En-
    glish Be the Official Language of the United
    States?" CQ Researcher 19 Jan. 1996: 65.
National Education Association. "NEA Statement on
    the Debate over English Only." Teacher's

College, U. of Nebraska, Lincoln. 27 Sept. 1999 <http://www.tc.unl.edu/enemeth/biling/engonly.html>.

Price, David. "English-Only Rules: EEOC Has Gone Too Far." <u>USA Today</u> 28 Mar. 1996, final ed.: A13.

Underwood, Robert A. "English-Only Legislation." U.S. House of Representatives, Washington, D.C., 28 Nov. 1995. 26 Sept. 1999 <http://www.house.gov/underwood/speeches/english.htm>.

Glossary of Useful Terms

Abstract   See *Concrete/Abstract.*

Allusion   An allusion is a passing reference to a familiar person, place, or thing, often drawn from history, the Bible, mythology, or literature. An allusion is an economical way for a writer to capture the essence of an idea, atmosphere, emotion, or historical era, as in "The scandal was his Watergate" or "He saw himself as a modern Job" or "The campaign ended not with a bang but a whimper." An allusion should be familiar to the reader; if it is not, it will add nothing to the meaning.

Analogy   Analogy is a special form of comparison in which the writer explains something unfamiliar by comparing it to something familiar: "A transmission line is simply a pipeline for electricity. In the case of a water pipeline, more water will flow through the pipe as water pressure increases. The same is true of electricity in a transmission line."

Anecdote   An anecdote is a short narrative about an amusing or interesting event. Writers often use anecdotes to begin essays as well as to illustrate certain points.

Argumentation   Argumentation is one of the four basic types of prose. (Narration, description, and exposition are the other three.) To argue is to attempt to persuade the reader to agree with a point of view, to make a given decision, or to pursue a particular course of action. There are two basic types of argumentation: logical and persuasive. See the introduction to Chapter 18 (pp. 420–26) for a detailed discussion of argumentation.

Attitude   A writer's attitude reflects his or her opinion of a subject. The writer can think very positively or very negatively about a subject, or somewhere in between. See also *Tone.*

Audience   An audience is the intended readership for a piece of writing. For example, the readers of a national weekly news magazine come from all walks of life and have diverse interests, opinions, and educational backgrounds. In contrast, the readership for an organic chemistry journal is made up of people whose interests and education are quite similar. The essays in *Models for Writers* are intended for general readers, intelligent people who may lack specific information about the subject being discussed.

Beginnings and Endings   A beginning is the sentence, group of sentences, or section that introduces an essay. Good beginnings usually identify the thesis or controlling idea, attempt to interest readers, and establish a tone.

An ending is the sentence or group of sentences that brings an essay to a close. Good endings are purposeful and well planned. They can be a summary, a concluding example, an anecdote, or a quotation. Endings satisfy readers when they are the natural outgrowths of the essays themselves and give the readers a sense of finality or completion. Good essays do not simply stop; they conclude. See the introduction to Chapter 4 (pp. 85–91) for a detailed discussion of beginnings and endings.

Cause and Effect   Cause-and-effect analysis is a type of exposition that explains the reasons for an occurrence or the consequences of an action. See the introduction to Chapter 17 (pp. 394–96) for a detailed discussion of cause and effect. See also *Exposition.*

Classification   See *Division and Classification.*

Cliché   A cliché is an expression that has become ineffective through overuse. Expressions such as *quick as a flash, jump for joy,* and *slow as molasses* are clichés. Writers normally avoid such trite expressions and seek instead to express themselves in fresh and forceful language. See also *Diction.*

Coherence   Coherence is a quality of good writing that results when all sentences, paragraphs, and longer divisions of an essay are naturally connected. Coherent writing is achieved through (1) a logical sequence of ideas (arranged in chronological order, spatial order, order of importance, or some other appropriate order), (2) the purposeful repetition of key words and ideas, (3) a pace suitable for your topic and your reader, and (4) the use of transitional words and expressions. Coherence should not be confused with unity. (See *Unity.*) See also *Transition.*

Colloquial Expression A colloquial expression is an expression that is characteristic of or appropriate to spoken language or to writing that seeks the effect of spoken language. Colloquial expressions are informal, as *chem, gym, come up with, be at loose ends, won't,* and *photo* illustrate. Thus, colloquial expressions are acceptable in formal writing only if they are used purposefully. See also *Diction.*

Combined Strategies By combining rhetorical strategies, writers are able to develop their ideas in interesting ways. For example, in writing a cause-and-effect essay about a major oil spill, the writer might want to describe the damage that the spill caused, as well as explain the cleanup process step by step.

Comparison and Contrast Comparison and contrast is a type of exposition in which the writer points out the similarities and differences between two or more subjects in the same class or category. The function of any comparison and contrast is to clarify — to reach some conclusion about the items being compared and contrasted. See the introduction to Chapter 16 (pp. 373–76) for a detailed discussion of comparison and contrast. See also *Exposition.*

Conclusions See *Beginnings and Endings.*

Concrete/Abstract A concrete word names a specific object, person, place, or action that can be directly perceived by the senses: *car, bread, building, book, John F. Kennedy, Chicago,* or *hiking.* An abstract word, in contrast, refers to general qualities, conditions, ideas, actions, or relationships that cannot be directly perceived by the senses: *bravery, dedication, excellence, anxiety, stress, thinking,* or *hatred.* See also the introduction to Chapter 8 (pp. 183–88).

Connotation/Denotation Both connotation and denotation refer to the meanings of words. Denotation is the dictionary meaning of a word, the literal meaning. Connotation, on the other hand, is the implied or suggested meaning of a word. For example, the denotation of *lamb* is "a young sheep." The connotations of *lamb* are numerous: *gentle, docile, weak, peaceful, blessed, sacrificial, blood, spring, frisky, pure, innocent,* and so on. See also the introduction to Chapter 8 (pp. 183–88).

Controlling Idea   See *Thesis.*

Coordination   Coordination is the joining of grammatical constructions of the same rank (e.g., words, phrases, clauses) to indicate that they are of equal importance. For example, *They ate hot dogs,* and *we ate hamburgers.* See the introduction to Chapter 7 (pp. 155–59). See also *Subordination.*

Deduction   Deduction is the process of reasoning from stated premises to a conclusion that follows necessarily. This form of reasoning moves from the general to the specific. See the introduction to Chapter 18 (pp. 420–26) for a discussion of deductive reasoning and its relation to argumentation. See also *Syllogism.*

Definition   Definition is one of the types of exposition. Definition is a statement of the meaning of a word. A definition may be either brief or extended, part of an essay or an entire essay itself. See the introduction to Chapter 14 (pp. 331–33) for a detailed discussion of definition. See also *Exposition.*

Denotation   See *Connotation/Denotation.*

Description   Description is one of the four basic types of prose. (Narration, exposition, and argumentation are the other three.) Description tells how a person, place, or thing is perceived by the five senses. See the introduction to Chapter 12 (pp. 287–88) for a detailed discussion of description.

Details   Details are the small elements that collectively contribute to the overall impression of a person, place, thing, or idea. For example, in the sentence "The *organic, whole-grain* dog biscuits were *reddish brown, beef flavored,* and in the *shape of a bone*" the italicized words are details.

Dialogue   Dialogue is the conversation of two or more people as represented in writing. Dialogue is what people say directly to one another.

Diction   Diction refers to a writer's choice and use of words. Good diction is precise and appropriate: the words mean exactly what the writer intends, and the words are well suited to the writer's subject, intended audience, and purpose in writing. The word-conscious writer knows that there are differences among *aged, old,* and *elderly; blue, navy,* and *azure;* and *disturbed, angry,* and *irritated.* Furthermore, this writer knows in which situation to use each word. See the introduction to Chapter 8 (pp. 183–88) for a detailed discussion of diction. See also *Cliché; Colloquial Expression; Connotation/Denotation; Jargon; Slang.*

Division and Classification   Division and classification is one of the types of exposition. When dividing and classifying, the writer first establishes categories and then arranges or sorts people, places, or things into these categories according to their different characteristics, thus making them more manageable for the writer and more understandable and meaningful for the reader. See the introduction to Chapter 15 (pp. 346–49) for a detailed discussion of division and classification. See also *Exposition.*

Dominant Impression   A dominant impression is the single mood, atmosphere, or quality a writer emphasizes in a piece of descriptive writing. The dominant impression is created through the careful selection of details and is, of course, influenced by the writer's subject, audience, and purpose. See also the introduction to Chapter 12 (pp. 287–88).

Emphasis   Emphasis is the placement of important ideas and words within sentences and longer units of writing so that they have the greatest impact. In general, what comes at the end has the most impact, and at the beginning nearly as much; what comes in the middle gets the least emphasis.

Endings   See *Beginnings and Endings.*

Evaluation   An evaluation of a piece of writing is an assessment of its effectiveness or merit. In evaluating a piece of writing, one should ask the following questions: What is the writer's purpose? Is it a worthwhile purpose? Does the writer achieve the purpose? Is the writer's information sufficient and accurate? What are the strengths of the essay? What are its weaknesses? Depending on the type of writing and the purpose, more specific questions can also be asked. For example, with an argument one could ask: Does the writer follow the principles of logical thinking? Is the writer's evidence sufficient and convincing?

Evidence   Evidence is the information on which a judgment or argument is based or by which proof or probability is established. Evidence usually takes the form of statistics, facts, names, examples or illustrations, and opinions of authorities.

Example   An example illustrates a larger idea or represents something of which it is a part. An example is a basic means of developing or clarifying an idea. Furthermore, examples enable writers to show and not simply to tell readers what they mean. See also the introduction to Chapter 10 (pp. 233–36).

Exposition   Exposition is one of the four basic types of prose. (Narration, description, and argumentation are the other three.) The purpose of exposition is to clarify, explain, and inform. The methods of exposition presented in *Models for Writers* are process analysis, definition, illustration, classification, comparison and contrast, and cause and effect. For a detailed discussion of these methods of exposition, see the appropriate chapter introductions.

Facts   Facts are pieces of information presented as having objective reality, that is, having actual existence. For example, water boils at 212°F, Bill Clinton won the 1996 presidential election, and the USSR no longer exists — these are all facts.

Fallacy   See *Logical Fallacy.*

Figure of Speech   A figure of speech is a brief, imaginative comparison that highlights the similarities between things that are basically dissimilar. Figures of speech make writing vivid, interesting, and memorable. The most common figures of speech are

> *Simile:* An explicit comparison introduced by *like* or *as.* "The fighter's hands were like stone."
> *Metaphor:* An implied comparison that makes one thing the equivalent of another. "All the world's a stage."
> *Personification:* A special kind of simile or metaphor in which human traits are assigned to an inanimate object. "The engine coughed and then stopped."

See the introduction to Chapter 9 (pp. 212–13) for a detailed discussion of figurative language.

Focus   Focus is the limitation that a writer gives his or her subject. The writer's task is to select a manageable topic given the constraints of time, space, and purpose. For example, within the general subject of sports, a writer could focus on government support of amateur athletes or narrow the focus further to government support of Olympic athletes.

General   See *Specific/General.*

Idiom   An idiom is a word or phrase that is used habitually with special meaning. The meaning of an idiom is not always readily apparent to nonnative speakers of that language. For example, *catch cold, hold a job, make up your mind,* and *give them a hand* are all idioms in English.

Illustration Illustration is the use of examples to explain, elucidate, or corroborate. Writers rely heavily on illustration to make their ideas both clear and concrete. See the introduction to Chapter 10 (pp. 233–36) for a detailed discussion of illustration.

Induction Induction is the process of reasoning to a conclusion about all members of a class through an examination of only a few members of the class. This form of reasoning moves from the particular to the general. See the introduction to Chapter 18 (pp. 420–26) for a discussion of inductive reasoning and its relation to argumentation.

Inductive Leap An inductive leap is the point at which a writer of an argument, having presented sufficient evidence, moves to a generalization or conclusion. See also *Induction.*

Introductions See *Beginnings and Endings.*

Irony Irony is the use of words to suggest something different from their literal meaning. For example, when Jonathan Swift suggested in "A Modest Proposal" that Ireland's problems could be solved if the people of Ireland fattened their babies and sold them to the English landlords for food, he meant that almost any other solution would be preferable. A writer can use irony to establish a special relationship with the reader and to add an extra dimension or twist to the meaning. See also the introduction to Chapter 8 (pp. 183–88).

Jargon Jargon, or technical language, is the special vocabulary of a trade, profession, or group. Doctors, construction workers, lawyers, and teachers, for example, all have a specialized vocabulary that they use on the job. See also *Diction.*

Logical Fallacy A logical fallacy is an error in reasoning that renders an argument invalid. See the introduction to Chapter 18 (pp. 420–26) for a discussion of the more common logical fallacies.

Metaphor See *Figure of Speech.*

Narration Narration is one of the four basic types of prose. (Description, exposition, and argumentation are the other three.) To narrate is to tell a story, to tell what happened. While narration is most often used in fiction, it is also important in expository writing, either by itself or in conjunction with other types of prose. See the introduction to Chapter 11 (pp. 259–61) for a detailed discussion of narration.

Opinion   An opinion is a belief or conclusion, which may or may not be substantiated by positive knowledge or proof. (If not substantiated, an opinion is a prejudice.) Even when based on evidence and sound reasoning, an opinion is personal and can be changed and is therefore less persuasive than facts and arguments.

Organization   Organization is the pattern or order that the writer imposes on his or her material. Some often-used patterns of organization include time order, space order, and order of importance. See the introduction to Chapter 3 (pp. 65–68) for a detailed discussion of organization.

Paradox   A paradox is a seemingly contradictory statement that is nonetheless true. For example, "We little know what we have until we lose it" is a paradoxical statement.

Paragraph   The paragraph, the single most important unit of thought in an essay, is a series of closely related sentences. These sentences adequately develop the central or controlling idea of the paragraph. This central or controlling idea, usually stated in a topic sentence, is necessarily related to the purpose of the whole composition. A well-written paragraph has several distinguishing characteristics: a clearly stated or implied topic sentence, adequate development, unity, coherence, and an appropriate organizational strategy. See the introduction to Chapter 5 (pp. 112–15) for a detailed discussion of paragraphs.

Parallelism   Parallel structure is the repetition of word order or grammatical form either within a single sentence or in several sentences that develop the same central idea. As a rhetorical device, parallelism can aid coherence and add emphasis. Franklin Roosevelt's statement "I see one-third of a nation ill-housed, ill-clad, and ill-nourished" illustrates effective parallelism.

Personification   See *Figure of Speech*.

Persuasion   Persuasion, or persuasive argument, is an attempt to convince readers to agree with a point of view, to make a decision, or to pursue a particular course of action. Persuasion appeals strongly to the emotions, whereas logical argument does not.

Point of View   Point of view refers to the grammatical person in an essay. For example, first-person point of view uses the pronoun *I* and is commonly found in autobiography and the personal essay; third-person point of view uses the pronouns *he, she,* or *it* and is commonly found in objective writing. See the introduction to Chapter 11 (pp. 259–61) for a discussion of point of view in narration.

Process Analysis   Process analysis is a type of exposition. Process analysis answers the question *how* and explains how something works or gives step-by-step directions for doing something. See the introduction to Chapter 13 (pp. 308–10) for a detailed discussion of process analysis. See also *Exposition.*

Purpose   Purpose is what the writer wants to accomplish in a particular piece of writing. Purposeful writing seeks to *tell* (narration), to *describe* (description), to *explain* (process analysis, definition, classification, comparison and contrast, and cause and effect), or to *convince* (argumentation).

Rhetorical Question   A rhetorical question is asked for its rhetorical effect but requires no answer from the reader. "When will nuclear proliferation end?" is such a question. Writers use rhetorical questions to introduce topics they plan to discuss or to emphasize important points. See the general introduction (pp. 1–25) and the introduction to Chapter 4 (pp. 85–91).

Sentence   A sentence is a grammatical unit that expresses a complete thought. It consists of at least a subject (a noun) and a predicate (a verb). See the introduction to Chapter 7 (pp. 155–59) for a discussion of effective sentences.

Simile   See *Figure of Speech.*

Slang   Slang is the unconventional, very informal language of particular subgroups in our culture. Slang terms, such as *bummed, coke, split, hurt, blow off,* and *cool,* are acceptable in formal writing only if used selectively for specific purposes.

Specific/General   General words name groups or classes of objects, qualities, or actions. Specific words, on the other hand, name individual objects, qualities, or actions within a class or group. To some extent the terms *general* and *specific* are relative. For example, *clothing* is a class of things. *Shirt,* however, is more specific than *clothing* but more general than *T-shirt.* See also *Diction.*

Strategy A strategy is a means by which a writer achieves his or her purpose. Strategy includes the many rhetorical decisions that the writer makes about organization, paragraph structure, sentence structure, and diction. In terms of the whole essay, strategy refers to the principal rhetorical mode that a writer uses. If, for example, a writer wishes to explain how to make chocolate chip cookies, the most effective strategy would be process analysis. If it is the writer's purpose to analyze why sales of American cars have declined in recent years, the most effective strategy would be cause-and-effect analysis.

Style Style is the individual manner in which a writer expresses his or her ideas. Style is created by the author's particular choice of words, construction of sentences, and arrangement of ideas.

Subordination Subordination is the use of grammatical constructions to make one part of a sentence dependent on, rather than equal to, another. For example, the italicized clause in the following sentence is subordinate: They all cheered *when I finished the race.* See the introduction to Chapter 7 (pp. 155–59). See also *Coordination.*

Supporting Evidence See *Evidence.*

Syllogism A syllogism is an argument that utilizes deductive reasoning and consists of a major premise, a minor premise, and a conclusion. For example,

All trees that lose leaves are deciduous. (major premise)
Maple trees lose their leaves. (minor premise)
Therefore, maple trees are deciduous. (conclusion)

See also *Deduction.*

Symbol A symbol is a person, place, or thing that represents something beyond itself. For example, the eagle is a symbol of the United States, and the maple leaf, a symbol of Canada.

Syntax Syntax refers to the way in which words are arranged to form phrases, clauses, and sentences, as well as to the grammatical relationship among the words themselves.

Technical Language See *Jargon.*

Thesis A thesis, also known as the controlling idea, is the main idea of an essay. A thesis may sometimes be implied rather than stated directly in a thesis statement. See the introduction to Chapter 1 (pp. 29–31) for a detailed discussion of thesis.

Title A title is a word or phrase set off at the beginning of an essay to identify the subject, to state the main idea of the essay, or to attract the reader's attention. A title may be explicit or suggestive. A subtitle, when used, explains or restricts the meaning of the main title.

Tone Tone is the manner in which a writer relates to an audience, the "tone of voice" used to address readers. Tone may be friendly, serious, distant, angry, cheerful, bitter, cynical, enthusiastic, morbid, resentful, warm, playful, and so forth. A particular tone results from a writer's diction, sentence structure, purpose, and attitude toward the subject. See the introduction to Chapter 8 (pp. 183–88) for several examples that display different tones.

Topic Sentence The topic sentence states the central idea of a paragraph and thus limits the content of the paragraph. Although the topic sentence normally appears at the beginning of the paragraph, it may appear at any other point, particularly if the writer is trying to create a special effect. Not all paragraphs contain topic sentences. See also *Paragraph.*

Transition A transition is a word or phrase that links sentences, paragraphs, and larger units of a composition in order to achieve coherence. Transitions include parallelism, pronoun references, conjunctions, and the repetition of key ideas, as well as the many conventional transitional expressions such as *moreover, on the other hand, in addition, in contrast,* and *therefore.* See the introduction to Chapter 6 (pp. 134–36) for a detailed discussion of transitions. See also *Coherence.*

Unity Unity is that quality of oneness in an essay that results when all the words, sentences, and paragraphs contribute to the thesis. The elements of a unified essay do not distract the reader. Instead, they all harmoniously support a single idea or purpose. See the introduction to Chapter 2 (pp. 47–49) for a detailed discussion of unity.

Verb Verbs can be classified as either strong verbs *(scream, pierce, gush, ravage,* and *amble)* or weak verbs *(be, has, get,* and *do).* Writers prefer to use strong verbs to make their writing more specific, more descriptive, and more action filled.

Voice   Verbs can be classified as being in either the active or the passive voice. In the active voice, the doer of the action is the grammatical subject. In the passive voice, the receiver of the action is the subject:

Active: Glenda questioned all of the children.
Passive: All of the children were questioned by Glenda.

(continued from copyright page)

Maya Angelou. "Momma, the Dentist, and Me." From *I Know Why the Caged Bird Sings* by Maya Angelou. Copyright © 1969 by Maya Angelou. Reprinted with the permission of Random House, Inc.

Isaac Asimov. "Intelligence." Reprinted with the permission of the Isaac Asimov Estate, c/o Ralph M. Vicinanza Ltd.

Russell Baker. "Becoming a Writer." From *Growing Up* by Russell Baker. Copyright © 1982 by Russell Baker. Published by Congdon & Weed, 1982. Reprinted with the permission of Don Congdon Associates, Inc. "The Plot against People." From the *New York Times,* January 1, 1968. Copyright © 1968 by The New York Times Company. Reprinted by permission.

Diana Bletter. "I Refuse to Live in Fear." From *Mademoiselle,* November 1996. Copyright © 1996 by The Conde Nast Publications, Inc. Reprinted by permission. All rights reserved.

Steve Brody. "How I Got Smart." From the *New York Times,* September 21, 1986. Copyright © 1986 by The New York Times Company. Reprinted by permission.

John Brooks. "The Effects of the Telephone." From *The Telephone: The First Hundred Years* by John Brooks. Copyright © 1975, 1976 by John Brooks. Reprinted with the permission of HarperCollins Publishers, Inc.

Lisa Brown. "Why I Want to Have a Family." From "My Turn," *Newsweek on Campus,* October 1984. Copyright © 1984 by Lisa Brown. Reprinted with the permission of the author.

Sandra Cisneros. "My Name." From *The House on Mango Street* by Sandra Cisneros. Copyright © 1984 by Sandra Cisneros. Published by Vintage Books, a division of Random House, Inc., and in hardcover by Alfred Knopf, 1994. Reprinted with the permission of Susan Bergholz Literary Services, New York. All rights reserved.

James Lincoln Collier. "Anxiety: Challenge by Another Name." From *Reader's Digest,* December 1986. Reprinted with the permission of the author and *Reader's Digest.*

Deborah Dalfonso. "Grammy Rewards." From *Newsweek,* special issue, Winter/Spring 1990. Copyright © 1990 by Newsweek, Inc. Reprinted with the permission of Newsweek.

Gary T. Dempsey. "The Myth of an Emerging Information Underclass." From *The Freeman,* April 1998. Published by the Foundation for Economic Education, Irvington-on-Hudson, New York. Reprinted with the permission of *The Freeman.*

Annie Dillard. "Hitting Pay Dirt" (editor's title). From *An American Childhood* by Annie Dillard. Copyright © 1987 by Annie Dillard. Reprinted with the permission of HarperCollins Publishers, Inc.

Lois Duncan. "How Not to Lose Friends over Money." From *Woman's Day 49,* May 25, 1989. Copyright © 1989 by Hachette Magazines. Reprinted with the permission of the author.

Jim Dwyer, Peter Neufeld, and Barry Scheck. "When Justice Lets Us Down." From *Newsweek,* February 14, 2000. Copyright © 2000 by Newsweek, Inc. Reprinted with the permission of Newsweek.

Lars Eighner. "On Dumpster Diving." From *Travels with Lizbeth* by Lars Eighner. Copyright © 1991, 1993 by Lars Eighner. This essay first appeared in *The Threepenny Review,* Fall 1991. Reprinted with the permission of St. Martin's Press, LLC.

Lynn Wenzel. "Reach Out and Write Someone." From *Newsweek on Campus,* Special Issue, "My Turn" column, January 9, 1984. Reprinted with the permission of the author.

Marianne Wiggins. "Grocer's Daughter." From *Herself in Love and Other Stories.* Copyright © 1987 by Marianne Wiggins. Reprinted with the permission of the Harry Dunow Literary Agency.

Diane Yen-Mei Wong. "Why 'Model Minority' Doesn't Fit." From *USA Weekend,* January 7–9, 1994: 24. Reprinted with the permission of the author.

William Zinsser. "Simplicity." From *On Writing Well,* Sixth Edition. Copyright © 1976, 1980, 1985, 1988, 1990, 1994, 1998 by William Zinsser. Published by HarperCollins Publishers, 1994. "The Right to Fail." From *The Lunacy Boom.* Copyright © 1969, 1970 by William Zinsser. Both reprinted with the permission of the author and Carol Brissie.

Art:
Nigel Holmes. "Hi, my name is BILL, but I'm changing it to LAW" illustration. Reprinted by permission.

Index

Research and Writing Online

Whether you want to investigate the ideas behind a thought-provoking essay or conduct in-depth research for a paper, the Web resources for *Models for Writers* can help you find what you need on the Web—and then use it once you find it.

The English Research Room for Navigating the Web

www.bedfordstmartins.com/english_research

The Web brings a flood of information to your screen, but it still takes skill to track down the best sources. Not only does *The English Research Room* point you to some reliable starting places for Web investigations, but it also lets you tune up your skills with interactive tutorials.

•Do you want to improve your skill at searching electronic databases, online catalogs, and the Web? Try the *Interactive Tutorials* for some hands-on practice.

•Do you need quick access on online search engines, reference sources, and research sites? Explore *Research Links* for some good starting places.

•Do you have questions on evaluating the sources you find, navigating the Web, or conducting research in general? Consult one of our *Reference Units* for authoritative advice.

Research and Documentation Online for Including Sources in Your Writing

www.bedfordstmartins.com/resdoc

Including sources correctly in a paper is often a challenge, and the Web has made it even more complex. This online version of the popular booklet *Research and Documentation in the Electronic Age,* by Diana Hacker, provides clear advice for the humanities, social sciences, history, and the sciences on—

•Which Web and library sources are relevant to your topic (with links to Web sources)

•How to integrate outside material into your paper

•How to cite sources correctly, using the appropriate documentation style

•What the format for the final paper should be

Instructor's Resource Manual
to Accompany

MODELS
for
WRITERS
Short Essays for Composition

Seventh Edition

ALFRED ROSA / PAUL ESCHHOLZ

Betsy Eschholz

Instructor's Resource Manual
to Accompany

Models
for
Writers

Instructor's Resource Manual
to Accompany

Models
for
Writers

Short Essays for Composition

SEVENTH EDITION

Alfred Rosa

Paul Eschholz

Prepared by

Betsy Eschholz

BEDFORD / ST. MARTIN'S

Boston ◆ *New York*

Manufactured in the United States of America.

6 5 4 3 2 1
f e d c b a

For information, write:
Bedford/St. Martin's, 75 Arlington Street, Boston, MA 02116
(617-399-4000)

ISBN: 0-312-25959-X

Preface

The purpose of this *Instructor's Resource Manual* is to help you use *Models for Writers* with the greatest effectiveness. We therefore provide for each selection in the book a fairly detailed analysis of the essay as a whole. In these sections of the manual, labeled *Essay Analysis and Discussion,* we try to share with you our experiences in teaching the essays—what to stress, what to explain, what to ask about, and what to expect generally from discussions. In addition, a typical analysis might do one or more of the following:

- explore one or more content issues
- point out stylistic features
- suggest classroom activities that reinforce rhetorical strategies
- suggest one or more other essays in the text that might be usefully taught in conjunction with the present one
- explain where students are likely to have difficulty understanding either content or rhetorical techniques

In addition, we provide in the section called *Questions for Study and Discussion* suggested responses to the questions following each selection. Our intent is to save you time, not to dictate answers. On occasion you may disagree with our interpretation or emphasis, but we trust that the suggested responses here will be useful at least as starting points. There are no substitutes for your own experience with each essay or for common sense about what will challenge and engage your students. Also included are definitions for the words featured in each *Vocabulary* exercise and detailed discussions of what you might expect from each of the *Classroom Activities.*

The essays in *Models for Writers* are grouped into eighteen chapters, each devoted to a separate rhetorical topic. The first seven chapters focus on specific elements of essays: thesis, unity, organization, beginnings and endings, paragraphs, transitions, and effective sentences. The next two chapters concern some uses and effects of language: diction and tone, and figurative language. The final nine chapters explore types of essays: illustration, narration, description, process analysis, definition, division and classification, comparison and contrast, cause and effect, and argument.

The arrangement of the chapters suggests a logical teaching sequence, from the elements of an essay through the language of an essay to the types of essays. An alternative teaching strategy is to structure your course according to the types of essays, teaching other chapters as necessary or having students use them for reference. Finally, because each chapter is self-contained, you can design your own teaching sequence, omitting or emphasizing particular chapters according to the special needs of your class.

To help you use the book effectively, we would like to call your attention to the following special features:

General Introduction. An enlarged introduction provides guidelines for reading and writing short essays and includes four sample student papers with annotations that highlight the elements of an essay that are emphasized in the text proper. The sample papers and the analyses that accompany them provide the opportunity to show and discuss with your class how four students went about completing typical writing assignments. Moreover, the sample papers give students a good idea of the length and quality of writing they should be striving to produce. We suggest, therefore, that you assign this introduction early in the course and that you spend as much time as possible discussing the student papers and their salient features.

Chapter Introductions. Before reading the essays in a particular chapter, students should read the chapter introduction. There they will find an explanation of the rhetorical principle under consideration and a discussion of how it can be used. The information in the introductions will also help students to answer the questions and do the writing assignments that accompany each selection.

Questions for Study and Discussion. The study questions for each selection focus on its content, its author's purpose, and the rhetorical principle used to achieve that purpose. Some of the questions require brief answers, and others are intended to stimulate class discussion. Because students' knowledge of rhetorical techniques and patterns will increase as the course proceeds, we have included for each essay one or more questions about rhetorical elements other than the one highlighted in the particular essay.

Vocabulary. We have tried to emphasize each author's choice of words and have included an exercise on vocabulary building for every essay. The vocabulary words in these exercises are defined in this manual and can be used for a vocabulary test for each essay or chapter.

Classroom Activities. These brief exercises (requiring fifteen to twenty minutes in most cases) enable students to work with each rhetorical element, technique, or pattern in the classroom, often in groups. The activities included here will help students develop thesis statements, organize sentences within paragraphs, use strong action verbs, work with connotation and denotation, use figurative language, use examples to document a generalization, use facts effectively, work with outlines for comparison and contrast, test cause-and-effect relationships, classify on the basis of distinctive characteristics, and build argumentative evidence. Frequently, these activities require students to engage in critical thinking and problem-solving. We have used all of these activities in our own writing classes, and our students have found them helpful.

Suggested Writing Assignments. At least two writing assignments accompany each essay in the textbook. They offer students the opportunity to apply the rhetorical principle at hand. Often these assignments are related to the content of the essays as well; but most can be assigned independently if you prefer not to assign all the readings.

Writing Documented Essays. An appendix on the documented research essay includes up-to-date instruction on using print sources and on using Internet sources as well as guidelines for evaluating the authority and reliability of print and Internet sources. Instruction is provided on note-taking—including summaries, paraphrases, and direct quotations—and on integrating borrowed material into papers. Also provided are models for using the most current Modern Language Association documentation style, including in-text citations and list of works cited.

Glossary of Useful Terms. This glossary is located at the end of the book and provides students with concise definitions of terms useful for discussing the readings and their own writing. Wherever we have felt that information in the glossary might assist students in answering a study question, we have placed a cross-reference to the appropriate glossary entry next to the question.

Thematic Contents. If a particular essay evokes strong student response, this alternative table of contents makes it easier for you to choose thematically related pieces in other sections of *Models for Writers*. Nearly all the readings are entered under at least one subject heading, and many appear under two or three. Admittedly, some of these classifications may seem a bit arbitrary, but we believe that none are misfits. Beyond calling attention to the content of individual essays, this listing also allows you to point out different rhetorical approaches to common themes.

Finally, we are very much interested in hearing from anyone who has constructive ideas about the content or use of either *Models for*

Writers or this manual. We can be reached at the Department of English, 400 Old Mill, University of Vermont, Burlington, Vermont 05405.

Alfred Rosa
Paul Eschholz
Betsy Eschholz

Contents

CHAPTER 1 **Thesis**

The Most Important Day (p. 32)
■ **Helen Keller**

Essay Analysis and Discussion

The first paragraph of this essay, though short, is vital to establishing focus and direction for the paragraphs that follow. The first sentence states the thesis, but without the two sentences following it, the essay would lose the unity Keller has achieved. To get students to see the connection between the thesis statement and the opening paragraph as a whole, and their relation to the rest of the essay, have them consider what each of the first three sentences accomplishes in regard to the other paragraphs. It may help to look at the stages of Keller's narration (as they are outlined in study question 6) to see if there is a correlation between those stages and the three sentences in the opening paragraph. The students' analysis should reveal that though the thesis statement focuses on a particular day, the essay can include discussion of other days and other events and remain unified because of the context established by the entire first paragraph.

Questions for Study and Discussion

1. Keller's thesis is the first sentence of the essay. Keller answers the question "What is the most important day in my life and why is that day important?" This question focuses Keller on a specific period in her life, that time when Anne Mansfield Sullivan opened up the world of words to her, which, in turn, let her think and communicate with others. Keller's thesis answers the first part of the question and her narrative explains the importance of that day.
2. Keller's purpose is to *tell* why the day that Anne Sullivan came to her was the most important day in her life.
3. For several weeks before Anne Sullivan arrived, Keller was angry and bitter. When that passed she fell into a "deep languor." She compared the feeling to being a ship in a fog of darkness groping its way to shore.
4. Every new name gave birth to a new thought. Words would "make the world blossom for me."

1

5. Keller understood the connection between words and the things they describe one day, after many such days, when her teacher placed one of Keller's hands under running water while she spelled the word *water* in the other. "Suddenly I felt a misty consciousness as of something forgotten—a thrill of returning thought; and somehow the mystery of language was revealed to me."
6. On the first day, she meets Anne Sullivan and they embrace. On the next day, Anne gives her a doll and spells the word *doll* on her hand until Keller is able to imitate the spelling. Several weeks later, Anne again tries to make the connection between objects and words (e.g., *mug* and *water* and *doll*) and is finally able to accomplish this at the well-house with the word *water* and the actual water.

Vocabulary

dumb (2) lacking the faculty of speech; mute
preyed (2) exerted an injurious effect
languor (2) sluggishness
passionate (2) expressing or revealing strong emotion
plummet (3) a weight tied to a line that is used to measure the depth of the sea
tussle (6) struggle or scuffle
vainly (8) unsuccessfully

Classroom Activity Using Thesis

Some questions that our students suggested include the following:

1. How serious is our campus wastepaper problem?
2. How much of our paper waste is currently being recycled?
3. How can our wastepaper be effectively used?
4. What is made from recycled paper?
5. What are the problems of collecting wastepaper on campus?
6. Is recycling paper waste an economic or an environmental issue, or both?
7. Does the campus newspaper use recycled newsprint?
8. What recycled paper products are currently being used on campus?
9. If we don't recycle wastepaper on campus, what will be the impact on our environment?
10. What other items, if any, are being recycled on campus?

Your students will come up with questions of their own, questions that perhaps focus on the situation on your campus. Ask students to discuss what information is needed and where they would be likely to obtain that information to answer each of their questions on recycling.

Anxiety: Challenge by Another Name (p. 37)
■ **James Lincoln Collier**

Essay Analysis and Discussion

Collier arranges his essay chronologically, beginning with his youth and coming into the present, to demonstrate his thesis that we can learn to overcome the stultifying effects of anxiety. At each era of his life, he pauses to use examples from philosophy, psychology, and other peoples' lives to illustrate and strengthen his argument. The examples he uses are common enough that the reader can sympathize with and relate to the author's point of view. At three different points, Collier also punctuates the essay with his rule and its corollaries, the conclusions he has drawn about anxiety and its relationship to learning. Ask students to think about some of the rules they have learned for themselves. Then ask them to describe, using examples, how these rules might have universal application. Remind them to use examples of situations that are easily identified by the other students in the class. They might try writing about lessons they learned over time, as well as ones they learned quickly, after one hapless episode. How would the arrangement of material differ in that case?

Questions for Study and Discussion

1. Collier states his thesis in paragraph 20: "The new, the different, is almost by definition scary. But each time you try something, you learn, and as the learning piles up, the world opens to you." Students will explain their own experience with Collier's thesis.
2. Collier explains extinction in paragraph 14.
3. Collier came up with his basic rule for himself after turning down an offer to work in Argentina one summer. He developed his first corollary as a result of reflecting upon what he went through while interviewing famous people. He developed his second corollary as a result of his hesitating to accept a three-month assignment to work in Europe. By sharing the three experiences that led him to develop his basic rule and the two corollaries, Collier makes it easy for readers to accept his thesis. By the time readers reach paragraph 20, they are already familiar with the life situations that gave Collier his insight and understanding.

3

4. Collier means to demonstrate, based on his own experience, that we can overcome anxiety and in so doing can live a richer, fuller life.
5. Collier uses personification to depict anxiety as a traveling companion.
6. These paragraphs contrast with the first paragraph in Collier's essay to show that over time he has learned to overcome the kind of anxiety that kept him "safe" at home when he was a young adult.

Vocabulary

daunted (2) lessened the courage of
proposition (3) something proposed for consideration
anxiety (5) abnormal apprehension and fear
depression (5) an emotional disorder marked by sadness, inactivity, or difficulty in concentration
butterflies (5) a fluttery sensation accompanying nervousness
crack (6) attempt; try
venture (10) an understanding involving chance or risk
corollary (15) a natural consequence, result, or conclusion

Classroom Activity Using Thesis

Sentences 1, 2, 4, and 6 identify the topic and make an assertion about that topic that the writer must document in the body of the essay. Sentences 3 and 5, however, are weak as thesis statements; both sentences are too general and opinionated. By way of discussion, have students talk about what they would expect to read in an essay about each topic. Students' expectations for sentences 1, 2, 4, and 6 should be clearer than their expectations for sentences 3 and 5.

Why "Model Minority" Doesn't Fit (p. 43)
■ **Diane Yen-Mei Wong**

Essay Analysis and Discussion

Using personal experience to bring immediacy to a general argument can be an effective technique to grab the reader's attention. It is often difficult to mesh the two elements into a unified essay, however. Wong's essay is effective and unified because she uses her personal experience to draw the reader in, then establishes it as a springboard to address the larger issues involved. Paragraph 4 leads the reader

4

smoothly from one point of view to the other. She adds paragraph 13 to put her general argument back in the context of her original story, yielding a more unified essay. How do your students react to Wong's assertion that there are no good stereotypes?

Questions for Study and Discussion

1. Wong begins with a personal anecdote to grab the reader's attention and to provide a motivation for her essay. By starting with a specific experience that backs up the general argument presented later, she makes the reader ready to accept her point of view. The paragraphs help unify her essay by allowing her to reference her personal experience again in paragraph 13. By doing this, she brings the essay together as she reveals the consequences of the problems in the Asian American community.

2. Wong's thesis is that it is wrong to stereotype the Asian American community. She states it in paragraph 5. The advantages of stating it so late in the essay are explored above.

3. Wong's audience is society as a whole; she states that people both in and out of the Asian American community perpetuate the model minority stereotype.

4. The model minority stereotype is harmful because it encourages people to ignore the increasing problems in the Asian American community. Wong illustrates her argument by identifying the problems that are present, such as poverty and violence.

5. In paragraph 13, Wong comments on the story she introduces in her opening four paragraphs, a story that frames her essay. At the end of paragraph 4, she says that this murder "has compelled me to rethink how I view my own community of Asian Americans." In paragraph 13, she returns to this thought, wondering how the acknowledgment of crime within the Asian American community affects the perception of that community at large.

6. Paragraph 14 summarizes Wong's argument by reviewing the commonly held myths about Asian Americans and the reality that Asian Americans "are more like everyone else than some of us ever thought." Wong restates her thesis in the last sentence of this paragraph. Most readers find this conclusion effective because it neatly summarizes the essence of her argument without repeating the details of the examples that she uses.

Vocabulary

render (2) give
septuagenarian (2) person in his or her seventies

extort (2) obtain through threats
valedictorians (7) high school academic leaders
espouses (7) advocates; supports
mantra (8) chant; prayer

Classroom Activity Using Thesis

Our students gave us these thesis statements as answers:

1. The "model minority" label has blinded Asian Americans and the public in general to the realities of life in the United States.
2. Asian Americans have been stereotyped because people equated Asians' respect for family, authority, hard work, and educational achievement with model behavior.
3. Asian Americans have to shed the stereotype of "model minority."

Your students, of course, will come up with other thesis statements or variations on the ones we have given. It's instructive to put all alternative theses on the board or overhead projector for analysis and discussion.

CHAPTER 2 **Unity**

My Name (p. 50)
■ **Sandra Cisneros**

Essay Analysis and Discussion

Cisneros's essay is at once very simple and very challenging. Despite its brevity, it should yield several excellent discussion topics. First, its unity may not be apparent to many students, especially in paragraph 3. Cisneros's great-grandmother is vital to the discussion of her name, however, because of the obvious connection they have, not just in their given names but in their personalities as well. Students should understand the irony that two such strong-willed women should be named "hope." Also discuss why Cisneros presents her name so late in her essay. What does the reader think while reading the essay before she states her name? How does it make the similes in the first paragraph more effective if you have to wait to consider why the name is like the number nine or a muddy color? Finally, students should enjoy the idea of choosing a new name. What does Zeze the X communicate to them about Cisneros?

Questions for Study and Discussion

1. Cisneros's thesis is that she has inherited her grandmother's name, with all of its associations, but she does not want to be trapped by it. She states the thesis at the end of paragraph 4.

2. Cisneros's essay is unified in that each paragraph is logically related to her thesis. There are no digressions and there is no unrelated information. In the first paragraph, she presents the meaning and associations of her name. In the second, third, and fourth paragraphs she presents the family history of her name, and of her identification with the personality of her great-grandmother, if not with her ultimate situation. In the fifth she establishes how she is unable to escape her name. In the sixth, she explains just how far she would go to escape it.

3. The name *Esperanza* is part of a culture that does not encourage strength in women. Using her name as the subject, Cisneros presents her heritage of cultural restrictions and her overwhelming desire to escape them.

4. The similes are open to interpretation, but students should demonstrate that some thought went into their answers. Most students, after having read the essay, will probably say that the similes give the impression that the narrator holds a negative opinion of the name, but other interpretations would be interesting.

5. Cisneros's tone is angry and defiant. She establishes it best in paragraph 2, where she attacks the Chinese for their view of women that parallels the Hispanic one. She also says bluntly that she will not be at all content with her great-grandmother's role in life. The tone helps her convey her desire to escape the associations that her name carries with it.

6. This is open to various interpretations, but Cisneros involves the reader by presenting intriguing similes and an intriguing personality associated with her name without revealing what the name is. The reader wonders what name is like a muddy color or the number nine, and by the time it is revealed, the reader is interested and aware of Cisneros's contempt for what her name implies.

7. Again, this is open to interpretation. Most students should pick up on the fact that it is unusual, dramatic, and hard-edged.

Vocabulary

sobbing (1) weeping or crying uncontrollably
chandelier (3) hanging light fixture, often very ornate

baptize (6)   perform the Christian ceremony of baptism by initiating with cleansing and water

Classroom Activity Using Unity

Before starting this exercise, students should reread the introduction to the Unity chapter. Students can analyze their own paragraphs individually or they can exchange paragraphs with each other. In testing paragraphs for unity, students should look for sentences or portions of sentences that stray from the subject. Have students read their paragraphs aloud to the class and explain why their paragraphs are unified or how they need to be revised.

Life under the Chief Doublespeak Officer (p. 53)
■ William Lutz

Essay Analysis and Discussion

Many students will find Lutz's essay entertaining, but they should be reminded that his topic is a very serious one—doublespeak. As Lutz says, "doublespeak is language that only pretends to say something; it's language that hides, evades or misleads." Such language misrepresents reality and allows what is unpleasant or even dangerous to be acceptable. Lutz himself reminds us in his pointed conclusion that "doublespeak can pay for the company, but usually not for the workers who lose their jobs." One of the real strengths of Lutz's essay is his use of examples from the world of business. These examples show how pervasive doublespeak is in America and clearly establish Lutz's authority as the "chief doublespeak officer."

Questions for Study and Discussion

1. Lutz states his thesis in the opening sentence. He argues that American business is the source of an extraordinarily high quantity of the doublespeak produced in this country.

2. In paragraph 2, Lutz explains the range of doublespeak by giving examples of words that "no one really understands" as well as words that try "to hide meaning." In paragraphs 3 through 12, Lutz provides examples of doublespeak from the worlds of truck driving, waste removal, and travel and banking, as well as from such business-related operations as job titles and personnel management including firings, downsizing, and plant closings. In paragraphs 13 and 14, Lutz draws his conclusion about doublespeak in the workplace.

3. In jumping from one business to another, Lutz runs the risk of having his essay sound choppy. The one unifying factor, however, is the subject doublespeak, and he is careful to use that word near the beginning of paragraphs 2, 3, 5, 7, and 13. He uses the coordinate conjunction "but" at the beginning of paragraph 9 to link that paragraph to the previous one. His line "let me count the ways" at the end of paragraph 9 transitions nicely into the list of corporate doublespeak at the beginning of paragraph 10. By beginning paragraphs 11 and 12 with "one company" and "an automobile company," Lutz indicates that these are both specific examples of the point made in paragraph 10. Ask students to suggest where Lutz might have used a transitional expression or repeated a key word or idea to make a stronger link between paragraphs.

4. Lutz ends his essay with quotations from two cartoon characters. While most students will be familiar with Dilbert, some may not know of Pogo, which was popular several generations ago. Each of these quotations causes us to smile but at the same time recognizes the serious import of what Lutz is saying about doublespeak in the business world. Together, these two quotations provide an effective reflection on his conclusion in paragraph 13.

5. Although students' language will vary, it should point to the way in which doublespeak deceives, manipulates, misrepresents, and misleads. Some students will feel that doublespeak deliberately lies. While we sometimes find the absurdity of some constructions humorous, we have to remember that doublespeak is both conscious and deliberate. This question offers you the opportunity to discuss whether doublespeak can ever be used in a positive way. For example, how do students feel about euphemisms that are used to avoid offensive labels and terms?

6. To combat doublespeak, people need to be aware of its existence and how it affects them. Without such awareness, people are vulnerable to the deceptive, manipulative power of those using doublespeak. As an expert on doublespeak, Lutz is fulfilling his obligation to inform the public. Educating the public is a first step toward a solution that, in turn, can lead to others.

Vocabulary

evades (1) to escape or avoid by cleverness or deceit
dismantlers (4) people who take apart or tear down
procurement (5) to obtain, acquire, or bring about
ethics (5) the rules or standards governing the conduct of the members of a profession

outplacement (6) locating new positions outside the company for employees to be terminated

rationalization (9) the act, process, or practice of devising self-satisfying but incorrect reasons for actions or policies

severance (12) a sum of money usually based on length of employment for which an employee is eligible upon termination

Classroom Activity Using Unity

This activity is meant to be somewhat amusing, but it should also be a good exercise for students who tend to get sidetracked in their writing. All of the extraneous sentences are closely related to the subject matter, but they add nothing to the essay's message, and most students will easily recognize the problem in someone else's writing, even if they have trouble identifying it in their own. The following sentences should be eliminated:

Paragraph 1 "Whether the walls . . ."
Paragraph 2 "Most of the students lived . . ."
           "Mr. Norant was known . . ."
Paragraph 3 "A cheerleader in college . . ."
           "Among those she fired . . ."

Discuss the reasons these sentences detract from the unity of the essay. Also, have students discuss what the other sentences contribute to the writer's argument.

The Meanings of a Word (p. 59)
■ Gloria Naylor

Essay Analysis and Discussion

In her essay, Naylor uses illustration to argue that there are two different definitions of the word *nigger*, depending on who is using it and to what purpose. In so doing, Naylor makes the larger point that all of language is similarly subject to interpretation and change depending on the "context." Readers will notice that Naylor concentrates most of her essay on illustrating the lesser-known meaning of the word *nigger* as it is used in African American culture. This imbalance is based on Naylor's assumption that most of her readers will be familiar with the racist connotation of the word as it is used in the white culture. Students can choose a word that has both a familiar and a lesser-known meaning to discuss in an essay. Then, using Naylor's essay as a guide, they can illustrate the ways in which the understanding of that word changes from culture to culture or from speaker to speaker.

Questions for Study and Discussion

1. The subject of Naylor's opening two paragraphs is language. While Naylor has the greatest respect for the written word, she considers the spoken word more powerful for coming at the instant of a thought and being expressed in the full dynamic interplay of all the senses. She points to the fact that words are simply arbitrary symbols that derive their meaning from the consensus of people who use them. She develops this thesis with a series of examples in the remainder of her essay.

2. Naylor best defines *nigger* in its role as a racial slur in paragraph 14: "a word that whites used to signify worthlessness or degradation." *Nigger* as used by African Americans is best expressed in the same paragraph: "Gathering there together, they transformed *nigger* to signify the varied and complex human beings they knew themselves to be."

3. Naylor means simply that the word *nigger* was used in her family in a context of love, admiration, and affection that allowed it to dwell there comfortably and unnoticed. In her third-grade class, she heard it expressed in a hostile context, for an altogether different purpose—as an insult. In other words, it was not the same word she had heard all her life and so she was hearing it for the first time.

4. Naylor includes details of her family's history, its structure, the neighborhood in which they all lived, the activities they enjoyed, the ways they earned their livings, and the substance of their conversations as a means of establishing the context in which their use of the word *nigger* arose. The little she offers in the way of a definition of the word *nigger* as used by the white community is disquieting to any reader who notices the omission and so is jolted to an awareness of not needing to be told what the word means.

5. Naylor could hardly have been faulted had she used an angry tone to describe the different meanings of the word *nigger*. However, she has chosen to use a level, objective tone—as if she were standing back casting a cold, educated glance at the phenomenon that has hurt so many of her people. In paragraph 3, when she recounts the moment she first heard the word *nigger* as a slur, Naylor describes the event rather matter-of-factly: "I remember the first time I heard the word *nigger*. . . . Had he called me a nymphomaniac or a necrophiliac, I couldn't have been more

puzzled." Throughout her essay she analyzes the meaning of the word *nigger* as an anthropologist might under the white light of science. It is not until her final sentence that Naylor reveals the sadness and fatigue that we can assume came after who knows how long an effort to assimilate her initial feelings of confusion, shock, anger, and betrayal.

6. Naylor's final sentence is effective for reminding the reader once again that "in America" the primary use of the word *nigger* will be as a racial slur and is one that most readers do not have to sit on their mothers' laps to have explained.

Vocabulary

transcendent (1) exceeding usual limits; passing beyond material existence

innocuous (2) harmless; inoffensive

consensus (2) collective opinion

nymphomaniac (3) a female with excessive sexual desire

necrophiliac (3) one who is sexually attracted to the dead

mecca (4) a place sought as a goal by many people, usually religious

clamor (5) vigorous, noisy protest or demand

anecdotes (5) brief stories of interesting, usually biographical, incidents

inflections (5) the changes in form that words undergo to make case, gender, number, tense, person, mood, or voice; changes in the tone or mood in speech that signal a word's connotations and the emotions it is being used to express

unkempt (10) disheveled; not combed

trifling (10) of little value or importance

internalization (14) the incorporation of an attitude into one's thinking

impotent (14) helpless; lacking in power or strength

Classroom Activity Using Unity

Paragraph 2 is the one that does not belong because it disrupts the unity of Gladstone's advice on building a fireplace fire. In paragraph 1 he gives the basic steps in building a fire. In paragraphs 3 through 5 he discusses three common mistakes that readers could make. Paragraph 2, which discusses the joys of a fireplace fire in winter and the need to properly maintain both the fireplace and the chimney, digresses from the writer's point. While the paragraph offers advice, the advice offered is not specifically about building a fire.

A *View from the Bridge* (p. 69)
■ **Cherokee Paul McDonald**

Essay Analysis and Discussion

McDonald's essay is remarkable not only for the story that he tells but also for the vivid description that he uses. He organizes his narration chronologically and lets his story unfold through the use of dialogue between the narrator (presumably McDonald himself) and the young boy fishing. This dialogue enables McDonald to show us that the child is blind instead of telling us. Interestingly, the events that McDonald recounts occur within a half hour. Finally, take the opportunity that this essay offers to discuss with your students what it means to "see." How, for example, are the narrator and the boy using the word "see" in paragraphs 42 and 43?

Questions for Study and Discussion

1. McDonald has organized his essay chronologically. The essay recounts an incident that took place in perhaps 30 minutes—certainly no more than an hour.
2. The kid wore wrap-around sunglasses (3). He was "fumbling" with his rod and reel (4); he could not see the shrimp by his foot (10); his fingers "felt" for the drag setting (16); he thought he had lost the fish when the line went slack (20); and he asked the narrator to tell him what the fish looked like (29). The narrator does not realize the kid is blind because he is preoccupied with his jogging and because the kid is a competent fisherman whose behavior does not arouse suspicion.
3. The narrator seeks to use words and phrases that are familiar to a child. He also looks for words that appeal to a sense other than sight. (For example, he starts to say that the fish is three feet long but then changes to the more concrete and sensory phrase, "as long as one of your arms" [33].) The effect is a description both accessible and vivid.
4. We learn that the kid is courteous; he says "please" (5 and 8) and "thanks" (12 and 42). He is, against all odds, a capable, determined fisherman (15, 24, and 47). Both the act of fishing and the fish itself give him tremendous delight. We see his joy in hooking and playing the fish (15 and 22), his pleasure in the narrator's description, and his desire to set the fish free (37).

5. The dialogue in this narrative plays up the shared interests between the narrator and the kid as well as their developing relationship. It gives the essay an informal tone. It brings the reader right into the scene, to see and overhear the event directly. Without the dialogue, the story would have lost its immediacy. The writer would have been reporting or telling us what happened instead of showing us.
6. The narrator is both acknowledging the kid's thanks and reciprocating them. As he describes the tarpon carefully to please the kid, the narrator comes to his own renewed sense of wonder and appreciation for the beauty of the fish.
7. A view is not just what is seen but a perspective, a way of seeing. The bridge spans the water, but it also represents the connection of respect and understanding that develops between the narrator and the kid.

Vocabulary

negotiate (1) to succeed in accomplishing or coping with
exasperated (9) irritated
tarpon (14) large game fish of tropical Atlantic waters
pilings (23) a structure of long, slender columns driven vertically into the ground or ocean floor

Classroom Activity Using Organization

Ask students if they see any patterns in the information presented or if they drew any conclusions about these seven states. Depending on their answers (their purposes), students could organize a discussion of these seven states in a number of ways: (1) chronologically according to the date each state entered the union; (2) spatially from east to west, north to south, etc.; (3) smallest to largest; (4) by population density; or (5) by impact on elections. This activity lets students discover that there are always several ways in which they can organize information, and that purpose is essential in making an appropriate choice.

Reach Out and Write Someone (p. 75)
■ **Lynn Wenzel**

Essay Analysis and Discussion

Wenzel offers the reasons we should cultivate and cherish the art of letter writing. She begins with historical reasons and finishes with the implications for our own lives, which she deems the most important. She argues that good writing demands all the components of good thinking. In presenting her case, Wenzel contrasts old-fashioned values with the ease and convenience of the modern world. She reminds her reader that modern technology exacts a toll—in this case, a literal monetary one as well as the loss of the art of personal correspondence. Students can discuss whether they agree with Wenzel. Then ask them to write letters to each other, specifically about topics they have recently discussed over the phone with friends or family. Have them read the letters aloud in class and discuss how, if at all, the quality and content of a letter differ from those of a phone call.

Questions for Study and Discussion

1. Wenzel states her thesis, that the talent of letter writing is being lost in this technological age in paragraph 2.

2. Other forms of creative writing such as fiction and poetry are alive and well in our culture. It is the art of letter writing that is in danger of becoming extinct.

3. "Much of our knowledge of events and of the people who lived them is based on such commonplace communication," Wenzel says in her essay. Without letters we would be left with dates and names but would be bereft of the causes and effects. Letters have also contributed enormously to our knowledge of women's lives and thus have given us much of the women's history that is taking its place alongside "weighty tomes about men's contributions to the changing world."

4. Letter writing requires thinking in a way that a phone call does not, because the words can never be taken back. It demands "thought, logic, organization and sincerity," qualities that Wenzel believes we must not lose but must cultivate and "bring to luster."

5. Wenzel uses chronological and logical order in developing her essay. Students will find examples from the early days of our history in the beginning of the essay, examples of recent history in the middle, and the shortcomings of the telephone at the end. Wenzel considers all of her reasons important; however, she labels "thinking" at the end of the essay as the most important reason of all.

6. Wenzel uses a common device in rhetoric. She begins and ends with the same thought. When we first read of the breaking up of the phone company and the resulting dependency on letter writing, we may feel panicky. By the end of the essay, we are convinced that we need to worry more about losing the gentle art of letter writing.

Vocabulary

exorbitant (1) exceeding what is usual or proper
fomenting (6) stirring up; instigating
tomes (8) books, especially large or weighty ones
accouterments (10) personal clothing, accessories, etc.
seal (10) a device having a raised design that can be stamped on clay
    or wax

Classroom Activity Using Organization

William Least Heat Moon organizes his paragraph spatially—he moves from the center of the store to the outside walls. After telling us how the store was lit and what it smelled like as one walks in, he takes us to the stove in the middle of the rectangular room. From that point he moves his description to the table to the right of the stove and then to the goods on the shelves around the walls.

In sketching Thurmond Watts's store, students will discover the telling details that Least Heat Moon provides to flesh out his description of the inside of the store: three fifty-watt bulbs, sagging oak floor, iron stove, wooden table, unfinished checkers game, apple-tree stump stool, shelving, earthen jugs with corncob stoppers, canned goods, and two thousand old clocks and clockworks.

The Corner Store (p. 80)
■ Eudora Welty

Essay Analysis and Discussion

Welty makes good use of detail and organization as she moves through the corner store of her childhood. In a few words, she manages to fill our minds as full as Mr. Sessions fills his shelves. Note how Welty uses sensory description to paint a picture that is real, without overusing detail. Also, students can analyze the way Welty acquaints us with Mr. Sessions without having him speak. Then students can discuss the author's use of hard detail as contrasted with her poetic impressions. The exercise will help them understand how difficult it is to say enough without saying too much.

Questions for Study and Discussion

1. Students will find examples of chronological and spatial organization throughout the essay. Welty organizes the essay chronologically through the sequence of events from the time she enters the store until she leaves. Her body movement around the store and

16

the movement of her eyes as she looks over the shelves and the counters are examples of spatial organization.

2. Welty realizes that a person who comes into a store out of the bright sunlight immediately feels almost blind. Therefore, the first things that a person would be aware of are the smells of licorice, dill pickle brine, ammonia, and untrapped mice.

3. Welty creates an impression of the old-fashioned plenty associated with a nineteenth-century country store by describing shelves, counters, and barrels stocked with the numberless goodies and smells available in such places.

4. Mr. Sessions is warm and friendly, a man who invites a child's hand to reach for a choice of penny candies, who knows what the child's favorite drink is, who weighs small children on his scale before they leave the store, and who will "remember what you weighed the last time."

5. Welty puts certain phrases in parentheses to set them apart. This information characterizes the era in even more detail than the rest of the essay. A personal quality, which identifies the things that were especially dear to the writer, would be lost if these asides to the reader were left out.

6. Students should give reasons that demonstrate their understanding of endings.

Vocabulary

frame (1) having a wood frame
tangible (2) perceptible, especially by the sense of touch
brine (2) water saturated with salt
motes (3) small particles
signet (3) a small intaglio seal
agates (4) children's marbles of agate or material resembling agate
concoction (8) a mixture prepared by combining diverse ingredients
scales (9) a weighing machine

Classroom Activity Using Organization

Using the principles of division and classification, students should establish general categories for the materials found in the desk and then distribute the specific items into the appropriate categories. The following is one possible arrangement:

> *writing/marking instruments:* no. 2 pencils, ballpoint pens, mechanical pencil, highlighting marker, felt-tip pen
> *personal items:* plastic comb, nail clipper, scissors, nail file, toothbrush

postage/mail supplies: book mailing bag, first-class stamps, post-cards, 8 × 10 manila envelopes, business envelopes, postcard stamps, airmail stamps

items to hold things together: rubber bands, adhesive tape, paper clips, clasps, thumbtacks, bottle of glue

correction materials: eraser, bottle of correction fluid

miscellaneous supplies: 3 × 5 cards

Students will come up with categories of their own. For example, someone could argue that the scissors from the second category above could be combined with the items in the fourth, fifth, and sixth categories to form the general category "desk supplies." There is no single correct answer; students should discuss the pros and cons of the various organizational plans put forth by the class.

CHAPTER 4 Beginnings and Endings

Of My Friend Hector and My Achilles Heel (p. 92)
■ Michael T. Kaufman

Essay Analysis and Discussion

Kaufman's first paragraph is unusual and grabs the reader's attention. Two short sentences admitting prejudice contrast sharply with the finger pointing, subtle or not, that forms the backbone of most essays about prejudice. Kaufman's story is not dramatic or even noteworthy until the end, but he hooks the reader into bearing with him to find out the nature of his so-called "prejudice and stupidity." Have your students write a short personal essay that uses a concise, attention-grabbing first paragraph. Have them discuss the essays and identify the type of essay for which it might be most effective and tell why. Kaufman's ending stays with the reader for two reasons. First, it is a situation that everyone can empathize with because getting back in touch with an old, wrongfully neglected friend is something that most of us should do—but haven't. Second, it is an open-ended conclusion. The reader hopes that perhaps Kaufman will reunite with Hector somehow. Have your students discuss their reaction to the ending. How effective would the essay have been with a resolution at the end?

Questions for Study and Discussion

1. Such an admission is unusual in a first-person essay, so it grabs the reader's attention and encourages the reader to finish the essay to find out what provoked such a statement. It also leads the reader to pay close attention to Kaufman's writing in hopes of discovering the roots of his stated stupidity. The second part of the question is personal experience.
2. Achilles was a Greek hero who had a weak spot on his heel, a fatal flaw that eventually killed him. Kaufman is referring to his own flaw, which is prejudice.
3. The essay is organized chronologically.
4. Kaufman's purpose is to demonstrate how easy it is to form prejudices and segregate oneself from other people based on assumptions. His organization helps him express his purpose by allowing him to trace when, why, and how his prejudice was formed.
5. Kaufman ignored Hector because he assumed him to be a physical laborer with whom he would have difficulty holding a conversation. It tells him that "tracking," as he calls it, may not be unusual, and it may be damaging to people from the entire range of socioeconomic "tracks."
6. Kaufman's ending is effective because it describes a painful situation that most people can identify with. By keeping the ending open-ended, he emphasizes the ongoing nature of his—and presumably many others'—problem.

Vocabulary

intellectually (6) concerning the ability to learn or the mind
perfunctory (9) short; without elaboration
contemporaries (10) people of the same age
acclaimed (13) praised; celebrated
concocted (14) made; manufactured

Classroom Activity Using Beginnings and Endings

Students readily pick the second paragraph as the one they would use to start an essay. They like the opening sentence, which piques their curiosity, and the anecdote used to introduce Hugh Troy. The first paragraph has the advantage of using one of Troy's stunts but suffers from an opening sentence that seems to come out of nowhere. The paragraph might make a good ending to an essay about Troy. The third paragraph is simply too dry, too matter-of-fact for a beginning. While a paragraph like this is sometimes necessary when writing a brief essay about a famous person, it should not come first.

How to Take a Job Interview (p. 97)
■ Kirby W. Stanat

Essay Analysis and Discussion

The ending of the essay makes use of a kind of evidence writers often use to provide effective support for personal opinions—the experiment. Students sometimes hesitate to draw conclusions in their essays, fearing that they lack the necessary objective information to back them up. The experiment is one way of putting those opinions to a test, while also providing a way to develop the body of an essay. When you approach Stanat's essay, have students look at the conclusion he reaches in paragraph 28. In the paragraph following it, he uses objective data to support that conclusion. Ask your students if those data are as effective as the experiment he goes on to describe in paragraphs 30 through 36. Though the information in paragraph 29 serves the same purpose as the experiment, most students will probably agree that the closing paragraphs finally convince readers that Stanat's opinion is correct. The specific case study gives authenticity to the generic description in paragraph 29 by presenting a more concrete and visual connection for the reader.

Questions for Study and Discussion

1. Stanat opens the essay by establishing a key point about his topic—the recruiter is coming from corporate headquarters—and uses the first three paragraphs to drive that point home. Paragraphs 4 through 11 illustrate how *not* to approach an interview, given the opening lesson; and, after a nice transition in paragraph 12, Stanat explains in detail how a recruiter operates (paragraphs 13 through 29). The last seven paragraphs present a fitting climax by once again providing a sample experience to illustrate his preceding lesson and, at the same time, reemphasize the point made at the beginning. The opening, in essence, provides the context for the entire essay. Stanat's whole point relies on this information.

2. Stanat's purpose is to provide information about the interview process to help college students succeed in campus job interviews. His thesis is that in order to succeed in an interview, one has to

know what the recruiter is looking for as well as where he or she is "coming from."

3. The sequence of steps in the process is as follows: (1) recruiter examines résumé or data sheet, (2) recruiter goes to lobby and calls for interviewee, (3) recruiter looks to see who moves, (4) recruiter waits for interviewee to approach, (5) recruiter scrutinizes interviewee's physical actions as well as dress and appearance, (6) recruiter introduces self and leads way to interviewing room, (7) recruiter opens door and gestures interviewee into room, (8) recruiter gives close-up inspection, (9) recruiter smells interviewee, (10) recruiter checks interviewee's backside, (11) recruiter asks interviewee to sit down (Stanat believes that at this point the decision on the interviewee is 75 to 80 percent made), and (12) recruiter talks to interviewee.

4. Body movement alerts the recruiter to the applicant's attitude. If you come across like a brisk, young professional hopping out of your seat, he will assume that will be your attitude on the job. If you slouch now, you'll probably slouch through the workday.

5. Most recruiters have made up their minds before the actual interview begins. The essay is useful for advising young job applicants that recruiters need to be impressed with the whole person, not just a résumé and a grade point average.

6. The structural and technical devices Stanat uses to establish this informal tone include: (a) the pronoun *you,* (b) contractions, (c) imperative mood, (d) informal diction, (e) active voice, and (f) loose (as opposed to periodic) sentences. Stanat's use of slang and colloquial expressions reinforces the informality. To make his tone more formal, Stanat could have used: (a) third-person pronouns, (b) passive constructions, (c) periodic sentences, (d) no contractions, and (e) no slang or colloquial expressions.

7. In the final seven paragraphs Stanat recounts an experiment he conducted with several recruiters. This story can be summarized in the following sentence: Recruiters make decisions not to recommend a candidate within the first minutes of an interview. This dramatic concluding story reiterates the point that Stanat makes in his opening paragraphs and thus brings his essay full circle.

Vocabulary

cubicle (3) any small compartment or room
deteriorates (10) decreases in quantity, character, or value
résumé (13) a summary of experience submitted with a job application
adamant (35) firm in purpose or opinion; unyielding

Classroom Activity Using Beginnings and Endings

Stanat's paragraph 29 has some merit—it summarizes what the interviewer knows about the interviewee before the "sit down" portion of the interview takes place. It allows Stanat to conclude with his main point: The recruiter's decision for all practical purposes has already been made by this point in the interview. But that's a hard point for readers to accept. Stanat felt that many would be saying "prove it" or "show me." And that's exactly what he does with the anecdote told in paragraphs 30–36. This paragraph block brings the essay to a snappy—no pun intended—conclusion that echoes the scenario Stanat presents at the beginning of his essay. Most students tell us that it's the anecdote that "convinces" them.

Intelligence (p. 103)
■ **Isaac Asimov**

Essay Analysis and Discussion

Students generally like this essay because of the repair man's joke at the end. Indeed, the essay's success rests on Asimov's use of the auto-repair man throughout, first as a way of introducing the nature of his thesis (paragraphs 3 and 4), and then to illustrate his point with an entertaining anecdote (paragraphs 5 through 7). In your classroom discussion of the essay, you may want to consider suitable alternatives for Asimov's repair man that fit the context of his thesis. Students should be able to offer a variety of examples to show that intelligence is relative, and you may have several examples of your own to share. Once the class has developed a list of possibilities, try to fit one or another of them into the structure of the essay, first, to state and clarify the thesis, and then to provide an extended illustrative example. Try, especially, to maintain the conversational aspect of paragraph 6, so that the impact of the last sentence is not diminished. This can be an oral or written exercise, with the emphasis on getting students to incorporate personal observations and experience into an essay, while maintaining unity, coherence, and a consistent tone.

Questions for Study and Discussion

1. The rhetorical question immediately engages readers and starts them thinking how they might answer the question. The question, especially Asimov's "anyway," seems to emphasize that there are perhaps multiple definitions of "intelligence." The story related in the remainder of paragraph 1 shows that a high score on an apti-

tude or intelligence test is just that, a high score that is not necessarily related to one's duties.

2. Asimov states his thesis in the last sentence of paragraph 4: "My intelligence, then, is not absolute but is a function of the society I live in and of the fact that a small subsection of that society has managed to foist itself on the rest as an arbiter of such matters." The last three paragraphs are an extended example that illustrates Asimov's point.

3. Paragraph 2 is linked to paragraph 1 with the transition "scores like that." The "For instance" that begins paragraph 3 indicates that an example will follow to illustrate a point made in paragraph 2. Paragraph 4 is linked to paragraph 3 by the transitional expression "then." The "Consider" in paragraph 5 indicates that an example will follow, and the reference to "auto-repair man" and "again" make the link to earlier paragraphs. "Indulgently" in paragraph 6 refers to the manner in which he responds to a request made in paragraph 5. The transition "And" makes the link to paragraph 7.

4. For most students, the word "moron" connotes a remarkably stupid person. The word's denotation is "a mentally retarded person having a mental age between 7 and 12 years or an intelligence quotient between 50 and 75." Asimov uses this strong emotion-packed word to emphasize his point that intelligence is relative.

5. Through the use of a joke, Asimov is able to show us rather than tell us what he means by intelligence. The auto-repair man makes the distinction between *educated* (meaning schooled) and *smart* (meaning commonsensical), which relates directly to Asimov's thesis in paragraph 4.

Vocabulary

aptitude (1) intelligence

complacent (2) self-satisfied

intellectual (2) of or pertaining to the ability to learn and reason as distinguished from the ability to feel

oracles (3) persons who deliver authoritative, wise, or highly regarded pronouncements

academician (4) a member of an art, literary, or scientific society or academy

foist (4) force upon or impose unjustifiably

arbiter (4) one who judges or decides a disputed issue

indulgently (6) in a tolerant manner

raucously (6) in a rough or hoarse manner

Classroom Activity Using Beginnings and Endings

Students should be able to complete this activity in less than fifteen minutes, and it will encourage them to internalize the possibilities open to them when beginning an essay. It does not matter which two techniques each student chooses as long as the sentences make sense and are likely to catch a reader's interest. Have students evaluate the beginnings—by working in pairs, in groups, or as a class—to help them better understand which beginnings work well and why they are effective.

Alternatively, have the class as a whole brainstorm about how each of the seven strategies for opening an essay might be used.

The Wounds That Can't Be Stitched Up (p. 107)
■ Ruth Russell

Essay Analysis and Discussion

Russell's essay offers the opportunity to discuss the issues of drinking and driving. Encourage students to share stories of how drunk driving has touched their lives or the lives of relatives and friends. These stories will help students empathize with the pain that Russell felt when a drunk driver almost killed members of her family over two decades ago. Several years ago, when that same drunk driver became her neighbor, the old emotional wounds were reopened. Her outrage was rekindled when she witnessed him roar down the street into their parking lot, drunk again. Russell's outrage is not directed only at the drunk driver but also at a system that is lenient on DWI (driving while intoxicated) offenders and a society that jumps to their defense with lame excuses. Ask students to describe how they might feel if they were treated the way Russell was in paragraphs 11 and 12 after their family or friends were victims of a drunk driver.

Questions for Study and Discussion

1. The details of what the day was like are important to the writer because this was a day that her life and that of her family changed dramatically. More importantly, by showing readers that nothing was unusual that December evening, she shows that there were no extenuating circumstances to account for the accident. Quite simply, the other driver was drunk. The title captures readers' attention by getting them to think about the emotional and psychological wounds that remain unhealed as a result of something that happened on a seemingly ordinary December evening.

24

2. In paragraph 5 Russell describes her youngest brother as sitting "in the bed, a lonely little figure in a darkened hospital room." Although the black eye that the eight-year-old suffered in the accident will heal, the picture of him sitting alone in a hospital room lets the reader wonder how long the emotional scars will remain. The emotional impact of this image on readers prepares them for the description of the near-fatal injuries incurred by Russell's sister and mother.

3. Russell's tone is one of restrained outrage. Readers see her restraint and anger most strikingly in paragraphs 4, 8, 9, 10, 11, 12, and 14 as she articulates the deep wounds left from the accident and shows how townspeople questioned her and defended the drunk driver. Twenty-three years after the accident, Russell had believed that "the accident was ancient history"; she wasn't prepared for the way an encounter with the driver would reopen those old wounds. The irony of the driver's concluding remark ("Did I scare you?") does not escape readers.

4. Russell is making the point that "good guys" don't drink and drive. And, more importantly, good guys don't continue to drink and drive after a first offense. This excuse or defense is like saying people are not responsible for their actions when they are drinking.

5. The encounter with the drunk driver recounted in the final paragraph happened on a December day much like the day of the accident. Implicit in Russell's telling of this bizarre incident is her outrage at society's treatment of repeat drunk drivers. The driver did not know when he made his offhand remark "Did I scare you?" that this question brought to the surface Russell's real pain over the accident twenty-three years earlier.

Vocabulary

confided (6) to tell private or personal matters in confidence
gaped (7) opened wide
distorted (9) twisted out of a proper or natural relation of parts; contorted
accusatory (11) containing or implying charges of an error or misdeed
apprehensive (13) anxious, fearful, or uneasy

Classroom Activity Using Beginnings and Endings

Having students write alternative beginnings to an essay is a wonderful way to get them back inside their own writing. If students are having difficulty coming up with ideas for alternative beginnings, suggest that they read the opening paragraphs of six to ten essays in *Models for Writers*. You might want to start this activity by asking some students to read these paragraphs aloud to the class.

Students have told us that this exercise has given them new perspectives on their topics, ideas for ways in which they could revise their essays, and ideas for reorganizing their materials. By sharing the alternative beginnings with others in the class, students discover that a good opening paragraph really does make a difference for readers, especially when students are not required to read the essay.

CHAPTER 5 **Paragraphs**

Simplicity (p. 116)
■ **William Zinsser**

Essay Analysis and Discussion

Freshmen are often surprised by Zinsser's suggestion to simplify, simplify. Many have come through high school writing courses believing that more is better and that the thesaurus is the basic tool for selecting vocabulary. To reinforce the notion of revising for simplicity's sake, have your students look over Zinsser's sample revision from manuscript on pages 121–22. Then, using examples from past student papers (or some other suitable source), present students with paragraphs needing simplifying. As students trim words or alter vocabulary or rearrange sentences, be sure they keep in mind the elements for an effective paragraph—controlling idea, unity, development, and coherence. When they've finished, analyze the deletions and changes and see if they can identify common types of clutter.

Questions for Study and Discussion

1. As Zinsser states in paragraph 1, clutter is a writing disease, the symptoms of which include "unnecessary words, circular constructions, pompous frills and meaningless jargon." In paragraph 2, Zinsser says that "the secret of good writing is to strip every sentence to its cleanest components." He then proceeds to give examples of "the thousand and one adulterants that weaken the strength of a sentence." Writers need to ask themselves "What am I trying to say?" and then "Have I said it?" in order to eliminate clutter.

2. Each of Zinsser's paragraphs relates to his topic of clutter in writing and to his purpose of making readers more aware of clutter and its effect on writing. The main idea of each paragraph is as follows:

1. "Clutter is the disease of American writing."
2. Most language of American commerce is unnecessarily complicated.
3. Words that serve no function need to be stripped from prose.
4. People need to express their thoughts in simple, straightforward language.
5. Roosevelt's example of clear English contrasts with the government memo.
6. Simplify as Thoreau does in his writing.
7. Clear thinking leads to clear writing and the freedom from clutter.
8. Clutter gives readers unnecessary trouble.
9. When readers are lost, it's usually because the writer hasn't been careful enough.
10. Although readers might be forgiving at first, they usually don't stay with writers who make them work too hard.
11. Writers need to know what they are trying to say and cut everything that doesn't contribute to the intended meaning.
12. Thinking clearly is a conscious act that writers must force on themselves.
13. "Writing is hard work."

3. Paragraphs 4 through 6 illustrate the points Zinsser makes in paragraph 3 by providing examples of cluttered writing by highly educated people, which demonstrate the need for simplicity. He then presents simplified versions to underscore what he advocates.

4. Writers must ask themselves constantly: What am I trying to say? Have I said it? Is it clear to someone encountering the subject for the first time? These questions are important to Zinsser because good writing doesn't come naturally or easily. And the clear thinking that precedes it "is a conscious act that writers must force on themselves."

5. The first paragraph introduces the essay by defining "clutter" and establishing what Zinsser hopes to eliminate by writing his essay. It provides a necessary context for his thesis about simplicity. The final paragraph is a reminder that good writing does not come naturally but is the result of hard work. It is effective because it reemphasizes the importance of revision to successful writing.

6. "Clear thinking becomes clear writing; one can't exist without the other. It's impossible for a muddy thinker to write good English."

Vocabulary

pompous (1) characterized by an exaggerated show of dignity or self-importance

decipher (2) to read or interpret something ambiguous, obscure, or illegible

adulterants (3) extraneous or improper ingredients that make something impure or inferior

mollify (4) allay anger; placate

enviable (7) desirable

tenacious (10) persistent

bearded (12) confronted boldly

Classroom Activity Using Paragraphs

Students should be immediately impressed by Zinsser's ability to ferret out and eliminate clutter in each of his paragraphs. This alone makes the paragraphs clearer and easier to follow because without the clutter Zinsser's craftsmanship shines through. At several points Zinsser edits out whole sentences—sentences that would have weakened the paragraph's unity. For example, in the first new paragraph he cuts the sentence "He *thinks* he knows what the writer is trying to say, but he's not sure," because it does not present an example of "carelessness" as each of the other sentences in the paragraph does. In that same paragraph, Zinsser uses the word "perhaps" to signal that he is presenting yet another example. Students should note how Zinsser uses the first sentence in each paragraph to refer back to a key idea in the last sentence of the previous paragraph.

One way to do this activity in class is to divide the class into groups of two or three and to have each group responsible for one of Zinsser's paragraphs. During class discussion have the groups that worked on the same paragraphs present their findings and conclusions about Zinsser's editing changes.

"I Just Wanna Be Average" (p. 123)
■ Mike Rose

Essay Analysis and Discussion

Students will likely find Rose's tribute to Jack MacFarland entertaining, but some may find it wordy or drawn out. Yet when they study the essay, they will find that each anecdote, each personal reference, and each seemingly casual statement directly relates to the topic Rose wants to present in a particular paragraph. Rose proves that you don't have to be overly concise or conservative in your writing to write an effective essay, but you do have to have a purpose and stick to it in each paragraph. Rose makes MacFarland and his own situation real to the reader while maintaining a flow in his essay that would be impossible to maintain with sloppy paragraphs. Have your students closely examine a paragraph of their choice and explain how each sentence relates to the paragraph's topic. If they write an essay about a teacher, emphasize the importance of using examples and anecdotes to liven up their essay—as long as those examples and anecdotes directly contribute to the paragraph containing them.

Questions for Study and Discussion

1. The title gives the reader a sense of just how much Rose's standards were raised by MacFarland. By the end of the essay Rose obviously goes well beyond the average in a number of areas—he has exceeded his academic dreams.

2. MacFarland is a slob with wrinkled pants, a sorry tie, and stained teeth. Obviously, his abilities as a teacher have nothing to do with the way he looks.

3. (1) Jack MacFarland looked awful, but he was a very good teacher. (2) MacFarland's lectures were well crafted and intellectually stimulating, and his course covered a lot of ground. (3) He was able to handle the difficult students and earn everyone's respect. (4) MacFarland inspired Rose to work hard and do well. (5) Good grades from MacFarland were things of value. (6) MacFarland encouraged Rose into working to get into college. (7) MacFarland succeeded in helping Rose go to college.

4. Rose's second paragraph can be divided into two parts. In the first four sentences he discusses how MacFarland built up his students' knowledge of Western intellectual history. This background or overview material is necessary preparation for the analytical work that is discussed in the next four sentences of the paragraph. Rose's use of the pronouns "he" (MacFarland) and "we" (students) show how the teacher led the way in the activities described in both parts of the paragraph. Rose's detailed accounting of authors, works, concepts, and activities prepares readers for the last sentence "The man immersed us in language."

5. The transition between paragraphs 2 and 3 has to do with language—Rose's somewhat idyllic view in paragraph 2 and the real world of Mercy High in paragraph 3. The transition between

paragraphs 3 and 4 brings the reader to what MacFarland did for Rose in particular. Rose shows what MacFarland did in class and how he interacted with others before he begins an in-depth account of his own relationship with MacFarland.

6. Rose introduces the reader to real people, kids like those everyone knows in high school. It makes the essay more entertaining, and it gives the reader a way to see what MacFarland had to contend with. By making them real people, Rose shows the interaction MacFarland had with a variety of students, and the respect he earned from all.

7. Rose has difficulty getting into college because his grades are awful. He makes it by doing well in MacFarland's class and having him pull strings at his alma mater.

Vocabulary

beatnik (1) hippie; counterculture person
curriculum (1) course of study
paradox (2) incongruity; puzzle
existentialism (2) philosophy focusing on human responsibility
rejoin (3) respond; counterattack
indomitable (3) dauntless; impossible to subdue
linguistic (3) relating to language
incipient (3) developing; budding
ministrations (4) attention; care
extrinsic (5) from outside
spectroscopic (5) concerning a spectroscope, an optical instrument
gangly (6) tall; lanky

Classroom Activity Using Paragraphs

Once students select their topic sentences, have them make a list of all the details that come to mind that could be used in a paragraph. For example, for the topic sentence "Signs of the sanitation strike were evident everywhere" a student's list might include "a discarded mattress, overflowing trash cans, littered streets, the smells of decaying garbage in dumpsters, piles of plastic trash bags curbside, rats venturing out in daylight, and flies everywhere." Next, have students write their paragraphs using only those details needed to show, demonstrate, or support the idea in the topic sentence. Finally, have several students read their paragraphs aloud—or better yet, put them on transparencies—for the class to discuss for unity, coherence, and development.

One Good Turn: How Machine-Made Screws Brought the World Together (p. 129)
■ Witold Rybczynski

Essay Analysis and Discussion

If asked to write about something as ordinary as a wood screw, nail, paper clip, or rubber band, most students would be at a loss for where to start. After all, what can someone say about commonplace objects that we can all take for granted? Rybczynski's essay shows students that there is a story behind even the most ordinary of objects. His paragraphs are developed with specific information, and he makes transitions between paragraphs seem effortless. He engages his readers at the start by telling how he and his wife built their own home with hand tools. Through this experience, Rybczynski learned the pleasures and satisfactions of working with hand tools ("really extensions of the human body"). His thoughts about his tool box of hand tools segues nicely into a discussion of how medieval artisans would have found most of these tools familiar. From here he provides a historical overview of screws from the time of Archimedes to the mass production of precise and standardized screws in the twentieth century. It is this historical overview—replete with numerous examples—that prepare readers for Rybczynski's claim that "accurately threaded screws changed the world" in the final paragraph.

Questions for Study and Discussion

1. The first three and one-half paragraphs engage readers by personalizing the experience of working with hand tools. In these paragraphs one gains an appreciation for the craftsmanship (and related pleasures and satisfactions) associated with using hand tools as well as with their history. Such an introduction adds both interest and importance to the screw and screwdriver, subjects that many readers take for granted.

2. In paragraph 2 Rybczynski explains that "hand tools are really extensions of the human body" and that they have been refined over the centuries so as to be closely related to the job being performed. When using a hammer or a hand saw one has the feeling that he or she is in control and in close contact with the materials being worked.

3. Rybczynski supports this claim with numerous examples in paragraphs 5 through 7. These examples enable him to say that "without screws, entire fields of science would have languished, naviga-

tion would have remained primitive and naval warfare as well as routine maritime commerce in the eighteenth and nineteenth centuries would not have been possible. Without screws there would have been no machine tools, hence no industrial products and no Industrial Revolution."

4. At the end of paragraph 4 Rybczynski says that screws as fixing devices were unknown in the Middle Ages. He starts the subsequent paragraph with both a reference to screws and the time they originated. He starts paragraph 6 with the statement "Inexpensive screws are quintessentially modern," a statement that repeats the key idea of the last sentence in paragraph 5. After showing what machined screws enabled people to accomplish in the last sentence of paragraph 7, Rybczynski starts paragraph 8 with his claim about the impact of "accurately threaded screws."

5. Rybczynski selects his examples carefully to develop the particular point(s) he is making in each paragraph. In paragraph 1, for example, he lists the various hand tools in his toolbox to help readers envision his equipment; in paragraph 3 he uses the example of the Roman carpenter to establish the history of the tools in his toolbox. Because many readers might not immediately think of the large wooden screw Archimedes invented, the author describes it in paragraph 4 and provides several examples of its successors. In paragraph 6 Rybczynski provides a catalog of household examples to remind us how versatile and useful the common wood screw is. Have students identify the examples they found most effective and explain why these examples worked for them. Our students tell us that the specificity of Rybczynski's examples adds interest and substance to his essay.

6. Although not so technical so as to intimidate or confuse a general readership, Rybczynski's diction reveals that he is an authority on his subject. He is comfortable with the names of various hand tools as well as the names of their Roman counterparts (*plana, regula*). He's familiar with the "Egyptian bow drill," "hand-forged spikes," and "turnscrews." In paragraph 6 he explains in clear, precise language how wood screws and bolts work.

Vocabulary

conscripted (1) enrolled or drafted
untutored (3) having no formal instruction; unsophisticated, unrefined
neophytes (3) beginners, novices
retractable (3) able to be drawn back or in
infer (3) to conclude from evidence or premises

quintessentially (6) purest or most typically
mundane (6) ordinary; commonplace
epic (7) large-scale; comparable to the feats of a legendary or traditional hero

Classroom Activity Using Paragraphs

The order should be 3, 5, 1, 6, 4, 2. Some students may argue that sentence 5 should be put at the end, but it introduces the topic of brain hemispheres, which needs to precede sentence 2 so sentence 2's content can be readily understood.

CHAPTER 6 **Transitions**

Why I Want to Have a Family (p. 137)
■ **Lisa Brown**

Essay Analysis and Discussion

Because students may find it intimidating to argue against Brown's thesis in class, try playing devil's advocate when considering this essay. Develop a series of points opposed to Brown's, paying particular attention to her reasons for wanting to raise a family, and present your own set of contrasting situations. See what kinds of reactions this generates. You may stimulate a discussion similar to one that has occurred more than once in the students' dorms and apartments, but one they are initially reluctant to broach in a classroom situation. Such a discussion could reveal aspects of the underlying motive in Brown's approach to her audience.

Questions for Study and Discussion

1. In the first sentence of paragraph 2, the transitional *though* sets up a contrast with the point made in paragraph 1; similarly, the "good news–bad news" transition at the beginning of paragraph 3 sets up a contrast with paragraph 2. Paragraph 4 begins with a transitional concession (*granted*) that provides a contrast between "now" and "then"; the final sentence in paragraph 4 is a summary (*in short*) that offers a transition into the writer's second reason that motherhood came to be seen as an obstacle. The fourth sentence in paragraph 6 uses *though* to point out a transi-

tion in the way Brown herself began to think about motherhood. In paragraph 8 the first sentence answers a question posed at the end of paragraph 7, providing a transition into Brown's concluding arguments. The first word in paragraph 9 (*today*) sets up a transitional contrast to the final sentence in paragraph 8.

2. Brown starts paragraph 10 with a reference to "fiercely independent women," which harkens back to the central idea of paragraph 9. In paragraph 11, she uses the words "college" and "student" to link to the word "educated" in paragraph 10. Brown's concluding paragraph echoes some of the key ideas presented earlier in her argument; for example, Brown states that she's in college because "I want to be a smart mommy" (8).

3. Brown argues for what she calls a "package deal"—the personal fulfillment of relationships and family life in conjunction with the individual awareness that a college education can produce. Her attitude began to change when her sister and a friend had babies, and she noticed the positive influence that raising children can have on parents.

4. Brown argues against those women whose obsessiveness in pursuing a career insulates them from the people around them and prevents them from seeing the inherent value of relationships and family life.

5. In paragraph 6 Brown discusses the "abstract happiness" associated with raising children and explains what children offer parents: (1) teaching them patience and sensitivity, (2) serving as clues to their own pasts, and (3) reminding them to ensure a quality future. The culmination of her reasoning appears in paragraph 7, when she states, "I want to be unselfish. But I've spent most of my life working in the opposite direction. . . ."

6. Children require patience and sensitivity if we care to see the world as they see it and want them to see our needs as well. Seeing the world through their eyes reminds us of how the world once looked to us, which in turn strengthens our sensitivity. It is a circle that points to the future. We give them the memories and quality of compassion that they will someday pass on to their children.

7. Though this essay is aimed at a female audience, especially those who have ruled out a family in their future plans (as evidenced by the questions at the end of paragraph 3), its arguments can be applied to males too. Brown's ideas about the roles of women, egocentrism, education, and what children can teach us transcend any limitations of gender.

Vocabulary

relegating (2) sending or consigning to an obscure place, position, or condition

autonomy (2) the condition or quality of being self-governing

insular (3) detached and isolated in outlook and experience

bravado (3) defiant or swaggering behavior

precepts (5) rules or principles that impose a particular standard of action or conduct

contingent (5) dependent

doting (6) showing excessive love or fondness

tandem (10) one behind the other; in partnership or conjunction

Classroom Activity Using Transitions

The correct order for the sentences in E. B. White's paragraph is 4, 2, 5, 1, 3. The sentences in the paragraph follow in chronological order from that first summer in 1904 to the present. Students will point to the time markers "1904," "returned," "since," and "a few weeks ago." White uses pronouns skillfully as well; he moves from the family experience ("we" and "us") to the personal experience ("I"). Finally, White uses subtle references to previous ideas to link sentences together. For example, when he states "We returned summer after summer," we know that the place he is referring to is "a lake in Maine." And that "this feeling" in sentence 3 relates back to his "wish for the placidity of a lake in the woods."

How I Got Smart (p. 142)
■ Steve Brody

Essay Analysis and Discussion

Brody uses the first three paragraphs of his essay to set up his point that sometimes a love of education is not born, it is made. The rest is a narrative presented chronologically to take us from his distaste for book learning to his "thirst" for it. This is a "one-joke" essay: The excerpts from the encyclopedia not only are used to support his thesis, they also form the bulk of the dialogue with the girl Brody wants to impress. His lengthy discourses are punctuated with her short responses, which moves the narrative along smoothly. Brody makes good use of transitions to keep his story easy to read. However, just as frequently, he gets readers from paragraph to paragraph by moving them in time and space with transitions like "a few days later," "one day I was," and "and so it went." Students can study Brody's essay to observe his movement from one paragraph or one sentence to another with and without the use of transitional words.

Questions for Study and Discussion

1. In each case, the following paragraph begins with a transitional term, such as *consequently, but, occasionally,* etc.

2. Dialogue always forces a writer to show and not tell. Brody's dialogue adds energy and life to his essay by letting the characters or players in this narrative speak for themselves. In witnessing the conversations between Debbie and the narrator and between Mrs. Larrivee and the narrator, we have a greater understanding of each person's personality and behavior and a greater appreciation of the humor in the situations than we would have had if Brody had simply reported what had happened. Notice that Brody is careful to start new paragraphs when speakers change and to use names or pronouns so that it's always clear who is speaking.

3. He had already "savored the heady wine of knowledge" and could not alter his course.

4. Brody's humor is affected by the stilted encyclopedia-style prose he tries to pass off as casual conversation.

5. Coleridge was an English poet (1772–1834). "The Rime of the Ancient Mariner" is probably his best-known work. It describes in "exotic and supernatural themes" the plight of a mariner, alone at sea with an albatross around his neck. Agamemnon, leader of the Greek forces in the Trojan War, was murdered by his wife Clytemnestra and her lover. Alexander Pope (1688–1744), was an English poet.

6. Brody's denial of any innate erudition at the beginning of his essay and his enthusiasm for learning at the end emphasize that the revelation of learning can happen to anyone and has little to do with higher intelligence. Also, by referring to Volume XIV, Brody reveals that he stuck to his resolve to read the encyclopedia.

7. Brody's substitution of encyclopedia entries for conversation is funny and contributes to the tone of the essay. His selections are also humorous for being outside the usual context of interest for most teenage boys and girls. They are dry and humorless, yet become funny when Debbie is kind and tolerant enough to take them as serious conversation. By including so many of them, Brody has several opportunities to elaborate on his joke.

Vocabulary

misconception (1) incorrect interpretation

prodigies (1) highly talented children

devotee (2) a zealous follower, supporter, or enthusiast

bearish (3) apt to sell securities or commodities in expectation of a price decline

dabbled (3) worked without serious effort

surge (9) move in waves

erudition (9) learning; scholarship

snout (16) a long, projecting muzzle

sidled (20) moved sideways or side foremost

forbidding (24) disagreeable; repellent

subsist (26) receive the means of maintaining life

amorous (32) being in love

expatiated (32) talked or wrote at length

adenoids (32) an enlarged mass of tissue near the opening of the nose into the throat

voracious (35) excessively eager

disgorging (39) discharging forcefully or confusedly

savored (43) tasted with pleasure

Classroom Activity Using Transitions

The correct order for the sentences is 6, 4, 8, 3, 9, 2, 11, 1, 12, 5, 10, 7. Engage students in a discussion of the language cues that helped them arrange the sentences in a logical order. Students will readily point to transitions like *first* and *however*, the pronoun *this*, the repetition of key ideas such as "wetting down the surface" and "foreign material," and the organizational device "three steps."

Becoming a Writer (p. 149)
■ Russell Baker

Essay Analysis and Discussion

Few have gone through school without knowing a teacher like Baker's Mr. Fleagle—earnest, interested in his subject, eager to teach, but unable to communicate the joy of the subject to the class. The effectiveness of Baker's essay rests on his ability to describe Mr. Fleagle, and his description in paragraphs 2 and 3 is amusing, devastating, and full of imagery. Students should have a very clear notion of Mr. Fleagle's appearance, personality, and mannerisms from the description, and it should communicate to them the lesson Baker himself learns in the course of the essay—good writing can be funny and informal if it is clear and written with a purpose. It is through having so thoroughly established Mr. Fleagle as inept that Baker can make the ending surprising and effective, and it is easy for the reader to share Baker's joy and surprise. The paragraph transitions become particularly important in the telling of the development of the essay and its subsequent fate. Baker ushers the reader along in chronological order, but it is not a plodding account by any means. Baker bases his transitions on emotions and feelings, going from the joy of writing the essay to the anxiety of waiting for it to come back, to the joy of having it read. The reader can easily follow the progression, and the emotion-based transitions carry the reader on the same roller coaster Baker endured to the end.

Questions for Study and Discussion

1. Baker's transitional expressions, repeated key words and ideas, and pronoun references have been underlined in the following transcription of paragraphs 1 and 2.

   The notion of becoming a writer had flickered off and on in my head . . . but it wasn't until my third year in high school that the possibility took hold. <u>Until then</u> I'd been bored by everything associated with English courses. I found <u>English grammar</u> dull and baffling. I hated the assignments to turn out "compositions," and went at <u>them</u> like heavy labor, turning out laden, lackluster <u>paragraphs</u> that were agonies for teachers to read and for me to write. The classics thrust on me to read seemed as deadening as chloroform.

   When our class was assigned to Mr. Fleagle for third-year English I anticipated another grim year in that dreariest of subjects. <u>Mr. Fleagle</u> was notorious among City students for dullness and inability to inspire. <u>He</u> was said to be <u>stuffy, dull, and hopelessly out of date</u>. To me he looked to be sixty or seventy and prim to a fault. He wore <u>primly</u> severe eyeglasses, his wavy hair was <u>primly</u> cut and <u>primly</u> combed. <u>He</u> wore <u>prim</u> vested suits with neckties blocked <u>primly</u> against the collar buttons of his <u>primly</u> starched white shirts. <u>He</u> had a <u>primly</u> pointed jaw, a <u>primly</u> straight nose, and a <u>prim</u> manner of speaking that was so correct, so gentlemanly, that he seemed a comic antique.

2. Make sure students note how Baker links the paragraphs to each other so that they flow chronologically without resorting to a plodding "Then I did this, then he did that" progression that

38

many students fall into. Baker uses some very basic transitions—"This title," "When I finished it," "And he started to read," for example—but they are skillfully woven into the emotion of the story, so they lead the reader on without interfering with the flow of the narrative.

3. Baker's description of Mr. Fleagle paints an extremely clear picture of a teacher who will have trouble communicating with adolescents. Stuffy, prim, correct, antique—all are damning adjectives for teenagers. The repeated use of the word *prim* emphasizes the character of someone who appears out of touch with students—he sounds like the male equivalent of a stuffy old aunt whom children never want to visit because they must dress in uncomfortable clothes and sit up straight for what seems like hours on end. The description is important for the essay because it maximizes the impact of the later revelation Baker has in Fleagle's class. The man described in paragraph 2 seems incapable of inspiring anyone to do anything.

4. Mr. Fleagle's use of "don't you see" is ironic because the students obviously don't see the significance of what he's trying to say. In the end, however, Baker does see what Mr. Fleagle is trying to teach him, and it makes his epiphany that much more poignant.

5. Baker writes about the art of eating spaghetti, based on a discussion he had with relatives. He writes about it because he wants to and because it brings back good memories for him. He doesn't want to turn it in because he thinks it violates all rules of formal composition—it is not respectable enough for Mr. Fleagle.

6. Baker repeats himself to communicate the sense of surprise and wonder he felt at the moment Mr. Fleagle read his essay. The reader understands the impact the event had on Baker much more clearly than if Baker had used a simple, emotionally neutral sentence.

7. Mr. Fleagle had demonstrated to Baker the power that his writing could have: It could make people laugh and enjoy the experience of reading or hearing it. Baker's prejudice that writing is not honest work made it difficult to think of writing as a career.

Vocabulary

laden (1) burdened; loaded with

chloroform (1) a chemical that puts one to sleep, used as an anesthetic

irrepressible (3) not able to be restrained or controlled

antecedent (5) a word, phrase, or clause that is subsequently referred to by a pronoun

reminiscence (9) a remembered experience

Classroom Activity Using Transitions

The lack of transitions between the three paragraphs in the exercise is painfully obvious, but writing them for text that is already there will teach students the kind of information and the techniques for linking paragraphs that are necessary for smooth transitions. There are no absolute right or wrong answers, but when a student reads the completed passage aloud, it should flow from paragraph to paragraph and be easy to follow. You might want to allow a little more time for this activity than usual, as it may take students a while to create effective transitions.

CHAPTER 7 **Effective Sentences**

Hitting Pay Dirt (p. 160)
■ **Annie Dillard**

Essay Analysis and Discussion

Dillard's essay charts two forms of childhood personal discovery. The more immediate is her discovery of the microscopic world, and the fascination that world holds for her. The more profound is her discovery of how she is to relate with her parents on matters of personal interest or passion. While Dillard's parents' reaction may strike some as aloof or uncaring—and probably would have been difficult for an extroverted child to handle—Dillard is careful to describe how it worked to open new avenues of exploration for her. With her curiosity and the right tools, "Anything was possible" for Dillard. Note how she uses both complex and simple sentences to make the essay easy to understand, yet interesting to read. Students who believe that every sentence must be complex and dotted with commas, semicolons, and em dashes for an essay to be considered good writing will see ample evidence contrary to that notion. For example, the sentence "Mother regarded me warmly" is vital to understanding her parents' good will and willingness to respond positively to Dillard on a personal level. By limiting the sentence to those four words, Dillard makes it carry more weight. The reader knows that her mother's warmth is important enough to set apart from the rest of the text. Students can be encouraged to look at previous examples of their own writing—are there places where simple sentences would be more suitable than complex sentences? Or are there too many short, choppy sentences that detract from the flow of the essay?

40

Questions for Study and Discussion

1. Dillard writes with a child's voice to communicate her experience to the reader without adult cynicism or worldliness getting in the way of her sense of wonder and enthusiasm. It also sharpens the contrast between her reaction and her parents' reaction to her discovery of the amoeba. Dillard learns that she is not dependent upon her parents for a life; in paragraph 12, she says, "My days and nights were my own to plan and fill."

2. Dillard mixes complex and simple sentences in her first four paragraphs, interspersing her lists of materials and descriptions with short, pithy sentences that emphasize important points and make the paragraphs easier to read. The short sentences are the following:

   "Everybody needed a microscope." This communicates her childhood enthusiasm, as discussed in question 1.

   "One of the test tubes contained 'hay infusion'" and "This did not work for me." These sentences are used for variety. The first is a simple topic sentence, and the second emphasizes the problems Dillard began having with the material provided with the microscope.

   "Another test tube contained 'diatomaceous earth'" and "The kit's diatomaceous earth was a bust." These sentences perform the same functions as the preceding ones, with the use of the word *bust* emphasizing Dillard's disappointment.

3. It is not directly stated why the microscope appeals to Dillard, but it is obvious that she was a very curious child and wished to see for herself the things she read about. She perseveres through her early disappointments and is patient enough to wait until the weather is warm enough to pursue the field experiments that ultimately succeed for her.

4. Students should answer yes, in that Dillard uses a very simple vocabulary—aside from the necessary scientific terms—that is appropriate for a child's point of view. Words such as *bust*, *blobby*, *chance of a lifetime*, and *fuss over* maintain the informal tone.

5. Paragraph 12 is among the longest in Dillard's essay, yet surprisingly it consists of only three sentences. In sentence 1 she announces that she'd "been handed my own life." In the second sentence she explains exactly what that meant. In the first half of the sentence she tells what her parents provided for her growing up, and in the second half she describes the freedom and independence that they gave her. The length of the second sentence

41

reinforces the enormity of the gift that Dillard's parents gave her. She concludes the paragraph with a short, punchy sentence that states she was now free to plan and fill her own days.

6. The three short sentences in Dillard's final paragraph ("I had hit pay dirt." "Anything was possible." "The sky was the limit.") dramatically capture her excitement and delight. These short sentences surprise readers and focus their attention on the life lesson that Dillard learns.

Vocabulary

infusion (3) solution that includes material steeped in water
friable (4) easily crumbled
siliceous (4) composed of silicon
iridescent (5) shiny; glittering
festering (7) rotting

Classroom Activity Using Effective Sentences

Although this paragraph describes a dramatic event, it is written in a way that makes it boring and difficult to read. The sentence structure is monotonously consistent, and, although all the necessary information is included, it is presented in such a way that the mundane has equal footing with the dramatic and unusual. You might wish to read the paragraph aloud to the class as it stands, then read the students' revised paragraphs aloud when they are done. Hearing the passage in both forms will give the students an auditory reference for what they need to do to create interesting and effective sentences.

Salvation (p. 165)
■ Langston Hughes

Essay Analysis and Discussion

In addition to Hughes's use of different sentence lengths and patterns in this essay, he varies the manner of his material, particularly for the scene at the church. To add a sense of the revival meeting's liveliness, he includes bits of conversation that enhance the essay's main idea. In paragraph 3 he presents the preacher's words; in paragraph 6, Westley's whispered mutterings; and in paragraphs 8 through 10, an exchange between the minister and Langston's aunt. To illustrate the effects of these passages, read the essay aloud to your students and ask them to pay attention to what the dialogue contributes. Your discussion should focus, especially, on the dialogue's relation to the first and last paragraphs, and on how the inclusion of conversation helps convey Hughes's central idea. Students should also note that he includes only enough dialogue to serve his purpose.

Questions for Study and Discussion

1. According to Hughes, salvation is being "saved from sin" when Jesus and the Holy Ghost come into your life. Young Langston "wanted to see Jesus." However, his salvation was more important to his aunt, who cared about his soul and didn't want to be embarrassed in front of the congregation by his being the only one left who had not been saved. Hughes expects to be saved because his aunt and the other townspeople had built up the expectation during the weeks of preparation for the revival meeting. In paragraph 3 we see the various appeals made by the preacher, and the preacher's appeals are reinforced by the prayers and songs of the congregation.

2. Have students read portions of Hughes's essay aloud so that they can hear the rhythms that his sentences create. They'll see how the short, dramatic sentences punctuate the events of the evening, engaging readers in the emotions of the moment. Longer sentences, such as the one that begins paragraph 3, reinforce the ebb and flow of the preaching and singing at the revival meeting. Others, such as the third sentence in paragraph 11, reflect the unfolding of Hughes's thinking as he tries to decide whether to stand up at the revival meeting or what the whole experience means in the end.

3. If these two sentences had been combined, the dramatic effect of the reversal of thought and statement would have been lost.

4. The coordinating conjunctions in paragraph 3 are *and, and, and, and,* and *but.* Hughes uses coordinating conjunctions throughout his essay. When he wants to link closely related actions and not give any one of them emphasis, he does so in a long sentence. When he wants to link closely related ideas but give emphasis to each idea, he uses short sentences that begin with coordinating conjunctions.

5. The subordinating conjunctions in paragraph 15 are *for, for, because, because, because, that, that, that, that, since.* In this last paragraph Hughes reflects on the experience, and, therefore, makes explicit connections.

6. Some of the words Hughes uses to remind us that we are at a revival meeting are *sin, mourners' bench, preached, sermon, hell, prayed, Jesus, congregation,* and *wail.* In addition, Hughes uses traditional religious figures of speech such as "to bring the young

lambs to the fold," "when you were saved you saw a light," "lower lights are burning," and "all the new young lambs were blessed in the name of God."

7. The boy cried because he had lied to the congregation about seeing Jesus, because he regretted not seeing Jesus, and because he now doubted that Jesus existed at all. The irony of the tale is that Langston's "salvation from sin" was based on a lie.

Vocabulary

dire (3) dreadful or terrible
gnarled (4) deformed; twisted
vain (11) without due respect or piety
punctuated (14) interrupted periodically
ecstatic (14) enraptured

Classroom Activity Using Effective Sentences

The six sets of short sentences can be rewritten as follows:

1. I can take the 6:30 express train or catch the 7:00 bus.
2. Miriam was tired after working all weekend on her research paper, for which she interviewed five people.
3. Juan did not have time to work out at the gym for over a month because his new job kept him busy every day.
4. Completely restored for the nation's 200th birthday, the Statue of Liberty, a gift of the French government over 120 years ago, welcomes newcomers to America.
5. The starting center on the basketball team, Carla is a tall, strong team player.
6. Betsy loves Bach's music, and she also likes Scott Joplin.

Have students put their rewrites on the board and discuss the ways in which each of the sets of sentences can be combined.

The Good Daughter (p. 170)
■ **Caroline Hwang**

Essay Analysis and Discussion

Caroline Hwang discusses a conflict many young adults can relate to, the conflict between their parents' hopes and dreams for them and their own aspirations and dreams. Her story has an added wrinkle, however—cultural differences that result from her being the child of immigrant parents. Caught between the Korean world of her parents

44

and the American world in which she grows up, she sees her life as a series of compromises, a "life of halfwayness." Have students discuss their feelings about having "to choose between pleasing their parents and being true to themselves." Stylistically, Hwang's essay is interesting for its use of dialogue and for its sentence variety. For example, the dialogue in the opening seven paragraphs makes Hwang's dilemma real and gives voice to the Korean woman's cultural stance. Many of her sentences capture the hesitation or conflict in Hwang's own thinking about her situation. As a child of immigrants she is quite literally torn between her parents' dreams and her own.

Questions for Study and Discussion

1. Hwang most clearly and succinctly states her thesis in paragraph 18: "Children of immigrants are living paradoxes."
2. The incident in the dry-cleaning store pointedly shows Hwang's dilemma; she is literally caught between two cultures. The dialogue gives action and life to the incident. By having the store owner speak in her own words—pronouncing "Fxuang" as Koreans would, Hwang avoids the need to explain the incident herself. In paragraph 9, Hwang listens as her mother responds to the incident over the pronunciation of the family name. In both instances dialogue allows Hwang to show not tell the reader the attitude differences between her mother and the store owner.
3. Both short sentences capture Hwang's feelings, first in response to the storekeeper's unexpected question, and the second to the woman's cruel taunt. The two short sentences enhance the confrontational nature of this encounter.
4. Each of the sentences in paragraph 13 is structured to highlight the conflicts and contrasts that Hwang is experiencing in regard to her own identity. For example, in the first sentence "sacrifices" are contrasted with "opportunities," and in the second sentence her parents' thinking is contrasted with her own.
5. In these sentences Hwang means that the children of immigrants are caught between two cultures—in this case, Korean and American. She is suggesting that these children are the only generation to have a split identity. If Hwang herself has children in America, the children will be more culturally American and further removed from their Korean heritage.

Vocabulary

obeisance (2) a gesture or movement of the body expressing deference or homage *ransacked* (6) searched or examined thoroughly

flippant (9) marked by disrespectful levity or indifference

assimilated (12) absorbed into the prevailing culture

rhapsodizing (12) expressing oneself in an immoderately enthusiastic manner

concessions (17) the act of yielding

paradoxes (18) seeming contradictions that may nonetheless be true

filial (18) befitting a son or daughter

Classroom Activity Using Effective Sentences

This activity is an exercise in combining sentences. Encourage students to discuss the various ways in which each set of sentences can be combined—some ways are better than others—so that they can appreciate the flexibility of the English language.

1. Bonnie wore red shorts with pockets.
2. The deer hunter awoke at 5:00 A.M.; ate a quick breakfast of coffee, juice, and cereal; and was in the woods before sunrise.
3. After playing golf every weekend for years, my grandparents stopped playing last year, and now they miss the game.
4. If you fly over any major city, you will be appalled at the number of tall smokestacks you will see.
5. Most farmers were on the brink of declaring bankruptcy because most crops in the region failed during the three-month dry spell.
6. After work, I exercise, shower, and relax, and eat a light low-fat dinner.

38 *Who Saw Murder Didn't Call Police* (p. 175)
■ Martin Gansberg

Essay Analysis and Discussion

Gansberg uses a third-person point of view in this essay because he was not involved in the events described. But third person is appropriate because it lets the facts speak for themselves. When you discuss this essay, mention that at no point does Gansberg editorialize about what happened to Kitty Genovese. Yet it is clear after reading the essay how he feels about the incident. Ask them how Gansberg manages to display his attitude about the lack of response to the attack, even though he uses third person and interjects no opinions of his own. Have students look closely at his selection of details and ordering of events, and at his choices of diction. His use of dialogue is another important element in the narrative. After they've examined these aspects, students should see that though the facts seem to speak for themselves, deliberate choices about which facts to present help the essay achieve its purpose.

Questions for Study and Discussion

1. Gansberg's purpose is to show how apathy and fear have gripped the lives of New Yorkers, making them indifferent to the suffering of others. His use of narration has the advantage of illustrating the stark results of such apathy and fear, but the disadvantage of relying on readers to draw their own conclusions about the incident— conclusions that might not reflect what Gansberg hoped to achieve.

2. Gansberg's narrative of Kitty Genovese's murder begins with paragraph 7. As with Dick Gregory's essay "Shame," the introductory paragraphs establish an appropriate context in which to consider the events of the narrated incident. Without that context, the neighbors' reactions to the attack on Genovese would not have as much emotional appeal.

3. The subordinate clauses that Gansberg uses include "who was called Kitty by almost everyone in the neighborhood," "although the railroad frowns on the practice," "which is in a Tudor building, with stores in the first floor and apartments on the second," "because the front is rented to retail stores," and "that marks most residential areas." The information that is essential to the story is contained in the main clause of each of the sentences in these three paragraphs.

4. Short sentences such as "She halted," "She screamed," "'Please help me!'" "Lights went out," "'I'm dying!'" "The assailant returned," and "It drove off" emphasize action and rivet the reader's attention to what's happening. Student responses about the impact of these sentences will vary. It is important, however, to have them explain why they selected the particular sentence that they did.

5. Quotes from eleven people in the essay lend authenticity to Gansberg's narrative and illustrate, through the words of those involved, exactly how appalling the situation is.

6. Gansberg uses a tone of controlled anger and subdued amazement. Though he describes events objectively in the third person, his arrangement of details and use of diction and dialogue hint at a more aggressive attitude toward his subject.

7. Gansberg might appear didactic if he were to analyze the meaning of his narrative at the end. Though he is forced to rely on readers to formulate an appropriate meaning for his essay, that is better than if he were to appear "preachy" and create hostility between himself and his audience. Students may or may not agree.

Vocabulary

stalk (1) pursue

recitation (4) the act of repeating or uttering aloud memorized materials

assailant (5) a person who attacks or assaults another

staid (6) prudently reserved and colorless in style, manner, or behavior

shrouded (9) concealed; hidden

sheepishly (21) in an embarrassed manner, as though conscious of a fault

apprehensive (28) anxious or fearful

Classroom Activity Using Effective Sentences

One possible rewrite of the paragraph is as follows:

> Day care centers should be available to all women who work and have no one to care for their children, and not just to women who are raising their children alone or to families whose income is below the poverty level. This care should be reliable, responsible, convenient, and relatively inexpensive. Women who work must demand more day care centers. No woman should be prevented from working because child care facilities are unavailable.

You might want to put the activity paragraph on an overhead transparency so that you can rework the paragraph with all your students participating.

CHAPTER 8 **Diction and Tone**

On Being 17, Bright, and Unable to Read (p. 189)
■ **David Raymond**

Essay Analysis and Discussion

This essay contains some good examples for demonstrating the use of abstract and concrete diction. For instance, in paragraphs 5, 11, and 13, Raymond makes abstract statements and then interprets their meanings by providing concrete supporting information. Before your students look at these paragraphs, ask them how they would define the following three terms: *dumb, change, problem*. Unless they use examples, their definitions will likely be general and abstract—intangible rather than concrete ideas. This is how Raymond uses the three words:

> "I just felt *dumb*. And *dumb* was how the kids treated me."
> "Life began to *change* for me then, because I began to feel better about myself."
> "Homework is a real *problem*."

In each case, Raymond goes on to show what he means in very concrete terms. Have students look over this concrete supporting information and discuss what distinguishes it from the statements above. Let them consider the elements of sensory perception and the identification of facts as they are described in the introductory section to this chapter. Once the distinction between concrete and abstract is clear, have them do a short writing exercise in which they develop a concrete representation for an abstract idea.

Questions for Study and Discussion

1. Other examples include "but from where I sit," "unless you've been there," "I wish I were dead," "I guess I couldn't read," and "I didn't talk as good as other kids." These colloquialisms are the authentic expressions of a seventeen-year-old youth, and they add to the realism and credibility of the essay.

2. In each instance, the word suggested as a substitute is inferior either because it is imprecise or because it lacks the rich connotative value of Raymond's diction.

3. Raymond's tone is intimate and sincere and, though informal, serious enough to establish his central point. The colloquial expression suggests that his reflections are honest.
4. Dyslexia is a learning disorder in which the brain cannot interpret spatial relationships or has trouble distinguishing the difference between aural and visual information. The definition is not included because the essay is not about dyslexia. Raymond is writing about the effect on a child of being labeled as different or stupid.
5. Raymond's purpose for telling his story is to tell teachers and parents what it is like to be dyslexic so that they will treat other children with this difficulty compassionately.
6. Raymond's story warns us that negative early-childhood experiences can have a devastating effect on a child's self-esteem, academic performance, and achievement, and that this effect can define us as adults.

Vocabulary

dyslexia (2) a learning disorder that impairs the ability to read
psychiatrists (6) persons whose profession is the study, diagnosis, treatment, or prevention of mental illness

Classroom Activity Using Diction and Tone

Our students have suggested the following menu descriptions:

tomato juice: spicy tomato juice; tomato juice with a wedge of lemon
onion soup: French onion soup; onion soup covered with cheese and slow-baked in a clay crock
ground beef: Salisbury steak; chopped sirloin smothered with onions and peppers
chicken: tender roasted chicken; lightly breaded, crispy chicken
peas: baby peas; petite farm-fresh peas
potatoes: tender, new potatoes; southern hash brown potatoes
salad: crisp salad greens; fresh garden greens lightly dressed with our house vinaigrette
bread and butter: fresh-baked, whole-grain breads and creamy butter
teas: all-natural herb teas; selection of finest teas from around the world
cake: sinfully delicious triple chocolate cake; delightfully light angel food cake with farm-fresh berries

Try to engage students in a discussion of what the various descriptions tell them about the foods as well as about the restaurants that have these descriptions on their menus. For example, what restaurants serve "hash browns" and "french fries" and which ones serve "tender new potatoes"?

La Vida Loca *(The Crazy Life):* *Two Generations of Gang Members* (p. 194)
■ Luis J. Rodriguez

Essay Analysis and Discussion

Rodriguez uses vivid imagery to communicate the despair associated with gang life and his pain at seeing his son follow the same destructive path. The first paragraph is a good example—Rodriguez shows the dreariness of winter in an urban neighborhood by juxtaposing the streets filled with "dark scum" and "the whiskers of old men" hanging from the buildings. Paragraph 6 is particularly poignant: "As Ramiro speeds off, I see my body enter the mouth of darkness, my breath cut the frigid flesh of night—my voice crack open the night sky." The choice of words is poetic and striking, and it effectively readies the reader for the tone of anger and despair found in the rest of the essay. It would be hyperbolic in a different context, but here it is very effective in conveying Rodriguez's passionate involvement in his topic. Have your students find other examples of unusual word choices and images. Has the essay helped them understand the motivations of gang members?

Questions for Study and Discussion

1. Words such as *scum, decay, whiskers of old men, bone-chilling,* and *fever* add to the description by painting a vivid image. The reader has a better sense of the hostile conditions Rodriguez faces both inside and outside of his apartment.
2. The tone is indicated in the first sentence of the passage—tired. Tired of the dying, tired of tiring his mother, tired of his pain. His escape from the streets is not a grand release, but a drawn-out battle against his pain and hopelessness. His use of phrases such as "post-traumatic syndrome," "fallen through the cracks," and wanting his "self-consuming hate to wither in the sunlight" gives the reader a sense of how deep his hopelessness was—and how difficult it must have been to climb out of it.

3. Rodriguez brought Ramiro to Chicago to escape the California gangs that he had joined when he was Ramiro's age.

4. Gangs offer their members a way to get both power and respect within a group. Rodriguez had been made to feel powerless in school and society, so he was very susceptible to the influence of gangs.

5. It often means "kill me." Gang murders involve members killing the people most like themselves—in killing someone like themselves, they are, in a way, committing suicide.

6. Rodriguez says that collective action by schools, parents, and the law is needed. He is vague about exactly what should be done, and he doesn't say it will be easy. The ending is optimistic because Ramiro is off the streets, but it is a tenuous optimism. The battle for Ramiro's future is not yet won.

Vocabulary

admixture (1) mixture; substance created by mixing
dissipating (3) disappearing; dissolving
kindred (10) similar; related
absolution (12) redemption; forgiveness
impotence (22) powerlessness; inability to change a situation
disenfranchised (24) displaced; outside of society
innate (35) natural; instinctive

Classroom Activity Using Diction and Tone

Synonyms for *eat*, *drink*, *sleep*, and *work* include the following:

> *eat:* devour, nibble, feast, gorge, gobble, pick, dine, wolf, consume
> *drink:* gulp, quaff, sip, chug, guzzle, imbibe, tipple
> *sleep:* snooze, nap, slumber, doze, take forty winks, turn in, hit the hay, crash
> *work:* toil, labor, perform, serve, slave, sweat

Make four lists of the verbs on the chalkboard. Classroom discussion should focus on the connotative differences between the verbs on each list. Students usually find it helpful to try using each verb in a sentence of their own. Also discuss how the verbs in each list convey more than the meaning contained in *eat*, *drink*, *sleep*, and *work*. For example, *to nibble* means *to eat delicately*. Have students translate the verbs on each list. The bottom line: strong, active verbs reduce the need to modify.

The Fourth of July (p. 201)

■ Audre Lorde

Essay Analysis and Discussion

Lorde's essay is a carefully crafted slow boil, her restraint at the beginning serving to emphasize the blazing anger at the end. She progresses from documenting the ingenuous pleasure of traveling as a young girl to the fury of confronting racism, and her tone follows suit. Yet even in the first four paragraphs, where she doesn't mention race, she foreshadows things to come with her disappointment at not seeing the Liberty Bell and the "violently yellow" cakes. See how many other details your students can find that foreshadow the rage at the end of the essay. The reader senses that she passively accepts her parents' method of shielding her from racism—it is a "new and crushing reality" for them, but it is private. It is not until she and the reader confront racism head-on in the essay that the tone becomes angry. Have your students reread the last paragraph, including the stinging "the ice cream I never ate . . . that summer I left childhood was white." Have them discuss it in the context of current racial issues. How have things changed since Lorde wrote her essay, and how have they stayed the same?

Questions for Study and Discussion

1. Lorde describes racism as *crushing*, but *private* for her parents. She describes her physical agony on the Fourth of July as a child, implying that it is now a mental agony for her because of the *travesty* of the holiday for black people. Lorde's repetition of *white* in the one-sentence final paragraph brings home the disgust and physical sickness she felt at confronting racism head-on for the first time.

2. Lorde writes an angry essay, but it is a restrained anger until the very end. The choice of words listed above shows the progression of her understanding and anger toward racism as it unfolds in the essay. Early on, she uses subtle and indirect methods to discuss racism, but in the last three paragraphs, detailing how she is confronting it for the first time, she is very direct and very angry.

3. Lorde describes the food to emphasize the celebrational nature of her family's trip. She also implies that the food—and her family— is very American and proper, at least when discussed outside of

53

the context of her family's color. Finally, her description of the food in paragraph 4 provides a natural lead-in to the next paragraph, where we get our first glimpse of racism in the essay.

4. Lorde found the bright sunlight and glare painful for her eyes as a child. As an adult, she dislikes it because it celebrates ideals about the United States that don't exist for her and her family.

5. The Fourth of July represents American ideals of liberty and equality, ideals that don't extend to black citizens in Lorde's essay. The second part of the question is a matter of opinion, but most students should find that the irony of the title contributes to the effectiveness of the essay.

6. Lorde's parents are probably people who don't like to cause trouble. Though they are dismayed by racism, their personalities lead them to avoid confronting it and to live in a way that allows them to be comfortable without conflict. Lorde is obviously a confrontational person, so she reacts in an aggressive, confrontational manner to the injustice she faces.

Vocabulary

ensconced (3) settled; firmly placed
measly (6) pathetic; unsatisfactory
injunction (7) order; command
corolla (10) circular arrangement; petals in a flower
travesty (10) ridiculous or farcical representation
pinafored (16) dressed in a pinafore (a sleeveless dress or apron)
emphatic (18) heated; strong

Classroom Activity Using Diction and Tone

Students' lists of words for each of the tones given will vary. Here are some of the words our students gave us:

> *humorous:* laugh, joke, funny, surprise
> *angry:* hate, sarcastic, fight, boil, humiliate
> *authoritative:* dictate, judge, rule, control
> *tentative:* hesitate, unsure, undecided, reluctant
> *triumphant:* win, victor, celebrate, party, hard work

After having students compare their lists, engage them in a discussion of the connotative values associated with the words in each list. Have them focus on the verbs in their lists, and point out how well-chosen verbs influence the tone of a piece of writing.

The Dance within My Heart (p. 207)
■ **Pat Mora**

Essay Analysis and Discussion

Almost everyone has had the experience of launching into a story or a joke with great enthusiasm, only to have it fall flat. "Well," we say into the embarrassing silence, "I guess you had to be there." And we wonder why we were not able to communicate the joy, beauty, humor, or drama that provided the impetus for telling the story in the first place. If Mora had not written her essay with skill and effective language, it would have fallen very flat indeed, for it is exceedingly difficult to communicate to a reading audience an enthusiasm for something as static and subjective as visiting museums. Notice how carefully she uses her words to convey her love of museums. What they do is "offer beauty," and their halls and rooms are "a pleasure maze." They give her hope—art "nourishes our parched spirits. It is essential." It provides "escape from the confines of the predictable." Even those who may have been bored out of their minds the last time they visited a museum will be drawn into the way Mora regards museums and will identify with the palpable pleasure that comes across in her language. What place do museums have in your students' lives? Do they enjoy going to them? How relevant do they find them?

Questions for Study and Discussion

1. The prevailing tone of Mora's essay is celebrational and joyous. It is achieved by her use of words that communicate how the museums make her feel. Paragraph 9 communicates this joy very well.
2. *Spriteliness* connotes liveliness, but it also connotes a magical quality, as in a sprite from folklore. Students will have various choices for the second part of the question.
3. Museums are "pleasure havens" and "attentive to life" (paragraph 4), celebrate "the strength and inventiveness of the human imagination" (paragraph 6), allow Mora to be "with humans I admire" (paragraph 9), and "provide escape from the confines of the predictable" (paragraph 13). She begins with exhibits of living things because they are more immediately pleasing to a variety of people—human art and artifacts are more of an acquired taste.
4. Museums are recognizing that artifacts and art should be accessible to all people, not just some, so they are making their displays more acceptable to those whom they might not have considered

"washed and worthy" in the past. It is clear that Mora views art as a basic part of life, not a luxury, as she states outright in paragraph 9.

5. The question is effective because the rest of the essay presents a unified and engaging answer to the question. The essay's thesis is stated outright at the end of paragraph 9.

6. The title is a direct reference to a display text that impresses Mora. In the context of the essay it refers to the emotional impact that museums have on Mora and foreshadows the celebratory nature of her essay.

Vocabulary

havens (4) refuges; safe places
grandeur (4) glory; magnificence
arboretums (4) places where plants, particularly trees and shrubs, are cultivated for display and educational purposes
penchant (5) inclination; tendency
cowrie (6) snail with bright shell
parched (9) dry, thirsty

Classroom Activity Using Diction and Tone

This activity might take more time than average, so be prepared to assign half of it as a homework assignment. When you introduce the activity, have the students think about how they speak to older and younger people, and, if possible, have them role-play the different ages and address each other in class, so that they can actually hear their tone. They will then have a good foundation from which to proceed with their paragraphs.

CHAPTER 9 **Figurative Language**

The Barrio (p. 214)
■ **Robert Ramirez**

Essay Analysis and Discussion

Ramirez points out the sights of the barrio from a moving train that emerges in the "deep sleep" of night in the opening paragraph, and reappears to the "yawns and restless stretchings" of a new dawn in the closing paragraph. Students can discuss this use of figurative language in the asking of four questions: Why does Ramirez use a train to establish a context for his description of the barrio? and why does he take us into the barrio only through the still hours of the night? What does he intend as the symbolism of the train and the street lamp? What do they add to his portrayal of the barrio?

Questions for Study and Discussion

1. *Barrio* is a Spanish word that refers to a chiefly Spanish-speaking neighborhood (typically in a city) in the southwestern United States. Ramirez generally describes barrios as isolated communities "fenced off by railroads, canals, and expressways." Because the barrio is a "refuge from the harshness and the coldness of the Anglo world," members of the barrio have no desire to leave. All their needs are met within its confines.

2. The Spanish phrases, spoken as if the reader understands them, lend an aura of authenticity and color to Ramirez's essay. These words allow us to "hear" the people of the barrio. The other words connote warmth, community, intimacy, and friendliness. They are meant to emphasize the positive feelings of life in the barrio that are known only to its inhabitants.

3. "[T]his pulsing light . . . beats slower, like a weary heartbeat" (1). "[F]rom the angry seeds of rejection grow the flowers of closeness between outcasts, not the thorns of bitterness" (4). "[T]he warmth of the tortilla factory is a wool *sarape*" (5). "Their houses, aged and bent, oozing children, are fissures in the horn of plenty" (17). These metaphors are particularly apt because they compare things common to the barrio with other things that are relevant to it. The wool *sarape* is as common as the factory. The horn of plenty, broken and empty, is also a metaphor for the people of the barrio.

4. Ramirez uses a number of words and phrases that attribute human characteristics to the barrio and the daily train. These include "blinks" (1), "pulsing" (1), "weary heartbeat" (1), "grumble" (2), "arrest" (13), "ignore" (13), and "greets a new dawn with yawns and restless stretchings" (20).

5. Ramirez intends his comparison of the fences in the barrio with the walls of the Anglo community to symbolize the easy interaction among the people of his culture as compared with the isolation and separation of the Anglo world.

6. Had Ramirez begun his description of the barrio with the negative aspects of life there he would have risked having readers misunderstand the intent of his essay. Ramirez wants us to understand that life in the barrio is integral, satisfying, and necessary. He saves the sadder aspects of life there until the end, so that we do not confuse his desire for our understanding with a desire for pity.

Vocabulary

paradoxical (2) seemingly contradictory
eludes (2) escapes or evades
permeated (3) pervaded
stoical (4) suffering silently and without complaint
pariahs (4) outcasts
complacently (9) with satisfaction or acceptance, especially self-satisfaction
Chicano (11) an American of Mexican descent
countenances (12) human faces, especially as an indication of mood or character
fissures (17) narrow openings or cracks
adverse (19) unfavorable
elusive (19) evasive; out of reach

Classroom Activity Using Figurative Language

Possible metaphors or similes for each of the items on the list include:

1. *a skyscraper:* huge glass needle
2. *the sound of an explosion:* rumble of distant thunder, cannon shot
3. *an intelligent student:* computer
4. *a crowded bus:* stuffed turkey, packed suitcase
5. *a slow-moving car:* snail, turtle, tank
6. *a pillow:* puffy cloud, flat pancake
7. *a narrow alley:* cave, tunnel
8. *greasy french fries:* slippery carrot sticks, glistening wet skin
9. *hot sun:* roasting oven, baking, sear like a flame
10. *a dull knife:* cutting with wooden utensil, frustrating as playing golf with the wrong club

Engage students in a discussion of the various figures of speech that they came up with for each item and have them decide which ones work best. They will see that good figures of speech are those that are fresh (not clichéd) and create a clear mental image.

A Hanging (p. 220)
■ George Orwell

Essay Analysis and Discussion

Many students will find Orwell's essay very disturbing, but they should also find it relevant. It is interesting that, although "A Hanging" was written more than sixty years ago, it addresses some very modern issues, most notably that of capital punishment. It is a narrative, but it is also an extremely powerful and eloquent testimonial against the practice of putting a fellow human being to death. Notice how Orwell uses the two events that break the routine of the morning—the arrival of the dog and the prisoner's crying "Ram" on the gallows—to emphasize the awful nature of what is taking place. Yet, without those two events, the reader realizes that it would have just been another morning at the jail, an early morning routine that concludes with someone's death. Orwell's use of figurative language reinforces the bestial nature of the proceedings from the start—the condemned cells are "like small animal cages" and the guards handle the prisoner "like men handling a fish which is still alive and may jump back into the water." Have your students look for other examples of figurative language. Also, discuss the ending with your students. Why do they think Orwell and the others felt so jovial and euphoric? What does the ending say about the jail workers and the jobs they must do?

Questions for Study and Discussion

1. The appearance of the dog is dreadful to the executioners because it disrupts the routine. The dog disrupts the effort of the magistrates and other officials to carry out the execution in an orderly, reasonable fashion and to devalue and dehumanize the prisoner before he dies.

2. Neither the narrator's role nor the prisoner's transgression matters because Orwell is commenting on the practice in general, not on the legal aspects of this one case.

3. Orwell realizes that the prisoner is a human, just like all the rest of them, and is experiencing life just as they are, even to the point of reasoning that puddles will make him wet, so they should be stepped around. The only difference is that his life is to be cut short. "One mind less, one world less" means that for every human who is removed from the earth, there is one less unique perspective and understanding about the world.

4. Francis's story about the troublesome prisoner is ironic in that he was remonstrating the prisoner for inconveniencing those who were about to kill him!
5. "A sickly light, like yellow tinfoil" (1), "like the moustache of a comic man in the films" (2), "[the gallows] was a brick erection like three sides of a shed" (11), "almost like the tolling of a bell" (12), and so on.
6. A pariah is an outcast from society, as the prisoner is. The variety of backgrounds underscores the universal approach to justice, and it points out that one culture or another is not particularly cruel, bloodthirsty, or callous toward what happens that day.
7. The group is somber, almost automaton-like before the hanging (3 through 8); and ebullient, almost manic after the hanging (17 through 24). The superintendent "moodily prodded the gavel with his stick" and had a gruff voice; all are "aghast" at the glee of the dog. Afterward, it is a homely, jolly scene; the men are garrulous and laugh without knowing why. The shift in mood can be explained by the fact that they have gotten through this terrible event. Some students will notice that the police need a drink after the hanging.

Vocabulary

magistrates (6) government officials
volley (6) a burst or emission of many things
gambolled (8) cavorted; ran around
erection (11) something erect; standing tall
servile (11) abject; submissive
abominable (13) awful; terrible
timorously (15) timidly; fearfully
oscillated (16) swung back and forth
garrulously (20) in an annoyingly talkative way; verbosely
refractory (22) resisting control or authority
genially (23) amicably; in a friendly way
amicably (24) genially; in a friendly way

Classroom Activity Using Figurative Language

This activity should not be terribly difficult for your students, but it will bring home how effective figurative language can be in communicating an image or atmosphere. Make sure they use familiar associations that communicate more to the reader than a simple description would. If you wish, have the students write a couple of similes or metaphors for the same actions on the part of those who are excited or pleased—how can they use figurative language to communicate a different mood from the same action?

The Flight of the Eagles (p. 227)
■ **N. Scott Momaday**

Essay Analysis and Discussion

The most noticeable aspect of Momaday's essay is, of course, his selection of words—particularly, strong, descriptive verbs—to help create the image of the eagles' flight. Not so noticeable, perhaps, but just as important to the essay's success, is his use of transitions. Because this selection is so short and there are many good examples to show the subtle ways that transitions can operate, it may be helpful to go through it sentence by sentence, looking at the ways transitions are integrated into a paragraph. There are examples to illustrate all three types of transitions described in the introduction to the Transitions chapter. Students should discover that Momaday's transitions help make his descriptive diction come alive.

Questions for Study and Discussion

1. Momaday's figures of speech include the following:
    1. The dead snake fell "like a bit of silver thread against the wide backdrop of the land." (Momaday suggests how insignificant and delicate the snake was against the wide expanse of the land.)
    2. The female was still, "her crop and hackles gleaming like copper in the sun." (Momaday suggests that the feathers around the throat and neck areas of the eagle were like shining copper.)
    3. The eagle hit the snake "cracking its long body like a whip." (The eagle hit one end of the snake with such force as to make a whip out of the snake; Momaday suggests further that the snake made the snapping noise of a whip.)
    4. The eagle "swung upward in a great pendulum arc, riding out his momentum." (Momaday describes the eagle coming out of a dive as if it were a pendulum on the upswing going only as far as its momentum would take it.)
2. The female was full-grown, had a broad wing span, and had great weight. The male was younger, half as large as the female, and "quicker, tighter in his moves."

3. The strong descriptive verbs that Momaday uses include *cavorting, spinning, spiraling, swooped, hovered, swung, fanned, flared, buoyed, swerved, sailed, rolled,* and *soared.* The two birds in this description are flying, but, instead of simply repeating that verb, Momaday uses verbs that create specific mental pictures of the birds' precise actions.
4. In this exercise students should consider both the denotative and connotative values of each of the italicized words and phrases. You may wish to suggest substitutions for each word or phrase to contrast them with Momaday's diction.
5. Examples of Momaday's concrete and specific language include *golden eagles, male, female, mating flight, rattlesnake, crop,* and *hackles.* Also see the specific descriptive verbs discussed in 3 above.

Vocabulary

cavorting: engaging in extravagant behavior
feinting: making a pretense of
spectral: ghostly

Classroom Activity Using Figurative Language

The first selection, "The Fading Season," is an example of what might be called "purple prose." The writer has made use of uncontrolled personification and metaphors, as well as pretentious diction, in such profusion that the reader is overwhelmed and the writer's message is lost.

The second selection, "October," is fashioned around the personification of "blond October," a consistent and easy-to-follow description. The diction in this selection is far more appropriate for the season being described. The comparison of these two passages provides you with an opportunity to identify those students who hold on to the notion that overwrought, highly modified prose is what English teachers are looking for.

CHAPTER 10 **Illustration**

A Crime of Compassion (p. 237)
■ **Barbara Huttmann**

Essay Analysis and Discussion

At the heart of Huttmann's dramatic and often shocking essay is the story of her young patient. In the beginning of her essay we meet him, a strong, confident, healthy young man. Then Huttmann proceeds in a chronological order to describe the rapid deterioration that ends in his death. Other things are happening as well: the falling apart of his family and the nurse's own evolution from rule-abiding health worker to mercy "killer." Yet as dramatic as Huttmann's tale is, it remains a model of "show, don't tell." For Huttmann never asks us to weep—she moves us to tears with the details of the events she witnessed and the emotions she experienced. Even those who condemn her actions would be hard pressed to remain unmoved by the horrors that the young family went through. Ask students to reread Huttmann's essay carefully to see how she sustains the dramatic atmosphere of her story. Which kinds of evidence were convincing and which were not? In the end, is she successful in convincing readers of the justness of her actions?

Questions for Study and Discussion

1. Huttmann did not have the legal right to end her patient's life. By that definition, she is a murderer. However, her defenders no doubt will point out that the definition of murder as premeditated and malicious killing of a human being does not fit the circumstances of Huttmann's deed. She killed out of love, not hate, and the decision to do so was painful given her attitude that life is something that must be sustained and nurtured. As Huttmann wondered at the right of doctors to sustain life beyond reasonable bounds, she no doubt questioned their right, and hers, to end it. That is why she argues so strenuously for a patient's right to make this terrible decision.

2. Huttmann's essay is as much a tale of her own struggle as it is the story of her patient's decline and death. She begins in paragraph 7 by telling us how often Mac had to be resuscitated and the terrible and grisly agony he went through. By paragraph 8, she is praying he will die but she has not yet thought of helping him to do it. In

paragraph 9 she asks for a "no-code order," which only a doctor can issue. In other words, it is not illegal for doctors to allow a patient to die, only for a nurse. When her request was refused she contemplated the implications of failing to press the button. By paragraph 10, when Mac had undergone fifty-two codes, she began appealing to a higher court, a spiritual judge to question the necessity of her actions. She began to be haunted by the question that modern technology has made inevitable—"do we have the right to play God," not in taking life, but in sustaining it beyond all hope? Finally she makes us witness her panic and fear as she makes the decision not to press the button. Her story is compelling and terrifying and she spares us little of the terror she experienced in making her final decision.

3. As Huttmann explains in paragraph 18, a doctor may legally issue a no-code order. The hypocrisy for her is that the charge of murder is based not on intent but on which uniform a person wears.

4. In paragraph 7 Huttmann describes the work a team of nurses had to do over Mac's body: "The nurses stayed to wipe the saliva that drooled from his mouth, irrigate the big craters of bedsores that covered his hips, suction the lung fluids that threatened to drown him, clean the feces that burned his skin like lye, pour the liquid food down the tube attached to his stomach, put pillows between his knees to ease the bone-on-bone pain, turn him every hour to keep the bedsores from getting worse, and change his gown and linen every two hours to keep him from being soaked in perspiration." Such graphic descriptions are necessary to force the reader to see what Huttmann saw and, however feebly, to feel what Mac felt. She knows it is easy to make philosophical decisions about life and death from a distance. She wants to rub the readers' noses in the truth.

5. As her essay moves forward, Huttmann intensifies the story by going into lengthier detail about shorter periods of time. No doubt this is meant to parallel as much as possible the way in which Mac's pain escalated, not only in intensity but in the horror of its detail.

6. Quite simply Huttmann means to say that as long as medical science and its practitioners have the means to keep patients alive and believe that they must do so, and as long as the decision not to resuscitate rests with the doctors, patients cannot legally choose to die.

Vocabulary

resuscitate (3) to revive from a condition resembling death
irrigate (7) to flush with liquid

lucid (10) clear-minded; alert
imperative (11) power to restrain, control, or direct
waxen (15) resembling wax (as in color or consistency)
pallor (15) paleness

Classroom Activity Using Illustration

This exercise has worked well in getting students to see the relationship between a thesis statement and what is necessary to make it credible and convincing. Of course, this exercise can also be used to have students generate a series of shorter examples, but here the focus is on the single example, which allows for some degree of depth and detail. You may want to have students think about possible examples and also compose one.

Be Specific (p. 243)
■ **Natalie Goldberg**

Essay Analysis and Discussion

Goldberg's message in this essay is simple and to the point—"Be specific." We all recognize when a writer is specific; the writing seems to come alive, to jump off the page. But beginning writers have difficulty being specific, using telling details. Goldberg offers some direct advice for students to start with: give people and things names and provide a specific context (month, day, moment, etc.) for the situation about which you're writing. Not only does Goldberg give writers advice about being specific but she also demonstrates that advice in her own writing. In her final paragraph, Goldberg asks readers to "learn the names of everything: birds, cheese, tractors, cars, buildings." As a class exercise, generate lists of names for items in each of the categories she suggests.

Questions for Study and Discussion

1. Goldberg practices what she preaches in this essay. She's careful to "be specific." She "give[s] things the dignity of their names." And she set out to learn the names of everything, concentrating first on "the names of plants and flowers in my environment."
2. The lists help define the word "specific" because each list is made up of particular members of a general category. They forcefully show that names do, in fact, convey very precise images; each name on the list removes a particular object from its category by

bringing to mind a picture of that object in a setting furnished by the reader's imagination.

3. A writer needs to know not only the name of a particular thing, but the month, day, and moment of the context in which it is important (4). Precision in time is as important as precision in identity in making a subject real and immediate to the reader.

4. To know the name of something connects us to the earth—it makes us more awake and friendly toward the environment (3). It allows us to "penetrat[e] more deeply" into what is in front of us and to learn from it (5); it grounds us and makes us more attentive in a group (6).

5. According to Goldberg's example (addressing a girl by her name rather than by "girl"), people—and by extension, things—are dignified when they are recognized by name as specific individuals instead of as members of a general class. "Integrity" implies uniqueness, wholeness, and self-worth.

6. Goldberg is addressing writers. In paragraph 4 she quotes William Carlos Williams: "Write what's in front of your nose." She mentions writing groups (6) and gives advice to "a writer" (7).

Vocabulary

pomegranate (1) a thick-skinned, reddish fruit with many seeds
integrity (4) a firm adherence to a code of moral or artistic values

Classroom Activity Using Illustration

Possible answers for the blanks in each ladder of abstraction are pen, food, Native American, *The American Heritage Dictionary*, Essex Vocational/Technical High School, Tylenol Gel Caps.

For additional practice with being more specific, have students create their own ladders of abstraction (with one step on the ladder blank) and exchange them with classmates.

The Case for Short Words (p. 247)
■ **Richard Lederer**

Essay Analysis and Discussion

Many writers lose track of what writing is all about somewhere along the way. Instead of a medium of communication, it becomes a medium of vanity—the writer is out to impress readers with craft, not clarity. One of the easiest ways to spot this problem in a piece of writing is the use of vocabulary, as *use* becomes *utilize*, *try* becomes *endeavor*, and so on. Lederer's essay addresses this problem in two ways. He presents a standard, though eloquent, plea for the use of short words when long ones are not necessary. He supports his argument with evidence—academic studies that demonstrate that short words provide the foundation for the English language—and examples of great writing and speeches composed entirely of one-syllable words. Much of the impact of his essay, however, comes from how he illustrates his point in a more immediate manner. First, his four paragraphs of single-syllable words do a wonderful job of making his point that you can write well with only short words. Second, by presenting the student essays, he drives home the point that it does not take a great writer to make good use of short words—anyone's writing will benefit from using them where and when appropriate. Ask your students how many saw what Lederer was doing before he told them in the fifth paragraph of his essay. Have them reread the paragraphs. How does Lederer's use of all one-syllable words differ from his standard prose, as seen in the middle of the essay? Which is easier to read and understand?

Questions for Study and Discussion

1. Such words can be called the "best" because everyone knows exactly what they are; if you use them, you do not have to worry about how advanced or specialized your audience is. The same advantage holds true for old versus new words.
2. Lederer says, "If a long word says just what you want to say, do not fear to use it." He is not trying to discourage the use of long words, but to encourage the use of more short ones where appropriate, as they can make essays easier to read and understand.
3. By having several quotes from those who are considered among the most effective writers and orators in history, Lederer proves that such great communicators do not seek to use long words just for the sake of showing off. Some of their best work is done with very simple tools. The inclusion of the ninth-grade essays demonstrates that it does not take the skill and polish of a great writer to use short words with great effectiveness.
4. Students have many choices, for example: "Big words can make the way dark for those who read what you write and hear what you say." This metaphor communicates that the use of long words can obscure the meaning of what a writer wants to say, not make it easier to understand. "Short words are bright like sparks that glow in the night" contrasts with the former piece of figurative language, communicating that short words are readily understood.

5. Students often feel pressure to come across as learned, formal, or smart in their writing, so they feel pressured to use fancy words. Lederer's point is that great writing often relies on short words, so the success the students have in completing the assignment supports his argument in favor of the use of short words.
6. Lederer's image of the sign will help readers retain the content of his essay. It is something that readers will remember even if they do not care to as they sit down to their next writing assignment.
7. Student responses will differ.

Vocabulary

cabined (5) confined; cramped
cribbed (5) confined; cramped
monosyllabic (6) consisting of one syllable
proverbs (7) short statements of folklore or wisdom
eloquence (10) fluency; persuasiveness
obligatory (10) requisite; mandatory
vitality (11) vigor; freshness

Classroom Activity Using Illustration

In a short piece of writing in which one is trying to explain or define a subjective or complex topic, an effective illustration is crucial to getting the point across. The ideal gift is a difficult thing to present to a reader, but the use of an example that captures the meaning of the ideal gift makes it concrete for the reader. You may wish to specify a particular situation—such as the birthday of a special friend, or a holiday with a relative—to help students narrow their choices.

Don't Let Stereotypes Warp Your Judgments (p. 253)
■ **Robert L. Heilbroner**

Essay Analysis and Discussion

Heilbroner's essay is an excellent example of how to make use of support—objective, gathered information—to convey an idea. When you discuss this essay, point out the references to persons and events outside of the author's immediate realm of experience. For example, in the first few paragraphs, as he describes the nature and scope of stereotyping, Heilbroner relies on the authority of questionnaires, university studies, and the findings of criminologists and optometrists rather than just his own observations. In later paragraphs, he incorporates quotes from persons noted for their observations on human behavior (William James, Walter Lippmann, S. I. Hayakawa, F. Scott Fitzgerald) to amplify his statements about stereotypes and prejudice. As you look at these references with students, discuss how Heilbroner makes sure they are consistent with his central point and, therefore, lend credibility and support. Heilbroner's essay can show students how to incorporate various types of supporting information into a clearly focused and tightly connected essay.

Questions for Study and Discussion

1. Heilbroner feels that stereotypes do an injustice to others and also impoverish those who think in terms of stereotypes.
2. Paragraph 6 is an example of our tendency to prejudge people. Paragraph 8 shows how stereotypes affect adults. Paragraph 15 shows how difficult it is to get rid of stereotypes. In each case the paragraph is directly related to the preceding paragraph. All three paragraphs illustrate Heilbroner's thesis about stereotypes.
3. Heilbroner uses a number of transitional devices: relative pronouns, repeated key words and ideas, conjunctions, transitional expressions. By indicating the relationships between paragraphs, these devices enhance the unity of the essay.
4. We stereotype for many reasons, beginning with childhood when we learn to tell the good guys from the bad guys on television. Later, as adults, we ingrain stereotypes through the jokes we listen to and repeat; we pick up other stereotypes in ads, books, and movies. Finally, "we tend to stereotype because it helps us make sense out of a highly confusing world." Stereotypes are dangerous, according to Heilbroner, because they become "substitutes for observation." Even when we do observe, "stereotypes get in the way of our judgment." In addition to the harm stereotypes do to others, "they impoverish ourselves," robbing us of the opportunity to see the world in our own, unique way. We can shed stereotypes on three fronts, according to Heilbroner. One, we can become aware of them in our thinking, in the thinking of others, and in the world around us. Two, we can become suspicious of all rules that we allow the exception to "prove." Three, "we can learn to be chary of generalizations about people."
5. Heilbroner uses the word *picture* as a near-synonym for a stereotype because a stereotype really is a mental image. His repetition of the word culminates in his gallery metaphor in the final paragraph.

Vocabulary

irrational (7) illogical; contrary to reason
perpetuated (8) continued without interruption
infinite (10) having no boundaries or limits
preconceptions (11) opinions formed in advance of actual knowledge
vindicated (11) cleared, as from suspicion
impoverish (12) deprive of natural richness or strength
chastening (18) refining or purifying
edifice (18) building
chary (19) cautious

Classroom Activity Using Illustration

It's always a good idea to emphasize the five senses when having students describe or provide details. It is important to the success of this exercise that students be allowed to compare their lists of details for the object in question so that those having trouble generating details can see what others who find the exercise easier have done. As far as names for items is concerned, students should be made aware of the fact that having names for things has both positive and negative aspects. Certainly, common and proper names are a kind of experiential shorthand; when we have a name for something (e.g., Coke can) we don't have to spend a lot of time and effort signifying what we mean. However, the name of something can, for the writer, put the object at some distance from experience and lessen the importance and power of specific details.

CHAPTER 11 **Narration**

Shame (p. 262)
■ **Dick Gregory**

Essay Analysis and Discussion

The heart of this essay is the incident Gregory relates about being shamed in front of Helene Tucker. Gregory chooses a chronological organization, but the chronology does not begin until the fourth paragraph because Gregory needs to establish a context for the incident in paragraphs 1 through 3. To give your students an indication of how vital such a context is to this essay, have them reexamine the first three paragraphs and consider what they contribute to Gregory's narration of the schoolroom incident in paragraphs 4 through 27, and what effect the removal of these three paragraphs would have on the essay. If you wish to narrow the focus of the discussion even further, ask them how the following sentences from those initial paragraphs interact with elements from Gregory's anecdote:

> "It was a lady's handkerchief, but I didn't want Helene to see me wipe my nose on my hand." (1)
>
> "Everybody's got a Helene Tucker, a symbol of everything you want." (2)
>
> "And she had a Daddy, and he had a good job." (2)
>
> "When I played the drums in high school it was for Helene and when I broke track records in college it was for Helene and when I started standing behind microphones and heard applause I wished Helene could hear it, too." (3)

After you've discussed the relationship between the opening paragraphs and the episode at school, have students analyze how those three paragraphs connect with Gregory's conclusion. The intent of your discussion should be to clarify what it means to establish a clear context for a narration.

Questions for Study and Discussion

1. For Gregory, *shame* means "disgrace," in this case disgrace in an environment where he least expected to find it. Gregory was ashamed of his poverty and of not having a father; however, that day in school was the day "I learned to be ashamed of myself."

2. In the first three paragraphs of the essay, Gregory introduces Helene Tucker and tells of his infatuation with her. This information provides the motivation for his later behavior.

3. Because Gregory lived the experience he is telling, it is most natural for him to narrate it in the first person. The third-person point of view would give the narrative an objective, perhaps even a sociological, bent.

4. The teacher thought Gregory was stupid, he said, but didn't stop to consider that he had trouble in school because he wasn't getting enough to eat at home. She also thought he was a troublemaker, again not taking time to consider that he was looking for attention he didn't get at home. Nevertheless, until the day of his shaming, he thought she liked him. "She always picked me to wash the blackboard on Friday, after school . . . it made me feel important." Ultimately she showed contempt for "you and your kind," and publicly humiliated him when she announced his secret to the class: "We know you don't have a daddy."

5. This is not a story about racism. In fact, there's nothing to indicate that his teacher wasn't black. The lack of money is the basis of Gregory's shame, just as it would be the having of money that erased it. Helene Tucker, the little girl who was light-complexioned, clean, and well-dressed, became the symbol of what he wasn't. "It wasn't until I was twenty-nine years old and married and making money that I finally got her out of my system."

6. Examples of Gregory's use of descriptive details abound in the essay. (By locating examples, students will become aware of how such details help to create vivid and interesting prose.)

7. There are three distinct time periods in which Gregory's narrative takes place:

    1. In paragraphs 1 through 3, Gregory talks about his twenty-two-year infatuation with Helene Tucker. Time references he uses include "seven years old," "by summertime," "next twenty-two years," "twenty-nine years old."

    2. In paragraphs 4 through 27, Gregory tells what happened on that "Thursday" when he was seven years old. After giving us some insight about his teacher's attitude toward him in paragraphs 5 and 6, Gregory starts narrating the crucial scene with the sentence, "It was on a Thursday, the day before the Negro payday."

    3. In paragraph 28 he discusses the importance of the aftermath of the events of that crucial Thursday. He starts the paragraph with the time reference "Now."

Vocabulary

nappy (2) shaggy or fuzzy
mackinaw (28) a short double-breasted coat of heavy woolen material

Classroom Activity Using Narration

Here is the rewrite of the first paragraph, using both the author's first name (the selection is autobiography) and the appropriate third-person pronouns (he, his, and him):

> Dick never learned hate at home, or shame. He had to go to school for that. He was about seven years old when he got his first big lesson. Dick was in love with a little girl named Helene Tucker, a light-complexioned little girl with pigtails and nice manners. She was always clean and she was smart in school. Dick thinks he went to school then mostly to look at her. He brushed his hair and even got himself a little old handkerchief. It was a lady's handkerchief, but he did-

n't want Helene to see him wipe his nose on his hand. The pipes were frozen again, there was no water in the house, but he washed his socks and shirt every night. Dick would get a pot, and go over to Mr. Ben's grocery store, and stick his pot down into the soda machine. Scoop out some chopped ice. By the evening the ice melted to water for washing. Dick got sick a lot that winter because the fire would go out at night before his clothes were dry. In the morning he'd put them on, wet or dry, because they were the only clothes he had.

Most students will find it easy to switch from first-person to third-person pronouns. They may not catch on so quickly to using the proper name. While rewriting a sentence like "She was always clean and she was always smart in school," students might ask how a third-person narrator could know this information. Finally, most students prefer the original to the rewrite because of the intimacy and immediacy of the subject matter.

The Dare (p. 268)
■ Roger Hoffmann

Essay Analysis and Discussion

Hoffmann begins his story with a description of the terrible, frightening thing he did to win the dare. Then he explains that he would never do it again as an adult. He allows the present, the lesson to be learned from all this, to interrupt his narrative only one other time—just after he accepts the dare. The author wants us to know two things: what the moment was like for a young boy and how it fit into his picture of himself as a man. Ask students to compare episodes of their lives that were significant when they happened and then took on even more significance in retrospect. How would they write such a story?

Questions for Study and Discussion

1. Hoffmann took the dare because he wanted to be accepted by the rest of the twelve-year-old boys in his class. He implies in paragraph 4 that by taking the dare at twelve, he doesn't have to prove anything to himself or anyone else at thirty-eight.
2. Paragraph 4 explains the author's purpose in telling us his story.
3. Hoffmann organizes his narration chronologically. He covers the first years of his schooling in the first five paragraphs. In the last seven he covers one day. A narration needs to spend less time

setting the scene or the context of the story than it does on the story itself.

4. Hoffmann uses several very effective figures of speech to convey his feelings of dread. And in the final sentences he tells us he has wet his pants.

5. Hoffmann uses the following figures of speech:

"The monkey clawing my back was Teacher's Pet." (3), metaphor
"a circle on another planet" (7), metaphor
"Their silhouette resembled a round-shouldered tombstone." (8), metaphor
"The train sounded like a cow going short of breath." (9), simile

Hoffmann uses the different figures of speech to sharpen his images and to present the world the way it seemed to a frightened boy.

6. Using the third person, whether from the perspective of O.T. or Dwayne or omnisciently, would fictionalize the narrative. It would also distance readers from the central action: We could not lie under the train with Hoffmann or experience his terror first-hand. In addition, using third person would limit Hoffmann's ability to reflect as an adult on his childhood experience. However, a third-person narrator *would* be able to give readers greater insight into the responses and motives of O.T. and Dwayne.

Vocabulary

shards (1) broken pieces; fragments
baited (1) nagged; teased; tempted
cronies (2) close friends, especially of long standing
escalated (2) increased in intensity
guerrilla (2) one who engages in irregular warfare
evaporating (3) disappearing quickly
implicit (4) understood though not directly stated
ambiguous (4) capable of being understood in more than one way
convulsive (11) violently disturbing

Classroom Activity Using Narration

Describing a movement in an interesting fashion is a difficult writing task, so this exercise is quite worthwhile in extending students' range of capabilities. Students will typically leave important aspects of the movements out of their descriptions and will need to have the benefit of a peer conference to have someone point out the incompleteness of their descriptions. Sometimes students actually have to make the movements and stand outside of themselves to objectify them before being able to render them accurately.

Momma, the Dentist, and Me (p. 273)
■ Maya Angelou

Essay Analysis and Discussion

The editors of this text placed their own title on this selection from Angelou's *I Know Why the Caged Bird Sings*. Their title is appropriate for the content of the essay, but, given the complexity of Angelou's narration, other suitable options may also exist. This essay can, therefore, serve as a catalyst for discussion of how to choose an effective title. Ask your students to reread the essay with an eye toward providing it with a new title. Then, have them write suggested titles on slips of paper and turn them in so you can compile an anonymous listing on the board. Once you've completed the list, ask the students to vote on which title they like best, and when they've indicated their preferences, discuss why some titles were chosen over others. You will want to consider originality, ability to stimulate interest, and appropriateness to the content of the essay, as well as other factors the students may see as significant.

Questions for Study and Discussion

1. Angelou's purpose is to show the kind of pain that bigotry and injustice inflict, and to show that such cruelty often fosters the desire for retribution in its victims.
2. The content of the two interchanges between Momma and the dentist is similar in that, in both cases, Momma exacts revenge on the dentist for his refusal to treat the young girl. But the way she achieves that revenge is different. In Maya's version, Momma "obliterates" the dentist with her angry words, rendering him weak and submissive under her power and authority. In Momma's version, although she speaks of the dentist and his nurse with contempt, the scene she describes is more subdued and less vengeful, but ultimately, more productive in getting Maya's toothache treated. The style of the two versions is very different. To use Angelou's words, the first displays an "eloquent command of English," both in the way Momma speaks and in Maya's de-

scription of events, while in the second, Momma uses her usual vernacular to recall the scene.

3. Angelou's chronological presentation helps her establish a clear and purposeful context for the scene at the dentist's office. In the narration leading up to the visit, she builds a sense of tension and frustration as she describes the pain of her toothache and her anxiety about approaching a white dentist. The chronological pattern also helps to juxtapose the two versions of what occurred between Momma and the dentist. The first-person point of view is crucial to the central idea of the essay because it shows Maya's desire for retribution firsthand, a desire that creates the fantasized version of the confrontation between Momma and the dentist. Her version becomes more poignant because readers come to feel what she is like and what motivates her, before they reach that scene. This makes the final statement more potent.

4. Angelou's essay contains the following similes: "as if a white-breeze blew off whitefolks and cushioned everything in their neighborhood" (6); "the way people hunt for shells" (18); "like little claps of thunder" (29); "like filling in a pie crust" (46); "like a piece of lint" (48); "thick as thieves" (48); and "like he was sitting on a pin" (48). Each simile works within its paragraph and all of the similes work together to provide a more vivid description of events.

5. Angelou's version of the episode describes what, for her, is a more just resolution of the situation: a Dodge City–style triumph over bigotry. The dentist is not only confronted, he is driven from town frightened and disgraced. To the child, it must have been a pale consolation that the dentist had to pay a few more dollars on his debt to the grandmother.

6. Angelou first uses exaggerated descriptions to indicate the magnitude of her pain: "I prayed earnestly that I'd be allowed to sit under the house and have the building collapse on my left jaw" (1); "seriously considering the idea of jumping in the well" (2); "I was certain that I'd be dead" (2); "the pain was more serious than that which anyone had ever suffered" (3). She then presents some startling metaphors to show her intimate connection to that pain: "I had frozen to the pain" (4); "the pain was my world, an aura that haloed me for three feet around" (5). These references are important because they establish the extent to which she suffers physically; yet the physical pain subsides when Maya confronts the psychic pain of bigotry and injustice described in paragraphs 9 through 26, culminating in the dentist's refusal to treat her.

Vocabulary

bailiwick (1) specific area of interest, skill, or authority
calaboose (7) jail
mite (22) a very small creature
vernacular (34) the nonstandard everyday speech of a country or region
varlet (39) rascal; knave
concoct (42) to prepare by mixing ingredients
snippety (49) impertinent
retributive (50) characterized by the giving or demanding of repayment, especially punishment

Classroom Activity Using Narration

Making a list rather than drafting is the important part of this activity. It's far easier for students to see a sequence of activities, and how it may be reordered, in list form than in a paragraph or essay. It is useful to discuss how drama is achieved through placement at the beginning or end of a sequence and what it takes to create a rising tension in a sequence of events.

The Story of an Hour (p. 282)
■ Kate Chopin

Essay Analysis and Discussion

Chopin lived in an era when women had few options. Those who did not marry and manage their family's household were referred to in pejorative terms such as "old maid" and "spinster" if they were known to be chaste, and as "eccentric" or worse if they had the hint of scandal about them. "The Story of an Hour" would not have much impact in these days of no-fault divorce and ever-increasing career opportunities for women, but, taken in the context of its time, it is a compelling story that raises many issues of the day. The journal prompt asks students to consider marriage on personal terms. It may be a good idea to discuss what marriage meant for both men and women in the early 1900s before students read the story. Some of them may know something about married life in that era, but they probably have not thought about it much as a reality. What is it like to be bound to someone with no hope of ever being released if the relationship sours? The swift progression of Mrs. Mallard's emotions—and she was married to a gentle man whom she was able to love at least some of the time—communicates how stifling the situation could be in Chopin's eyes.

Questions for Study and Discussion

1. Mrs. Mallard's friends and relatives see nothing other than pure grief at first, and they assume that she remains in that state. Her actual feelings are much more complicated. They include grief but are mixed with large portions of relief and joy.
2. Chopin is setting the scene in which Mrs. Mallard's epiphany is to occur. The descriptions distance the reader from the strong emotional nature of the situation. They establish that life is going on around her, even though she is in a state of suspended thought. The section effectively bridges the gap between the abrupt beginning of the story and the dominant reaction Mrs. Mallard has to her husband's supposed death, and it allows Chopin to acquaint the reader with Mrs. Mallard's physical setting.
3. Her feeling of freedom is improper. One is not supposed to feel great joy so soon after the death of a spouse, so the natural reaction would be to fight it, at least initially.
4. The swift progression of Mrs. Mallard's emotions communicates the stifling effect marriage had on women. A more gradual, thought-out reaction would not have the same impact, because, once the grief has passed, the pleasure of regaining personal freedom is not a startling thing for the widow to feel. For her to feel it within an hour is startling, and by using the time element in her title, Chopin ensures that the reader does not miss the point.
5. The fictional narrative allows her to place thoughts in Mrs. Mallard's head, and it allows her to manipulate the events of the story to present her point. The psychology of marriage is something that would have been difficult for her to write about on a factual basis—especially in such a patriarchal society—but fiction is a medium in which she can present her point of view clearly and dramatically.
6. On an obvious level, Chopin couldn't have Mrs. Mallard narrate her own story because she is dead at the end. Chopin uses a third-person narrator so that we can observe Mrs. Mallard's reactions to the news of her husband's apparent death and her subsequent realization that she was now "free, free, free!" The third-person narrator's description of Louise Mallard as "a goddess of Victory" sets readers up for Brently Mallard's surprise appearance and for the final irony in Chopin's concluding sentence.

Vocabulary

afflicted (1) suffering from; possessing a detrimental condition
aquiver (5) quivering all over
bespoke (8) told of; indicated
tumultuously (10) violently; with upheaval
exalted (12) glorified; elevated
imploring (17) asking; begging
elixir (18) a medicinal concoction
importunities (20) urgent or rude requests or demands

Classroom Activity Using Narration

The sentence progression is 3, 5, 2, 1, 4. Students may need to revise their first try at writing their own paragraph, because the exercise demands that the sentences be linked strongly to one another before they are scrambled. Writing about a progression of events without falling into a plodding, monotonous style of writing can be difficult, but students should try to make their paragraphs as interesting and smoothly linked as possible.

CHAPTER 12 **Description**

Subway Station (p. 289)
■ **Gilbert Highet**

Essay Analysis and Discussion

Highet's description of a subway station is an arresting piece to read because of the way he takes delight in the nauseating place. It is almost as though taking the time to examine it closely has imparted an interest value to the filth, the grime, and the murk. A good descriptive essay does the same thing for readers—no matter what it describes, it takes the time to examine something closely and carefully, and it communicates an impression that the reader may not have paused long enough to notice before. Highet's use of adjectives such as *leprous* and *abominable* gives the station an atmosphere that goes beyond dark and grimy—it makes it a place of interest because of its almost evil and unhealthy air. Students are asked to describe their classroom and other relatively familiar places in the exercises for this selection. Instruct them to take their time when they observe the places they choose to write about. After they make their lists of objects and adjectives, have them sit still for a while and just observe the details of their surroundings—they will probably notice more than they did in the process of writing things down.

Questions for Study and Discussion

1. The dominant impression that Highet creates is one of dirt, gloom, and neglect. The detail list will include light bulbs "coated with filth," tiles coated with fifty years of soot, paint "peeling off like scabs from an old wound," and so on.

2. Students will give different responses to why Highet observes the subway station with zest and relish; he provides no explicit discussion of reasons in the essay itself. Perhaps he enjoys it because it yields such a rich tapestry of filth to observe—the closer one looks, the more dirt and neglect one can see.

3. The similes and metaphors are

   "as though it were a bolt hole in an abandoned coal mine"
   "paint was peeling off like scabs from an old wound"
   "looked like the hallway of a condemned slum building"

   All of these descriptions convey powerful imagery and emphasize the disgusting nature of Highet's surroundings.

4. The advertisements include text from the Bible, a half-naked girl, a woman wearing a hat in the form of a hen sitting on a nest full of eggs, and a pair of girl's legs walking up the keys of a cash register. Allow students to have fun thinking of products that each of these might be advertising.

5. Highet is probably a regular rider of the subways. His eye for detail is acute, but his positive reaction to his surroundings indicates he is taking pleasure in observing familiar surroundings. If he were seeing it for the first time, he would likely recoil in horror and vow, when his train came, not to repeat the experience if at all possible. Instead he says that the experience was over for the time, indicating he will soon be back to repeat it.

Vocabulary

perfunctory hasty; cursory
leprous resembling leprosy; scaly
defilement material that makes unclean or corrupts
dubious doubtful
abominable terrible; awful

Classroom Activity Using Description

When you work on this activity with students, you may want to have them list the objects they see and connect them with adjectives that come to mind to describe them. When they decide what dominant impression they wish to communicate, they can use the objects that are related to the adjectives that best suit their purpose. Have the students compare their lists once they edit them down. It is likely that the students will be surprised that one room can yield such a large variety or range of dominant impressions.

The Sounds of the City (p. 292)
■ James Tuite

Essay Analysis and Discussion

Tuite's images appeal to the reader's sense of hearing, which is a common source for descriptive details. To round out your students' consideration of sensory images, ask them to do some writing in which they appeal to the senses of smell, taste, and touch as well. They should spend ten to twelve minutes on each of the three senses, trying to evoke corresponding images by choosing appropriate descriptive details. For example, to convey an image through smell, a student might describe a carnival or festival at which ethnic foods send off an array of distinctive aromas. Because these three senses are appealed to infrequently, when a successful image directed to one of them does appear, it is all the more effective. Read some of the students' selections aloud and see if they bear this out.

Questions for Study and Discussion

1. Tuite's main purpose is to show that New York is a city of sounds and that these sounds are part of the life of the city. He points out that New Yorkers don't hear these sounds because they are constantly surrounded by them.
2. The dominant impression that Tuite creates is one of ceaseless, discordant sound.
3. Among the sounds Tuite includes are "tinseled honky-tonk" (3), "firm beat of rock 'n' roll" (3), "frenzied outbursts of the discotheque" (3), "shrill laughter" (4), "bottle shatters" (4), "whine of a police siren" (4), "guttural halt" (4), "snarling, arrogant bickering of automobile horns" (7), "Taxicabs blaring" (7), "Trash cans rattle" (9), "satisfied groan of gears" (9), "rat-a-tat-tat" (10),

81

and "whistles . . . chirp" (11). With each of the adjectives and verbs that he uses, Tuite gets at the essence of the sound and so enlivens his description.

4. Visitors are more sensitive to city sounds because they do not hear them all the time, whereas for "cliff dwellers" the sounds are "constant and eternally urban." City people who do not stop to listen are asphalt-kin to those who do not stop to smell the roses. Noises are the life of the city and people ought to stop to listen, "to think about them, to be appalled or enchanted."

5. Among the metaphors and similes Tuite uses are "The cliff dwellers of Manhattan" (1), "Somewhere in the canyons below" (4), "The growl of a predatory monster" (8), "Metallic jaws . . . gulp and masticate . . . then digest" (9), "as jarring as the glare of a sun" (10), and "like birds calling for their mates" (11). Each of these figures of speech gives a naturalistic picture of the city.

6. Tuite has organized his essay chronologically. He starts in the nighttime, moves through the daylight hours, and ends with nightfall. This organization is effective because it gives readers an overview of the city's sounds on a typical day.

Vocabulary

muted (1) muffled; softened
inaudible (2) incapable of being heard
restive (2) restless, uneasy
raucous (4) rough-sounding or harsh
tentative (5) not definite or positive
precocious (8) prematurely developed
taunts (8) challenges
vibrant (9) resonant or resounding
perpetuate (10) to continue without interruption

Classroom Activity Using Description

Different students will seek different pleasures from their favorite place. Communicate to them that while the appeal of the place may be obvious to them, it may not be obvious to other people, so they need to be careful in how they describe it. "Danger" may not be something that other people will understand as appealing, but the thrill and satisfaction of overcoming it is. "Serenity" is readily understandable, but what is it about the place that makes serenity possible there in a way that it is not possible elsewhere?

Unforgettable Miss Bessie (p. 296)
■ Carl T. Rowan

Essay Analysis and Discussion

Rowan's essay offers students the opportunity to analyze the effective use of the dash. Many students have problems recognizing the proper place for this helpful form of punctuation and either use it too much or not at all. Rowan uses it in seven of his paragraphs, and for various purposes. Look over these instances with your students and have them identify which of the two most common reasons for using a dash each case falls under.

1. Use dashes to highlight parenthetical material, informal explanations, and afterthoughts that warrant emphasis.
2. Use dashes to signal a dramatic reversal of thought or tone.

When you've finished with Rowan's examples, have the students develop sentences of their own, using dashes in each of the ways described.

Questions for Study and Discussion

1. In paragraph 1 Rowan describes Miss Bessie as about 5 feet tall and never more than 110 pounds. In paragraph 4 he notes that she had large brown eyes and in paragraph 12 that she was "frail-looking." Though these characteristics do not seem to fit the image of the tough and towering figure from Rowan's school days, by the end of the essay they seem less inconsistent with the warm-hearted and compassionate teacher he looks back on as an adult.
2. A firm, committed, wise, and caring individual emerges from Rowan's description of Miss Bessie. Some of the words used to convey this are *towering, tough* (1); *informed, dedicated, blessing, asset* (8); *essence of pride and privacy* (9); *bearing of dignity* (11); *softness and compassion* (22); *love and motivation, wisdom and influence* (25); and *wise, educated, warm-hearted* (28).
3. The details of Miss Bessie's background appear in paragraphs 9 and 10. Rowan delays presenting this information so that he can first describe what Miss Bessie was like and why he is writing about her. This provides a stimulating opening and establishes a context for the biographical details because it helps to know what role Miss Bessie will play in the essay before being given information about her background.

4. Rowan's use of dialogue presents a more vivid picture of Miss Bessie's personality. Rather than rely on only a subjective, third-person description of her, Rowan allows the dialogue to provide a few more realistic glimpses into her character.
5. Students' opinions may vary as to whether Miss Bessie's drinking influences their view of her. Rowan's feeling of a "new sense of equality" suggests that his discovery that she drank made Miss Bessie more lifelike, dispelling some of the larger-than-life images from his grade-school perception of her, while not diminishing her significance to his life.
6. Miss Bessie gave her students a sense of pride and self-worth by encouraging their talent and curiosity. In opening to them the world of literature, writing, self-expression, and a solid notion of this country's time in history, Miss Bessie taught young black children to stretch beyond the limits a segregated world had set for them.

Vocabulary

civics (1) the branch of political science that deals with civic affairs

barrios (16) chiefly Spanish-speaking communities or neighborhoods within U.S. cities

conscience (18) the faculty of recognizing the distinction between right and wrong, coupled with a sense that one should act accordingly

cajoling (20) coaxing gently and persistently

osmotic (20) characterized by a gradual, often unconscious process of assimilation or absorption

measure (25) an evaluation or basis of comparison

Classroom Activity Using Description

It's fun to see the variety of alternative terms the students are capable of producing, and it's helpful for some students to see that choosing the right word can make a very big difference in the effectiveness of their writing. Depending on the amount of time you have, this can also be a good time to do some direct instruction in the proper use of a thesaurus, especially now that many students have this resource built into their word-processing programs. Students should be made aware of both the usefulness and the pitfalls associated with using a thesaurus.

Grocer's Daughter (p. 302)

■ Marianne Wiggins

Essay Analysis and Discussion

Wiggins's personal description of her father flows like most memories—disjointed and sometimes rambling. In fact, the essay often seems disorganized and not well crafted. It is held together by a consistent focus, however, established in the very first sentence: "I am shameless in the way I love my father." That opening propels the reader through an intimate description of a man who was probably seen as unsuccessful by his peers and who must have been, at times, difficult to live with. Yet Wiggins shows so many facets of her father that, by the end of the essay, the reader knows him and the reasons behind Wiggins's difficult love for him far better than he or she would from a stiffer, more formal written presentation. Have your students emulate Wiggins's technique in their personal essays, concentrating less on form than on creating a complete portrait of their chosen subject.

Questions for Study and Discussion

1. The first sentence emphasizes that despite all the faults and struggles Wiggins describes later on, John Wiggins was a good father and a man who earned his daughter's respect and love. The last sentence "I write longhand, and in ink" suggests that Wiggins is leaving her mark (a "stain" in ink), a mark that perpetuates her father's memory.
2. The list indicates that he was a simple, honest, and hard-working man, who probably had more success in keeping his customers happy than in running a profitable business.
3. Wiggins's writing emulates memory, in that it describes her father in a series of fragments that add up to a complete picture. It should be effective for most students, but some may be put off by the lack of readily seen organization.
4. The Wiggins family moved so often because John Wiggins's small grocery stores kept getting squeezed out by the larger suburban supermarkets.
5. He taught his daughter important values, including perseverance and honesty. He obviously loved her and both educated and entertained her. And it is obvious that his legacy lives on in her.
6. Wiggins explores the impact her father had on her both while he was alive and after his death, so what is important to her is how

he lived, not how he died. Perhaps, too, the event of his death is a painful memory that she prefers to leave out of her description. It is obvious that he died suddenly, but students will need to use some creative research to answer the rest of the question.

Vocabulary

pathology (2) referring to disease
concocted (4) developed; made
germinated (4) sprouted; emerged from a seed
charisma (7) personal charm; appeal
portenting (10) disturbing
novitiate (11) beginner; novice
piecemeal (13) in pieces; broken into bits

Classroom Activity Using Description

Here's an example of what students usually come up with for a person who loves sports: never misses *Monday Night Football*; reads the sports page every day; uses dialogue with sports facts, comparisons, allusions; makes references to having played on teams in high school and college; gets *Sports Illustrated* or other sports magazines; has sports-related injuries; goes to sporting events; coaches Little League baseball; etc.

CHAPTER 13 **Process Analysis**

How to Write a Personal Letter (p. 311)
■ **Garrison Keillor**

Essay Analysis and Discussion

Keillor has written the directional type of process analysis. He is instructing us in the art of letter writing. However, it suits the nature of the task that Keillor waits five paragraphs before he begins to list the actual steps in the process. First he wants to answer our silent questions: Why should I write? Who cares? What is a letter? Why is it important? Even as he takes us step by step from the first thoughts we give to our letter, to our signing it and stuffing it in an envelope, Keillor attends to the very personal, aesthetic nature of the task. Students can compare Keillor's approach to the organization and points of persuasion used by Lynn Wenzel in her essay "Reach Out and Write Someone," in Chapter 3. Ask students to underline the topic sentences in both articles and to map out the route each takes in his or her argument. Does one approach seem more effective than the other?

Questions for Study and Discussion

1. Keillor thinks of a letter as a gift because it is given freely (or ought to be) and because it offers our friends a glimpse of the "real" us.
2. Keillor suggests that the first step in writing is to "get over the guilt of not writing. You don't owe anybody a letter. Letters are a gift." Large stationery is intimidating to the writer who thinks he has nothing to say just as a plate filled with too much is apt to take away a diner's appetite.
3. Keillor is writing a directional process analysis. He tells his readers that "We need to write." Not only does he give us steps to follow when writing a letter, but also he anticipates problems that we might encounter and advises how to deal with them.
4. At the point that the writer's friend becomes real, he should write the salutation, take a deep breath, and plunge in.
5. Keillor is referring specifically to shy people who are unable to present themselves and their ideas in conversation.
6. Keillor addresses first the problem of not knowing where to begin. He suggests starting with the present. Next he says it isn't necessary to worry about form: "When you come to the end of one episode, just start a new paragraph." Finally Keillor advises the writer to ignore mistakes and keep going: "Let the letter cook along and let yourself be bold." The three problems and their solutions are discussed in the order in which they would occur: the beginning, the middle, and the end of the letter.
7. By the end of the letter, the writer should know something he didn't know when he began, because "writing is a means of discovery, always. . . ."

Vocabulary

trudges (2) walks or marches steadily and usually laboriously
wahoos (2) any of several American trees or shrubs; slang for weirdos
anonymity (4) unknown or undeclared identity
sensuous (7) voluptuous
crank (11) to produce in a mechanical manner
episode (12) an incident in a course of events
relic (14) souvenir, memento

Classroom Activity Using Process Analysis

Preface this activity by telling your class that they need to avoid assuming knowledge on the part of the reader. Students are usually surprised at how difficult it is to write a process analysis so that a true novice can follow it. Even directing a simple task, like scrambling eggs, is a challenge when the directions are for someone who has never been in a kitchen. The student reviews should be stringent— "beat the eggs" could lead to disastrous results if not properly explained in the paper.

The Beekeeper (p. 316)
■ Sue Hubbell

Essay Analysis and Discussion

Hubbell personalizes her description of the process used to desensitize a person to bee stings by using the example of David, the son of one of her friends. She also has her audience in mind when she minimizes the repetition of certain steps in the process. Point out to students how she moves from two stings a day to six stings a day to ten a day almost effortlessly. An informational process analysis does not relieve the writer of the necessity to be specific even though there isn't the expectation that readers will replicate the act. Notice, for example, how many details Hubbell uses in her description of the first bee sting and what happens afterward in paragraphs 2 through 4.

Questions for Study and Discussion

1. According to Hubbell, on day one a bee sting is administered, but only half the venom is allowed to enter the person's body. On day two the venom sac is allowed to empty. The person continues at one sting a day until there is no redness or swelling. At that point the dose is increased to two stings a day until there is again no reaction. This process is repeated until the person can tolerate ten stings a day with no reaction. Hubbell's process analysis is informational. While she gives some clear directions on how to apply the first sting—numbing the arm with ice, holding the bee by its head, allowing the stinger to remain in the flesh a short time, and scraping it out—her purpose seems to be to describe or explain the process and not to give directions that can be replicated.
2. Hubbell is cautious with David at first because of the possibility that David could have an allergic reaction to the bee stings.

3. "The spot where the stinger went in grew red and began to swell," and later David felt itchy. Hubbell's attention to the details of David's reaction lets the reader know exactly what a normal reaction is and that any other reaction should be treated as an emergency.
4. The reiterating of each step that increases the number of stings would become repetitious, slowing down the pace of the article. The reader might lose interest and disengage before Hubbell made her final point.
5. Students should analyze paragraphs 5 and 6 to arrive at an estimate of how long it took to desensitize David. The first seven days are laid out carefully, but Hubbell's use of the words "few days" and "soon" make it difficult to estimate exactly how long it took David to tolerate ten stings a day. Our students usually gauge the process as taking between three and four weeks.

Vocabulary

barbed (2) having a sharp point projecting in reverse direction to the main point of the stinger
bulbous (2) resembling a bulb in shape; rounded or swollen
anaphylactic (3) a serious toxic reaction caused in an unsensitized person by an excessive dose of a substance
coaxed (5) to gently persuade
tolerate (6) to endure

Classroom Activity Using Process Analysis

Students have fun with this activity. It's an exercise in following written directions. Even though each student is following the same set of directions, don't be surprised if their Astro Tubes don't look alike. Ask students if any of the directions were difficult to follow, and, if so, how those directions might be improved. Ask students whether they relied primarily on the written or visual directions. Finally, recalling the specific directions in steps 6 and 9, have students fly their tubes.

Why Leaves Turn Color in the Fall (p. 320)
■ Diane Ackerman

Essay Analysis and Discussion

In her description of the process by which leaves change color in the fall, Ackerman makes skillful use of metaphor and simile to enhance her writing. Her vivid descriptions achieve two ends: one, they enable readers to see, smell, and feel the splendor of autumn as Ackerman does; and, two, they demonstrate with wonderful clarity that informational writing does not have to be flat and uninteresting. Students can try writing their own process analysis, one that not only informs but through the use of figurative language also enhances the reader's appreciation of something familiar. Examples of possible subjects would be the annual winter migration of geese or the ebb and flow of the ocean tides as they respond to the pull of the moon. Such an essay can give voice to a writer's aesthetic appreciation of nature at the same time that it demands the attention to details required of any informational writing.

Questions for Study and Discussion

1. According to Ackerman, leaves change color because they produce no new pigment in autumn: "no new pigment is produced, and so we notice the other colors that were always there, right in the leaf, although chlorophyll's shocking green hid them from view." She attributes the brightest colors, geographically, to a "rich climate," and, meteorologically, explains, "The fiercest colors occur in years when the fall sunlight is strongest and the nights are cool and dry."

2. Paragraphs 2 and 3 of the essay give the steps of the process by which the leaves change color.

3. In addition to describing the process by which leaves change color, Ackerman also explains what causes leaves to be particularly bright some years (4); she lists the different colors that different species of trees assume in the fall (5); she explains why trees turn color at different rates (5); and she describes what makes leaves finally lose their grip and fall from the trees (9). She also explains the function of leaves underfoot (10). This wealth of information, contained in a short essay, enriches her description by explaining that the turning of color is part of a cycle and not an isolated act of nature.

4. Ackerman has organized this essay in chronological order because it mimics the action taking place—the season of autumn arrives, progresses, and ends, as does this selection.

5. Two similes are "hidden like a vivid secret" (3) and "damp, stuccolike mortar of decayed leaves" (10). Two metaphors are "the shuddering pink of a blush" (6) and "soft unruly mattresses [of leaves]" (8). Ackerman's phrasing—use of simile and metaphor included—gives the essay a lush texture. Ackerman uses personification when she likens autumn to a quiet, perhaps at first unwel-

come, intruder that arrives bit-by-bit while summer is looking the other way. It brings frost, a magician that sits upon the grass and magically transforms barbed wire fences into stars. Later, when autumn is dried up and nearly spent, leaves "roll up in clenched fists before they actually fall off" (1).

6. Ackerman ends the essay by looking at death. Death is traditionally understood as an end, but in nature death, as in the decaying leaves, gives rise to a new life. Ackerman plays with this irony in closing her essay.

Vocabulary

stealth (1) proceeding furtively, secretly, or imperceptibly
clenched (1) held tightly
gushing (1) flowing quickly and uncontrollably
camouflage (3) protective coloring
tawny (6) light, golden brown
figments (8) components; small parts
stuccolike (10) in the manner of a durable plaster or cementlike finish
vibrant (10) full of energy and vigor; lively

Classroom Activity Using Process Analysis

This activity is an exercise in prewriting, and it lends itself to small group work. Divide the class into groups of three or four students and assign each group one of the activities listed in the text (or activities of your own choosing). Instruct each group to compile two lists—one list of any materials they might need and a second of the steps they would follow in completing the task. After fifteen or twenty minutes have each group report their information to the rest of the class.

On Dumpster Diving (p. 326)
■ **Lars Eighner**

Essay Analysis and Discussion

It is hard for anyone who has never faced homelessness to imagine life on the streets. Eighner, who became homeless after working and having a home for ten years, understands this. His essay about one aspect of homeless life, Dumpster diving—what he likes to call *scavenging*—incorporates concrete examples of the dangers and rewards of Dumpster diving. The image of pristine, still-frozen ice cream in a Dumpster is a powerful one, and one Eighner uses to explain the odd appeal of

91

Dumpster diving. Discuss the final five paragraphs with your students, and how Eighner's essay may have changed the way they look at the material things that clutter everyone's life.

Questions for Study and Discussion

1. Dumpster diving quite literally is the jumping into large trash receptacles to find useful articles. Eighner says that he likes "the frankness of the word *scavenging*" (3). It does not mislead in the way "foraging" does—it does not imply a gathering of natural goods; it implies living directly from refuse. He considers it a valid niche in society. A definition of scavenging is important enough for Eighner to include at the beginning because it establishes his view of this subject and because it establishes the frank tone maintained throughout the rest of the essay.

2. Eighner discusses the three main stages: the stage of shame and self-loathing; the stage of discovery, in which the scavenger discovers the wealth to be found in Dumpsters; and the stage of "professionalism," defined as being willing and able to eat from Dumpsters. Eighner provides vivid examples of the goods to be found in the Dumpsters that move scavengers through their period of shame. Such things as a working calculator and still-frozen ice cream indicate the thoughtlessness with which people throw things away (6). The discussion of food to be found and consumed in Dumpsters is more prosaic, but Eighner again provides specific examples.

    Students will have different connotations for "dilettanti" and "professional," but they should indicate that there is a strong contrast between the two. Eighner establishes just how big a step it is to eat from Dumpsters by using these terms. Also, "professional" should imply that the person makes his or her living from it—that he or she is very good at it and that it is how he or she survives.

3. In paragraphs 4 through 12 Eighner describes the process of retrieving useable items from dumpsters. Quickly new divers discover that "people do throw away perfectly good stuff," and later they realize that "they must restrict themselves to items of relatively immediate utility." Eighner emphasizes the caution that is needed in evaluating edible items and confesses that even he makes an occasional mistake, resulting in dysentery. Eighner's title suggests a reflective, philosophical treatment of the subject. "How to Dumpster Dive," on the other hand, has the wrong feel; this title suggests that Eighner is giving practical advice or directions, which he isn't.

92

4. Eighner has learned to take what he can use and let the rest go (13) and that material being is transient (14). He learned not to grab for objects just for the sake of having them, and he has found a peace that he believes eludes the "rat-race millions," confounded as they are by their consumer society (16). Eighner believes that Dumpster diving "has serious drawbacks as a way of life" (12). He gets dysentery at least once a month.

5. Eighner discusses the concrete aspects of Dumpster diving to teach readers what it is like—what can be found in Dumpsters, how scavenging affects its practitioners, in what ways scavenging is a potential hazard, and so on. It is only from this base of knowledge that Eighner can then discuss the abstract, particularly the transience of material objects. For those who have never found such things as new running shoes or working calculators in Dumpsters, a discussion of transience may have little meaning. Eighner's concrete experiences give his abstract lessons credence.

6. Dumpster diving is a process. If the reader is able to understand how it is done, including its inherent challenges, problems, and rewards, it is then far easier to understand any lessons that may be learned from it. It is therefore a very effective strategy for Eighner to provide readers with a process analysis of Dumpster diving before presenting his conclusions or arguments regarding what he has learned from it. Students will give various answers to the second part of the question, but they should explain why it is important to present the process they choose before presenting a related conclusion or argument. Why is it important to present exactly what happens or how to do something before proposing an argument based on the process?

Vocabulary

refuse (3) garbage
niche (3) specialized role or place
pristine (6) clean; unblemished
bohemian (8) nonconformist; eccentric
qualms (10) misgivings; apprehensions
transience (14) lack of permanence
sated (16) satisfied

Classroom Activity Using Process Analysis

Recipes offer wonderful examples of directional process analyses, and Frances Mayes's recipe for lemon cake is no exception. Students will have various responses to reading this recipe depending on their interest or experience with cooking and food in general. Most will find it interesting to read because of its conversational tone and the writer's enthusiasm for the cake, but it's clear that the author assumes that the reader knows something about cooking. Although Mayes's recipe is interesting to read in paragraph form, it would be easier to follow if the ingredients were listed together followed by the individual steps for making the cake. Have students divide Mayes's paragraph into the individual steps they would follow if they were to make the cake. In the context of this analysis students might discover the need for directions such as preheating the oven or softening the butter and the need for an explanation on how the doneness test works, for example. Finally, this activity is sure to be a hit if you bring a lemon cake to class for a taste test.

CHAPTER 14 **Definition**

A Jerk (p. 334)
■ **Sydney J. Harris**

Essay Analysis and Discussion

Harris's essay, though short, contains a good number of delightfully expressed ideas. The entire piece can serve as a case study in choosing the right words to get the job done. His unique use of words and images combined with his ease and naturalness of expression makes Harris's subject matter more interesting and entertaining than it might otherwise be. To illustrate, have your students consider the following fragments from the essay:

> "I *fluffed* her off with some *inane* answer" (2)
> "It is a *marvelously apt* word" (3)
> "it is, rather, a kind of *subtle but persuasive aroma emanating from the inner part of the personality*" (4)
> "he is totally incapable of *looking into the mirror of his soul and shuddering at what he sees there*" (5)
> "most of us—unlike the jerk—are *perfectly and horribly aware of it when we make asses of ourselves*" (6)

Noting, especially, the italicized portions, discuss why these fragments are so effective in conveying Harris's ideas. In their responses, students should recognize the role that originality of expression plays in arousing the appropriate connotations and mental imagery for an essay. In this respect, Harris's manipulation of language is "mar-

velously apt," and demonstrates the need for students, also, to make
the language they use in their writing uniquely their own.

Questions for Study and Discussion

1. *Jerk* is a widely used slang word, and people use it without really
   knowing what it means. The question from Harris's son Michael
   prompts him to define the word. According to Harris, "a jerk . . .
   is a man (or woman) who is utterly unable to see himself as he appears to others" (6).
2. According to Harris, boobs and simps are lovable, and jerks never
   are; fools and dopes lack intelligence, and a jerk may not.
3. Harris sees no relationship between the two.
4. The example of the college president shows that being a jerk has
   little to do with intelligence.
5. The episode points out our tendency to use words that we cannot
   easily define. We intuit the meaning of words such as *jerk*. The
   anecdote works because it gets the reader thinking about not only
   the meaning of the word *jerk* (how would I define it for one of my
   children?), but other similarly slippery words in our vocabulary.

Vocabulary

inane (2) empty; lacking sense or substance
apt (3) appropriate
coined (3) invented
emanating (4) coming from
amenities (5) courtesies, pleasantries, or civilities
tactless (6) offensively blunt; undiplomatic

Classroom Activity Using Definition

This is a simple exercise in critical thinking, requiring students to see a
given item as being both a part of some larger class of items that share
certain characteristics as well as differentiated from the other members of that class by certain distinguishing features. Not all students
will be able to differentiate a tenor saxophone from other types of
saxophones in the woodwind instrument class, so it may be necessary
to have someone in the class who knows this narrower subject area
offer assistance. You may want to prepare yourself for the possibility
that no one knows that the saxophone is a nineteenth-century invention of Adolphe Sax and that there are eight types of saxophone, each
representing a different tonal range. Of these eight types, only four are
widely used: the B-flat soprano, the E-flat alto, the B-flat tenor, and
the E-flat baritone.

The Company Man (p. 337)
■ **Ellen Goodman**

Essay Analysis and Discussion

Ellen Goodman's essay, like W. H. Auden's poem "The Unknown Citizen," uses irony and sarcasm to expose Americans' penchant to become workaholics. She develops her definition of "company man" by carefully showing readers what Phil is as well as what he is not. Ask students if they make a distinction between a *company man* and a *workaholic*. Have them share their own experiences with a parent, relative, or friend who is a "company man" or workaholic and to describe the defining personality traits of that person. Explore the reasons why some people become overinvolved with their schooling or careers to the exclusion of other facets of their lives (for example, recreation, relationships, health, and so on). Finally, ask students what they think will be their own priorities after they graduate and take a job.

Questions for Study and Discussion

1. Although some people look at a *company man* in a positive light—an employee who is reliable and shows extreme loyalty to his employer—Goodman does not. She calls Phil—the company man in this case—a "workaholic." For Goodman, the two terms are synonymous. A workaholic is someone for whom work is a compulsion, one who takes the behavior of the workplace to an extreme, who never has a quitting time, and who sacrifices everything in life for the sake of a job. Ask students about the suffix *-aholic;* where else have they seen it used?

2. The phrase "Important People" ironically implies those who spend all their time on work and work-related events, trying to reach the importance of money, position, and power.

3. Goodman uses this selection to issue a warning to those who are in danger of falling prey to the same circumstances that eventually killed Phil. The cold, detached tone of the essay matches the cold, detached attitude of Phil toward what really should have been the most important things in his life—his wife and children.

4. Goodman's unemotional tone enhances the irony and sarcasm of the essay. Her diction of irony and sarcasm is encapsulated in her descriptions of Phil. She writes about how Phil acknowledged weekends by wearing a "sports jacket" to the office instead of a

suit. He is described matter-of-factly, being "of course, over-weight by 20 or 25 pounds." He always ate lunch—"egg salad sandwiches"—at his desk. Have your students find other examples of Goodman's sarcastic and ironic diction.

5. Phil's survivors are distanced from him. In paragraphs 7 through 12, Goodman describes the nonrelationships that Phil had with his wife Helen, his two sons, and his daughter. He seems to be one who works and brings home money and little else. One gets the feeling that Phil's fellow workers do not really have the time to think about Phil's family duties (or their own family duties). This train of thought is important in the context of the selection because Goodman draws a close eye on Phil's effect on the family while her apparent focus is mostly on Phil's career. Phil's oldest son canvassed the neighborhood—much to the neighbors' embarrassment—to find out about his father because he had never really known him, his father being too busy and preoccupied with work. Yet, by being an executive in a plant elsewhere, this son is repeating virtually the same pattern that alienated his father from the family and ultimately took his life. His daughter, while close to her mother, had nothing to talk about with her father when they were together. Although Phil worried about his youngest son, he didn't spend time with his son. The boy tried unsuccessfully to mean something to his father.

6. The time of Phil's death is repeated to drive home the irony that he died because of the work at 3:00 A.M. on Sunday, a time when hardly anyone is working at all.

Vocabulary

obituary (2) brief bibliographic death notice
extracurricular (4) outside the usual duties of a job or profession
discreetly (16) showing prudence and self-restraint

Classroom Activity Using Definition

This activity encourages students to explore how connotations work, how different people have different associations with some words. For example, some people think that a "go-getter" is a self-motivated, determined person, while others might see such a person as pushy, aggressive, or selfish. As writers, we all need to be aware of the connotations that our audience might bring to the words we use.

Who Wins? Who Cares? (p. 341)
■ Mariah Burton Nelson

Essay Analysis and Discussion

In this essay Nelson, a former professional basketball player, stipulates her own definition of "competition," a definition that reflects the meaning of the word's Latin root *competere*. She believes that women and men view competition differently and takes every opportunity to contrast the two positions. For Nelson, men are too intent on winning whatever the cost while women value competition for the opportunity "to get to know other people, to be challenged, and to have fun in a close and caring environment. To seek together" (12). As an athlete, Nelson draws on personal experiences in sports to support and illustrate various parts of her definition of *competition*. Our students respond to this essay with lively discussion. Some students believe that the tone of women's sports has changed dramatically in the decade since Nelson wrote this article. Other students want to take the discussion outside the world of sports to talk about competition in the classroom and in the workplace. Ask your students whether they believe women and men have different attitudes or styles when it comes to competition and working with people. Have them share specific examples from their own experiences.

Questions for Study and Discussion

1. Nelson believes that people lose sight of the original meaning of *to compete* when they put too much emphasis on winning. When people take to heart the original meaning "to seek together," they come to understand "that competition can be a way to get to know other people, to be challenged, and to have fun in a close and caring environment" (12).
2. According to Nelson, men have "killer instincts" and are primarily interested in "who won." In paragraph 4 she implies that men equate "trying to win" with "trying to belittle," believe that winning is wonderful, and consider losing a sign of failure.
3. Although Nelson's opening statement that "competition can damage self-esteem, create anxiety and lead to cheating and hurt feelings" casts a negative light on competition, it certainly captures our attention. The comparison to romantic love not only surprises but also prepares readers for Nelson's suggestion that if we can perfect our understanding of what love means, we can do the same for competition.

4. According to Nelson, many women shied away from competition because they were intent on avoiding the pitfalls of men's sports. In paragraph 9 she says, "Some women, scarred by childhood exclusion, shamed by early 'defeats,' or sickened by abuses such as cheating and steroid use, still avoid competition."

5. The examples that Nelson uses are all recognizable stars in the world of women's professional tennis (although names like Lindsey Davenport, Venus Williams, and Martina Hingis might be more recognizable today ten years after Nelson wrote her article). One reason why Nelson focused on tennis for her examples might be that tennis is a popular lifelong sport to which many readers can relate.

6. Nelson uses this often-heard cliché because she knows that it's familiar, but she doesn't want us to use it as a quick and easy summary to her argument. Many young people who hear this cliché from adults often don't buy it. They believe that it isn't true and that adults are just trying to make them feel good when they lose. In anticipating what some readers will think of the cliché, Nelson can then proceed to amplify and provide her own interpretation. In paragraph 12 she says that we should not "just parrot that cliché, but demonstrate our commitment to fair, participatory competition by paying equal attention to skilled and unskilled children; by allowing all children to participate fully in games, regardless of the score; and by caring more about process than results."

Vocabulary

ritualistic (2) a detailed method of procedure faithfully or regularly followed

tantamount (4) an equivalent

empathy (7) identification with and understanding of another's situation, feelings, and motives

eschew (8) to avoid

polarize (8) to cause to concentrate about two conflicting or contrasting positions

myriad (9) constituting a very large, indefinite number; innumerable

bulimia (9) insatiable appetite

parrot (12) to mindlessly imitate the words or actions of another

intuit (12) to know or sense by intuition or sharp insight

Classroom Activity Using Definition

You can start this exercise by having the class generate a list of words that women and men view differently. Words suggested by our students include *accomplishment, love, leadership, conflict, intimacy, conversation, feelings, commitment, beauty, harassment, sexism, control, independence,* and *power.* Have students in small groups of either all men or all women write definitions for two or three words from the perspective of their gender. Then ask students to share their definitions with the class. Discuss gender differences.

CHAPTER 15 **Division and Classification**

The Ways of Meeting Oppression (p. 350)
■ **Martin Luther King Jr.**

Essay Analysis and Discussion

In addition to being an excellent example of division and classification, King's essay is a model of how to achieve unity between paragraphs. To illustrate this, have students identify the topic sentence in each of King's paragraphs and make a list of those statements. They should come up with the following:

1. "One way is acquiescence: the oppressed resign themselves to their doom."
2. "There is such a thing as the freedom of exhaustion."
3. "So acquiescence—while often the easier way—is not the moral way."
4. "A second way that oppressed people sometimes deal with oppression is to resort to physical violence and corroding hatred."
5. "Violence as a way of achieving racial justice is both impractical and immoral."
6. "Violence is not the way."
7. "The third way open to oppressed people in their quest for freedom is the way of nonviolent resistance."
8. "It seems to me that this is the method that must guide the actions of the Negro in the present crisis in race relations."
9. "Nonviolent resistance makes it possible for the Negro to remain in the South and struggle for his rights."
10. "By nonviolent resistance, the Negro can also enlist all men of good will in his struggle for equality."

This list demonstrates how tightly King's ideas are connected as he moves from paragraph to paragraph. The supporting information that surrounds these topic sentences explains and strengthens the main idea of each paragraph, but it is the close connection between those main ideas that gives the essay its unity and makes King's logical argument, and the presentation of the ways to meet oppression, so easy to follow and understand.

Questions for Study and Discussion

1. King's purpose in writing this essay is to argue for nonviolent resistance. By classifying the types of resistance, King makes clear that there are essentially three ways to deal with oppression, and that for him only one of these options, nonviolent resistance, is viable.

2. The principle of division that King uses is the way oppressed people react to the oppression.

3. The order that King uses runs from the option that is easiest and least effective for the oppressed to the option that is most difficult and most effective.

4. Slaves become accustomed to being slaves. They will bear the ills slavery offers rather than risk other, unknown ills.

5. The "freedom of exhaustion" refers to a kind of giving up that engulfs the slave to the extent that he doesn't even "mind" his slavery any more, and if he doesn't mind, then he is "free" to do nothing about it.

6. For King, one who acquiesces "increases the oppressors's arrogance and contempt." One who resorts to violence uses a means that "never brings permanent peace." King shows that he does not favor acquiescence by using the following words and phrases: *resign* (1), *doom* (1), *prefer to remain oppressed* (1), *slaves* (1), *fleshpots of Egypt* (1), *worn down* (2), *give up* (2), *negative freedom* (2), *cooperate* (3), *evil* (3), *coward* (3), *inferiority* (3), *sell* (3). King shows that he does not favor violent resistance by using the following words and phrases: *resort* (4), *corroding hatred* (4), *momentary* (4), *temporary* (4), *impractical* (5), *immoral* (5), *humiliate* (5), *annihilate* (5), *thrives* (5), *bitterness* (5), *brutality* (5), *cluttered* (5), *wreckage* (5), *succumb* (6), *temptation* (6), *desolate night of bitterness* (6), *endless reign of meaningless chaos* (6). King shows that he favors nonviolent resistance by using the following words and phrases: *quest* (7), *truths* (7), *guide* (8), *rise to the noble height* (8), *loving* (8), *passionately* (8), *unrelentingly* (8), *full stature as a citizen* (8), *great opportunity* (9), *lasting contribution* (9), *sublime example of courage* (9).

Vocabulary

acquiescence (1) passive assent or agreement
tacitly (1) quietly without open expression
corroding (4) consuming
annihilate (5) destroy utterly
desolate (6) barren; miserable
synthesis (7) the combining of separate elements to form a new, coherent whole
sublime (9) inspiring or impressive

Classroom Activity Using Division and Classification

Here are some possible classification criteria for the first group, Hobbies:

sports	sedentary activities
spectator sports	physical activities
participatory sports	

The Three Faces of Stress (p. 355)
■ Sarah Federman

Essay Analysis and Discussion

The dialogue in Federman's opening paragraphs immediately engages readers in the topic of stress. While most readers think that they experience stress in their lives, they are unable to identify the sources of this stress. Federman states that it's important for people to be able to identify and understand the physical, chemical, and emotional stress because they will be better able to take control of their lives and thereby eliminate or reduce the levels of stress they experience. Federman's organization is interesting in this essay. She could have chosen to divide the body of her essay into three main parts, one devoted to each of the three types of stress. In that scheme she would have discussed Megan's, Howie's, and Jen's physical stresses in one section before moving on to their chemical and emotional stresses in the other two sections. Instead, Federman chose to focus on each of the three people, showing the three types of stress in their daily activities. In doing so, she has created three mini divisions and classifications in her essay. Finally, Federman restates her thesis in the last paragraph and offers readers some advice about what they can do the next time they feel stressed out.

Questions for Study and Discussion

1. In paragraph 8 Federman identifies the three types of stress—physical stress, chemical stress, and emotional stress. Students' examples will vary depending on their own personal experience. While the three types of stress are easy to understand, students sometimes have difficulty linking a particular symptom—fatigue, for example—with a particular type of stress (emotional, physical, or chemical).

2. In paragraph 8 Federman states her belief that only when people can identify and understand the different types of stress in their lives can they begin to do something about it. In reducing stress, people can avoid disease and "alleviate fatigue, sluggishness, moodiness, headaches, irritability, allergies, and nausea." Sometimes it is difficult to identify a particular stress. For example, if a person exercises to reduce emotional stress, the cure—exercise—can itself become a stressor (physical) if overdone.

3. The definitions given by three friends help Federman make the point (in paragraph 10) that people tend to identify emotional stresses in their lives and not the physical or chemical stresses.

4. Federman uses division and classification to organize each example that she uses in the body of her essay. She classifies the various activities in each individual's life into the three categories of physical, chemical, and emotional stress.

5. The dialogue in Federman's opening seven paragraphs reveals that Megan does not understand the effects that stress can have on her well-being. This real-life conversation effectively leads into Federman's thesis (paragraph 8) and discussion of the confusion surrounding stress (paragraphs 9 and 10). These paragraphs together effectively introduce the examples of Megan, Howie, and Jim in paragraph 11 and following.

6. At the end of paragraph 26, Federman suggests that "The next time you feel overwhelmed by 'stress,' pain, or discomfort, try listing all of the possible emotional, chemical, and physical stresses you might be experiencing. Then, decide which ones can be eliminated. Reducing these stresses will help you move toward greater balance and control over your own experience."

Vocabulary

symptoms (8) phenomena experienced by individuals indicating disorder or disease
chronic (12) of long duration; continuing; constant
pesticides (14) chemicals used to kill insects and rodents

laudable (19) deserving praise
phenomenal (19) extraordinary; outstanding; remarkable
predisposition (22) a tendency or inclination
carcinogens (24) cancer-causing substances
enhance (24) to increase or make greater in value

Classroom Activity Using Division and Classification

This exercise works well as a small-group activity. After discussing the example of pets provided in the text, assign each group one of the items suggested in the activity or an item that you determine. After ten to fifteen minutes of work, have several groups present their divisions and classifications to the class or write them on the board for discussion.

Friends, Good Friends—and Such Good Friends (p. 362)
■ Judith Viorst

Essay Analysis and Discussion

An analysis of the division-and-classification section of this essay will reveal two important features: its consistency in structure and its variety in development. For the most part, Viorst uses a three-step approach in her categories of friends: first, she defines the type of friend being discussed; second, she offers examples of the type; and third, she provides further clarification to reinforce her definition. The consistency of this pattern makes it easier to follow along as she goes down her list of numerous kinds of friends. She achieves variety in the ways she presents the further clarification in step three. She makes use of examples from women friends, dialogue from women friends, her own additional analysis, examples from her own experience, and various combinations of these to clarify the main points of her categories. Discuss this method of organization and development with your students and, when you've finished, see if they can offer additional supporting evidence for any of Viorst's categories, based on their own experiences. Then have them decide where that evidence would fit within the three-step structure of her essay.

Questions for Study and Discussion

1. Viorst has come to see that friendships are "conducted at many levels of intensity, serve many different functions, meet differ-

ent needs and range from . . . soul sisters to . . . casual play-mates."

2. Viorst's purpose in this essay is to make her readers understand the many different kinds of relationships that fall into the general class of friendship. Classification is clearly an appropriate strategy because it helps to clarify the distinct types of friends.

3. Viorst's categories are: convenience friends; special-interest friends; historical friends; crossroads friends; cross-generational friends; part-of-a-couple friends; men who are friends; and medium friends, pretty good friends, and very good friends.

4. Viorst states in paragraph 3 the principles of division that she uses in this essay.

5. Viorst numbers each category, labels each category ("convenience friends," "special-interest friends," etc.), and provides at least one memorable example of each type of friendship.

6. Viorst's tone is informal, almost conversational. It is certainly appropriate given her subject matter—friends—and her audience—*Redbook* readers, women twenty-five to thirty-five years old.

Vocabulary

ardor (2) passion
nonchalant (3) appearing casual, unconcerned, indifferent
sibling (16) brother or sister
forge (18) make or fashion
dormant (19) inactive
perspective (20) point of view

Classroom Activity Using Division and Classification

This exercise works wonderfully when students work in small groups to divide and classify the figures. Review the division-and-classification tree diagram on page 348 in the introduction to this chapter. Students can start by identifying all the variables—hair, eyebrows, position of mouth, necktie type, necktie shape, necktie design. Next, they need to decide which feature they want to use first as a basis for division. For example, one group might start by dividing the fifteen heads into two groups—one with hair, the other without. Then, they would divide these two groups, based on another category—say, necktie type. Students continue dividing and classifying until they exhaust the variables. Have students compare their division-and-classification tree diagrams. What conclusions, if any, can they draw from their diagrams?

The Plot against People (p. 369)
■ Russell Baker

Essay Analysis and Discussion

The hallmark of Baker's essay is his humor, the way he looks at inanimate objects' methods "to resist man and ultimately to defeat him." Things that do not work when most people need them are, according to Baker, in the "highest state possible" for inanimate objects. By "conditioning" people to know that they will not work, and thereby defeating them, people are necessarily at "peace" with them. Speaking about inanimate objects as though they were alive is a means to making these objects more understandable; they come to be more in our control—or so we think. If an object can be made personable, we think it starts to make more sense (as if it works like we do). Most of Baker's examples hold up today, with the exception of the toy locomotive perhaps (nowadays, we talk about video games breaking down). It is not so much the examples used that date Baker but the examples he does not use. He makes no mention of television, computers, or cell phones (three objects that have become part of our everyday lives. Although we do not pretend that science can explain all our questions, we have not strayed far from Baker's tongue-in-cheek explanations about inanimate objects. Ask students to list the inanimate objects they encounter every day, and find out which ones seem to be talked back to the most. Vending machines, computers, printers, televisions, stereos, and cars are among the most popular objects with students.

Questions for Study and Discussion

1. Baker says that the three major categories of inanimate objects are those that break down, those that get lost, and those that do not work. He probably arrived at these categories from being frustrated in his own experiences with inanimate objects. There are many ways that objects can be classified, such as by weight, height, use, material, and so forth.
2. Baker organizes this essay from least significant to most significant. The objects that "don't work" are the pinnacle of inanimate objects, the rulers of the inanimate world. Thus the essay must work up to the introduction of the most important elements.
3. Paragraph 5 serves as a transition to move into the introduction of the second category—objects that "get lost."

4. Personification allows the reader to see his or her own emotions mirrored by the very objects that have caused him or her such frustration, aggravation, time, and money. Paragraphs 3, 4, and 7 all contain excellent examples of personification. The word *plot* in Baker's title is in keeping with this personification. Inanimate objects are out to get people.

5. Paragraph 7 is actually an extended example of paragraph 6. Paragraph 3 is another instance of an extended example (the statements of paragraph 2 are elaborated through the use of examples by Baker in the following paragraph). Baker uses this form of organization—a statement followed by supporting examples—to persuade the reader that the inanimate may be animate. The examples that Baker chooses show the differences among the objects in each of the three categories. Automobiles and washing machines extend the classification he makes about things that break down. Keys and missing purses clarify the classification he makes about things that get lost. Finally, barometers and car clocks show the difference between the other categories and things that do not work.

6. By personifying the objects and their actions—anthropomorphization—such as when he says "keys . . . burrow three feet under mattresses," or "a pair of pliers climb all the way from the cellar to the attic in its single-minded determination to raise its owner's blood pressure" (7), Baker lets his readers know that this essay is intended to be humorous. Yet for all the humor, Baker touches on a common problem.

Vocabulary

cunning (3) sly; clever
league (4) allied with
plausible (6) possible
conciliatory (10) placating; overcoming the distrust or animosity of
baffled (13) confused; nonplussed

Classroom Activity Using Division and Classification

Students like this exercise because it is a very real one for them. They have all had experiences in supermarkets trying to figure out if the Sweet 'n Low and Equal are in the diet section or in the sweetener section with sugar. It drives home the point that the process of dividing and classifying is really an essential life skill, whether one is establishing the system or just having to work within someone else's system. If students have been unable to visit a supermarket, you can always use the general class soft drinks and beverages because students are already familiar with the various types and sizes of these products.

CHAPTER 16 **Comparison and Contrast**

Two Ways of Seeing a River (p. 377)
■ Mark Twain

Essay Analysis and Discussion

This selection from Twain's *Life on the Mississippi* is remarkable for the way that it shows how one's perception of something—in this case, Twain's perception of the river—can change with education. With Twain's knowledge of steamboat piloting comes the ability to differentiate between the "appearance" of the river and the "reality" of the river. What once appeared as "graceful circles and radiating lines" on the river's surface are now for Twain "a warning that that troublesome place is shoaling up dangerously." Extend the discussion of Twain's experience to other arenas, and ask students to share times when knowledge has changed their views of something.

Questions for Study and Discussion

1. Block organization is used in this essay. The only other option in a comparison and contrast selection would be a point-by-point organization, which would involve constantly going back and forth between the two views to show specific examples. This would ruin the narrative flow.
2. The analogy of a doctor being unable to appreciate human beauty because he or she has gained too much knowledge about the practicalities of human beings and their illnesses is effective and appropriate. In addition, by providing an example that is vastly different from his own experience—doctor and steamboater—Twain shows the reader a broad spectrum of examples. The reader realizes that, with almost everything, the acquisition of knowledge comes at the cost of losing an elemental—and innocent—response to beauty.
3. The appearance of the river is one of beauty, poetry, and grace in the first paragraph, but in the second paragraph Twain describes the reality of the river. Now that he works on the river, Twain sees

the river in a practical way, translating previously ethereal images into guidelines used by steamboaters.

4. "Long, ruffled trail," "shone like silver," "boiling tumbling rings . . . as many-tinted as an opal," and "splendor that was flowing from the sun" are examples of simile and metaphor found in this essay. Have your students find others—all of paragraph 2 directly compares and contrasts with the views expressed in paragraph 1.

5. According to Twain, there are two ways to see the river, but one option is removed once the river becomes his place of "business." Becoming an adept steamboater was a triumph for Twain, but there was a trade-off. "I had made a valuable acquisition. But I had lost something, too . . . which could never be restored to me. . . . All the grace, the beauty, the poetry, had gone out of the majestic river!"

Vocabulary

acquisition (1) to gain something
hue (1) shade of color
opal (1) translucent semiprecious stone
rapture (2) ecstasy
romance (3) a quality suggestive of adventure and idealized exploits

Classroom Activity Using Comparison and Contrast

The key to this activity is to have students compile lengthy lists of descriptive details for each of the places they are comparing and contrasting. The more exhaustive their lists, the more they will see similarities and differences, and it is from the similarities and differences that they will draw conclusions. This exercise works well when students work in pairs. After fifteen to twenty minutes have the students present their lists and preliminary conclusions to the class for discussion.

Grammy Rewards (p. 381)
■ Deborah Dalfonso

Essay Analysis and Discussion

Dalfonso's essay is short, to the point, and does an excellent job of presenting the characters, personalities, and beliefs of two people who, as she says, are "as different as chalk and cheese." In the very short time it takes to read the essay, the reader gets to know both grandmothers rather well and appreciate the vastly different views of the world they present to their grandchild. Note how Dalfonso avoids unnecessary explanations and discussions of the two grandmothers. Simply presenting certain preferences, interactions, and ways of dealing with situations is enough to establish the subjects as nearly polar opposites of one another. Also, Dalfonso presents the information without any opinion or judgment on her part, even at the end, where it would be tempting to insert it. It is rare to find a comparison-and-contrast essay about two such disparate subjects without some indication of which philosophy the author agrees with—and it is likely even more rare when the subjects are a mother and a mother-in-law. Yet, as she promises to do for her daughter, she makes no judgment for the reader and, because of this, her last paragraph rings true.

Questions for Study and Discussion

1. Dalfonso likely chose a point-by-point method of organization to highlight the differences between the two. By juxtaposing how each would react to the same situation, Dalfonso makes it easy to see just how different the two women are.

2. The better metaphor has the proper grandmother as chalk and the eccentric one as cheese. Chalk is hard, monochromatic, and exhibits little or no variety. Cheese has a large number of tastes and appearances, depending on the variety, and is likable but not good for you as a steady diet. The alliteration of *chalk* and *cheese* also enhances the effectiveness of the metaphor because the words begin with the same sounds yet have quite different meanings— just as both women are grandmothers but have very different personalities.

3. Dalfonso does not need to identify the grandmothers, and that is testimony to how different they are. That one can readily tell which grandmother she is talking about throughout the essay is a telling statement about the fundamental differences in their philosophies and personalities, and it helps to make the concluding paragraphs more powerful.

4. Dalfonso's purpose is to show that each of the grandmothers has something worthwhile to share with their granddaughter, Jill. Dalfonso's refusal to judge indicates that she has respect for both grandmothers. By writing the essay in the manner that she does, she is saying that both women have valid outlooks on the world, even if their outlooks are extreme. Instead of judging them, her daughter should learn from them. From her question, it is clear that Jill has already started to learn.

5. The metaphors are very effective at putting the grandmothers' influence into an easily identifiable context. The metaphors also communicate the worth of both outlooks—both anchors and mainsails are vital on a sailboat but perform opposite tasks. One can infer, however, that Dalfonso does not expect her daughter to embrace either extreme—a boat without an anchor soon washes ashore, while a boat without a sail goes nowhere. The metaphoric ending is effective because it is brief and it causes readers to reflect back on the qualities that the two grandmothers pass onto Jill.

Vocabulary

impervious (2) impenetrable
regal (3) kinglike, royal
taupe (4) brownish gray
expletive (5) exclamatory word or phrase
ions (6) atom(s) with a net positive or negative charge

Classroom Activity Using Comparison and Contrast

Dalfonso's essay is effective because she paints such clear images of each grandmother as she contrasts the two of them. This is very important if the essay is to be effective, but it is not easily done. Before you have students work on this activity, you might wish to have the class brainstorm about other situations that they can add to the list. This activity should be relatively easy for students to complete once the situations have been chosen, but it should also be fun and interesting, and it is a good lesson about how to write a concise yet informative sentence.

A Case of "Severe Bias" (p. 384)
■ Patricia Raybon

Essay Analysis and Discussion

Prejudice is often strengthened by stereotypes, by members of a certain group being lumped together. When the negative stereotypes of a small segment of a group are transferred to the whole group, as often happens, the whole group suffers the consequences. Raybon argues that the U.S. media does exactly this to African Americans by slanting its coverage of blacks strongly toward images of poverty, crime, drug addiction, and other problems. As a result, the millions of African Americans who are responsible citizens are unfairly saddled

111

with negative associations. To make her point, Raybon begins her essay by listing what she is not—her life, she asserts, is not dysfunctional, unlike the lives so often depicted in media stories about African Americans. What is accepted as the norm for African Americans contrasts sharply with reality, which Raybon argues leads to problems for all of American society. Discuss with your students the disadvantages of being associated with a negative stereotype. How would they feel if they saw a group they identify with portrayed in a bad light much of the time?

Questions for Study and Discussion

1. Raybon uses the comparison and contrast technique to work toward overcoming the stereotypes that have been presented by the media, because she perceives that there is a huge difference between the media image and reality. She wants more balanced coverage of African Americans in the media, and she would like her readers to work toward achieving this.

2. Raybon establishes the contrast between the stereotype of African Americans and the life she and her friends actually lead. She gives examples of images used by the media to depict African Americans.

3. By saying who she is not, Raybon is directly arguing against what she perceives is the image that the media constructs about African Americans. She perceives that readers will wonder: If she is not this, not that, and does not do that, how can she still be an African American? It underscores the absurdity, and the harm, of the media's depictions.

4. Both paragraphs 1 and 6 say what she and African Americans are not. She repeats this style to reinforce her debunking of media myths.

5. Her thesis is that the news media presents an image of African Americans that is misleading and damaging. She presents it in paragraph 3. The final part of the question is personal opinion, but the answers should be defended.

6. Raybon's tone is angry and frustrated. It can be readily seen in the way she describes the media's actions, such as her use of the word *insidious*, and in the way she concludes her essay by saying that "it's time to let the truth be known."

Vocabulary

tenement (1) crowded housing unit, usually run-down or cramped
dysfunctional (3) unable to function in society

insidious (3) underhanded; harmful
myopic (7) with poor vision
besetting (8) plaguing; provoking
scenario (9) script; imagined scene
aberrant (9) irregular; unconventional
pervasive (10) widespread; extensive
subtleness (16) indirectness; implication
enterprise (16) undertaking; project

Classroom Activity Using Comparison and Contrast

This activity reinforces some of the fundamental tasks that need to be considered before continuing with the writing itself. It's good to stress yet again that time spent at this preliminary stage considering such important questions is not wasted but is an effort that will actually save time and ensure a better result in the long run. It is true for most of us that as we become more and more familiar with the writing process we think we can cut corners and not put the necessary time into prewriting activities.

A Battle of Cultures (p. 389)
■ K. Connie Kang

Essay Analysis and Discussion

Kang's comparison-and-contrast piece is based on conflict. The presence of the conflict implies right in the first sentence that differences exist between African Americans and Korean Americans. Kang then contrasts the two cultures to explain the root causes of the conflict. Kang organizes her essay very effectively. Paragraphs 1 through 5 are used to establish the surface problems. Note how Kang makes paragraph 6 a very effective one-sentence transition into the cultural contrasts that underlie the problem. She can then explore what these differences are and how they contribute to the misunderstanding, such as the Korean cultural bias against smiling, in paragraphs 7 through 14. Paragraphs 15 through 20 suggest simple solutions to the problem, and comment on the role of everyone in an ethnically diverse democracy. Have your students write a comparison-and-contrast essay based on conflict. Direct them to follow Kang's organization by beginning with the surface conflict, then making a transition to the contrasts that contribute to the conflict.

Questions for Study and Discussion

1. The "battle of cultures" referred to in the title is the clash between the Korean American and African American cultures in the Flatbush area of Brooklyn, New York, that "started with cultural misunderstanding and was compounded by a lack of bilingual and bicultural community leaders to intervene quickly." Kang believes that "cultural insight" is missing in this drama. Three of the differences between Korean Americans and African Americans that Kang points to are (1) attitudes toward smiling, (2) attitudes toward money, and (3) the value of social conscience.

2. Kang states her thesis in paragraph 3. Her comparison and contrast of the Korean American and African American communities provides the "cultural insight" to understand this inter-ethnic, inner-city drama. In her concluding paragraph, Kang reiterates the point of her essay: "making democracy work in a multicultural society is difficult but we have no choice but to strive for it."

3. After a long period of tension between the two groups, the African Americans are boycotting the Korean American grocers because a black customer said that she was attacked by a store employee.

4. Most Asian immigrants are ill-equipped to run businesses in the United States because they lack cultural and social knowledge of their new country. They are indebted to African Americans because of the civil-rights work done by them, which means that Korean Americans face less discrimination today.

5. Kang is writing from the point of view of a Korean American, so she understands many of the elements of Korean culture that make it difficult to assimilate into American neighborhoods. She also understands the American point of view toward new Korean immigrants.

6. One element that makes it difficult for Koreans to adapt is that the "Confucian ethos lacks the value of social conscience." Koreans tend to focus on themselves and their own success. They are not tolerant of other cultures and they don't reach out to people from other cultures, which has helped to exacerbate the situation in New York.

Vocabulary

volatile (1) dangerous; explosive
boycotting (1) protesting by not buying from
bilingual (3) able to speak two languages
intervene (3) step in; come between

brusque (4) rude; curt
sporadic (4) occasional; infrequent
gregarious (9) friendly; comfortable in groups
inclination (10) tendency
ethos (16) guiding beliefs of a person, group, or institution

Classroom Activity Using Comparison and Contrast

Analogy can be a difficult strategy for students to understand and even more difficult to work with. It is good to stress, however, that a good analogy can be highly effective. Points to stress include the following:

1. The analogy normally relates a fairly abstract concept to a much more concrete and immediate subject.
2. An analogy is used to clarify, not to mystify.
3. The subjects of both sides of the analogy are not usually in the same class.
4. It is better not to create an analogy than to create one that is so bizarre or laughable that the reader is distracted by it.

Recently, one of our local television interviewers was heard attempting to clarify the difference between a proposal for a widespread tax increase and a proposal for a targeted increase as the difference between dust on everything and dirt in a flowerpot—a concrete analogy, all right, but hardly an effective one.

CHAPTER 17 **Cause and Effect**

The Effects of the Telephone (p. 397)
■ **John Brooks**

Essay Analysis and Discussion

As Brooks states toward the end of his essay, few ponder the effects of technological innovations that become part of the fabric of our society. We take certain things so much for granted that it is difficult if not impossible to imagine life without them. We go to Amish country to look upon these stalwarts who exist without modern conveniences, yet they only forgo the innovations of the past one hundred years or so—in 1860, everybody lived so deprived. Now the effects of the telephone and of electricity are so profound that they cannot be adequately identified or quantified. It is likely that for children in grade school, computers will occupy a similar role, used every day and part of the very fabric of their lives. Note how Brooks admits that his causal chain is partial and inadequate. When dealing with a topic such as this, it is better to introduce several effects, some familiar and some that most readers will not have considered, and leave it at that than to try to write a long, exhaustive list that leaves the reader flat. Brooks wants to communicate how deeply the telephone affects our lives, and his first paragraph is an adequate representation of this. Discuss with your students the effects of a more recent innovation that has swiftly become an important part of our society, such as microwave ovens, computers, or cell phones.

Questions for Study and Discussion

1. Brooks opens with the question, then supplies a partial answer to it in the rest of the paragraph. At the beginning of paragraph 2 he identifies why the question may be impossible to answer—the crucial effects of the telephone are evanescent and unmeasurable because they impact every individual in different ways at different times.

2. Telephones eliminate the importance of physical proximity. One can do business from any nook of any building without needing couriers and face-to-face contact. Because of this, buildings and, eventually, entire cities could be built with little or no regard for where much of their commerce takes place. Elevators obviously make it possible for those who work high in the buildings to get to and from their offices without having to be trained athletes.

3. The effects of personal use of the telephone are difficult to chart because they change so much depending on the person and on the situation. As "our nerve-end to society," the telephone changes character millions of times every day for millions of people, but its importance to these people is constant.

4. These times are characterized by immediacy and speed of interaction, and the telephone represents the essence of these factors. Communication is instantaneous and independent of distance. It is also remote—although telephone conversations can be intimate, they can also be coldly efficient and distant, as anyone dealing with a telemarketer knows all too well.

5. Brooks is perhaps hyperbolic in comparing telephones with parts of the body, but he makes the point that it is impossible to separate the effects of the telephone on the society it helped create and shape from the society itself. Students will have differing reactions to his assessment.

Vocabulary

quantum (1) large, significant
impartially (1) without bias; objectively
disseminates (1) distributes; disperses
mechanistic (2) mechanically determined
evanescent (2) fleeting; ephemeral
paradox (3) contradiction; incongruity
polar (3) relating to one or more poles, as in a magnet

Classroom Activity Using Cause and Effect

One of the difficult things about writing a cause-and-effect essay similar to Brooks's is that the effects are felt on many levels. The effect the
item has on you may not be at all the same as the effect it has on your
neighbor, and it may affect society in ways that few people stop to
think about in their daily lives. The discussion suggested at the end of
the essay analysis section would be a good way to preface this activity
as well. Have students identify the different effects television has on
individuals, communities, and society as a whole.

I Refuse to Live in Fear (p. 401)
■ Diana Bletter

Essay Analysis and Discussion

It is hard for Americans to imagine living in a country where any unattended parcel, such as a shoe box, has the potential to cause death and
destruction. Bletter's status as an expatriate American living in Israel
makes her particularly aware of what that can mean in daily life, and
her opening anecdote is very effective at communicating to the reader
that living in such a place requires a way of thinking far different from
what is currently needed in the United States. The policeman is right—
in the Middle East, you cannot be careless. If you are, at best you can
cause fear and consternation, and at worst, you can become a good
target for the terrorists. As Bletter's essay goes on to say, the effects of
terrorism depend on the resilience of those being targeted. It is impossible to fight back against a group of fanatics who might blow themselves up along with passersby, except by carrying on the normal patterns of life in defiance of the terrorist threat. The goal of terrorists is to
disrupt and upset the general population, so if those effects take hold,
they have won. Discuss the article with your students in reference to
the terrorist acts that have hit close to home in recent years, including
the ones Bletter mentions. What can one do to overcome the helpless

117

fear and anger that such actions provoke? Do students think that the United States is likely to see the frequency of these events increase to the point that we need to start thinking the way the Israelis now do?

Questions for Study and Discussion

1. A shoe box, like any unattended parcel, may be a bomb set up by terrorists. No one will touch it, and, if the owner leaves it for too long, he or she may find an innocuous pair of shoes imploded for safety. In the United States, people will assume that someone forgot a purchase, and they will be likely to ignore it or, perhaps, pick up the package and drop it at a lost and found.
2. Bletter quotes the policeman because his words are important to her essay. He is angry, and rightfully so, and his quote demonstrates the common attitude in the Middle East—you cannot be careless, you must always play it safe. It is better that a whole squad of policemen blow up a pair of shoes than run the risk that the box might blow up on its own.
3. Daydreaming is dangerous in Israel because one always needs to be alert to the possibility of something being awry and to where emergency exits are located, what can be used as a weapon for self-defense, where the windows are, and so on.
4. Zina's dream symbolizes the ability of people under fire to work together to defeat those who want to beat them down. As an Arab, Zina is part of a cooperative effort on the part of people in Nahariyya to look out for each other, not just their own kind, to better keep the terrorists at bay.
5. Terrorism is defeated by resisting the temptation to become paranoid and isolated and by sticking up for each other. The most beneficial effect terrorism can have on the population is for it to bring people together to work to defeat it. If it has the effect of disrupting people's lives, the terrorists have been successful.
6. Bletter is fatalistic about the need to be careful, but she is quietly defiant toward the terrorists. Her stated resolve to prove again and again to terrorists that she and her fellow citizens are not giving in to their fears, and her last statement, "by sticking up for one another, we remain undefeated," are the best examples of this defiance.

Vocabulary

imploded (6) underwent violent compression
suburbia (7) suburban environment
vanquished (12) defeated; overcome

prophetic (13) clairvoyant; correct in predicting future events
paranoid (15) fearful; distrustful

Classroom Activity Using Cause and Effect

The cause-and-effect pairs listed here are meant to provide students with familiar causal chains. All of them should be easy to develop along familiar pathways. The second part of the activity allows students to be a bit more creative. Have them develop as general a chain as possible for the mixed pair. An airplane having engine trouble on a specific vacation can definitely have the effect of making a vacationer nervous, but what elements of all vacations tend to make people nervous?

Why We Crave Horror Movies (p. 406)
■ Stephen King

Essay Analysis and Discussion

In his first sentence, King tells us we are all mentally ill; then he suggests that our love of horror movies helps us feel balanced because those movies provide a psychic release for our darker feelings. In paragraphs 8 through 10 King defines the nature of our insanity in more detail and explains how society forces us to deal with our darker emotions. Next, King suggests that because we cannot flaunt our meaner feelings, we need an outlet for them, through horror movies and the "sick" joke. He has gone through his argument twice, with more emphasis on explaining the nature of our illness the second time through. He presents a thesis—that we are all mentally ill—and then carefully uses our love of horror movies and the sick joke to prove it. The horror movie gives us permission to express our dark feelings; those dark feelings are forbidden; they are forbidden because they are (this is where he gets us) "crazy." Can students refute King's position using a cause-and-effect argument of their own? Or is he right?

Questions for Study and Discussion

1. We crave horror movies to show that we are not afraid, to reestablish our feelings of being normal, and to have fun. Some people go to satisfy a morbid curiosity about how the horror will be effected or because they are aficionados of the macabre.
2. King compares the thrills and chills of the roller-coaster ride with the thrills and chills of the horror movie. Each propels you along, promising to reward your terror at the next turn; and each fulfills that promise, but when you least expect it.

3. The horror movie maintains the status quo of the nature of good and evil and beauty and ugliness in our minds. It does not ask us to rework our values.
4. Society applauds love, friendship, loyalty, and kindness because they "maintain the status quo of civilization itself." King labels emotions that are mean and murderous as "anticivilization."
5. The sick joke and the horror movie both must appeal "to all that is worst in us."
6. King gives examples of strange behavior that occurs in all of us, moving from the innocence of people who talk to themselves to the potentially murderous "lyncher." His last line suggests, as Freud did, that a darker, more menacing creature lies in wait beneath the civilized exterior we present to the world.
7. King's tone is humorously menacing. He, like the horror movie, likes to lead the viewer along, and then without warning spring at the viewer with a grisly thought or a shocking idea. His first and final sentences are meant to bring the reader up short. In between, students will find numerous examples: "If your insanity leads you to carve up women" (8), "The potential lyncher is in almost all of us" (9), "But if we deliberately slam the rotten little puke of a sister's fingers in the door, sanctions follow" (10). King also goes so far as to repeat for us one of the more horrifying of the "sick" jokes.

Vocabulary

grimaces (1) facial expressions showing disgust or disapproval
hysterical (1) marked by uncontrollable fear or emotion
voyeur's (6) of one who habitually seeks sexual satisfaction by visual stimulation
penchant (7) a strong inclination, liking
rein (7) restraining rope ("free rein" implies complete freedom from restraint)
exalted (9) raised in rank, power, or dignity
status quo (9) the existing state of affairs
puke (10) vomit; (slang) brat
sanctions (10) measures designed to enforce a law or standard
remonstrance (10) an act of arguing against
recoil (11) shrink; flinch; wince
anarchistic (11) believing that all government is unnecessary and undesirable
morbidity (12) gloomy or unwholesome ideas or feelings
subterranean (12) lying or being underground

Classroom Activity Using Cause and Effect

This activity, which our first-year students have found eye-opening, is useful in demonstrating for your students how easy it is to make assumptions while reading that are based on little or no evidence. The activity is also useful in alerting the writer to the care that must be taken not to imply more than he or she knows.

Answers:

1. T	4. T	7. ?
2. ?	5. ?	8. F
3. ?	6. ?	9. ?

How Not to Lose Friends over Money (p. 412)
■ **Lois Duncan**

Essay Analysis and Discussion

Duncan presents a cause-and-effect relationship that can take many different forms but has two things in common—money and tension between friends. Almost everyone can identify with the frustrations of having a petty money problem with someone they like, and it can look like a no-win situation when one is trying to figure out what to do about it. Duncan presents her essay in a way that is easy to follow. She begins with a personal anecdote to illustrate the kind of problem she is going to discuss, then presents a variety of different scenarios that are generally related to the central theme. She returns to her anecdote to discuss how she would like to resolve it, which unifies the essay and gives immediacy to the advice that is presented. It is interesting that she relied on lay friends rather than experts not only for the extensive examples she presents but for the advice she gives the reader as well. Do your students think this is an effective way to present the information? Discuss with them why Duncan may have chosen her friends' advice over the expert advice of psychologists and counselors.

Questions for Study and Discussion

1. Duncan's anecdote about Olivia effectively demonstrates that even minor problems with money can take on a greater importance as time goes on. Resentment over the perceived unfairness of the treatment one has received can build to the point that the friendship can be jeopardized.

2. Money is a volatile topic between friends because it can represent so much more than a simple amount of cash. It represents power and worth, and perceived unfairness in how it is handled can communicate to one party that the other party does not hold them in high esteem or worth. It may have been useful to include some theory in this essay, but Duncan probably chose to use her friends' advice because it is all based on direct involvement with applicable situations. Such advice may not work all the time but, because it worked in the case mentioned, it is likely that the reader will think that it is worth a try.

3. This question might be a good one to answer as a class. Choose five of the money problems and identify the causal chain with them on the board. Then assign the other four for the students to do on their own.

4. Duncan organizes her essay by opening with an anecdote, then presenting ten common money problems and their solutions, then using the solution to the final problem as a basis for concluding her anecdote. As her presentation is easy to follow and the information is easy to understand, most students should find her organization to be effective.

5. Duncan offers more than one solution for problems 5, 6, and 10. The choices should be a help to those who want to follow her advice, because one choice may be more appropriate than another in certain situations. Because money is such a difficult topic, presenting different solutions, where possible, will allow readers to choose the style—and, perhaps, the level of aggressiveness—with which they feel the most comfortable.

6. Most students will find the ending effective, because it brings resolution to the decades-old problem that Duncan has had. That she feels she could now go up to Olivia and ask for her money back also indicates that she is ready to take the advice that she has been presenting to the reader.

Vocabulary

inequities (9) inequality; unfairness
disparity (11) contrast; discrepancy
reciprocation (13) returning of a favor or gesture
milestone (23) landmark; occasion
impasse (30) standoff; deadlock
crass (34) rude; boorish

Classroom Activity Using Cause and Effect

Causal chains can be confusing at first, and it is often difficult to distinguish between the ultimate cause, the immediate cause, and one or more of the effects when first developing the chain. As was suggested for question 3 in the Questions for Study and Discussion, it would probably help students to develop some chains as a class before they attempt to do so on their own. Take fifteen or twenty minutes and have the students work together to come up with causal chains that are relevant to their own lives, then have them take another ten minutes or so to develop one on their own.

CHAPTER 18 **Argument**

As They Say, Drugs Kill (p. 427)
■ **Laura Rowley**

Essay Analysis and Discussion

Rowley arranges her argument into four sections: an opening statement, in which she presents the subject of her essay; the narrative, in which she gives an eyewitness account of the young man's death; her reaction to his death; and the conclusions she draws from the experience. The first three sections argue persuasively; by telling us her feelings and by forcing us to witness the man's agonizing and sudden death, Rowley makes an emotional case for not using drugs. In her conclusion, she is more logical, almost saying that it is unreasonable to witness or hear about an incident such as this and remain unconvinced. Students can go through the different sections to see what emotions Rowley inspires and what effect those feelings have on the reader. She says in her essay that friends remained unconvinced and thought it could not happen to them. What has Rowley done to ensure that her written narrative will be more convincing than her spoken one?

Questions for Study and Discussion

1. Rowley uses very emotional, graphically disturbing language in her dialogue, her diction, and her choice of details. For example, "His face was grayish blue, his mouth hung open, rimmed with

blood, and his eyes were rolled back with a yellowish color on the rims." The dialogue adds drama, realism, and immediacy to her argument. The emotional graphic language and the disturbing details are intended to shock readers into believing that drugs kill, that it can happen to anyone, and that they should change their behavior accordingly if they are using drugs.

2. Rowley wants us to consider that death by drugs can happen to anyone; she wants us to think about this fact and, if we are users, she wants us to stop.

3. Rowley is able to shock the reader and force our attention to the issue with her eyewitness account of the death. Her friend seemed to agree with Rowley that witnessing such a death would be convincing enough to prevent anyone's using drugs again. Others saw no special meaning in the incident. They considered it a "freak accident" and learned little if anything from the young man's death.

4. Rowley may have chosen not to violate the man's privacy. However, his anonymity also gives an "everyman" quality to the story and underlines her proposition that what happened to him could happen to anyone. The young man's ordinariness distinguishes him from celebrity victims such as Len Bias.

5. Rowley shares openly her sense of helplessness and sorrow for the man who died and her concern for others who might die the same way. "It seemed irreverent to talk as the ambulance pulled away." "My hands began to shake and my eyes filled with tears for someone I didn't know." "If this death cannot make people think and change, that will be an even greater tragedy."

6. Rowley's opening paragraph is apparently glib, which makes it shocking and grabs the reader's attention. The impact would have been diluted if the reader could have continued reading into the next sentence.

7. Rowley wants to reach drug users, of course. However, she wants everyone to think about the issue, so that a general complacency may be destroyed. Some students will feel that, as with many such events, the impact eventually dissolves and people resume their old habits. Whether someone is convinced may depend on how that person feels about drug use to begin with.

Vocabulary

ambivalence (2) simultaneous attraction toward and repulsion by a person, object, or action

stupefied (3) made dull, torpid, or numb by or as if by drugs

convulse (6) to agitate violently

semicoherent (11) not completely logical or consistent
audibly (20) in a way capable of being heard
gnashing (21) grinding together
irreverent (26) showing lack of reverence
unravel (28) solve, especially a mystery
speculated (29) reasoned; thought; deliberated
tragedy (30) a disastrous event

Classroom Activity Using Argument

Much of the success of any argument depends on the quantity and quality of the material brought to bear on it. Yet, even before going to the library or the Internet to search for information, students should be encouraged to engage in some essential critical thinking. While it is perfectly legitimate sometimes to cast a wide net in any search for information and issues, there are times when the search can be narrowed to save time and effort. Knowing how to ask questions related to the topic will get the search started more easily. In item 2, for example, the student might ask the following questions:

1. Isn't English the official language of the United States?
2. What is an official language anyhow?
3. What good is an official language?
4. Who wants an official language? For what reason?
5. Might it be the case that an official language is not desirable?
6. Do any states have state laws about an official language?
7. If so, which ones? What was the reasoning behind enacting such laws?

These same questions can be asked of just about any topic: Who? What? Why? Where? and When? So what? These are always excellent starting points.

As far as the question of where to obtain the desired information is concerned, it is good to remind students that it is sometimes helpful to use an encyclopedia as a way of gaining the most fundamental information in the quickest manner. Also, students should be cautioned to use only the most recently published information. An encyclopedia may be several years old and may not be accurate in stating how many states have passed English-Only laws. Newspaper indexes are a good way to get the most up-to-date statistics, but they should be checked for their accuracy. Finally, any information obtained from the Internet should be used cautiously, as the accuracy of such information is not always scrupulously checked. Using known authorities and disseminators, whether institutions or individuals, is always wise.

Against the Great Divide (p. 433)
■ Brian Jarvis

Essay Analysis and Discussion

Jarvis presents a scenario that is familiar to many people. Efforts at integration brought students from different races into the same building, but in many cases this did not result in students from different races mingling and learning from one another. Jarvis's essay eloquently presents such a situation at his school, but he further illustrates it with a very telling personal anecdote. Even his close friend from grade school gradually drifts away, until they no longer spend any time together. Discuss with your students why they think this occurred. What, other than sports, keeps them apart? Why do they think this voluntary separation is so pervasive? Jarvis uses persuasive argumentation to propose ways to improve the situation. Although he presents no evidence to back up his arguments, he gains credibility by being in a situation in which he must confront the problem daily. Still, he admits that the multiracial leadership camp was an idyllic setting, and the question remains how well his solutions would work with a broad range of students, many of whom will not be as bright and open-minded as he. Do your students believe a class that taught black and white students "how to get along" and enforced intra-class integration would work to bridge the gap between the two races? What is their reaction to the camp?

Questions for Study and Discussion

1. Jarvis's personal experiences speak directly to his point that school teachers and administrators need to make the mixing of whites and blacks in school activities a priority. His experience at Camp Miniwanca in Michigan shows what is possible when white and black youths are brought together in a leadership setting. This experience makes Jarvis hopeful. Some readers might not be persuaded by Jarvis's experiences and would have liked him to buttress the example of his St. Louis high school with examples of the racial situation in other schools or of national or regional surveys about the voluntary separation of the races in our nation's "integrated" schools. Most readers, however, find the thoroughness of Jarvis's story from his childhood African American friend to his experiences in the commons, classrooms, and camp, and his two-country analogy compelling.

2. Students will have various reactions to this question. At least some of them will probably question the applicability of the camp experience to life in an urban or suburban high school.

3. Jarvis and his friend do not interact in large part because they do not share a single class or activity. This effectively illustrates the separation between the races—he had been friends with the African American boy in grade school, but they were pulled in different directions by the time they reached high school. Jarvis is participating in classes and sports that are predominantly white, and his friend is involved with sports and, presumably, studies that are predominantly "black." Jarvis also mentions peer pressure—interaction between the races is unusual enough that it comes across as being difficult to achieve.

4. The two groups stay apart through their own choice, and efforts to bring them closer together have failed because the situation *is* voluntary, so attempts to encourage the two groups to interact are almost sure to fail.

5. Students will have various responses to this question.

6. Jarvis wants adults to read his essay. His peers already know the situation; it is the adults who thought they had accomplished their ends by integrating the schools that he wants to reach. It is also concerned adults—parents, teachers, administrators—whom he is asking to establish the courses and the camps he proposes.

Vocabulary

commons (1) area where all can gather
proponents (7) those in favor of
desegregation (7) removal of segregation; mixing
idyllic (11) pastoral; pleasing in rural simplicity
multicultural (12) made up of members or influences from more than one culture

Classroom Activity Using Argument

To choose the best quote for their paragraph, students will need to decide if they will use mostly persuasive arguments, logical arguments, or a mix of the two. The first quote will fit a mostly persuasive argument, the second a logical argument (let students know they can make up other statistics if they wish), and the third can be used for both. Make sure the students integrate the quote into the paragraph so that it directly supports their argument and suits their tone. Students may enjoy reading their finished paragraphs aloud—have them discuss which method of presenting the argument is the most effective for each subject.

Exposing Media Myths: TV Doesn't Affect You as Much as You Think (p. 438)
■ **Joanmarie Kalter**

Essay Analysis and Discussion

Facing the task of arguing against accepted truths, Kalter organizes her essay well. She brings up each so-called myth, states the actual situation as she sees it, then backs up her statements with statistics and expert opinions. Also note how she chooses her words. Researchers do not find data, they find "an eye-opening collection of myth-busters." An accepted truth becomes a "little canard" or "fable." Kalter does not overdo it, but her choice of words helps build the reader's confidence in the new research and erode confidence in the old accepted truths. This essay should promote a good discussion in your class. Although Kalter addresses only TV news, there is a strong suggestion that many other accepted truths about other forms of programming may in fact be false. Have your students write about how they think TV has affected them and their friends. Do they believe that the current concern over the strong sexual and violent content of some shows is merited?

Questions for Study and Discussion

1. Kalter is able to focus on a particular body of research about TV news, the impact of which has probably been studied more intensively than that of other television programs. By limiting her argument to the news, she is able to make a clearly organized argument, and she does not need to make any potentially questionable extrapolations of the data she presents.

2. In paragraph 16 Kalter introduces the myth that TV news is easily understood and explains that studies have shown it is not. She uses the next four paragraphs to detail why it is not always an effective medium. Thus the reader is not only convinced about the veracity of what she is saying, he or she also understands the reasons behind it. Paragraph 17 states why the visual medium is not always clear. Paragraph 18 explains how the content and structure of news stories do not correlate with normal viewing habits. Paragraph 19 differentiates between the public's reaction to the

extraordinary, which is remembered, and the ordinary, which is not. Paragraph 20 concludes that TV news is useful to a select few but lost on the general public.

3. The word *myth* has come to be associated with old stories that rely more on imagination than fact. Kalter uses it to imply that certain assumptions about TV news rely more on imagination than fact.

4. General survey questions can yield skewed results because they can be confusing or very difficult to answer correctly. The Roper polls indicated that people received most of their news from television, thus increasing the perceived importance of TV news, but when more specific questions were asked, the responses indicated that fewer people watch TV news each day than read a newspaper.

5. Kalter says that public opinion helped shape TV coverage of the Vietnam War, not vice versa. The tone of the coverage of the war followed public opinion trends. The perceived ability of TV media to shape public opinion about conflicts has been used as a rationale for censoring some coverage of recent battles.

6. Television reaches a larger audience than do other types of media and it can be improved. It can be changed by improving the writing and by studying how people watch news and what they want to get from watching it. Television news has not changed because journalists and networks, under pressure to produce, have not sufficiently analyzed how best to present the news.

Vocabulary

truism (1) something held to be a true statement
canard (3) false story
succinctly (7) without wasting words
brevity (8) conciseness; briefness
rapt (13) entranced; paying close attention
rationale (15) reasoning; explanation
gist (17) essence; meaning
glitzed (21) jazzed up; made shiny or fancy

Classroom Activity Using Argument

Audience is an abstraction for most writers. They have a vague sense of why it might be more helpful to say this or that, with such and such diction, but they don't really study the issue, the importance of not missing the target at every point in the writing. We find this exercise helpful in getting students to think more practically about the audience for their work. Types of evidence students should consider include the following:

1. A lot of basic information is conveyed if the audience is deemed by the writer to be uninformed on the subject.
2. Key terms and concepts are defined if the audience is uninformed.
3. Technical language is used if the audience is presumed to be familiar with the subject.
4. Unexamined assumptions that would not pass muster with less friendly readers would be offered if the audience is like-minded or sympathetic.

The Merits of Failure

In Praise of the F Word (p. 445)
■ **Mary Sherry**

Essay Analysis and Discussion

Anything that involves short-term sacrifice to achieve long-term benefits is hard to sell in our society, and Mary Sherry knows it. But she also knows that her perspective as an adult literacy teacher carries weight when it comes to addressing those who would argue that failing is too traumatic for kids. In particular, note how she organizes paragraphs 2 through 4. She begins by saying what she does, she progresses to what she has learned about her school and what difficulties students and teachers there face, and only at the end of paragraph 4 does she bring up the word "failure." By the time she gets to that word, she has established her experience and credibility. She has also implied that the schools have, in some cases, failed their students by not being willing to fail them. Also note how paragraphs 10 through 12 comprise what is essentially a three-paragraph conclusion. Much of the text in the three paragraphs would be repetitive and unnecessary if Sherry felt she were addressing sympathetic readers, but it is clear that she feels that it is important to drive her point home. Discuss these and other techniques Sherry uses to persuade her presumably reluctant audience.

Questions for Study and Discussion

1. Sherry's thesis is that flunking kids—or even the possibility of flunking them—can motivate many of them in the short term and prevent many long-term problems. She uses her experience as both an adult literacy program teacher and a parent as evidence.

2. Sherry acknowledges the opposition to flunking in paragraphs 8 and 11, but her strong language—"cheats" and "excuses"— clearly shows how she thinks. She does not detail the reasons— mostly economic and social—for a policy of passing students probably because she believes that such a discussion would get her argument off track by focusing on issues other than the students themselves. Sherry's experiences with students in her adult literacy program who have been "passed along" without mastering basic materials while in school argue strongly for a system that gets "tough" with students and encourages them with the threat of failure to make school a priority.

3. The "F word" can mean either failure or flunking. By calling it the "F word," Sherry implies that it has now become a taboo concept to flunk kids.

4. Sherry's audience is presumably educators and parents. It does not appear to be receptive to the "F word." Students should note the gradual introduction of the concept of failure, the long conclusion, and the personal examples.

5. Sherry establishes her adult literacy students' dissatisfaction with the laissez-faire attitude of their schools.

6. Sherry has seen the results of passing marginally literate and illiterate students—severe problems after graduation and a need to go back to school. The second part is a matter of personal opinion.

7. Flunking gets the attention of the students in the classroom, it can be used as a long-term motivator, and it prevents the integration of incapable high-school graduates into society.

Vocabulary

validity (1) justifiability; correctness
semiliterate (1) barely able to read and write
impediments (4) obstacles
trump (4) powerful; especially valuable
testimony (9) statement; description

Classroom Activity Using Argument

The reliability of evidence is, of course, what drives writers, scholars, doctors, lawyers, and researchers to do what they do. Finding more than one authority who agrees with the assumption of the reliability of a body of evidence sometimes can make a case for accuracy; sometimes such reliance only proves that scholars rely too heavily on the unexamined and untested work of their predecessors. A writer we know, for example, has been working on a book on the covered bridges of Vermont. Finding some discrepancies in the measurements of those bridges in source materials, he thought it necessary to take his own measurements. He found that not only were early published statistics inaccurate but subsequent researchers and writers had relied on that information and republished it. The issue of reliability turns on the question, very often, of how much time a writer or other professional has to accomplish a given task. It should be made clear, however, that writing based on questionable information may so distort the conclusions that the whole endeavor becomes a waste of time.

The Right to Fail (p. 450)
■ **William Zinsser**

Essay Analysis and Discussion

For such a fluid and diverse society, America has long had narrow and rigid capitalistic definitions of what it means for young people to succeed. The path can be varied, but the goal of affluence and professional standing is assumed to always be in the sights of students and young professionals, and any divergence from these goals is viewed with suspicion. Any step that is not directed toward these goals is a step back, whatever it may represent to the person making it. Zinsser's essay argues that such steps, usually labeled as failures for those who take them, are often nothing of the sort. As he says, "We need mavericks and dissenters and dreamers far more than we need junior vice-presidents." Taking risks, even if they are of the type not smiled upon by society, is one way to grow stronger, even if the path chosen turns into a dead end. Note how Zinsser uses art, in the character of Holden Caulfield, and artists, whose work always involves risks, to illustrate this point. Artists are people who must succeed on their own terms, not those of society, and Zinsser applies this sensibility to all young people struggling to define what success ultimately means to them. How much pressure do your students feel to follow a traditional educational and vocational path? How supportive do they think their families and friends would be if they were to step sideways and try something new and not goal-oriented?

Questions for Study and Discussion

1. Zinsser argues a two-part thesis. He argues that taking risks, or side trips, is an important way in which young people grow. He also argues that society is making a mistake by branding such side trips as failures and by trying to funnel young people along a nar-

row path to what it defines as success. He presents his thesis most clearly in paragraphs 4 through 6.

2. Zinsser's use of the word *fluid* suggests he considers young adulthood a time when young men and women should be flexible, pliable, and easily changed. It is a time when young people should explore and experiment, taking risks that include the possibility of failure. As Zinsser says, "the only way for boys and girls to find their proper road is often to take a hundred side trips, poking out in different directions, faltering, drawing back, and starting again" (4). The word *fluid* reinforces this line of argument.

3. Zinsser's essay has held up extremely well, but words that date it include *VISTA volunteers, dropping in, hippies,* and *vapid* (as a word to describe college educations).

4. A *fink* is an informant or, more loosely, someone who betrays someone else. In Zinsser's use, a fink is someone who betrays society by "dropping out." Finks are not following the expected path, so society views them as troublemakers and as being detrimental to the workings of society.

5. Movie directors and other artists rarely know what will "succeed" from a popular standpoint, so they need to work on projects that they believe in and do their best. Even if the results do not meet with acclaim or succeed financially, the experience is something that they can learn from, and they need to push on and try something else. Artists make good examples for Zinsser because they do not always succeed. But to be ultimately successful they must look upon their "failures" as learning experiences and not become discouraged by them. It is the way artists grow, and Zinsser applies it to young people in general, who must be able "to take the risks in life that artists take in art."

6. VISTA volunteers are not pursuing material wealth, but they are certainly not lazy. They are working hard at something they believe in, and it is work that fulfills them. Therefore, instead of dropping out, they could be said to be dropping in on something more useful to society and more suitable to their own happiness than the path society expects of them.

Vocabulary

dissenters (4) those who disagree with an established regime or idea
strewn (6) scattered; thrown without pattern
eminent (6) esteemed; famous
coddle (9) spoil; overindulge
affluent (12) wealthy; prosperous
vapid (14) boring; inane

Classroom Activity Using Argument

1. An effective syllogism establishes a connection between the major and minor premises. No such connection has been established in this attempt at a syllogism, therefore the conclusion may or may not be true.
2. This syllogism is valid and true.
3. This syllogism is valid and true.
4. The conclusion to this syllogism is not necessarily true because writers are not the only people who enjoy reading books.
5. The conclusion to this syllogism is not necessarily true because all incredibly sticky candy is not cotton candy.

When inexperienced writers become involved with presenting an argument, it is easy for them to lose track of logic as they write. The argument may seem to be clear in their heads, but it can become garbled on paper. When isolated and pointed out, the breakdowns in logic are easy to see, as this activity will demonstrate to students. They should have an easy time writing their own effective syllogisms, and the exercise will help them to think more about maintaining a logical presentation of their arguments as they write.

Examining the Death Penalty

Cruel and Unusual (p. 456)
■ **Sherwin B. Nuland**

Essay Analysis and Discussion

At a time when the death penalty is being debated by the American public, Sherwin B. Nuland offers an argument against the electric chair as a means of execution. Because so few people have a clear understanding of what happens when a person is electrocuted or have incomplete information about the process, Nuland, a physician, describes in detail what happens to the human body when it is given three 2,000-volt jolts of electricity. To persuade readers that the electric chair is indeed cruel and unusual punishment, he knows that he must demonstrate the barbarity of this method. His detailed description in paragraphs 4 through 8 prepare the reader for Nuland's conclusion in paragraph 9 that "the electric chair should be forbidden."

1. Nuland prefaces his argument with the question of providing murderers a quiet death because that very question establishes a context for his argument about the electric chair. He tells us that the Supreme Court will soon consider "whether Florida's use of the electric chair constitutes cruel and unusual punishment," and he wants us to focus on the electric chair as a method of execution.

2. Nuland describes death in the electric chair in gruesome detail because he is arguing that the electric chair constitutes cruel and unusual punishment. His mention of the now widely used lethal injection in the final paragraph is intended to contrast with what he feels is the barbarity of electrocution. Because Nuland's purpose is not to argue the merits of the death penalty or to argue for lethal injection over electrocution, he felt no need to provide additional support for his claim.

3. Nuland's diction in paragraphs 4 through 8 is intended to reinforce the idea that "electrocution is a barbaric way to kill someone." A clinical professor of surgery, Nuland describes the functions of the electric chair and the physiological effects of electric current on the human body in objective scientific terms. When coupled with words and phrases such as "brutal killer," "botched," "exquisitely painful," and "appallingly obvious," electrocution becomes something that we wouldn't wish on any human being.

4. In paragraph 7 Nuland lists the three ways in which electrocution can cause death. But he cautions that "all of these mechanisms take more than two minutes to cause brain death, the legal definition of the end of life." When the initial shock fails to render the person unconscious, he or she retains awareness of what's happening to his or her body. Nuland notes that an awareness of being asphyxiated is particularly cruel and unusual punishment.

5. Nuland's argument is with the electric chair as a means of execution; he believes electrocution is "cruel and unusual punishment." In arguing against the electric chair, Nuland is arguing against revenge as a motive for the death penalty. While Nuland does not explicitly state his position on the death penalty, he does not give any indication that he is against it. His main concern seems to be with the method of execution, favoring one like lethal injection that can be carried out effectively and with as little pain as possible.

Vocabulary

trauma (1) a wound produced by sudden physical injury
paradoxical (2) seemingly contradictory
quietus (3) a release from life; death
botched (5) to bungle or perform clumsily
asphyxiates (7) to smother or suffocate
ventricular (7) relating to heart chambers

Classroom Activity Using Argument

This exercise offers your students the chance to review the logical fallacies discussed in the introduction to the argument chapter on pages
420–26. The answers for the five short passages are as follows:

1. false analogy
2. post hoc, ergo propter hoc
3. oversimplification
4. non sequitur
5. hasty generalization

When Justice Lets Us Down (p. 461)
■ Jim Dwyer, Peter Neufeld, and Barry Scheck

Essay Analysis and Discussion

This essay offers a number of interesting points for discussion. The
story of Ron Williamson retold in the first five paragraphs engages
readers in the topic of capital punishment because it shows how imperfect our justice system can be and makes readers ask what can be
done about it. Next, look at the factual information ("Since 1976, Illinois has executed 12 people—and freed 13 from death row as innocent," for example) and the quotations from Governor George Ryan,
Justice Learned Hand, and Judge Frank Seay to see how the authors
have used these materials to build their argument. Stylistically, the authors vary their sentence structure so that when they use short sentences the effect is dramatic. Focus your students' attention on the
sentence that opens paragraph 6, the series of short sentences that end
paragraph 7, and the final sentence of the essay.

Questions for Study and Discussion

1. The opening anecdote about Ron Williamson gives a human face
   to the argument about capital punishment. This case shows read-

ers what can go wrong in capital cases. The thought of executing an innocent person is most Americans' worst fear. The story of an innocent man who was almost executed is a powerful way to lead off an essay arguing for reforms in the current justice system, especially as it pertains to capital cases.

2. The two ways that this quotation strengthens the authors' argument are (1) it's an admission that Governor Ryan cannot think of a way to prevent the execution of an innocent person, and (2) it's a statement of support from a "death-penalty supporter."

3. The American public is being enlightened about the flaws in our country's justice system and how these flaws can send innocent people to their deaths. For example, "In the last decade, DNA tests have provided stone-cold proof that 69 people were sent to prison and death row in North America for crimes they did not commit."

4. The authors use the metaphor of the "fabric of false guilt" with its "vivid threads" to show how people from all regions and walks of life are bound together by the problems of our justice system. All of these cases are cut from the same cloth. The authors use this image to remind readers that capital cases are connected and should not be considered in isolation when studying the problem of wrongful convictions.

5. The authors believe that DNA testing reveals that "eyewitnesses make mistakes. Snitches tell lies. Confessions are coerced or fabricated. Racism trumps the truth. Lab tests are rigged. Defense lawyers sleep. Cops lie." While it seems perfectly logical to offer any person DNA testing if it can prove his or her innocence, people seem reluctant to authorize it without litigation. Reasons why it is so difficult to obtain DNA testing may include (1) fear of being exposed for one of the problems listed in paragraph 7, (2) possible economic implications, and (3) fear that if you offer it in one case it will open the floodgates of DNA testing. Ask students to offer their own thinking of why DNA testing is difficult to obtain.

Vocabulary

litany (3) a repetitive phrase or saying
stay (2) to delay or stop the effect of an order by legal action
inept (4) incompetent
moratorium (5) a suspension of action
vivid (7) bright, distinct, intense, and strong
coerced (7) forced through pressure, threats, or intimidation
statutory (8) authorized by law
exonerations (8) freedom from blame

Classroom Activity Using Argument

This exercise works well as a group activity. Before setting students free on one of the suggested topics or a topic of your own choosing, make sure they understand the dog leash law example provided in the text. This exercise gets students to focus on the essential pieces of an argument—in this case, three key points in favor of the writer's position (two logical and one emotional) and one point held by the opposition. After fifteen or twenty minutes have several groups write their key points on the board or present their thoughts orally.

Is There Equity in Cyberspace?

Cyberghetto: Blacks Are Falling through the Net (p. 466)
■ **Frederick L. McKissack**

Essay Analysis and Discussion

McKissack's argument is interesting for the wide range of sources that he uses to support his position. He uses personal experience, a study published in the journal *Science,* a letter to the editor of the *New York Times,* a book about science in the twenty-first century, an online magazine, a State of the Union address, a consulting firm, the U.S. Department of Education, a monthly magazine, a computer magazine, a foundation study, and a newspaper article. He appears to be well read and well informed on his topic. In paragraph 14 and again in paragraphs 20 and 21 McKissack addresses the opposition arguments and quickly responds with his own counterarguments.

Have your students read the following article by Gary T. Dempsey, "The Myth of an Emerging Information Underclass," and ask them to compare these opposing arguments, paying particular attention to how each writer uses facts, statistics, and quotations to best serve their respective arguments. For example, you can start by comparing paragraph 4 of McKissack's article with paragraph 4 of Dempsey's. Or, you might look at the differences between McKissack's claims in paragraph 5 about households that don't have telephones with Dempsey's claims in paragraphs 6 and 7 about cable and local multipoint distribution systems.

Questions for Study and Discussion

1. McKissack's opening two paragraphs not only engage readers but also suggest the urgency of his argument. He begins this way because he knows that computers and the Internet are a powerful

force today, a force that will dominate the world that our children and young adults will inherit. The example of the teenager who wrote a book about Web design and programming is appropriate because the heart of McKissack's argument speaks to educational opportunities and reform that are needed to close the technology gap in the future.

2. In paragraph 7 McKissack presents his thesis: "The gulf between technological haves and have-nots is the difference between living the good life and surviving in what some technologists and social critics term a 'cyberghetto.'" As McKissack himself says, "I am one of the few African Americans in this country who has a computer at home, uses one at work, and can use a lot of different kinds of software on multiple platforms" (3). McKissack now works for an Internet development firm.

3. According to McKissack, cyberghetto "suggests that minorities have barely passable equipment to participate in tech culture." This can be misleading because, as McKissack notes, "most minorities aren't even doing that well."

4. According to Jon Katz, politicians and journalists have focused their attention on the wrong problem when they worry about Internet pornography. Katz suggests that the real problem is a "technological gap" that is dividing society into two groups—those who have computer and Internet skills and those who do not.

5. McKissack quotes from a Markle Foundation–Bellcore Labs study to support his claim that dropping prices for computers and specialized Web accessing devices do not translate into increased Internet use by minorities (24).

6. While it would be ideal for every black student to have a computer at school and at home, McKissack doubts that that will "obliterate all racial obstacles to success." McKissack fears that if we are not vigilant about putting computers and Internet access into the hands of minorities, we will create a "silicon ceiling" in our society.

Vocabulary

Luddite (1) a person who believes that labor-saving machinery diminishes employment; after Ned Ludd, a legendary British leader
exacerbate (8) to increase the severity of
disseminate (10) to spread or distribute
menial (12) appropriate for a servant
allocated (19) designated or set apart for
affluent (22) rich; wealthy

Classroom Activity Using Argument

Letters to the editor of a newspaper are usually very opinionated and do not rely on new information or the correction of erroneous evidence. Thoughtful, interesting letters, however, do present new information and new perspectives while recognizing other points of view. For this reason, students should be encouraged to go beyond their own opinions and bring new material or perspectives to light for the readers of the newspaper. Their work will have a much better chance of being considered for publication when they send them to the newspaper.

The Myth of an Emerging Information Underclass (p. 473)
■ Gary T. Dempsey

Essay Analysis and Discussion

Dempsey's organization is interesting for students to analyze. Dempsey's title announces his topic and position: An emerging information underclass is a myth. In the opening two paragraphs, he presents the claims of the opposition and identifies two false assumptions he believes they make. In paragraph 3 he presents his thesis. Dempsey uses paragraphs 4 through 11 to give five reasons for his stance and to document reasons where he deems necessary. He concludes his argument in paragraph 12 with a restatement of his thesis. Ask students to analyze the facts, statistics, and quotations that Dempsey uses to buttress his thinking and to consider ways that they might counter his arguments.

Questions for Study and Discussion

1. Some students will argue that Dempsey makes a hasty generalization from the information given in paragraph 4. People could counter Dempsey's arguments by questioning his statistics. For example, how does a 160 percent increase among low-income people compare to the percentage increase for Internet use by the public at large? Also it could be argued that Eric Schmidt's prediction is vague; being "connected to the Internet" or having access to the Internet doesn't necessarily mean that people will use the Internet.

2. To argue that low-income people will have access to the Internet without government subsidies, Dempsey is obliged to present strong evidence supporting this position. In paragraph 2 Dempsey

quickly dispatches the opposition by questioning the assumptions underlying their position. He then turns to present his own argument. In paragraphs 4 through 11 he enumerates five reasons—together with supporting documentation—to support his contention that an information underclass will not emerge.

3. In paragraph 2 Dempsey likens access to an Internet connection to living next door to a public library. Just as an Internet connection doesn't make a person "information rich" close proximity to a library doesn't make a person "more knowledgeable." This analogy is appropriate in the context of Dempsey's argument because the two things being compared involve access, information, and knowledge.

4. Dempsey argues that the wider availability of LMDSs will make the Internet more accessible at a lower cost because cable "is now available to 97 percent of U.S. homes." Dempsey assumes that low-income Americans will be connected to cable and that LMDS technologies will "with competition" provide Internet access that is cheaper than current telephone technology.

5. *The American Heritage Dictionary* defines underclass as "the lowest societal stratum usually composed of the disadvantaged." In the context of Dempsey's article, the "information underclass" is equated with low-income households in America. The connotations of the word *underclass* will vary; possible connotations include poor, uneducated, socially disadvantaged, and minority groups.

Vocabulary

advocacy (1) supporting a cause, idea, or policy
proponents (2) people who argue in support of something
diversified (7) varied or spread out
inevitable (12) incapable of being avoided or prevented

Classroom Activity Using Argument

Direct students—either individually or in pairs—to construct one list of Internet benefits and another of its drawbacks or dangers. Benefits that students might mention include having scholarly information at your fingertips, 24-hour-a-day access, shopping online, investing online, email, and chat-room exchanges. Drawbacks or dangers include spreading pornography and hate literature; inaccurate, biased, or unfounded information; and commercial fraud.

Research and Writing Online

Whether you want to investigate the ideas behind a thought-provoking essay or conduct in-depth research for a paper, the Web resources for *Models for Writers* can help you find what you need on the Web—and then use it once you find it.

The English Research Room for Navigating the Web

www.bedfordstmartins.com/english_research

The Web brings a flood of information to your screen, but it still takes skill to track down the best sources. Not only does *The English Research Room* point you to some reliable starting places for Web investigations, but it also lets you tune up your skills with interactive tutorials.

•Do you want to improve your skill at searching electronic databases, online catalogs, and the Web? Try the *Interactive Tutorials* for some hands-on practice.

•Do you need quick access on online search engines, reference sources, and research sites? Explore *Research Links* for some good starting places.

•Do you have questions on evaluating the sources you find, navigating the Web, or conducting research in general? Consult one of our *Reference Units* for authoritative advice.

Research and Documentation Online for Including Sources in Your Writing

www.bedfordstmartins.com/resdoc

Including sources correctly in a paper is often a challenge, and the Web has made it even more complex. This online version of the popular booklet *Research and Documentation in the Electronic Age*, by Diana Hacker, provides clear advice for the humanities, social sciences, history, and the sciences on—

•Which Web and library sources are relevant to your topic (with links to Web sources)

•How to integrate outside material into your paper

•How to cite sources correctly, using the appropriate documentation style

•What the format for the final paper should be